OPERA AND SONG BOOKS
PUBLISHED IN ENGLAND
1703-1726

OPERA AND SONG BOOKS

PUBLISHED IN ENGLAND

1703-1726

a descriptive bibliography

DAVID HUNTER

LONDON
BIBLIOGRAPHICAL SOCIETY
1997

© The Bibliographical Society 1997

Published by the Bibliographical Society

ISBN 0 948170 10 7
A CIP catalogue record for this book is
available from The British Library

Designed by David Chambers
Printed and bound by The Alden Press, Oxford.

To my parents

' "The only exact knowledge there is," said Anatole France, "is the knowledge of the date of publication and the format of books".'
  Quoted by Walter Benjamin in 'Unpacking My Library', translated by Harry Zohn, *Illuminations* (New York: Schocken Books, 1969), 59-67 (60).

Bibliographers' corollary: there is no knowledge without error.

Abstract

This bibliography offers descriptions of almost 200 issues of secular vocal music published in England 1703-1726, including works by Giovanni Bononcini, Henry Purcell, John Weldon, Attilio Ariosti and Richard Leveridge. The only exclusions are 'reprints' or subsequent volumes of books first published before 1703, books comprising solely the work of Handel, and the issues of the *Monthly Mask of Vocal Music*. The book indexes 2296 song first lines. The books described here represent the first extended effort to issue entirely commercial printed versions of musical stage works and they are also the first song books to be printed by engraving on a systematic basis. The book is a sequel to Day and Murrie's *English Song Books 1651-1702*, published by the Bibliographical Society in 1940, and augments David Foxon's *English Verse 1701-1750*.

In addition to clarifying the bibliographic history of the books through examination of 863 within-scope copies (91.3% of those identified), the bibliography tests and extends the standard concepts of bibliographical description. Several new descriptive features are introduced. There are over 200 illustrations of title-pages, frontispieces and music engraving styles. By permitting access to material that is not currently widely available in print, the bibliography will be of assistance to musicians, music and theatre historians, and literary scholars, as well as to librarians and bibliographers.

Table of Contents

Acknowledgements

The initial research for this bibliography was part of my dissertation. Many thanks to the committee—Donald W. Krummel (chairman), Walter C. Allen, N. Frederick Nash, Robert Rogers, and Nicholas Temperley—for their example, continued advice, and support.

Financial assistance for dissertation research was provided by the University of Illinois at Urbana-Champaign, the Bibliographical Society of America, and the University of California Research Grants for Librarians Program. Subsequently, research funding was provided by the Music Library Association, the National Endowment for the Humanities, and the ERMULI Trust.

I am grateful to Henry L. Snyder, Director, and my colleagues at the Eighteenth-Century Short Title Catalogue/North America, and to Harold Billings, Director, and my colleagues in the General Libraries at the University of Texas at Austin, for their understanding and forbearance of research trips and talk.

Maria X. Wells, Harry Ransom Humanities Research Center, University of Texas at Austin, provided assistance with the Italian texts. Dell Hollingsworth, who catalogues in the same Center, checked the French.

Without the support of the Council of the Bibliographical Society and the successive editors of monographs, Peter Isaac, Michael Perkin, and David Chambers, this book would not have appeared in this form. David Chambers transformed brute bytes into typographical beauty, for which I am most grateful.

Many librarians, book dealers and collectors in Britain, the United States of America, France, Germany, Belgium, Canada, Austria, the Netherlands, and Denmark have expedited my search for song books. Their efforts were invaluable. Particularly helpful in answering queries were: Olive Baldwin and Thelma Wilson, John Bidwell, Chris Bornet, Sheila Craik, Mrs M.V. Cranmer, Peggy Daub, Miss Mary Ellison, Virginia Gifford, Laura Gowdy, William Guthrie, Michael Halls, Barbara Henry, John Howard, Meryl Jancey, Peter Ward Jones, Ian Ledsham, Rosamond McGuinness, Richard Macnutt, Catherine Massip, Ruthann McTyre, Roger Norris, Elizabeth Orton, John Roberts, John Shepard, Margaret Sherry, Bart Smith, M.N. Thacker, Judy Tsou, Raymond van der Moortell, John Wagstaff, Brad Young, and last but not least, O.W. Neighbour, Hugh Cobbe, Malcolm Turner and the rest of the staff at the Music Library, the British Library.

My family and friends offered board and lodging during travels, and constant encouragement. Many thanks.

Acknowledgements for Plates

Photographs of title-pages were kindly supplied by the following libraries:

Austria	Vienna	Musiksammlung, Nationalbibliothek
France	Paris	Bibliothèque nationale
Germany	Hamburg	Staats- und Universitätsbibliothek
United Kingdom		
England	Cambridge	Fitzwilliam Museum
		Rowe Music Library, King's College
	Durham	Cathedral Library
	London	British Library
		Gresham College Collection, Guildhall Library
		Royal Academy of Music
		Royal College of Music
		Vaughan Williams Library, Cecil Sharp House
	Oxford	Bodleian Library
Scotland	Edinburgh	National Library of Scotland
		Reid Music Library, University of Edinburgh
	Glasgow	Euing Music Library, University of Glasgow
Wales	Cardiff	Cardiff Public Library
		University of Wales, College of Cardiff
United States of America		
California	Los Angeles	Clark Library, University of California, Los Angeles
	San Marino	Huntington Library
District of Columbia		
	Washington	Folger Shakespeare Library
		Library of Congress
Illinois	Chicago	Newberry Library
	Urbana	University of Illinois
Massachusetts	Boston	Boston Public Library
	Cambridge	Houghton Library, Harvard University
		Music Library, Harvard University
Michigan	Ann Arbor	University of Michigan
New York	New York	New York Public Library
	Rochester	Sibley Music Library, Eastman School of Music
Pennsylvania	Philadelphia	University of Pennsylvania

Introduction

This study provides detailed bibliographical descriptions of extant books of opera and other secular songs published in England between 1703 and 1726, and lists the first line of each song in those books together with information on composer, author, literary or stage work, and performer. Its pattern is Cyrus L. Day and Eleanore B. Murrie, *English Song-Books 1651-1702*, to which it forms a sequel.[1] The first-line index permits the identification and, consequently, the dating of the single songs and songs in binders' volumes that prove so troublesome to scholars and librarians. As the contents of a work can vary between issues, and copies vary within an issue, it is only by listing the contents of each issue and by examining as many copies as possible that we can establish what publishers actually published. 198 issues have been identified, and 2296 song first lines listed.

The first obligation of a bibliography is to provide all the information necessary to make unequivocal identification of each book described, through the presentation of that information in a standard form. Once that obligation is discharged, the information can be combined with other research to explore printing and publishing history. Elsewhere I have provided a fairly comprehensive picture of the publishing of secular vocal music during the early years of the eighteenth century.[2] Similarly, I have discussed the various techniques and materials used to print song books.[3] These books represent the first extended effort to issue entirely commercial printed versions of musical stage works and they are also the first song books to be printed by engraving on a systematic basis.[4] In another article I have considered the problems raised by the bibliographical descriptions in light of current norms of descriptive bibliography with a view to seeing how those norms both influence and are influenced by a type of material not frequently subject to standard description.[5] The bibliographical description of engraved material has considerable impact on several concepts of analytical bibliography, particularly 'ideal copy', 'composite books', and the terms of bibliographical classification.[6] Song books and their printing raise questions that assist our understanding of those terms and may lead to re-interpretation.[7]

---

[1] Cyrus L. Day and Eleanore B. Murrie, *English Song-Books 1651-1702* (London: Bibliographical Society, 1940).
[2] See David Hunter, 'The Publishing of Opera and Song Books in England, 1703-1726', *Notes* 47(3) (March 1991): 647-685.
[3] See David Hunter, 'The Printing of Opera and Song Books in England, 1703-1726', *Notes* 46(2) (December 1989): 328-351.
[4] See Richard Macnutt, 'Publishing', in *The New Grove Dictionary of Opera*, ed. Stanley Sadie (London: Macmillan, 1992), 3:1154-1166, for a fine survey of opera printing and publishing.
[5] See David Hunter, 'The Bibliographical Description of Opera and Song Books issued in England 1703-1726', *Papers of the Bibliographical Society of America* 83(3) (September 1989): 311–335.
[6] See David Hunter and N. Frederick Nash, 'Composite Books', *The Book Collector* 39(4) (Winter 1990): 504-528.
[7] Some specific cases are considered below.

DEFINITIONS

The scope of the study is dependent upon definition of the phrase 'opera and song books', consideration of existing bibliographical coverage, and the setting of chronological limits. The definition of 'song book' employed by Day and Murrie has been adopted: 'any publication containing the words and music of two or more secular songs. This definition embraces two rather different types of publication: (1) song-books proper, or books devoted exclusively to songs and vocal music; and (2) a number of miscellaneous works which would not ordinarily be called song-books, but which happen to contain the words and music of two or more secular songs'.[8] As the largest group of books, favourite songs from operas, falls in the second category, the words 'opera and' have been added to 'song books' to better indicate the scope. Place of publication is limited to England. Though there was music publishing in other parts of the British Isles (including Ireland) during the early eighteenth century no secular song books appear to have been published outside London from 1703 to 1726.[9] Songs were written by composers from several countries to words in French and Italian in addition to English.

As in Day and Murrie, five classes of material are excluded: '(1) manuscript music; (2) collections of songs which do not contain any music; (3) collections of song-tunes which do not contain any words; (4) collections of sacred songs [such as hymns or metrical psalms]; and (5) so-called single songs (i.e. songs, either engraved or type-set, printed on folio sheets or half-sheets, and separately published and sold)'.[10] Three more categories have been added to this list here: (6) bespoke books, tract or binders' volumes; in other words, volumes put together at the behest of a purchaser that lack a printed title-page or that have been assembled since the original time of publication; (7) odes and other academic exercises such as William Croft's *Musicus apparatus academicus*; and (8) playing cards, such as the sets published by Cluer and Creake.[11]

Day and Murrie rationalize their exclusions in quantitative terms; 'A separate volume would be required for the adequate treatment of each of these categories

---

[8] Day and Murrie, xi.
[9] Edinburgh's active cultural milieu included the publication of several books with the words of songs, such as Allan Ramsay's *Tea-Table Miscellany* vols. 1 (1723) and 2 (1725), a book of tunes, *Musick for Allan Ramsay's Collection of Scots Songs set by Alexr. Stuart* (1726), and Thomas Bruce, *The Common Tunes* (1726), which is chiefly a book of psalm tunes, though seven secular tunes are added at the end to illustrate different modes. See Thomas Crawford, *Society and the Lyric: A Study of the Song Culture of Eighteenth-Century Scotland* (Edinburgh: Scottish Academic Press, 1979), which includes a 'Select list of song books and miscellanies published in Scotland (1662-1786)'.
[10] Day and Murrie, xi.
[11] Examples of bespoke books are *Joyful Cuckoldom*, (British Library, K.5.b.15), and Francis Horton's *A Choice Collection of Songs by Several Masters 1704*, (British Library, K.7.i.2), and song collections at King's College, Cambridge (Rowe 110.22), Durham Cathedral (Mus. M.98), and St. Andrews University. Cluer and Creake described their 'New Musical Cards [as] a compleat Song on each Card. Compos'd by the most eminent Masters, the Words being engrav'd to the Musick, and the Songs entirely new. Price 3s. 6d. per Pack. Note, With these Cards you may play any Game, as well as you can with common Cards.' *Daily Post*, 28 December 1724.

[1-5 above]'.[12] While that remains partially true for the period 1703-1726, it is also the case that the practice of publishing changed, at least in relation to single songs. Five reasons suggest why the availability of single songs was de-emphasized during the period. First, the government made the sheets subject to stamp duty (introduced in 1712), thus limiting their profitability.[13] Second, songs gradually became longer, so that one would not fit on one side of a half sheet, even in the reduced form for voice, keyboard and flute. Third, composers, while unable to enjoy the full protection of the 1709/10 Copyright Act, were conscious of its helpful purpose; they had no desire to see whole works issued song by song, in unauthorized editions. Fourth, music sellers could not hope to organize and maintain huge stocks of single sheets. Fifth, for consumers who wished to acquire all of an opera's published songs, the purchase of a volume rather than individual sheets made economic and organizational sense. Publishers responded by producing collected volumes. From the bibliographical viewpoint there is little need to inventory collections of loose sheets because the phenomenon of separate publication became supplementary. All such collections examined as part of this study comprised sheets otherwise issued in volume form. This bibliography will enable scholars and librarians to identify the volumes to which the loose sheets pertain.[14]

One problem that Day and Murrie hardly had to face was the definition of song. Neither through-composed solo songs nor multi-voice choruses were frequently published in England before the advent of Italianate (i.e. all-sung) opera.[15] For the purposes of this study a song is defined as a 'free-standing' single musical work, with or without additional verses, comprising any number of vocal parts, with or without instrumental accompaniment. Written-out second and subsequent verses (i.e. through-composed songs) are as acceptable as strict strophic form. In one instance the definition leads to a somewhat arbitrary decision. Opera songs, whether arias or choruses, are included, while the aria-like portions of cantatas are not.[16] The published form of the works helps justify the decision. Opera songs were published as discrete items in volumes and, for a while, were available as single sheets. Cantatas were generally published with accompanying recitatives as whole works.[17]

[12] Day and Murrie, ibid.
[13] See Hunter, 'Publishing', 670-671, for details.
[14] For materials excluded from this bibliography, see pp. xv-xvii.
[15] J.R. Goodall, 'English Chamber Cantata and Through-Composed Solo Song 1660-c.1780' (D. Phil. diss., Oxford University, 1979), published in revised form as Richard Goodall, *Eighteenth-Century English Secular Cantatas*, Outstanding Dissertation in Music from British Universities (New York: Garland, 1989).
[16] For cantatas see Malcolm Boyd, 'English Secular Cantatas in the Eighteenth Century', *Music Review* 30(2) (May 1969): 85-97.
[17] The following books of cantatas have been excluded in their entirety:
J.C. Pepusch, *Six English Cantatas* [1710];   D. Purcell, *Six Cantatas* [1713];
J.E. Galliard, *Six English Cantatas* [1716];   G. Hayden, *Three Cantata* [1717];
J.C. Pepusch, *Six English Cantatas*, book two, [1720];   *Twelve Cantatas in English* [c.1720];
G. Bononcini, *Cantate e duetti* [1721];   A. Ariosti, [*Six Cantatas and Six Lessons*, 1724].
   Henry Carey's *Cantatas for a Voice with Accompanyment* is included in this study because it contains some songs. These only have been indexed.

Consideration of the existing bibliographical coverage suggested the need for a detailed and scholarly bibliography. Brief particulars of most of the items in the bibliography are to be found in the music union catalogues—*British Union-Catalogue of Early Music* and *Répertoire international des sources musicales*—and in the *National Union Catalog Pre-1956 Imprints*, but the descriptions are so limited that accurate identification of individual copies is often impossible.[18] The union catalogues of eighteenth-century materials exclude most music.[19] The books of Smith and Humphries on the publications of the firm of John Walsh, while providing a useful checklist, do not concern themselves with detailed listing of contents, nor do they provide unambiguous bibliographical descriptions.[20] Not all song books were published by Walsh's firm but among those that were, greater variety has been found than Smith and Humphries indicate. Copies of some works that they knew of only from advertisements have been uncovered and new information is available for dating. Revision and expansion of their work is therefore appropriate. David Foxon's monumental bibliography, *English Verse 1701-1750*, does not cover song books with music.[21] Lowell Lindgren's dissertation on the music of the brothers Bononcini bases its bibliographical descriptions on the work of Smith and Humphries.[22] Thus, while the achievements of prior scholars are admirable within their terms of reference, these terms are no longer adequate.

The starting point for the study was fixed by the conclusion of Day and Murrie's work at 1702. As the authors point out, the year in which Henry Playford published the second volume of Henry Purcell's *Orpheus Britannicus* marked the end of an era, for 'although [Playford] did not retire from business until 1707, his subsequent publications were merely new editions of earlier books'.[23] Walsh was establishing himself as the most prolific London publisher at this time. He employed engraving rather than type-setting and thus his books (and those of other music publishers

[18] *British Union-Catalogue of Early Music*, ed. Edith Schnapper (London: Butterworth, 1957).

Répertoire international des sources musicales, Series A/I, Einzeldrucke vor 1800 (Kassel: Bärenreiter, 1971-); Series B/II, Recueils imprimés XVIIIe siècle (München-Duisburg: G. Henle Verlag, 1964).

National Union Catalog Pre-1956 Imprints, 754 vols. (London: Mansell, 1968-81).

[19] *Eighteenth-Century British Books: An Author Union Catalogue*, 5 vols. (Folkestone: Dawson, 1981).

Eighteenth-century Short Title Catalogue, online file, available in the U.S.A. and Canada on RLIN and in the U.K. on BLAISE-LINE.

[20] William C. Smith, *A Bibliography of the Musical Works Published by John Walsh During the Years 1695-1720* (London: Bibliographical Society, 1948; 2d ed., 1968), and William C. Smith and Charles Humphries, *A Bibliography of the Musical Works Published by the Firm of John Walsh During the Years 1721-1766* (London: Bibliographical Society, 1968), cited hereafter as Walsh i and Walsh ii.

[21] David Foxon, *English Verse 1701-1750*, 2 vols. (London: Cambridge University Press, 1975), 1:xiii.

[22] Lowell Lindgren, 'A Bibliographic Scrutiny of Dramatic Works Set by Giovanni and his brother Antonia Maria Bononcini' (Ph.D. diss., Harvard University, 1972).

[23] Day and Murrie, xii.

who followed the trend) were made very differently and look quite different from the majority of those of the preceding era. In musical terms, the Italian influence was increasing.

The final terminus of 1726 anticipates the inception of English ballad operas, beginning with *The Beggar's Opera* in 1728. Ballad opera publications exist in so many copies, display such complex bibliographical problems and have a bibliographical form so different from the other song books of the period that they deserve separate study.[24] The date also takes cognizance of the advertising battle in 1725-26 between Cluer and Creake, publishers of *A Pocket Companion*, and Peter Fraser, whose *The Delightful Musical Companion* appeared in January 1726. It seemed only reasonable that both books be represented. Thirdly, Walsh was involved in a legal case concerning stamp duty in 1726.[25] This, and other factors, seems to have lessened his hold on the market during the mid-1720s. Fourthly, 1726 saw the premiere of the highly popular afterpiece *Apollo and Daphne* and a revival of *Camilla*. Such events suggested the end of 1726 as the appropriate chronological terminus.

One further consideration has a bearing on the question of scope. Whenever possible duplication of scholarly effort has been avoided. Thus publications consisting solely of works by Handel have been excluded from the bibliography. (See Table I.) The publications as publications differ little from those of other composers. They have been examined by Deutsch, Smith, Dean and Knapp, and by the editors of the *Hallische Händel-Ausgabe*.[26] They have been listed in the *Händel-Handbuch*.[27] The song first lines were listed by A. Craig Bell.[28] Handel songs found in general collections or pasticcios are included in the present study.

Secondly, the books published from 1703 to 1726 that are listed in Day and Murrie are excluded. (See Table II.) These comprise editions of books first published 1651-1702 and were all printed letterpress. Thirdly, the periodical *The Monthly Mask of Vocal Music*, published by John Walsh from November 1702 to September 1711 and intermittently from July 1717 to September 1727, has been excluded because it is to be republished in facsimile in the series 'Music for London Entertainment', with a detailed introduction and index by Olive Baldwin

---

[24] See, for example, James Sutherland, '*Polly* among the Pirates', *Modern Language Review* 37 (July 1942): 291-303. Yvonne Noble is working on the editions of *The Beggar's Opera*.

[25] William C. Smith, "New Evidence Concerning John Walsh and the Duties on Paper, 1726", *Harvard Library Bulletin* 6(2) (Spring 1952): 252-5.

[26] Otto E. Deutsch, *Handel: a Documentary Biography* (New York: Norton, 1955).

William C. Smith, *Handel: a Descriptive Catalogue of the Early Editions* (London: Cassell, 1960; 2d ed., Oxford: Blackwell, 1970).

Winton Dean and J. Merrill Knapp, *Handel's Operas 1704-1726* (Oxford: Clarendon Press, 1987).

Hallische Händel-Ausgabe (Kassel: Bärenreiter, 1957-).

[27] *Händel-Handbuch*, 5 vols. (Kassel: Bärenreiter, 1978-). For a summary listing of Handel's works see Bernd Baselt, *Verzeichnis der Werke Georg Friedrich Händels (HWV)* (Leipzig: Deutscher Verlag für Musik, 1986).

[28] A. Craig Bell, *Handel: Chronological Thematic Catalogue* (Darley, Yorkshire: Grian-Aig Press, 1972).

TABLE I

Publications Issued 1711-26 Comprising Secular Vocal Music Solely by Handel

		Publishers			
Year	Title	Walsh	Meares	Cluer & Creake	Musick Shops
1711	Rinaldo	e			
1720	Radamisto		e A		
1722	Floridant	e A	e		
	Additional Songs in Floridant	e A	e		
	Acis and Galatea	e			
1723	Flavius	e A	e		
	Otho	e A	e		
	Additional Songs in Otho	e		e A	e
1724	Julius Caesar			e A	e e
	Tamerlane			e A	e e
1725	Rodelinda			e A	e
1726	Alexander			e A	e e
	Scipio				
	Apollo's Feast, vol. 1	e			

e = Published and extant.
e e = Two editions extant.
A = Authorized (i.e., published expressly by/for Handel).
Some Musick Shops' editions can be identified as having been issued by Walsh or Cooke.

TABLE II

Books Published 1703-26 that are Listed in Day and Murrie, *English Song-Books*

The Compleat French Master, [1703], 1707, 1710, [1713], 1717, 1721, [1725].
An Introduction to the Skill of Musick, 1703, 1706, 1713, 1718, 1724.
Orpheus Britannicus, printed by William Pearson, 1706, 1711, 1712, 1721.
Pleasant Musical Companion, 1703, 1707, 1709, 1720, [1722], 1724, 1726.
Songs Compleat, Pleasant and Divertive, 1719.
Wit and Mirth, or, Pills to Purge Melancholy, 1705, 1706, 1707, 1709, 1712, 1714, 1719, 1720.

and Thelma Wilson.[29] The complex overlap between the *Monthly Mask* and other Walsh publications needs a brief summary. Some songs first published in the *Monthly Mask* appeared subsequently as parts of other works. Occasionally the opposite is to be found: songs first published elsewhere were included in the *Monthly Mask*. In some cases it is impossible to tell which came first. For example, Walsh sold favourite songs from *Elisa* and from *Calphurnia* in volume form as independent publications and as issues of the *Monthly Mask*. Such *Monthly Mask* issues have been excluded from the bibliography.

Also excluded are books for which no contemporary copies exist, but which can be posited from advertisements.[30] Subsequent editions are not used to create a description of an earlier edition. For example, copies of the ca. 1733 edition of Walsh's *Catch Club* exist but none are known for the ca. 1725 edition.[31] Twelve books were identified from catalogues as warranting inclusion but further research showed that they did not meet the criteria.[32]

[29] *The Monthly Mask of Vocal Music 1702-1711*, ed. Olive Baldwin and Thelma Wilson (London: Stainer and Bell, forthcoming).

[30] Walsh's advertisements and catalogues list editions of Dr. Blow's 'Songs' (1720), Eccles's 'Birthday Songs' (1716), Carey's 'Songs' (1720), and the 'Catch Club' (1725). Other missing books are William Richardson's 'A Collection of Songs' listed in Cullen's edition of *Camilla* (1707); Pippard's edition of G. Hayden, 'Six New Songs', advertised in the *Guardian*, 20 June 1713, and issues of W. Smith's 'Quarterly Collection of Songs' advertised in the *Evening Post*, 25 July 1721, and the *Post Boy*, 9 December 1721.

The Musick Shops' edition of *Darius*, 1725, (161), probably published by Walsh, lists fourteen titles, including works by Handel, not known to exist now in Musick Shop editions: 'Flavius', 'Otho', 'Additional Songs in Otho', 'Floridant', 'Additional Songs in Floridant', 'Acis and Galatea', 'Muzio Scaevola', 'Aquilio', 'Calphurnia', 'Vespasian', 'Pharnaces', 'Cyrus', 'Griselda', and 'Crispus'. As all these titles were published by Walsh from 1721-24 it seems unlikely that Musick Shops' editions were ever issued.

[31] See Walsh ii, nos. 338-39.

[32] Books deliberately excluded (published in London, unless noted otherwise) with the reason for their exclusion, arranged chronologically by actual or revised publication date:

A Collection of New Songs Sett by Several Masters. Thomas Shephard, 17--? Copy at Bibliothèque nationale, Paris. Shephard was in operation ca. 1686-96.

Purcell, H. *A Collection of the Most Celebrated Songs and Dialogues*. R. Meares, ca. 1705. Contains songs from *Orpheus Britannicus* book 1 (1698) and book 2 (1702), in editions engraved by Thomas Cross. I suggest 1702?, pending more research on the firm of Meares.

Apollo's Feast. H. Playford, 1703. Words only.

Ramsay, Allan. *The Gentle Shepherd*. Edinburgh: Thomas Ruddiman, 1725. Words only.

Galliard, J. *The Rape of Proserpine*. Rawlins, 1723? The 'new entertainment' opened in 1727.

A Collection of Songs with a Through Bass. Walsh, ca. 1715. Actually published 1727 or later, as volume contains songs from *Admetus*, (1727).

Leveridge, Richard. *A Collection of Songs*. Walsh, ca. 1723/25. Actually published in 1728.

Mottley, John. *Penelope*. Green and Davis, 1718. Date misprinted; should read 1728.

A Collection of Songs on Various Subjects. William Smith, 1720. On the only copy, at the British Library, the date is slightly mutilated, but it is probably 1729.

The Merry Musician. Wright, 1720? Copy at Duke University, Durham, North Carolina. Contains song from *Hurlothrumbo*, first performed in 1729.

Vanbrugh, G. *Mirth and Harmony*. Walsh, 1715? Dated 1730 by William C. Smith, on basis of a newspaper advertisement.

[Drinking Songs. Walsh, undated.] Copy at British Library (H.1610). Probably dates from ca. 1750.

Though Lindgren titled his dissertation 'A Bibliographic Scrutiny', his purpose was to show the development of the Bononcini brothers' works rather than to examine the publishing record of a particular time and place. Lindgren combined very brief bibliographical descriptions of the Bononcinis' publications and manuscripts with a first-line index to all the arias of all the versions from all of Europe. The emphasis here is rather the opposite—to indicate a publishing record and not, directly, the history of works—and thus requires extensive bibliographical descriptions with a listing of the first lines of all the songs by any composer published in England from 1703 to 1726.

One result of studying these books as physical objects is that I do not trace the origins of the texts. Scholars interested in this aspect of musical works, such as Lindgren and Reinhard Strohm, have already uncovered the sources for the words and music. I have not reproduced or reexamined their analyses.[33]

The limits of a study—whether chronological, geographical or linguistic, by subject, genre or species, by medium, material or form—can produce what may seem to be an unnecessarily artificial set of ideas or things, a set so circumscribed that observations of broader significance cannot be made. One danger is that the delimited set lacks cohesion in itself. Song books provide good counters to this criticism, from both the musical and the bibliographical aspects. Secular vocal music obviously is differentiated from its sacred counterpart by the origin and import of the texts and by the purpose of the compositions. Less obvious is the effect of adaptation of opera songs for publication. Apart from demotic music such as catches and rounds, the most common form of secular vocal music was settings for voice, keyboard, and recorder (and later flute). Opera songs, as originally written for the stage, had accompaniments for strings, woodwinds, and brass. Adaptation for domestic use made them indistinguishable from non-operatic solo song.

Bibliographically, the majority of song books of the early eighteenth century are differentiated by their upright shape and size ('folio') from the generally oblong format of instrumental music, and the smaller format of sacred music, though there are exceptions in all categories. The minority of song books, chiefly the reissued letterpress ones first published before 1703, retained their conventional size, usually octavo. The so-called single sheet song, usually a half-sheet printed on one side, was recognized in the 1690s as the typical bibliographical form for secular vocal music.[34] Originally conceived as a genuine single sheet, like the letterpress ballad, the half sheets were soon incorporated in volumes, then issued simultaneously in volume and sheet form, and then issued only in volume

---

[33] See Lowell Lindgren, 'A Bibliographic Scrutiny'; 'Ariosti's London Years, 1716-29', *Music & Letters* 62(3-4) (July-October 1981): 331-351; 'The Accomplishments of the Learned and Ingenious Nicola Francesco Haym (1678-1729)', *Studi Musicali* 16(2) (1987): 247-380; 'Venice, Vivaldi, Vico and Opera in London, 1705-17: Venician Ingredients in English Pasticci', in *Nuovi Studi Vivaldiani*, ed. Antonio Fanna and Giovanni Morelli, 2 vols. (Firenze: Olschki, 1988), 2:633-666; and Reinhard Strohm, *Italienische Opernarien des frühen Settecento (1720-1730)*, 2 vols. *Analecta Musicologica*, 16 (Köln: Arno Volk, 1976).

[34] For exploration of this aspect of bibliographical form see Donald W. Krummel, 'Musical Functions and Bibliographical Forms', *The Library* 5 ser., 31(4) (December 1976): 327-350.

form. Not until 1724, when Cluer and Creake issued the first of their 'new method' books—which eschewed one song per page and 'folio' orientation—did engraved song books become more like the pocket-sized letterpress ones. Song books display a surprisingly high degree of musical and bibliographical cohesion and thus their delimitation is less artificial than might be expected.

In short, this study is an examination of opera and other secular song books published in England from 1703 to 1726, excluding those books that have been studied in detail elsewhere, namely, editions of works first published before 1703, works of Handel and the *Monthly Mask*. It provides a sequel to Day and Murrie and constitutes a detailed bibliographical analysis of a distinctive publishing medium, early eighteenth-century English engraved music.

METHOD

A preliminary list of song books published between 1703 and 1730—including the works of Handel—and the location of current copies was drawn up from examination of the Harding Collection in the Bodleian Library, Oxford, from a reading of the Walsh bibliographies and the *British Union-Catalogue of Early Music*, and through consultation of *NUC* and *RISM*.[35] Once the scope had been narrowed chronologically to the end of 1726, and books containing solely the works of Handel excluded, the catalogues of particular collections were consulted, most notably those of the British Library, St. Andrews University Library, the Newberry Library, Durham Cathedral, and the Huntington Library.[36] Further information on books suitable for inclusion was gained from a reading of newspapers published 1720-1726 and from Michael Tilmouth's 'Calendar'.[37]

---

[35] The Harding Collection, Bodleian Library, Oxford, is being included in the supplementary volumes of *RISM*, Series A/I. Part of the Collection previously belonged to Sir John Stainer, who had a catalogue compiled that was published as *Catalogue of English Song Books* (London: Novello, Ewer, 1891; republished Boston, MA: Longwood Press, 1978).

[36] *Catalogue of Printed Music in the British Library to 1980*, 62 vols. (London: Saur, 1981-87).

Cedric T. Davie, *Catalogue of the Finzi Collection in the St. Andrews University Library* (St. Andrews: St. Andrews University Library, 1982).

Donald W. Krummel, *Bibliographical Inventory to the Early Music in the Newberry Library* (Boston, MA: G.K. Hall, 1977).

R. Alec Harman, *A Catalogue of the Printed Music and Books on Music in Durham Cathedral Library* (London: Oxford University Press, 1968).

Edythe N. Backus, *Catalogue of Music in the Huntington Library Printed before 1801* (San Marino, CA: Huntington Library, 1949).

[37] The newspapers were read from microfilms in the series *Early English Newspapers 1660-1800* (Woodbridge, CT: Research Publications Inc., 1978-83). Titles consulted, with years of pertinent coverage in the microfilm series, were:

British Journal 1722-26; *Daily Courant* 1720-26; *Daily Journal* 1721-26;
Daily Post 1720-26; *Evening Post* 1720-26; *London Journal* 1725-26;
Mist's Weekly Journal 1720-26; *Original Weekly Journal* 1720; *Parker's Penny Post* 1725;
Post Boy 1720-23; *Post Man* 1720; *Weekly Journal* 1720-26.

Michael Tilmouth, 'A Calendar of References to Music in Newspapers published in London and the Provinces (1660-1719)', *Royal Musical Association Research Chronicle* 1 (1961), reprinted with amendments in 1968; and 2 (1962), reprinted in 1975.

The *Monthly Catalogue* was also read for references to song books.[38] In addition, private collectors and a dealer permitted copies in their possession to be examined. Two libraries not listed in the standard union catalogues were visited, the National Maritime Museum, Greenwich, and the Britten-Pears Library, Aldeburgh. One library listed in the *British Union-Catalogue of Early Music* and *RISM*, at St. Michael's College, Tenbury, is now at the Bodleian Library, Oxford, though some items have been sold. Some of the materials now at the Bodleian or the Faculty of Music Library may have come from the Oxford University Music Club, though no copies within scope from the Music Club were reported in the *British Union-Catalogue of Early Music*. The rare music at Cardiff Public Library, has been transferred to the University of Wales, College of Cardiff. Ten years ago a search of the international bibliographic utilities such as OCLC (Online Computer Library Center) and RLIN (Research Libraries Information Network) would not have revealed many copies due to the lack of conversion of existing manual or local system records and the low priority given to cataloguing antiquarian printed music. Retrospective conversion projects and the cataloguing of new acquisitions or backlogs have brought improvements, for a search in 1993 allowed me to identify 14 copies of which I was previously unaware. Continuing bibliographical labour on behalf of *RISM* has recently uncovered a cache of eighteenth-century printed and manuscript scores at the Benedictine Abbey of Maredsous, Denée, Belgium, yielding six additional copies.[39]

For biographical and other information the following sources have proved of particular utility: *The London Stage*, Humphries and Smith's *Music Publishing*, *A Biographical Dictionary of Actors*, *The New Grove Dictionary of Music and Musicians*, Donovan Dawe's *Organists of the City of London*, and *The New Grove Dictionary of Opera*.[40]

A summary of the distribution of copies is displayed in Table III, which is arranged by the number of copies actually found in collections and not on reports, except in the case of libraries not visited. On occasion the report of a copy in a union catalogue was found to be groundless. The corollary was also true; libraries often contained copies not reported. Three copies were sold or missing and presumed lost. All collections with eight or more copies were visited, and, whenever possible, those collections with only 1-7 copies in convenient locations, such as in a city with

[38] *The Monthly Catalogue*, 1714-1717, 1723-1730, ed. David Foxon (London: Gregg-Archive, 1964).

[39] Marie Cornaz, 'Le fonds musique ancienne de l'abbaye de Maredsous', *Fontes Artis Musicae* 42(3) (July-September 1995): 246-270.

[40] *The London Stage, 1700-1729*, ed. Emmett L. Avery, 2 vols. (Carbondale: Southern Illinois University Press, 1960).

Charles Humphries and William C. Smith, *Music Publishing in the British Isles* (London: Cassell, 1954; 2d ed., Oxford: Blackwell, 1970).

A Biographical Dictionary of Actors, Actresses, Musicians, Dancers, Managers and Other Stage Personnel in London, 1660-1800, 16 vols. (Carbondale: Southern Illinois University Press, 1973-93).

The New Grove Dictionary of Music and Musicians, ed. Stanley Sadie, 20 vols. (London: Macmillan, 1980).

Donovan Dawe, *Organists of the City of London 1660-1850* (Padstow: Donovan Dawe, 1983).

TABLE III

Summary of Library Collections and Copies

Table IIIa—Libraries Visited

Library Codes[1]	Copies Examined		Copies Unexamined					
	In Scope	Out of Scope[2]	Part of *MMVM*[3]	Frag-ment[4]	Probably In Scope[5]	Lost	Sold	False Reports[6]
Lbl	115							
Ob + Obh + Obt	64	1		1	6			2
Ckc	61							
Lcm	44	3						
F-Pn + F-Pc	35		1					
CLU-C	32	1						
DLC	31	5			1			
NN	26	1						
CSfst	24							
DFo	23							1
En	22	1						
TWm	22			1				
Mp	20							1
D-Hs	19		1					
ICN	17							
Lam	16	1	1					1
NjP	16	1						1
CU-MUSI	15	1						
CaOLU	14							
NRU-Mus	14							
CDp	13							
MB	13							
Lgc	11							
MiU	11			1				1
B-Bc	10							2
Cfm	10							
CSt	10							
Ge	10	1						
A-Wn + A-Wn-h	9		1		1			
MH-H + MH-Mu	9	1			1			
BWbw	8							
B-Br	7							
CtY + CtY-Mus	7				1			1
DRc	7		1	1				
WaU	7							
Er	6							
NL-DHgm	6							
Coke	5	1			1			
CSmH	5							
Eu	5							
ICU	5							
NIC	5							
ALb	4		1					
Gu	4							

	In Scope	Out of Scope[2]	Part of MMVM[3]	Fragment[4]	Probably In Scope[5]	Lost	Sold	False Reports[6]
IU	4							
Gm	3							
HAdolmetsch	3							
Lsc	3							
LVp	3							
Ouf	3							
Bu	2							
Cpl	2							
LEp	2							
PU	2							1
TxDN	2							
TxU	2							
Bp	1				2			
CaOHM	1							1
Cpc	1							
Ctc	1							
Cu	1							
DK-Kk	1							
DU	1							2
INS[7]	1							
Lcml	1							
Lcs	1	1						
MiD	1							
MnU	1							
NcU[7]	1							
NPV	1							
P	1							
DCU[7]	0	1						
Lco	0						1	
OClW	0							1
Ooc	0	1						
ViWC[7]	0			1				
Totals 76	863	21	6	3	13	2	1	15

Notes to Table III

[1] For library codes see pp. xxxvii-xliii. Separate collections at a single institution are combined for Table IIIa (A-Wn and A-Wn-h, CtY and CtY-Mus, F-Pc and F-Pn, MH-H and MH-Mu, Ob and Obh and Obt).

[2] Out of scope includes editions or issues published after 1726 and manuscript copies wrongly identified in the union catalogues (*RISM*, *NUC*). Such copies are listed in the Notes of pertinent entries and in the Libraries index in parentheses.

[3] Issues of the *Monthly Mask of Vocal Music* are out of scope. Copies are listed in the Notes of pertinent entries and in the Libraries index in parentheses.

[4] Fragments and single sheets are out of scope. The difference between an incomplete copy and a fragment is one of degree. Books or folders with less than a third of the songs from the same bibliographical entity are regarded as fragmentary. Three such copies are listed in the Notes of pertinent entries and in the Libraries index in parentheses.

[5] These copies were not examined due to lack of time or to oversight.

[6] Bibliographic ghosts bedevil large union catalogue projects. Some errors are corrected silently.

[7] A single item was examined by librarians on my behalf at each of these four locations.

Table IIIb—Libraries Not Visited

Library Codes	Copies Reported	Collections	Copies Unexamined
I-Rsc, S-Skma	7	2	14
B-MAR, D-B	6	2	12
SA	5	1	5
I-BGi, RF-Mrg	4	2	8
H-Bn, J-Tn	3	2	6
CZ-Pu, I-MOe, InU, MBMH	2	4	8
CaBVaU, D-BMs, D-DL, D-Gs, D-Mbs, D-SWl, FMU, I-Gi(l), I-Vc, IaU, MdBPC, NcD, Omc, OU, PSt, TU	1	16	16
Totals		29	69

another, larger collection.[41] With copies reported or uncovered at 105 collections widely dispersed on three continents and travel funds being limited it was not possible to examine all copies.[42] Nevertheless, of a total of 945 copies definitely or probably in scope, 863 were examined (91.3%) and these form the basis of the ideal copy descriptions.[43] Thirty copies were examined and excluded due to their being out of scope, part of the *Monthly Mask of Vocal Music*, or fragmentary. Copies of thirty books not part of the study were also seen. Microfilm was not an acceptable substitute for personal inspection as it could not yield all the information necessary for such a study.[44]

Each copy was examined in person and the information gleaned was noted on specially designed large cards. Two databases, one for bibliographical information and one for song first lines, were constructed using R:base System V. R:base was used to compile the indexes. The introduction, descriptions and indexes were edited using WordPerfect 5.0. The book was typeset using the text supplied by the author on diskettes.

[41] For information on the origins and contents of some of the collections visited see *Handel Collections and their History*, ed. Terence Best (Oxford: Clarendon Press, 1993), and Richard G. King, 'The *Fonds Schoelcher*: history and Contents', *Notes* 53(3) (March 1997): 697–721.

[42] I would be grateful if any librarian, collector or dealer with copies not noted in the Libraries index could contact me at the Fine Arts Library, University of Texas at Austin, P.O. Box P, Austin, TX 78713-8916, U.S.A.

[43] The 82 unexamined copies definitely or probably in scope are likely to yield an additional 6-10 entries. See David Shaw, 'A Sampling Theory for Bibliographical Research', *The Library* 5th ser., 27(4) (December 1972): 310-19, for an important aspect of bibliographical work, the ramifications of which have yet to be fully explored.

[44] For astute commentary on the inefficacy of microfilm for bibliographical research see G. Thomas Tanselle, 'Reproduction and Scholarship', *Studies in Bibliography* 42 (1989): 25-54.

BIBLIOGRAPHICAL DESCRIPTION

Bibliographers of music, with a few exceptions, have imagined that because engraved and lithographed material is not frequently described by bibliographers of conventional letterpress material, they are exempted from utilizing the standard techniques of bibliographical description and the concepts of analytical bibliography. One purpose of this bibliography is to demonstrate that those techniques and concepts are applicable to non-letterpress material. Admittedly the special features of engraved opera and song books have required the development of some new descriptive techniques, but this has been done within the context of standard descriptive principles. The basic analytical concepts of ideal copy, composite books, and bibliographical classification have all been tested and have been found to apply. Indeed, this study has extended their use and bibliographers' understanding of them. The following sections discuss the arrangement of the bibliography and the parts of the descriptions in light of the detail found in the books examined, the concepts of analytical bibliography, and the modifications of standard bibliographical technique.[45]

Arrangement of the Bibliography

Chronological arrangement of the bibliographical descriptions highlights the historical development. While very few song books have the year of publication on them, accurate chronological arrangement is not so difficult to achieve as advertisements and other sources establish day, month and year of possible first publication. Books for which such accurate dates are known are listed at those dates. The dates of newspapers and other sources are accurate on their own terms, but they may misrepresent the actual date of publication, for reasons such as the failure of the publisher to have copies available on the stated day, or the fact that complete runs of newspapers have not survived and therefore we may be lacking issues with appropriate advertisements. 'Undated' books—'undated' in this context meaning that the day and month of issue cannot be established—are gathered together at the end of the appropriate year, and are sub-arranged alphabetically by short title. There are five exceptions to this.

First, any undated issues of an edition are listed immediately following its datable issue. One effect of this exception is to bring copies reissued by independent sellers adjacent with the original issue, when appropriate. Without it, related issues would be scattered unnecessarily. In some cases, when the sellers are known not to have been in business in the year of original issue, the reissue has been dated at a later year. In cases when the year of issue is unknown but the imprint suggests a span of possible dates, the book is listed under the earliest year.

Second, monthly publications are usually listed under the last day of their month. Included at the same date are editions of a musical work from different

---

[45] For the application of relatively unmodified descriptive techniques to this material see *Studies in Music* 4 (1979). The first three issues (pp. 1-487) comprise a catalogue of the collection of opera materials 1600-1750 now in the Music Library at the University of Western Ontario, London, Canada. These descriptions can be compared with those in this book to judge the efficacy of the techniques used here for the first time.

publishers (see *Necromancer*, 135a, 135b, 135c), and re-issues of the same work (see *Jupiter and Europa* 127a and 127b). Two modifications of this exception are the *Monthly Apollo* (146) and *Monthly Collection* (173), where in both cases three months' issues are listed together at the latest date.

Third, *A Collection of the Choicest Songs & Dialogues* (5) has all copies listed at the earliest known date, despite the widely differing contents and some evidence for other dates. Copies of this book seem to have been issued on demand for an extended period. The complexity of the book in terms of its origin (publishers' intention), contents and publishing history, and the lack of accurate dates of issue for most copies make the single entry the practical solution.

Fourth, copies that represent intermediate stages of completion, such as those with partial pagination, are assigned an inferred date (see 19, 33a, 40a) even though not all copies listed are identical.

Fifth, in the case of *Pyrrhus and Demetrius*, issued by Walsh in 1709, all examined copies have the altered title-page with the text 'also he hath made words to 17 [*recte* 27] of ye Italian songs', but not all the copies have the Italian words. On 20 January Walsh advertised the title as available but without mentioning the Italian words, so copies lacking Italian words are assigned that date (48a, 48b). Walsh advertised on 9 February the 'second edition', one having Italian words (49-52).

Each entry has been allocated a unique number in a single series based on the chronological arrangement. The original sequence of 180 numbers established in my dissertation (January 1989) has had to be modified in light of subsequent research for a net gain of 18 entries. These entries have been incorporated into existing entries and the first number vacated: 17→15, 27→26, 28→29, 39→38, 48→22, 61→177, 165→164. These entries have been moved to new numbers and the first number vacated: 36→33a, 60→78a, 66→76a, 67→76a, 131→55a, 132→127a, 133→127b, 154→135a, 155→135b, 156→135c. These entries have been added: 12a, 21a, 22a, 24a, 32a, 34a, 40a, 43a, 44a, 47a, 48a, 48b, 74a, 75a, 78b, 79a, 79b, 80a, 90a, 90b, 114a, 114b, 126a, 145a, 178a. The additions are indicated by letter suffix. The use of the number plus suffix need not reflect a direct relationship with the entry identified only by the number. One hundred and twenty-six copies have been examined since 1988 thus indicating that evidence from relatively few additional copies (an increase of 17% beyond the initial 737 copies seen) can produce significant alterations.

The degressive principle has been applied to the display of information.[46] Second and subsequent issues of a work from the same publisher and reissues by different publishers generally do not receive the full level of description accorded to the first issue. The kinds of detail omitted include title-page photograph, plate sizes, and song information.

The standard definitions of the hierarchy of bibliographical classification—

[46] For a summary of the literature on the degressive principle see Donald W. Krummel, *Bibliographies: their Aims and Methods* (London: Mansell, 1984): 63-64, and for the principle's application see G. Thomas Tanselle, 'The Arrangement of Descriptive Bibliographies', *Studies in Bibliography* 37 (1984): 1-38.

edition, impression, issue, state—have been applied. The most pertinent standard criteria used here are:

edition   different engraving of work

impression (printing)   (usually not possible to distinguish from edition or issue, but see below)

issue   imprint differs either by change of title-page or through application of new seller's label

state   minor textual differences such as the addition of dynamic markings or bass figures.

The following additional criteria have been isolated as part of this study:

edition   partial publication (e.g., the first act of an opera)

impression (printing)

    one or both sides of each leaf printed

    use of modified passe-partout title-page for several works

issue

    lack of all or most pagination

    addition of Italian translation

state

    variant leaf order (typically reversal)

    lack of page numbers on fewer than half the pages.

With a very few exceptions each entry represents a single issue. On occasion issue is coterminous with edition and impression. No attempt has been made to establish all differences of state for every issue, primarily because such differences do not alter the classification. Scholars interested in particular texts now have access to an organized body of musical literature, have information on the whereabouts of most copies, and can themselves pursue the detail of minor textual differences.

In a few cases an entry knowingly presents more than a single issue; for example, 5 *A Collection of the Choicest Songs & Dialogues*, 19 *Camilla*, 146 *Monthly Apollo*, and 173 *Monthly Collection*. The reasons vary according to the specific situation. Even though the copies listed in entries 5 and 19 differ considerably (in contents and pagination, respectively), treating them individually would scatter them, which seems foolish as we lack any means of dating them more accurately. Entries 146 and 173 each provide details of three monthly issues of short-lived periodicals. In each case the pragmatic solution of the single entry both eases searching and points to the evident problems.

Other examples of the difficulties of bibliographical classification and therefore of proper chronological placement are numerous but have been resolved. *Rosamond*, published by Walsh, is one. Entry 37 comprises the first collection (act) only. In the single copy extant there is an appropriately short contents page, and the pages themselves are numbered. Entry 38 comprises the complete work (as published), the list of contents is long, but of 19 copies, 9 are lacking pagination on pages 3-18. Does this group constitute a separate impression or state? One copy (of two known) of a later issue, 81, also lacks the pagination of pages 3-18. In these cases, with fewer than half the pages affected, the decision was made not to create a separate entry for the sets of copies partially lacking pagination. In contrast, see entries 55 and 55a, where two copies of *Jovial Companions* entirely lack pagination (55). As this difference applies to the whole book and not just a portion, separate entries were created. Three cases illustrate the difficulties caused by incomplete pagination. In entry 19 a variety of incomplete and incompletely paginated copies of *Camilla* are brought together. The copies suggest Walsh was caught by demanding customers in the midst of production. Entry 33a comprises the almost identical situation with the Cullen edition of *Camilla*. Entry 40a is the same situation with two copies of the Cullen edition of *Thomyris*. The dates on these three entries are estimates and there is less assurance than usual that the dates apply to all copies.

Another problematic case is Morley and Isum's *A Collection of New Songs*, 'Printed for the Authors' themselves (24 and 24a). Two copies lack the imprint and the engraver's name on the title-page. Is this a difference of impression, issue or state? If it is a difference of impression or issue a separate entry is required; if it is a difference of state then no separate entry is required. Without going into a lengthy argument, we can see that as the plate must have been taken from the press for some time in order for the imprint and Cross's name to be engraved on it, the difference is one of impression. The lack of an imprint also constitutes a difference of issue. Though separate records have been created for these impressions, they are given the same date of publication as there is no way at present of determining whether it was the impression with or without imprint that was made available on 1 August 1706 (see advertisement in the *London Gazette*).

Does the lack of the overture from some copies constitute a different issue? One example is *Camilla*, 22 and 22a. Ten copies of 16 examined lack the overture. Three copies remain unexamined. Admittedly, in two of the copies lacking the overture, the entire preliminary leaves are missing. Nonetheless, the sheer number of copies without the overture suggests a deliberate attempt by Walsh to make distinct issues. But even if we disregard producer intention, the bibliographer's responsibility to report the physical evidence would require two entries as the contents of the two groups of copies differ. While the quantity of evidence is less in other cases (21, 21a, 34, 34a, 44, 44a, 48a, 48b) the same reasoning has been applied. Similarly, the presence or absence of a dedication leaf in *Temple of Love* (32, 32a) has led to the creation of two entries.

Contrast the above cases of the presence or absence of internal pages with that of illustrated title-pages. As these most decorative of pages were placed at the beginning of copies, their absence may be as attributable to wear and tear as deliberate omission by the publisher. Thus their absence is copy-specific rather than issue-specific. On the other hand, when in some copies of a book the only title-page is the illustrated title-page then we have a case of separate issue and I have made two entries (see *Arsinoe*, 26 and 29).

Lastly, we have a curious situation in which the words 'The Additionall' have been engraved on a passe-partout title-page for a legitimately additional collection of songs (74) issued in January 1711 but the title-page is subsequently used for impressions of other works that do not comprise additional songs, sometimes with the words partially, almost entirely or completely not printed (which was achieved by not inking that part of the plate, or by covering it over), or obscured with a plain paper paste-over (74a, 76a, 77, 78, 78a, 78b, 79, 79a, 79b, 80, 80a, 91, 93). Is impression the correct classification for these copies? The fact that a different printing of the title-page is used distinguishes one group of copies from another and is the strongest factor in favour of impression. While time is a possible differentiating factor for issues, in this instance such a significant delay is indicated—a year or more—that it suggests reprinting of the whole work. That the altered title-page was only used for reprints after January 1711 can be demonstrated by:

1) the existence of three works first published 1709-10 in a bound-with still in its original binding that dates from no earlier than May 1711 (it also contains *Etearco*, March 6, and *Rinaldo* April 24) which have the altered title-page. This evidence, owned by Richard Macnutt and seen by me in 1991, has clarified the picture considerably and resulted in the renumbering of three entries, as well as the creation of four new entries.

2) the fact that the title-page was not used after its alteration for any new work.

3) the presumption that Walsh wanted to reuse the title-page for re-impressions of works of which it had been a part even though that meant disguising the alteration.

The practical difficulty arises in the cases where the words are partially, almost entirely, or completely not printed or are obscured: should they be included in the transcription? Again, it is the bibliographer's duty to report the physical evidence. Thus the words have been included in the transcriptions even though the publisher presumably did not intend them to be read if they were visible.

PARTS OF THE DESCRIPTION

1 Heading

Each entry starts at the top of a new page. The heading comprises the unique identification number, the surname of the composer(s) or arranger, the short title, and the date of possible first publication. Composer/arranger attributions are derived from title-pages, caption headings, advertisements and the latest scholarly research as presented in *The New Grove Dictionary of Opera*. A single name often distorts the creative contributions of composers, librettists and arrangers to particular works, especially for pasticcios. Only in three cases (24, 119, and 178) are two or three names given. Brackets are used to indicate editorial clarification of titles, inverted commas to indicate title-page assertions that are misleading. The date is usually derived from the earliest known advertisement. Occasionally registration with the Stationers' Company is used. When only the month of publication is known the last day of that month is used. Similarly, when only the year is known, then 31 December is used.

2 Illustration and Caption

The illustrative plate or plates pertinent to an entry precede it. Caption information relating to the copy used for illustration follows the heading. I give a plate number or numbers (keyed to the entry number), page size of the copy, the location of the copy and its call number (shelfmark). In cases where the title-pages of different issues of the same work are identical only one example is reproduced. Descriptions of the issues that lack illustrations have references to the appropriate plates in other entries. In four cases there are no plates due to the difficulty of obtaining photographs.

3 Title-page Description

Photographic reproduction of title-pages is used in combination with simplified transcription to satisfy the triple needs of identification, visualization, and ideal copy.[47] Three aspects of transcription deserve comment. Firstly, capitalization sometimes poses problems in the transcription of early eighteenth-century song book title-pages. Words printed entirely in upper-case and those with the initial letter capitalized are transcribed with the initial letter capitalized. Secondly, manuscript annotations—such as composer or librettist attributions, owners' names, library shelf-marks or call numbers, dates, prices or other notes—or library stamps are not transcribed. If the marks seem significant a note is made. Thirdly, two new symbols have been introduced to clarify the transcription of engraved title-pages: ⌠ and ⌡ indicate the beginning and end of blank areas in passe-partout title-pages. Text was printed in these blank areas from small, additional plates, or occasionally supplied in manuscript. Not only do these symbols help to interpret the plate marks, they also allow the correct comparison of title-pages and show which alterations apply to a particular plate and which are the result of passe-partout changes.

Is it necessary to reproduce so many passe-partout title-pages? After all, the mere fact of being passe-partout makes the title-pages of a group of editions and issues almost identical with one another. Reference cannot simply be made to a single reproduction of a passe-partout title-page for these reasons: firstly, there may be more than one version of the specific title information, and it may not be possible to indicate differences between the versions using simple transcription; secondly, without the reproduction in each case the particular visual arrangement of the specific title information would not be conveyed; thirdly, the imprint information on the passe-partout portion may vary; fourthly, without the reproduction the integrity of the bibliographical description of the individual edition or issue would be compromised.

By utilizing both photographs and simplified transcription the bibliographer can allow visualization, fulfil ideal copy requirements, and achieve identification.[48] The last is perhaps the most important. Typographic transcription has never been particularized to the extent necessary to solve the difficulties of distinguishing between roman and italic script and upper- and lower-case letters, of indicating calligraphic flourishes that are integral parts of engraved letters, and of showing particularly awkward cases where the title is not laid out in a linear way.

[47] For justification of this technique see Hunter, 'Bibliographical Description', 312-317.
[48] In theory digital image processing could permit the creation of a single ideal copy title-page image. Simplified transcription would still be necessary to clarify obscure letters or punctuation. For one application see Paul R. Sternberg and John M. Brayer, 'Composite Imaging: A New Technique in Bibliographical Research', *Papers of the Bibliographical Society of America* 77(4) (1983): 431-445.

4 Pagination

Every printed page is assigned a number. Frequently this involves the allocation of roman numerals to preliminary pages. Occasionally it means the interpolation of additional numbers, identified by a letter suffix, into an existing series. All assigned pagination is bracketed thus: [ ]. All pages are included in the pagination statement, either with their own or with inferred or assigned pagination. Zero is occasionally used by a publisher (see 54, for example). Pages numbered in what is apparently contemporary manuscript are not considered numbered, but copy-specific notes are given on the detail. All blank pages are also noted. Blank end-papers are ignored. The number of leaves is given first, followed by the statement of pagination.

The twin considerations of brevity and clarity bear on the form of expression of song book pagination selected. Brevity suggests the use of a symbol at the end of the pagination statement to indicate whether one or both sides of each leaf carried printing, thereby removing the need for frequent employment of a new sign in the statement itself. The symbol at the end would act like the $ sign in the descriptions of letterpress books that indicates the number of leaves per gathering that are signed. Unfortunately, the variety of numeration sequences within books precludes the easy application of such a terminal symbol. Clarity suggests that the most immediate expression of the books' actual and assigned pagination would provide the best formulation for comparison. Therefore, page numbers in combination with some symbols are used.

The occurence of so many blank pages suggested adoption of a symbol first recommended by Allan Stevenson, the upright rectangle: □.[49] This is the first time the symbol has been used in music bibliography. It always appears with a numbered page, be that numeration actual, inferred, or assigned. These pairs of sign and number indicate the individual leaves that comprise the books. Leaves may or may not be conjoint.

The single back slash (\) is used between two blank pages to indicate a blank opening. It signifies separation and is an aid to the readability of the pagination statements. □1 2□\□3 4□ (see 22) is short-hand for recto blank, verso printed 1, recto printed 2, verso blank, recto blank, verso printed 3, recto printed 4, verso blank. Such blank openings are common.

The hyphen is used to indicate series. Thus in the example 20□-35□, all the leaves from page number 20 to 35 carry the correct page numbering on their rectos and all are blank on their versos. Pairs of leaves are regarded as a series and therefore are hyphenated. Pairing relates to printing and leaf orientation,[50] not to

[49] *Catalogue of Botanical Books in the Collection of Rachel McMasters Miller Hunt*, 2 vols. (Pittsburgh: The Hunt Botanical Library, 1961), v.2, pt.1, Printed Books 1701-1800, compiled by Allan Stevenson, p. cxlvii.

[50] I use 'orientation' rather than the expected 'imposition' because the latter refers to the act of laying out type pages, and, by extension, the variety of possible arrangements of type pages. It does not refer to the arrangement of actual pages (folded paper sheets), which is a function of binding. Publishers/printers of engraved books had greater flexibility in terms of how the pages in their books could be oriented, due to printing on single half sheets. Indeed, the concept of imposition is foreign as there was, generally, only one way of placing the printed image vis-à-vis the sheet, with the long axes of paper and plate parallel. Imposition remains valid in the context of the books published by Cluer that have four pages engraved per plate.

contents. For example, 17□-18□ is a pair because both rectos are numbered, the numbering is consecutive and both leaves are identically oriented (printed recto, blank verso). The statement □17 18□ identifies the absence of a pair insofar as the leaves are not identically oriented. Even if the text of a single song is spread over pages 17 and 18, □17 18□ would not be a pair. The hyphen does not necessarily indicate the conjugacy of two leaves.

Back-slashes are used in conjunction with hyphens, page numbers and □ to indicate groups of identically arranged leaves. Typically these groups have blank openings between them. For example, \□3-4□\-\□7-8□\ signifies a blank recto, its verso printed 3, recto printed 4, blank verso, blank recto, verso printed 5, recto printed 6, blank verso, blank recto, verso printed 7, recto printed 8, blank verso.

The creation of statements of pagination of ideal copies of engraved song books has demanded the application of a rule of thumb. If only a single copy exists or has been examined, the pagination of that copy is followed. When two to four copies have been examined and the pagination found to differ, the statement draws on all the evidence but ultimately reflects the bibliographer's conception of the most perfect form of the book. It is not necessarily equal to any particular copy. When five or more copies have been examined the pagination of the majority or largest single group is adopted. All differences from the ideal pagination are given in the Note area.

As the distinction between printing on one or both sides of the leaves of a book is a determinant of impression, the fact in each case is specified even though it can be inferred from the pagination statement. A few leaves may differ from the predominent case. See Index 9 for a summary list of books published in versions with one or both sides of each leaf printed.

5 Signatures

Signatures are not common features of engraved music of this or any other period. Books comprising single half-sheet or folio sheets would hardly require signatures, at least for most purposes, provided that pagination was supplied and was accurate. Only in cases where leaves had to be folded more than once would we expect to find signatures. The 'new method' books of Cluer and Creake, and others of similar size, do, indeed, use signatures. Cross's use of them in *The Opera Miscellany* (**159**) differs from conventional employment in letterpress books inasmuch as the signatures appear on the first two and last two pages of each quarto gathering, thus indicating the beginning and end of the 'inner' and 'outer' plates (to adapt letterpress terminology).

As the registers to be found in a few engraved song books differ in expression from each other and from standard letterpress registers they have not been given in the Signature field. Details of such registers have been reported in the Note area. This avoids confusion with the two letterpress books (**41, 99**), which have their signature registers given in the standard formulary as enunciated by Fredson Bowers.[51] Signature registers have not been created for books that do not carry them.

[51] Fredson Bowers, *Principles of Bibliographical Description* (Princeton: Princeton University Press, 1949; reissued, Winchester: St Paul's Bibliographies, 1986).

6 Format, Size, Paper and Binding

Determination of format is a Sisyphean task for engraved materials. No sooner has one worked out a comprehensive scheme than a group of as yet unexamined materials throws the whole into confusion. The crux of the problem is that printers and publishers of engraved materials generally did not conceive of format as letterpress printers did. There are early eighteenth-century song books described by publishers in advertisements as 'quartos' with either vertical or horizontal chain lines, and 'folios' with vertical *and* horizontal chain lines. Indeed, the very term 'folio' is probably a misnomer insofar as books comprised of single half sheets are not folios in the sense of being constructed from single sheets folded once. In the descriptions format is omitted in favour of the measurements of the leaf size of the tallest extant copy and an indication of the direction of chain lines. The tallest copy was selected to be the representative of each group of copies because it is the closest we can get to the uncut sheet. The original binding and any subsequent rebinding usually reduce the size of each leaf, particularly along the fore-edge. Evidence of leaf conjugacy is noted, if available.[52]

The difficulties of establishing with certainty the origins of the paper used in printing the song books of the early eighteenth century are legion. Although copies were examined for presence of watermarks and the general type noted, no comprehensive study was undertaken.[53] The initial evidence indicates that paper stocks of surviving copies of an issue were surprisingly consistent. No instances were found of large and regular issue copies or of other distinctions such as fine and ordinary paper. Rather than mislead the user of the bibliography by giving partial and untested information, no comments on paper stocks are made in the descriptions.[54]

Bibliographies of books published prior to the advent of trade bindings do not generally accommodate any discussion of the binding of the books examined as the bindings are assumed to have been supplied, in the vast majority of cases, to the specification of the purchaser. Little is known of the binding of music publications. When a form of trade binding seems to have been adopted or advertisements say 'price bound', a note is provided. Copies of different publications were bound together forming 'bound-withs'. For the purposes of this bibliography each publication is considered individually, except in the cases of periodicals, and of *Camilla* when it was issued with additional songs in 1726 (**177**).

7 Engraving

The number of text pages engraved per plate is indicated. There is no necessary correlation between plate size, the number of pages engraved, and the format of the book but it is true that books with one page engraved per plate usually

---

[52] In the case of the two letterpress books format has been included as part of the signature register.
[53] Such a study would require a panoply of modern radiographical techniques and should not be done in isolation from other musical publications.
[54] See Frederick Hudson, 'Musicology and Paper Study—A Survey and Evaluation', in *Essays in Paper Analysis*, ed. Stephen Spector (Washington, DC: Folger Shakespeare Library, 1987): 34-60, for application of watermark analysis to music manuscripts and publications.

comprise folio leaves or single half sheets, whereas those with four pages per plate are quartos (in the strict sense). The name of an engraver or engraving style is given in almost all cases. Whenever possible the actual engraver of the music plates is identified. Other instances cite the name of the publisher when known to be an engraver or, in the case of Walsh punch sets, a number. Each readily distinguishable engraving style (except Parker) is illustrated. Consult the index to engravers and engraving styles for a list by name and an indication of the location of the illustration, or see Table V, Summary of Descriptions, for a chronological list.

The sizes of the plates used to print title-pages, contents and dedication leaves are given. The measurements are to the nearest millimeter measured across the centre of the plate, height before width. As in measurement of any malleable material, allowance must be made for differences between copies. Furthermore, differences in the printing of individual sheets—resulting from the placement of the plate, paper, or blanket—and the technique of the printer, make the exact location of the platemark variable. In the case of early eighteenth-century half sheets ±8 mm is probably acceptable. Only the *engraved* area is here reproduced, which is slightly smaller than the *plate* area.

The books described here comprise the earliest sustained employment of passe-partout title-pages. Each passe-partout has been given a number; Table IV provides a summary of the title-pages and their usage.[55]

8 Bibliographical References

References to numbers in the Walsh bibliographies are provided ('Walsh i' indicates William C. Smith, *A Bibliography of the Music Works Published by John Walsh During the Years 1695-1720*; 'Walsh ii' indicates William C. Smith and Charles Humphries, *A Bibliography of the Musical Works Published by the Firm of John Walsh During the Years 1721-1766*). Smith and Humphries did not intend their bibliographies to act as union catalogues so their descriptions list copies in only a few locations. They were not aware of the existence of copies of all the items they listed, nor was their dating always correct. A single item in this bibliography may match more than one Walsh number but only one is cited. *RISM* numbers are not cited because of possible confusion. As a union catalogue *RISM* A/I is reliant upon the records supplied by libraries and published catalogues— which vary greatly in detail—and is not based on examination of sources. Thus it cannot usually distinguish editions, impressions and issues. One or more *RISM* numbers for the same work often apply to several impressions or issues in this bibliography. Some editions or issues are not listed in *RISM* at all.

9 Advertisements and Price

As with most other musical publications early eighteenth-century English song books are undated. Thankfully, newspaper advertisements, registrations with the Stationers' Company, and other external sources often provide precise information. The date of the possible first publication for a complete work and the name of

---

[55] For further information see Hunter, 'Printing'.

TABLE IV

Passe-partout Title-pages Used in Song Books Published 1703-26

Passe-partout Number	Identification	Type of Title-Page[1]	Date of First Use	User 1703-26	Examples of Use[2]
1	Engraved by Collins	illus.	ca.1690	Walsh	1-2, 4-7, 26, 29
2	Designed by Berchet and engraved by Hulsbergh	illus.	1704	Walsh	8-10, 19, 21, 22
3	Songs in the new opera[3]	lettered	1697	Walsh	12-16, 18-22, 23
4	Engraved by Van der Gucht[4]	illus.	1702	Walsh	32-32a
5	Royal Arms[5]	illus.	1690	Walsh	46-47a,
6	Musical canopy	illus.	1710	Walsh & Hare	75-75a, 83-85, 88
7	Collection of new songs	lettered	1697	Walsh & Hare	95
8	Royal Arms	illus.	1717?	Wright	100, 135c
9	Favourite songs[6]	lettered	1721	Walsh & Hares	113, 121-122, 130
10	Masque of songs	lettered	1723	Walsh & Hares	127a-127b, 135b
11	Favourite songs	lettered	1723	Musick Shops	128-29, 161-62
12	Favourite songs	lettered	1724	Walsh & Hare	145a, 153
13	Monthly Apollo	lettered	1724	Cluer & Creake	146
14	Favourite songs	lettered	1724	Cooke	152, 158
15	Favourite songs (rough)	lettered	1725	Musick Shops	163
16	Quarterly Collection	lettered	1725	Walsh & Hare	167
17	Monthly Collection	lettered	1726	Wright	173

Notes

[1] All plates are 'folio' size, and are either illustrated (illus.) or lettered.

[2] See Index 8 Passe-partout Title-pages for the complete list of uses.

[3] Modified in 1711, so that the title begins, 'The Additionall Songs in the'; see nos. 74-74a, 76a-80a, 91, 93.

[4] Title-page plate first used for D. Purcell, *The Judgment of Paris*, Walsh, 1702 (see Walsh i, no. 89). Subsequent to modification in 1702 and 1706, it was used as a passe-partout for the first issue of the revived *Monthly Mask of Vocal Music*, July 1717 (see Walsh i, no. 517). Prior to 1717 title changes were engraved directly on the plate.

[5] Plate not used by Walsh from its initial employment on G. Finger, *VI Sonatas* (1690-1702) until 1708, when the imprint was altered from 'his Majesty' to 'her Majesty' (Walsh i, no. 82a). Realtered back to 'his Majesty' in 1714.

[6] Modified in 1726 by substituting 'Additional' for 'Favourite'.

the newspaper are given when uncovered. These dates are derived from searches of *Early English Newspapers* microfilm series published by Research Publications Inc., from the Walsh bibliographies, and from Michael Tilmouth's 'Calendar'. Advertisements and the item itself are the best sources of information on price, which is given when known.

10 Contents and List of Songs

In addition to providing a summary account of contents, most entries in the bibliography also give a complete list of songs. The exceptions are those issues that have contents identical with a previous issue; in such cases a reference is given to the appropriate complete entry. Each song is assigned a number within each book. The pagination, whether original, inferred, or assigned, is given in both the contents summary and the list of songs.

The first lines are transcribed using their original spelling. In the cases of pairs of letters that were used for each other (i and j, u and v) I transcribe the letter as printed except when the letter comes at the beginning of the line and does not conform to today's convention. Swash J is transcribed as I. Repeated words or phrases are omitted. Initial articles in English texts are placed at the end of the lines following a comma. Those in Italian and French retain their original placement. Spacing between words and letters is conventionalized. Accents and apostrophes were used by publishers when unnecessary and not used when needed; they have been regularized in Italian and French texts only. Eighteenth-century irregular capitalization is conventionalized so that only proper names (etc.) and initial words are capitalized. Punctuation is modified only slightly but terminal punctuation is omitted. These practices are maintained in the first line index. In short, the song first lines are not transcribed literally. Rather, following the practice of Day and Murrie, I have attempted to provide a readable indication of the verbal text.

Any translation on the page is transcribed following the first line, and is enclosed with parentheses. Information on composer, librettist, adaptor, literary or stage work, and singer(s) is given in conventional spelling when supplied as a caption to the song itself. Again, it has not been my intention to adjudicate claims concerning the identification of the individuals responsible either for each song text or for each monographic text as a whole. Initials or forenames follow surnames when necessary to identify different individuals, such as Purcell, H., and Purcell, D. Day and Murrie's abbreviations for the different roles are used: m for composer, v for librettist, s for singer, < for from or out of; with the addition of: a for adaptor of the literary text. References to Day and Murrie song numbers are given when appropriate, and are indicated by: D&M.

By combining the expression of ideal pagination and contents with the information given in the notes it is possible to identify the physical form of every copy examined.

11 Notes

Notes are primarily used to indicate the ways in which individual copies differ from the ideal. Also given here is the rationale for dating, when complex, and additional information not provided elsewhere in the description, such as on binding. The reasons for the exclusion of particular copies (due to loss, for example) are given.

Some terms are used in special ways:

1) *reversed*   refers to leaf orientation. Reversal typically occurs with leaves printed on one side, where the orientation of the printed side is opposite to the norm.

2) *transposed*   placement of two unadjacent leaves is opposite to the norm.

3) *inverted*   placement of two adjacent leaves is opposite to the norm.

4) *duplicated*   two copies of a leaf are present.

Songs present in one copy of an issue that do not pertain to the ideal copy are mentioned in a note.

12 Copies

Each description is completed by a list of extant copies. Libraries in the United States of America and in Canada are indicated by *National Union Catalog* sigla (as in *The New Grove Dictionary of American Music*). United Kingdom collections are indicated by *RISM* sigla without the GB prefix. For the two private collections—of Richard Macnutt (TWm) and of Olive Baldwin and Thelma Wilson (BWbw), which are not included in *RISM*—I have created sigla. The siglum for the collection of St. Michael's College, Tenbury, I changed from T to Obt. The siglum for the Harding Collection, Bodleian Library, Oxford, I shortened to Obh. Libraries in other parts of the world are indicated by full *RISM* sigla, with hyphens between country and city, as used in *The New Grove* dictionaries. *RISM* sigla are those current at the end of 1996. See the following Library Codes list for all the codes and their libraries. Copies in entries are recorded in alphabetical order by code.

The call numbers (shelfmarks) of examined copies are given. Copies that have no call number are indicated thus: —. Copies in unvisited locations (indicated by italicization of the sigla) are derived from *RISM*, *NUC*, OCLC, RLIN, and reports to the Eighteenth-century Short Title Catalogue/North America project, and must be regarded as provisional. Information on unexamined copies (also indicated by italicized sigla) in visited libraries is derived from library catalogues, OCLC and RLIN.

Indexes

The volume concludes with ten indexes: first lines and translations; composers, librettists, adaptors; singers; literary or dramatic works, operas, occasions; short-titles, publishers and dates; printers, publishers, sellers, with short-titles and dates; engravers and engraving styles; passe-partout title-page uses; books published in versions with one or both sides of each leaf printed; and libraries.

Library Codes

D-SWl	Wissenschaftliche Allgemeinbibliothek, Schwerin, Germany
DCU	Catholic University, Washington, DC, USA
DFo	Folger Shakespeare Library, Washington, DC, USA
DK-Kk	Royal Library, Copenhagen, Denmark
DLC	Library of Congress, Washington, DC, USA
DRc	Durham Cathedral Library, England
DU	Dundee Public Library, Scotland
En	National Library of Scotland, Edinburgh, Scotland
Er	Reid Music Library, University of Edinburgh, Scotland
Eu	Rare Book Room, University of Edinburgh, Scotland
F-Pc	Fonds du Conservatoire, Bibliothèque nationale, Paris, France
F-Pn	Bibliothèque nationale, Paris, France
FMU	University of Miami, Coral Gables, FL, USA
Ge	Euing Music Library, University of Glasgow, Scotland
Gm	Mitchell Library, Glasgow, Scotland
Gu	Special Collections, University of Glasgow, Scotland
H-Bn	National Library, Budapest, Hungary
HAdolmetsch	Dolmetsch, Private Collection, Haslemere, England
I-BGi	Civico Istituto musicale, Bergamo, Italy
I-Gi(l)	Biblioteca dell'Istituto (Liceo) Musicale 'Paganini', Genova, Italy
I-MOe	Biblioteca Estense, Modena, Italy
I-Rsc	Conservatorio di Santa Cecilia, Rome, Italy
I-Vc	Biblioteca del Conservatorio 'Benedetto Marcello', Venice, Italy
IaU	University of Iowa, Iowa City, IA, USA
ICN	Newberry Library, Chicago, IL, USA
ICU	University of Chicago, IL, USA
INS	Illinois State University, Normal, IL, USA
InU	Indiana University, Bloomington, IN, USA
IU	University of Illinois, Urbana, IL, USA
J-Tn	Nanki Library, Tokyo College of Music, Japan
Lam	Royal Academy of Music, London, England
Lbl	British Library, London, England
Lcm	Royal College of Music, London, England
Lcml	Westminster Music Library, London, England
Lco	Royal College of Organists, London, England
Lcs	Vaughan Williams Library, Cecil Sharp House, London, England
LEp	Leeds Public Library, England
Lgc	Gresham College Collection, Guildhall Library, London, England
Lsc	Sion College, London, England
LVp	Liverpool Public Library, England
MB	Boston Public Library, MA, USA
MBMH	Harvard Musical Association, Boston, MA, USA
MdBPC	Peabody Conservatory, Baltimore, MD, USA
MH-H	Houghton Library, Harvard University, Cambridge, MA, USA

MH-Mu	Music Library, Harvard University, Cambridge, MA, USA
MiD	Detroit Public Library, MI, USA
MiU	University of Michigan, Ann Arbor, MI, USA
MnU	Music Library, University of Minnesota, Minneapolis, MN, USA
Mp	Henry Watson Music Library, Manchester Public Library, England
NcD	Duke University, Durham, NC, USA
NcU	University of North Carolina, Chapel Hill, NC, USA
NIC	Cornell University, Ithaca, NY, USA
NjP	Princeton University, Princeton, NJ, USA
NL-DHgm	Gemeente Museum, The Hague, The Netherlands
NN	New York Public Library, NY, USA
NPV	Vassar College, Poughkeepsie, NY, USA
NRU-Mus	Sibley Music Library, Eastman School of Music, Rochester, NY, USA
Ob	Bodleian Library, Oxford, England
Obh	Harding Collection, Bodleian Library, Oxford, England
Obt	St. Michael's College, Tenbury, Collection, Bodleian Library, Oxford, England
OClW	Case Western Reserve University, Cleveland, OH, USA
Omc	Magdalen College, Oxford, England
Ooc	Oriel College, Oxford, England
OU	Ohio State University, Columbus, OH, USA
Ouf	Faculty of Music Library, Oxford University, England
P	Perth Public Library, Scotland
PSt	Pennsylvania State University, University Park, PA, USA
PU	University of Pennsylvania, Philadelphia, PA, USA
RF-Mrg	Rossiyskaya Gosudarstvennaya Biblioteka, Moscow, Russia
S-Skma	Music Academy, Stockholm, Sweden
SA	St. Andrews University Library, Scotland
TU	University of Tennessee, Knoxville, TN, USA
TWm	Macnutt, Private Collection, Tunbridge Wells, England
TxDN	University of North Texas, Denton, TX, USA
TxU	Harry Ransom Humanities Research Center, University of Texas, Austin, TX, USA
ViWC	Colonial Williamsburg Foundation, VA, USA
WaU	University of Washington, Seattle, WA, USA

BY COUNTRY AND PLACE

Austria
  Vienna   A-Wn Musiksammlung, Nationalbibliothek
                    A-Wn-h Hoboken Collection, Musiksammlung,
                                  Nationalbibliothek

Belgium
  Brussels   B-Bc Conservatoire Royal de Musique
                    B-Br Bibliothèque Royale Albert 1er
  Denée   B-MAR Abbaye de Maredsous
Canada
  Hamilton   CaOHM McMaster University, Ontario
  London   CaOLU University of Western Ontario
  Vancouver   CaBVau University of British Columbia
Czech Republic
  Prague   CZ-Pu Music Department, University of Prague
Denmark
  Copenhagen   DK-Kk Royal Library
France
  Paris   F-Pc Fonds du Conservatoire, Bibliothèque nationale
                    F-Pn Bibliothèque nationale

Germany
  Berlin   D-B Staatsbibliothek zu Berlin—Preussischer
                                Kulturbesitz
  Bremen   D-BMs Staats- und Universitätsbibliothek
  Delitzsch   D-DL Bibliothek, Museum
  Göttingen   D-Gs Staats- und Universitätsbibliothek
  Hamburg   D-Hs Staats- und Universitätsbibliothek
  München   D-Mbs Bayerische Staatsbibliothek
  Schwerin   D-SWl Wissenschaftliche Allgemeinbibliothek
Hungary
  Budapest   H-Bn National Library
Italy
  Bergamo   I-BGi Civico Istituto musicale
  Genova   I-Gi(l) Biblioteca dell'Istituto (Liceo) Musicale 'Paganini'
  Modena   I-MOe Biblioteca Estense
  Rome   I-Rsc Conservatorio di Santa Cecilia
  Venice   I-Vc Biblioteca del Conservatorio 'Benedetto Marcello'
Japan
  Tokyo   J-Tn Nanki Library, Tokyo College of Music
Netherlands
  The Hague   NL-DHgm Gemeente Museum
Russia
  Moscow   RF-Mrg Rossiyskaya Gosudarstvennaya Biblioteka

Sweden
  Stockholm   S-Skma Music Academy
United Kingdom
England
  Aldeburgh   ALb Britten-Pears Library
  Bentley   Coke Coke Private Collection
  Birmingham   Bp Public Library
                       Bu Barber Institute, University of Birmingham
  Brentwood   BWbw Baldwin-Wilson Private Collection
  Cambridge   Cfm Fitzwilliam Museum
                       Ckc Rowe Music Library, King's College
                       Cpc Pembroke College
                       Cpl Pendlebury Library, Music Faculty
                       Ctc Trinity College
                       Cu Cambridge University Library
  Durham   DRc Cathedral Library
  Haslemere   HAdolmetsch Dolmetsch Private Collection
  Leeds   LEp Leeds Public Library
  Liverpool   LVp Liverpool Public Library
  London   Lam Royal Academy of Music
                       Lbl British Library
                       Lcm Royal College of Music
                       Lcml Westminster Music Library
                       Lco Royal College of Organists
                       Lcs Vaughan Williams Library, Cecil Sharp House
                       Lgc Gresham College Collection, Guildhall Library
                       Lsc Sion College
  Manchester   Mp Henry Watson Music Library, Manchester Public
                             Library
  Oxford   Ob Bodleian Library
                       Obh Harding Collection, Bodleian Library
                       Obt St. Michael's College, Tenbury, Collection
                       Omc Magdalen College
                       Ooc Oriel College
                       Ouf Faculty of Music Library, Oxford University
  Tunbridge Wells   TWm Macnutt Private Collection
Scotland
  Dundee   DU Dundee Public Library
  Edinburgh   En National Library of Scotland
                       Er Reid Music Library, University of Edinburgh
                       Eu Rare Book Room, University of Edinburgh
  Glasgow   Ge Euing Music Library, University of Glasgow
                       Gm Mitchell Library
                       Gu Special Collections, University of Glasgow

Perth	P Perth Public Library
St. Andrews	SA St. Andrews University Library
Wales	
Cardiff	CDp Cardiff Public Library (now at the University of Wales, College of Cardiff, Library)
United States of America	
California	
Berkeley	CU-MUSI Music Library, University of California, Berkeley
Los Angeles	CLU-C Clark Library, University of California, Los Angeles
San Francisco	CSfst de Bellis Collection, San Francisco State University
San Marino	CSmH Huntington Library
Stanford	CSt Stanford University
Connecticut	
New Haven	CtY Yale University
	CtY-Mus Music Library, Yale University
District of Columbia	
Washington	DCU Catholic University
	DFo Folger Shakespeare Library
	DLC Library of Congress
Florida	
Coral Gables	FMU University of Miami
Illinois	
Chicago	ICN Newberry Library
	ICU University of Chicago
Normal	INS Illinois State University
Urbana	IU University of Illinois
Indiana	
Bloomington	InU Indiana University
Iowa	
Iowa City	IaU University of Iowa
Maryland	
Baltimore	MdBPC Peabody Conservatory
Massachusetts	
Boston	MB Boston Public Library
	MBHM Harvard Musical Association
Cambridge	MH-H Houghton Library, Harvard University
	MH-Mu Music Library, Harvard University
Michigan	
Ann Arbor	MiU University of Michigan
Detroit	MiD Detroit Public Library
Minnesota	
Minneapolis	MnU Music Library, University of Minnesota

New Jersey
  Princeton   NjP Princeton University
New York
  Ithaca   NIC Cornell University
  New York   NN New York Public Library
  Poughkeepsie   NPV Vassar College
  Rochester   NRU-Mus Sibley Music Library, Eastman School of
                       Music
North Carolina
  Chapel Hill   NcU University of North Carolina
  Durham   NcD Duke University
Ohio
  Cleveland   OClW Case Western Reserve University
  Columbus   OU Ohio State University
Pennsylvania
  Philadelphia   PU University of Pennsylvania
  University Park PSt Pennsylvania State University
Tennessee
  Knoxville   TU University of Tennessee
Texas
  Austin   TxU   Harry Ransom Humanities Research Center, Uni-
                       versity of Texas
  Denton   TxDN University of North Texas
Virginia
  Williamsburg   ViWC Colonial Williamsburg Foundation
Washington
  Seattle   WaU University of Washington

Summary of Descriptions

TABLE V

Book No.	Short Title	Composer or Adaptor	Publisher(s)	Date of Publication[1]	Engraving Style
1	New Year's Day Songs	Eccles, J	Walsh	23 Feb. 1703	Walsh 1
2	New Year's Day Songs	Eccles	Walsh, Hare	23 Feb. 1703	Walsh 1
3	New Year's Day Songs	Eccles	[Walsh]	23 Feb. 1703	Walsh 1
4	Third Book of Songs	Weldon, J	Walsh	11 May 1703	Walsh 1
5	Collection of the Choicest Songs & Dialogues		Walsh	31 Oct. 1703	Walsh[2] and Cross[3]
6	Birthday Songs	Eccles	Walsh	4 Nov. 1703	Walsh 1
7	Collection of New Songs	Weldon	Walsh	31 Dec. 1703	Walsh 1
8	Collection of Songs	Eccles	Walsh	14 Nov. 1704	Walsh 1, 2
9	Collection of Songs	Eccles	Walsh	14 Nov. 1704	Walsh 1, 2
10	Collection of Songs	Eccles	Walsh, Hare	14 Nov. 1704	Walsh 1, 2
11	Collection of Songs	Eccles	Young	14 Nov. 1704	Walsh 1, 2
12	Arsinoe [First Collection]	Clayton, T	Walsh	2 Apr. 1706	Walsh 1
12a	Arsinoe [First Collection]	Clayton	Walsh	2 Apr. 1706	Walsh 1
13	Camilla [First Collection]	Bononcini, G	Walsh	2 Apr. 1706	Walsh 1
14	Camilla, Second Collection	Bononcini	Walsh	17 Apr. 1706	Walsh 1
15	Camilla [Third Collection]	Bononcini	Walsh	30 Apr. 1706	Walsh 1
16	Camilla, 'Second Collection'	Bononcini	Walsh	1 May 1706	Walsh 1
17	Deleted (see 15)				
18	Camilla [First Collection]	Bononcini	Walsh	11 May 1706	Walsh 1
19	Camilla	Bononcini	Walsh	11 May 1706	Walsh 1
20	Camilla	Bononcini	Walsh	16 May 1706	Walsh 1
21	Camilla, 'Third Collection'	Bononcini	Walsh, Hare	16 May 1706	Walsh 1
21a	Camilla, 'Third Collection'	Bononcini	Walsh, Hare	16 May 1706	Walsh 1
22	Camilla	Bononcini	Walsh, Hare	16 May 1706	Walsh 1
22a	Camilla	Bononcini	Walsh, Hare	16 May 1706	Walsh 1
23	Camilla	Bononcini	Young	16 May 1706	Walsh 1
24	Collection of New Songs	Morley & Isum	[Authors]	1 Aug. 1706	Cross
24a	Collection of New Songs	Morley & Isum	Authors	1 Aug. 1706	Cross
25	Wonders in the Sun	Smith, J.	Walsh, Hare	7 Aug. 1706	Walsh 1
26	Arsinoe	Clayton	Walsh	5 Oct. 1706	Walsh 1
27	Deleted (see 26)				
28	Deleted (see 29)				
29	Arsinoe	Clayton	Walsh, Hare	5 Oct. 1706	Walsh 1
30	Arsinoe	Clayton	Young	5 Oct. 1706	Walsh 1
31	Arsinoe	Clayton	Rawlins	5 Oct. 1706	Walsh 1
32	Temple of Love	Fedelli, G	Walsh, Hare	18 Oct. 1706	Walsh 1
32a	Temple of Love	Fedelli	Walsh, Hare	18 Oct. 1706	Walsh 1
33	Comical Songs		Walsh	31 Dec. 1706	Walsh and Cross
33a	Camilla	Bononcini	[Cullen]	22 Feb. 1707	Cross
34	Camilla	Bononcini	Cullen	1 Mar. 1707	Cross
34a	Camilla	Bononcini	Cullen	1 Mar. 1707	Cross
35	Camilla	Bononcini	Rawlins	1 Mar. 1707	Cross
36	Deleted (see 33a)				
37	Rosamond [First Collection]	Clayton	Walsh, Randall	10 Mar. 1707	Walsh 1, 3
38	Rosamond	Clayton	Walsh, Randall	29 Apr. 1707	Walsh 1, 3
39	Deleted (see 38)				
40	Thomyris [First Collection]	Pepusch, J	Rawlins	31 May 1707	Walsh 1, 3
40a	Thomyris	Pepusch	Cullen	1 June 1707	Cross
41	Collection of New Songs	Young, A	Author	5 June 1707	Letterpress
42	Thomyris	Pepusch	Cullen	5 June 1707	Cross
43	Thomyris [Second & Third Collections]	Pepusch	Rawlins	7 June 1707	Walsh 1, 3

Book No.	Short Title	Composer or Adaptor	Publisher(s)	Date of Publication[1]	Engraving Style
43a	Thomyris	Pepusch	Walsh, Randall	14 June 1707	Walsh 1, 3
44	Thomyris	Pepusch	Walsh, Randall	19 June 1707	Walsh 1, 3
44a	Thomyris	Pepusch	Walsh, Randall	19 June 1707	Walsh 1, 3
45	Thomyris	Pepusch	Young	19 June 1707	Walsh 1, 3
46	Love's Triumph	Dieupart, C	Walsh, Hare	28 Apr. 1708	Walsh
47	Love's Triumph	Dieupart	Walsh, Randall, Hare	28 Apr. 1708	Walsh
47a	Love's Triumph	Dieupart	Walsh, Randall, Hare	28 Apr. 1708	Walsh
48	Deleted (see 22)				
48a	Pyrrhus and Demetrius	Scarlatti, A	Walsh, Randall, Hare	20 Jan. 1709	Walsh 1
48b	Pyrrhus and Demetrius	Scarlatti	Walsh, Randall, Hare	20 Jan. 1709	Walsh 1
49	Pyrrhus and Demetrius	Scarlatti	Walsh, Randall, Hare	9 Feb. 1709	Walsh 1
50	Pyrrhus and Demetrius	Scarlatti	Walsh, Hare	9 Feb. 1709	Walsh 1
51	Pyrrhus and Demetrius	Scarlatti	Walsh, Randall, Hare	9 Feb. 1709	Walsh 1
52	Pyrrhus and Demetrius	Scarlatti	Rawlins	9 Feb. 1709	Walsh 1
53	Clotilda	Conti, F	Walsh, Randall, Hare	15 Apr. 1709	Walsh 1
54	Clotilda	Conti	Walsh, Randall, Hare	15 Apr. 1709	Walsh 1
55	Jovial Companions		Walsh, Randall, Hare	20 May 1709	Walsh 1, 3, Cross
55a	Jovial Companions		Walsh, Randall, Hare	20 May 1709	Walsh 1, 3, Cross
56	Bottle Companions		Walsh, Randall, Hare	26 May 1709	Walsh 1, 2, 3
57	Pyrrhus and Demetrius	Scarlatti	Cullen	25 June 1709	Cross
58	Pyrrhus and Demetrius	Scarlatti	Cullen	25 June 1709	Cross
59	Clotilda	Conti	Young	29 Nov. 1709	Pippard
60	Deleted (see 78a)				
61	Deleted (see 177)				
62	Camilla	Bononcini	Walsh, Randall, Hare	31 Dec. 1709	Walsh 1
63	Camilla	Bononcini	Walsh	31 Dec. 1709	Walsh 1
64	Almahide	Heidegger, J	Walsh, Randall, Hare	16 Feb. 1710	Walsh and Cross
65	Almahide	Heidegger	Walsh, Randall, Hare	16 Feb. 1710	Walsh and Cross
66	Deleted (see 76a)				
67	Deleted (see 76a)				
68	Almahide	Heidegger	Rawlins	16 Feb. 1710	Walsh and Cross
69	Hydaspes	Mancini, F	Walsh, Randall, Hare	30 May 1710	Walsh and Cross
70	Musa et Musica		Pippard	13 June 1710	Pippard
71	Book of New Songs	Reading, J	Author	8 Nov. 1710	?
72	Book of New Songs	Reading	Author	8 Nov. 1710	?
73	[Collection of Catches]		[Pippard]	31 Dec. 1710	Pippard
74	Hydaspes, Additional Songs	Mancini	Walsh, Randall, Hare	27 Jan. 1711	Walsh 1
74a	Hydaspes, 'Additional Songs'	Mancini	Walsh, Randall, Hare	27 Jan. 1711	Walsh and Cross
75	Etearco	Bononcini	Walsh, Hare	6 Mar. 1711	Walsh and Cross
75a	Etearco	Bononcini	Walsh, Hare	6 Mar. 1711	Walsh and Cross
76	New Book of Songs	Leveridge, R	Leveridge	29 Nov. 1711	?
76a	Almahide, 'Additional Songs'	Heidegger	Walsh, Randall, Hare	31 Dec. 1711	Walsh and Cross
77	Almahide, 'Additional Songs'	Heidegger	Walsh, Hare	31 Dec. 1711	Walsh and Cross
78	Almahide, 'Additional Songs'	Heidegger	Walsh, Hare	31 Dec. 1711	Walsh and Cross
78a	Arsinoe, 'Additional Songs'	Clayton	Walsh, Randall, Hare	31 Dec. 1711	Walsh 1
78b	Arsinoe, 'Additional Songs'	Clayton	Walsh, Randall, Hare	31 Dec. 1711	Walsh 1
79	Camilla, 'Additional Songs'	Bononcini	Walsh, Hare	31 Dec. 1711	Walsh 1
79a	Camilla, 'Additional Songs'	Bononcini	Walsh, Randall, Hare	31 Dec. 1711	Walsh 1
79b	Clotilda, 'Additional Songs'	Conti	Walsh, Randall, Hare	31 Dec. 1711	Walsh 1
80	Hydaspes, 'Additional Songs'	Mancini	Walsh, Hare	31 Dec. 1711	Walsh and Cross
80a	Hydaspes, 'Additional Songs'	Mancini	Walsh, Randall, Hare	31 Dec. 1711	Walsh and Cross
81	Rosamond	Clayton	Walsh, Hare	31 Dec. 1711	Walsh 1, 3

Book No.	Short Title	Composer or Adaptor	Publisher(s)	Date of Publication[1]	Engraving Style
82	Thomyris	Pepusch	Walsh, Hare	31 Dec. 1711	Walsh 1, 3
83	Antiochus	Gasparini, F	Walsh, Hare	21 Feb. 1712	Walsh and Cross
84	Hamlet	Gasparini	Walsh, Hare	21 Apr. 1712	Walsh and Cross
85	Calypso and Telemachus	Galliard, J	Walsh, Hare	28 June 1712	Walsh and Cross
86	Musa et Musica		Pippard	31 Dec. 1713	Pippard
87	New Book of Songs	Ramondon, L	Walsh, Hare	31 Dec. 1713	Walsh 1
88	Croesus	Polani, G	Walsh, Hare	1 May 1714	Walsh 1
89	Arminius	Ziani, M	Walsh, Hare	1 June 1714	Walsh and Cross
90	Arsinoe	Clayton	Walsh, Hare	31 Dec. 1714	Walsh 1
90a	Croesus	Polani	Walsh, Hare	31 Dec. 1714	Walsh 1
90b	Etearco	Bononcini	Walsh, Hare	31 Dec. 1714	Walsh and Cross
91	Hydaspes, 'Additional Songs'	Mancini	Walsh, Hare	31 Dec. 1714	Walsh and Cross
92	Hydaspes	Mancini	Walsh, Hare	31 Dec. 1714	Walsh and Cross
93	Love's Triumph, 'Additional Songs'	Dieupart	Walsh, Hare	31 Dec. 1714	Walsh
94	Pyrrhus and Demetrius	Scarlatti	Walsh, Hare	31 Dec. 1714	Walsh 1
95	New Songs with a Through Bass		Walsh, Hare	31 Dec. 1715	Walsh
96	Venus and Adonis	Pepusch	Walsh, Hare	10 May 1716	Walsh 1
97	Venus and Adonis	Pepusch	Walsh	10 May 1716	Walsh 1
98	Venus and Adonis	Pepusch	Young	10 May 1716	Walsh 1
99	Merry Musician, vol. 1		Walsh, Hare, etc.	31 Dec. 1716	Letterpress
100	Three Songs	Marshall, S	Wright	20 July 1717	Wright
101	Twenty New Songs	Graves, J	Wright	19 Sept. 1717	Wright
102	Collection of Songs	Graves	Walsh, Hare	26 Oct. 1717	Walsh
103	Calypso and Telemachus	Galliard	Walsh, Hare	31 Dec. 1717	Walsh and Cross
104	Twenty New Songs	Turner, W	Author, Wright	29 Apr. 1718	Wright
105	Thomyris and Camilla, Additional Songs	Pepusch	Walsh, Hare	14 May 1719	Walsh
106	Yearly Subscription		Jones	5 Dec. 1719	Jones
107	Numitor	Porta, G	Walsh, Hare	18 June 1720	Walsh 1
108	Narcissus	Scarlatti, D	Walsh, Hare	6 Oct. 1720	Walsh 1
109	Sea Songs		Walsh, Hare	1 Dec. 1720	Walsh 1, 2
110	Modern Harmony	Vanbrugh, G	Walsh, Hare	31 Dec. 1720	Walsh 1
111	Astartus	Bononcini	Walsh, Hare	1 Apr. 1721	Walsh 1, 3
112	Astartus	Bononcini	Young	1 Apr. 1721	Walsh 1, 3
113	Cyrus	Bononcini	Walsh, Hares	31 Dec. 1721	Walsh 1
114	Griselda	Bononcini	Author	22 May 1722	Walsh 1, 3
114a	Griselda	Bononcini	Author	22 May 1722	Walsh 1, 3
114b	Griselda	Bononcini	Author	22 May 1722	Walsh 1, 3
115	Griselda	Bononcini	Meares	3 June 1722	Cross
116	Griselda	Bononcini	Meares	3 June 1722	Cross
117	Griselda	Bononcini	Cooke[4]	3 June 1722	Cross
118	Griselda	Bononcini	Rawlins	3 June 1722	Cross
119	Muzio Scaevola	Amadei et al.	Meares	23 Aug. 1722	Cross
120	Muzio Scaevola	Amadei et al.	Rawlins	23 Aug. 1722	Cross
121	Crispus	Bononcini	Walsh, Hares	25 Aug. 1722	Walsh 1
122	Muzio Scaevola	Amadei et al.	Walsh, Hares	25 Aug. 1722	Walsh
123	Clotilda	Conti	Cooke	31 Dec. 1722	Walsh 1
124	Collection of Songs	Sheeles, J	Walsh, Hares	31 Dec. 1722	Walsh 3, 4
125	Crispus	Bononcini	Meares	23 Aug. 1722	Cross
126	Crispus	Bononcini	Meares	23 Aug. 1722	Cross
126a	Thomyris	Pepusch	Cooke	31 Dec. 1722	Walsh 1, 3
127	Coriolano	Ariosti	Author	23 May 1723	Cross
127a	Jupiter and Europa	Galliard	Walsh, Hares	30 Sept. 1723	Walsh
127b	Jupiter and Europa	Galliard	Young	30 Sept. 1723	?

Book No.	Short Title	Composer or Adaptor	Publisher(s)	Date of Publication[1]	Engraving Style
128	Erminia	Bononcini	Musick Shops	31 Dec, 1723	Musick Shops[5]
129	Erminia	Bononcini	Barret	31 Dec. 1723	Musick Shops
130	Erminia	Bononcini	Walsh, Hares	31 Dec. 1723	Walsh 1
131	Deleted (see 55a Notes)				
132	Deleted (see 127a)				
133	Deleted (see 127b)				
134	Recueil d'airs françois	Gillier, J	Edlin	31 Dec. 1723	Walsh
135	Union of the Three Sister Arts	Pepusch	Walsh, Hares	31 Dec. 1723	Walsh 1
135a	Necromancer	Galliard	Cooke	28 Feb. 1724	Parker
135b	Necromancer	Galliard	Walsh, Hares	28 Feb. 1724	Walsh
135c	Necromancer	Galliard	Wright	28 Feb. 1724	Wright
136	Cantatas	Carey, H	Author	3 Mar. 1724	Bates
137	Coriolano	Ariosti	Walsh, Hares	23 Mar. 1724	Walsh 1, 4
138	Vespasian	Ariosti	Author	23 Mar. 1724	Walsh 1, 3
139	Vespasian	Ariosti	Walsh, Hares	23 Mar. 1724	Walsh 1, 3
140	Vespasian	Ariosti	Barret	23 Mar. 1724	Walsh 1, 3
141	Vespasian	Ariosti	Young	23 Mar. 1724	Walsh 1, 3
142	Vespasian	Ariosti	Meares	28 Mar. 1724	Cross
143	Pharnaces	Bononcini	Walsh, Hares	31 Mar. 1724	Walsh
144	Pocket Companion, [vol.1]		Cluer, Creake	2 May 1724	Cobb
145	Pocket Companion, [vol.1], ed.2		Cluer, Creake	8 June 1724	Cobb
145a	Calphurnia	Bononcini	Walsh, Hares	31 July 1724	Walsh 4, 5
146	Monthly Apollo		Cluer, Creake	14 Sept. 1724	Cobb
147	Aquilio	Ariosti	Walsh, Hares	30 Sept. 1724	Walsh 3, 4
148	Aquilio	Ariosti	Barret	30 Sept. 1724	Walsh 3, 4
149	Aquilio	Ariosti	Cooke	30 Sept. 1724	Walsh 3, 4
150	Artaxerxes	Ariosti	Musick Shops [Walsh?]	31 Dec. 1724	Musick Shops
151	Artaxerxes	Ariosti	Barret	31 Dec. 1724	Musick Shops
152	Calphurnia	Bononcini	Cooke	31 Dec. 1724	Bates
153	Calphurnia	Bononcini	Walsh, Hares	31 Dec. 1724	Walsh 4, 5
154	Deleted (see 135a)				
155	Deleted (see 135b)				
156	Deleted (see 135c)				
157	Orpheus Brittanicus	Purcell, H	Walsh, Hares	31 Dec. 1724	Walsh and Cross
158	Vespasian	Ariosti	Cooke	31 Dec. 1724	Bates
159	Opera Miscellany		Browne	27 Apr. 1725	Cross
160	Pocket Companion, vol.2		Cluer, Creake	23 Dec. 1725	Cobb
161	Darius	Ariosti	Musick Shops [Walsh?]	31 Dec. 1725	Musick Shops
162	Darius	Ariosti	Barret	31 Dec. 1725	Musick Shops
163	Elpidia	Vinci, L	Musick Shops	31 Dec. 1725	Musick Shops
164	Elpidia	Vinci	Musick Shops [Walsh?]	31 Dec. 1725	Musick Shops
165	Deleted (see 164)				
166	Elpidia, [Additional Songs]		[Barret?]	31 Dec. 1725	Mixed[6]
167	Quarterly Collection of Vocal Musick		Walsh, Hare	31 Dec. 1725	Walsh 4, 6
168	Orpheus Caledonius	Thomson, W	Author	5 Jan. 1726	Mixed
169	Delightful Musical Companion		Fraser	8 Jan. 1726	Cole
170	Delightful Musical Companion		Fraser	8 Jan. 1726	Cole
171	Diamonds Cut Diamonds	Carey	Wright & Wright	31 Jan. 1726	Cross
172	Apollo's Feast, vol.2		Walsh, Hare	16 Sept. 1726	Walsh
173	Monthly Collection of Songs		Wright	31 Oct. 1726	Mixed

OPERA AND SONG BOOKS PUBLISHED IN ENGLAND 1703-1726

Book No.	Short Title	Composer or Adaptor	Publisher(s)	Date of Publication[1]	Engraving Style
174	Apollo and Daphne	Galliard	Rawlins	31 Dec. 1726	Rawlins
175	Apollo and Daphne	Galliard	Walsh, Hare	31 Dec. 1726	Walsh
176	Astartus	Bononcini	Walsh, Hare	31 Dec. 1726	Walsh 1, 3
177	Camilla, Additional Songs	Bononcini	Walsh, Hare	31 Dec. 1726	Walsh 1, 5, 6, Cross
178	Elisa, and Additional Songs to Rodelinda	Porpora, N & Handel	Walsh, Hare	31 Dec. 1726	Walsh 4, 6
178a	Elisa, and Additional Songs to Rodelinda	Porpora & Handel	Walsh, Hare	31 Dec. 1726	Walsh 4, 6
179	Griselda	Bononcini	Author	31 Dec. 1726	Walsh 1, 3
180	Works	Carey	[Author]	31 Dec. 1726	Bates, Walsh

1. See pp. xxiv-xxviii for comments on dating.
2. When the particular Walsh style has not been identified or the copies display a variety of styles, 'Walsh' is used. Some books published by Walsh include sheets engraved prior to 1703 by different engravers, including the so-called 'London Music Engraver'. These styles have not been differentiated. For information on the 'London Music Engraver' see Miriam Miller, 'London Music Printing c1641-c1700' (M.A. Librarianship thesis, University College, University of London, 1971), 68, and Walsh i, 29.
3. 'Cross' is not a single style. As the variations are not like those between different set of punches, no attempt has been made to distinguish the styles.
4. Benjamin Cooke took over the shop of John Jones, the Golden Harp, New Street, Covent Garden, following Jones's death in 1722. On 2 July 1723 Cooke married Jones's widow, Phillipa. See Donovan Dawe, *Organists of the City of London*, 88.
5. 'Musick Shops' includes several different styles, even some of Walsh's.
6. 'Mixed' means several unidentified engraving styles are to be found in the item.

Descriptions

Plate 1.1   Eccles, *New Year's Day Songs*, 1703

1   Eccles, *New Year's Day Songs*, 23 February 1703

Caption: plate 1.1. 322 × 206 mm. Lcm: II.J.15a.

[within cartouche] (The Songs and Symphonys Perform'd before Her Majesty at her Palace of St. James, on New=years day, Compos'd by Mr. J. Eccles Master of her Majestys Musick, Published for Febrvary. 1703 price. 1s. 6d ♩ [at foot] London Printed for & Sould by I: Walsh Musicall Instrument maker in Ordinary to his Majesty at the Golden Harp & Ho=boy in Catherine=street near Summerset=house in ye strand

14 leaves. Pp. [i]□ 1□-13□.
Leaves printed on 1 side.
Tallest copy 322 × 206 mm. Vertical chain lines.

One page engraved per plate. Engraving style Walsh 1.
Title-page plate 256 × 190 mm. Passe-partout no. 1.

Walsh i: 117.
Advertised in *Post Boy*, 23 February 1703. Price 1/6.

Contents: title-page [i]; songs 1-13.

Songs:

No.	Page	First Line
1	1-4	Hark how the muses call aloud (m Eccles, s Robert, Elford)
2	5	They call and bid the spring appear (m Eccles, s Elford)
3	6-7	Like you the goddess thus replies (m Eccles, s Elford)
4	8-9	Sound thy loudest trumpet fame (m Eccles, s Elford)
5	10-12	War's angry voice be heard no more (m Eccles, s Cook)
6	13	Let thus thy prosp'rous minutes glide (m Eccles, s Robert)

Notes:
1. In title, 'Febrvary' is a label pasted over 'January'.
2. 'his' in imprint altered to 'her' in MS.
3. Copy at ALb issued as part of annual volume of *Monthly Mask of Vocal Music*.

Copy: Lcm II.J.15a.

Plate 2.1 Eccles, *New Year's Day Songs*, 1703

Caption: plate 2.1. 338 x 210 mm. Lbl: K.7.e.4.

[within cartouche] ⌠ The Songs and Symphonys Perform'd before Her
Majesty at her Palace of St. James, on New=years day, Compos'd by Mr. J.
Eccles Master of her Majestys Musick, Published for Febrvary. 1703 price. 1s.
6d ⌡ I: Collins. sculp [at foot] London Printed for & Sould by I: Walsh
Musicall Instrument maker in Ordinary to his Majesty at the Golden Harp &
Ho=boy in Catherine=street near Summerset=house in ye strand [on separate
engraved plate beneath] and I. Hare at the Golden Viol in St. Pauls Church=
yard, and at his shop in Freemans=yard near ye Royal Exchange

14 leaves. Pp. [i]⎵ 1⎵-13⎵.
Leaves printed on 1 side.
Tallest copy 367 x 238 mm. Vertical chain lines.

One page engraved per plate. Engraving style Walsh 1.
Title-page plate 256 x 190 mm. Passe-partout no. 1.

Walsh i: 117.
Advertised in *Post Boy*, 23 February 1703. Price 1/6.

Contents: title-page [i]; songs 1-13.

Songs: see 1.

Notes:
1. In title, 'Febrvary' is a label pasted over 'January'.
2. Ge: in imprint, 'his' altered to 'her' in MS.
3. Lbl: - pp. 12-13; 'Febrvary' lacks 'F'.

Copies: Ge R.x.17; Lbl K.7.e.4.

Plate 3.1   Eccles, *New Year's Day Songs*, 1703

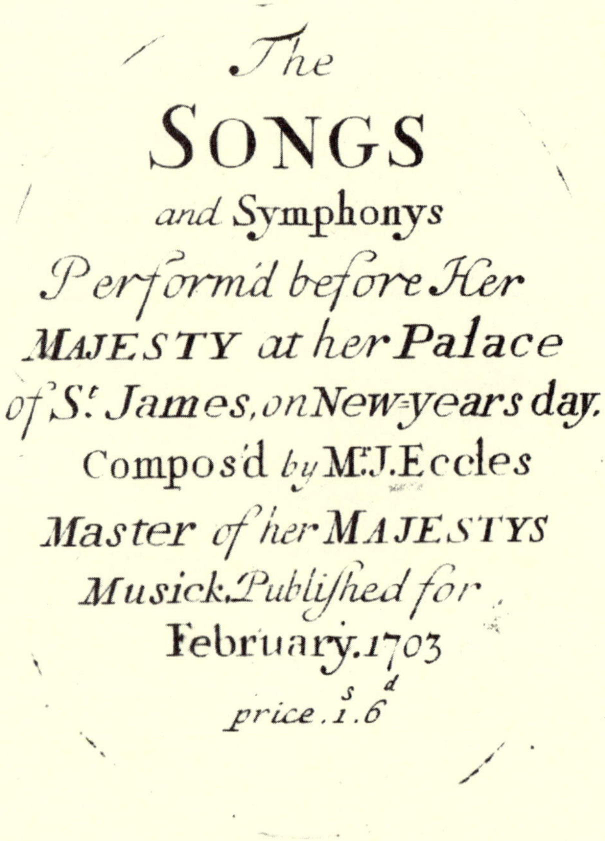

The

SONGS

and Symphonys

P erform'd before Her

MAJESTY at her Palace

of S.ᵗ James, on New-years day.

Compos'd *by* M.ᵗ J. Eccles

Master of her MAJESTYS

Musick. Published for

February. 1703

price . 1 . 6 ˢ ᵈ

6

3   Eccles, *New Year's Day Songs*, 23 February 1703

Caption: plate 3.1. 320 x 202 mm. Lbl: Hirsch IV.740.

[on small plate to fit within cartouche] The Songs and Symphonys Perform'd before Her Majesty at her Palace of St. James, on New=years day, Compos'd by Mr. J. Eccles Master of her Majestys Musick, Published for February. 1703 price. 1s. 6d

14 leaves. Pp. [i]▯ 1▯-13▯.
Leaves printed on 1 side.
Tallest copy 365 x 240 mm. Vertical chain lines.

One page engraved per plate. Engraving style Walsh 1.
Title-page plate 93 x 71 mm.

Walsh i: 117.
Advertised in *Post Boy*, 23 February 1703. Price 1/6.

Contents: title-page [i]; songs 1-13.

Songs: see 1.

Notes:
1. Text of title only; no outer passe-partout title-page; 'February' engraved on plate.
2. Copies at Lam and DRc were issued as parts of *Monthly Mask of Vocal Music* volumes.
3. Lbl: - p. 13.

Copies: Lbl Hirsch IV.740; Ob Don.c.66(1); Obh Mus. E.126; TWm —.

Plate 4.1   Weldon, *Third Book of Songs*, 1703

8

Caption: plate 4.1. 326 x 195 mm. Lbl: G.301.a.

[within cartouche] ⌠ Mr. Weldons Third Book of Songs Begining with single Songs Perform'd at the Consorts in York Buildings and at ye Theatres as also Symphony Songs for Violins and Flutes never before Publish'd Carefully Corrected by ye Author price 2s-6d ⌡ I: Collins. sculp [at foot] London Printed for & Sould by I: Walsh Musicall Instrument maker in Ordinary to her Majesty at the Golden Harp & Ho=boy in Catherine=street near Summerset=house in ye strand

20 leaves. Pp. [i]⬚ 1⬚-19⬚.
Leaves printed on 1 side.
Tallest copy 337 x 215 mm. Vertical chain lines.

One page engraved per plate. Engraving style Walsh 1.
Title-page plate 253 x 185 mm. Passe-partout no. 1.

Walsh i: 123.
Advertised in *Post Man*, 11 May 1703. Price 2/6.

Contents: title-page [i]; songs 1-19.

Songs:

No.	Page	First Line
1	1	Young Mirtillo brisk and gay, The (m Weldon, s Campion, < *Fair Example*)
2	2-3	My cruell fair one has the art (m Weldon, s Lindsey)
3	4-6	See how pleasantly yon fawn (m Weldon, s Campion)
4	7-9	Cupid instruct an amorous swain (m Weldon, s Campion)
5	10-14	In vain we say, that love's the best (m Weldon, s Lindsey)
6	15-19	Sue to Cælia for the favor (m Weldon, s Laroon)

Note:
1. Lcm: - p. 19.

Copies: Lbl G.301.a; Lcm II.F.22(3).

Plate 5.1   *Collection of Choicest Songs & Dialogues, 1703*

Caption: plate 5.1. 319 x 204 mm. Lbl: G.151.

[within cartouche] ⌠ A Collection of the Choicest Songs & Dialogues Composd By the most Eminent Masters of the Age ⌡ I: Collins. sculp [at foot] London Printed for & Sould by I: Walsh Musicall Instrument maker in Ordinary to his Majesty at the Golden Harp & Ho=boy in Catherine=street near Summerset=house in ye strand

Pp. See note under Contents.
Leaves printed on 1 side.
Tallest copy 320 x 210 mm. Vertical chain lines.

One page engraved per plate. Engraving style Walsh and Cross
Title-page plate 254 x 184 mm. Passe-partout no. 1.

Walsh i: 463.
Price £1 10s.

Contents: the complexity of *Choicest Songs* precludes creation of a standard summary of contents. Therefore I have listed all the songs in all the copies under Songs. Four copies—DFo, ICU, Lbl (G.151.a.), Obh (Mus. E.119)—contain the 'Cattaloge', the full title of which is 'A Cattaloge of the Choicest SONGS and DIALOGUES by the most Eminent Masters Printed for I WALSH'. There are a few differences between these 'Cattaloge' listings. Obh (Mus. E.119) is the fullest and has been used as the basis for the list of the first 234 songs. A short section of 6 songs follows; it lists songs that are omitted from the 'Cattaloge' but which are printed on a few of those same sheets. The third section comprises the additional (non-'Cattaloge') songs in each book. No copy contains all the songs and no copy contains all the songs listed in the 'Cattaloge'.

The copy of Bononcini's *Etearco* (75) issued in 1711 now at NRU-Mus contains a 'second edition' of the 'Cattaloge'. Completely re-engraved the page is titled, 'A Cattaloge of the Choicest Songs and Dialogues by the most Eminent Masters Printed for I Walsh & Randall' and lists 272 songs, one of which is a duplication.

As only a few of the song sheets are paginated and that pagination refers to the location of other copies of the sheets in different books, I indicate the contents of the copies of *Choicest Songs* by listing the song numbers for each song before Table VI, which summarizes in broad terms the quantities of songs in each copy.

The Song list comprises:
1 songs from the 'Cattaloge', first edition, pp. 12-16,
2 six songs on sheets of other songs listed in the 'Cattaloge', p. 16,
3 songs not in the 'Cattaloge' or on its song sheets, pp. 16-20.
Copy contents are listed on pp. 21-22 and summarized on pp. 24-25.
The 'Cattaloge' songs are listed in the order of the 'Cattaloge', which is semi-alphabetical. Similarly, the additional songs are not quite in strict alphabetical order, as they follow their arrangement in the books themselves. First lines are transcribed as they appear on the song sheets and not as listed in the 'Cattaloge'.
Copies in the list of songs are arranged by date of examination, an order that does not accord with date of publication or quantities of 'Cattaloge' contents.

Songs:

Song   First Line

Songs listed in 'Cattaloge'

1   Amorous swain to Juno pray'd, An (m Weldon)
2   Ah whither shall I fly (m Sweet, v Congreve)
3   Gentle warmth comes o're my heart, A (m Clarke, J.)
4   Bonny lad there was, A (s Prince, < *Maid in the Mill*)
5   Lass there lives upon the green, A (m Courteville, D&M 1925)
6   Awake my eyes awake (m Leveridge)
7   Ah! how sweet it is to love (m Purcell, H., s Ayliff, < *Tyrannic Love, or the Royal Martyr*, D&M 57)
8   Albacinda, drew the dart (D&M 102)
9   Ah Silvia never baulk my pleasure (D&M 79)
10 Lusty young smith at his vice stood a filing, A (m Leveridge, D&M 2145)
11 Bonny northern ladd, A (m Croft)
12 Ah how sweet are the cooling breeze (m Croft, v D'urfey, D&M 59)
13 Advance, gay tenants of the plain (m Eccles, s Bracegirdle, < *Mad Lover* D&M 13)
14 Ah fly those little charming arts (m Clarke, J.)
15 Ah sweet inchantress who canst throw (m Clarke, T.)
16 As Cupid rogishly one day (m Eccles, D&M 204)
17 At noon in a sultry summer's day (m Weldon, D&M 268)
18 And in each track of glory (m Purcell, H., D&M 168)
19 Amongst the pure ones all (s Willis, D&M 160)
20 As Oyster Nan stood by her tub (D&M 230)
21 By moonlight on the green (s Lucas, D&M 449)
22 Blythe Jockey, young and gay (s Boy)
23 Black and gloomy as ye grave
24 Behold the man that with gigantick might (m Purcell, H., s Leveridge, Lindsey, D&M 345)
25 Bellinda's pretty pleasing form (m Eccles, s Gouge, < *Women Will Have Their Wills*, D&M 352)
26 Blowzabella my bouncing doxie (v D'urfey, D&M 385)
27 Blow Boreas blow (m Bradley, Robert, D&M 384)
28 Beneath a gloomy shade (m Purcell, D., s Bowen, J., < *Humours of the Age*, D&M 356)
29 Cupid instruct an amorous swain (m Weldon)
30 Celladon when spring came on (v D'urfey, s Leveridge, < *Country Miss with her Furbeloe*, D&M 505)
31 Cælia let not pride undoe you (m Weldon)
32 Cloe thou goddess of my youth (m Weldon)
33 Cou'd a man be secure (m Clarke, J., s Leveridge, < *Committee*)
34 Cloe brisk and gay appears (m Leveridge, D&M 543)
35 Cupid make your virgins tender (m Purcell, D., D&M 771)
36 Come let us leave the town (m Purcell, H., D&M 673)
37 Cloe found love for his Psyche in tears (m Eccles, s Prince, < *Agreeable Disappointment*, D&M 545)
38 Charming creature look more kindly (m Barrett)
39 Celias bright beautys all other's transcend (m Keen, v Keen, < *Heiress or the Sallamanca Doctor*, D&M 519)
40 Corinna with a gracefull air (m Purcell, D., s Cooper, < *Reformed Wife, or the Lady's Cure*)
41 Cease your amrous pipes, and flutes (m Purcell, D., s Erwin, < *Grove*, D&M 502)
42 Clarinda urg'd by your disdain (m Weldon)
43 Come bring us wine in plenty (D&M 612)
44 Celia my heart has often rang'd (m Weldon, s Campion, < *She Would and She Would Not*, D&M 514)
45 Celia you in vain deceive me (m Weldon)
46 Celia has a thousand charms (m Purcell, H., D&M 511)

47 Celebrate this festival (m Purcell, H., D&M 506)
48 Crown your bowles, loyall soul's (m Purcell, H., v D'urfey, D&M 760)
49 Celestiall harmony is in her tongue (m Purcell, D.)
50 Come fill up the bowl (D&M 630)
51 Celinda's beauty voice and witt (m Barrett)
52 Dear, pretty youth (m Purcell, H., < *Tempest*, D&M 821)
53 Drink, my boys (D&M 890)
54 Dulcibella when e'er I sue for a kiss (m Purcell, H., D&M 899)
55 Draw Cupid draw, and make fair Sylvia know (m Motley, D&M 885)
56 Enticeing love my vows has broke (m Gorton)
57 Early in ye dawning of a winters morn (s Pinkethman, D&M 902)
58 Fye Amarillis cease to greive (m Eccles, s Hodgson, D&M 986)
59 Farewell my bonny, witty pretty, Moggy (v D'urfey, s Leveridge, D&M 965)
60 Fly ye lazy hours (m Eccles, s Bracegirdle, D&M 1031)
61 From rosie bow'rs where sleeps the god of love (m Purcell, H., D&M 1091)
62 Fixt on ye fair Miranda's eies (m Purcell, H., s Bowen, J., < *Humours of the Age*, D&M 1012)
63 Forth from my dark and dismall cell (D&M 1064)
64 Frank what shall we do (m Willis)
65 Farewell vaine nymph (m Gillier)
66 From silent shad's and the Elizium groves (m Purcell, H., D&M 1093)
67 Fye, Damon leave this foolish passion (D&M 991)
68 Fly from his charming language fly (m Leveridge, s Lindsey, D&M 1020)
69 Fond woman with mistaken art (m Purcell, D., s Erwin, < *Reformed Wife, or the Lady's Cure*)
70 For rurall and sincerer joys (m Purcell, D., s Shaw, < *Love Makes the Man*)
71 Fill all the glasses, fill e'm high (m Eccles, < *Harry the Fifth*)
72 Fair Cloe my breast so alarms (m Purcell, H., D&M 933)
73 Gloriana is engaging fair (m Barrett)
74 Hear ye midnight fantomes (m Eccles, s Cook, Davis, < *Fair Penitent*)
75 Hark the trumpet sounds alarms (m Berenclow)
76 Hark the cock crow'd (m Clarke, J., D&M 1264)
77 Happy wee who free from love (s Lindsey, < *Imposture Defeated*, D&M 1246)
78 How calm Elesa are these groves (s Lindsey, < *Imposture Defeated*, D&M 1397)
79 How vain and false a woman is (m Barrett)
80 How wretched is our fate, to love (m Barrett, D&M 1472)
81 How severe is my fate (m Croft, v Martin, s Freeman)
82 How long shall I pine, for love (s Prince, < *Maid in the Mill*, D&M 1438)
83 Hold Iohn e're you le've me (m Leveridge, s Leveridge, Pate, < *Island Princess*, D&M 1385)
84 Hark Prince Eugine com's along (m Shore, v Person of Quality)
85 How insipid were life (m Croft)
86 He that has whom he lov'd possest (m Eccles, s Hodgson, < *As you Find it*. Leaf exists in two states, one with and one without the composer's name at the top right-hand corner.)
87 If wine and musick have the pow'r (m Eccles, s Hodgson)
88 I'o Victoria (m Finger)
89 Insulting rivall doe not boast (m Weldon, D&M 1826)
90 I gently touch't her hand (m Eccles, D&M 1522)
91 If Celia you had youth at will (D&M 1670)
92 Ienny long resisted Wully's fierce desire (m Leveridge, s Campion, D&M 1858)
93 Iogging on from yonder green (m Leveridge, s Lindsey, D&M 1876)
94 I burn, my brain consumes to ashes (m Eccles, < *Don Quixote*, D&M 1497)
95 Is'e no more to shady coverts (m Clarke, J., s Temple, D&M 1653)
96 Iocky was as brisk & blith a lad (m Clarke, J., s Cross, D&M 1874)
97 In vain I seek for ease (m Gillier)
98 It tis not that I love you less (m Cox, D&M 1845)
99 I'm, like inconstant chance (s Prince, < *Maid in the Mill*)
100 If I hear Orinda swear (m Eccles, s Bracegirdle, < *Love Betrayed*, D&M 1681)
101 Jemmy told his passion, in a courtly phrase (m Keen)
102 I'll hurry thee hence (m Eccles, s Bracegirdle, < *Justice Buisy*)

157 Since times are so bad (m Purcell, H., < *Don Quixote*, D&M 2968)
158 Stop o ye waves (m Weldon, s Lindsey, D&M 3078)
159 Stay, ah stay, ah turn, ah whither wou'd you fly (m Eccles, s Hodgson, < *Fair Penitant*, D&M 3058)
160 Sound fame, thy brazen trumpet sound (m Purcell, H., < *Dioclesian*, D&M 3041)
161 Slaves to London I'll deceive you (m Berenclow, D&M 2993)
162 Sing ye muses (m Farinel, v D'urfey)
163 Sing all ye muses (D&M 2973). Not in any copy.
164 Shou'd I once change my heart (m Leveridge, < *Aesope*)
165 Sue to Cælia for the favor. Not in any copy.
166 Since Celia 'tis not in our power (m Purcell, D., s Hughes, < *Inconstant or the Way to Win him*)
167 Stay lovely youth, delay thy choice (m Eccles, < *Prize Musick*, D&M 3060)
168 See how pleasantly yon fawn (m Weldon, s Campion)
169 Twelve hundred years at least (m Clarke, J.)
170 Thou gay, thou cruel maid (m Purcell, D., s Bowen, J., < *Fop's Fortune*)
171 Take not a womans anger ill (m Purcell, H., s Leveridge, < *Rival Sisters*, D&M 3145)
172 This way mortall bend thy eyes (m Eccles, < *Prize Musick*, D&M 3287)
173 Old wife she sent to the miller her daughter, The (v D'urfey, D&M 2602)
174 Thô Cælia you my story hear
175 'Twas when summer was rosie (v D'urfey, D&M 3498)
176 Valliant Eugene to Vienna is gone, The (m D'urfey, s Leveridge, < *Country Miss with her Furbeloe*, D&M 3541)
177 Wakefull nightingale that takes no rest, The (m Weldon, D&M 3564)
178 To meet her Mars, the queen of love (m Eccles, s Hodgson, D&M 3431)
179 Charms of bright beauty, The (m Courteville, D&M 531)
180 Appointed hour of promis'd bliss, The (m Weldon, v Horace)
181 Tis sultry weather pretty maid (m Clarke, J., s Leveridge, Lindsey, < *Island Princess*)
182 Jolly breeze that comes whistling, The (m Eccles, < *Rinaldo and Armida*, D&M 1880)
183 Tis done, the pointed arrow's in my heart (m Purcell, D., s Shaw, < *Humours of the Age*, D&M 3377)
184 Jolly swains, The (m Purcell, D., < *Island Princess*)
185 Tell me Bellinda, prithee doe (D&M 3155)
186 Sun was just setting, The (v Person of Quality, s Leveridge, D&M 3107)
187 Fair Aurelias gon astray, The (m Leveridge, D&M 930)
188 Tho over all mankind (m Leveridge, s Lindsey, < *Tragedy of Calligula* D&M 3319)
189 Thou flask once filld (m Blow, D&M 3294)
190 To touch your heart (m Courteville, s Hughes)
191 To thee o gentle sleep alone (m Elford, s Hodgson, < *Tamerlane* (Rowe))
192 Take o take those lips away (m Weldon, v Shakespear, D&M 3147)
193 Twas in the month of May Jo (m Purcell, D., D&M 3496)
194 Twas within a fourlong of Edenborough town (m Purcell, H., s Girl, < *Mock Marriage*, D&M 3500)
195 Young Mirtillo brisk and gay, The (m Weldon, s Campion, < *Fair Example*)
196 Bonny gray ey'd morn, The (m Clarke, J., s Willis, < *Fond Husband or the Plotting Sisters*, D&M 394)
197 Tell me ye softer powers above (m Leveridge, s Campion, D&M 3180)
198 Thus Damon knock't at Celias door (s Leveridge, D&M 3351)
199 Jolly bowle, The (D&M 1879)
200 Ulme is gon, but basely won (m Clarke, J., v D'urfey, D&M 3506)
201 Virtumnus Flora you that bless the feilds (m Courteville, D&M 3546)
202 Underneath a gloomy shade (m Purcell, D., s Shaw, < *Grove*, D&M 3514)
203 What pain Corinna he endures (m Weldon, s Elford)
204 Whilst the French their arms discover (m Clarke, J., v D'urfey, D&M 3892)
205 When Cloe I your charms survey (m Leveridge, < *Plot and no Plot*)
206 Why de'you with disdain refuse (m Leveridge, v Person of Quality)

207 Was it a dream or did I hear (m Clarke, J., s Lindsey, < *Fool in Fashion*)
208 What beauty doe I see (m Akeroyde, v D'urfey, s Bourdon, Lucas, < *Bath, or the Western Lass*, D&M 3626)
209 When your angellick face I'd seen (m Weldon)
210 When Cupid from his mother fled (s Allinson, < *Love and a Bottle*, D&M 3702)
211 When Myra sings (m Purcell, H., D&M 3774)
212 When Cloe sings (m Barrett)
213 What wou'd Europa whose shrill cryes (s Leveridge, D&M 3673)
214 When loves sick Mars (m Leveridge, s Willis, < *Fool in Fashion*)
215 Wou'd bright Celinda favour me (m Croft)
216 When Daphne first her shepherd saw (m Purcell, D.)
217 Whilst Phillis is drinking (D&M 3864)
218 Whilst wretched fools sneak up and down (m Purcell, D., s Leveridge, Pate, < *Massaniello*, D&M 3895)
219 When Thirsis did Dorinda woe (m Martin, v Chocke)
220 When Phillida with Jockey (v D'urfey, D&M 3780)
221 Why will Clemene when I gaze (m Weldon, D&M 3963)
222 Wine does wonders ev'ry day (m Eccles, s Gouge, Curco, Spalding, < *Morose Reformer*)
223 When Sawny first did woe me (m Leveridge, D&M 3785)
224 What garrs th' feulish mayde complain (m Purcell, D.)
225 With horns, & with hounds (m Purcell, D., s Erwin, < *Pilgrim*, D&M 3994)
226 Within an arbor of delight (v D'urfey, D&M 4006)
227 You twice ten hundred deities (m Purcell, H., D&M 4111)
228 You ladyes who are young and gay (m Eccles, s Hodgson, < *Morose Reformer*, D&M 4086)
229 Ye gentle gales that fan the air (m Eccles, s Haines, D&M 4040)
230 Ye minutes bring ye happy hour (m Purcell, D., s Campion, < *Funeral*)
231 Young Corydon and Phyllis (m Clarke, J., D&M 4123)
232 You fly and yet you love me too (m Barrett, D&M 4074)
233 You the glorious sons of honour (m Barrett, v D'urfey, D&M 4110)
234 You laugh to see me fond appear (m Purcell, D., s Leveridge)

Songs on song sheets listed above but not included in 'Cattaloge'

235 Ah how lovely sweet and dear (< *Mad Lover*, D&M 55)
236 Cease of Cupid to complain (m Eccles, s Bracegirdle, D&M 497)
237 Come ye nymphs and ev'ry swain (s Bracegirdle, < *Mad Lover*, D&M 719)
238 Fear no danger to insue (m Purcell, H., < *Measure for Measure*)
239 Here Tom here's a health (m Willis)
240 Here's a health to the Queen

Songs from Obh Mus. E.119

241 Glory our martial paradice (m Purcell, D., s Freeman, < *Massaniello*)
242 Where, where's my Pan, my lord, my love (m Purcell, D., s Lindsey, < *Grove*)
243 Ye men and maids who cut the ear (m Purcell, D., s Lindsey, < *Grove*)

Songs from Lbl G.151

244 All things seem deaf to my complaints (m Eccles, s Boman, E. < *Pretenders, or the Town Unmasked*, D&M 134)
245 Awake Cordelia, let your listning ear (m Robart, v Chocke)
246 All ye pleasures Himen brings (m Purcell, D., s Boy, < *Island Princess*, D&M 131)
247 Calms appear when storms are past (m Finger, s Campion, < *Pilgrim*)
248 Come all away, you must not stay (m Purcell, D., s Freeman, < *Grove*, D&M 586)
249 Divine Astrea hither flew (m Clarke, J., s Cross, D&M 862)
250 Great Jove look down (s Lindsey, D&M 1200)

251 Happy mansions pleasant shades (m Purcell, D., s Erwin, < *Grove*, D&M 1240)
252 Happy ever, happy wee (m Purcell, D., s Boy, < *Grove*, D&M 1237)
253 How shall a lover come to know (m Robart)
254 He led her by the milk-white hand (m Akeroyde, s Campion, < *Massaniello*, D&M 1295)
255 Jockey was a dowdy lad (m Clarke, J., v D'urfey, s Campion, < *Campaigners* D&M 1873)
256 Let it be stout old hock (m Graves)
257 Lead on brave nimphs (m Leveridge, D&M 1944)
258 Leave ye mountain vale (s Hughes, D&M 1947)
259 Love's but the frailty of the mind (m Eccles, v Congreve, s Hodgson, < *Way of the World*)
260 Now the maids and the men are making their hay (m Purcell, H., s Reading, J., Pate, < *Fairy Queen*, D&M 2419)
261 Now to you yee dry wooers (m Clarke, J., s Lindsey, Boy, < *Island Princess*)
262 Oh! the mighty pow'r of love (m Eccles, s Boman, E., < *Self Conceit*, D&M 2539)
263 Oh! love what a torment art thou (m Robart, v Chocke)
264 Oh! Iris let my sleeping hours (m Robart)
265 Philander, do not think of arms (m Blow, s Boy, D&M 2676)
266 Shee that wou'd gain a faithfull lover (m Finger, s Hodgson, D&M 2901)
267 She walks as she dreams in a garden of flow'rs (m Purcell, D., s Pate, < *Alexander the Great*)
268 See the trembling sheep revive (m Purcell, D., s Pate, < *Grove*, D&M 2883)
269 See oh see dear cruell boy (m Isum)
270 To Cynthia then our homage pay (m Purcell, D., s Magnus Boy, D&M 3418)
271 Two nymphs insulted Damon's heart (m Robart, v Person of Quality, D&M 3504)
272 Charming Phyllis brisk and gay, The (m Robart)
273 Devil he pull'd off his jacket of flame, The (m Akeroyde, s Campion, < *Massaniello*, D&M 842)
274 Whilst I with greif did on you look (m Purcell, H., < *Spanish Fryar*, D&M 3880)
275 While here for the fair Amarillis I dye (m Finger, D&M 3861)
276 Whilst Galatea you design (m Courteville)
277 We with coldness and disdain (m Purcell, D., s Erwin)
278 Ye birds that in our forrests sing (m Purcell, D., s Boy, < *Grove*, D&M 4030)
279 You've been with dull prologues here banter'd so long (m Leveridge, s Leveridge, < *Island Princess*, D&M 4118)

Songs from Obh Mus. E.118

280 Awake thy spirits raise (< *Judgment of Paris*, D&M 287)
281 Celia is soft, she's charming too (m Clarke, J., s Erwin, D&M 513)
282 Celemene, pray tell me (m Purcell, H., v D'urfey, s Boy, Girl, < *Conquest of Granada*, D&M 507). There are two editions of this leaf. Obh Mus. E.118 contains the Cross edition, while the DLC copy has the Walsh edition.
283 De'el take ye warr yt hurrid Willy from me (D&M 831)
284 Far from thee be anxious care (m Purcell, D., < *Prize Musick*)
285 Forbear o goddess of desire (m Purcell, D., < *Prize Musick*)
286 Fear not mortall none shall harm thee (m Eccles, < *Prize Musick*, D&M 982)
287 Go perjur'd man (m Blow, D&M 1148)
288 In the pleasant month of May (m Barrett, D&M 1779)
289 In vain poor Damon prostrate lies (m Leveridge, v Lady, s Shaw, D&M 1802)
     Mercurius Musicus for October 1702, printed by William Pearson for Henry Playford.
290 Let the dreadfull engines of eternall will (m Purcell, H., s Boman, J., < *Don Quixote*, D&M 1998)
291 Olinda turne & through thy eys (m Purcell, D., s Boy, < *Unhappy Conquerer*)
292 She comes, my goddess comes (s Cibber, D&M 2896)
293 Tho Jockey su'd me long (m Lord Biron, D&M 3315)
294 Then come, kind Damon, come away (m Purcell, D., s Lindsey, D&M 3202)

Songs from Lbl G.304

295 Tory a Whigg & a moderate man, A (v D'urfey, D&M 3470)
296 Ah my fickle Jenny
297 Love thou art best of human joys (m Courteville, D&M 2115)
298 Phyllis has such charming graces (m Purcell, D., s New Boy, < *Campaigners*)
299 Phillis wou'd her charms improve (m Courteville, s Robert, Mrs)
300 To cullies and bullies of country and town (m Person of Quality, v D'urfey, D&M 3417)
301 To convent streams and shady groves (m Courteville, s Ayliff, < *Duke and no Duke*, D&M 3416)
302 That you alone my heart posses (m Eccles, s Fowell, < *Sir Fopling Flutter*, D&M 3196)
303 Your hay is mow'd and your corn is reap'd (m Purcell, H., v Dryden)

Songs from DLC M1620.C7 Case

304 Alass my dear Phyllis (m Simmons)
305 Alass when charming Sylvia's gon (m Purcell, D., s Bowen, J., < *Spanish Wives*)
306 Ah cruel Damon, cease to teaze (m Elford, s Hodgson)
307 Brightest nymph and fairest creature (m Elford)
308 Brisk and gay as blooming May (m Elford, v Scudamor)
309 Custom alass does partial prove (m Barrett)
310 Charming, fair Amoret (m Hall, v Hall, D&M 530)
311 Cælia with mournful pleasure hears (m Eccles, s Hodgson, < *Sir Fopling Flutter*, D&M 518)
312 Come away fellow saylors (m Purcell, H., s Wiltshire, < *Measure for Measure*)
313 Come yee inhabitants of heaven (m Morgan)
314 Celemene is both fair and young (m Garee)
315 Chloe is divinely fair, and sings (m Gillier, s Haines, < *Ladies Visiting Day*)
316 E'er since you came into my sight (m Eccles, s Bracegirdle, < *Justice Buisy*)
317 Fly from Dorinda's beauteous face (m Gillier, v Aliff)
318 For mighty Loves unerring dart (m Gillier, s Hodgson, < *Ladies Visiting Day*)
319 For Iris I sigh and hourely dye (m Purcell, H., v Dryden, s Butler, < *Amphitryon*, D&M 1046)
320 Fly ye winged cupids fly (m Courteville)
321 Her eyes are like the morning bright (m Eccles, s Boman, J., < *Novelty* D&M 1341)
322 Hold and no further advance (m Graves)
323 Hee, oh! pray father (m Eccles, s Boy, Girl, < *Novelty*)
324 Hence ye curst infernal train (m Purcell, D., s Lindsey, < *Amalasont*)
325 I humbly intreat you for charity's sake (m Brown, R.)
326 Barnaby's dead and laid in his tomb
327 I am come to lock all fast (m Purcell, H., s Dyer, < *Fairy Queen*, D&M 1487)
328 If doubts and fears my passion feed (m Corbett, s Gouge)
329 I bles'd his memory that first (m Brown, R.)
330 If loves a sweet passion (s Dyer, < *Fairy Queen*, D&M 1691)
331 I'm vex'd to think that Damon woes me (m Clarke, J., D&M 1650)
332 I attempt from love's sickness to fly (m Purcell, H., s Cross, < *Indian Queen*, D&M 1495)
333 Love is a god whose charming sway (m Eccles, s Knapp, < *Women Will Have Their Wills*)
334 Let us revel and roar (m Eccles, s Reading, J., Curco, < *Lovers' Luck*, D&M 2020)
335 Lucinda is bewitching fair (m Purcell, H., < *Abdelazar, or the Moor's Revenge*, D&M 2141)
336 Live Charles, King Williams friend (m Franck, v Bancks)
337 Lads and lasses blith and gay (m Purcell, H., s Hodgson, < *Don Quixote*, D&M 1920)
338 My dear cockadoodle (m Purcell, D., v D'urfey, s Lindsey, < *Campaigners*, D&M 2244)
339 My lover has an inconstant mind (m Eccles, s Bracegirdle, < *Justice Buisy*)
340 Musick allays the tempests of the soul (m Croft, v Toland)
341 New reformation, begins thro the nation (m Purcell, H., v D'urfey, < *Campaigners*, D&M 2314)
342 Nature her gifts us'd wisely to dispense (m Williams, v Jansons)

343 No, ev'ry morning my beauties renew (m Eccles, s Bracegirdle, < *Justice Buisy*, D&M 2320)
344 No I shan't envy him who e'er he be (m Brown, R., v Norris)
345 No more his brain possess (m Purcell, D., s Pate, < *Massaniello*)
346 Once more love's mighty chains are broak (m Elford)
347 Oh how you protest and solemly swear (m Purcell, H., s Knight, < *Mock Marriage*, D&M 2479)
348 Oh fye what mean I foolish maid (m Eccles, s Doggett, < *Married Beau*, D&M 2467)
349 O raree show, o brave show (m Eccles, s Laroche, D&M 2519)
350 Oh! lovely Syron now give o'er (m Wilford, v Child, D&M 2502)
351 She flies in vain from love (m Eccles, s Hodgson, < *Country Wake*)
352 Sleep shepherd sleep (s Cross, < *Imposture Defeated*, D&M 2998)
353 See in the smiling month of May (m Purcell, D., s Girl, D&M 2874)
354 Smile then with a beam devine (m Clarke, J., s Cross, D&M 3002)
355 Eagle evry night Prometheus spares, The (m Corbett, v Lord D., s Cross, < *Female Wits*) *Female Wits* was written by 'W. M.'
356 Twas when the sheep were shearing (m Morgan, s Doggett, < *Cynthia and Endymion*, D&M 3499)
357 Till now I suppress'd, the fire in my breast (m Eccles, s Bracegirdle < *Justice Buisy*)
358 Happy page, the lovely boy, The (m Purcell, D.)
359 What beauty is, let Strephon tell (m Eccles, s Hodgson, < *Fate of Capua*, D&M 3627)
360 Warr and battle, now no more (m Barrett, D&M 3568)
361 What ungrateful devil moves you (m Purcell, D., s Crofts, < *Love's Last Shift*, D&M 3668)
362 Whilst thus our calmer pleasure flow (m Clarke, J., s Freeman, Leveridge, D&M 3894)
363 Wasted with sighs I sigh'd & pin'd (m Eccles, v Howard, s Wiltshire, < *Chances*, D&M 3575)

Songs from CU-MUSI M1619.C6558 Case X

364 Must I a girl for ever be (m Clarke, J., s Campion, Mr Magnus' Boy, < *Island Princess*, D&M 2230)
365 One holliday last summer (v D'urfey, D&M 2627)
366 Phyllis the witty gay and fair (m Courteville)
367 Celia now is all my song (v Gentleman)

Song from DFo M1497.C43

368 In vain we say, that love's the best (m Weldon, s Lindsey)

Songs from B-Bc W472

369 Chronos mend thy pace (m Purcell, D., s Freeman, < *Pilgrim*, D&M 566)
370 Cease that inchanting song (m Clarke, J.)
371 Ha! well hast thou done (m Purcell, D., s Pate, < *Pilgrim*, D&M 1215)
372 Jockey loves his Moggey dearly (m Brown, R., D&M 1871)
373 In Cynthia's face and brightest eyes (m Nicola, D&M 1742)
374 Long has Pastora rul'd the plain (m Clarke, J., s Campion, < *Relapse, or Virtue in Danger*, D&M 2063)
375 Philander was a jolly swain (m Nickson, v Nickson)
376 Since Momus comes to laugh below (m Purcell, D., s Freeman, < *Pilgrim*, D&M 2948)
377 To you I gave a virgin heart (m Nicola, D&M 3454)
378 Wully and Georgy now beath are gean (m Akeroyde, D&M 4028)
379 When Jockey first I saw (m Cox, D&M 3761)
380 What life can compare with the jolly town rakes (m Purcell, D., s Edwards, < *Younger Brother*, D&M 3649)

Songs from CSmH 474197

381 Ah cruel nymph (D&M 41)
382 All beauty were a foolish toy (s Hodgson, < *City Lady*)
383 Alass you strive to heal in vain (m Weldon, D&M 100)
384 Alass here lies poor Alonzo slain (m Clarke, J., s Hodgson, < *Timon of Athens*)
385 But how can I live (m Clayton, s Tofts, < *Arsinoe*)
386 Boiling passions rage no more (m Clayton, s Leveridge, < *Arsinoe*)
387 Britains strike home (m Purcell, H., < *Bonduca*, D&M 437)
388 By purling streams (m Croft, s Elford)
389 Charming creature, every feature (m Clayton, s Hughes, < *Arsinoe*)
390 Conscious dungeon walls of stone (m Clayton, < *Arsinoe*)
391 Cruel stars who all conspire (m Clayton, s Cross, < *Arsinoe*)
392 Conqu'ring o but cruel eyes (m Clayton, s Cross, < *Arsinoe*)
393 Charming fair for thee I languish (s Boy, < *Camilla*)
394 Cease cruel tyrannising (s Hughes, < *Camilla*)
395 Cease cruell to deceive me
396 Come lovely charmer let's retire (s Hodgson)
397 Cloe blush't and frown'd and swore (m Eccles, s Cook, < *Biter*, D&M 542)
398 Fair Amoret is gone astray (v Congreve, D&M 927)
399 From grave lessons and restraint (m Weldon, s Bradshaw, < *Subscription Musick*)
400 Greatness leave me, undeceive me (m Clayton, s Tofts, < *Arsinoe*)
401 Hither turn thee (m Weldon, < *Prize Musick*, D&M 1378)
402 I see she flyes me (m Purcell, H., s Ayliff, < *Aureng-Zebe*, D&M 1596)
403 In Cloes sparkling eyes (m Croft, s Hodgson, D&M 1739)
404 Inspire me love to raise thee (m Weldon, D&M 1820)
405 Julia your unjust disdain (m Purcell, H., D&M 1892)
406 Love is an empty airy name (m Eccles, s Boman, E., < *City Lady*)
407 Love thou tyrant of the fair (m Croft)
408 My dearest, my fairest, I languish (m Purcell, H., s Cook, Hodgson)
409 Phillis not all your charms (m Weldon)
410 Queen of darkness sable night (s Hughes, < *Arsinoe*)
411 Sleep Ormondo void of fear (m Clayton, s Tofts, < *Arsinoe*)
412 So well Corinna likes the joy (m Eccles, s Little Boy, < *She Gallants*, D&M 3014)
413 Take heed Bellinda how you lend an ear (m Weldon, s Campion)
414 Thus sinking mariners (m Clayton, s Hughes, < *Arsinoe*)
415 To warr my thoughts to warr (m Clayton, s Tofts, < *Arsinoe*)
416 Thou soft machine, that dost her hand obey (m Croft)
417 Tell me wanton god of love (m Weldon, s Campion)
418 To arms your ensigns strait display (m Purcell, H., < *Bonduca*, D&M 3411)
419 Tell me why my charming fair (m Purcell, H., < *Prophetess*, D&M 3175)
420 Wanton zephy'rs softly blowing (s Tofts, < *Arsinoe*)
421 When charming Teraminta sings (m Weldon, D&M 3694)
422 Yee stars that rule my birth
423 Yee gods I only wish to die (m Clayton, s Leveridge, < *Arsinoe*)

The copies are arranged in order—from most to least songs they contain that are listed in the 'Cattaloge'—as in Table VI that follows. The contents are given as they are to be found in each book using the song numbers from the list.

Obh Mus. E.119: title-page, 1, 2, 3, 4, 5, 6, 7, 8, 9, 10, 11, 12, 13, 237, 14, 15, 16, 17, 18, 19, 20, 21, 22, 23, 24, 25, 26, 27, 28, 29, 30, 31, 32, 33, 34, 35, 36, 37, 236, 38, 39, 40, 41, 42, 43, 44, 45, 46, 47, 48, 49, 50, 51, 52, 53, 54, 56, 57, 58, 59, 60, 178, 61, 62, 63, 64, 239, 238, 65, 66, 67, 68, 69, 70, 71, 72, 241, 73, 74, 75, 76, 79, 80, 81, 82, 83, 84, 85, 86, 87, 88, 89, 90, 91, 92, 93, 94, 95, 96, 97, 98, 99, 240, 100, 101, 102, 103, 104, 105, 107, 108, 109, 110, 111, 112, 113, 114, 115, 117, 118, 119, 120, 121, 122, 123, 124, 125, 126, 127, 128, 130, 131, 132, 235, 133, 134, 135, 136, 138, 139, 140, 141, 142, 143, 144, 146, 147, 148, 149, 150, 151, 152, 153, 154, 155, 156, 157, 158, 159, 160, 161, 162, 164, 166, 167, 168, 169, 172, 173, 174, 175, 176, 177, 179, 180, 181, 182, 184, 185, 186, 187, 188, 189, 190, 191, 192, 193, 195, 196, 198, 199, 200, 201, 202, 203, 204, 205, 206, 208, 209, 210, 211, 212, 213, 214, 215, 216, 217, 218, 219, 220, 221, 223, 242, 243, 226, 227, 228, 229, 230, 231, 232, 233, 234, 'Cattaloge', *Monthly Mask* tables.

Lbl G.151.a: title-page, 1, 2, 3, 4, 5, 6, 7, 8, 9, 10, 11, 12, 13, 237, 14, 15, 16, 17, 19, 20, 21, 22, 23, 24, 25, 26, 27, 28, 29, 30, 31, 32, 33, 34, 35, 36, 37, 236, 38, 40, 41, 42, 43, 44, 45, 46, 47, 48, 50, 51, 52, 53, 54, 55, 56, 57, 58, 59, 60, 178, 61, 62, 63, 64, 239, 238, 65, 66, 67, 68, 69, 70, 71, 73, 241, 74, 75, 76, 79, 80, 81, 82, 83, 84, 85, 86, 87, 88, 89, 90, 91, 92, 93, 94, 95, 96, 98, 99, 240, 100, 101, 102, 103, 104, 105, 107, 109, 110, 111, 112, 113, 114, 115, 116, 117, 118, 119, 120, 123, 124, 125, 126, 127, 128, 130, 131, 132, 235, 133, 134, 136, 138, 139, 140, 141, 142, 143, 144, 146, 147, 148, 149, 150, 151, 152, 153, 154, 155, 156, 157, 158, 159, 161, 162, 164, 166, 167, 168, 169, 172, 173, 174, 175, 176, 177, 179, 180, 181, 182, 184, 185, 186, 187, 188, 190, 191, 192, 193, 196, 198, 199, 200, 202, 203, 204, 205, 208, 209, 210, 211, 214, 215, 216, 217, 218, 219, 220, 221, 223, 242, 243, 226, 227, 228, 229, 230, 231, 232, 233, 234, 'Cattaloge', *Monthly Mask* tables.

DFo M1497.C43: title-page, *Monthly Mask* tables, 'Cattaloge', 1, 2, 3, 4, 5, 6, 7, 8, 9, 10, 11, 12, 13, 237, 14, 15, 16, 17, 18, 19, 20, 21, 22, 23, 24, 25, 26, 27, 28, 29, 30, 31, 32, 33, 34, 35, 36, 37, 236, 38, 39, 40, 41, 42, 43, 44, 45, 46, 47, 48, 49, 50, 51, 52, 53, 54, 55, 56, 57, 58, 59, 60, 178, 61, 62, 63, 64, 239, 238, 65, 66, 67, 68, 69, 70, 71, 73, 74, 75, 76, 78, 79, 80, 81, 82, 83, 246, 84, 85, 86, 87, 88, 89, 90, 91, 92, 93, 94, 96, 98, 99, 240, 100, 101, 102, 103, 104, 106, 267, 107, 368, 109, 110, 111, 112, 113, 114, 115, 117, 118, 120, 121, 122, 123, 124, 125, 127, 130, 132, 235, 133, 134, 136, 138, 139, 140, 141, 142, 146, 147, 148, 149, 150, 151, 152, 153, 154, 155, 156, 157, 158, 159, 161, 162, 164, 166, 167, 169, 170, 172, 173, 174, 175, 176, 177, 179, 180, 181, 182, 183, 184, 185, 186, 187, 188, 189, 190, 191, 192, 193, 196, 198, 199, 200, 202, 203, 204, 205, 208, 209, 210, 211, 213, 216, 217, 218, 219, 220, 221, 224, 226, 227, 228, 229, 232, 233, 234.

ICU M1738.C79: title-page, 1, 2, 3, 4, 5, 6, 7, 8, 9, 10, 11, 12, 13, 237, 14, 15, 16, 17, 19, 20, 21, 22, 24, 25, 26, 27, 28, 29, 30, 31, 32, 33, 34, 35, 36, 37, 236, 38, 40, 41, 42, 43, 44, 45, 46, 47, 48, 50, 51, 52, 53, 54, 56, 57, 58, 59, 60, 178, 61, 62, 63, 64, 239, 238, 65, 66, 67, 68, 69, 70, 71, 73, 241, 73, 75, 76, 78, 79, 80, 81, 82, 83, 84, 85, 86, 87, 88, 89, 90, 91, 92, 93, 94, 95, 98, 99, 240, 100, 101, 102, 103, 104, 107, 109, 110, 111, 112, 113, 114, 115, 117, 118, 119, 120, 123, 124, 125, 126, 127, 128, 130, 131, 132, 235, 133, 134, 136, 138, 139, 140, 141, 142, 143, 144, 146, 147, 148, 149, 150, 151, 152, 153, 154, 155, 156, 158, 159, 161, 162, 164, 166, 167, 168, 169, 172, 173, 174, 175, 176, 177, 179, 180, 181, 182, 184, 185, 186, 187, 188, 190, 191, 192, 193, 196, 198, 199, 200, 202, 203, 205, 208, 209, 210, 211, 214, 215, 216, 217, 218, 219, 220, 221, 223, 226, 227, 228, 229, 230, 231, 232, 233, 234, 'Cattaloge', *Monthly Mask* tables.

Obh Mus. E.118: title-page, 16, 3, 4, 19, 17, 11, 10, 9, 15, 14, 13, 237, 12, 18, 8, 7, 6, 244, 280, 28, 25, 22, 26, 27, 21, 23, 46, 41, 40, 36, 32, 43, 51, 44, 42, 39, 247, 281, 35, 34, 33, 48, 282, 55, 53, 249, 52, 283, 54, 57, 56, 61, 59, 67, 64, 239, 238, 69, 62, 284, 285, 286, 70, 71, 68, 287, 250, 73, 79, 75, 78, 76, 80, 82, 251, 252, 85, 84, 83, 246, 81, 100, 99, 240, 98, 105, 103, 96, 93, 288, 101, 91, 104, 92, 97, 289, 89, 90, 110, 114, 111, 115, 116, 112, 290, 123, 120, 127, 122, 121, 126, 125, 124, 130, 129, 131, 260, 136, 138, 133, 139, 291, 132, 235, 143, 140, 146, 147, 149, 148, 144, 150, 152, 155, 153, 156, 154, 161, 160, 162, 269, 292, 167, 157, 158, 166, 164, 169, 189, 191, 188, 182, 184, 190, 187, 186, 193, 171, 198, 199, 293, 294, 192, 172, 181, 270, 185, 200, 202, 209, 219, 210, 204, 223, 220, 206, 205, 276, 217, 222, 225, 216, 274, 221, 214, 208, 211, 218, 232, 228, 230, 233, 229, 227.

CU-MUSI M1619.C6558 Case X: title-page, 1, 2, 3, 16, 4, 19, 17, 11, 15, 14, 12, 18, 8, 7, 6, 244, 9, 5, 280, 21, 28, 23, 25, 22, 26, 27, 21, 44, 42, 39, 33, 247, 48, 50, 43, 35, 34, 46, 41, 40, 36, 32, 55, 53, 249, 52, 283, 54, 56, 59, 61, 64, 239, 238, 62, 69, 67, 286, 71, 70, 320, 68, 250, 79, 75, 82, 76, 78, 80, 85, 84, 251, 252, 83, 246, 81, 100, 99, 240, 92, 98, 93, 101, 104, 102, 103, 91, 255, 89, 90, 94, 114, 111, 112, 337, 115, 259, 110, 123, 122, 121, 126, 127, 120, 125, 124, 364, 130, 129, 341, 260, 365, 136, 138, 133, 139, 291, 132, 235, 140, 143, 146, 147, 366, 298, 144, 150, 149, 155, 153, 152, 156, 154, 161, 157, 166, 167, 158, 160, 162, 164, 177, 169, 191, 189, 188, 184, 182, 199, 301, 187, 186, 193, 198, 270, 190, 192, 179, 181, 185, 302, 172, 200, 202, 209, 219, 204, 220, 210, 205, 276, 217, 222, 225, 214, 208, 242, 243, 221, 216, 367, 211, 218, 230, 232, 233, 228, 279, 229, 227.

Lbl G.151: title-page, 3, 4, 16, 19, 20, 12, 11, 14, 13, 237, 15, 17, 244, 8, 10, 18, 245, 5, 9, 21, 27, 28, 22, 25, 23, 26, 32, 33, 42, 39, 48, 43, 34, 46, 40, 41, 248, 258, 53, 52, 249, 54, 56, 57, 59, 62, 64, 239, 238, 69, 67, 71, 61, 68, 70, 241, 250, 73, 79, 75, 84, 76, 78, 80, 85, 251, 252, 253, 81, 83, 246, 254, 98, 89, 105, 91, 93, 92, 97, 96, 255, 101, 103, 95, 104, 106, 267, 94, 90, 114, 256, 116, 115, 111, 257, 112, 110, 259, 123, 121, 122, 126, 127, 120, 124, 125, 260, 129, 261, 141, 133, 262, 139, 138, 263, 132, 235, 134, 143, 140, 264, 148, 146, 265, 147, 145, 150, 144, 149, 155, 152, 153, 156, 154, 161, 158, 166, 266, 268, 269, 157, 162, 164, 191, 180, 169, 198, 189, 270, 182, 185, 197, 188, 187, 186, 184, 193, 170, 183, 181, 179, 272, 272, 273, 200, 202, 222, 204, 220, 223, 225, 214, 274, 210, 205, 206, 217, 275, 276, 277, 242, 243, 216, 211, 218, 233, 230, 232, 228, 278, 279, 229, 227.

Lbl G.304: title-page, 295, 296, 16, 4, 19, 17, 11, 10, 15, 14, 13, 237, 12, 18, 7, 6, 244, 5, 21, 28, 25, 22, 26, 51, 44, 42, 39, 32, 33, 43, 48, 41, 247, 36, 40, 46, 35, 282, 55, 52, 249, 54, 283, 56, 57, 59, 61, 64, 239, 238, 62, 69, 71, 70, 250, 73, 79, 82, 75, 76, 78, 80, 85, 84, 83, 246, 251, 252, 81, 100, 105, 93, 101, 99, 104, 92, 98, 90, 94, 114, 116, 111, 112, 115, 297, 290, 123, 122, 121, 126, 127, 120, 125, 124, 130, 129, 260, 134, 133, 139, 291, 138, 132, 235, 140, 143, 147, 148, 298, 299, 144, 150, 149, 155, 153, 152, 156, 154, 157, 166, 160, 269, 162, 164, 177, 169, 191, 189, 182, 199, 184, 186, 193, 196, 300, 301, 171, 198, 270, 302, 190, 192, 181, 179, 200, 202, 209, 219, 220, 205, 204, 210, 223, 276, 217, 222, 225, 221, 216, 211, 242, 243, 274, 218, 232, 230, 233, 228, 303, 229, 231, 227.

B-Bc W472: title-page, 16, 12, 11, 15, 17, 245, 5, 9, 64, 239, 240, 60, 54, 57, 10, 8, 13, 237, 6, 14, 28, 22, 307, 23, 25, 26, 281, 369, 370, 248, 247, 48, 43, 41, 40, 34, 33, 249, 68, 67, 62, 70, 69, 241, 250, 73, 84, 371, 253, 254, 81, 85, 251, 252, 83, 246, 80, 78, 76, 105, 96, 106, 267, 90, 104, 103, 102, 101, 97, 95, 93, 92, 91, 372, 373, 94, 114, 116, 374, 257, 259, 115, 112, 111, 110, 121, 126, 240, 122, 125, 124, 261, 345, 346, 129, 263, 264, 143, 291, 138, 346, 350, 139, 134, 365, 140, 133, 299, 375, 146, 145, 149, 148, 147, 154, 153, 155, 152, 351, 376, 352, 268, 158, 166, 353, 354, 164, 169, 191, 177, 272, 183, 170, 198, 377, 271, 300, 197, 301, 187, 188, 271, 273, 196, 294, 270, 186, 185, 184, 182, 181, 179, 202, 220, 223, 378, 379, 214, 277, 224, 242, 243, 208, 207, 225, 222, 276, 359, 275, 218, 360, 217, 362, 380, 213, 210, 206, 205, 204, 230, 232, 233, 231, 228, 227, 229, 216, 71.

DLC M1620.C7 Case: title-page, 12, 11, 5, 9, 304, 14, 305, 306, 7, 245, 25, 22, 307, 308, 48, 26, 281, 40, 33, 34, 41, 247, 309, 43, 310, 311, 312, 313, 36, 314, 315, 282, 52, 249, 283, 53, 316, 69, 317, 318, 319, 70, 67, 68, 320, 62, 72, 64, 239, 238, 73, 250, 241, 251, 78, 80, 77, 114, 252, 321, 322, 323, 324, 254, 273, 83, 246, 84, 103, 91, 97, 105, 104, 95, 96, 101, 93, 102, 325, 326, 327, 328, 329, 330, 331, 332, 94, 90, 112, 111, 115, 333, 334, 335, 336, 337, 290, 110, 116, 338, 339, 124, 125, 340, 129, 341, 342, 343, 261, 344, 345, 260, 346, 136, 138, 139, 291, 347, 262, 348, 349, 263, 350, 140, 143, 134, 133, 148, 146, 147, 265, 299, 153, 155, 152, 154, 160, 351, 268, 266, 352, 353, 292, 354, 164, 189, 198, 182, 187, 270, 193, 272, 355, 184, 196, 356, 301, 357, 177, 358, 272, 171, 294, 186, 194, 188, 185, 179, 302, 217, 242, 243, 205, 276, 359, 206, 224, 274, 360, 361, 274, 213, 362, 275, 210, 225, 222, 214, 218, 363, 278, 228.

CSmH 474197: title-page, 385, 411, 389, 38, 422, 390, 391, 386, 423, 414, 420, 400, 410, 415, 392, 393, 394, 395, 396, 115, 88, 146, 382, 86, 323, 406, 412, 159, 90, 363, 398, 94, 229, 244, 126, 25, 397, 12, 85, 416, 403, 407, 388, 142, 112, 164, 188, 187, 68, 34, 198, 205, 8, 125, 289, 152, 179, 381, 320, 5, 190, 17, 401, 399, 221, 368, 156, 149, 42, 44, 192, 168, 417, 409, 119, 158, 31, 413, 177, 144, 404, 421, 383, 103, 147, 62, 124, 35, 28, 111, 114, 40, 181, 384, 287, 405, 227, 66, 61, 46, 341, 52, 136, 47, 418, 387, 402, 290, 211, 54, 18, 36, 157, 24, 408, 419.

Notes:
1. Date of first issue based on inclusion of contents list of October 1703 issue of *Monthly Mask of Vocal Music* in DFo copy. All copies are listed here though all others must date from later. The three copies (Obh Mus. E.118, Lbl G.151.a. and ICU M1738.C79) with *Monthly Mask* tables are from 1704. The DLC copy was issued before 1711 as it contains drafts of documents written aboard H.M.S. Cumberland in 1711.
2. 'The Generall Collection containing 250 of the choisest Songs and Dialogaes Composed by the Eminents Masters of the Age Price Bound. £1. 10s. od.' is listed on the catalogue bound in the Bodleian Library copy of the 1703 complete volume of the *Monthly Mask of Vocal Music*, which was advertised in the *Post Man*, 4 December 1703. See Walsh i, nos. 140 and 142c.
3. Some leaves printed on both sides in a few copies.
4. The 1703/4 'Cattaloge' in Obh Mus. E.119 is reproduced in my 'The Publication and Dating of an Early Eighteenth-Century English Song Book' *Bodleian Library Record* 11(4) (May 1984): 231-240.
5. B-Bc, CSmH, CU-MUSI, DLC: contain MS. indexes.

Copies: B-Bc W472; CSmH 474197; CU-MUSI M1619.C6558 Case X; DFo M1497.C43; DLC M1620.C7 Case; ICU M1738.C79; Lbl G.151; Lbl G.151.a; Lbl G.304; Obh Mus. E.118; Obh Mus. E.119.

Copy Contents

Table VI.—Summary of collation of
A Collection of the Choicest Songs & Dialogues (London, John Walsh)

	Maxima	Obh	Lbl	DFo	ICU	Obh
Call number	—	Mus. E.119	G.151. a	M1497 .C43	M1738 .C79	Mus. E.118
Total songs[1]	250[2]	224	210	209	204	197
Songs in '1703/4 Cattaloge'	234[6]	215	201	200	197	165
Songs on song sheets listed in 1703/4 'Cattaloge'	6	6	6	6	6	5
Songs not in 1703/4 'Cattaloge' or on its song sheets	183	3	3	3	1	27
Songs in 1711 'Cattaloge'	271[7]	2	1	1	1	9
Unique songs[8]	120	4	0	0	0	5
Cross songs[9]	97	2	0	0	0	12
Unique Cross songs	53	0	0	0	0	3
1703/4 'Cattaloge' present	—	y	y	y	y	—
Advertisement present dated	—	—	—	Oct 1703	—	—
Monthly Mask Tables latest date	—	June 1704	April 1704	—	April 1704	—
Assigned dates	1704-15	1704?	1705	ca. 1715	1704?	1710?
Bibliography dates	1703-	1704	1704	1703	1704	—
Original binding	—	y	y	—	—	y

CU-MUSI M1619 .C6558 Case X	Lbl G.151	Lbl G.304	B-Bc W472	DLC M1620 .C7 Case	CSmH 474-197
193	199	173	188[3]	193[4]	116[5]
160	156	142	125	94	64[5]
4	4	4	3	2	0
29	39	27	60[3]	97[4]	52
11	9	9	9	8	16
3	2	4	13	46	43
14	18	11	28	65[4]	12
2	0	0	7	36	5
—	—	—	—	—	—
—	—	—	—	—	—
—	—	—	—	—	—
ca. 1715	ca. 1715[10]	ca. 1715[10]	—	1715?	ca. 1715?
—	—	—	—	1711	—
y	—	—	—	—	y

Notes to Table VI.

Copies are in order of 'Cattaloge' contents, from most to least.

y = yes

[1] Since some songs are printed on more than one leaf and some leaves contain more than one song this figure does not necessarily indicate the number of leaves in the book.

[2] As advertised. The total repertory in the eleven copies numbers 423 songs.

[3] Figure includes two songs that are duplicated. One copy of one of these songs is in a Cross edition.

[4] Figure includes two songs that are duplicated. Both copies of one of these songs are in a Cross edition.

[5] Figure includes one song that is duplicated.

[6] Three songs are not in any copy, 137, 163, 165.

[7] 271 includes 5 songs listed in 1703/4 'Cattaloge'. Does not include one song listed twice.

[8] 'Unique' means not in another copy.

[9] 'Cross songs' includes Cross editions of songs in the 'Cattaloge' but not unsigned songs engraved in his style.

[10] Walsh i, no. 463, gives '*c.* 1715 or later'.

Plate 6.1   Eccles, *Birthday Songs*, 1703

The
SONGS
and Symphonys
Perform'd before Her
MAJESTY at her Palace
of St James's on her Birth Day 1703
Composed by Mr Eccles
Master of Her MAJESTYS
Musick
price 1 s

I: Collins Sculp

London Printed for & sould by I: Walsh Musicall Instrument maker in Ordinary to her Majesty at the
Golden Harp & Ho-boy in Catherine street near Summersethouse in ye strand

6 Eccles, *Birthday Songs*, 4 November 1703

Caption: plate 6.1. 309 x 194 mm. Lbl: H.111.b.

[within cartouche] ſ The Songs and Symphonys Perform'd before Her Majesty at her Palace of St. Jame's on her Birth Day. 1703 Composed by Mr: Eccles Master of Her Majestys Musick price 1s. 6d. ♩ I: Collins. sculp [at foot] London Printed for & Sould by I: Walsh Musicall Instrument maker in Ordinary to her Majesty at the Golden Harp & Ho=boy in Catherine=street near Summerset= house in ye strand

13 leaves. Pp. [i]⬚ 1⬚-12⬚.
Leaves printed on 1 side.
Tallest copy 324 x 200 mm. Vertical chain lines.

One page engraved per plate. Engraving style Walsh 1.
Title-page plate 255 x 175 mm. Passe-partout no. 1.

Walsh i: 139.
Advertised in *Post Man*, 4 November 1703. Price 1/6.

Contents: title-page [i]; songs 1-12.

Songs:

No.	Page	First Line
1	1-2	Inspire us genius of the day (m Eccles, s Elford, Cook, Damascene)
2	3	Blest day arise in state (m Eccles, s Elford)
3	4-7	From this happy day (m Eccles, s Robert, Cook)
4	8	No Albion thou canst ner'e repay (m Eccles, s Elford)
5	9-12	Firm as a rock above the ocean seen (m Eccles, s Cook)

Notes:
1. Lbl: - p. 7.
2. Lcm: has additional pagination in MS. (68-79), partially obscuring printed pagination.

Copies: Lbl H.111.b; Lcm I.G.16.

Plate 7.1   Weldom, *Collection of New Songs*, 1703

A
Collection of New
SONGS
Accompagni'd with
VIOLINS *and* FLUTES
with a Thorow BASS
to Each Song *for y* ORGAN
or HARPSICORD *Composed*
by
M*r* John Weldon

I: Collins. *sculp*

London Printed for & sould by I. Walsh *Musicall Instrument maker in Ordinary to her Majesty at the*
Golden Harp & Ho-boy in Catherine street near Summersethouse in y strand

7   Weldon, *Collection of New Songs*, 31 December 1703

Caption: plate 7.1. 320 x 199 mm. Lbl: G.301.(1.).

[within cartouche] ⌠ A Collection of New Songs Accompagni'd with Violins and Flutes with a Thorow Bass to Each Song for ye Organ or Harpsicord Composed by Mr John Weldon ⌡ I: Collins. sculp [at foot] London Printed for & Sould by I: Walsh Musicall Instrument maker in Ordinary to her Majesty at the Golden Harp & Ho=boy in Catherine=street near Summerset=house in ye strand

21 leaves. Pp. [i]□-[ii]□ 1□-19□.
Leaves printed on 1 side.
Tallest copy 339 x 218 mm. Vertical chain lines.

One page engraved per plate. Engraving style Walsh 1.
Title-page plate 255 x 176 mm. Passe-partout no. 1.
Dedication plate 196 x 170 mm.

Walsh i: 124.

Contents: title-page [i]; dedication [ii]; songs 1-19.

Songs: see **4**.

Notes:
1. Lbl: price in MS. title-page: 2/6.
2. Obh: - p. [i]; pp. 2, 4, 7, 10, 12, 15, 17 reversed in rebinding.
3. Copy at Bp lost.

Copies: Lbl G.301.(1.); Lcm I.A.11.(2.); Obh Mus. E.63.

Plate 8.1   Eccles, *Collection of Songs*, 1704

Plate 8.2   Eccles, *Collection of Songs*, 1704

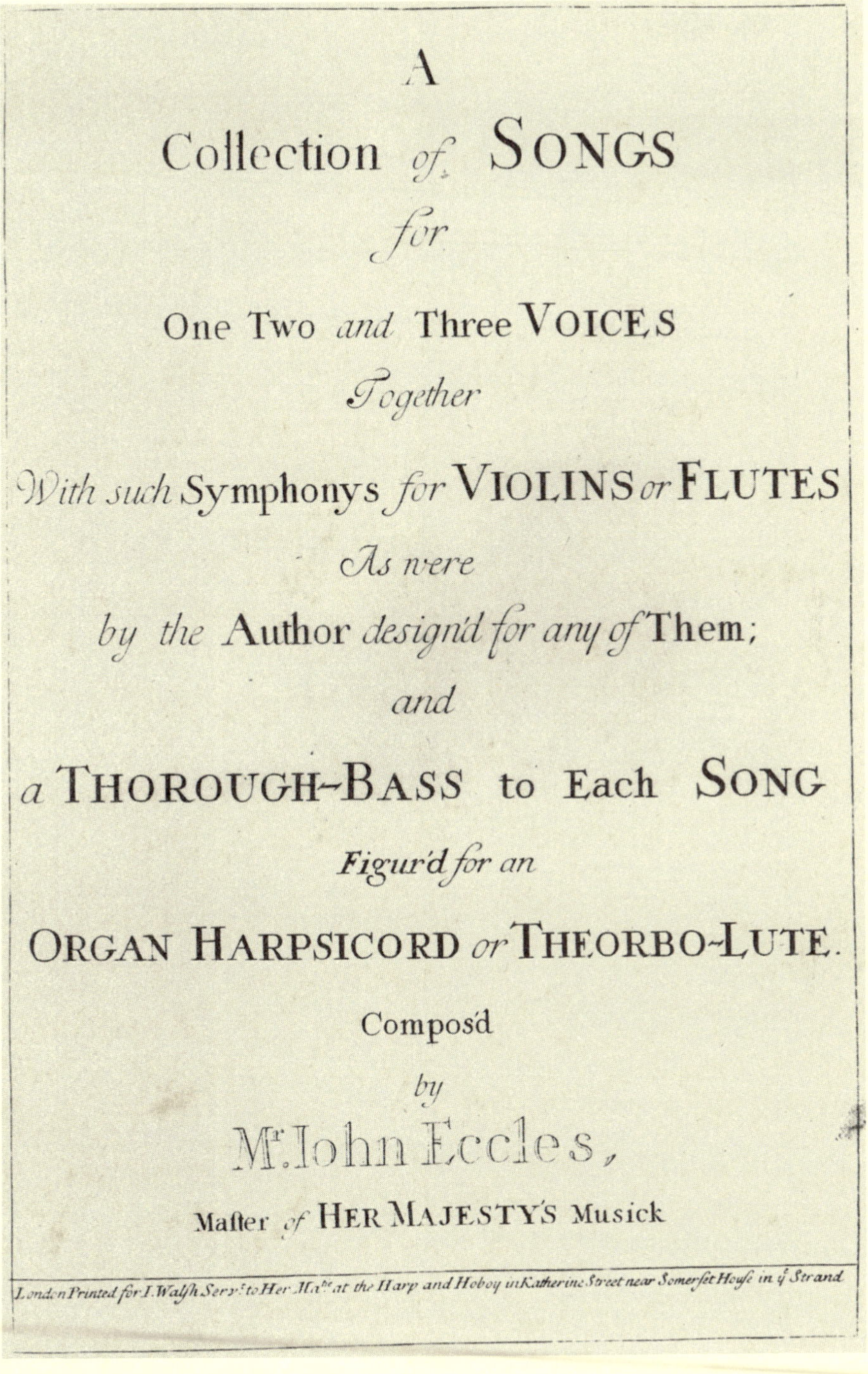

A

Collection *of* SONGS

for

One Two *and* Three VOICES

Together

With such Symphonys *for* VIOLINS *or* FLUTES

As were

by the Author *design'd for any of* Them;

and

a THOROUGH-BASS to Each SONG

Figur'd for an

ORGAN HARPSICORD *or* THEORBO-LUTE.

Compos'd

by

Mr. Iohn Eccles,

Mafter *of* HER MAJESTY'S Musick

London Printed for I. Walfh Servt to Her Mat at the Harp and Hoboy in Katherine Street near Somerfet Houfe in ye Strand.

Plate 8.3   Eccles, *Collection of Songs*, 1704

Plate 8.4   Eccles, *Collection of Songs*, 1704

Caption: plates 8.1-8.4. 320 x 205 mm. Lbl: G.300.

[within cartouche] ⌠ Mr. Ino. Eccles General Collection of Songs ⌡ Berchet
Inventor. H. Hulsbergh Sculpsit. [at foot] London Printed for I. Walsh Servt. to
Her Matie. at the Harp and Hoboy in Katherine Street near Somerset House in
the Strand.

A Collection of Songs for One Two and Three Voices Together With such
Symphonys for Violins or Flutes As were by the Author design'd for any of
Them; and a Thorough-Bass to Each Song Figur'd for an Organ Harpsicord or
Theorbo-Lute. Compos'd by Mr. John Eccles, Master of Her Majesty's
Musick [at foot] London Printed for I. Walsh Servt. to Her Matie. at the
Harp and Hoboy in Katherine Street near Somerset House in ye Strand

87 leaves. Pp. [i]□-[iv]□ 1-164 165□.
Leaves printed on 2 sides.
Tallest copy 365 x 237 mm. Vertical chain lines.

One page engraved per plate. Engraving style Walsh 1 (plate 8.3), 2 (plate 8.4).
Illus. title-page plate 292 x 200 mm. Passe-partout no. 2.
Title-page plate 277 x 180 mm.
Contents plate 303 x 176 mm.
Dedication plate 277 x 180 mm.

Walsh i: 156.
Advertised in *Post Man*, 14 November 1704. Price 18s.

Contents: illus. title-page [i]; title-page [ii]; dedication [iii]; contents [iv]; songs 1-165.

Songs:

No.	Page	First Line
1	1	Cease of Cupid to complain (s Bracegirdle, < *Mad Lover*, D&M 497)
2	2-3	Restless in thought disturb'd in mind (s Hodgson, < *She Ventures and He Wins*, D&M 2800)
3	4-5	Thou only goddess first could'st tell (v Congreve, < *Cecilia song 1701*)
4	6-7	Why, oh! why shou'd the world mistake (< *Princess of Persia*, D&M 3938)
5	8	Stay, ah stay, ah turn, ah whither wou'd you fly (v Congreve, s Hodgson, < *Fair Penitent*, D&M 3058)
6	9	Thus you may be as happy as we (v Doggett, < *Lancashire Witches*, D&M 3360)
7	10	How sweet how lovely when return'd (< *Sham Doctor*, D&M 1463)
8	11-14	From this happy day (s Robert, Cook, < *Her Majesty's Birthday 1702/3*)
9	15-16	All things seem deaf to my complaints (< *Pretenders, or the Town Unmasked*, D&M 134)
10	17	Blest day arise in state (s Elford, < *Her Majesty's Birthday 1702/3*)
11	18-19	Daphne to prove my heart is true (D&M 798)
12	20-21	Inspire us genius of the day (s Elford, Cook, Damascene, < *Queen's Birthday Song 1703/4*)

Notes:
1. Issued by subscription. Proposal published in *Post Man*, 28 October 1703.
2. Mp: - pp. [i-ii]. With three additional songs bound in at the end: 'All in the Downs', 'Stop o ye waves', and 'Oh the charming month of May'.
3. NN (Mus.Res.): additional p. 112 in place of p. 102.

Copies: CtY-Mus Rare Ms14.Ec27; Cu Mr290.a70.III; DFo M1497.E5C4 Cage; DLC M1620.A2E2; Ge R.x.67; *I-Rsc*; Lam —; Lbl G.300; Lbl Mad.Soc.28; Lcm II.J.13; Mp BR f410Ec32; NN Drexel 4122; NN Mus.Res. *MP+ English; Obh Mus. E.13; OU.

Caption: see plates 8.1-8.2.

[within cartouche] ⌈ Mr. Ino. Eccles General Collection of Songs ⌋ Berchet Inventor. H. Hulsbergh Sculpsit. [at foot] London Printed for I. Walsh Servt. to Her Matie. at the Harp and Hoboy in Katherine Street near Somerset House in the Strand.

A Collection of Songs for One Two and Three Voices Together With such Symphonys for Violins or Flutes As were by the Author design'd for any of Them; and a Thorough-Bass to Each Song Figur'd for an Organ Harpsicord or Theorbo-Lute. Compos'd by Mr. Iohn Eccles, Master of Her Majesty's Musick [at foot] London Printed for I. Walsh Servt. to Her Matie. at the Harp and Hoboy in Katherine Street near Somerset House in ye Strand

163 leaves. Pp. [i]□-[iv]□ 1□-18□ 19-20 21□-110□ 111-114 115□-120□ 121-122 123□-140□ 141-142 143□-160□ 161-162 163□-165□.
Leaves printed on 1 side.
Tallest copy 349 x 220 mm. Vertical chain lines.

One page engraved per plate. Engraving style Walsh 1, 2.
Illus. title-page plate passe-partout no. 2.

Walsh i: 156.

Contents: illus. title-page [i]; title-page [ii]; dedication [iii]; contents [iv]; songs 1-165.

Songs: see 8.

Notes:
1. Leaf count, sides printed and pagination are of DFo copy.
2. Lcm: - pp. [i-iv], 1-17, 20-66, 73-94, 103-104, 107-130, 137-165. Pp. 95-100, 131-136 printed using both sides of leaves.
3. TWm: - pp. 33-34; p. [i] reversed; pp. 1-18, 21-32, 35-36, 39-88, 91-92, 95-102, 105-120, 123-126, 131-140, 143-152, 157-164 printed using both sides of leaves. Cartouche on p. [i] empty.

Copies: DFo M1497.E5C3 Cage; Lcm II.J.13a; TWm —.

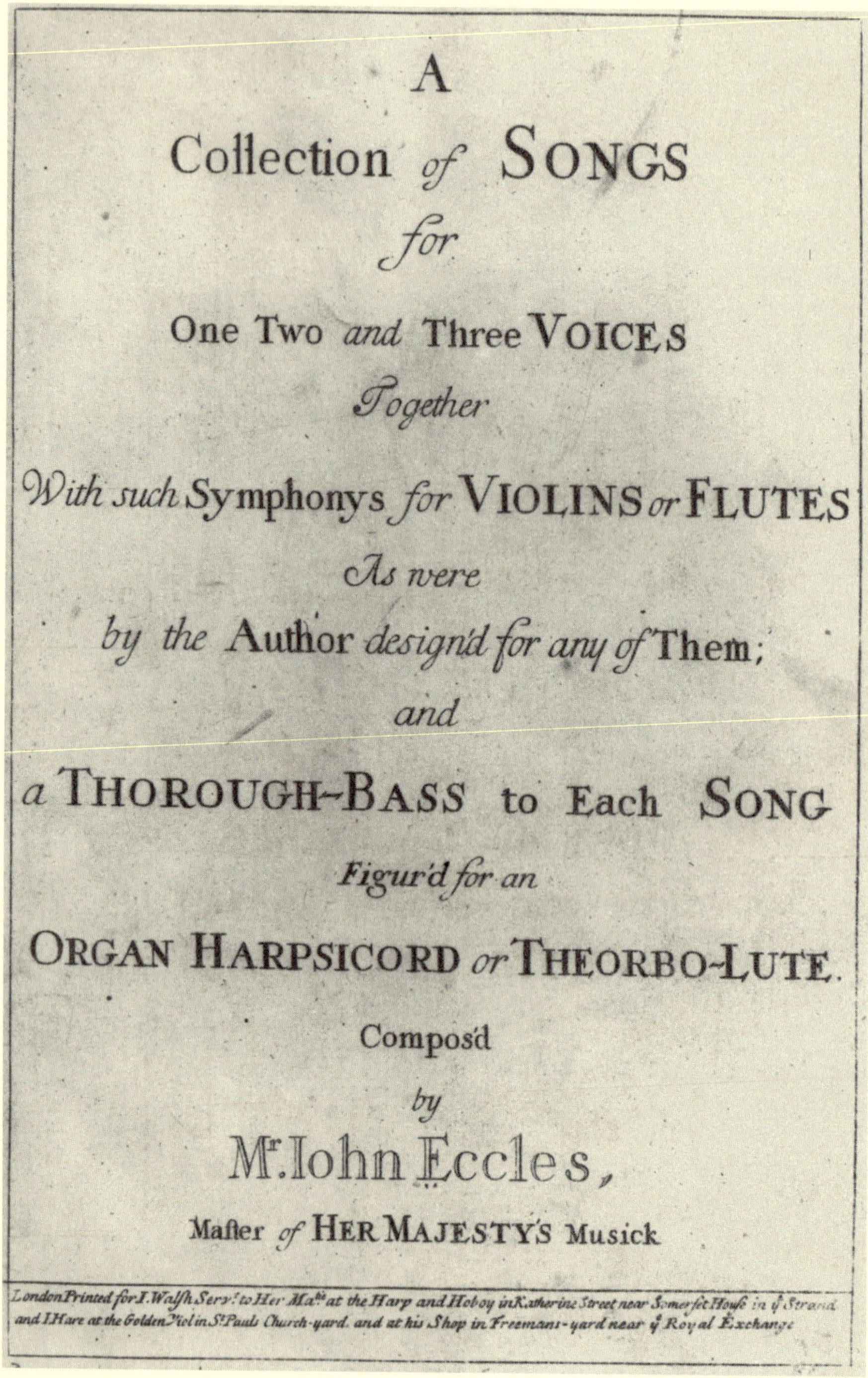

Plate 10.1   Eccles, *Collection of Songs*, 1704

A
Collection *of* SONGS
for

One Two *and* Three VOICES

Together

With such Symphonys *for* VIOLINS *or* FLUTES

As were

by the Author *design'd for any of* Them;

and

a THOROUGH-BASS *to* Each SONG

Figur'd for an

ORGAN HARPSICORD *or* THEORBO-LUTE.

Compos'd

by

M^r.Iohn Eccles,
Mafter *of* HER MAJESTYS Mufick

London Printed for I.Walfh Servt to Her Matie at the Harp and Hoboy inKatherine Street near Somerfet Houfe in ye Strand and I.Hare at the Golden Viol in St Pauls Church-yard. and at his Shop in Freemans-yard near ye Royal Exchange

Caption: see plate 8.1. Plate 10.1. 325 x 204 mm. MB: **M.Cab.1.65.

[within cartouche] ⌠ Mr. Ino. Eccles General Collection of Songs ⌡ Berchet Inventor. H. Hulsbergh Sculpsit. [at foot] London Printed for I. Walsh Servt. to Her Matie. at the Harp and Hoboy in Katherine Street near Somerset House in the Strand.

A Collection of Songs for One Two and Three Voices Together With such Symphonys for Violins or Flutes As were by the Author design'd for any of Them; and a Thorough-Bass to Each Song Figur'd for an Organ Harpsicord or Theorbo-Lute. Compos'd by Mr. Iohn Eccles, Master of Her Majesty's Musick London Printed for I. Walsh Servt. to Her Matie. at the Harp and Hoboy in Katherine Street near Somerset House in ye Strand and I. Hare at the Golden Viol in St. Pauls Church-yard, and at his Shop in Freemans-yard near ye Royal Exchange

87 leaves. Pp. [i]▯-[iv]▯ 1-164 165▯.
Leaves printed on 2 sides.
Tallest copy 325 x 204 mm. Vertical chain lines.

One page engraved per plate. Engraving style Walsh 1, 2.
Illus. title-page plate passe-partout no. 2.
Title-page plate 276 x 180 mm

Contents: illus. title-page [i]; title-page [ii]; dedication [iii]; contents [iv]; songs 1-165.

Songs: see 8.

Copy: MB **M.Cab.1.65.

Plate 11.1   Eccles, *Collection of Songs*, 1704

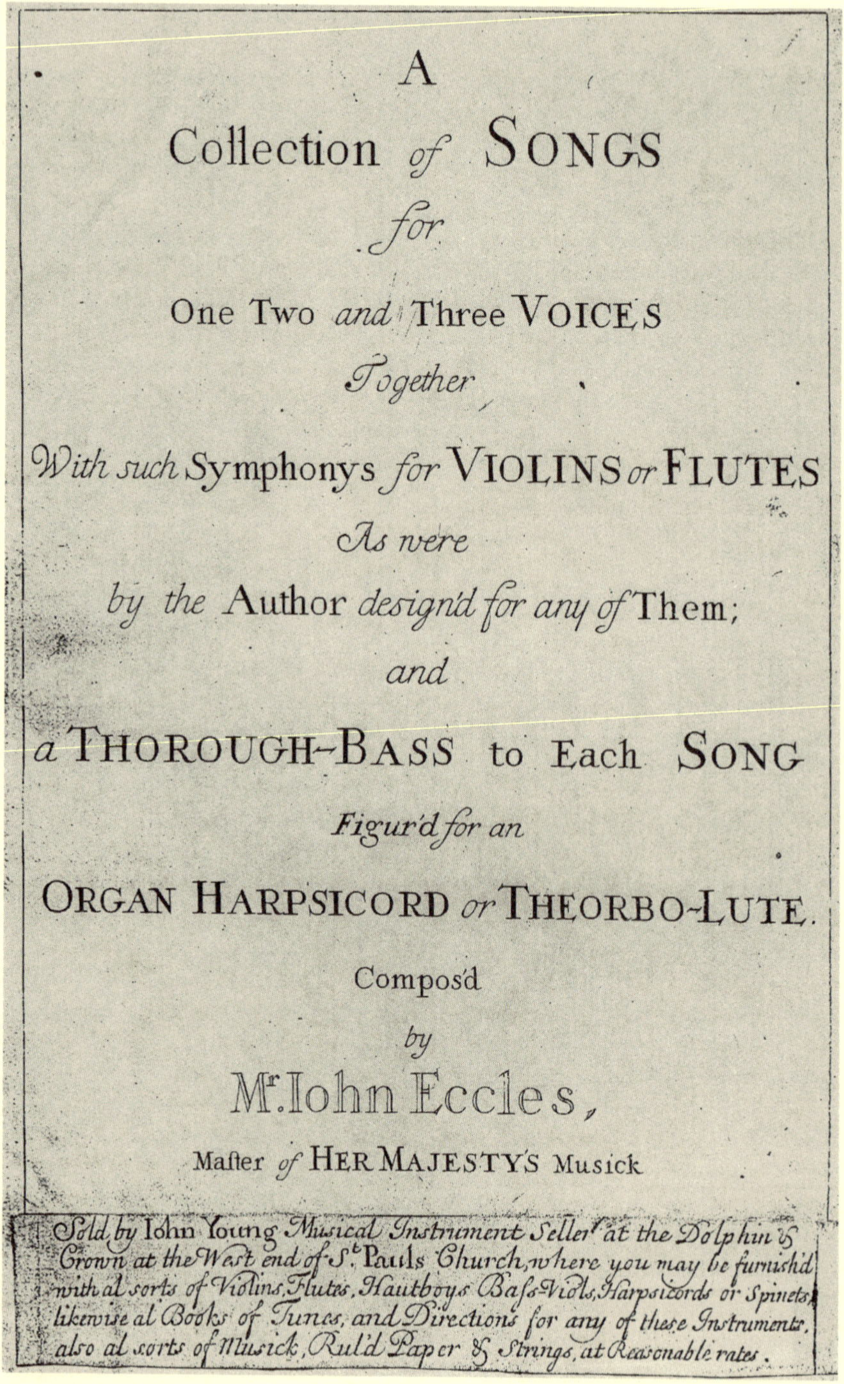

A

Collection *of* SONGS

for

One Two *and* Three VOICES

Together

With such Symphonys *for* VIOLINS *or* FLUTES

As were

by the Author *design'd for any of* Them;

and

a THOROUGH-BASS to Each SONG

Figur'd for an

ORGAN HARPSICORD *or* THEORBO-LUTE.

Compos'd

by

Mr. Iohn Eccles,

Mafter *of* HER MAJESTY'S Musick

Sold by Iohn Young *Musical Instrument Seller at the Dolphin &*
Crown at the West end of S^t*. Pauls Church, where you may be furnish'd*
with al sorts of Violins, Flutes, Hautboys Bass Viols, Harpsicords or Spinets,
likewise al Books of Tunes, and Directions for any of these Instruments,
also al sorts of Musick, Rul'd Paper & Strings, at Reasonable rates.

Caption: plate 11.1. 321 x 202 mm. Lcs: MP25.3.

A Collection of Songs for One Two and Three Voices Together With such Symphonys for Violins or Flutes As were by the Author design'd for any of Them; and a Thorough-Bass to Each Song Figur'd for an Organ Harpsicord or Theorbo-Lute. Compos'd by Mr. Iohn Eccles, Master of Her Majesty's Musick [engraved label over Walsh imprint] Sold by Iohn Young Musical Instrument Seller at the Dolphin & Crown at the West end of St. Pauls Church, where you may be furnish'd with al sorts of Violins, Flutes, Hautboys Bass-Viols, Harpsicords or Spinets; likewise al Books of Tunes, and Directions for any of these Instruments, also al sorts of Musick, Rul'd Paper & Strings, at Reasonable rates.

166 leaves. Pp. [i]□-[iii]□ 1-2 3□-154□ 155-156 157□-165□.
Leaves printed on 1 side.
Tallest copy 321 x 202 mm. Vertical chain lines.

One page engraved per plate. Engraving style Walsh 1, 2.

Contents: title-page [i]; dedication [ii]; contents [iii]; songs 1-165.
Title-page plate ? x 180 mm. (See note 1.)

Songs: see 8.

Note:
1: Label obscures lower edge of plate.

Copy: Lcs MP25.3.

Plate 12.1 Clayton, *Arsinoe*, [First Collection], 1706

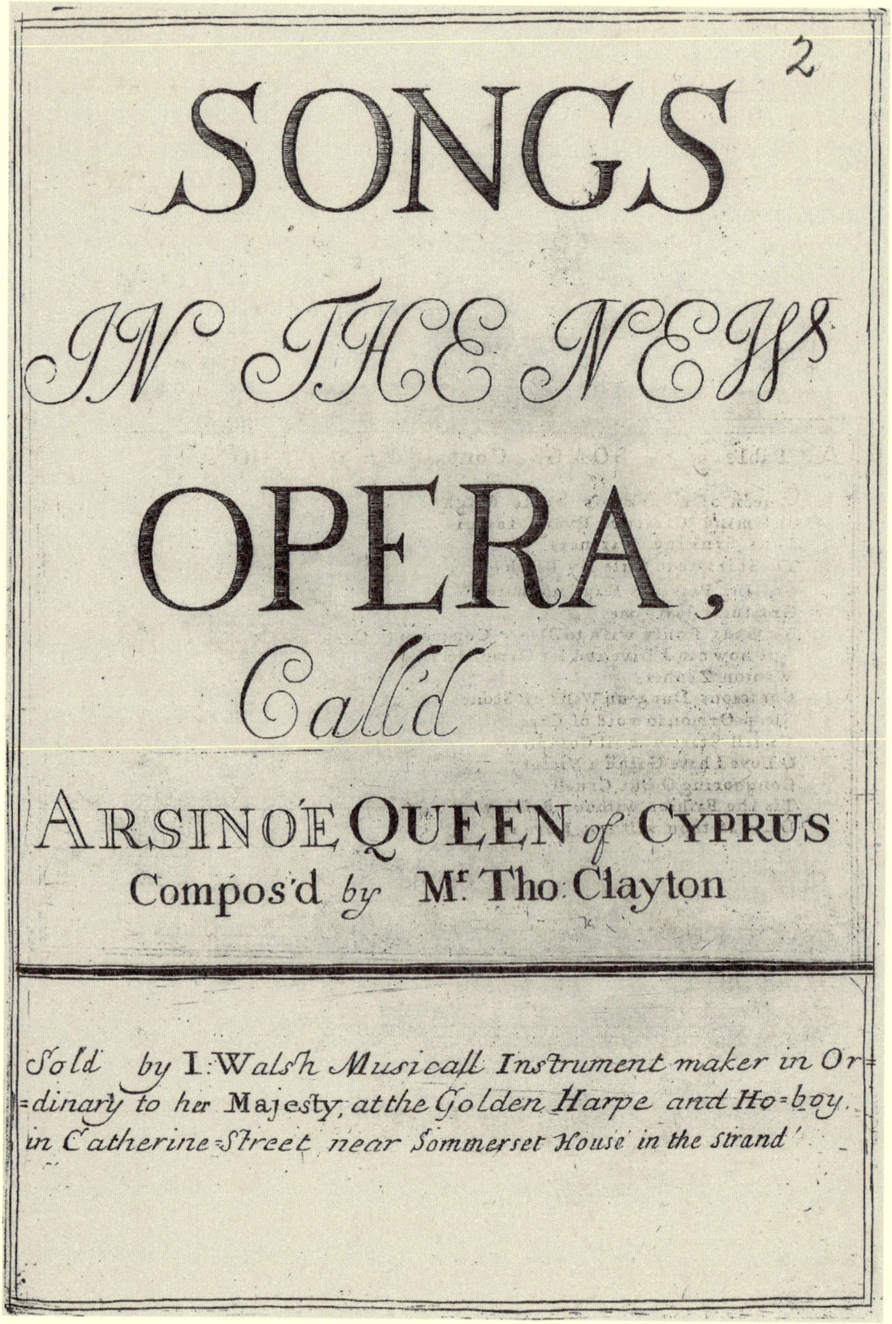

SONGS

IN THE NEW

OPERA,

Call'd

ARSINOÉ QUEEN of CYPRUS

Compos'd by Mr Tho. Clayton

*Sold by I. Walsh Musicall Instrument maker in Or-
=dinary to her Majesty, at the Golden Harpe and Ho-boy,
in Catherine-Street near Sommerset House in the strand*

Caption: plate 12.1. 318 x 200 mm. Lbl: RM. 15.c.12.(2.).

Songs In The New Opera, Call'd ʃ Arsino'e Queen of Cyprus Compos'd by
Mr. Tho: Clayton ʃ Sold by I: Walsh Musicall Instrument maker in Or==dinary
to her Majesty, at the Golden Harpe and Ho=boy, in Catherine=Street near
Sommerset House in the Strand

20 leaves. Pp. [i]-[ii] [1]□-[19]□.
Leaves printed on 1 side.
Tallest copy 331 x 225 mm. Vertical chain lines.

One page engraved per plate. Engraving style Walsh 1.
Title-page plate 270 x 184 mm. Passe-partout no. 3.
Contents plate 115 x 181 mm.

Walsh i: 203.
Advertised in *Post Man*, 2 April 1706. Price 3s.

Contents: title-page [i]; contents [ii]; songs [1-19].

Songs:

No.	Page	First Line
1	[1]	Queen of darkness sable night (s Hughes, < *Arsinoe*)
2	[2]	Charming creature, every feature (m Clayton, s Hughes, < *Arsinoe*)
3	[3]	Thus sinking mariners (m Clayton, s Hughes, < *Arsinoe*)
4	[4]	Yee stars that rule my birth (m Clayton, s Cross, < *Arsinoe*)
5	[5-6]	Boiling passions rage no more (m Clayton, s Leveridge, < *Arsinoe*)
6	[7]	Greatness leave me, undeceive me (m Clayton, s Tofts, < *Arsinoe*)
7	[8]	Yee gods I only wish to die (m Clayton, s Leveridge, < *Arsinoe*)
8	[9]	But how can I live (m Clayton, s Tofts, < *Arsinoe*)
9	[10]	Wanton zephy'rs softly blowing (m Clayton, s Tofts, < *Arsinoe*)
10	[11-12]	Conscious dungeon walls of stone (m Clayton, < *Arsinoe*)
11	[13]	Sleep Ormondo void of fear (m Clayton, s Tofts, < *Arsinoe*)
12	[14-15]	Cruel stars who all conspire (m Clayton, s Cross, < *Arsinoe*)
13	[16]	O love I have gain'd a victory sure (m Clayton, s Tofts, < *Arsinoe*)
14	[17]	Conqu'ring o but cruel eyes (m Clayton, s Cross, < *Arsinoe*)
15	[18]	Tis the fashion, without passion (m Clayton, s Lindsey, <*Arsinoe*)
16	[19]	Delbo if thou wilt not woe, me (m Clayton, s Lindsey, Good, < *Arsinoe*)

Notes:
1. These are the songs given on the contents list and found in Lbl.
2. Some songs originally issued as part of *Monthly Mask of Vocal Music*.
3. Ckc Mn.18.13: - pp. [i]-[1], [9], [16], [18]-[19]; p. [17] bound between pp. [8] and [10].
4. Ckc Mn.18.13A: - pp. [i]-[ii], [5]-[6], [9], [16]-[19]. Loose leaves. Song 3 in different engraving
style.

Copies: Ckc Mn.18.13; Ckc Mn.18.13A; Lbl RM.15.c.12.(2.).

Caption: see plate 12.1.

Songs In The New Opera, Call'd ⌠ Arsino'e Queen of Cyprus Compos'd by Mr. Tho: Clayton⌡ Sold by I: Walsh Musicall Instrument maker in Or==dinary to her Majesty, at the Golden Harpe and Ho=boy, in Catherine=Street near Sommerset House in the Strand

23 leaves. Pp. [i]-[ii] [1]▯-[22]▯.
Leaves printed on 1 side.
Tallest copy 323 x 202 mm. Vertical chain lines.

One page engraved per plate. Engraving style Walsh 1.
Title-page plate 270 x 184 mm. Passe-partout no. 3.
Contents plate 113 x 176 mm.

Walsh i: 203.
Advertised in *Post Man*, 2 April 1706. Price 3s.

Contents: title-page [i]; contents [ii]; songs [1-22].

Songs:

No.	Page	First Line
1	[1]	Queen of darkness sable night (s Hughes, < *Arsinoe*)
2	[2]	Charming creature, every feature (m Clayton, s Hughes, < *Arsinoe*)
3	[3]	Thus sinking mariners (m Clayton, s Hughes, < *Arsinoe*)
4	[4]	Yee stars that rule my birth (m Clayton, s Cross, < *Arsinoe*)
5	[5-6]	Boiling passions rage no more (m Clayton, s Leveridge, < *Arsinoe*)
6	[7]	Greatness leave me, undeceive me (m Clayton, s Tofts, < *Arsinoe*)
7	[8]	Yee gods I only wish to die (m Clayton, s Leveridge, < *Arsinoe*)
8	[9]	But how can I live (m Clayton, s Tofts, < *Arsinoe*)
9	[10]	Wanton zephy'rs softly blowing (m Clayton, s Tofts, < *Arsinoe*)
10	[11-12]	Conscious dungeon walls of stone (m Clayton, < *Arsinoe*)
11	[13]	Sleep Ormondo void of fear (m Clayton, s Tofts, < *Arsinoe*)
12	[14-15]	Cruel stars who all conspire (m Clayton, s Cross, < *Arsinoe*)
13	[16]	O love I have gain'd a victory sure (m Clayton, s Tofts, < *Arsinoe*)
14	[17]	Conqu'ring o but cruel eyes (m Clayton, s Cross, < *Arsinoe*)
15	[18]	Tis the fashion, without passion (m Clayton, s Lindsey, <*Arsinoe*)
16	[19]	Delbo if thou wilt not woe, me (m Clayton, s Lindsey, Good, < *Arsinoe*)
17	[20]	Lillies roses pearly dew (m Clayton, s Hughes, < *Arsinoe*)
18	[21]	As roses shew more pale with dew (m Clayton, s Hughes, < *Arsinoe*)
19	[22]	To warr my thoughts to warr (m Clayton, s Tofts, < *Arsinoe*)

Notes:
1. Three songs (17-19) added to the initial contents list (see 12).
2. Some songs originally issued as part of *Monthly Mask of Vocal Music*.
3. BWbw: - pp. [i]-[12].
4. CU-MUSI: - p. [22].

Copies: BWbw —; CaOLU MZ.527; CU-MUSI M1505.C55A71720 Case X; En Newb.4297(2); WaU M1503 B7T7 1706.

The attempt to construct a publishing history of the Walsh editions and issues of *Camilla* is handicapped by the absence of publishers' records, by the lack of newspapers for some months or years thus eliminating advertisements, and by the complexity of the combinations of title-pages, lists of contents, overtures and songs. Nonetheless it is necessary to explore the evidence that exists in order not only to assign dates whenever possible, but to understand how an early eighteenth-century English music printer and publisher handled a popular work.

The early days are the easiest. The first song to be published was 'Sen vola il dio,' which appeared in the December 1703 issue of the *Monthly Mask of Vocal Music*. The first collection (13) was advertised in the *Post Man* on 2 April 1706, only three days after the London première. To judge from advertisements Walsh appears to have worked only on *Camilla* during April, publishing the second collection (14) on 17 April (*Daily Courant*), and the third (15) on 30 April (*Daily Courant*). As Walsh pointed out, the third collection 'together with the 1st and 2d Collections compleats all the Songs'. The advertisement also appeared in the *Post Man* 4 May, with Hare's new address. These early editions are all unpaginated.

Did Walsh immediately paginate the plates and issue the paginated 'complete' first edition on 16 May (*Daily Courant*) or did he issue only unpaginated 'complete' copies at that time? (The first 'complete' edition does not contains the overture nor the two songs added later.) Copies of the 'complete' first edition exist with varying degrees of pagination. Entry 16 has no pagination and is led by the title-page to the second collection. Other entirely unpaginated copies were issued but with the illustrated and lettered title-pages (19). The same lettered title-page leads copies with a variety of pages numbered. These obviously represent an intermediate stage and suggest that demand was necessitating the collation of leaves in whatever state was available.

There are two copies (Lbl I.354.e. and Ob Mus. 22.c.749) that comprise the three collections (separate editions) each with their own title-pages. For the purposes of bibliographical description each part of the collection has been considered a separate entry. The justification for this is that Walsh is unlikely to have issued the three collections together once he had all the plates engraved. A more likely scenario is that purchasers bought the individual collections as they were published and had them bound together. Walsh would probably have been willing to supply collections or individual songs to complete sets. This would explain 18 which comprises the songs of the first collection but with songs 4 and 14 paginated 39 and 32. A date around 11 May is suggested for 18, being between completion of the plates and their possible issue with pagination.

'Complete' first edition copies with pagination throughout exist with a variety of title-pages. 20 lacks the illustrated title-page. Its title-page names Walsh only. 21 and 21a combine the illustrated title-page with the Walsh and

Hare imprint on the title-page to the third collection. 22 and 22a combine the illustrated title-page with the Walsh and Hare imprint on the regular title-page. 23 has the same title-pages as 22 but with the label of Young pasted over both imprints. Presumably 22 is the ideal, 20 and 21 representing the using up of already printed title-pages that were no longer strictly accurate, either in terms of imprint or of title.

The first advertisement for the whole work appeared on 16 May. That date is used here for publication of the first 'complete' paginated edition. An alternative chronology, and the one suggested in Walsh i, is that the paginated 'complete' edition did not appear until 18 October (*Daily Courant*). The May 16 advertisement would be taken to refer to the unpaginated 'complete' edition. Did Walsh need two weeks to engrave the overture, to slightly reorder the songs, and to paginate the whole, or did he leave those tasks for five and a half months until he had finished engraving other works including *Wonders in the Sun*, and instrumental versions of *Camilla* and *Arsinoe*? (Smith considers that the overture was not available until 1709.) The alternative does not seem very likely, so the October advertisement has been taken to represent merely a restatement of availability.

Plate 13.1   Bononcini, *Camilla*, [First Collection], 1706

SONGS

IN THE NEW

OPERA,

Call'd

CAMILLA

as they are perform'd at the
Theatre Royall

*Sold by I. Walsh Musicall Instrument maker in Or-
=dinary to her Majesty, at the Golden Harpe and Ho=boy,
in Catherine-Street near Sommerset House in the strand*

13 Bononcini, *Camilla*, [First Collection], 2 April 1706

Caption: plate 13.1. 327 x 210 mm. Obh: Mus. D.6.

Songs In The New Opera, Call'd ſ Camilla as they are perform'd at the
Theatre Royall ſ Sold by I: Walsh Musical Instrument maker in Or==dinary
to her Majesty, at the Golden Harpe and Ho=boy, in Catherine=Street near
Sommerset House in the Strand

16 leaves. Pp. [i-ii] [1]☐-[15]☐.
Leaves printed on 1 side.
Tallest copy 327 x 210 mm. Vertical chain lines.

One page engraved per plate. Engraving style Walsh 1.
Title-page plate 270 x 186 mm. Passe-partout no. 3.
Contents plate 84 x 155 mm.

Walsh i: 201.
Advertised in *Post Man*, 2 April 1706. Price 2s. 6d.

Contents: title-page [i]; contents [ii]; songs [1-15].

Songs:

No.	Page	First Line
1	[1]	I was born of royall race (s Tofts, < *Camilla*)
2	[2]	O nymph of race divine (s Boy, < *Camilla*)
3	[3]	In vain I fly from sorrow (s Boy, < *Camilla*)
4	[4]	Cupid o at lenght reward me (s Boy, < *Camilla*)
5	[5]	Love darts are in your eyes (s Ramondon, < *Camilla*)
6	[6]	Since you from death thus save me (s Boy, < *Camilla*)
7	[7]	Ungratefull you fly me, unkindly (s Boy, < *Camilla*)
8	[8]	Linco's grown another creature (s Leveridge, < *Camilla*)
9	[9]	Fair Dorinda happy may'st thou ever be (s Baroness, < *Camilla*)
10	[10]	These eyes are made so killing (s Lindsey, < *Camilla*)
11	[11]	Fortune like a wanton gipsye (s Tofts, < *Camilla*)
12	[12]	Tho fierce the lightning flyes (s Ramondon, < *Camilla*)
13	[13]	I love but dare not my flame discover (s Ramondon, < *Camilla*)
14	[14]	All I'le venture to restore ye (s Ramondon, < *Camilla*)
15	[15]	Something is in my face so alluring (s Lindsey, < *Camilla*)

Notes:
1. Ob: bound with second and third collections.
2. Obh: pages numbered in MS. 31-45.

Copies: Ob Mus. 22.c.749; Obh Mus. D.6.

Plate 14.1   Bononcini, *Camilla*, Second Collection, 1706

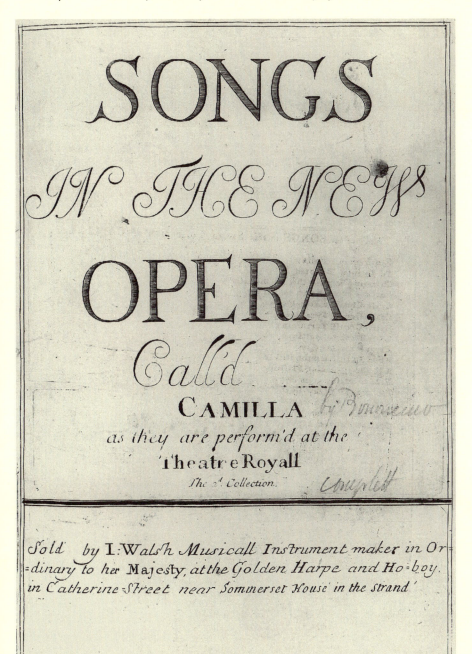

Caption: plate 14.1. 324 x 203 mm. Lbl: I.354.e.

Songs In The New Opera, Call'd ⌠ Camilla as they are perform'd at the Theatre Royall The 2d. Collection. ⌡ Sold by I: Walsh Musicall Instrument maker in Or==dinary to her Majesty, at the Golden Harpe and Ho=boy, in Catherine=Street near Sommerset House in the Strand

17 leaves. Pp. [i-ii] [1]◻-[16]◻.
Leaves printed on 1 side.
Tallest copy 324 x 203 mm. Vertical chain lines.

One page engraved per plate. Engraving style Walsh 1.
Title-page plate 270 x 187 mm. Passe-partout no. 3.
Contents plate 140 x 154 mm.

Walsh i: 204.
Advertised in *Daily Courant*, 17 April 1706. Price 2s. 6d.

Contents: title-page [i]; contents [ii]; songs [1-16].

Songs:

No.	Page	First Line
1	[1]	Fly and follow your idol beauty (s Baroness, < *Camilla*)
2	[2]	To beauty devoted (s Boy, < *Camilla*)
3	[3]	Charming fair for thee I languish (s Boy, < *Camilla*)
4	[4]	Fortune ever known to vary (s Tofts, < *Camilla*)
5	[5]	Cease cruell tirannizing (s Hughes, < *Camilla*)
6	[6]	Cease cruell to deceive me (s Baroness, < *Camilla*)
7	[7]	Cease cruell tirannizing (s Hughes, Baroness, < *Camilla*)
8	[8]	Love leads to battle, who dares oppose (s Ramondon, < *Camilla*)
9	[9]	Fly ye virgins th' unfaithfull lover (s Baroness, < *Camilla*)
10	[10]	Aged Phillis, wanton still is (s Leveridge, < *Camilla*)
11	[11]	Let the lightening flashing flying (s Boy, < *Camilla*)
12	[12]	Tender maids your pity show (s Baroness, < *Camilla*)
13	[13]	Revenge I summon (s Tofts, < *Camilla*)
14	[14]	Yes t'is all I want (s Boy, < *Camilla*)
15	[15]	Wellcome sorrow death attending (s Baroness, < *Camilla*)
16	[16]	Frail are a lovers hopes (s Hughes, < *Camilla*)

Notes:
1. Bound with first and third collections.
2. Ob: pp. [5]-[6] inverted.

Copies: Lbl I.354.e; Ob Mus. 22.c.749; *Obh*.

15 Bononcini, *Camilla*, [Third Collection], 30 April 1706

Caption: see plate 13.1.

Songs In The New Opera, Call'd ⌠ Camilla as they are perform'd at the
Theatre Royall ⌡ Sold by I. Walsh Musicall Instrument maker in Or==dinary
to her Majesty, at the Golden Harpe and Ho=boy, in Catherine-Street near
Sommerset House in the Strand

20 leaves. Pp. [i-ii] [1]□-[19]□.
Leaves printed on 1 side.
Tallest copy 324 x 203 mm. Vertical chain lines.

One page engraved per plate. Engraving style Walsh 1.
Title-page plate 270 x 187 mm. Passe-partout no. 3.
Contents plate 253 x 163 mm.

Walsh i: 206.
Advertised in *Daily Courant*, 30 April 1706. Price 3s.

Contents: title-page [i]; contents [ii]; songs [1-19].

Songs:

No.	Page	First Line
1	[1]	See the just gods of innocence (s Tofts, < *Camilla*)
2	[2]	Floods shall quit the ocean, The (s Hughes, < *Camilla*)
3	[3]	Among women they for certain know (s Lindsey, < *Camilla*)
4	[4]	I languish, I sorrow (s Leveridge, Lindsey, < *Camilla*)
5	[5]	Ah never yet was known (s Hughes, < *Camilla*)
6	[6]	Now Cupid or never be kind (s Hughes, < *Camilla*)
7	[7]	Not so much cruelty, I prethee now (s Lindsey, < *Camilla*)
8	[8]	Joys are attending those cares (s Baroness, < *Camilla*)
9	[9]	Around her see Cupid flying (s Hughes, < *Camilla*)
10	[10]	Love and ambition strive (s Tofts, < *Camilla*)
11	[11]	Tullia I feell thy charms (s Leveridge, < *Camilla*)
12	[12]	O tyrannous jealousy, fly far away (s Hughes, < *Camilla*)
13	[13]	Happy I love and haste to enjoy her (s Hughes, Boy, < *Camilla*)
14	[14-15]	Thou art he my dearest creature (s Leveridge, Lindsey, < *Camilla*)
15	[16]	Wretched am I, that I gain him (s Tofts, < *Camilla*)
16	[17]	Be cruel and be jealous (s Turner, < *Camilla*)
17	[18]	Angers for war declaring (s Baroness, < *Camilla*)
18	[19]	Fate the more it does depress me (s Tofts, < *Camilla*)

Notes:
1. Bound with first and second collections.
2. Lbl: song order: 1, 15, 3, 5, 4, 7, 6, 8-14, 2, 16-18.

Copy: Lbl I.354.e; Ob Mus. 22.c.749.

Caption: see plate 14.1.

Songs In The New Opera, Call'd ⌠ Camilla as they are perform'd at the Theatre Royall The 2d. Collection. ⌡ Sold by I: Walsh Musicall Instrument maker in Or==dinary to her Majesty, at the Golden Harpe and Ho=boy, in Catherine=Street near Sommerset House in the Strand

53 leaves. Pp. [i-ii] [1]▯-[37]▯\▯[38] [38A]▯ [39]▯-[51]▯.
Leaves printed on 1 side.
Tallest copy 319 x 195 mm. Vertical chain lines.

One page engraved per plate. Engraving style Walsh 1.
Title-page plate passe-partout no. 3.
Contents plate 113 x 155 mm.

Contents: title-page [i]; contents [ii]; songs [1-38], [38A], [39-51].

Songs:

No.	Page	First Line
1	[1]	I was born of royall race (s Tofts, < *Camilla*)
2	[2]	O nymph of race divine (s Boy, < *Camilla*)
3	[3]	Since you from death thus save me (s Boy, < *Camilla*)
4	[4]	Love darts are in your eyes (s Ramondon, < *Camilla*)
5	[5]	Fortune ever known to vary (s Tofts, < *Camilla*)
6	[6]	Tender maids your pity show (s Baroness, < *Camilla*)
7	[7]	Frail are a lovers hopes (s Hughes, < *Camilla*)
8	[8]	Wellcome sorrow death attending (s Baroness, < *Camilla*)
9	[9]	All I'le venture to restore ye (s Ramondon, < *Camilla*)
10	[10]	See the just gods of innocence (s Tofts, < *Camilla*)
11	[11]	Fair Dorinda happy may'st thou ever be (s Baroness, < *Camilla*)
12	[12]	Charming fair for thee I languish (s Boy, < *Camilla*)
13	[13]	Wretched am I, that I gain him (s Tofts, < *Camilla*)
14	[14]	Among women they for certain know (s Lindsey, < *Camilla*)
15	[15]	Aged Phillis, wanton still is (s Leveridge, < *Camilla*)
16	[16]	I languish, I sorrow (s Leveridge, Lindsey, < *Camilla*)
17	[17]	Ah never yet was known (s Hughes, < *Camilla*)
18	[18]	Revenge I summon (s Tofts, < *Camilla*)
19	[19]	In vain I fly from sorrow (s Boy, < *Camilla*)
20	[20]	To beauty devoted (s Boy, < *Camilla*)
21	[21]	I love but dare not my flame discover (s Ramondon, < *Camilla*)
22	[22]	Now Cupid or never be kind (s Hughes, < *Camilla*)
23	[23]	Fortune like a wanton gipsye (s Leveridge, < *Camilla*)
24	[24]	Not so much cruelty, I prethee now (s Lindsey, < *Camilla*)
25	[25]	No love was ever known that (s Baroness, < *Camilla*)
26	[26]	Joys are attending those cares (s Baroness, < *Camilla*)
27	[27]	Around her see Cupid flying (s Hughes, < *Camilla*)
28	[28]	Love leads to battle, who dares oppose (s Ramondon, < *Camilla*)
29	[29]	Ungratefull you fly me, unkindly (s Boy, < *Camilla*)
30	[30]	Love and ambition strive (s Tofts, < *Camilla*)
31	[31]	Tullia I feell thy charms (s Leveridge, < *Camilla*)
32	[32]	Something is in my face so alluring (s Lindsey, < *Camilla*)

33	[33]	Fly and follow your idol beauty (s Baroness, < *Camilla*)
34	[34]	O tyrannous jealousy, fly far away (s Hughes, < *Camilla*)
35	[35]	Happy I love and haste to enjoy her (s Hughes, Boy, < *Camilla*)
36	[36]	Fly ye virgins th' unfaithfull lover (s Baroness, < *Camilla*)
37	[37]	These eyes are made so killing (s Lindsey, < *Camilla*)
38	[38-38A]	Thou art he my dearest creature (s Leveridge, Lindsey, < *Camilla*)
39	[39]	Cupid o at lenght reward me (s Boy, < *Camilla*)
40	[40]	Yes t'is all I want (s Boy, < *Camilla*)
41	[41]	Floods shall quit the ocean, The (s Hughes, < *Camilla*)
42	[42]	Dangers ev'ry way surround me (s Tofts, < *Camilla*)
43	[43]	Be cruel and be jealous (s Turner, < *Camilla*)
44	[44]	Angers for war declaring (s Baroness, < *Camilla*)
45	[45]	Tho fierce the lightning flyes (s Ramondon, < *Camilla*)
46	[46]	Linco's grown another creature (s Leveridge, < *Camilla*)
47	[47]	Cease cruell tirannizing (s Hughes, < *Camilla*)
48	[48]	Cease cruell to deceive me (s Baroness, < *Camilla*)
49	[49]	Cease cruell tirannizing (s Hughes, Baroness, < *Camilla*)
50	[50]	Fate the more it does depress me (s Tofts, < *Camilla*)
51	[51]	Let the lightening flashing flying (s Boy, < *Camilla*)

Notes:
1. Date an estimate based on earliest possible gathering of all leaves prior to addition of pagination for issuance as complete edition.
2. Contents list gives only 'Second Collection' contents.

Copy: DLC M1508 Case.

17   Deleted. See 15.

Caption: see plate 13.1.

Songs In The New Opera, Call'd ⌠ Camilla as they are perform'd at the Theatre Royall ⌡ Sold by I: Walsh Musicall Instrument maker in Or==dinary to her Majesty, at the Golden Harpe and Ho=boy, in Catherine-Street near Sommerset House in the Strand

16 leaves. Pp. [i-ii] 1□ [2]□-[3]□ 39□ [5]□-[14]□ 32□.
Leaves printed on 1 side.
Tallest copy 324 x 203 mm. Vertical chain lines.

One page engraved per plate. Engraving style Walsh 1.
Title-page plate 270 x 187 mm. Passe-partout no. 3.
Contents plate 82 x 154 mm.

Contents: title-page [i]; contents [ii]; songs 1, [2-3], 39, [5-14], 32.

Songs:

No.	Page	First Line
1	1	I was born of royall race (s Tofts, < *Camilla*)
2	[2]	O nymph of race divine (s Boy, < *Camilla*)
3	[3]	In vain I fly from sorrow (s Boy, < *Camilla*)
4	39	Cupid o at length reward me (s Boy, < *Camilla*)
5	[5]	Love darts are in your eyes (s Ramondon, < *Camilla*)
6	[6]	Since you from death thus save me (s Boy, < *Camilla*)
7	[7]	Ungratefull you fly me, unkindly (s Boy, < *Camilla*)
8	[8]	Linco's grown another creature (s Leveridge, < *Camilla*)
9	[9]	Fair Dorinda happy may'st thou ever be (s Baroness, < *Camilla*)
10	[10]	These eyes are made so killing (s Lindsey, < *Camilla*)
11	[11]	Fortune like a wanton gipsye (s Tofts, < *Camilla*)
12	[12]	Tho fierce the lightning flyes (s Ramondon, < *Camilla*)
13	[13]	I love but dare not my flame discover (s Ramondon, < *Camilla*)
14	[14]	All I'le venture to restore ye (s Ramondon, < *Camilla*)
15	32	Something is in my fare so alluring (s Lindsey, < *Camilla*)

Notes:
1. Contains songs of the first collection with songs 1, 4 and 14 paginated 1, 39 and 32 respectively, as in the complete edition. Bound with second and third collections.
2. Date an estimate based on inclusion of numbered and unnumbered pages.

Copy: Lbl I.354.e.

Plate 19.1   Bononcini, *Camilla*, 1706

Caption: plate 19.1. 314 x 200 mm. Ob: Mus. 22.c.28. See plate 13.1.

[within cartouche] ⸢ Songs in the Opera of Camilla ⸥ Berchet Inventor. H Hulsbergh Sculpsit. [at foot] London Printed for I. Walsh Servt. to Her Matie. at the Harp and Hoboy in Katherine Street near Somerset House in the Strand.

Songs In The New Opera, Call'd ⸢ Camilla as they are perform'd at the Theatre Royall ⸥ Sold by I. Walsh Musicall Instrument maker in Or==dinary to her Majesty, at the Golden Harpe and Ho=boy, in Catherine-Street near Sommerset House in the Strand

54 leaves. Pp. [i]⬚ [ii-iii] [1]⬚-[38]⬚ [38A]⬚ [39]⬚-[51]⬚.
Leaves printed on 1 side.
Tallest copy 320 x 200 mm. Vertical chain lines.

One page engraved per plate. Engraving style Walsh 1.
Illus. title-page plate 293 x 195 mm. Passe-partout no. 2.
Title-page plate 271 x 187 mm. Passe-partout no. 3.
Contents plate 253 x 162 mm.

Contents: illus. title-page [i]; title-page [ii]; contents [iii]; songs [1-38], [38A], [39-51].

Songs: see **16**.

Notes:
1. No single date is applicable to these copies because the copies exhibit various combinations of unpaginated and paginated pages. A point roughly mid-way between completion of the third collection (30 April 1706) and issuance of the complete work paginated throughout (16 May 1706) was chosen. Similarly, a single pagination statement can only be a rough guide. The most complete form with no numeration has been given.
2. Ckc: - pp. [i], [1-9], [11-12], [15], [18-21], [23], [25], [28-29], [32-33], [36-37], [39-40], [42], [45-49], [51]. Pp. [13] and [41] transposed.
3. En: - pp. [25], [42].
4. MH-H: - pp. [i], [25], [42]. P. [38A] bound at end.
5. Ob ([MS.] Mus. Sch. c.97(21)): - p. [i]. Pp. 1-9, 11-12, 15, 18-21, 23, 25, 28-29, 32-33, 36-37, 39-40, 42, 45-49, 51 paginated. The parallel with the Ckc copy is striking. It suggests that Walsh had no copies available of the pages missing from the Ckc copy and that the plates were being paginated and printed at the moment the purchaser obtained the Ckc copy.
6. Ob (Mus. 22.c.28): - pp. [25], [37], [42], [46]. Pp. 1, 4, 9, 11, 19, 21, 23, 29, 32, 39, 45 paginated.
7. WaU: pp. 1-12, 14-16, 18-23, 25, 28-29, 32-33, 36-37, 39-42, 45-51 paginated.

Copies: Ckc 85.26; En Newb. 4297; MH-H *fMus.P9713.6980ba (B)(2); Ob [MS.] Mus. Sch. c.97(21); Ob Mus. 22.c.28; *Omc*; WaU M1503 B7T7 1706.

Caption: see plate 13.1.

Songs In The New Opera, Call'd ⌠ Camilla as they are perform'd at the Theatre Royall ⌡ Sold by I. Walsh Musicall Instrument maker in Or==dinary to her Majesty, at the Golden Harpe and Ho=boy, in Catherine-Street near Sommerset House in the Strand

53 leaves. Pp. [i-ii] 1□-38□ [38A]□ 39□-51□.
Leaves printed on 1 side.
Tallest copy 355 x 222 mm. Vertical chain lines.

One page engraved per plate. Engraving style Walsh 1.
Title-page plate passe-partout no. 3.

Advertised in *Daily Courant*, 16 May 1706.

Contents: title-page [i]; contents [ii]; songs 1-38, [38A], 39-51.

Songs:

No.	Page	First Line
1	1	I was born of royall race (s Tofts, < *Camilla*)
2	2	O nymph of race divine (s Boy, < *Camilla*)
3	3	Since you from death thus save me (s Boy, < *Camilla*)
4	4	Love darts are in your eyes (s Ramondon, < *Camilla*)
5	5	Fortune ever known to vary (s Tofts, < *Camilla*)
6	6	Tender maids your pity show (s Baroness, < *Camilla*)
7	7	Frail are a lovers hopes (s Hughes, < *Camilla*)
8	8	Wellcome sorrow death attending (s Baroness, < *Camilla*)
9	9	All I'le venture to restore ye (s Ramondon, < *Camilla*)
10	10	See the just gods of innocence (s Tofts, < *Camilla*)
11	11	Fair Dorinda happy may'st thou ever be (s Baroness, < *Camilla*)
12	12	Charming fair for thee I languish (s Boy, < *Camilla*)
13	13	Wretched am I, that I gain him (s Tofts, < *Camilla*)
14	14	Among women they for certain know (s Lindsey, < *Camilla*)
15	15	Aged Phillis, wanton still is (s Leveridge, < *Camilla*)
16	16	I languish, I sorrow (s Leveridge, Lindsey, < *Camilla*)
17	17	Ah never yet was known (s Hughes, < *Camilla*)
18	18	Revenge I summon (s Tofts, < *Camilla*)
19	19	In vain I fly from sorrow (s Boy, < *Camilla*)
20	20	To beauty devoted (s Boy, < *Camilla*)
21	21	I love but dare not my flame discover (s Ramondon, < *Camilla*)
22	22	Now Cupid or never be kind (s Hughes, < *Camilla*)
23	23	Fortune like a wanton gipsye (s Leveridge, < *Camilla*)
24	24	Not so much cruelty, I prethee now (s Lindsey, < *Camilla*)
25	25	No love was ever known that (s Baroness, < *Camilla*)
26	26	Joys are attending those cares (s Baroness, < *Camilla*)
27	27	Around her see Cupid flying (s Hughes, < *Camilla*)
28	28	Love leads to battle, who dares oppose (s Ramondon, < *Camilla*)
29	29	Ungratefull you fly me, unkindly (s Boy, < *Camilla*)
30	30	Love and ambition strive (s Tofts, < *Camilla*)
31	31	Tullia I feell thy charms (s Leveridge, < *Camilla*)

32	32	Something is in my face so alluring (s Lindsey, < *Camilla*)
33	33	Fly and follow your idol beauty (s Baroness, < *Camilla*)
34	34	Happy I love and haste to enjoy her (s Hughes, Boy, < *Camilla*)
35	35	Happy I love and haste to enjoy her (s Hughes, Boy, < *Camilla*)
36	36	Fly ye virgins th' unfaithfull lover (s Baroness, < *Camilla*)
37	37	These eyes are made so killing (s Lindsey, < *Camilla*)
38	38-[38A]	Thou art he my dearest creature (s Leveridge, Lindsey, < *Camilla*)
39	39	Cupid o at lenght reward me (s Boy, < *Camilla*)
40	40	Yes t'is all I want (s Boy, < *Camilla*)
41	41	Floods shall quit the ocean, The (s Hughes, < *Camilla*)
42	42	Dangers ev'ry way surround me (s Tofts, < *Camilla*)
43	43	Be cruel and be jealous (s Turner, < *Camilla*)
44	44	Angers for war declaring (s Baroness, < *Camilla*)
45	45	Tho fierce the lightning flyes (s Ramondon, < *Camilla*)
46	46	Linco's grown another creature (s Leveridge, < *Camilla*)
47	47	Cease cruell tirannizing (s Hughes, < *Camilla*)
48	48	Cease cruell to deceive me (s Baroness, < *Camilla*)
49	49	Cease cruell tirannizing (s Hughes, Baroness, < *Camilla*)
50	50	Fate the more it does depress me (s Tofts, < *Camilla*)
51	51	Let the lightening flashing flying (s Boy, < *Camilla*)

Copy: CU-MUSI M1505.B65T7 1706 Case X.

Plate 21.1   Bononcini, *Camilla*, 'Third Collection', 1706

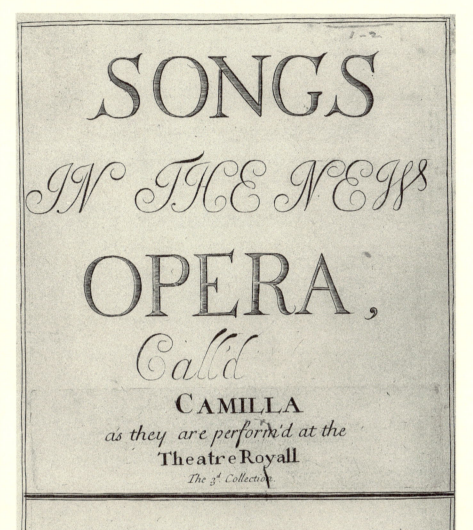

Caption: see plate 22.1. Plate 21.1. 327 x 213 mm. Lcm: XXXII.A.1.(1.).

[within cartouche] ⌠ Songs in the Opera of Camilla ⌡ Berchet Inventor. H. Hulsbergh Sculpsit. [at foot] London Printed for I. Walsh Servt. to Her Matie. at the Harp and Hoboy in Katherine Street near Somerset House in the Strand.

Songs In The New Opera, Call'd ⌠ Camilla as they are perform'd at the Theatre Royall The 3d. collection. ⌡ Sold by I:Walsh Musicall Instrument maker in Or==dinary to her Majesty, at the Golden Harpe and Ho=boy, in Catherine=Street near Sommerset House in the Strand and I. Hare Musick Instrument maker at ye Golden Viol and Flute in Cornhill near ye Royal Exchange.

55 leaves. Pp. [i]□-[ii]□\□[iii] 1□-38□ [38A]□ 39□-51□.
Leaves printed on 1 side.
Tallest copy 327 x 213 mm. Vertical chain lines.

One page engraved per plate. Engraving style Walsh 1.
Illus. title-page plate 294 x 197 mm. Passe-partout no. 2.
Title-page plate 273 x 190 mm. Passe-partout no. 3.
Contents plate 253 x 164 mm.

Contents: illus. title-page [i]; title-page [ii]; contents [iii]; songs 1-38, [38A], 39-51.

Songs: see 20.

Note:
1. Date based on advertisement in *Daily Courant* for issuance of complete edition. 'The 3d. collection' title-page, presumably remaining from an earlier issue, was used in place of the usual title-page (22).

Copy: Lcm XXXII.A.1.(1.)

Bononcini, *Camilla*, 'Third Collection', 16 May 1706

Caption: see plates 22.1-22.2.

[within cartouche] ⌠ Songs in the Opera of Camilla ⌡ Berchet Inventor. H. Hulsbergh Sculpsit. [at foot] London Printed for I. Walsh Servt. to Her Matie. at the Harp and Hoboy in Katherine Street near Somerset House in the Strand.

Songs In The New Opera, Call'd ⌠ Camilla as they are perform'd at the Theatre Royall The 3d. collection. ⌡ Sold by I:Walsh Musicall Instrument maker in Or==dinary to her Majesty, at the Golden Harpe and Ho=boy, in Catherine=Street near Sommerset House in the Strand and I. Hare Musick Instrument maker at ye Golden Viol and Flute in Cornhill near ye Royal Exchange.

59 leaves. Pp. [i]▢-[ii]▢\▢[iii] ▢1 2▢-4▢ 1▢-38▢ [38A]▢ 39▢-51▢.
Leaves printed on 1 side.
Tallest copy 344 x 206 mm. Vertical chain lines.

One page engraved per plate. Engraving style Walsh 1.
Illus. title-page plate 295 x 199 mm. Passe-partout no. 2.
Title-page plate 275 x 190 mm. Passe-partout no. 3.
Contents plate 253 x 164 mm.

Contents: illus. title-page [i]; title-page [ii]; contents [iii]; overture 1-4; songs 1-38, [38A], 39-51.

Songs: see **20**.

Notes:
1. Date based on advertisement in *Daily Courant* for issuance of complete edition. 'The 3d. collection' title-pages, presumably remaining from an earlier issue, were used in place of the usual title-page (**22**).
2. CaOLU: contains pp. [52-53] first issued in 1709 printed on slightly smaller paper and lacking stab holes, suggesting that an owner and/or dealer added the songs at a later date (a sophisticated copy).
3. Ckc: - p. [i]; p. 1 (overture) reversed.

Copies: CaOLU MZ.526; Ckc 85.4.(2.).

Plate 22.1   Bononcini, *Camilla*, 1706

Plate 22.2   Bononcini, *Camilla*, 1706

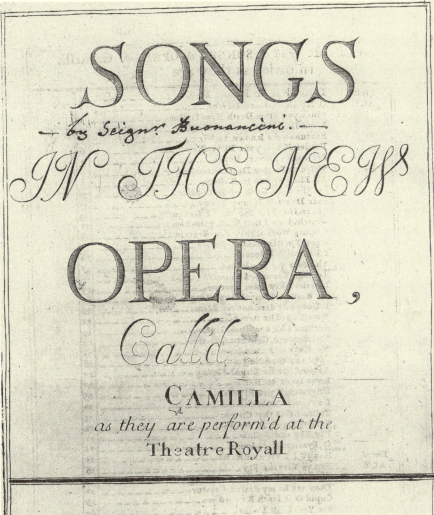

Caption: plates 22.1-22.2. 363 x 217 mm. Lbl: I.354.

[within cartouche] ⌠ Songs in the Opera of Camilla ⌡ Berchet Inventor. H. Hulsbergh Sculpsit. [at foot] London Printed for I. Walsh Servt. to Her Matie. at the Harp and Hoboy in Katherine Street near Somerset House in the Strand.

Songs In The New Opera, Call'd ⌠ Camilla as they are perform'd at the Theatre Royall ⌡ Sold by I: Walsh Musicall Instrument maker in Or==dinary to her Majesty, at the Golden Harpe and Ho=boy, in Catherine-Street near Sommerset House in the Strand and I. Hare Musick Instrument maker at ye Golden Viol and Flute in Cornhill near ye Royal Exchange.

54 leaves. Pp. [i]□ [ii-iii] 1□-38□ [38A]□ 39□-51□.
Leaves printed on 1 side.
Tallest copy 363 x 217 mm. Vertical chain lines.

One page engraved per plate. Engraving style Walsh 1.
Illus. title-page plate 294 x 200 mm. Passe-partout no. 2.
Title-page plate 272 x 187 mm. Passe-partout no. 3.
Contents plate 254 x 163 mm.

Walsh i: 221.
Advertised in *Daily Courant*, 16 May 1706.

Contents: illus. title-page [i]; title-page [ii]; contents [iii]; songs 1-38, [38A], 39-51.

Songs: see 20.

Notes:
1. BWbw: - p. [i]; p. 38 reversed.
2. F-Pc (D.1529): - p. [i]. P. 42 unnumbered.
3. F-Pc (Rés V.S. 1274): p. [i] coloured.
4. Ge: - pp. [i], 1, 51. P. [38A] bound after p. 39.
5. IU: - pp. [i-iii], 1-4.
6. Lbl (Hirsch II.92): - p. [i].
7. TWm: Italian text in red MS. above staff on pp. 2, 3, 12, 17, 19, 20, 27, 29, 39, 40, 41, 47, 51.
8. TWm (disbound): - pp. [i-iii], 51.
9. Copy reported at DLC comprises instrumental parts only.

Copies: BWbw —; *D-B*; F-Pc D.1529; F-Pc Rés. V.S. 1274; Ge P.b.46; IU Fraenkel 691; Lbl Hirsch II.92; Lbl I.354; *MdBPC*; NRU-Mus Vault M1503.B7192c; TWm —; TWm (disbound); *RF-Mrg*.

Caption: see plates 22.1-22.2.

[within cartouche] ⌠ Songs in the Opera of Camilla ⌡ Berchet Inventor. H. Hulsbergh Sculpsit. [at foot] London Printed for I. Walsh Servt. to Her Matie. at the Harp and Hoboy in Katherine Street near Somerset House in the Strand.

Songs In The New Opera, Call'd ⌠ Camilla as they are perform'd at the Theatre Royall ⌡ Sold by I: Walsh Musicall Instrument maker in Or==dinary to her Majesty, at the Golden Harpe and Ho=boy, in Catherine-Street near Sommerset House in the Strand and I. Hare Musick Instrument maker at ye Golden Viol and Flute in Cornhill near ye Royal Exchange.

58 leaves. Pp. [i]⬚ [ii-iii] ⬚1 2⬚\⬚3 4⬚ 1⬚-38⬚ [38A]⬚ 39⬚-51⬚.
Leaves printed on 1 side.
Tallest copy 357 x 215 mm. Vertical chain lines.

One page engraved per plate. Engraving style Walsh 1.
Illus. title-page passe-partout no. 2.
Title-page plate passe-partout no. 3.

Walsh i: 221.
Advertised in *Daily Courant*, 16 May 1706.

Contents: illus. title-page [i]; title-page [ii]; contents [iii]; overture 1-4; songs 1-51.

Songs: see 20.

Notes:
1. CSfst (de Bellis 820): - p. 41; p. 12 unnumbered and in Cullen edition.
2. CSfst (de Bellis 821): - pp. [i]-[iii], 50-51; supplied in photographs from Lbl R.M. 11.b.20.(2.) (see 177).
3. NjP and Obh: p. 42 numbered in MS.
4. NN: overture bound 1-4.
5. TWm: overture printed on smaller leaves, guarded out, and bound 1-4.

Copies: CSfst de Bellis 820; CSfst de Bellis 821; NjP (Ex) M1508.2.C14B6q; NN Drexel 4854.1; Obh Mus. D.8; TWm —.

Plate 23.1   Bononcini, *Camilla*, 1706

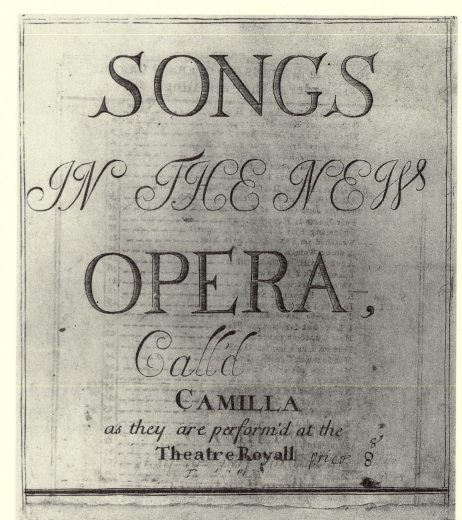

Caption: see plate 22.1. Plate 23.1. 348 x 220 mm. CLU-C: *fM1621.B72c.

[within cartouche] ⌠ Songs in the Opera of Camilla ⌡ Berchet Inventor. H. Hulsbergh Sculpsit. [at foot] London Printed for I. Walsh Servt. to Her Matie. at the Harp and Hoboy in Katherine Street near Somerset House in the Strand.

Songs In The New Opera, Call'd ⌠ Camilla as they are perform'd at the Theatre Royall ⌡ [engraved label over Walsh and Hare imprint] Sold by Iohn Young Musical Instrument Seller at the Dolphin & Crown at the West end of St. Pauls Church, where you may be furnish'd with al sorts of Violins, Flutes, Hautboys Bass-Viols, Harpsicords or Spinets; likewise al Books of Tunes, and Directions for any of these Instruments, also al sorts of Musick, Rul'd Paper & Strings, at Reasonable rates.

54 leaves. Pp. [i]▢ [ii-iii] 1▢-38▢ [38A]▢ 39▢-51▢.
Leaves printed on 1 side.
Tallest copy 348 x 220 mm. Vertical chain lines.

One page engraved per plate. Engraving style Walsh 1.
Illus. title-page plate passe-partout no. 2.
Title-page plate passe-partout no. 3.

Contents: illus. title-page [i]; title-page [ii]; contents [iii]; songs 1-38, [38A], 39-51.

Songs: see 20.

Copy: CLU-C *fM1621.B72c.

Plate 24.1   Morley and Isum, *Collection of New Songs*, 1706

Caption: plate 24.1. 310 x 202 mm. Lbl: G.117.

A Collection Of New Songs set to Musick By Mr Wm: Morley and Mr: Iohn Isum With A Thorough-bass to each Song, All transpos'd for the Flute: And Fairly Engraven on Copper Plates.

23 leaves. Pp. [i]▢\▢[1] [2]▢\▢[3] [4]▢-[6]▢\▢[7] [8]▢-[10]▢\▢[11] [12]▢-[14]▢\▢[15] [16]▢\▢[17] [18]▢-[22]▢
Leaves printed on 1 side.
Tallest copy 319 x 206 mm. Vertical chain lines.

One page engraved per plate. Engraving style Cross.
Title-page plate 274 x 176 mm.

Walsh i: 379.
Advertised in *London Gazette*, 1 August 1706. Price 3s.

Contents: title-page [i]; songs [1-18]; flute parts [19-22].

Songs:

No.	Page	First Line
1	[1-2]	With how much grace her swelling sighs (m Morley)
2	[3-4]	Ah Gratiania help your swain (m Isum)
3	[5]	Instruct me gentle Cupid (m Morley)
4	[6]	Born to surprize the world (m Morley, D&M 402)
5	[7-8]	Astrea by her conqu'ring charms (m Morley)
6	[9]	In vain ye god I ask (m Isum, D&M 1806)
7	[10]	Celia's charms are past expressing (m Isum, D&M 520)
8	[11-12]	When first I saw ye lovely charming fair (m Morley)
9	[13]	Corinna if my fates to love you (m Isum, D&M 733)
10	[14]	Drink a bottle with your friend (m Morley)
11	[15-16]	'Tis vain fond Strephon to complain (m Morley)
12	[17-18]	From love from thought from business free (m Isum)

Notes:
1. DLC: - pp. [17-18].
2. Lbl: - pp. [7-8].
3. OClW is wrongly given in *NUC* as the location of the copy actually at DLC.

Copies: DLC M1619.M86 Case; Lbl G.117.

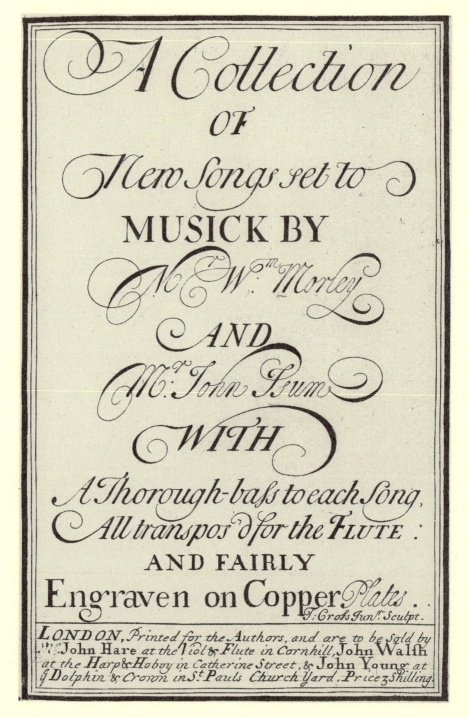

Caption: plate 24a.1. 321 x 200 mm. Lbl: H.1601.h.(1.).

A Collection Of New Songs set to Musick By Mr Wm: Morley and Mr: Iohn Isum With A Thorough-bass to each Song, All transpos'd for the Flute: And Fairly Engraven on Copper Plates. T: Cross Junr. Sculpt. London, Printed for the Authors, and are to be Sold by John Hare at the Viol & Flute in Cornhill, John Walsh at the Harp & Hoboy in Catherine Street, & John Young at ye Dolphin & Crown in St. Pauls Church Yard, Price 3 Shilling.

23 leaves. Pp. [i]□\□[1] [2]□\□[3] [4]□-[6]□\□[7] [8]□-[10]□\□[11] [12]□-[14]□\□[15] [16]□\□[17] [18]□-[22]□
Leaves printed on 1 side.
Tallest copy 336 x 230 mm. Vertical chain lines.

One page engraved per plate. Engraving style Cross.
Title-page plate 274 x 178 mm.

Walsh i: 379.
Advertised in *London Gazette*, 1 August 1706. Price 3s.

Contents: title-page [i]; songs [1-18]; flute parts [19-22].

Songs:

No.	Page	First Line
1	[1-2]	With how much grace her swelling sighs (m Morley)
2	[3-4]	Ah Gratiania help your swain (m Isum)
3	[5]	Drink a bottle with your friend (m Morley)
4	[6]	Instruct me gentle Cupid (m Morley)
5	[7-8]	Astrea by her conqu'ring charms (m Isum)
6	[9]	Born to surprize the world (m Morley, D&M 402)
7	[10]	In vain ye god I ask (m Isum, D&M 1806)
8	[11-12]	When first I saw ye lovely charming fair (m Morley)
9	[13]	Celia's charms are past expressing (m Isum, D&M 520)
10	[14]	Corinna if my fates to love you (m Isum, D&M 733)
11	[15-16]	'Tis vain fond Strephon to complain (m Morley)
12	[17-18]	From love from thought from business free (m Isum)

Notes:
1. Lbl: pp. [5] and [6], and [13] and [14] transposed.
2. Lcm: - pp. [9], [17-18].
3. Obh (Mus. E.35): - pp. [5], [17-22], + [6A] 'I thought you'd charms but now I find' (m Isum, chain lines horizontal). Leaves arranged: [i]□\□[11] [12]□\□[1] [2]□\□[15] [16]□ [6]□-[6A]□ [9]□\□[7] [8]□ [13]□-[14]□\□[3] [4]□ [10]□.

Copies: Lbl H.1601.h.(1.); Lcm I.A.11.(1.); Obh Mus. E.35; Obh Mus. E.36.

Plate 25.1   Smith, *Wonders in the Sun*, 1706

SONGS²

IN THE NEW

OPERA,

Call'd

WONDERS *in the* SUN

or

The KINGDOM *of the* BIRDS

Sold by I: Walsh Musicall Instrument maker in Or=
=dinary to her Majesty, at the Golden Harpe and Ho=boy
in Catherine-Street near Sommerset House in the strand
and I Hare Musick Instrument maker at ÿ Golden Viol and Flute in
Cornhill near ÿ Royal Exchange.

25 Smith, *Wonders in the Sun*, 7 August 1706

Caption: plate 25.1. 321 x 200 mm. Lbl: H.1601.h.(2.).

Songs In The New Opera, Call'd ⌠ Wonders in the Sun or The Kingdom of the Birds. ⌡ Sold by I: Walsh Musicall Instrument maker in Or==dinary to her Majesty, at the Golden Harpe and Ho=boy, in Catherine-Street near Sommerset House in the Strand and I. Hare Musick Instrument maker at ye Golden Viol and Flute in Cornhill near ye Royal Exchange.

11 leaves. Pp. [i-ii] 1-10.
Leaves printed on 1 side.
Tallest copy 322 x 200 mm. Vertical chain lines.

One page engraved per plate. Engraving style Walsh 1.
Title-page plate 272 x 187 mm. Passe-partout no. 3.
Contents plate 129 x 165 mm.

Walsh i: 212.
Advertised in *Daily Courant*, 7 August 1706. Price 1s. 6d.

Contents: title-page [i]; contents [ii]; songs 1-10.

Songs:

No.	Page	First Line
1	1	Oh love if a god thou wilt be (s Pack, Bradshaw, < *Wonders in the Sun*, D&M 2499)
2	2	In the fields in frost and snows (s Mrs Willis's Girl, < *Wonders in the Sun*)
3	3	What are these ideots doing (s Pack, < *Wonders in the Sun*, D&M 3622)
4	4	Since now the worlds turn'd upside down (s Willis, < *Wonders in the Sun*, D&M 2950)
5	5-6	Last night when Phæbus went to bed (< *Wonders in the Sun*)
6	7-10	Down from the towring rock (s Pack, Boman, J., < *Wonders in the Sun*)

Note:
1. Caption title uses the subtitle 'Kingdom of the Birds'.

Copy: Lbl H.1601.h.(2.).

Plate 26.1   Clayton, *Arsinoe*, 1706

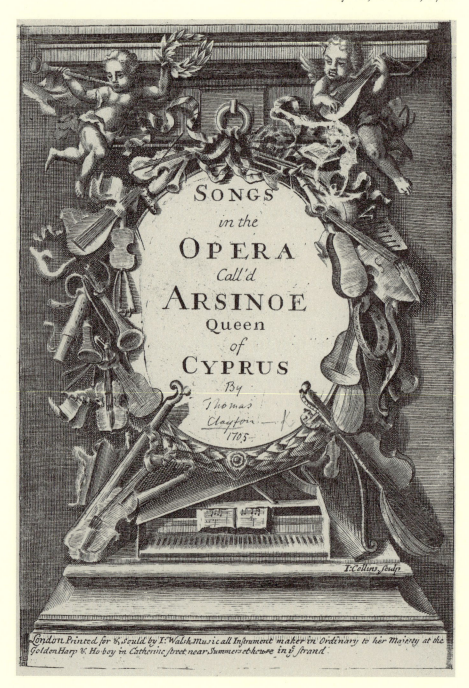

SONGS
in the
OPERA
Call'd
ARSINOE
Queen
of
CYPRUS
By
Thomas
Clayton
1705

I: Collins, sculp

London Printed for & sould by I: Walsh Musicall Instrument maker in Ordinary to her Majesty at the
Golden Harp & Ho-boy in Catherine street near Summerset house in ȳ strand.

Caption: plate 26.1. 330 x 202 mm. Lbl: H.124.(1.).

[within cartouche] ⌠ Songs in the Opera Call'd Arsinoe Queen of Cyprus ⌡ I:
Collins. sculp. [at foot] London Printed for & Sould by I: Walsh Musicall
Instrument maker in Ordinary to her Majesty at the Golden Harp & Ho=boy
in Catherine=street near Summerset=house in ye strand

51 leaves. Pp. [i]☐-[ii]☐ 1☐-49☐.
Leaves printed on 1 side.
Tallest copy 374 x 237 mm. Vertical chain lines.

One page engraved per plate. Engraving style Walsh 1.
Title-page plate 252 x 189 mm. Passe-partout no. 1.
Contents plate 206 x 146 mm.

Walsh i: 220.
Advertised in *Post Man*, 5 October 1706.

Contents: title-page [i]; contents [ii]; overture 1-2; songs 3-49.

Songs:

No.	Page	First Line
1	3	Queen of darkness sable night (s Hughes, < *Arsinoe*)
2	4	Lillies roses pearly dew (m Clayton, s Hughes, < *Arsinoe*)
3	5	As roses shew more pale with dew (m Clayton, s Hughes, < *Arsinoe*)
4	6-7	So sweet an air (s Tofts, Hughes, < *Arsinoe*)
5	8	For thy ferry boat Charon (s Ramondon, < *Arsinoe*)
6	9-10	And you Dorisbe (s Hughes, < *Arsinoe*)
7	11-12	Happy he who void of love (s Leveridge, < *Arsinoe*)
8	13	Tis the fashion, without passion (m Clayton, s Lindsey, < *Arsinoe*)
9	14	But pitty shou'd move you (s Cross, Hughes, < *Arsinoe*)
10	15	Rise Alecto, rise rejoyce and see with me (s Cross, < *Arsinoe*)
11	16-17	Ungratefull so to deceive me (s Hughes, Leveridge, < *Arsinoe*)
12	18-19	Wounded I, and sighing lye (s Tofts, < *Arsinoe*)
13	20	O love I have gain'd a victory sure (m Clayton, s Tofts, < *Arsinoe*)
14	21	Charming creature, every feature (m Clayton, s Hughes, < *Arsinoe*)
15	22	Eies that kill me with disdain (m Clayton, s Hughes, < *Arsinoe*)
16	23	Hated strife, and rebells life, A (s Hughes, Leveridge, < *Arsinoe*)
17	24	Yee gods I only wish to die (m Clayton, s Leveridge, < *Arsinoe*)
18	25	Blind god from your chains I am free (m Clayton, s Hughes, < *Arsinoe*)
19	26	Conqu'ring o but cruel eyes (m Clayton, s Cross, < *Arsinoe*)
20	27-28	Assist ye furys from the deep (m Clayton, s Cross, < *Arsinoe*)
21	29	Doubtfull heart oh tell me why (s Tofts, Hughes, < *Arsinoe*)
22	30	Doubtfull heart oh tell me why (s Tofts, Hughes, < *Arsinoe*)
23	31	Was ever fate so hard as mine (s Tofts, Hughes, < *Arsinoe*)
24	32	Thus sinking mariners (m Clayton, s Hughes, < *Arsinoe*)
25	33	Yee stars that rule my birth (m Clayton, s Cross, < *Arsinoe*)
26	34	Delbo if thou wilt not woe, me (m Clayton, s Lindsey, Good, < *Arsinoe*)
27	35	To warr my thoughts to warr (m Clayton, s Tofts, < *Arsinoe*)
28	36-37	Boiling passions rage no more (m Clayton, s Leveridge, < *Arsinoe*)

29	38	Greatness leave me, undeceive me (m Clayton, s Tofts, < *Arsinoe*)
30	39	But how can I live (m Clayton, s Tofts, < *Arsinoe*)
31	40	Wanton zephy'rs softly blowing (m Clayton, s Tofts, < *Arsinoe*)
32	41-42	Conscious dungeon walls of stone (m Clayton, s Tofts, < *Arsinoe*)
33	43	Sleep Ormondo void of fear (m Clayton, s Tofts, < *Arsinoe*)
34	44-45	Cruel stars who all conspire (m Clayton, s Cross, < *Arsinoe*)
35	46	My dear my joy (s Tofts, Hughes, < *Arsinoe*)
36	47-48	Hail happy pair, great Pelops and Arsinoe (m Clayton, s Leveridge, < *Arsinoe*)
37	49	Then tell it in the Cyprian groves (m Clayton, s Hughes, < *Arsinoe*)

Notes:
1. TWm: pp. 6, 16, 18, 41 reversed.
2. Copy reported at ViWC comprises 3 songs only.

Copies: Ckc 85.1.(5); CLU-C *fM1624.7.C62; CZ-*Pu*; *D-B*; F-Pc Rés. V.S.1279; Lbl H.124.(1.); LVp 785.2; MH-Mu Mus 639.182.606 (Cage); NjP (Ex) M1503.C5A7q; NN Drexel 4854; Obh Mus. D.8(3); *SA*; *S-Skma*; TWm —.

27   deleted (see 26).

28   deleted (see 29).

Plate 29.1   Clayton, *Arsinoe*, 1706

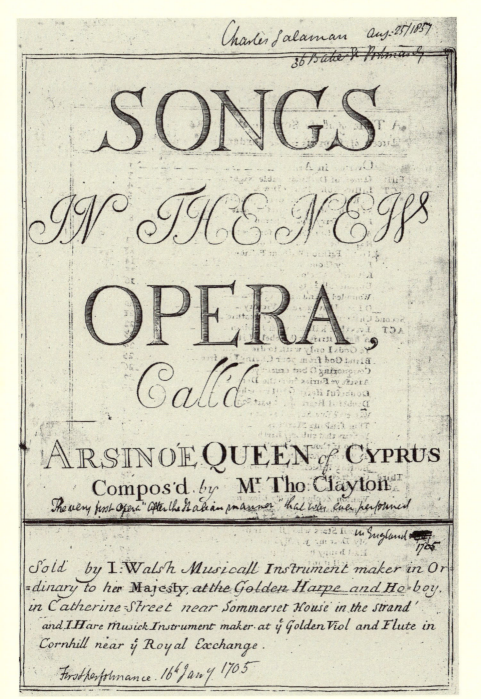

Caption: see plate 26.1. Plate 29.1. 355 x 215 mm. CSmH: 139672.

[within cartouche] (Songs in the Opera Call'd Arsinoe Queen of Cyprus) I: Collins. sculp [at foot] London Printed for & Sould by I: Walsh Musicall Instrument maker in Ordinary to her Majesty at the Golden Harp & Ho=boy in Catherine=street near Summerset=house in ye strand

Songs In The New Opera, Call'd (Arsino'e Queen of Cyprus Compos'd by Mr. Tho: Clayton) Sold by I: Walsh Musicall Instrument maker in Or==dinary to her Majesty, at the Golden Harpe and Ho=boy, in Catherine Street near Sommerset House in the Strand and I. Hare Musick Instrument maker at ye Golden Viol and Flute in Cornhill near ye Royal Exchange.

51 leaves. Pp. [i]☐ [ii-iii] 1☐-49☐.
Leaves printed on 1 side.
Tallest copy 360 x 228 mm. Vertical chain lines.

One page engraved per plate. Engraving style Walsh 1.
Illus. title-page plate 253 x 189 mm. Passe-partout no. 1.
Title-page plate 270 x 187 mm. Passe-partout no. 3.
Contents plate 206 x 146 mm.

Contents: illus. title-page [i]; title-page [ii]; contents [iii]; overture 1-2; songs 3-49.

Songs: see **26**.

Notes:
1. B-Br: - p. [i]; p. 1 reversed.
2. Cfm: p. 1 reversed.
3. Ckc, CSmH, NRU-Mus, TWm: - p. [i].
4. CtY-Mus: - p. [i]; pp. 4, 24, 33, 38 lack pagination.
5. DLC: - p. [i]; pp. 3-5, 13, 20-21, 24, 26, 32-39, 43-45 lack pagination; pp. 6, 9, 11, 16, 18, 27, [36], 41, [44], 47 reversed; '2d part' in MS. on title-page.
6. ICN: pp. 6, 16, 18, 41 reversed and contents on separate leaf.
7. Lgc: - p. [i]; short contents plate listing only 19 songs; pp. 6, 9, 11, 16, 18, 27, 36, 41, 44, 47 reversed.
8. NL-DHgm: - p. [i]; price in MS. on title-page, 'pr. 7s=od'.

Copies: B-Br Fétis 2850; Cfm MU.MS. 1283; Ckc 85.4.(1.); CSmH 139672; CtY-Mus Rare Mq20.C57a; DLC M1500.C685A6; ICN VM1505.C62a no. 1; Lgc G.Mus.112(3); NL-DHgm 24 A 31; NN Drexel 4965.1; NRU-Mus Vault M1500.C622A; Ob Mus. 22.c.158(2); TWm —.

Plate 30.1   Clayton, *Arsinoe*, 1706

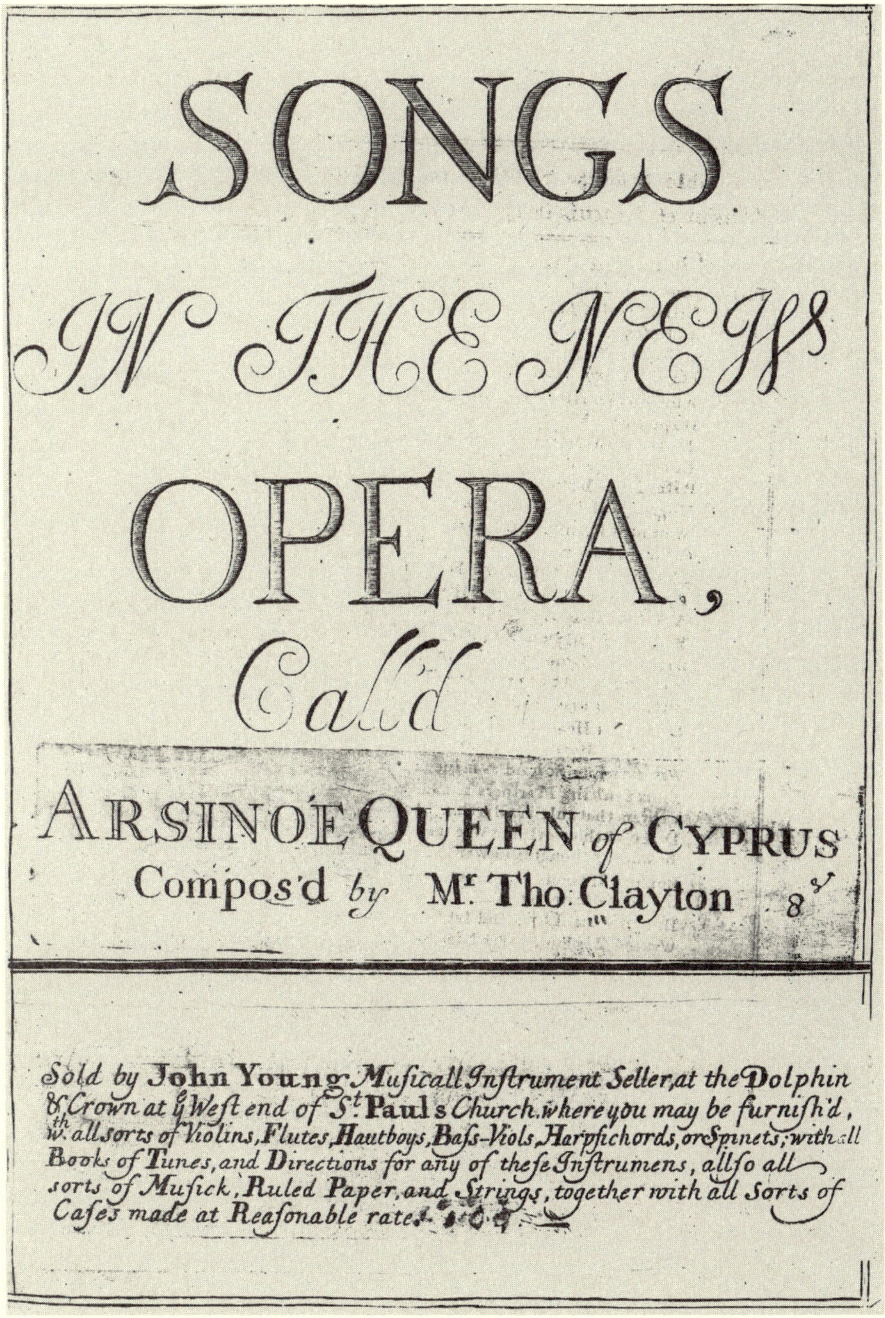

SONGS

IN THE NEW

OPERA,

Call'd

ARSINOÉ QUEEN *of* CYPRUS

Compos'd *by*   Mr Tho: Clayton   8^s

Sold by **John Young**. Musicall Instrument Seller, at the **Dolphin**
& Crown at ye West end of St **Paul** s Church, where you may be furnish'd,
w.th all sorts of Violins, Flutes, Hautboys, Bass-Viols, Harpsichords, or Spinets, with all
Books of Tunes, and Directions for any of these Instrumens, allso all
sorts of Musick, Ruled Paper, and Strings, together with all Sorts of
Cases made at Reasonable rate.

Caption: plate 30.1. 348 x 226 mm. PU: RB Folio Music M1500.C55A7.

Songs In The New Opera, Call'd ⌠ Arsino'e Queen of Cyprus Compos'd by
Mr. Tho: Clayton ⌡ [engraved label over Walsh imprint] Sold by Iohn Young
Musicall Instrument Seller, at the Dolphin & Crown at ye West end of St. Pauls
Church. where you may be furnish'd, wth. all sorts of Violins, Flutes,
Hautboys, Bass-Viols, Harpsichords, or Spinets; withall Books of Tunes,
and Directions for any of these Instrumens, allso all sorts of Musick, Ruled
Paper, and Strings, together with all Sorts of Cases made at Reasonable rate.

49 leaves. Pp. [i-ii] 1☐-23☐ 25☐-49☐.
Leaves printed on 1 side.
Tallest copy 348 x 226 mm. Vertical chain lines.

One page engraved per plate. Engraving style Walsh 1.
Title-page plate 271 x 185 mm. Passe-partout no. 3.
Contents plate 206 x 147 mm.

Contents: title-page [i]; contents [ii]; overture 1-2; songs 3-23, 25-49.

Songs: see 26.

Notes:
1. Price 8s. in MS. on title-page.
2. Wanting p. 24.

Copy: PU RB Folio Music M1500.C55A7.

Plate 31.1   Clayton, *Arsinoe*, 1706

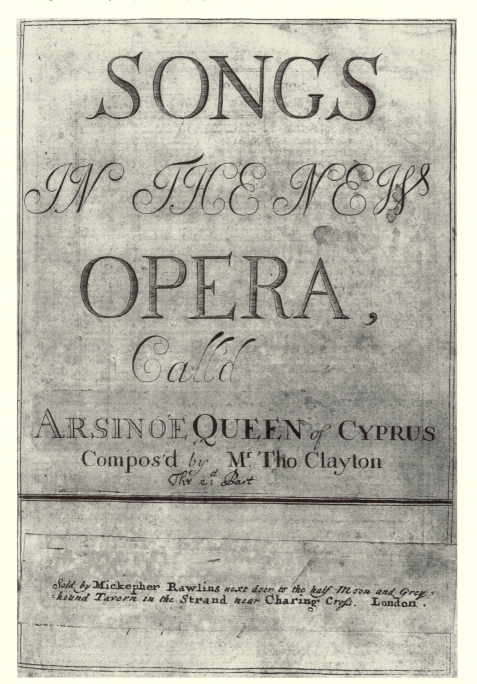

31   Clayton, *Arsinoe*, 5 October 1706

Caption: plate 31.1. 313 x 199 mm. Ge: R.x.17.

Songs In The New Opera, Call'd ⌠ Arsino'e Queen of Cyprus Compos'd by Mr. Tho: Clayton ⌡ [engraved label over Walsh imprint] Sold by Mickepher Rawlins next door to the half-Moon and Grey==hound Tavern in the Strand near Charing Cross. London.

50 leaves. Pp. [i-ii] 1□-4□ [5]□ 6□-12□ [13]□ 14□-19□ [20]□ 21□-23□ [24]□ 25□ [26]□ 27□-33□ [34]□ 35□-49□.
Leaves printed on 1 side.
Tallest copy 313 x 199 mm. Vertical chain lines.

One page engraved per plate. Engraving style Walsh 1.
Title-page plate 271 x 185 mm. Passe-partout no. 3.

Contents: title-page [i]; contents [ii]; overture 1-2; songs 3-49.

Songs: see **26**.

Note:
1. 'The 2d: Part' in MS. on title-page.

Copy: Ge R.x.17.

Plate 32.1   Fedelli, *Temple of Love*, 1706.

Plate 32.2   Fedelli, *Temple of Love*, 1706

SONGS

IN THE NEW

OPERA,

Call'd

The TEMPLE of LOVE,

Compos'd by

Sign: Gioseppe Fedelli Saggione

Sold by I: Walsh *Musicall Instrument maker in Or=*
=dinary to her Majesty, at the Golden Harpe and Ho=boy,
in Catherine=Street near Sommerset House in the strand
and I.Hare Musick Instrument maker at y̓ Golden Viol and Flute in
Cornhill near y̓ Royal Exchange.

84

32   Fedelli, *Temple of Love*, 18 October 1706

Caption: plates 32.1-32.2. 351 x 223 mm. Lbl: Hirsch IV.1582.

⌠ The Temple Of Love [within cartouche] Songs in the Opera Call'd the Temple of Love ⌡ M Vander Gucht Sculp [at foot] London Printed for I. Walsh Servt to Her Matie. at the Harp and Hoboy in Katherine Street near Somerset House in ye Strand

Songs In The New Opera, Call'd ⌠ The Temple of Love Compos'd by Signr: Gioseppe Fedelli Saggione ⌡ Sold by I: Walsh Musicall Instrument maker in Or==dinary to her Majesty; at the Golden Harpe and Ho=boy, in Catherine=Street near Sommerset House in the Strand and I. Hare Musick Instrument maker at ye Golden Viol and Flute in Cornhill near ye Royal Exchange.

34 leaves. Pp. [i]◻ [ii-iii] 1◻-32◻.
Leaves printed on 1 side.
Tallest copy 389 x 245 mm. Vertical chain lines.

One page engraved per plate. Engraving style Walsh 1.
Illus. title-page plate 324 x 195 mm. Passe-partout no. 4.
Title-page plate 272 x 185 mm. Passe-partout no. 3.
Contents plate 202 x 176 mm.

Walsh i: 222.
Advertised in *Daily Courant*, 18 October 1706.

Contents: illus. title-page [i]; title-page [ii]; contents [iii]; songs 1-30; setting of last song for 2 flutes and bass 31-32.

Songs:

No.	Page	First Line
1	1-2	Charming roses flowry treasures (s Gallia, < *Temple of Love*)
2	3-4	E're I change or make advances (s Lawrence, < *Temple of Love*)
3	5-6	I'll ever be loving (s Gallia, < *Temple of Love*)
4	7	Ne'er leave me more my treasure (s Bracegirdle, < *Temple of Love*)
5	8	Pow'rs immortall your riddle clearing (s Laroon, < *Temple of Love*)
6	9-10	Love's fire in my eyes is shining (s Laroon, < *Temple of Love*)
7	11-12	Sleep in body, wake in mind (s Boman, E., < *Temple of Love*)
8	13	Ev'ry man in love's a traitor (s Bracegirdle, < *Temple of Love*)
9	14	More we fondly run, The (s Cook, < *Temple of Love*)
10	15-16	Contenting of a lover, The (s Gallia, < *Temple of Love*)
11	17	Ne'er deceive me (s Bracegirdle, < *Temple of Love*)
12	18	Loves blind and strikes our heart's (s Gallia, < *Temple of Love*)
13	19-20	If I ever encline to complying (s Gallia, < *Temple of Love*)
14	21	Lovers for their harvest staying (s Laroon, < *Temple of Love*)
15	22-23	Warbling the birds enjoying (s Gallia, < *Temple of Love*)
16	24-25	If love claims no return (s Lawrence, < *Temple of Love*)
17	26-27	Come all yee tender swains (s Gallia, < *Temple of Love*)
18	28-30	I grasp thee (s Gallia, Laroon, < *Temple of Love*)

Notes:
1. Titles engraved directly on illustrated title-page, though the plate was used as a passe-partout.
2. B-Br: - pp. [i], 30-32.
3. DLC, Lbl (Hirsch III.741), Ob: - p. [i].

Copies: B-Br Fétis 2852; Ckc 85.2.(11.); CLU-C *fM1508.T285; CSfst de Bellis 878; CZ-Pu; D-B; DLC M1503.F293T4 Case; Lbl H.124.(2.); Lbl Hirsch III.741; Lbl Hirsch IV.1582; Lcm XXXII.A.2.(2.); NjP (Ex) M1508.F3T2q; NN Drexel 4854.3; Ob Mus. 22c.158(4); Obh Mus. D.8(5); S-Skma.

32a Fedelli, *Temple of Love*, 18 October 1706

Caption: see plates 32.1-32.2.

⌠ The Temple Of Love [within cartouche] Songs in the Opera Call'd the Temple of Love ⌡ M Vander Gucht Sculp [at foot] London Printed for I. Walsh Servt to Her Matie. at the Harp and Hoboy in Katherine Street near Somerset House in ye Strand

Songs In The New Opera, Call'd ⌠ The Temple of Love Compos'd by Signr: Gioseppe Fedelli Saggione ⌡ Sold by I: Walsh Musicall Instrument maker in Or==dinary to her Majesty; at the Golden Harpe and Ho=boy, in Catherine=Street near Sommerset House in the Strand and I. Hare Musick Instrument maker at ye Golden Viol and Flute in Cornhill near ye Royal Exchange.

35 leaves. Pp. [i]▯ [ii-iii] [iv]▯ 1▯-32▯.
Leaves printed on 1 side.
Tallest copy 361 x 225 mm. Vertical chain lines.

One page engraved per plate. Engraving style Walsh 1.
Illus. title-page plate 327 x 194 mm. Passe-partout no. 4.
Title-page plate 272 x 188 mm. Passe-partout no. 3.
Contents plate 203 x 178 mm.
Dedication plate 247 x 190 mm.

Walsh i: 222.
Advertised in *Daily Courant*, 18 October 1706.

Contents: illus. title-page [i]; title-page [ii]; contents [iii]; dedication [iv]; songs 1-30; setting of last song for 2 flutes and bass 31-32.

Songs: see 32.

Notes:
1. Titles engraved directly on illustrated title-page, though the plate was used as a passe-partout.
2. Dedication dated 7 October 1706.
3. Gu: - pp. [i], 7, 32.
4. NN, NRU-Mus: pp. 1, 3, 9, 11, 19, 29 reversed so that songs can be seen entire at a single opening. NRU-Mus: p. 31 also reversed.

Copies: F-Pc Rés.V.S.1281; Gu Ca.13-y.22; ICN VM1505.C62a no.4; Mp BRf200.Sa37; NN Drexel 4965.3; NRU-Mus Vault M1508.S129; TWm —.

Plate 33.1   *Comical Songs*, 1706

COMICAL
Songs, and Songs of
HUMOUR.
as also
two part Songs.,
AND
Dialogues

T:Collins sculp

London Printed for & sould by I: Walsh Musicall Instrument maker in Ordinary to his Majesty at the
Golden Harp & Ho-boy in Catherine street near Summersethouse in y strand.

Caption: plate 33.1. 318 x 201 mm. Lbl: K.8.k.19.

[within cartouche; in MS.] ⌠ Comical songs, and songs of Humour, as also two part Songs ..,. And Dialogues. ⌡ I: Collins. sculp [at foot] London Printed for & Sould by I: Walsh Musicall Instrument maker in Ordinary to his Majesty at the Golden Harp & Ho=boy in Catherine=street near Summerset=house in ye strand

137 leaves. Pp. [i]□-[iii]□ [1]□-[86]□ [86A]□ [87]□-[94]□\□[95] [96]□-[97]□\□[98] [99]□-[111]□ [111A]□ [112]-[113] [114]□-[117]□\□[118] [119]□-[133]□. Leaves printed on 1 side. Tallest copy 318 x 201 mm. Vertical chain lines.

One page engraved per plate. Engraving style Walsh and Cross. Title-page plate 254 x 194 mm. Passe-partout no. 1.

Walsh i: 358. Advertised in *Post Man*, 8 August 1710.

Contents: title-page [i]; contents [ii-iii]; songs [1-86]; title-page [86A]; songs [87-111]; title-page [111A]; songs [112-133].

Songs:

No.	Page	First Line
1	[1]	Bonny lad there was, A (s Prince, < *Maid in the Mill*)
2	[2]	Ah tell me noe more of your duty (v D'urfey, D&M 81)
3	[3]	Ah sweet inchantress who canst throw (m Clarke, T.)
4	[4]	As Oyster Nan stood by her tub (D&M 230)
5	[5]	Amongst the pure ones all (s Willis, Faire, D&M 160)
6	[6]	Lusty young smith at his vice, A (m Leveridge, D&M 2145)
7	[7]	Lavia would but dare not venture (m Townsend, v Rolfe, D&M 1937)
8	[8]	Cloe blush't and frown'd and swore (m Eccles, s Cook, < *Biter*, D&M 542)
9	[9]	Celias bright beautys all other's transcend (m Keen, v Keen, s Willis, < *Heiress or the Sallamanca Doctor*, D&M 519)
10	[10]	Blow Boreas blow (m Bradley, Robert, D&M 384)
11	[11-12]	Blowzabella my bouncing doxie (a D'urfey, D&M 385)
12	[13]	Blythe Jockey, young and gay (m Leveridge, s Boy, D&M 382)
13	[14]	By moonlight on the green (s Lucas, D&M 449)
14	[15]	Cupid would you exert your pow'r (s Davis)
15	[16]	Celia's smiles will quite undoe me (m Davis)
16	[17]	Cloe found love for his Psyche in tears (s Prince, < *Agreeable Disappointment*, D&M 545)
17	[17]	Cease of Cupid to complain (s Bracegirdle, D&M 497)
18	[18-19]	Come all ye little Cupids now (m Wilford, s Wilford)
19	[20]	Crown your bowles, loyall soul's (m Purcell, H., v D'urfey, D&M 760)
20	[21]	Cupid make your virgins tender (m Purcell, D., D&M 771)
21	[22]	Celladon when spring came on (v D'urfey, s Leveridge, D&M 505)
22	[23]	Cou'd a man be secure (m Clarke, J., s Leveridge, < *Committee*)
23	[24]	Dear Celena lovely creature (m White)
24	[25]	Drunk I was last night (m Purcell, H., D&M 896)
25	[26]	Draw Cupid draw, and make fair Sylvia know (m Motley, D&M 885)

26	[27]	Fond woman with mistaken art (m Purcell, D., s Erwin, < *Reformed Wife, or the Lady's Cure*)
27	[28]	Fye Damon leave this foolish passion (D&M 991)
28	[29]	Frank what shall we do (m Willis)
29	[29]	Here Tom here's a health
30	[29]	Fear no danger to insue (m Purcell, H., < *Measure for Measure*)
31	[30]	Fareweell my bonny, witty pretty, Moggy (v D'urfey, s Leveridge, D&M 965)
32	[31]	Hide me in some lonely den (m Berenclow)
33	[32]	How insipid were life (m Croft)
34	[33]	Hark Prince Eugine com's along (m Shore, v Person of Quality)
35	[34]	Hark the cock crow'd (m Clarke, J., D&M 1264)
36	[35]	Just comeing from sea (m Weldon, s Doggett, < *Subscription Musick*, D&M 1895)
37	[36]	I'll stick to my bottle (m Garee, v Garee)
38	[37]	In vain we dispair (m Wilford, v Aliff)
39	[38]	Jolly Roger Twangdillo of Plowden Hill (v D'urfey, D&M 1881)
40	[39]	I'll hurry thee hence (m Eccles, s Bracegirdle, < *Justice Buisy*)
41	[40]	Jockey was as brisk & blith a lad (m Clarke, J., s Cross, D&M 1874)
42	[41]	It tis not that I love you less (m Cox, D&M 1845)
43	[42]	Is'e no more to shady coverts (m Clarke, J., s Temple, D&M 1653)
44	[43]	Jogging on from yonder green (m Leveridge, s Lindsey, D&M 1876)
45	[44]	Jenny long resisted (m Leveridge, s Campion, D&M 1858)
46	[45-46]	Like you the goddess thus replies (s Elford)
47	[47]	Let me not always ask in vain (m Berenclow)
48	[48]	Let's sing of stage coaches (m Eccles, s Doggett, < *Stage Coach*, D&M 2033)
49	[49]	Lord! what's come to my mother (m Clarke, J., v D'urfey, s Lucas, < *Bath, or the Western Lass*, D&M 2083)
50	[50]	Martillo whilst you patch your face (m Clarke, T.)
51	[51]	No more let Damons eyes persue (m Eccles, H., v Wall, D&M 2335)
52	[52-53]	Now let Bellona Albion's minds inspire (m Willis)
53	[54]	Now my freedom's regain'd (m Willis, D&M 2403)
54	[55]	On Brandon Heath (D&M 2605)
55	[56]	O! Strephon court no more in vain (m Cox)
56	[57]	On Sunday after Mass (m Leveridge, s Mills)
57	[58]	Of all the worlds enjoyments (m Leveridge, s Leveridge, < *Massaniello*, D&M 2574)
58	[59]	Oh! my panting heart (s Baldwin, D&M 2508)
59	[60]	Phillis the fairest of loves powr's (m Eminent Master, v Person of Quality)
60	[61]	Phillis talk not more of passion (m Purcell, D., < *Alexander the Great*, D&M 2689)
61	[62]	Of late I was so much in love (m Cox)
62	[63]	Room for a rover (m Paisible, D&M 2819)
63	[64]	See sirs, see here, a doctor rare (m Leveridge, s Leveridge, < *Quacks, or Farewell Folly*, D&M 2878)
64	[65]	Strike up drowsy gutts scrapers (m Lane, v D'urfey, D&M 3090)
65	[66]	To beauty born a willing slave (m Ximenes)
66	[67]	Twas within a fourlong of Edinborough town (m Purcell, H., s Girl, < *Mock Marriage*, D&M 3500)
67	[68]	Twas in the month of May Jo (m Purcell, D., D&M 3496)
68	[69]	Sun was just setting, The (m Leveridge, D&M 3107)
69	[70]	Twas when summer was rosie (v D'urfey, D&M 3498)
70	[71]	Thô Cælia you my story hear
71	[72]	Old wife she sent to the miller her daughter, The (v D'urfey, D&M 2602)
72	[73]	Bane of all pleasure, The
73	[74]	Take not a womans anger ill (m Purcell, H., s Leveridge, < *Rival Sisters*, D&M 3145)
74	[75]	While on those lovely looks I gaze (m Hayden)
75	[76]	When Celia was learning (m Isum, v Chocke, D&M 3692)
76	[77]	Why de'you with disdain refuse (m Leveridge, v Person of Quality)
77	[78]	Within an arbor of delight (m D'urfey, v D'urfey, D&M 4006)
78	[79]	When Sawny first did woe me (m Leveridge, D&M 3785)
79	[80]	Why shou'd women be so coy (m Ximenes, v Estcourt)

80	[81]	When Phillida with Jockey (v D'urfey, D&M 3780)
81	[82]	When Thirsis did Dorinda woe (m Martin, v Chocke)
82	[83]	What wou'd Europa whose shrill cryes (s Leveridge, < *Music of the Peace*, D&M 3673)
83	[84]	Whilst the French their arms discover (m Clarke, J., v D'urfey, D&M 3892)
84	[85]	You the glorious sons of honour (m Barrett, v D'urfey)
85	[86]	Young Corydon and Phyllis (m Clarke, J., D&M 4123)
86	[87]	Bury delights my roving eye
87	[88-89]	Come let us howle some heavy note (< *Duchess of Malfey*)
88	[90-91]	Daphne to prove my heart is true (D&M 798)
89	[92-93]	For you who are rid by the fury, Love (< *Unnatural Brother*)
90	[94-95]	Fill all the glasses, fill e'em high (< *Harry the Fifth*)
91	[96]	How sweet how lovely when return'd (< *Sham Doctor*, D&M 1463)
92	[97-98]	Farewell vaine nymph (m Gillier)
93	[99]	Go perjur'd man (m Blow, D&M 1148)
94	[100]	Happy Britains, seated here (m Weldon, < *Britain's Happiness*)
95	[101-102]	Hear ye midnight fantomes (v Rowe, s Cook, Davis, < *Fair Penitent*)
96	[103]	Let us revell and roar (< *Lovers' Luck*, D&M 2020)
97	[104]	Melancholy look's and whining (m Weldon, s Laroon, Hughes)
98	[105]	Nothing adds to your fond fire (m Hickes, s Cook, Davis)
99	[106]	Plenty mirth & gay delights (m Purcell, D., s Lindsey, Laroon, < *Grove*, D&M 2707)
100	[107]	Wine does wonders ev'ry day (m Eccles, s Gouge, Curco, Spalding, < *Morose Reformer*)
101	[108-109]	What's love (< *Libertine*)
102	[110]	When Cloe sings (m Barrett)
103	[111]	Wise nature owns, thy undisputed sway (v Congreve, < *Cecilia song 1701*)
104	[112-114]	Ah how lovely sweet and dear (s Bracegirdle, Boman, E., D&M 55)
105	[115-116]	What beauty doe I see (m Akeroyde, v D'urfey, s Bourdon, Lucas, < *Bath, or the Western Lass*, D&M 3626)
106	[117]	Where oxen do low (m Purcell, D., v D'urfey, D&M 3846)
107	[118-119]	Whilst wretched fools sneak up and down (m Purcell, D., s Leveridge, Pate, < *Massaniello*, D&M 3895)
108	[120-121]	You damzells who sleep, devoid of all care (< *Midnight Mistakes*)
109	[122-125]	Shou'd I not lead a happy life (s Reading, J., Lee, < *Love's a Jest*, D&M 2922)
110	[126-131]	Proud women I scorn you (s Boman, J., Doggett, < *Mad Lover*, D&M 2441)
111	[132-133]	By those pigsneyes that starrs do seem (s Doggett, Bracegirdle, < *Richmond Heiress*, D&M 453)

Notes:

1. Text of main title and of titles to second ('Two Part Songs') and third ('Dialogues.') parts is in MS. These internal title-pages also use the Collins passe-partout title-page with the same imprint.
2. Contents list, pp. [ii-iii], is in MS. Songs paginated in MS., in top right-hand corner.
3. One leaf (pp. [112]-[113]) printed on both sides.
4. Dating: volume contains songs published in *Monthly Mask of Vocal Music* during 1705; texts of two songs were published in *Wit & Mirth*, 1706; texts of three songs were published in *Wit & Mirth*, 1707. Several songs are not known from other sources. Imprint of all title-pages reads 'his Majesty', and therefore must date from 1702 or earlier. The advertisement noted in Walsh i (358), that appeared in the *Post Man*, 8 August 1710, announces 'A Collection of Comical Songs and songs of Humour, by Mr. D'Urfey'. In the same issue there was also an advertisement for 'Several Dialogues and 2 and 3 Part Songs' (Walsh i, 359). The works of other authors are to be found in the extant volume suggesting that either the advertisement refers to some other book or Walsh did not adhere strictly to his description when putting this copy together. 'D'Urfey's Songs' were available in 1721 for 2s., a price that is far too low for this volume. Smith suggests that Walsh's advertisement may have been a response to Pippard's *Musa et Musica*, published on 13 June 1710, and containing songs by D'urfey. That does not preclude the possibility that *Comical Songs* had been available earlier. 1706 seems a reasonable compromise, if we assume that Walsh was using left-over title-pages and that none of the songs actually date from a later year.

Copy: Lbl K.8.k.19.

33a Bononcini, *Camilla*, 22 February 1707

No title-page.

50 leaves. Pp. □[1] [2]□-[3]□ [1]□-[26]□ [26, i.e.27]□ [28]□-[44]□ [44, i.e.45]□ [46]□-[47]□.
Leaves printed on 1 side.
Tallest copy 358 x 230 mm. Vertical chain lines.

One page engraved per plate. Engraving style Cross.

Contents: overture [1-3], songs [1-26], [26, i.e.27], [28-44], [44, i.e.45], [46-47].

Songs:

No.	Page	First Line
1	[1]	I was born of royall race (s Tofts, < *Camilla*)
2	[2]	O nymph of race divine (s De L'Épine, < *Camilla*)
3	[3]	Since you from death thus save me (s De L'Épine, < *Camilla*)
4	[4]	Love darts are in your eyes (s Ramondon, < *Camilla*)
5	[5]	Fortune ever known to vary (s Tofts, < *Camilla*)
6	[6]	Tender maids your pity show (s Baroness, < *Camilla*)
7	[7]	Frail are a lovers hopes (s Hughes, < *Camilla*)
8	[8]	Wellcome sorrow death attending (s Baroness, < *Camilla*)
9	[9]	All I'll venture to restore ye (s Ramondon, < *Camilla*)
10	[10]	See ye just gods of innocence (s Tofts, < *Camilla*)
11	[11]	Fair Dorinda happy mays't thou ever be (s Baroness, < *Camilla*)
12	[12]	Charming fair for thee I languish (s De L'Épine, < *Camilla*)
13	[13]	Wretched am I, that I gain him (s Tofts, < *Camilla*)
14	[14]	Among women they for certain know (s Lindsey, < *Camilla*)
15	[15]	Aged Phillis, wanton still is (s Leveridge, < *Camilla*)
16	[16]	I languish, for whom
17	[16]	Care is fled dispairs no more
18	[17]	Ah never yet was known (s Hughes, < *Camilla*)
19	[18]	Revenge I summon (s Tofts, < *Camilla*)
20	[18]	Now Cupid or never be kind (s Hughes)
21	[19]	In vain I fly from sorrow (s De L'Épine, < *Camilla*)
22	[20]	To beauty devoted (s De L'Épine, < *Camilla*)
23	[21]	I love but dare not my flame discover (s Ramondon, < *Camilla*)
24	[22]	Fortune like a wanton gipsy (s Leveridge, < *Camilla*)
25	[23]	Not so much cruelty, I prethee now (s Lindsey, < *Camilla*)
26	[23]	Joys are attending those cares (s Baroness)
27	[24]	No love was ever known that (s Baroness, < *Camilla*)
28	[25]	Around her see Cupid flying (s Hughes, < *Camilla*)
29	[26]	Love leads to battle, who dares oppose (s Ramondon, < *Camilla*)
30	[26, i.e.27]	Ungratefull you fly me, unkindly (s De L'Épine, < *Camilla*)
31	[28]	Love & ambition strive (s Tofts, < *Camilla*)
32	[29]	Tullia I feel thy charms (s Leveridge, < *Camilla*)
33	[30]	Something is in my face so alluring (s Lindsey, < *Camilla*)
34	[31]	Fly and follow your idol beauty (s Baroness, < *Camilla*)
35	[32]	Oh tyranous jealousy (s Hughes, < *Camilla*)
36	[33]	Happy I love & haste to enjoy her (< *Camilla*)
37	[34]	Fly ye virgins th' unfaithfull lover (s Baroness, < *Camilla*)
38	[35]	These eyes are made so killing (s Lindsey, < *Camilla*)
39	[36]	Thou art he my dearest creature
40	[37]	Cupid oh at length reward me (s De L'Épine, < *Camilla*)

41	[38]	Yes 'tis all I want (s Boy, < *Camilla*)
42	[39]	Flood shall quit ye ocean, The (s Hughes, < *Camilla*)
43	[40]	Dangers ev'ry way surround me (s Tofts, < *Camilla*)
44	[41]	Angers for war, declaring (s Baroness, < *Camilla*)
45	[42]	Tho' fierce ye light'ning flys (s Ramondon, < *Camilla*)
46	[43]	Linco's grown another creature (s Leveridge, < *Camilla*)
47	[44]	Cease cruel tyrannising (s Hughes, < *Camilla*)
48	[44]	Cease cruell to deceive me
49	[44, i.e.45]	Cease cruel tyranizing
50	[44, i.e.45]	Be cruel & be jealous (s Turner)
51	[46]	Fate the more it does depress me (s Tofts, < *Camilla*)
52	[47]	Let ye lightning flashing flying (s De L'Épine, < *Camilla*)

Notes:
1. Date is an estimate. For paginated impression with preliminaries see **34**, published by Cullen 1 March 1707. The pagination and contents statements represent the overture and full list of songs found in **34**. Both copies lack song 6.
2. MB: comprises songs 1-5, 7-8, 10-12, 14-15, 18, 21-24, 27-32, 34, 36-38, 40-42, 44-48. Initial leaf lists contents in MS. with page numbers, but pages themselves lack pagination. Original blue paper front cover carries title 'Songs in Camilla' in MS. Songs 2 and 3 not engraved by Cross, sung by the Boy.
3. NjP: - pp. [6], [44]; p. 44[i.e.45] duplicated; song pages paginated: 2-3, 5, 9, 11, 13, 15-16, 18, 23, 26, 30-32, 35-36, 44[i.e.45], 46-47.

Copies: MB **M.400.53(1); NjP (Ex) Oversize M1508.2 C14 B6 1707q.

Plate 34.1   Bononcini, *Camilla*, 1 March 1707

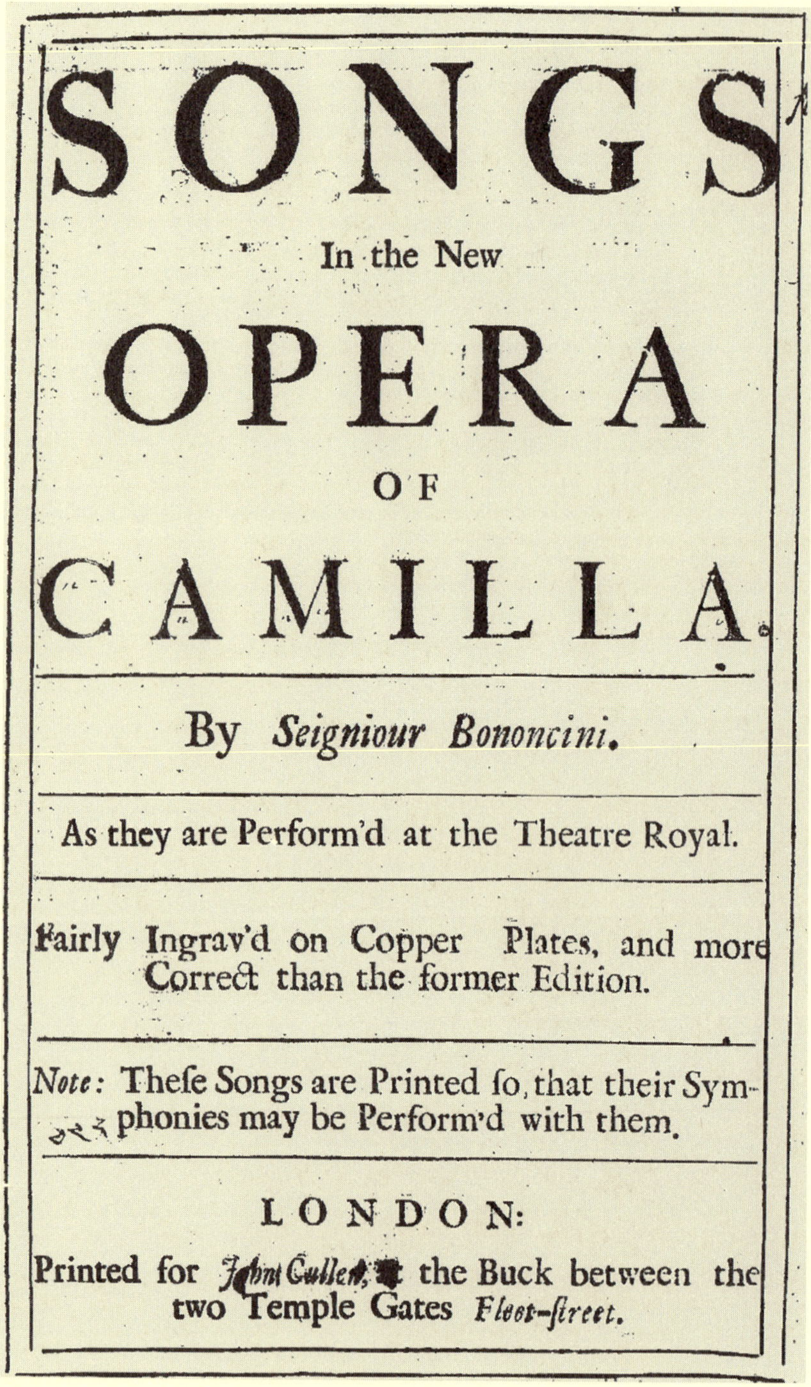

SONGS

In the New

OPERA

OF

CAMILLA.

By *Seigniour Bononcini.*

As they are Perform'd at the Theatre Royal.

Fairly Ingrav'd on Copper   Plates, and more
Correct than the former Edition.

Note: These Songs are Printed so that their Symphonies may be Perform'd with them.

LONDON:

Printed for *John Cullen,* at the Buck between the
two Temple Gates *Fleet-street.*

Caption: plate 34.1. 350 x 210 mm. Ckc: 85.13.

[letterpress, in red and black] Songs In the New Opera of Camilla. By Seigniour Bononcini. As they are Perform'd at the Theatre Royal. Fairly Ingrav'd on Copper Plates, and more Correct than the former Edition. Note: These Songs are Printed so, that their Sym-phonies may be Performed with them. London: Printed for John Cullen, at the Buck between the two Temple Gates Fleet-street.

51 leaves. Pp. [i-ii] □[1] [2]□-[3]□ 1□-5□ [6]□ 7-□26□ 26[i.e.27]□ 28□-44□ 44[i.e.45]□ 46□-47□.
Leaves printed on 1 side.
Tallest copy 350 x 210 mm. Vertical chain lines.

One page engraved per plate. Engraving style Cross.
Title-page letterpress.

Walsh i: 221.
Advertised in *Post Man*, 1 March 1707.

Contents: title-page [i]; contents and advertisement [ii]; overture [1-3]; songs 1-5, [6], 7-26, 26[i.e.27], 28-44, 44[i.e.45], 46-47.

Songs:

No.	Page	First Line
1	1	I was born of royall race (s Tofts, < *Camilla*)
2	2	O nymph of race divine (s De L'Épine, < *Camilla*)
3	3	Since you from death thus save me (s De L'Épine, < *Camilla*)
4	4	Love darts are in your eyes (s Ramondon, < *Camilla*)
5	5	Fortune ever known to vary (s Tofts, < *Camilla*)
6	[6]	Tender maids your pity show (s Baroness, < *Camilla*)
7	7	Frail are a lovers hopes (s Hughes, < *Camilla*)
8	8	Wellcome sorrow death attending (s Baroness, < *Camilla*)
9	9	All I'll venture to restore ye (s Ramondon, < *Camilla*)
10	10	See ye just gods of innocence (s Tofts, < *Camilla*)
11	11	Fair Dorinda happy mays't thou ever be (s Baroness, < *Camilla*)
12	12	Charming fair for thee I languish (s De L'Épine, < *Camilla*)
13	13	Wretched am I, that I gain him (s Tofts, < *Camilla*)
14	14	Among women they for certain know (s Lindsey, < *Camilla*)
15	15	Aged Phillis, wanton still is (s Leveridge, < *Camilla*)
16	16	I languish, for whom
17	16	Care is fled dispairs no more
18	17	Ah never yet was known (s Hughes, < *Camilla*)
19	18	Revenge I summon (s Tofts, < *Camilla*)
20	18	Now Cupid or never be kind (s Hughes)
21	19	In vain I fly from sorrow (s De L'Épine, < *Camilla*)
22	20	To beauty devoted (s De L'Épine, < *Camilla*)
23	21	I love but dare not my flame discover (s Ramondon, < *Camilla*)
24	22	Fortune like a wanton gipsy (s Leveridge, < *Camilla*)

25	23	Not so much cruelty, I prethee now (s Lindsey, < *Camilla*)
26	23	Joys are attending those cares (s Baroness)
27	24	No love was ever known that (s Baroness, < *Camilla*)
28	25	Around her see Cupid flying (s Hughes, < *Camilla*)
29	26	Love leads to battle, who dares oppose (s Ramondon, < *Camilla*)
30	26 [i.e.27]	Ungratefull you fly me, unkindly (s De L'Épine, < *Camilla*)
31	28	Love & ambition strive (s Tofts, < *Camilla*)
32	29	Tullia I feel thy charms (s Leveridge, < *Camilla*)
33	30	Something is in my face so alluring (s Lindsey, < *Camilla*)
34	31	Fly and follow your idol beauty (s Baroness, < *Camilla*)
35	32	Oh tyranous jealousy (s Hughes, < *Camilla*)
36	33	Happy I love & haste to enjoy her (< *Camilla*)
37	34	Fly ye virgins th' unfaithfull lover (s Baroness, < *Camilla*)
38	35	These eyes are made so killing (s Lindsey, < *Camilla*)
39	36	Thou art he my dearest creature
40	37	Cupid oh at length reward me (s De L'Épine, < *Camilla*)
41	38	Yes 'tis all I want (s Boy, < *Camilla*)
42	39	Flood shall quit ye ocean, The (s Hughes, < *Camilla*)
43	40	Dangers ev'ry way surround me (s Tofts, < *Camilla*)
44	41	Angers for war, declaring (s Baroness, < *Camilla*)
45	42	Tho' fierce ye light'ning flys (s Ramondon, < *Camilla*)
46	43	Linco's grown another creature (s Leveridge, < *Camilla*)
47	44	Cease cruel tyrannising (s Hughes, < *Camilla*)
48	44	Cease cruell to deceive me
49	44 [i.e.45]	Cease cruel tyranizing
50	44 [i.e.45]	Be cruel & be jealous (s Turner)
51	46	Fate the more it does depress me (s Tofts, < *Camilla*)
52	47	Let ye lightning flashing flying (s De L'Épine, < *Camilla*)

Notes:
1. Only CSfst has song 6, 'Tender maids your pity show', and that in the Walsh edition, even though the song is listed on p. [ii].
2. Cfm: - pp. [6], 33.
3. Ckc: - p. [6].
4. Lgc: - p. [6]; has Walsh edition of overture (4 pp.) in place of Cross's.

Copies: Cfm MU.MS.1278; Ckc 85.13; CSfst de Bellis 819; *J-Tn*; Lgc G.Mus.112(4).

34a Bononcini, *Camilla*, 1 March 1707

Caption: see plate 34.1.

[letterpress, in red and black] Songs In the New Opera of Camilla. By Seigniour Bononcini. As they are Perform'd at the Theatre Royal. Fairly Ingrav'd on Copper Plates, and more Correct than the former Edition. Note: These Songs are Printed so, that their Sym-phonies may be Performed with them. London: Printed for John Cullen, at the Buck between the two Temple Gates Fleet-street.

47 leaves. Pp. [i-ii] 1□-5□ 7□-26□ 26[i.e.27]□ 28□-44□ 44[i.e.45]□ 46□-47□.
Leaves printed on 1 side.
Tallest copy 342 x 213 mm. Vertical chain lines.

One page engraved per plate. Engraving style Cross.
Title-page letterpress.

Walsh i: 221.
Advertised in *Post Man*, 1 March 1707.

Contents: title-page [i]; contents and advertisement [ii]; songs 1-5, 7-26, 26[i.e.27]; 28-44, 44[i.e.45], 46-47.

Songs: see **34**.

Note:
1. Verso of p. 5 carries in MS. 'Tender maids your pity show', with caption 'Lavinia Sung by the Barrns: in ye Opera of Camilla.' This song, no. 6 in **34**, is listed on p. [ii].

Copy: CLU-C *fM1621.B72c 1707.

Plate 35.1   Bononcini, *Camilla*, 1707

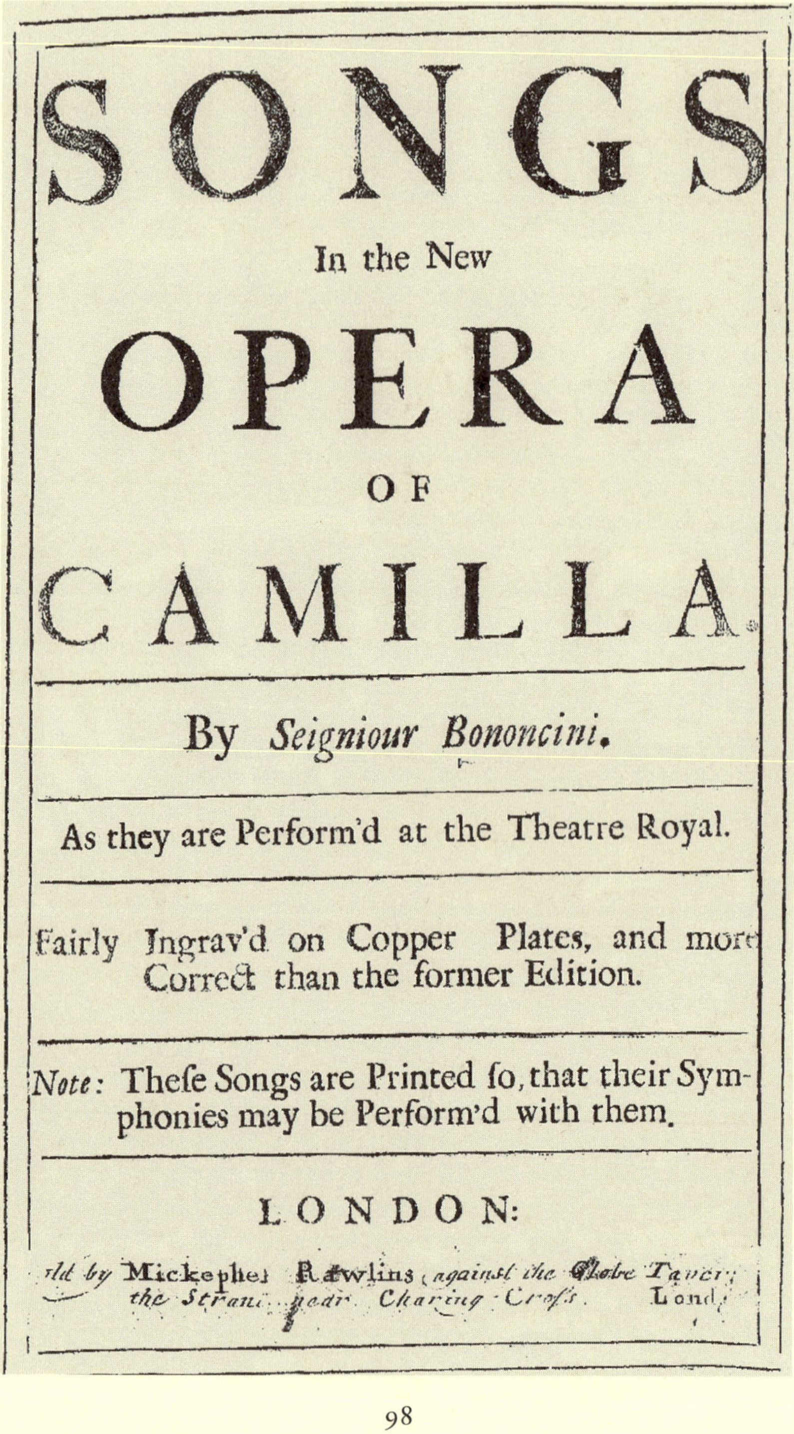

SONGS

In the New

OPERA

OF

CAMILLA.

By *Seigniour Bononcini.*

As they are Perform'd at the Theatre Royal.

Fairly Ingrav'd on Copper   Plates, and more
Correct than the former Edition.

Note: These Songs are Printed so, that their Symphonies may be Perform'd with them.

LONDON:

...ld by Mickepher Rawlins (against the Globe Tavern
the Strand near Charing-Cross.   Lond...

Plate 35.2 Bononcini, *Camilla*, 1707

35 Bononcini, *Camilla*, 1 March 1707

Caption: plates 35.1-35.2. 360 x 225 mm. Lbl: I.354.d.

[letterpress, in red and black] Songs In the New Opera of Camilla. By Seigniour Bononcini. As they are Perform'd at the Theatre Royal. Fairly Ingrav'd on Copper Plates, and more Correct than the former Edition. Note: These Songs are Printed so, that their Sym-phonies may be Perform'd with them. London: [engraved label over Cullen imprint] [S]old by Mickepher Rawlins against the Globe Taver[n] the Strand near Charing-Cross. Lond[on.]

51 leaves. Pp. [i-ii] □[1] [2]□-[3]□ 1□-5□ [6]□ 7□-26□ 26[i.e.27]□ 28□-44□ 44[i.e.45]□ 46□-47□.
Leaves printed on 1 side.
Tallest copy 360 x 225 mm. Vertical chain lines.

One page engraved per plate. Engraving style Cross.
Title-page letterpress.

Contents: title-page [i]; contents and advertisement [ii]; overture [1-3]; songs 1-5, [6], 7-26, 26[i.e.27], 28-44, 44[i.e.45], 46-47.

Songs:

No.	Page	First Line
1	1	I was born of royall race (s Tofts, < *Camilla*)
2	2	O nymph of race divine (s De L'Épine, < *Camilla*)
3	3	Since you from death thus save me (s De L'Épine, < *Camilla*)
4	4	Love darts are in your eyes
5	5	Fortune ever known to vary
6	[6]	Tender maids your pity show (s Baroness, < *Camilla*)
7	7	Frail are a lovers hopes (s Hughes, < *Camilla*)
8	8	Wellcome sorrow death attending (s Baroness, < *Camilla*)
9	9	All I'll venture to restore ye (s Ramondon, < *Camilla*)
10	10	See ye just gods of innocence (s Tofts, < *Camilla*)
11	11	Fair Dorinda happy mays't thou ever be (s Baroness, < *Camilla*)
12	12	Charming fair for thee I languish (s De L'Épine, < *Camilla*)
13	13	Wretched am I, that I gain him (s Tofts, < *Camilla*)
14	14	Among women they for certain know (s Lindsey, < *Camilla*)
15	15	Aged Phillis, wanton still is (s Leveridge, < *Camilla*)
16	16	I languish, for whom
17	16	Care is fled dispairs no more
18	17	Ah never yet was known (s Hughes, < *Camilla*)
19	18	Revenge I summon (s Tofts, < *Camilla*)
20	18	Now Cupid or never be kind (s Hughes)
21	19	In vain I fly from sorrow (s De L'Épine, < *Camilla*)
22	20	To beauty devoted (s De L'Épine, < *Camilla*)
23	21	I love but dare not my flame discover (s Ramondon, < *Camilla*)
24	22	Fortune like a wanton gipsy (s Leveridge, < *Camilla*)
25	23	Not so much cruelty, I prethee now (s Lindsey, < *Camilla*)
26	23	Joys are attending those cares (s Baroness)
27	24	No love was ever known that (s Baroness, < *Camilla*)

28	25	Around her see Cupid flying (s Hughes, < *Camilla*)
29	26	Love leads to battle, who dares oppose (s Ramondon, < *Camilla*)
30	26	[i.e.27] Ungratefull you fly me, unkindly (s De L'Épine, < *Camilla*)
31	28	Love & ambition strive (s Tofts, < *Camilla*)
32	29	Tullia I feel thy charms (s Leveridge, < *Camilla*)
33	30	Something is in my face so alluring (s Lindsey, < *Camilla*)
34	31	Fly and follow your idol beauty (s Baroness, < *Camilla*)
35	32	Oh tyranous jealousy (s Hughes, < *Camilla*)
36	33	Happy I love & haste to enjoy her (< *Camilla*)
37	34	Fly ye virgins th' unfaithfull lover (s Baroness, < *Camilla*)
38	35	These eyes are made so killing (s Lindsey, < *Camilla*)
39	36	Thou art he my dearest creature
40	37	Cupid oh at length reward me (s De L'Épine, < *Camilla*)
41	38	Yes 'tis all I want (s Boy, < *Camilla*)
42	39	Flood shall quit ye ocean, The (s Hughes, < *Camilla*)
43	40	Dangers ev'ry way surround me (s Tofts, < *Camilla*)
44	41	Angers for war, declaring (s Baroness, < *Camilla*)
45	42	Tho' fierce ye light'ning flys (s Ramondon, < *Camilla*)
46	43	Linco's grown another creature (s Leveridge, < *Camilla*)
47	44	Cease cruel tyranizing
48	44	Be cruel & be jealous (s Turner)
49	44 [i.e.45]	Cease cruel tyrannising (s Hughes, < *Camilla*)
50	44 [i.e.45]	Cease cruell to deceive me
51	46	Fate the more it does depress me (s Tofts, < *Camilla*)
52	47	Let ye lightning flashing flying (s De L'Épine, < *Camilla*)

Notes:
1. In comparison with 34, the order of the two page 44s is inverted.
2. Songs 4-5 lack captions.
3. Song 6 is Walsh edition.

Copy: Lbl I.354.d.

36   deleted (see 33a).

Caption: see plate 38.2.

Songs in the New Opera Call'd Rosamond as they are perform'd at the Theatre Royall Compos'd by Mr. Tho. Clayton London Printed for I. Walsh Servt. to Her Matie. at ye Harp & Hoboy in Katherine Streed near Somerset House in ye Strand — and P. Randall at ye Violin & Lute by Paulsgrave head Court without Temple Barr —

17 leaves. Pp. [i-ii] 3☐-18☐.
Leaves printed on 1 side.
Tallest copy 330 x 215 mm. Mixed chain lines.

One page engraved per plate. Engraving style Walsh 1, 3.
Title-page plate 262 x 186 mm.
Contents plate 120 x 159 mm.

Walsh i: 237.
Advertised in *Daily Courant*, 10 March 1707.

Contents: title-page [i]; contents [ii]; songs 3-18.

Songs:

No.	Page	First Line
1	3	As o'er the hollow valts we walk (m Clayton, s Tofts, < *Rosamond*)
2	4-5	Behold on yonder rising ground (m Clayton, s Holcomb, < *Rosamond*)
3	6	I feel my heart relent (m Clayton, s Tofts, < *Rosamond*)
4	7	He comes victorious Henry comes (m Clayton, s Holcomb, < *Rosamond*)
5	8	No 'tis decreed the traytress shall bleed (m Clayton, s Tofts, < *Rosamond*)
6	9	How unhappy is he (m Clayton, s Leveridge, < *Rosamond*)
7	10	O Grideline consult thy glass (m Clayton, s Leveridge, < *Rosamond*)
8	11	O how blest were Grideline (m Clayton, s Lindsey, < *Rosamond*)
9	12-13	Thou art ugly and old (m Clayton, s Leveridge, Lindsey, < *Rosamond*)
10	14	Was ever passion cross'd like mine (m Clayton, s Gallia, < *Rosamond*)
11	15	Ye pow'rs I rave, I bleed, I dye (m Clayton, s Gallia, < *Rosamond*)
12	16	Beneath some hoary mountain (m Clayton, s Gallia, < *Rosamond*)
13	17	Was ever nymph like Rosamond (m Clayton, s Hughes, < *Rosamond*)
14	18	O the pleasing anguish (m Clayton, s Hughes, < *Rosamond*)

Note:
1. Contents = contents list.

Copy: Ouf —.

Plate 38.1   Clayton, *Rosamond*, 1707

W: Sykes Junior Inventor. ———————————————— H: Hulsbergh Fecit.

SONGS
in the New OPERA *Called*
ROSAMOND
Compos'd by
Mr Tho: Clayton

London Printed for I Walsh Serv! to Her Ma.ty at y Harp and Hoboy in Katherine Street near Somerset House
in y Strand - and P. Randall at y Violin and Lute by Paulsgrave head Court without Temple Barr.

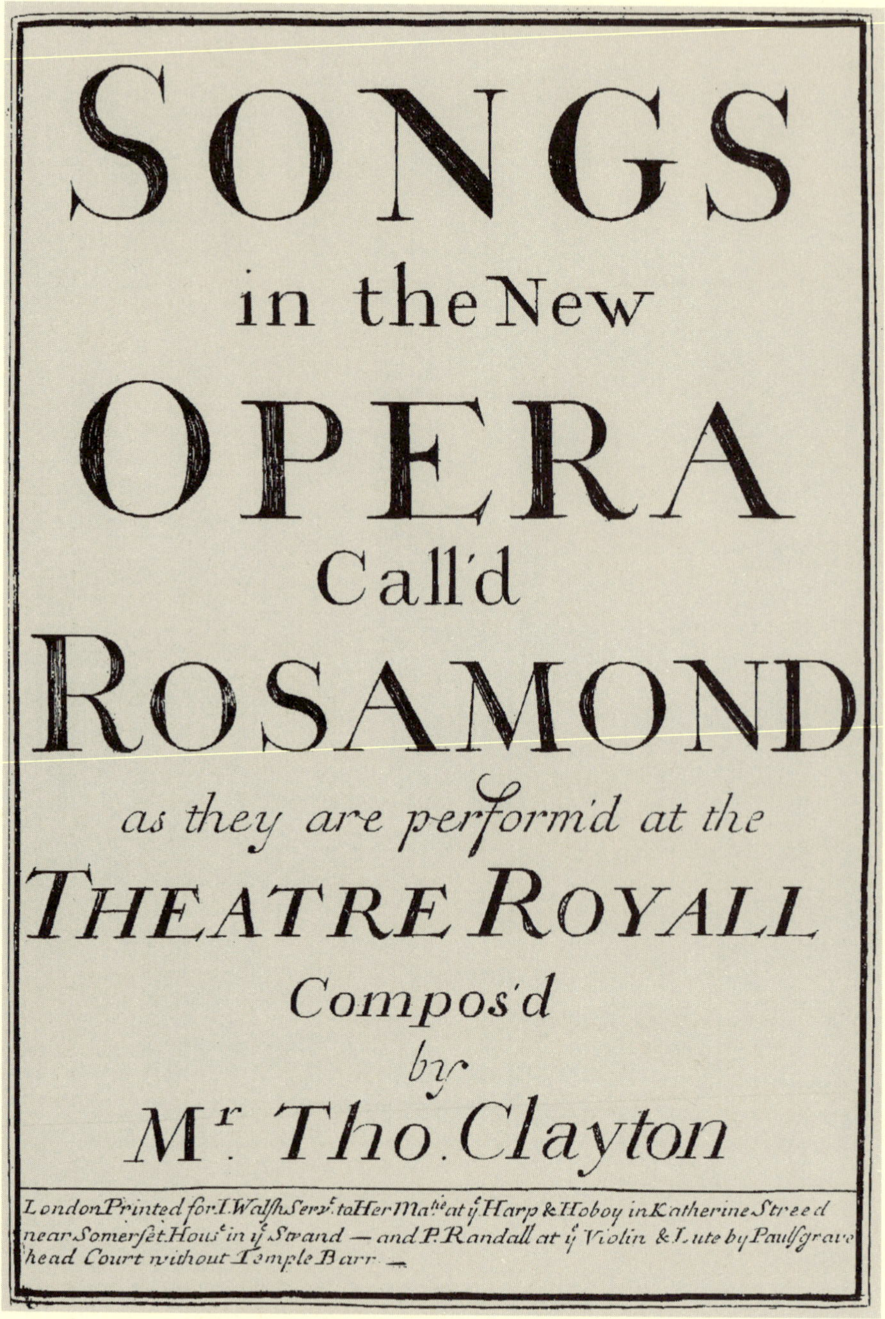

Plate 38.2   Clayton, *Rosamond*, 1707

SONGS

in the New

OPERA

Call'd

ROSAMOND

as they are perform'd at the

THEATRE ROYALL

Compos'd

by

Mr *Tho. Clayton*

London Printed for I. Walsh Servt to Her Matie at y.^e Harp & Hoboy in Katherine Stree d near Somerset Hous.^e in y.^e Strand — and P. Randall at y.^e Violin & Lute by Paulsgrave head Court without Temple Barr.

Plate 38.3   Clayton, *Rosamond*, 1707

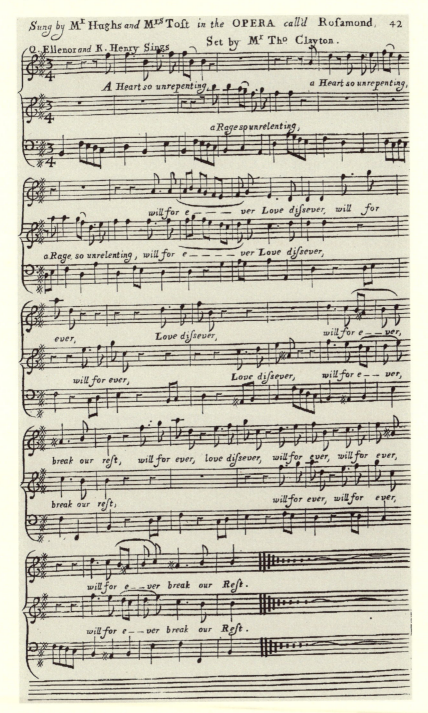

Caption: plates 38.1-38.3. 338 x 210 mm. MiU: RBR M1507.E12 v.1 no.3.

W: Sykes Iunior Inventor. H: Hulsbergh Fecit. [within cartouche] Songs in the New Opera Called Rosamond Compos'd by Mr. Tho: Clayton [at foot] London Printed for I. Walsh Servt. to Her Matie. at ye Harp and Hoboy in Katherine Street near Somerset House in ye Strand — and P Randall at ye Violin and Lute by Paulsgrave head Court without Temple Barr.

Songs in the New Opera Call'd Rosamond as they are perform'd at the Theatre Royall Compos'd by Mr. Tho. Clayton London Printed for I. Walsh Servt. to Her Matie. at ye Harp & Hoboy in Katherine Streed near Somerset House in ye Strand — and P. Randall at ye Violin & Lute by Paulsgrave head Court without Temple Barr —

49 leaves. Pp. [i]⬚ [ii-iii] ⬚1 2⬚-20⬚ [21]⬚ 22⬚-23⬚ [24]⬚ 25⬚-47⬚.
Leaves printed on 1 side.
Tallest copy 354 x 214 mm. Mixed chain lines.

One page engraved per plate. Engraving style Walsh 1, 3 (plate 38.3).
Illus. title-page plate 301 x 193 mm.
Title-page plate 264 x 186 mm.
Contents plate 255 x 155 mm.

Walsh i: 247.
Advertised in *Post Man*, 29 April 1707.

Contents: illus. title-page [i]; title-page [ii]; contents [iii]; overture 1-2; songs 3-20, [21], 22-23, [24], 25-47.

Songs:

No.	Page	First Line
1	3	As o'er the hollow valts we walk (m Clayton, s Tofts, < *Rosamond*)
2	4-5	Behold on yonder rising ground (m Clayton, s Holcomb, < *Rosamond*)
3	6	I feel my heart relent (m Clayton, s Tofts, < *Rosamond*)
4	7	He comes victorious Henry comes (m Clayton, s Holcomb, < *Rosamond*)
5	8	No 'tis decreed the traytress shall bleed (m Clayton, s Tofts, < *Rosamond*)
6	9	How unhappy is he (m Clayton, s Leveridge, < *Rosamond*)
7	10	O Grideline consult thy glass (m Clayton, s Leveridge, < *Rosamond*)
8	11	O how blest were Grideline (m Clayton, s Lindsey, < *Rosamond*)
9	12-13	Thou art ugly and old (m Clayton, s Leveridge, Lindsey, < *Rosamond*)
10	14	Was ever passion cross'd like mine (m Clayton, s Gallia, < *Rosamond*)
11	15	Ye pow'rs I rave, I bleed, I dye (m Clayton, s Gallia, < *Rosamond*)
12	16	Beneath some hoary mountain (m Clayton, s Gallia, < *Rosamond*)
13	17	Was ever nymph like Rosamond (m Clayton, s Hughes, < *Rosamond*)
14	18	O the pleasing anguish (m Clayton, s Hughes, < *Rosamond*)
15	19	Oh may the present bliss endure (s Hughes, Gallia, < *Rosamond*)
16	20	They're phantoms all I'le think no more (m Clayton, s Gallia, < *Rosamond*)
17	[21]	Prithee Cupid no more (m Clayton, s Lindsey, < *Rosamond*)

18	22	Thousand fairy scenes appear, A (m Clayton, s Holcomb, < *Rosamond*)
19	23	I cannot see my lord repine (m Clayton, s Tofts, < *Rosamond*)
20	[24]	Wild and frantick is my grief (m Clayton, s Tofts, < *Rosamond*)
21	25	Transporting pleasure who can tell it (m Clayton, s Gallia, < *Rosamond*)
22	26	Oh how dreadfull 'tis to dye (m Clayton, s Gallia, < *Rosamond*)
23	27	Think on the soft the tender fires (m Clayton, s Gallia, < *Rosamond*)
24	28	Moveing language, shining tears (m Clayton, s Tofts, < *Rosamond*)
25	29	Accept great queen like injur'd heav'n (m Clayton, s Gallia, < *Rosamond*)
26	30	Think not thou author of my woe (m Clayton, s Gallia, < *Rosamond*)
27	31	When vanquish'd foes beneath us lay (m Clayton, s Tofts, < *Rosamond*)
28	32	Bow'r turns round, The (m Clayton, s Leveridge, < *Rosamond*)
29	33	My Henry shall be mine alone (m Clayton, s Tofts, < *Rosamond*)
30	34-35	Behold th'afflicted monarch there (m Clayton, s Lawrence, Reading, Mrs, < *Rosamond*)
31	36	Glory strives the field is won (m Clayton, s Lawrence, Reading, Mrs, < *Rosamond*)
32	37	Love may plead (m Clayton, s Lawrence, Reading, Mrs, < *Rosamond*)
33	38	Adieu ye wanton shades and bow'r (m Clayton, s Hughes, < *Rosamond*)
34	39	Rise glory rise in all thy charms (m Clayton, s Hughes, < *Rosamond*)
35	40	Mysterious love uncertain treasure (m Clayton, s Tofts, < *Rosamond*)
36	41	Distracted with woe (m Clayton, s Hughes, < *Rosamond*)
37	42	Heart so unrepenting, A (m Clayton, s Hughes, Tofts, < *Rosamond*)
38	43	So bright a bloom (m Clayton, s Hughes, < *Rosamond*)
39	44	If 'tis joy to wound a lover (m Clayton, s Tofts, < *Rosamond*)
40	45	No more I'le change (m Clayton, s Hughes, Tofts, < *Rosamond*)
41	46	Since conjugal passion (m Clayton, s Leveridge, Lindsey, < *Rosamond*)
42	47	Who to forbidden joys would rove (m Clayton, s Hughes, Tofts, < *Rosamond*)

Notes:
1. The first part (Walsh i, 237) was advertised in *Daily Courant* 10 March 1707; the second part (Walsh i, 245) was advertised in *Post Man* 22 April 1707. *Rosamond* was listed on title-page of *Thomyris*, which was itself advertised 29 April 1707.
2. B-Br: - p. [i]; pp. 3-13, 15-18 unpaginated; pp. 1 and 34 reversed; leaves forming pp. [ii-iii] glued together.
3. BWbw, Cfm, DRc, F-Pc, Lcm, MH-H: pp. 3-18 unpaginated (except BWbw and MH-H: p. 14 paginated).
4. BWbw, CU-MUSI, DRc, NjP: p. 1 reversed.
5. CLU-C: - p. [i]; pp. 3-18 unpaginated.
6. DLC: - p. [i]; p. 24 paginated.
7. Lbl: p. [i] bound after pp. [ii-iii]; p. 1 reversed; p. 14 duplicated; pp. [21] and [24] transposed.
8. NN: - p. [16]; p. 1 reversed; pp. 3-18 unpaginated.
9. Ob: - p. [i]; pp. 1 and 34 reversed; leaves forming pp. [ii-iii] glued together.
10. Obh: - pp. [ii-iii].
11. TxDN: price in MS. on illus. title-page, '5s 6d'. Pagination for pp. 21 and 24, in MS.

Copies: B-Br Fétis 2851; BWbw —; Cfm MU. MS.1280; Ckc 85.25; CLU-C *fM1624.7.C62r; CU-MUSI M1505.C55R5 1707 Case; DFo M1503.C38R6 Cage; DLC M1500.C685R5; DRc Mus.D.41; F-Pc Rés. V.S.1280; Lbl H.105.(1.); Lcm XXXII.A.2(1.); MH-H Typ 705.07.288F; MiU RBR M1507.E12 v.1 no.3; NjP (Ex) M1503.C5R7q; NN Drexel 4965.2; Ob Mus. 22.c.158(3); Obh Mus. D.8(4); TxDN M784.8 C579rs.

39 deleted (see 38).

Plate 40.1   Pepusch, J, *Thomyris*, [First Collection], 1707

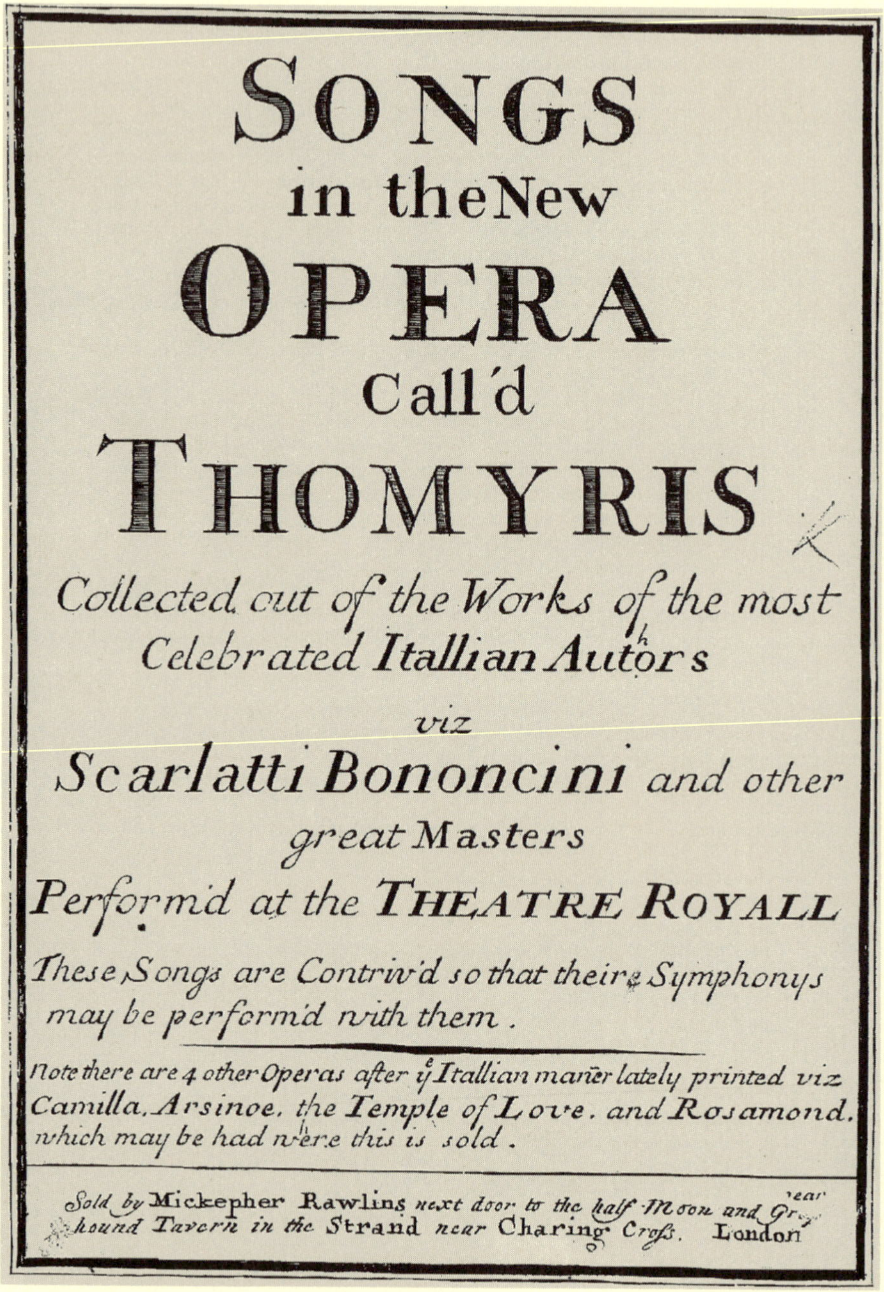

SONGS
in the New
OPERA
Call'd
THOMYRIS

*Collected out of the Works of the most
Celebrated Itallian Autors*

viz

*Scarlatti Bononcini and other
great Masters*

Perform'd at the THEATRE ROYALL

*These Songs are Contriv'd so that their Symphonys
may be perform'd with them.*

*Note there are 4 other Operas after ÿ Itallian maner lately printed viz
Camilla, Arsinoe, the Temple of Love, and Rosamond,
which may be had n'ere this is sold.*

*Sold by Mickepher Rawlins next door to the half Moon and Grey-
hound Tavern in the Strand near Charing Cross. London*

40 Pepusch, J, *Thomyris*, [First Collection], 31 May 1707

Caption: plate 40.1. 362 x 225 mm. Lbl: H.114.(4.).

Songs in the New Opera Call'd Thomyris Collected out of the Works of the most Celebrated Itallian Autors viz Scarlatti Bononcini and other great Masters Perform'd at the Theatre Royall These songs are Contriv'd so that theire Symphonys may be perform'd with them. Note there are 4 other Operas after ye Itallian maner lately printed viz Camilla, Arsinoe, the Temple of Love, and Rosamond, which may be had were this is sold. [engraved label over Walsh and Randall imprint] Sold by Mickepher Rawlins next door to the half-Moon and Gr[ey==]hound Tavern in the Strand near Charing Cross. London[.]

19 leaves. Pp. [i-ii] [1]☐-[18]☐.
Leaves printed on 1 side.
Tallest copy 362 x 225 mm. Vertical chain lines.

One page engraved per plate. Engraving style Walsh 1, 3.
Title-page plate 265 x 185 mm.
Contents plate 99 x 177 mm.

Walsh i: 246.
Advertised in *Daily Courant*, 31 May 1707. Price 1s.

Contents: title-page [i]; contents [ii]; songs [1-18].

Songs:

No.	Page	First Line
1	[1]	Freedom thou greatest blessing (s Tofts, < *Thomyris*)
2	[2]	Ever merry gay and airy (s Lindsey, < *Thomyris*)
3	[3]	What shoud alarm me, no foe (s Tofts, < *Thomyris*)
4	[4]	Strike me fate, now no danger allarms (s Lawrence, < *Thomyris*)
5	[5]	Gently treat my sorrow (s Tofts, < *Thomyris*)
6	[6]	Shoud er'e the fair disdain you (s Lindsey, < *Thomyris*)
7	[7]	Bright wonder of nature (s Valentini, < *Thomyris*)
8	[8]	Never let your heart despair (s Lindsey, < *Thomyris*)
9	[9]	Can you leave ranging (s Lindsey, < *Thomyris*)
10	[10]	My delight, my dear my princess (s Leveridge, < *Thomyris*)
11	[11]	Away you rover, for shame give over (s Lindsey, < *Thomyris*)
12	[12-13]	Prethee leave me (s Leveridge, Lindsey, < *Thomyris*)
13	[14]	Joy and empire are no more (s Lawrence, < *Thomyris*)
14	[15]	In vain is complaining (s Lawrence, < *Thomyris*)
15	[16]	Halt when love and honour call you (s Leveridge, < *Thomyris*)
16	[17]	Let us fly, our undoing love allures me (s Tofts, < *Thomyris*)
17	[18]	Farewell love and all soft pleasure (s Leveridge, < *Thomyris*)

Note:
1. Contents = contents list. Copy combines early state of title-page with songs from acts 1-3. Reissue of what is presumed to be the first collection of Walsh, advertised in *Daily Courant*.

Copy: Lbl H.114.(4.).

40a Pepusch, *Thomyris*, 1 June 1707

No title-page.

51 leaves. Pp. [1]◻-[20]◻ [21-21A] [22]◻-[51]◻.
Leaves printed on 1 side.
Tallest copy 346 x 222 mm. Vertical chain lines.

One page engraved per plate. Engraving style Cross.

Contents: songs [1-21]; flute part [21A]; songs [22-51].

Songs:

No.	Page	First Line
1	[1]	Freedom thou greatest blessing (s Tofts)
2	[2]	Ever merry, gay & airy (s Lindsey, < *Thomyris*)
3	[3]	What shou'd allarm me, no foe (s Tofts, < *Thomyris*)
4	[4]	Rouse yee brave for fame and glory (s De L'Épine, < *Thomyris*)
5	[5]	Gently treat my sorrow (s Tofts, < *Thomyris*)
6	[6]	No more let sorrow pain you (s De L'Épine, < *Thomyris*)
7	[7]	Bright wonder of nature (s Valentini, < *Thomyris*)
8	[8]	Never let your heart despair (s Lindsey, < *Thomyris*)
9	[9]	Love wd invade me (s Tofts, < *Thomyris*)
10	[10]	My delight, my dear, my princess (s Leveridge, < *Thomyris*)
11	[11]	Away you rover, for shame give over (s Lindsey, < *Thomyris*)
12	[12]	Prethee leave me (< *Thomyris*)
13	[13]	Joy and empire are no more (s Lawrence, < *Thomyris*)
14	[14]	In vain is complaining (s Lawrence, < *Thomyris*)
15	[15]	Cares on a crown attending (s De L'Épine, < *Thomyris*)
16	[16]	Lover near despairing, A (s Valentini, < *Thomyris*)
17	[17]	Let us fly our undoing (s Tofts, < *Thomyris*)
18	[18]	Ne'er torment me (s De L'Épine, < *Thomyris*)
19	[19]	I grieve to see your sorrow (s Valentini, < *Thomyris*)
20	[20]	You who for wedlock importune (s Lindsey, < *Thomyris*)
21	[21]	What lover ever can hope for favour (s Lindsey, < *Thomyris*)
22	[22]	Who can bear tho' of late (s Leveridge, < *Thomyris*)
23	[23]	Strike me fate, now no danger allarms (s Lawrence, < *Thomyris*)
24	[24]	Oh, in pitty cease to greive me (< *Thomyris*)
25	[25]	Say must I then dispair (< *Thomyris*)
26	[26]	Ye horrors of this hollow grave (s Lawrence, < *Thomyris*)
27	[26]	Slaves to the fashion (s Leveridge)
28	[27]	Oh I must fly, cease to try to charm me (s Tofts, < *Thomyris*)
29	[28]	While tho' conquest charms me, A (s De L'Épine , < *Thomyris*)
30	[29]	Shou'd e'er the fair disdain you (s Lindsey, < *Thomyris*)
31	[30]	What wou'd I not do to gain you (s Leveridge, < *Thomyris*)
32	[31]	Chains of love I wear, The (s Hughes, < *Thomyris*)
33	[32]	Ye pow'rs oh let me know (s Tofts, < *Thomyris*)
34	[33]	Since in vain I strive to gain you (s Lawrence, < *Thomyris*)
35	[34]	Again be victorious, be glorious (s De L'Épine, < *Thomyris*)
36	[35]	Pritty warbler cease to hover (s Tofts, < *Thomyris*)
37	[36]	In vain is delay (s Tofts, < *Thomyris*)
38	[37]	When duty's requiring
39	[38]	Halt when love & honour call you (s Leveridge, < *Thomyris*)
40	[39]	Can you leave ranging (s Lindsey, < *Thomyris*)
41	[40]	Wou'd you charme us (s Lindsey, < *Thomyris*)

42	[41]	Farewell love & all soft pleasure (s Leveridge, < *Thomyris*)
43	[42]	Unhappy lovers are ne'er contented (s Lawrence, < *Thomyris*)
44	[43]	I cease to love her (s Hughes, < *Thomyris*)
45	[44]	Why must sorrow (s Tofts, < *Thomyris*)
46	[45]	When one's gone ner'e keep a pother (s Lindsey, < *Thomyris*)
47	[46]	Humble sheperds greif may pain you (s De L'Épine, < *Thomyris*)
48	[47]	Like ye thunder guilt alarming (s De L'Épine, < *Thomyris*)
49	[47]	Ye pow'rs my welcome death forgive (s Tofts)
50	[48]	Sally before you they're falling (s De L'Épine, < *Thomyris*)
51	[49]	Vain ambition tho still you try (s Lawrence, < *Thomyris*)
52	[50]	I revive now you're turning (s Tofts, < *Thomyris*)
53	[51]	Pleasure calls fond hearts recover (s De L'Épine, < *Thomyris*)

Notes:
1. Date is an estimate. For paginated impression with preliminaries see **42**, published 5 June 1707. The pagination and contents statements represent the full list of songs found in **42** as the two copies between them contain all the songs.
2. Song 1 has drophead title 'Songs in the opera of Thomyris' and an imprint at the foot 'Printed for John Cullen at ye Buck between ye two Temple-gates, Fleet-Street'.
3. NjP: - pp. [3], [9], [11], [21], [21A], [33]; p. 28 bound between pp. 30-31; duplicate p. 30 in place of p. [3]; pp. 1, 4, 7, 12, 14-16, 19-20, 22, 26[i.e.24], 25-31, 34-35, 37-45, 47-48, 50 carry printed pagination; p. 46 paginated in MS.
4. Obh: comprises songs 1-3, 5, 7-8, 10-14, 17, 23, 30, 39-40, 42, 47, 4, 41, 19, 16, 29, 51, 18, 9, 52, 37, 34, 36, 32, 53, 21, 28, all leaves unpaginated.

Copies: NjP (Ex) Oversize M1508.2 C14 B6 1707q; Obh Mus. D.16(1).

Plate 41.1   Young, *Collection of New Songs*, 1707

K.5.c.25.

A
COLLECTION
OF NEW
SONGS,
For One and Two
VOICES:
WITH A
Thorow-BASS to Each SONG.

Compos'd by Mr. *ANTHONY YOUNG,*
Organist of *St. Clement Danes.*

Several of the S O N G S that are not in the Compass, are
Transpos'd for the F L U T E, at the End of the Book.

L O N D O N :

Printed by **William Pearson**, for the Author; And Sold by
J. Walsh, and *M. Rawlins* in the *Strand, J. Young* at the Dolphin in St. *Pauls-Church-Yard, J. Hare* in *Cornhill,* and *J.Cullen* at the Buck in *Fleet-street* 1707.

Caption: plate 41.1. 318 x 198 mm. Lbl: K.5.c.25.

[Letterpress] A Collection Of New Songs, For One and Two Voices: With A Thorow-Bass to Each Song. Compos'd by Mr. Anthony Young, Organist of St. Clement Danes. Several of the Songs that are not in the Compass, are Transpos'd for the Flute, at the End of the Book. London: Printed by William Pearson, for the Author; And Sold by J. Walsh, and M. Rawlins in the Strand, J. Young at the Dolphin in St. Pauls-Church-Yard, J. Hare in Cornhill, and J. Cullen at the Buck in Fleet-street 1707.

14 leaves. Pp. [i]□ 1-26.
Leaves printed on 2 sides.

Letterpress throughout. 2° π1 B-G² χ1.
Tallest copy 322 x 196 mm. Vertical chain lines.

Walsh i: 252.
Advertised in *Post Boy*, 5 June 1707.

Contents: title-page [i]; songs 1-24; flute parts 25-26.

Songs:

No.	Page	First Line
1	1	Ease whining Damon to complain
2	2-4	You fair but peevish (v Young Gentleman)
3	5-7	When first I saw Larinda's face
4	8-9	Whilst I am scorch'd with warm desire
5	10-11	Cupid designing to disarm
6	12-13	Damon restrain your wand'ring eyes (s Davis)
7	14-15	Oh tell me gentle god of love
8	16-17	I lately vow'd but 'twas in haste
9	18-19	Alas in vain I strive
10	20-21	Strephon forbear you strive in vain (v Young Lady)
11	21-22	What put off with one denial
12	23-24	Come fill me a glass fill it high

Copies: Lbl K.5.c.25; Lcm II.J.20.(b)(30.).

Plate 42.1   Pepusch, *Thomyris*, 1707

SONGS

In the New

OPERA

OF

THOMIRIS,

Queen of Scythia.

Collected out of the WORKS of the most
Celebrated Italian AUTHORS, *viz.*

Scarlait; Bononchini, Albinoni, &c.

As they are Perform'd at the Theatre Royal.

Fairly Ingrav'd on Copper – Plates, and more
Correct then the former Edition.

Note: These Songs are Printed so, that their
Symphonies may be Plaid with them.

LONDON:

Printed for *John Cullen,* at the Buck between the Two *Temple-
Gates, Fleet-street.*

Caption: plate 42.1. 357 x 220 mm. Lbl: H.113.a.

[Letterpress, in red and black] Songs In the New Opera Of Thomiris, Queen of Scythia. Collected out of the Works of the most Celebrated Italian Authors, viz. Scarlait, Bononchini, Albinoni, &c. As they are Perform'd at the Theatre Royal. Fairly Ingrav'd on Copper-Plates, and more Correct then the former Edition. Note: These Songs are Printed so, that their Symphonies may be Plaid with them. London: Printed for John Cullen, at the Buck between the Two Temple-gates, Fleet-street.

52 leaves. Pp. [i-ii] 1□-20□ 21 [21A] 22□-23□ 26[i.e.24]□ 25□-51□.
Leaves printed on 1 side.
Tallest copy 367 x 230 mm. Vertical chain lines.

One page engraved per plate. Engraving style Cross.
Title-page letterpress.

Advertised in *Daily Courant*, 5 June 1707.

Contents: title-page [i]; contents and advertisement [ii]; songs 1-21; flute part [21A]; songs 22-51.

Songs:

No.	Page	First Line
1	1	Freedom thou greatest blessing (s Tofts)
2	2	Ever merry, gay & airy (s Lindsey, < *Thomyris*)
3	3	What shou'd allarm me, no foe (s Tofts, < *Thomyris*)
4	4	Rouse yee brave for fame and glory (s De L'Épine, < *Thomyris*)
5	5	Gently treat my sorrow (s Tofts, < *Thomyris*)
6	6	No more let sorrow pain you (s De L'Épine, < *Thomyris*)
7	7	Bright wonder of nature (s Valentini, < *Thomyris*)
8	8	Never let your heart despair (s Lindsey, < *Thomyris*)
9	9	Love wd invade me (s Tofts, < *Thomyris*)
10	10	My delight, my dear, my princess (s Leveridge, < *Thomyris*)
11	11	Away you rover, for shame give over (s Lindsey, < *Thomyris*)
12	12	Prethee leave me (< *Thomyris*)
13	13	Joy and empire are no more (s Lawrence, < *Thomyris*)
14	14	In vain is complaining (s Lawrence, < *Thomyris*)
15	15	Cares on a crown attending (s De L'Épine, < *Thomyris*)
16	16	Lover near despairing, A (s Valentini, < *Thomyris*)
17	17	Let us fly our undoing (s Tofts, < *Thomyris*)
18	18	Ne'er torment me (s De L'Épine, < *Thomyris*)
19	19	I grieve to see your sorrow (s Valentini, < *Thomyris*)
20	20	You who for wedlock importune (s Lindsey, < *Thomyris*)
21	21	What lover ever can hope for favour (s Lindsey, < *Thomyris*)
22	22	Who can bear tho' of late (s Leveridge, < *Thomyris*)
23	23	Strike me fate, now no danger allarms (s Lawrence, < *Thomyris*)
24	26 [i.e.24]	Oh, in pitty cease to greive me (< *Thomyris*)
25	25	Say must I then dispair (< *Thomyris*)

26	26	Ye horrors of this hollow grave (s Lawrence, < *Thomyris*)
27	26	Slaves to the fashion (s Leveridge)
28	27	Oh I must fly, cease to try to charm me (s Tofts, < *Thomyris*)
29	28	While tho' conquest charms me, A (s De L'Épine , < *Thomyris*)
30	29	Shou'd e'er the fair disdain you (s Lindsey, < *Thomyris*)
31	30	What wou'd I not do to gain you (s Leveridge, < *Thomyris*)
32	31	Chains of love I wear, The (s Hughes, < *Thomyris*)
33	32	Ye pow'rs oh let me know (s Tofts, < *Thomyris*)
34	33	Since in vain I strive to gain you (s Lawrence, < *Thomyris*)
35	34	Again be victorious, be glorious (s De L'Épine, < *Thomyris*)
36	35	Pritty warbler cease to hover (s Tofts, < *Thomyris*)
37	36	In vain is delay (s Tofts, < *Thomyris*)
38	37	When duty's requiring
39	38	Halt when love & honour call you (s Leveridge, < *Thomyris*)
40	39	Can you leave ranging (s Lindsey, < *Thomyris*)
41	40	Wou'd you charme us (s Lindsey, < *Thomyris*)
42	41	Farewell love & all soft pleasure (s Leveridge, < *Thomyris*)
43	42	Unhappy lovers are ne'er contented (s Lawrence, < *Thomyris*)
44	43	I cease to love her (s Hughes, < *Thomyris*)
45	44	Why must sorrow (s Tofts, < *Thomyris*)
46	45	When one's gone ner'e keep a pother (s Lindsey, < *Thomyris*)
47	46	Humble sheperds greif may pain you (s De L'Épine, < *Thomyris*)
48	47	Like ye thunder guilt alarming (s De L'Épine, < *Thomyris*)
49	47	Ye pow'rs my welcome death forgive (s Tofts)
50	48	Sally before you they're falling (s De L'Épine, < *Thomyris*)
51	49	Vain ambition tho still you try (s Lawrence, < *Thomyris*)
52	50	I revive now you're turning (s Tofts, < *Thomyris*)
53	51	Pleasure calls fond hearts recover (s De L'Épine, < *Thomyris*)

Notes:

1. Song 1 has drophead title 'Songs in the opera of Thomyris' and an imprint at the foot 'Printed for John Cullen at ye Buck between ye two Temple-gates, Fleet-Street'.
2. Cfm: - p. 37.
3. Lam: - pp. [i-ii], [21A].
4. Lbl: - pp. 36-37; pp. 13, 23 unpaginated.
5. Lcm: - p. 41.
6. Lgc: + overture from Walsh edition 44 (4 leaves, printed one side only, paginated 1-4) bound between pp. [ii] and 1; pp. 19, 27, 49 unpaginated.
7. MH-Mu: pp. 2-3, 8, 12-13, 17, 33, 35 unpaginated.

Copies: Cfm MU.MS.1282; Er Cupb.T.782.8(46)THO; Lam —; Lbl H.113.a; Lcm XCV.D.25; Lgc G.Mus.112(5); MH-Mu Mus 800.3.636 (Cage).

Plate 43.1   Pepusch, *Thomyris*, [Second and Third Collections], 1707

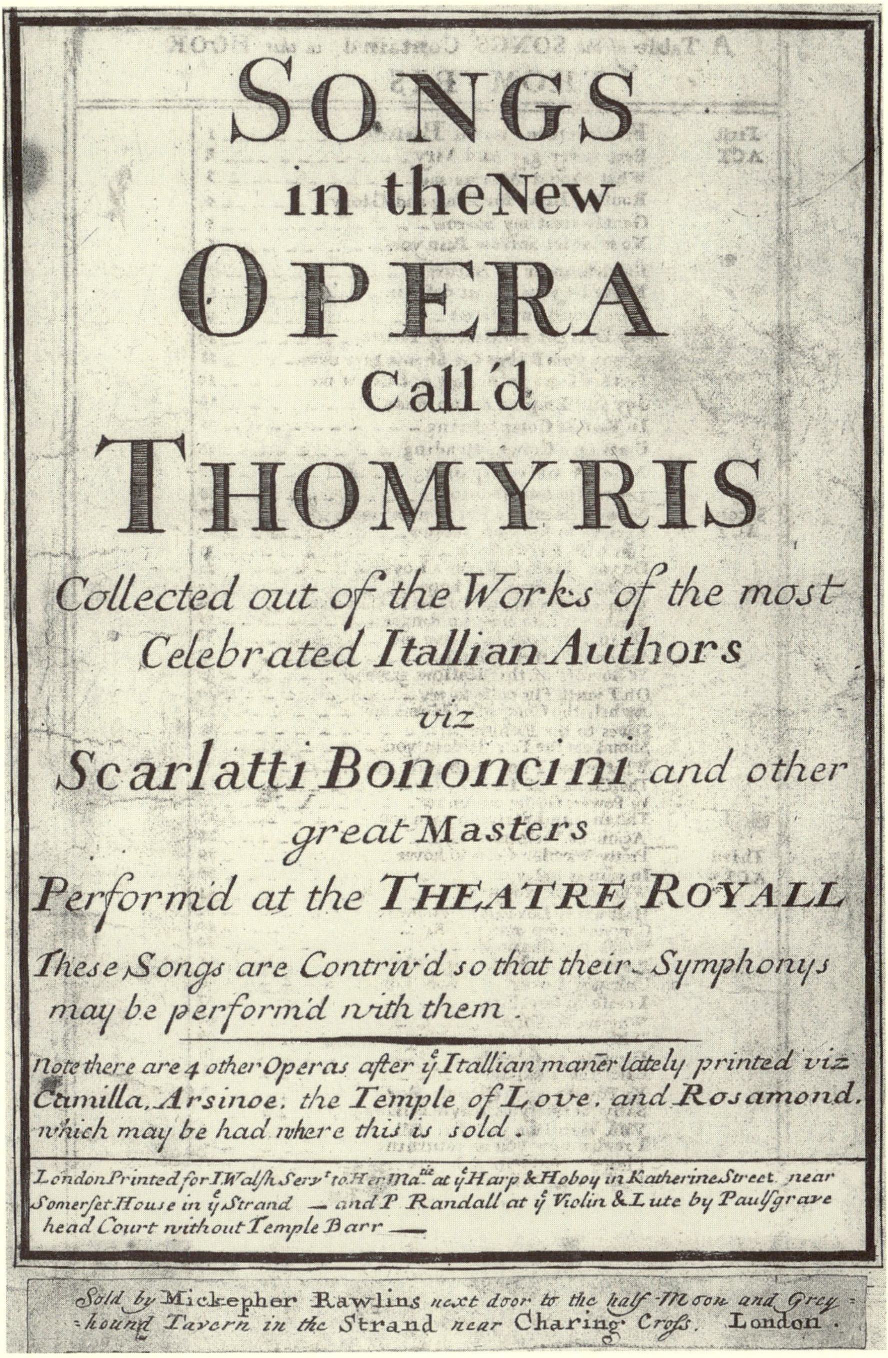

SONGS
in the New
OPERA
Call'd
THOMYRIS

Collected out of the Works of the most
Celebrated *Itallian Authors*

viz

Scarlatti Bononcini and other
great Masters

Perform'd at the THEATRE ROYALL

These Songs are Contriv'd so that their Symphonys
may be perform'd with them.

Note there are 4 other Operas after *ỹ Itallian* maner lately printed *viz*
Camilla, Arsinoe. the Temple of Love. and Rosamond.
which may be had where this is sold.

London Printed for I.Walsh Serv.t to Her Ma.tie at *ỹ* Harp & Hoboy in Katherine Street near
Somerset House in *ỹ* Strand ——— and P. Randall at *ỹ* Violin & Lute by Paulsgrave
head Court without Temple Barr ———

Sold by Mickepher Rawlins next door to the half Moon and Grey-
-hound Tavern in the Strand near Charing Cross. London.

43   Pepusch, *Thomyris*, [Second and Third Collections], 7 June 1707

Caption: plate 43.1. 347 x 220 mm. Ob: [MS.] Mus. Sch. c.97(23).

Songs in the New Opera Call'd Thomyris Collected out of the Works of the most Celebrated Itallian Authors viz Scarlatti Bononcini and other great Masters Perform'd at the Theatre Royall These Songs are Contriv'd so that their Symphonys may be perform'd with them. Note there are 4 other Operas after ye Itallian maner lately printed viz Camilla, Arsinoe, the Temple of Love, and Rosamond, which may be had where this is sold. [engraved label, previously pasted over Walsh and Randall imprint, now stuck below it] Sold by Mickepher Rawlins next door to the half-Moon and Grey==hound Tavern in the Strand near Charing Cross. London.

37 leaves. Pp. [i-ii] 4□ 6□ 9□ 16□ 16[i.e.17]□ 19□-24□ 26□-32□ 34□-41□ 44□ 47□-55□. Leaves printed on 1 side.
Tallest copy 347 x 220 mm. Vertical chain lines.

One page engraved per plate. Engraving style Walsh 1, 3.
Title-page plate 265 x 185 mm.

Walsh i: 253.
Advertised in *Post Man*, 7 June 1707. Price 6s.

Contents: title-page [i]; contents [ii]; 4, 6, 9, 16, 16[i.e.17], 19-24, 26-32, 34-41, 44, 47-55.

Songs:

No.	Page	First Line
1	4	Rouse yee brave for fame and glory (s De L'Épine, < *Thomyris*)
2	6	No more let sorrow pain you (s De L'Épine, < *Thomyris*)
3	9	Love woud invade me (s Tofts, < *Thomyris*)
4	16	Cares on a crown attending (s De L'Épine, < *Thomyris*)
5	16 [i.e.17]	Lover near despairing, A (s Valentini, Hughes, < *Thomyris*)
6	19	Ner'e torment me, but content me (s De L'Épine, < *Thomyris*)
7	20	I grieve to see your sorrow (s Hughes, < *Thomyris*)
8	21	You who for wedlock importune (s Lindsey, < *Thomyris*)
9	22	Do you think so warm a lover (s Leveridge, < *Thomyris*)
10	23	What lover ever can hope for favour (s Lindsey, < *Thomyris*)
11	24	Who can bear tho of late tis so common (s Leveridge, < *Thomyris*)
12	26	Oh in pity cease to grieve me (s Lawrence, Tofts, < *Thomyris*)
13	27-28	Say must I then despair (s Hughes, Tofts, < *Thomyris*)
14	29	Ye horrors of this hollow grave (s Lawrence, < *Thomyris*)
15	30	Oh I must fly, cease to try to charm me (s Tofts, < *Thomyris*)
16	31	While tho conquest charms me, A (s De L'Épine, < *Thomyris*)
17	32	Slaves to the fashion (s Leveridge, < *Thomyris*)
18	34	What woud I not do to gain you (s Leveridge, < *Thomyris*)
19	35	Chains of love I wear, The (s Hughes, < *Thomyris*)
20	36	Yee Powr's oh let me know what reason (s Tofts, < *Thomyris*)
21	37	Since in vain I strive to gain you (s Lawrence, < *Thomyris*)

22	38	Again be victorious, be glorious (s De L'Épine, < *Thomyris*)
23	39	Pretty warbler cease to hover (s Tofts, < *Thomyris*)
24	40	In vain is delay (s Tofts, < *Thomyris*)
25	41	When duty's requiring (s Tofts, < *Thomyris*)
26	44	Woud you charme us (s Lindsey, < *Thomyris*)
27	47	I cease to love her (s Hughes, < *Thomyris*)
28	48	Why must sorrow for ever attend (s Tofts, < *Thomyris*)
29	49	When one's gone ner'e keep a pother (s Lindsey, < *Thomyris*)
30	50	Humble sheperds greif may pain you (s De L'Épine, < *Thomyris*)
31	51	Like the thunder guilt aming (s De L'Épine, < *Thomyris*)
32	52	Yee powr's my welcome death forgive (s Tofts, < *Thomyris*)
33	53	Sally before you they're falling (s De L'Épine, < *Thomyris*)
34	54	Vain ambition tho still you try to soar (s Lawrence, < *Thomyris*)
35	55	I revive now you're turning (s Tofts, < *Thomyris*)

Note:
1. Presumed to be a reissue of the collection of songs from the second and third acts of *Thomyris* advertised by Walsh in the *Post Man* (Walsh i, 253).

Copy: Ob [MS.] Mus. Sch. c.97(23).

43a Pepusch, *Thomyris*, 14 June 1707

Caption: see plate 44.2.

Songs in the New Opera Call'd Thomyris Collected out of the Works of the most Celebrated Itallian Authors viz Scarlatti Bononcini and other great Masters Perform'd at the Theatre Royall These Songs are Contriv'd so that their Symphonys may be perform'd with them. Note there are 4 other Operas after ye Itallian maner lately printed viz Camilla, Arsinoe, the Temple of Love, and Rosamond, which may be had where this is sold. London Printed for I. Walsh Servt to Her Matie. at ye Harp & Hoboy in Katherine Street near Somerset House in ye Strand—and P Randall at ye Violin & Lute by Paulsgrave head Court without Temple Barr—

33 leaves. Pp. [i]□ [2]□-[3]□ 4□ 6□ [8]□ 9□ 14□ 16□-17□ [18]□ 19□ 25□ 27□-29□ 31□ 33□-34□ 36□-39□ 41□ 44□-45□ 47□-49□ 51□-52□ 54□ 56□.
Leaves printed on 1 side.
Tallest copy 322 x 222 mm. Vertical chain lines.

One page engraved per plate. Engraving style Walsh 1, 3.

Contents: title-page [i]; songs [2]-[3], 4, 6, [8], 9, 14, 16-17, [18], 19, 25, 27-29, 31, 33-34, 36-39, 41, 44-45, 47-49, 51-52, 54, 56.

Songs:

No.	Page	First Line
1	[2]	Ever merry gay and airy (s Lindsey, < *Thomyris*)
2	[3]	What should alarm me, no foe (s Tofts, < *Thomyris*)
3	4	Rouse yee brave for fame and glory (s De L'Épine, < *Thomyris*)
4	6	No more let sorrow pain you (s De L'Épine, < *Thomyris*)
5	[8]	Never let your heart despair (s Lindsey, < *Thomyris*)
6	9	Love woud invade me (s Tofts, < *Thomyris*)
7	14	Joy and empire are no more (s Lawrence, < *Thomyris*)
8	16	Cares on a crown attending (s De L'Épine, < *Thomyris*)
9	17	Lover near despairing, A (s Valentini, Hughes, < *Thomyris*)
10	[18]	Let us fly, our undoing love allures me (s Tofts, < *Thomyris*)
11	19	Ner'e torment me, but content me (s De L'Épine, < *Thomyris*)
12	25	Strike me fate, now no danger allarms (s Lawrence, < *Thomyris*)
13	27-28	Say must I then despair (s Hughes, Tofts, < *Thomyris*)
14	29	Ye horrors of this hollow grave (s Lawrence, < *Thomyris*)
15	31	While tho conquest charms me, A (s De L'Épine, < *Thomyris*)
16	33	Shoud er'e the fair disdain you (s Lindsey, < *Thomyris*)
17	34	What woud I not do to gain you (s Leveridge, < *Thomyris*)
18	36	Yee Powr's oh let me know what reason (s Tofts, < *Thomyris*)
19	37	Since in vain I strive to gain you (s Lawrence, < *Thomyris*)
20	38	Again be victorious, be glorious (s De L'Épine, < *Thomyris*)
21	39	Pretty warbler cease to hover (s Tofts, < *Thomyris*)
22	41	When duty's requiring (s Tofts, < *Thomyris*)
23	44	Woud you charme us (s Lindsey, < *Thomyris*)
24	45	Farewell love and all soft pleasure (s Leveridge, < *Thomyris*)
25	47	I cease to love her (s Hughes, < *Thomyris*)

26	48	Why must sorrow for ever attend (s Tofts, < *Thomyris*)
27	49	When one's gone ner'e keep a pother (s Lindsey, < *Thomyris*)
28	51	Like the thunder guilt aming (s De L'Épine, < *Thomyris*)
29	52	Yee powr's my welcome death forgive (s Tofts, < *Thomyris*)
30	54	Vain ambition tho still you try to soar (s Lawrence, < *Thomyris*)
31	56	Pleasure calls fond hearts recover (s De L'Épine, < *Thomyris*)

Note:
1. Date is an estimate, a week following advertisement of second and third collections.

Copy: HAdolmetsch II E 34.

Plate 44.1   Pepusch, *Thomyris*, 1707

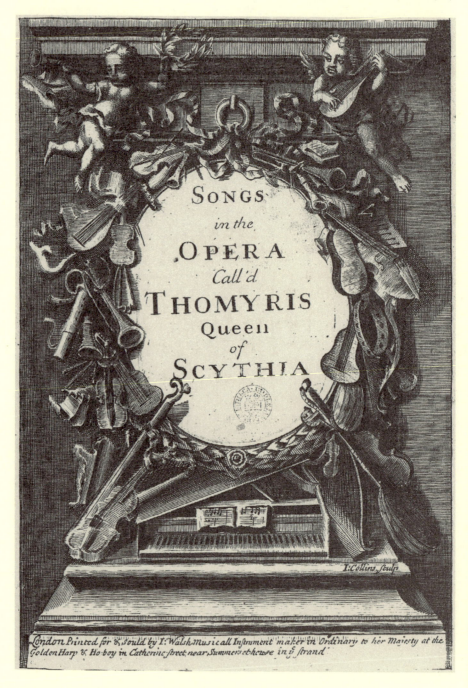

SONGS

in the

OPERA

Call'd

THOMYRIS

Queen

of

SCYTHIA

T. Collins *sculp*

London Printed for & Sould by I. Walsh Musicall Instrument maker in Ordinary to her Majesty at the Golden Harp & Ho-boy in Catherine street near Summerset house in ye strand

Plate 44.2   Pepusch, *Thomyris*, 1707

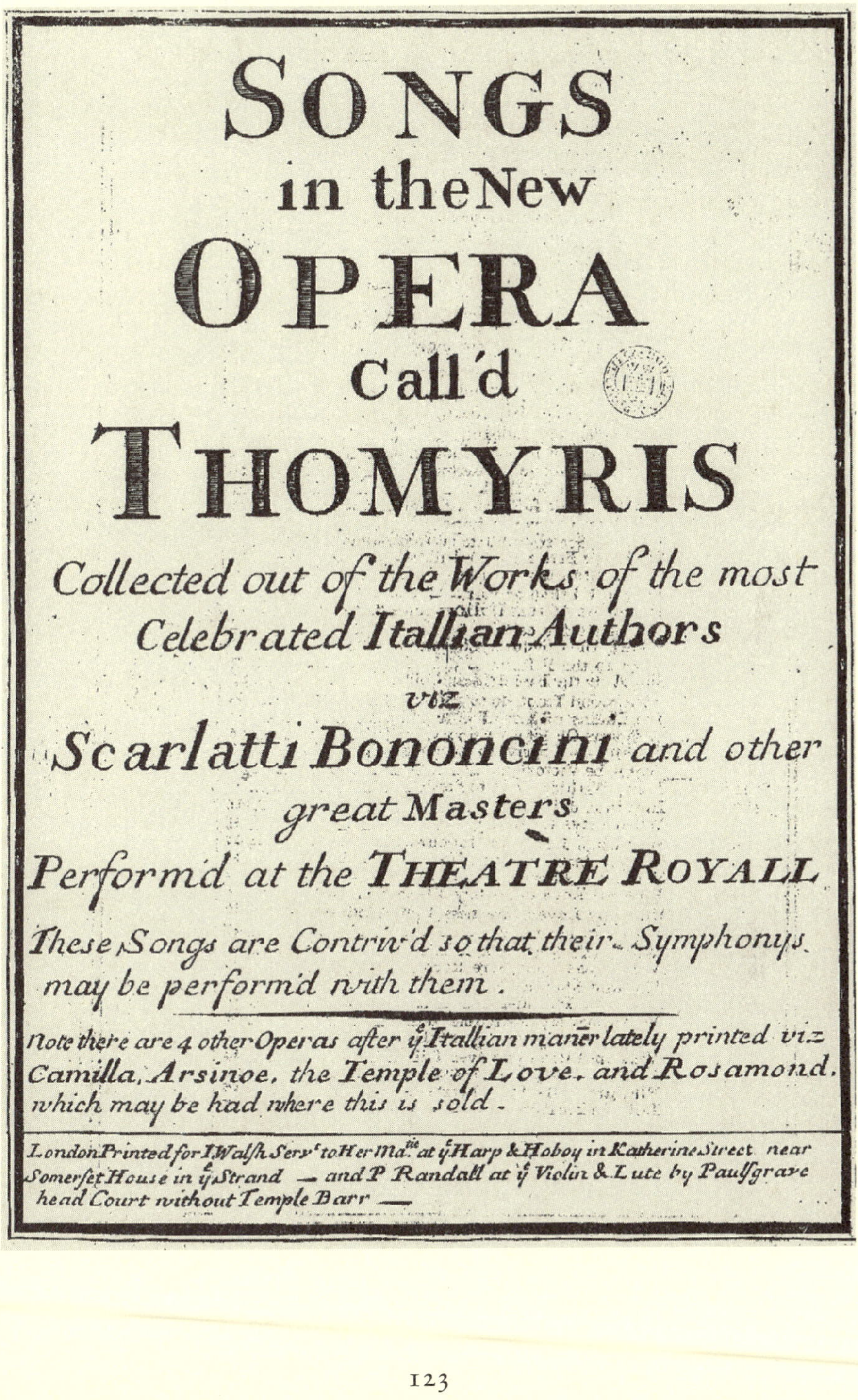

SONGS
in the New
OPERA
Call'd
THOMYRIS

*Collected out of the Works of the most Celebrated **Itallian Authors***

viz

Scarlatti Bononcini *and other great Masters*

Perform'd at the **THEATRE ROYALL**

These Songs are Contriv'd so that their Symphonys may be perform'd with them.

Note there are 4 other Operas after ŷ Itallian maner lately printed viz Camilla, Arsinoe, the Temple of Love, and Rosamond, which may be had where this is sold.

London Printed for I. Walsh Serv't to Her Ma.st at ŷ Harp & Hoboy in Katherine Street near Somerset House in ŷ Strand — and P Randall at ŷ Violin & Lute by Paulfgrave head Court without Temple Barr —

Caption: plates 44.1-44.2. 355 x 218 mm. Ob: Mus. 22.c.27.

[within cartouche] ⌠ Songs in the Opera Call'd Thomyris Queen of Scythia ⌡ I: Collins. sculp [at foot] London Printed for & Sould by I: Walsh Musicall Instrument maker in Ordinary to her Majesty at the Golden Harp & Ho=boy in Catherine-street near Summerset=house in ye strand

Songs in the New Opera Call'd Thomyris Collected out of the Works of the most Celebrated Itallian Authors viz Scarlatti Bononcini and other great Masters Perform'd at the Theatre Royall These Songs are Contriv'd so that their Symphonys may be perform'd with them. Note there are 4 other Operas after ye Itallian maner lately printed viz Camilla, Arsinoe, the Temple of Love, and Rosamond, which may be had where this is sold. London Printed for I. Walsh Servt to Her Matie. at ye Harp & Hoboy in Katherine Street near Somerset House in ye Strand—and P Randall at ye Violin & Lute by Paulsgrave head Court without Temple Barr—

62 leaves. Pp. [i]◻ [ii-iii] 1◻-4◻ 1◻-56◻.
Leaves printed on 1 side.
Tallest copy 355 x 218 mm. Vertical chain lines.

One page engraved per plate. Engraving style Walsh 1, 3.
Illus. title-page plate 255 x 195 mm. Passe-partout no. 1.
Title-page plate 260 x 186 mm.
Contents plate 263 x 153 mm.

Walsh i: 254, ii: 1443.
Advertised in *Post Man*, 19 June 1707.

Contents: illus. title-page [i]; title-page [ii]; contents [iii]; overture 1-4; songs 1-56.

Songs:

No.	Page	First Line
1	1	Freedom thou greatest blessing (s Tofts, < *Thomyris*)
2	2	Ever merry gay and airy (s Lindsey, < *Thomyris*)
3	3	What should alarm me, no foe (s Tofts, < *Thomyris*)
4	4	Rouse yee brave for fame and glory (s De L'Épine, < *Thomyris*)
5	5	Gently treat my sorrow (s Tofts, < *Thomyris*)
6	6	No more let sorrow pain you (s De L'Épine, < *Thomyris*)
7	7	Bright wonder of nature (s Valentini, < *Thomyris*)
8	8	Never let your heart despair (s Lindsey, < *Thomyris*)
9	9	Love woud invade me (s Tofts, < *Thomyris*)
10	10	My delight, my dear my princess (s Leveridge, < *Thomyris*)
11	11	Away you rover, for shame give over (s Lindsey, < *Thomyris*)
12	12-13	Prethee leave me (s Leveridge, Lindsey, < *Thomyris*)
13	14	Joy and empire are no more (s Lawrence, < *Thomyris*)
14	15	In vain is complaining (s Lawrence, < *Thomyris*)

15	16	Cares on a crown attending (s De L'Épine, < *Thomyris*)
16	16[i.e.17]	Lover near despairing, A (s Valentini, Hughes, < *Thomyris*)
17	18	Let us fly our undoing love allures me (s Tofts, < *Thomyris*)
18	19	Ner'e torment me, but content me (s De L'Épine, < *Thomyris*)
19	20	I grieve to see your sorrow (s Hughes, < *Thomyris*)
20	21	You who for wedlock importune (s Lindsey, < *Thomyris*)
21	22	Do you think so warm a lover (s Leveridge, < *Thomyris*)
22	23	What lover ever can hope for favour (s Lindsay, < *Thomyris*)
23	24	Who can bear tho of late tis so common (s Leveridge, < *Thomyris*)
24	25	Strike me fate, now no danger allarms (s Lawrence, < *Thomyris*)
25	26	Oh in pity cease to grieve me (s Lawrence, Tofts, < *Thomyris*)
26	27-28	Say must I then despair (s Hughes, Tofts, < *Thomyris*)
27	29	Ye horrors of this hollow grave (s Lawrence, < *Thomyris*)
28	30	Oh I must fly, cease to try to charm me (s Tofts, < *Thomyris*)
29	31	While tho conquest charms me, A (s De L'Épine, < *Thomyris*)
30	32	Slaves to the fashion (s Leveridge, < *Thomyris*)
31	33	Shoud er'e the fair disdain you (s Lindsey, < *Thomyris*)
32	34	What woud I not do to gain you (s Leveridge, < *Thomyris*)
33	35	Chains of love I wear, The (s Hughes, < *Thomyris*)
34	36	Yee powr's oh let me know what reason (s Tofts, < *Thomyris*)
35	37	Since in vain I strive to gain you (s Lawrence, < *Thomyris*)
36	38	Again be victorious, be glorious (s De L'Épine, < *Thomyris*)
37	39	Pretty warbler cease to hover (s Tofts, < *Thomyris*)
38	40	In vain is delay (s Tofts, < *Thomyris*)
39	41	When duty's requiring (s Tofts, < *Thomyris*)
40	42	Halt when love and honour call you (s Leveridge, < *Thomyris*)
41	43	Can you leave ranging (s Lindsey, < *Thomyris*)
42	44	Woud you charme us (s Lindsey, < *Thomyris*)
43	45	Farewell love and all soft pleasure (s Leveridge, < *Thomyris*)
44	46	Unhappy lovers are ne'er contented (s Lawrence, < *Thomyris*)
45	47	I cease to love her (s Hughes, < *Thomyris*)
46	48	Why must sorrow for ever attend (s Tofts, < *Thomyris*)
47	49	When one's gone ner'e keep a pother (s Lindsey, < *Thomyris*)
48	50	Humble sheperds grief may pain you (s De L'Épine, < *Thomyris*)
49	51	Like the thunder guilt aming (s De L'Épine, < *Thomyris*)
50	52	Yee powr's my welcome death forgive (s Tofts, < *Thomyris*)
51	53	Sally before you they're falling (s De L'Épine, < *Thomyris*)
52	54	Vain ambition tho still you try to soar (s Lawrence, < *Thomyris*)
53	55	I revive now you're turning (s Tofts, < *Thomyris*)
54	56	Pleasure calls fond hearts recover (s De L'Épine, < *Thomyris*)

Notes:

1. Alternative arrangements of overture leaves: 1 2 3-4; 1 2-4.

2. The last song—'Lost in pleasure'—listed on Contents as p. 57, was apparently never published.

3. B-Br: p. 3 (second sequence) duplicated.

4. CaOHM, CSfst, ICN: contents printed on separate leaf, reversed, and p. 2 (overture) and p. 12 reversed; pp. [i]□-[iii]□ 1□\□2 3□-□4 1□-11□\□12 13□-56□.

5. CaOLU, CLU-C: contents printed on separate leaf, reversed; pp. [i]□-[ii]□\□[iii] etc.

6. Ckc (85.4.(3)): - pp. [i], [iii]. 'First treble' part to each song pasted on verso. Walsh published 'The Symphonys or Instrumental Parts' to *Thomyris* in October 1707 (see Walsh i, 256).

7. CSt, DFo: - p. [i].

8. CU-MUSI: p. 8 unpaginated.

9. Lbl: - pp. [i], 52-56.

10. MB: - p. [i]; contents printed on separate leaf and p. 12 reversed; pp. [ii]□\□[iii] 1□-4□ 1□-11□\□12 13□-56□.

11. NL-DHgm: - p. [i]; contents printed on separate leaf; pp. [ii]□\□[iii] etc.

12. Ob: - p. 30.

13. Obh: - p. 46. P. 17 mispaginated p. 16. P. 45 paginated in MS.
14. Obt: contents printed on separate leaf; pp. [i]□-[ii]□\□[iii] 1□\□2 3□-4□ 1□-11□\□12 13□-56□. Copy sold.

Copies: B-Bc 13,397; CaOHM RB Disbd; CaOLU MZ.534; Ckc 85.4.(3.); Ckc 85.15; CLU-C *fM1621.B72c 1707; CSfst de Bellis 1157; CSt SpC MLM 936; CU-MUSI M1503.P4T45 Case X; *D-B*; DFo M1500.T5 Cage; F-Pc Rés. V.S.1275; F-Pn Vm.3 215; ICN VM1505.C62a no.3; *InU*; Lbl H.113; MB **M.293.30; MiU RBR M1507.E12 v.1 no.1; NL-DHgm 24 D 14; Ob Mus. 22.c.27; Obh Mus. D.8(2); Obt F.IV.5; *TU*.

Caption: see plates 44.1-44.2.

[within cartouche] ⌠ Songs in the Opera Call'd Thomyris Queen of Scythia ⌡ I: Collins. sculp [at foot] London Printed for & Sould by I: Walsh Musicall Instrument maker in Ordinary to her Majesty at the Golden Harp & Ho=boy in Catherine=street near Summerset=house in ye strand

Songs in the New Opera Call'd Thomyris Collected out of the Works of the most Celebrated Itallian Authors viz Scarlatti Bononcini and other great Masters Perform'd at the Theatre Royall These Songs are Contriv'd so that their Symphonys may be perform'd with them. Note there are 4 other Operas after ye Itallian maner lately printed viz Camilla, Arsinoe, the Temple of Love, and Rosamond, which may be had where this is sold. London Printed for I. Walsh Servt to Her Matie. at ye Harp & Hoboy in Katherine Street near Somerset House in ye Strand—and P Randall at ye Violin & Lute by Paulsgrave head Court without Temple Barr—

58 leaves. Pp. [i] [ii-iii] 1-56.
Leaves printed on 1 side.
Tallest copy 358 x 223 mm. Vertical chain lines.

One page engraved per plate. Engraving style Walsh 1, 3.
Illus. title-page plate 254 x 195 mm. Passe-partout no. 1.
Title-page plate 260 x 187 mm.
Contents plate 265 x 155 mm.

Walsh i: 254, ii: 1443.
Advertised in *Post Man*, 19 June 1707.

Contents: illus. title-page [i]; title-page [ii]; contents [iii]; songs 1-56.
Songs: see **44**.

Notes:
1. The last song—'Lost in pleasure'—listed on Contents as p. 57, was apparently never published.
2. Ckc (85.2.(7)): - pp. [i-iii], 46, 54-56.
3. CSfst: - pp. [i], 46. Pp. 2, 3, 8, 11, 17 paginated in MS.
4. Lcm: - p. [i].
5. LEp: - pp. [i], 39. 'Price 8s.' in MS. on title-page; copy cropt at top with loss of some song titles and pagination.
6. NjP: - pp. [i], 46; + 'Diogenes surly and proud' set and sung by Leveridge (p. [58]), a two-page version of the overture (not engraved by Walsh, pp. [59-60]), and 'How blest is a solder when lifted to rove' (p. 1) from *The additional songs in the opera's of Thomyris & Camilla*, published by Walsh and Hare in 1719 (105). These four leaves are poorer quality paper than the rest of the volume.
7. NPV: pp. 2, 5, 7, 8, 10, 15, 18 and 42 from Cullen edition engraved by Cross and paginated in MS.

Copies: Ckc 85.2.(7.); CSfst de Bellis 1156; IU xq782.15P39ts; Lcm XXXII.A.3.(4.); LEp Taphouse F782.1.M858; NjP (Ex) M1503.T356q; NPV 978 P397t/s.

Plate 45.1   Pepusch, *Thomyris*, 1707

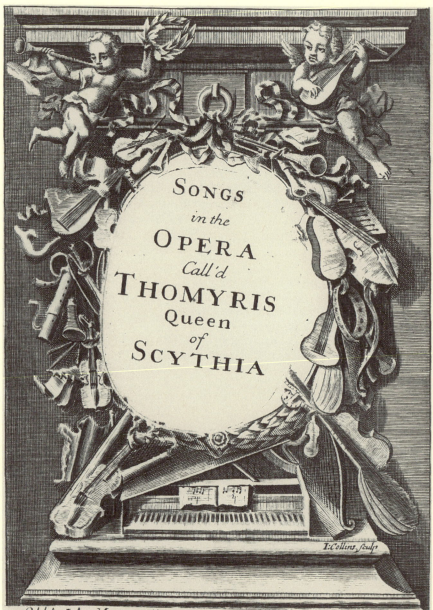

SONGS
in the
OPERA
Call'd
THOMYRIS
Queen
of
SCYTHIA

T. Collins, sculp.

Sold by Iohn Young, Musical Instrument Seller at the Dolphin &
Crown at the West end of S.t Pauls Church, where you may be furnish'd
with al sorts of Violins, Flutes, Hautboys, Bass Viols, Harpsicords or Spinets,
likewise al Books of Tunes, and Directions for any of these Instruments,
also al sorts of Musick, Rul'd Paper & Strings, at Reasonable rates.

Plate 45.2   Pepusch, *Thomyris*, 1707

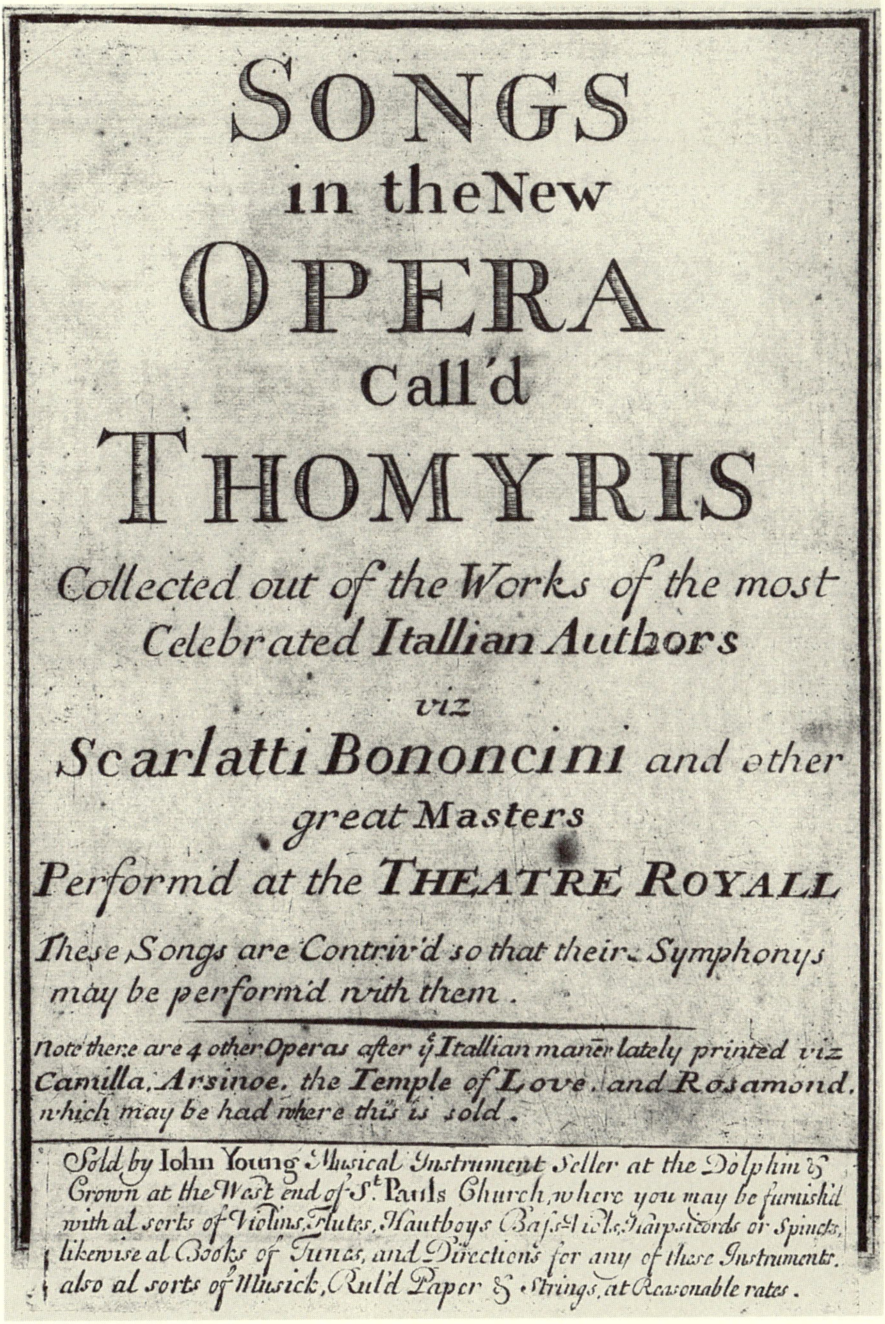

SONGS
in the New
OPERA
Call'd
THOMYRIS

*Collected out of the Works of the most
Celebrated Itallian Authors*

viz

Scarlatti Bononcini *and other*
great Masters

Perform'd at the THEATRE ROYALL

*These Songs are Contriv'd so that their Symphonys
may be perform'd with them .*

---

*Note there are 4 other Operas after ỹ Itallian maner lately printed viz
Camilla, Arsinoe, the Temple of Love and Rosamond,
which may be had where this is sold .*

Sold by Iohn Young *Musical Instrument Seller at the Dolphin ỹ
Crown at the West end of St Pauls Church, where you may be furnish'd
with al sorts of Violins, Flutes, Hautboys Bass Viols, Harpsicords or Spinets,
likewise al Books of Tunes, and Directions for any of these Instruments,
also al sorts of Musick, Rul'd Paper & Strings at Reasonable rates .*

45 Pepusch, *Thomyris*, 19 June 1707

Caption: plates 45.1-45.2. 341 x 218 mm. NRU-Mus: Vault M1500.T486.

[within cartouche] ⌠ Songs in the Opera Call'd Thomyris Queen of Scythia ⌡ I: Collins. sculp [engraved label over Walsh imprint] Sold by Iohn Young Musical Instrument Seller at the Dolphin & Crown at the West end of the St. Pauls Church, where you may be furnish'd with al sorts of Violins, Flutes, Hautboys Bass-Viols, Harpsicords or Spinets; likewise al Books of Tunes, and Directions for any of these Instruments, also al sorts of Musick, Rul'd Paper & Strings, at Reasonable rates.

Songs in the New Opera Call'd Thomyris Collected out of the Works of the most Celebrated Itallian Authors viz Scarlatti Bononcini and other great Masters Perform'd at the Theatre Royall These Songs are Contriv'd so that their Symphonys may be perform'd with them. Note there are 4 other Operas after ye Itallian maner lately printed viz Camilla, Arsinoe, the Temple of Love, and Rosamond, which may be had where this is sold. [engraved label over Walsh and Randall imprint] Sold by Iohn Young Musical Instrument Seller at the Dolphin & Crown at the West end of St. Pauls Church, where you may be furnish'd with al sorts of Violins, Flutes, Hautboys Bass-Viols, Harpsicords or Spinets; likewise al Books of Tunes, and Directions for any of these Instruments, also al sorts of Musick, Rul'd paper & Strings, at Reasonable rates.

63 leaves. Pp. [i]□-[iii]□ 1□-4□ 1□-56□.
Leaves printed on 1 side.
Tallest copy 341 x 218 mm. Vertical chain lines.

One page engraved per plate. Engraving style Walsh 1, 3.
Illus. title-page plate ? x 195 mm. Passe-partout no. 1. (See note 1.)
Title-page plate ? x 186 mm. (See note 1.)

Contents: illus. title-page [i]; title-page [ii]; contents [iii]; overture 1-4; songs 1-56.

Songs: see **44**.

Note:
1: Label obscures lower edge of plates.

Copy: NRU-Mus Vault M1500.T486.

Plate 46.1   Dieupart, *Love's Triumph*, 1708

Plate 46.2   Dieupart, *Love's Triumph*, 1708

SONGS

IN THE NEW

OPERA,

Call'd

LOVE'S TRIUMPH

as they are Perform'd at the
QUEENS Theatre

Sold   by I. Walsh Musicall Instrument maker in Or=
=dinary to her Majesty, at the Golden Harpe and Ho=boy.
in Catherine=Street near Sommerset House in the strand'
and I. Hare Musick Instrument maker at ÿ Golden Viol and Flute in
Cornhill near ÿ Royal Exchange.

46   Dieupart, *Love's Triumph*, 28 April 1708

Caption: plates 46.1-46.2. 341 x 215 mm. En: Mus.E.l.153.

[within cartouche] ⟨ Songs in the Opera Calld Loves Triumph ⟩ [at foot] London Printed for & Sold by Iohn Walsh Servant to his Majesty at the Harp and Hautboy in Katherine Street near Somerset House in the Strand

Songs In The New Opera, Call'd ⟨ Love's Triumph as they are Perform'd at the Queens Theatre ⟩ Sold by I: Walsh Musicall Instrument maker in Or==dinary to her Majesty, at the Golden Harpe and Hoboy, in Catherine-Street near Sommerset House in the Strand and I. Hare Musick Instrument maker at ye Golden Viol and Flute in Cornhill near ye Royal Exchange.

74 leaves. Pp. [i]□-[ii]□ □[iii] 1□-58□ [58A]□ 59□-70□.
Leaves printed on 1 side.
Tallest copy 347 x 223 mm. Vertical chain lines.

One page engraved per plate. Engraving style Walsh.
Illus. title-page plate 238 x 190 mm. Passe-partout no. 5.
Title-page plate 274 x 190 mm. Passe-partout no. 3.
Contents plate 311 x 111 mm.

Walsh i: 272.
Advertised in *Daily Courant*, 28 April 1708.

Contents: illus. title-page [i]; title-page [ii]; contents [iii]; songs 1-58, [58A], 59-70.

Songs:

No.	Page	First Line
1	1	Spare my sorrow rurall pleasure (s Baroness, < *Love's Triumph*)
2	2	Lets laugh, and dance, & play (s Leveridge, < *Love's Triumph*)
3	3	Do like the rest (s Leveridge, < *Love's Triumph*)
4	4	Be gay my eyes regain a heart (s Baroness, < *Love's Triumph*)
5	5	I love a plain lass (s Leveridge, < *Love's Triumph*)
6	6	Sweet lillies and roses (s Lindsey, < *Love's Triumph*)
7	7	My dear lett us wed (s Lindsey, Leveridge, < *Love's Triumph*)
8	8	Secret joy I share, A (s Valentini, < *Love's Triumph*)
9	9	My fatal charmer chains me before her (s Valentini, < *Love's Triumph*)
10	10	Tho coy my charmer (s De L'Épine, < *Love's Triumph*)
11	11	Kindly thus my treasure (s Tofts, < *Love's Triumph*)
12	12	Young and charming (s De L'Épine, < *Love's Triumph*)
13	13	Give way to pleasure (s Lindsey, < *Love's Triumph*)
14	14	Him I love, no longer try me (s Baroness, De L'Épine, < *Love's Triumph*)
15	15	Charmer why do you fly me (s Baroness, < *Love's Triumph*)
16	16	How great is my blessing (s Tofts, Valentini, < *Love's Triumph*)
17	17	Dare not oh dare not talke of love (1, s Tofts, < *Love's Triumph*)
18	18	Go sheperd you're a rover (s Tofts, < *Love's Triumph*)
19	19	Sweet and gay, like rosy may (s Valentini, < *Love's Triumph*)
20	20	No more tryall, nor deniall (s Leveridge, < *Love's Triumph*)
21	21	My poor heart says dally (s Lindsey, < *Love's Triumph*)
22	22	Tho to conquer proud love is preparing (s Tofts, < *Love's Triumph*)
23	23	Gay kind and airy (s Lindsey, < *Love's Triumph*)
24	24	Blest with freedom peace and leisure (s Lindsey, Leveridge, < *Love's Triumph*)
25	25	Now is the time for sporting (s Lindsey, < *Love's Triumph*)
26	26	Wanton rovers winds now sporting (s Tofts, < *Love's Triumph*)

27	27	In my brest what disorder so rages (s Baroness, < *Love's Triumph*)
28	28	Remember o disembler (s Tofts, < *Love's Triumph*)
29	29	Why are you kind to late (s Valentini, < *Love's Triumph*)
30	30	Oh love now hopes no more (s Baroness, < *Love's Triumph*)
31	31	If ever tis my fortune (s Lindsey, < *Love's Triumph*)
32	32	So form'd to charm (s De L'Épine, < *Love's Triumph*)
33	33	How inviting how smiling a rose (s Tofts, < *Love's Triumph*)
34	34	Shall I hear you (s De L'Épine, < *Love's Triumph*)
35	35	Charmer at last be kind (s Tofts, De L'Épine, < *Love's Triumph*)
36	36	While every creature loves free by nature (s Valentini, < *Love's Triumph*)
37	37	In vain you keep a pother (s Lindsey, < *Love's Triumph*)
38	38	Who cou'd think we loveing noddies (s Leveridge, < *Love's Triumph*)
39	39	Love oh spare me (s Valentini, < *Love's Triumph*)
40	40	Where's my rover (s Baroness, < *Love's Triumph*)
41	41	Again you say you love me (s Baroness, < *Love's Triumph*)
42	42	Vain is my art (s De L'Épine, < *Love's Triumph*)
43	43	Swains wing the day (s De L'Épine, < *Love's Triumph*)
44	44	Lover discover no sorrow (s Tofts, < *Love's Triumph*)
45	45	No sorrow we discover (s De L'Épine, < *Love's Triumph*)
46	46-47	Delights all around smile on our leisure (s Tofts, < *Love's Triumph*)
47	48	Kind hope dawn of pleasure (s Baroness, < *Love's Triumph*)
48	49	Fond love has gain'd my heart (s Baroness, < *Love's Triumph*)
49	50	Air a shape a face, An (s De L'Épine, < *Love's Triumph*)
50	51	Be wiser ne'er betray us (s De L'Épine, < *Love's Triumph*)
51	52	Dare not oh dare not talke of love (2, s Valentini, < *Love's Triumph*)
52	53	Fond moments false pleasure (s Tofts, < *Love's Triumph*)
53	54	Now my dear, all is clear (s Leveridge, < *Love's Triumph*)
54	55	Why so fast, why in haste (s Lindsey, Leveridge, < *Love's Triumph*)
55	56	You're so pretty airy witty (s Lindsey, < *Love's Triumph*)
56	57	You scorn a tender heart (s Leveridge, < *Love's Triumph*)
57	58-[58A]	When I am ranging (s Valentini, Baroness, < *Love's Triumph*)
58	59	Come my charmer (s Valentini, Leveridge, < *Love's Triumph*)
59	60	Ne're complain tho' ne're contented (s Tofts, < *Love's Triumph*)
60	61	Love and Hymen are combining (< *Love's Triumph*)
61	62	Why vainly am I calling (s Tofts, < *Love's Triumph*)
62	63	Oh no more with love torment me (s Tofts, De L'Épine, < *Love's Triumph*)
63	64	My love bright creature (s De L'Épine, < *Love's Triumph*)
64	65	Come now my dear be gay (s Leveridge, < *Love's Triumph*)
65	66	You say you love me (s Lindsey, < *Love's Triumph*)
66	67	Serpetta my pleasure (s Lindsey, Leveridge, < *Love's Triumph*)
67	68	Yee loves and pleasure (s Valentini, < *Love's Triumph*)
68	69-70	True love alone can never cloy (s De L'Épine, < *Love's Triumph*)

Notes:

1. Although issued after Randall joined partnership, his name does not appear in title-page imprint as Walsh was using up previously printed passe-partout title-pages.

2. There are two versions of 'Dare not oh dare not talke of love', songs 17 and 51.

3. BWbw: - p. [i], 21, 66; pp. 22 and 23 inverted.

4. CDp: pp. 66 and 70 unpaginated. 'his' in imprint on illus. title-page altered in MS. to 'her'.

5. Ckc (85.4.(4.)): - p. [i], 68.

6. Ckc (85.11): pp. 66 and 70 unpaginated.

7. CLU-C: p. [iii] reversed. Illus. title-page imprint 'her' not 'his'.

8. CU-MUSI: - p. [i], pp. 66 and 70 unpaginated.

9. NN: - p. [i].

10. NRU-Mus: p. [i] reversed.

11. Copy reported by *RISM* at DRc comprises 4 songs (11, 23, 18, 5) in a composite volume.

Copies: BWbw —; CDp M.C.3.23; Ckc 85.4.(4.); Ckc 85.11; CLU-C *fM1508.L91; CU-MUSI M1503.C3L61708* Case B; En Mus.E.l.153; NN Drexel 4809; NRU-Mus Vault M1500.V421L.

Plate 47.1   Dieupart, *Love's Triumph*, 1708

Plate 47.2   Dieupart, *Love's Triumph*, 1708

SONGS

IN THE NEW

OPERA,

Call'd

LOVE'S TRIUMPH

as they are Perform'd at the
QUEENS Theatre

Sold   by I. Walsh Musicall Instrument maker in Or=
=dinary to her Majesty, & P. Randall at the Harp and Ho=boy.
in Catherine=Street near Sommerset House in the Strand
and I. Hare Musick Instrument maker at y Golden Viol and Flute in
Cornhill near y Royal Exchange.

Caption: plates 47.1-47.2. 338 x 210 mm. MiU: RBR M1507.E12 v.1 no.2.

[within cartouche] ⌠ Songs in the Opera Calld Loves Triumph ♩ [at foot] London Printed for & Sold by Iohn Walsh Servant to her Majesty at the Harp and Hautboy in Katherine Street near Somerset House in the Strand

Songs In The New Opera, Call'd ⌠ Love's Triumph as they are Perform'd at the Queens Theatre ♩ Sold by I: Walsh Musicall Instrument maker in Or==dinary to her Majesty, & P. Randall at the Harp and Ho=boy, in Catherine=Street near Sommerset House in the Strand and I. Hare Musick Instrument maker at ye Golden Viol and Flute in Cornhill near ye Royal Exchange.

74 leaves. Pp. [i]□-[iii]□ 1□-58□ [58A]□ 59□-70□.
Leaves printed on 1 side.
Tallest copy 351 x 220 mm. Vertical chain lines.

One page engraved per plate. Engraving style Walsh.
Illus. title-page plate 238 x 185 mm. Passe-partout no. 5.
Title-page plate 271 x 186 mm. Passe-partout no. 3.
Contents plate 312 x 111 mm.

Walsh i: 272.
Advertised in *Daily Courant*, 28 April 1708.

Contents: illus. title-page [i]; title-page [ii]; contents [iii]; songs 1-58, [58A], 59-70.

Songs: see **46**.

Notes:
1. B-Br: - pp. [i-ii], 33.
2. CSfst: - p. 23.
3. CtY-Mus: - pp. [i-iii].
4. MiU: - p. 52.
5. Ob: p. 55 reversed.
6. Obh: - pp. 6, 23.

Copies: B-Br Fétis 2849; CSfst de Bellis 812; CtY-Mus Rare M1506.5.C421L89+; ICN VM1505.C62a no.6; MiU RBR M1507.E12 v.1 no.2; Ob Mus. 22.c.158(1); Obh Mus. D.13.

47a   Dieupart, *Love's Triumph*, 28 April 1708

Caption: see plates 47.1-47.2.

[within cartouche] ⌠ Songs in the Opera Calld Loves Triumph ⌡ [at foot] London Printed for & Sold by Iohn Walsh Servant to her Majesty at the Harp and Hautboy in Katherine Street near Somerset House in the Strand

Songs In The New Opera, Call'd ⌠ Love's Triumph as they are Perform'd at the Queens Theatre ⌡ Sold by I: Walsh Musicall Instrument maker in Or==dinary to her Majesty, & P. Randall at the Harp and Ho=boy, in Catherine=Street near Sommerset House in the Strand and I. Hare Musick Instrument maker at ye Golden Viol and Flute in Cornhill near ye Royal Exchange.

38 leaves. Pp. [i]▯ [ii-iii] 1▯ 2-58 [58A] 59-70.
Leaves printed on 2 sides.
Tallest copy 359 x 227 mm. Vertical chain lines.

One page engraved per plate. Engraving style Walsh.
Illus. title-page plate 236 x 186 mm. Passe-partout no. 5.
Title-page plate 270 x 186 mm. Passe-partout no. 3.
Contents plate 308 x 111 mm.

Walsh i: 272.
Advertised in *Daily Courant*, 28 April 1708.

Contents: illus. title-page [i]; title-page [ii]; contents [iii]; songs 1-58, [58A], 59-70.

Songs: see **46**.

Copy: TWm —.

48   deleted (see 22).

48a Scarlatti, A, *Pyrrhus and Demetrius*, 20 January 1709

Caption: see plates 49.1-49.2.

[within cartouche] ⌠ Songs in the Opera Call'd Pyrrhus and Demetrius ⌡ [at foot] London Printed for & Sold by Iohn Walsh Servant to her Majesty at the Harp and Hautboy in Katherine Street near Somerset House in the Strand

Songs In The New Opera, Call'd ⌠ Pyrrhus and Demetrius All ye Singing Parts being transpos'd into ye G: Cliff & put into such Keys that brings them into ye Compass of Treble or Tenor Voices. The whole being done from ye Original by that Compleat writer of Musick Mr. Armstrong, and by him carefully corrected, also he hath made words to 17 of ye Italian songs, thus mark'd †⌡ Sold by I: Walsh Musicall Instrument maker in Or==dinary to her Majesty, & P. Randall at the Harp and Ho=boy, in Catherine=Street near Sommerset House in the Strand and I. Hare Musick Instrument maker at ye Golden Viol and Flute in Cornhill near ye Royal Exchange.

63 leaves. Pp. [i]□-[ii]□\□[iii] □[1] [2]□ 1□-16□\□17 18□-19□\□20 21□-31□\□32 33□-41□\□42 43□-58□.
Leaves printed on 1 side.
Tallest copy 348 x 223 mm. Vertical chain lines.

One page engraved per plate. Engraving style Walsh 1.
Illus. title-page plate 237 x 186 mm. Passe-partout no. 5.
Title-page plate 272 x 187 mm. Passe-partout no. 3.
Contents plate 302 x 87 mm.

Walsh i: 292.
Advertised in *Daily Courant*, 20 January 1709.

Contents: illus. title-page [i]; title-page [ii]; contents and advertisement [iii]; overture [1-2]; songs 1-58.

Songs:

No.	Page	First Line
1	1	Come o sleep and gently ease me (s Nicolini, < *Pyrrhus and Demetrius*)
2	2	Rise o sun, (s Tofts, < *Pyrrhus and Demetrius*)
3	3	Thus in a solitary grove (s Tofts, < *Pyrrhus and Demetrius*)
4	4	Heal o heal the wounds you gave her (s Tofts, < *Pyrrhus and Demetrius*)
5	5	If of my sorrow she has compassion (s Nicolini, < *Pyrrhus and Demetrius*)
6	6	My sorrows unrelenting (s Baroness, < *Pyrrhus and Demetrius*)
7	7	We knaves that wait upon the great (m Haym, s Cook, < *Pyrrhus and Demetrius*)
8	8	Too lovely cruel fair (m Haym, s De L'Épine, < *Pyrrhus and Demetrius*)
9	9	In vain ye cruel fair (s Ramondon, < *Pyrrhus and Demetrius*)
10	10	Tho nature strives t'oppose (m Haym, s Baroness, < *Pyrrhus and Demetrius*)
11	11	I feel my doubtfull mind (m Haym, s De L'Épine, < *Pyrrhus and Demetrius*)
12	12	If for me the fates ordain her (m Haym, s Valentini < *Pyrrhus and Demetrius*)
13	13	Appear all ye graces (m Haym, s Valentini, < *Pyrrhus and Demetrius*)

14	14	Great love I adore thee (s Valentini, < *Pyrrhus and Demetrius*)
15	15	Gentle sighs awhile releive us (m Haym, s Tofts, < *Pyrrhus and Demetrius*)
16	16	Her bright eyes are starrs that charm us (s Nicolini, < *Pyrrhus and Demetrius*)
17	17-18	Kindly Cupid o exert thy power (s Baroness, Tofts, < *Pyrrhus and Demetrius*)
18	19	Shepherds fortune who must keep, The (s Nicolini, < *Pyrrhus and Demetrius*)
19	20-21	Her lovely face enchains me (m Haym, s Nicolini, Valentini, < *Pyrrhus and Demetrius*)
20	22	Blushing violetts sweetly smelling (s De L'Épine, < *Pyrrhus and Demetrius*)
21	23	No forces shall scare me (m Haym, s De L'Épine, < *Pyrrhus and Demetrius*)
22	24	Cruel charmer fair ungratefull (m Haym, s Ramondon, < *Pyrrhus and Demetrius*)
23	25	In vain are sighs to move us (m Haym, s Baroness, < *Pyrrhus and Demetrius*)
24	26	Let ev'ry lover his care give over (s Ramondon, < *Pyrrhus and Demetrius*)
25	27	Thus with thirst my soul expiring (m Haym, s Tofts, < *Pyrrhus and Demetrius*)
26	28	Dying still I love (m Haym, s Valentini, < *Pyrrhus and Demetrius*)
27	29	Hast o sun, o quickly fly (m Haym, s Valentini, < *Pyrrhus and Demetrius*)
28	30	Than friendship ye are dearer (m Haym, s Nicolini, < *Pyrrhus and Demetrius*)
29	31	Give or take my life my dear (s Tofts, < *Pyrrhus and Demetrius*)
30	32-33	Charmer if faithfull thou'lt beleive me (s Tofts, Nicolini, < *Pyrrhus and Demetrius*)
31	34	Tho the god of love assail me (s Nicolini, < *Pyrrhus and Demetrius*)
32	35	That which love denyes me (m Haym, s Ramondon, < *Pyrrhus and Demetrius*)
33	36	May I tell you that I'me dyeing (s De L'Épine, < *Pyrrhus and Demetrius*)
34	37	O destinys, what would ye with me have (s De L'Épine, < *Pyrrhus and Demetrius*)
35	38	Something bloody and unexpected (s Nicolini, < *Pyrrhus and Demetrius*)
36	39	Fortune boldly aims at all (s Nicolini, < *Pyrrhus and Demetrius*)
37	40	O ungratefull, how couldst thou deceive me (s Tofts, < *Pyrrhus and Demetrius*)
38	41	Barbarous, insolent, nere see my face again (s Tofts, < *Pyrrhus and Demetrius*)
39	42-43	I'me contented, nere tormented (s Nicolini, Valentini, < *Pyrrhus and Demetrius*)
40	44	Our hopes to joys aspiring (m Haym, s De L'Épine, < *Pyrrhus and Demetrius*)
41	45	Love thou airy vain illusion (s Ramondon, < *Pyrrhus and Demetrius*)
42	46	Ungratefull traytor go (m Haym, s Baroness, < *Pyrrhus and Demetrius*)
43	47	Furyes infernal quickly come teare me (m Haym, s De L'Épine, < *Pyrrhus and Demetrius*)
44	48	Murmm'ring zephyr's sweetly singing (s Nicolini, < *Pyrrhus and Demetrius*)
45	49	Moveing soft breezes charm me (s Nicolini, < *Pyrrhus and Demetrius*)
46	50	Strike deep and kill a hopeless lover (s De L'Épine, < *Pyrrhus and Demetrius*)
47	51	Soft ioys young loves gay pleasure (m Haym, s Baroness, < *Pyrrhus and Demetrius*)
48	52	For me love has decreed her (m Haym, s De L'Épine, < *Pyrrhus and Demetrius*)
49	53	I will fly tho I dye (s Valentini, < *Pyrrhus and Demetrius*)
50	54	When o cruel fortune (s Nicolini, < *Pyrrhus and Demetrius*)
51	55	Dear brother adieu t'yee (s Baroness, < *Pyrrhus and Demetrius*)
52	56	My heart I feel now languish (s Valentini, < *Pyrrhus and Demetrius*)
53	57	My dear I feel with pleasure (s Nicolini, < *Pyrrhus and Demetrius*)
54	58	Live great Thames

Notes:
1. No Italian texts are present in this issue despite the title-page statement.
2. Ckc: - p. [i]; p. 39 unpaginated.
3. CLU-C: pp. 17, 20 reversed.
4. CU-MUSI: - pp. 29, 39.
5. Gu: - pp. [i], 58; leaves of pp. 1-57 arranged so that all versos are blank.
6. NN: p. 17 reversed.

Copies: Ckc 85.4.(5.); CLU-C *fM1508.P99; CU-MUSI M1503.S29P5 1708 Case X; Gu Ca.13-y.23; NN Drexel 4809.2.

Caption: see plates 49.1-49.2.

[within cartouche] ⌠ Songs in the Opera Call'd Pyrrhus and Demetrius ⌡ [at foot] London Printed for & Sold by Iohn Walsh Servant to her Majesty at the Harp and Hautboy in Katherine Street near Somerset House in the Strand

Songs In The New Opera, Call'd ⌠ Pyrrhus and Demetrius All ye Singing Parts being transpos'd into ye G: Cliff & put into such Keys that brings them into ye Compass of Treble or Tenor Voices. The whole being done from ye Original by that Compleat writer of Musick Mr. Armstrong, and by him carefully corrected, also he hath made words to 17 of ye Italian songs, thus mark'd † ⌡ Sold by I: Walsh Musicall Instrument maker in Or==dinary to her Majesty, & P. Randall at the Harp and Ho=boy, in Catherine=Street near Sommerset House in the Strand and I. Hare Musick Instrument maker at ye Golden Viol and Flute in Cornhill near ye Royal Exchange.

61 leaves. Pp. [i]□-[ii]□\□[iii] 1□-16□\□17 18□-19□\□20 21□-31□\□32 33□-41□\□42 43□-58□.
Leaves printed on 1 side.
Tallest copy 348 x 225 mm. Vertical chain lines.

One page engraved per plate. Engraving style Walsh 1.
Illus. title-page plate passe-partout no. 5.
Title-page plate passe-partout no. 3.

Walsh i: 292.
Advertised in *Daily Courant*, 20 January 1709.

Contents: illus. title-page [i]; title-page [ii]; contents and advertisement [iii]; songs 1-58.

Songs: see **48a**.

Notes:
1. No Italian texts are present in this issue despite the title-page statement.
2. Eu: - p. 13; p. 32 reversed.

Copies: Eu SpC S*17.61.(3); MiU RBR M1507.E12 v.2 no.4.

Plate 49.1   Scarlatti, A, *Pyrrhus and Demetrius*, 1709

Plate 49.2 Scarlatti, A, *Pyrrhus and Demetrius*, 1709

SONGS

IN THE NEW

OPERA,

Call'd

PYRRHUS and DEMETRIUS

All ÿ Singing Parts being transpos'd into ÿ G: Cliff & put into such Keys that brings them into ÿ Compaß of Treble or Tenor Voices. The whole being done from ÿ Original by that Compleat writer of Musick Mr. Armstrong. and by him carefully corrected. also he hath made words to 17 of ÿ Italian Songs. thus mark'd †

Sold by I: Walsh Musicall Instrument maker in Ordinary to her Majesty, & P. Randall at the Harp and Ho=boy. in Catherine=Street near Sommerset House in the strand. and I. Hare Musick Instrument maker at ÿ Golden Viol and Flute in Cornhill near ÿ Royal Exchange.

49 Scarlatti, A, *Pyrrhus and Demetrius*, 9 February 1709

Caption: plates 49.1-49.2. 338 x 223 mm. Lbl: Hirsch II.841.

[within cartouche] ⌠ Songs in the Opera Call'd Pyrrhus and Demetrius ⌡ [at foot] London Printed for & Sold by Iohn Walsh Servant to her Majesty at the Harp and Hautboy in Katherine Street near Somerset House in the Strand

Songs In The New Opera, Call'd ⌠ Pyrrhus and Demetrius All ye Singing Parts being transpos'd into ye G: Cliff & put into such Keys that brings them into ye Compass of Treble or Tenor Voices. The whole being done from ye Original by that Compleat writer of Musick Mr. Armstrong, and by him carefully corrected, also he hath made words to 17 of ye Italian songs, thus mark'd † ⌡ Sold by I: Walsh Musicall Instrument maker in Or==dinary to her Majesty, & P. Randall at the Harp and Ho=boy, in Catherine=Street near Sommerset House in the Strand and I. Hare Musick Instrument maker at ye Golden Viol and Flute in Cornhill near ye Royal Exchange.

63 leaves. Pp. [i]□-[ii]□\□[iii] □[1] [2]□ 1□-16□\□17 18□-19□\□20 21□-31□\□32 33□-41□\□42 43□-58□.
Leaves printed on 1 side.
Tallest copy 366 x 230 mm. Vertical chain lines.

One page engraved per plate. Engraving style Walsh 1.
Illus. title-page plate 239 x 187 mm. Passe-partout no. 5.
Title-page plate 270 x 185 mm. Passe-partout no. 3.
Contents plate 305 x 88 mm.

Walsh i: 293.
Advertised in *Daily Courant*, 9 February 1709.

Contents: illus. title-page [i]; title-page [ii]; contents and advertisement [iii]; overture [1-2]; songs 1-58.

Songs:

No.	Page	First Line
1	1	Come o sleep and gently ease me (Vieni o sonno e l'alma in petto) (s Nicolini, < *Pyrrhus and Demetrius*)
2	2	Rise o sun, (s Tofts, < *Pyrrhus and Demetrius*)
3	3	Thus in a solitary grove (Tortorella) (s Tofts, < *Pyrrhus and Demetrius*)
4	4	Heal o heal the wounds you gave her (Bello tu bello sei) (s Tofts, < *Pyrrhus and Demetrius*)
5	5	If of my sorrow she has compassion (S'ha pietà del mio dolore) (s Nicolini, < *Pyrrhus and Demetrius*)
6	6	My sorrows unrelenting (s Baroness, < *Pyrrhus and Demetrius*)
7	7	We knaves that wait upon the great (m Haym, s Cook, < *Pyrrhus and Demetrius*)
8	8	Too lovely cruel fair (m Haym, s De L'Épine, < *Pyrrhus and Demetrius*)
9	9	In vain ye cruel fair (s Ramondon, < *Pyrrhus and Demetrius*)
10	10	Tho nature strives t'oppose (m Haym, s Baroness, < *Pyrrhus and Demetrius*)
11	11	I feel my doubtfull mind (m Haym, s De L'Épine, < *Pyrrhus and Demetrius*)

12	12	If for me the fates ordain her (Se non fosse la speranza) (m Haym, s Valentini < *Pyrrhus and Demetrius*)
13	13	Appear all ye graces (O'gratie accorete) (m Haym, s Valentini, < *Pyrrhus and Demetrius*)
14	14	Great love I adore thee (Beltà più vezzosa) (s Valentini, < *Pyrrhus and Demetrius*)
15	15	Gentle sighs awhile releive us (m Haym, s Tofts, < *Pyrrhus and Demetrius*)
16	16	Her bright eyes are starrs that charm us (Due pupille che sono due stelle) (s Nicolini, < *Pyrrhus and Demetrius*)
17	17-18	Kindly Cupid o exert thy power (s Baroness, Tofts, < *Pyrrhus and Demetrius*)
18	19	Shepherds fortune who must keep, The (Per le campagne pascendo l'agne) (s Nicolini, < *Pyrrhus and Demetrius*)
19	20-21	Her lovely face enchains me (m Haym, s Nicolini, Valentini, < *Pyrrhus and Demetrius*)
20	22	Blushing violetts sweetly smelling (s De L'Épine, < *Pyrrhus and Demetrius*)
21	23	No forces shall scare me (m Haym, s De L'Épine, < *Pyrrhus and Demetrius*)
22	24	Cruel charmer fair ungratefull (m Haym, s Ramondon, < *Pyrrhus and Demetrius*)
23	25	In vain are sighs to move us (m Haym, s Baroness, < *Pyrrhus and Demetrius*)
24	26	Let ev'ry lover his care give over (s Ramondon, < *Pyrrhus and Demetrius*)
25	27	Thus with thirst my soul expiring (m Haym, s Tofts, < *Pyrrhus and Demetrius*)
26	28	Dying still I love (Son ferito e cerco i dardi) (m Haym, s Valentini, < *Pyrrhus and Demetrius*)
27	29	Hast o sun, o quickly fly (Corri o sole, per pieta cori) (m Haym, s Valentini, < *Pyrrhus and Demetrius*)
28	30	Than friendship ye are dearer (Più cara, cara del'core) (m Haym, s Nicolini, < *Pyrrhus and Demetrius*)
29	31	Give or take my life my dear (Dammi o'prendi o'caro almèn) (s Tofts, < *Pyrrhus and Demetrius*)
30	32-33	Charmer if faithfull thou'lt beleive me (Caro se fido tu mi credi) (s Tofts, Nicolini, < *Pyrrhus and Demetrius*)
31	34	Tho the god of love assail me (Son'guerriero e son amante) (s Nicolini, < *Pyrrhus and Demetrius*)
32	35	That which love denyes me (m Haym, s Ramondon, < *Pyrrhus and Demetrius*)
33	36	May I tell you that I'me dyeing (s De L'Épine, < *Pyrrhus and Demetrius*)
34	37	O destinys, what would ye with me have (Destin che vuoi da'me destin) (s De L'Épine, < *Pyrrhus and Demetrius*)
35	38	Something bloody and unexpected (Veder parmi un'ombra nera) (s Nicolini, < *Pyrrhus and Demetrius*)
36	39	Fortune boldly aims at all (La fortuna è un pronto ardir che tutto) (s Nicolini, < *Pyrrhus and Demetrius*)
37	40	O ungratefull, how couldst thou deceive me (M'ingannasti, o crudo ingrato) (s Tofts, < *Pyrrhus and Demetrius*)
38	41	Barbarous, insolent, nere see my face again (s Tofts, < *Pyrrhus and Demetrius*)
39	42-43	I'me contented, nere tormented (s Nicolini, Valentini, < *Pyrrhus and Demetrius*)
40	44	Our hopes to joys aspiring (m Haym, s De L'Épine, < *Pyrrhus and Demetrius*)
41	45	Love thou airy vain illusion (s Ramondon, < *Pyrrhus and Demetrius*)
42	46	Ungratefull traytor go (m Haym, s Baroness, < *Pyrrhus and Demetrius*)
43	47	Furyes infernal quickly come teare me (Furie del'Erebo, sù laceratemi) (m Haym, s De L'Épine, < *Pyrrhus and Demetrius*)
44	48	Murmm'ring zephyr's sweetly singing (Sussurando il Zefiretto) (s Nicolini, < *Pyrrhus and Demetrius*)
45	49	Moveing soft breezes charm me (Sento più dolce il vento) (s Nicolini, < *Pyrrhus and Demetrius*)
46	50	Strike deep and kill a hopeless lover (s De L'Épine, < *Pyrrhus and Demetrius*)
47	51	Soft ioys young loves gay pleasure (m Haym, s Baroness, < *Pyrrhus and Demetrius*)
48	52	For me love has decreed her (m Haym, s De L'Épine, < *Pyrrhus and Demetrius*)
49	53	I will fly tho I dye (Fugirò la spietata crudele) (s Valentini, < *Pyrrhus and Demetrius*)
50	54	When o cruel fortune (Quando o'cruda forte sarai) (s Nicolini, < *Pyrrhus and Demetrius*)

51	55	Dear brother adieu t'yee (Germano addio) (s Baroness, < *Pyrrhus and Demetrius*)
52	56	My heart I feel now languish (Per te già sento in petto) (s Valentini, < *Pyrrhus and Demetrius*)
53	57	My dear I feel with pleasure (Per te cara nel petto sento brillarmi il cor) (s Nicolini, < *Pyrrhus and Demetrius*)
54	58	Live great Thames

Notes:

1. The 17 songs with Italian texts mentioned on the title-page are indicated using an obelus on the contents' list, but three songs thus marked (19, 39, and 54) have no Italian. In actuality there are 27 songs with Italian texts; marked by Walsh: 5, 16, 18, 30, 34, 36, 37, 43-45, 49, 50, 52, 53; not marked: 1, 3, 4, 12-14, 26-29, 31, 35, 51.
2. Some copies have the earlier state of one or more songs, lacking the Italian texts.
3. CaOLU, CSt: Italian texts added in MS. to a few songs.
4. CaOLU, Ckc (both), DRc, ICN: p. [iii] reversed and p. 39 unnumbered.
5. CSfst: pp. [iii], 17 reversed.
6. INS: - p. [i].
7. Lbl (H.109): - pp. [i]-[ii], 58.
8. Copy reported at DLC comprises instrumental parts only.

Copies: *B-MAR*; CaOLU MZ.525; Ckc 85.5.(4.); Ckc 85.12; CSfst de Bellis 1161; CSt Mus Lib *M1508.S28P62a; *CtY-Mus*; DRc Mus.D.36; ICN Case VM1505.S28p no.1; INS M1505 S3P5; Lbl H.109; Lbl Hirsch II.841; Mp BRf200Sf36; NcU M1508.S33 P57; NN Drexel 4914.

Plate 50.1   Scarlatti, A, *Pyrrhus and Demetrius*, 1709

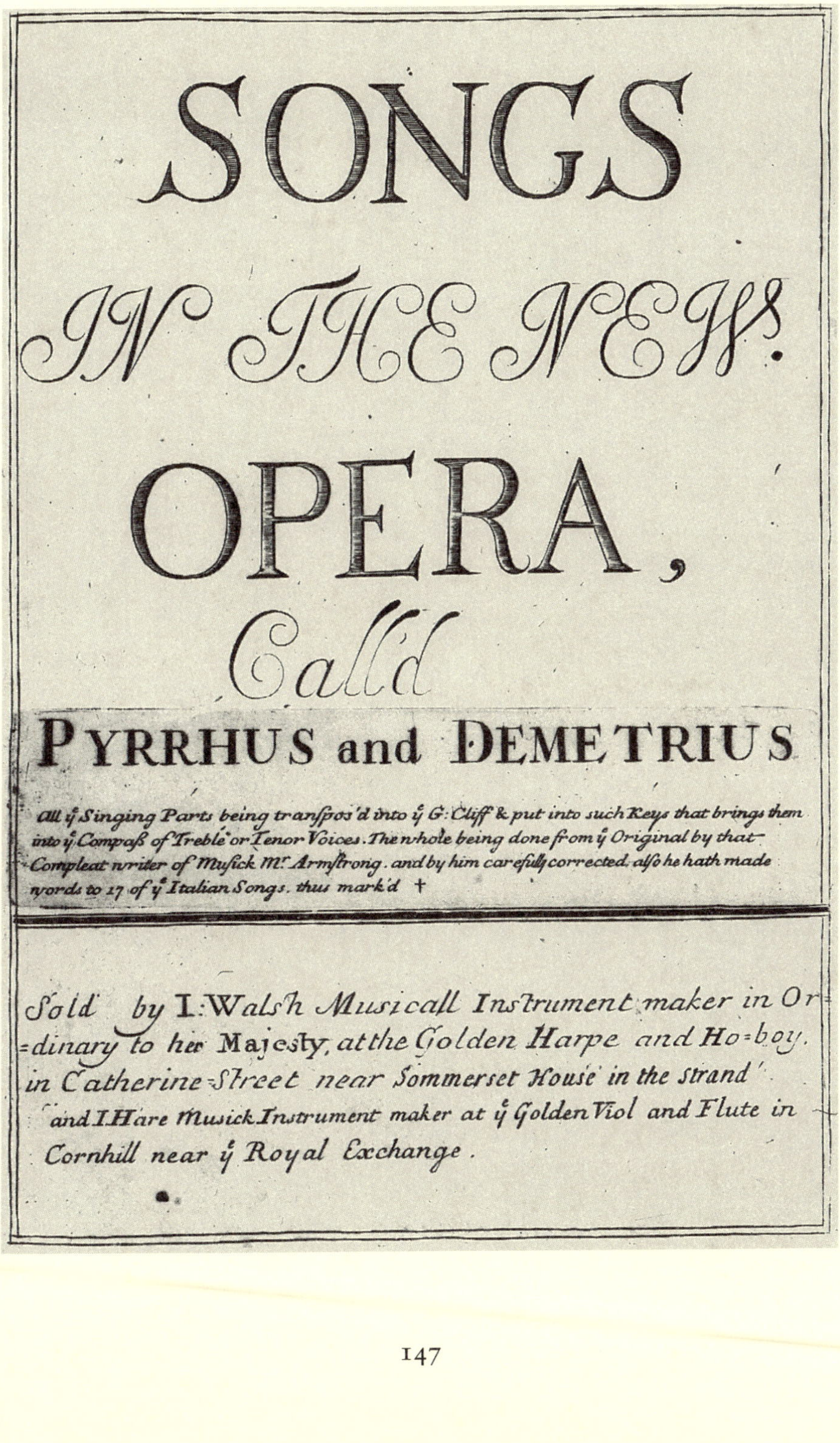

SONGS

IN THE NEW:

OPERA,

Call'd

PYRRHUS and DEMETRIUS

All y̆ Singing Parts being transpos'd into y̆ G: Cliff & put into such Keys that brings them
into y̆ Compaſs of Treble or Tenor Voices. The whole being done from y̆ Original by that
Compleat writer of Muſick M.ʳ Armſtrong. and by him carefully corrected. alſo he hath made
words to 17 of y̆ Italian Songs. thus mark'd †

Sold   by I. Walsh Muſicall Inſtrument maker in Or
=dinary to her Majesty, at the Golden Harpe and Ho=boy.
in Catherine Street near Sommerset Houſe in the strand'
and I. Hare Muſick Inſtrument maker at y̆ Golden Viol and Flute in
Cornhill near y̆ Royal Exchange.

Caption: see plate 49.1. Plate 50.1. 350 x 225 mm. NRU-Mus: Vault M1508.S286P.

[within cartouche] ⌠ Songs in the Opera call'd Pyrrhus and Demetrius ⌡ [at foot] London Printed for & Sold by Iohn Walsh Servant to her Majesty at the Harp and Hautboy in Katherine Street near Somerset House in the Strand

Songs In The New Opera, Call'd ⌠ Pyrrhus and Demetrius All ye Singing Parts being transpos'd into ye G: Cliff & put into such Keys that brings them into ye Compass of Treble or Tenor voices. The whole being done from ye Original by that Compleat writer of Musick Mr. Armstrong, and by him carefully corrected, also he hath made words to 17 of ye Italian Songs, thus mark'd †
⌡ Sold by I: Walsh Musicall Instrument maker in Or==dinary to her Majesty, at the Golden Harpe and Ho=boy, in Catherine=Street near Sommerset House in the Strand and I. Hare Musick Instrument maker at ye Golden Viol and Flute in Cornhill near ye Royal Exchange.

63 leaves. Pp. [i]□-[ii]□\□[iii] □[1] [2]□ 1□-16□\□17 18□-19□\□20 21□-31□\□32 33□-41□\□42 43□-58□.
Leaves printed on 1 side.
Tallest copy 350 x 225 mm. Vertical chain lines.

One page engraved per plate. Engraving style Walsh 1.
Illus. title-page plate passe-partout no. 5.
Title-page plate 270 x 185 mm. Passe-partout no. 3.

Contents: illus. title-page [i]; title-page [ii]; contents and advertisement [iii]; overture [1-2]; songs 1-58.

Songs: see **49**.

Notes:
1. Though published after Randall had joined the partnership, Walsh issued these copies with old passe-partout title-pages lacking Randall's name.
2. Song 30 in both copies lacks Italian words.
3. TWm: - p. [i].

Copies: NRU-Mus Vault M1508.S286P; TWm —.

51   Scarlatti, A, *Pyrrhus and Demetrius*, 9 February 1709

Caption: see plates 49.1-49.2.

[within cartouche] ⌠ Songs in the Opera Call'd Pyrrhus and Demetrius ⌡ [at foot] London Printed for & Sold by Iohn Walsh Servant to her Majesty at the Harp and Hautboy in Katherine Street near Somerset House in the Strand

Songs In The New Opera, Call'd ⌠ Pyrrhus and Demetrius All ye Singing Parts being transpos'd into ye G: Cliff & put into such Keys that brings them into ye Compass of Treble or Tenor Voices. The whole being done from ye Original by that Compleat writer of Musick Mr. Armstrong, and by him carefully corrected, also he hath made words to 17 of ye Italian songs, thus mark'd †
⌡ Sold by I: Walsh Musicall Instrument maker in Or==dinary to her Majesty, & P. Randall at the Harp and Ho=boy, in Catherine=Street near Sommerset House in the Strand and I. Hare Musick Instrument maker at ye Golden Viol and Flute in Cornhill near ye Royal Exchange.

33 leaves. Pp. [i]▢ [ii-iii] ▢[1] [2] 1-38 [39] 40-57 58▢
Leaves printed on 2 sides.
Tallest copy 361 x 232 mm. Vertical chain lines.

One page engraved per plate. Engraving style Walsh 1.
Illus. title-page plate 237 x 186 mm. Passe-partout no. 5.
Title-page plate 270 x 187 mm. Passe-partout no. 3.
Contents plate 304 x 87 mm.

Walsh i: 293.
Advertised in *Daily Courant*, 9 February 1709.

Contents: illus. title-page [1]; title-page [ii]; contents and advertisement [iii]; overture [1-2]; songs 1-38, [39], 40-58.

Songs: see **49**.

Copy: Lcm XCV.D.15.(4.).

Plate 52.1   Scarlatti, A, *Pyrrhus and Demetrius*, 1709

Plate 52.2   Scarlatti, A, *Pyrrhus and Demetrius*, 1709

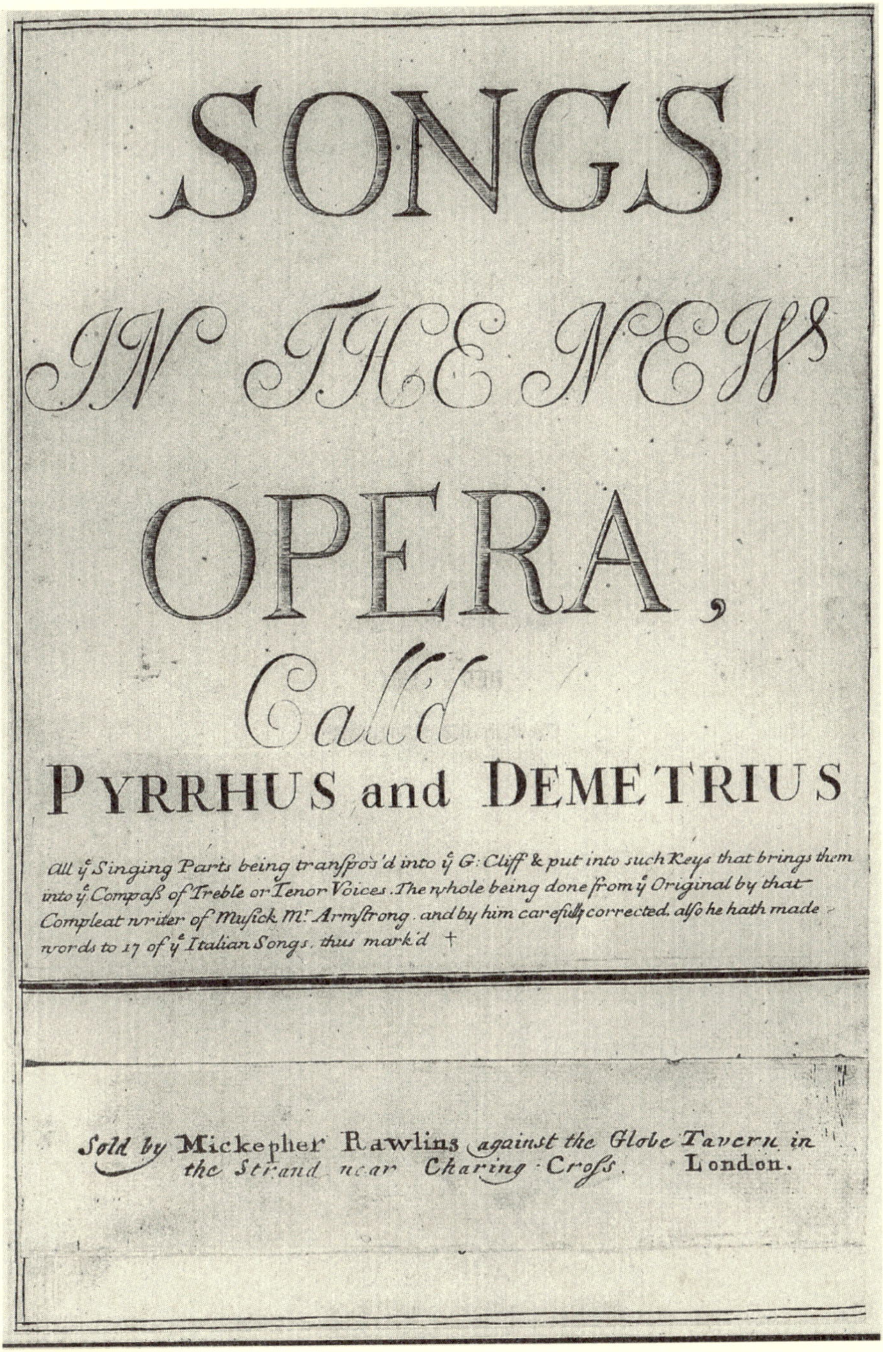

SONGS

IN THE NEW

OPERA,

Call'd

PYRRHUS and DEMETRIUS

All ye Singing Parts being transpos'd into ye G: Cliff & put into such Keys that brings them
into ye Compaß of Treble or Tenor Voices. The whole being done from ye Original by that
Compleat writer of Musick Mr. Armstrong, and by him carefully corrected. also he hath made
words to 17 of ye Italian Songs. thus mark'd †

Sold by Mickepher Rawlins against the Globe Tavern in
the Strand near Charing-Cross.   London.

52 Scarlatti, A, *Pyrrhus and Demetrius*, 9 February 1709

Caption: plates 52.1-52.2. 356 x 210 mm. MH-Mu: Mus 800.3.636 (Cage).

[within cartouche] ⌠ Songs in the Opera Call'd Pyrrhus and Demetrius ⌡ [engraved label over Walsh imprint] Sold by Mickepher Rawlins against the Globe Tavern the Strand near Charing-Cross. London.

Songs In The New Opera, Call'd ⌠ Pyrrhus and Demetrius All ye Singing Parts being transpos'd into ye G: Cliff & put into such Keys that brings them into ye Compass of Treble or Tenor voices. The whole being done from ye Original by that Compleat writer of Musick Mr. Armstrong, and by him carefully corrected, also he hath made words to 17 of ye Italian songs, thus mark'd † ⌡ [engraved label over Walsh imprint] Sold by Mickepher Rawlins against the Globe Tavern the Strand near Charing-Cross. London.

63 leaves. Pp. [i]□-[ii]□\□[iii] □[1] [2]□ 1□-16□\□17 18□-19□\□20 21□-31□\□32 33□-41□\□42 43□-58□.
Leaves printed on 1 side.
Tallest copy 356 x 210 mm. Vertical chain lines.

One page engraved per plate. Engraving style Walsh 1.
Illus. title-page plate 239 x 187 mm. Passe-partout no. 5.
Title-page 270 x 185 mm. Passe-partout no. 3.

Contents: illus. title-page [i]; title-page [ii]; contents and advertisement [iii]; overture [1-2]; songs 1-58.

Songs: see **49**.

Note:
1. Song 4 lacks its Italian text.

Copy: MH-Mu Mus 800.3.636 (Cage).

Plate 53.1   Conti, *Clotilda*, 1709

Plate 53.2   Conti, *Clotilda*, 1709

SONGS
IN THE NEW
OPERA,
Call'd
CLOTILDA
The Songs *done in* Italian *and* English
as they are Perform'd at y̆ QUEENS *Theatre*
The whole Carefully Corected

Sold by I: Walsh *Musicall Instrument maker in Or=
=dinary to her Majesty, & P. Randall at the Harp and Ho=boy,
in Catherine Street near Sommerset House in the strand,
and I. Hare Musick Instrument maker at y̆ Golden Viol and Flute in
Cornhill near y̆ Royal Exchange .*

53 Conti, *Clotilda*, 15 April 1709

Caption: plates 53.1-53.2. 350 x 223 mm. Lbl: H.328.

[within cartouche] ʃ Songs in the Opera Call'd Clotilda ♩ [at foot] London Printed for & Sold by Iohn Walsh Servant to her Majesty at the Harp and Hautboy in Katherine Street near Somerset House in the Strand

Songs In The New Opera, Call'd ʃ Clotilda The Songs done in Italian and English as they are Perform'd at ye Queens Theatre The whole Carefully Corected ♩ Sold by I: Walsh Musicall Instrument maker in Or==dinary to her Majesty, & P. Randall at the Harp and Ho=boy, in Catherine=street near Sommerset House in the Strand and I. Hare Musick Instrument maker at ye Golden Viol and Flute in Cornhill near ye Royal Exchange.

60 leaves. Pp. [i]□-[ii]□\□[iii] □1 2□\□3 4□ o□-12□\□13 14□-20□\□21 22□-26□\□27 28□-29□\□30 31□\□32 33□-37□\□38 39□\□40 41□-43□\□44 45□-47□\□48 49□-50□\□51 52□.
Leaves printed on 1 side.
Tallest copy 372 x 220 mm. Vertical chain lines.

One page engraved per plate. Engraving style Walsh 1.
Illus. title-page plate 240 x 185 mm. Passe-partout no. 5.
Title-page plate 270 x 186 mm. Passe-partout no. 3.
Contents plate 307 x 89 mm.

Walsh i: 296.
Advertised in *Daily Courant*, 15 April 1709.

Contents: illus. title-page [i]; title-page [i]; contents and advertisement [iii]; overture 1-4; songs 0-52.

Songs:

No.	Page	First Line
1	0	Deh venite a'consolarmi (s De L'Épine, < *Clotilda*)
2	1	Cupid go seek the rover (Voglio morir ma voglio) (s De L'Épine, < *Clotilda*)
3	2	What is a crown, if you deceive me (s De L'Épine, < *Clotilda*)
4	3	Ti stringo o mio tesoro o mio diletto (Bright charmer flying to thy arms receive me) (s Valentini, < *Clotilda*)
5	4	Hor sì m'insegna il ciel (Ungratefull cruel maid) (s Nicolini, < *Clotilda*)
6	5	Fortune bright queen o'th skies (s Tofts, < *Clotilda*)
7	6	Honour is a virgins treasure (s Tofts, < *Clotilda*)
8	7	Non è bella la vittoria (When ye fair too soon believe us) (s Valentini, < *Clotilda*)
9	8	Woud you free and easy (s Lindsey, < *Clotilda*)
10	9	Still I follow still she fly's me (s Lawrence, < *Clotilda*)
11	10	Lascia di sospirar (Fool me fond hope no more) (s Nicolini, < *Clotilda*)
12	11	Rimirarvi e non amarvi (Think not that I will allways love ye) (s Nicolini, < *Clotilda*)
13	12	Cease to love me (s Tofts, < *Clotilda*)

14	13-14	Vorrei ma non posso (Great love is immortal) (s Nicolini, < *Clotilda*)
15	15	Tho sworn to despise me (s De L'Épine, < *Clotilda*)
16	16	Pria ch'il sole s'imerga nell'onda (Phebus rising shall see me adore her) (s Valentini, < *Clotilda*)
17	17	Cease o Cupid thus to obraid me (s Tofts, < *Clotilda*)
18	18	Let other beauties (s Tofts, < *Clotilda*)
19	19	Ditemi dolci aurete (Fan me ye gentle zephyrs) (s Nicolini, < *Clotilda*)
20	20	Whilst distrust my souls assailing (Deh ritorna o sonno amato) (s De L'Épine, < *Clotilda*)
21	21-22	Luccioletta fra gl'orrori (When a blind unhappy passion) (s Nicolini, < *Clotilda*)
22	23	When loves inciting and pow'r inviteing (s Lawrence, < *Clotilda*)
23	24	Man in imagination (s Lindsey, < *Clotilda*)
24	25	Compassion leave me (s Tofts, < *Clotilda*)
25	26	Soft blessing descending (s Ramondon, < *Clotilda*)
26	27-28	Gioia e contento (To joys that delight us) (s Tofts, Valentini, < *Clotilda*)
27	29	Vieni o morte a consolarmi (Pity a lover ye virgins tender) (s De L'Épine, < *Clotilda*)
28	30-31	Belle fonti che correte (Bubling fountains daily flowing) (s Nicolini, Valentini, < *Clotilda*)
29	32-33	La gioa m'abonda (Ah who can discover) (s Valentini, < *Clotilda*)
30	34	Si crudel barbara forte (Since ungratefull still you shun me) (s Nicolini, < *Clotilda*)
31	35	Dye Clotilda, thy death will secure me (s Tofts, < *Clotilda*)
32	36	How sweet is love (s Lindsey, < *Clotilda*)
33	37	Non han core (Tho' yon waters) (s De L'Épine, < *Clotilda*)
34	38-39	S'armi pur amor superbo (Tho' fierce love ye war is waging) (s Nicolini, < *Clotilda*)
35	40-41	La forte 'ed il destin (Since heav'n & earth combine) (s Tofts, < *Clotilda*)
36	42	Del fallo sul camin (s Valentini, < *Clotilda*)
37	43	Let virgins ev'ry year (s De L'Épine, < *Clotilda*)
38	44-45	Del piacer ch'io sento in petto (s De L'Épine, Valentini, < *Clotilda*)
39	46	Destin se vuoi (s Nicolini, < *Clotilda*)
40	47	Non dar pui pene o cara (No more thou dearest creature) (s Nicolini, < *Clotilda*)
41	48-49	Prendi l'alma prend il core (Take a heart you long have wanted) (s Tofts, Nicolini, < *Clotilda*)
42	50	Cares when they'r over (s De L'Épine, < *Clotilda*)
43	51-52	Tutto rida in si bel

Notes:

1. CSfst (de Bellis 864): some leaves printed on both sides; 54 leaves, pp. [i]□ [ii]-[iii] □1 2-o 1□-12□\□13 14□-18□ 19-20 □21 22□-26□\□27 28□-29□\□30 31□\□32 33□-35□ 37□\□38 39□\□40 41□-43□\□44 45□-47□\□48 49□-50□\□51 52□; - p. 36.
2. Lcm: p. 42 unpaginated.
3. Mp: p. 40 reversed.

Copies: CaOLU MZ.531; CLU-C *fM1508.C64; CSfst de Bellis 863; CSfst de Bellis 864; DFo M1503.C58C7 Cage; Eu SpC S* 17.61.(1); *H-Bn*; ICN Case VM1505.S28p no.3; Lbl H.328; Lcm XXXII.A.3.(5.); MiU RBR M1507.E12 v.2 no.3; Mp BR f200Cq32; NjP (Ex) M1508.C7C6q; NN Drexel 4809.1; TWm —.

54   Conti, *Clotilda*, 15 April 1709

Caption: see plates 53.1-53.2.

[within cartouche] ʃ Songs in the Opera Call'd Clotilda ♩ [at foot] London Printed for & Sold by Iohn Walsh Servant to her Majesty at the Harp and Hautboy in Katherine Street near Somerset House in the Strand

Songs In The New Opera, Call'd ʃ Clotilda The Songs done in Italian and English as they are Perform'd at ye Queens Theatre The whole Carefully Corected ♩ Sold by I: Walsh Musicall Instrument maker in Or==dinary to her Majesty, & P. Randall at the Harp and Ho=boy, in Catherine=Street near Sommerset House in the Strand and I. Hare Musick Instrument maker at ye Golden Viol and Flute in Cornhill near ye Royal Exchange.

31 leaves. Pp. [i]▯ [ii-iii] ▯1 2-4 0-52.
Leaves printed on 2 sides.
Tallest copy 361 x 232 mm. Vertical chain lines.

One page engraved per plate. Engraving style Walsh 1.
Illus. title-page plate passe-partout no. 5.
Title-page plate passe-partout no. 3.

Walsh i: 296.
Advertised in *Daily Courant*, 15 April 1709.

Contents: illus. title-page [i]; title-page [ii]; contents and advertisement [iii]; overture 1-4; songs 0-52.

Songs: see 53.

Notes:
1. BWbw: - pp. [i-ii], 19, 43-52; pp. [iii], 2-4, 0, 20 printed on single leaves; 27 leaves in all.
2. Lgc: - p. [i].
3. MB: pp. 47-48, each printed on one side of leaf; p. 48 duplicated (33 leaves in all). Price on illustrated title-page in MS.: £0-9s-0d.

Copies: BWbw —; Ckc 85.5.(3.); Lcm XCV.D.15(1); Lgc G.Mus.61(1); MB **M.400.53(2).

Caption: see plate 55a.2.

The Iovial Companions or Merry Club being A Choice Collection of the Newest and most Diverting Catches for three & four Voices Together with the most Celebrated Catches Compos'd by the late Mr. Henr. Purcell & Dr. Blow all fairly Engraven & Carefully Corrected London Printed for I. Walsh & P. Randall at the Harp and Hoboy in Katherine Street by Somerset House in the Strand, and at the Violin and Lute by Paulsgrave Court without Temple Barr, and I. Hare at the Golden Viol and Flute in Cornhill near ye Royal Exchange

25 leaves. Pp. [][i] [ii]□-[iii]□ [1]□-[22]□.
Leaves printed on 1 side.
Tallest copy 334 x 217 mm. Vertical chain lines.

One page engraved per plate. Engraving style Walsh 1, 3, Cross.
Frontispiece plate 284 x 192 mm.
Title-page plate 255 x 180 mm.
Contents plate 260 x 173 mm.

Walsh i: 303.
Advertised in *Daily Courant*, 20 May 1709.

Contents: frontispiece [i]; title-page [ii]; contents [iii]; songs [1]-[22].

Songs:

No.	Page	First Line
1	[1]	Ding dong bell hark great Marlborough is come (m Eccles)
2	[2]	Said Sr John to his lady (m Brown, R.)
3	[2]	Was ever mortal man so fitted, (m Brown, R.)
4	[2]	Good indeed the herb's good weed, (D&M 1173)
5	[3]	Duke sounds to horse boyes, The (m Brown, R.)
6	[3]	O're Neptune's dominions, brave Ormond (m Brown, R.)
7	[4]	From Aud'nard fam'd battel (m Brown, R.)
8	[4]	Tis pitty poor Barnet a vigilant curr (m Brown, R.)
9	[4]	Hark Harry tis late (m Eccles, D&M 1251)
10	[5]	Frank what shall we do (m Willis)
11	[5]	Here Tom here's a health (m Willis)
12	[5]	Here's a health to Queen Anne (m Clarke, J., D&M 1360)
13	[5]	Quoth Jack on a time (m Morgan, D&M 2777)
14	[6]	Come take of your liquor (m Hall, v Hall)
15	[7]	Come good sober Jacob (m Brown, R.)
16	[7]	Of honest malt liquor lets English boys sing (m Brown, R.)
17	[7]	All wee here whose names sir (m Brown, R.)
18	[7]	Would you know how we meet (m Purcell, H., v Otway, D&M 4025)
19	[8]	Now we are met and humours agree (m Purcell, H., D&M 2434)
20	[8]	Who comes there, stand, who comes there (m Purcell, H., D&M 3906)
21	[8]	Hark the bonny Christ Church bells (D&M 2534)
22	[8]	You may talk of brisk claret (m Tudway, D&M 4095).
23	[9]	Fy nay prithee John (D&M 993)

24	[9]	Here's that will challenge all the fair (m Purcell, H., D&M 1366)
25	[9]	Sum up all the delights (m Purcell, H., D&M 3103)
26	[10]	Ah sorry poor French men (m Brown, R.)
27	[10]	Intombed here lyes good Sr Harry (m Brown, R.)
28	[10]	Come drink about Tom (m Day)
29	[11]	Pox on you for a fop (m Purcell, H., D&M 2733)
30	[11]	Will you go by water (D&M 3975)
31	[11]	Tom making a manteua for a lass (m Purcell, H., D&M 3458)
32	[12]	Tis too late for a coach (m Purcell, H., D&M 3397)
33	[12]	Young Collen cleaving of a beam (m Purcell, H., D&M 4121)
34	[12]	Once twice thrice I Julia try'd (m Purcell, H., D&M 2621)
35	[12]	Lets live good honest lives (m Purcell, H., D&M 2030)
36	[13]	Millers daughter riding to the fair, The (m Purcell, H., D&M 2199)
37	[13]	Come let us drink (m Purcell, H., D&M 670)
38	[13]	True English men drink a good health (m Purcell, H., D&M 3480)
39	[14]	Drink on till night be spent (m Purcell, H., D&M 893)
40	[14]	Under this stone lies Gabriel John (m Purcell, H., D&M 3512)
41	[14]	Once in our lives (m Purcell, H., D&M 2615)
42	[14]	If all be true that I do think (m Purcell, H., D&M 1661)
43	[14]	Ape, a lyon, a fox and an ass, An (m Purcell, H., D&M 179)
44	[15]	When Celia was learning (m Isum, v Chocke, D&M 3692)
45	[16]	In seventeen hundred, and three (m Eccles, v D'urfey, D&M 1764)
46	[17]	Room for th'express (m Purcell, H., D&M 2823)
47	[17]	Here where is my landland (D&M 1354)
48	[17]	Confusion to the pow'r of Cupid (m Eccles, D&M 726)
49	[17]	Hogshead was offer'd, A (m Reading, D&M 1383)
50	[17]	Whose three hoggs are these (D&M 3915)
51	[18]	Jack thou'rt a toper (m Purcell, H., D&M 1852)
52	[18]	Bring the bowl and cool Nantz (m Purcell, H., D&M 432)
53	[18]	Pale faces stand by (m Purcell, H., D&M 2656)
54	[18]	Soldier take off thy wine (m Purcell, H., D&M 3020)
55	[19]	Had she not care enough (D&M 1220)
56	[19]	Tinking Tom was an honest man (m Akeroyde, D&M 3367)
57	[19]	In drinking full bumper there is no deceit (m Clarke, J., D&M 1744)
58	[19]	Say good master Bacchus (D&M 2853)
59	[20]	I know brother tar (m Purcell, H., D&M 1537)
60	[20]	Here are the rarities of the whole fair (m Blow, D&M 1346)
61	[20]	God preserve her Majesty (m Blow, D&M 1165)
62	[20]	Joan has been galloping (m Blow, D&M 1867)
63	[20]	How shall we speak thy praise (m Blow, D&M 1457)
64	[21]	Thus while the eight goes merrily round (m Hall)
65	[22]	Wee catts when assembl'd at midnight (m Brown, R.)
66	[22]	Prophets old dog, The
67	[22]	Lets drink to all our wives

Note:
1. Lbl: - p. [i].

Copies: Lbl G.108; Obh Mus. E.91.

The
Iovial Companions
or
MERRY CLUB
being
A Choice Collection of the Newest
and most
Diverting CATCHES
for
three & four Voices
Together with
the most Celebrated

CATCHES
Compos'd by the
late Mr. Henr. Purcell & Dr. Blow
all fairly Engraven & Carefully Corrected

London Printed for I.Walsh & P.Randall at the Harp and Hoboy in Katherine
Street by Somerset House in the Strand, and at the Violin and Lute by Paulsgrave Court
without Temple barr, and I.Hare, at the Golden Viol and Flute in Cornhill near ye Royal Exchange

Caption: plates 55a.1-55a.2. 379 x 227 mm. Ob: Mus. 2.b.3.

The Iovial Companions or Merry Club being A Choice Collection of the Newest and most Diverting Catches for three & four Voices Together with the most Celebrated Catches Compos'd by the late Mr. Henr. Purcell & Dr. Blow all fairly Engraven & Carefully Corrected London Printed for I. Walsh & P. Randall at the Harp and Hoboy in Katherine Street by Somerset House in the Strand, and at the Violin and Lute by Paulsgrave Court without Temple Barr, and I. Hare at the Golden Viol and Flute in Cornhill near ye Royal Exchange

25 leaves. Pp. ◻[i] [ii]◻-[iii]◻ 1◻-15◻ [16]◻ 17◻-22◻.
Leaves printed on 1 side.
Tallest copy 379 x 227 mm. Vertical chain lines.

One page engraved per plate. Engraving style Walsh 1, 3, Cross.
Frontispiece plate 284 x 188 mm.
Title-page plate 255 x 180 mm.
Contents plate 254 x 177 mm.

Walsh i: 303.
Advertised in *Daily Courant*, 20 May 1709.

Contents: frontispiece [i]; title-page [ii]; contents [iii]; songs 1-15, [16], 17-22.

Songs:

No.	Page	First Line
1	1	Ding dong bell hark great Marlborough is come (m Eccles)
2	2	Said Sr John to his lady (m Brown, R.)
3	2	Was ever mortal man so fitted, (m Brown, R.)
4	2	Good indeed the herb's good weed, (D&M 1173)
5	3	Duke sounds to horse boyes, The (m Brown, R.)
6	3	O're Neptune's dominions, brave Ormond (m Brown, R.)
7	4	From Aud'nard fam'd battel (m Brown, R.)
8	4	Tis pitty poor Barnet a vigilant curr (m Brown, R.)
9	4	Hark Harry tis late (m Eccles, D&M 1251)
10	5	Frank what shall we do (m Willis)
11	5	Here Tom here's a health (m Willis)
12	5	Here's a health to Queen Anne (m Clarke, J., D&M 1360)
13	5	Quoth Jack on a time (m Morgan, D&M 2777)
14	6	Come take of your liquor (m Hall, v Hall)
15	7	Come good sober Jacob (m Brown, R.)
16	7	Of honest malt liquor lets English boys sing (m Brown, R.)
17	7	All wee here whose names sir (m Brown, R.)
18	7	Would you know how we meet (m Purcell, H., v Otway, D&M 4025)
19	8	Now we are met and humours agree (m Purcell, H., D&M 2434)
20	8	Who comes there, stand, who comes there (m Purcell, H., D&M 3906)
21	8	Hark the bonny Christ Church bells (D&M 2534)
22	8	You may talk of brisk claret (m Tudway, D&M 4095)
23	9	Fy nay prithee John (D&M 993)

24	9	Here's that will challenge all the fair (m Purcell, H., D&M 1366)
25	9	Sum up all the delights (m Purcell, H., D&M 3103)
26	10	Ah sorry poor French men (m Brown, R.)
27	10	Intombed here lyes good Sr Harry (m Brown, R.)
28	10	Come drink about Tom (m Day)
29	11	Pox on you for a fop (m Purcell, H., D&M 2733)
30	11	Will you go by water (D&M 3975)
31	11	Tom making a manteua for a lass (m Purcell, H., D&M 3458)
32	12	Tis too late for a coach (m Purcell, H., D&M 3397)
33	12	Young Collen cleaving of a beam (m Purcell, H., D&M 4121)
34	12	Once twice thrice I Julia try'd (m Purcell, H., D&M 2621)
35	12	Lets live good honest lives (m Purcell, H., D&M 2030)
36	13	Millers daughter riding to the fair, The (m Purcell, H., D&M 2199)
37	13	Come let us drink (m Purcell, H., D&M 670)
38	13	True English men drink a good health (m Purcell, H., D&M 3480)
39	14	Drink on till night be spent (m Purcell, H., D&M 893)
40	14	Under this stone lies Gabriel John (m Purcell, H., D&M 3512)
41	14	Once in our lives (m Purcell, H., D&M 2615)
42	14	If all be true that I do think (m Purcell, H., D&M 1661)
43	14	Ape, a lyon, a fox and an ass, An (m Purcell, H., D&M 179)
44	15	When Celia was learning (m Isum, v Chocke, D&M 3692)
45	[16]	In seventeen hundred, and three (m Eccles, v D'urfey, D&M 1764)
46	17	Room for th'express (m Purcell, H., D&M 2823)
47	17	Here where is my landland (D&M 1354)
48	17	Confusion to the pow'r of Cupid (m Eccles, D&M 726)
49	17	Hogshead was offer'd, A (m Reading, D&M 1383)
50	17	Whose three hoggs are these (D&M 3915)
51	18	Jack thou'rt a toper (m Purcell, H., D&M 1852)
52	18	Bring the bowl and cool Nantz (m Purcell, H., D&M 432)
53	18	Pale faces stand by (m Purcell, H., D&M 2656)
54	18	Soldier take off thy wine (m Purcell, H., D&M 3020)
55	19	Had she not care enough (D&M 1220)
56	19	Tinking Tom was an honest man (m Akeroyde, D&M 3367)
57	19	In drinking full bumper there is no deceit (m Clarke, J., D&M 1744)
58	19	Say good master Bacchus (D&M 2853)
59	20	I know brother tar (m Blow, D&M 1537)
60	20	Here are the rarities of the whole fair (m Blow, D&M 1346)
61	20	God preserve her Majesty (m Blow, D&M 1165)
62	20	Joan has been galloping (m Blow, D&M 1867)
63	20	How shall we speak thy praise (m Blow, D&M 1457)
64	21	Thus while the eight goes merrily round (m Hall)
65	22	Wee catts when assembl'd at midnight (m Brown, R.)
66	22	Prophets old dog, The
67	22	Lets drink to all our wives

Notes:
1. CLU-C: + pp. 57-59 from H. Purcell, *Don Quixote,* bound between pp. 3-4.
2. DFo: - pp. [i-iii], 15, 20-21; p. [16] bound at end.
3. En, NN, Obh: - p. [i].
4. Lgc: - pp. [i], 6.
5. Copies at MH-H (*52-1268) and Obt (Mus. c.41) have Walsh imprint from about 1730. MH-H also has Barret label.

Copies: CLU-C Temp.; DFo M1547.J6 Cage; En Inglis 172; Lgc G.Mus.276; MB **M.Cab.1.18; NN Drexel 4285.4; Ob Mus. 2.b.3; Obh Mus. E.92.

Plate 56.1 *Bottle Companions*, 1709

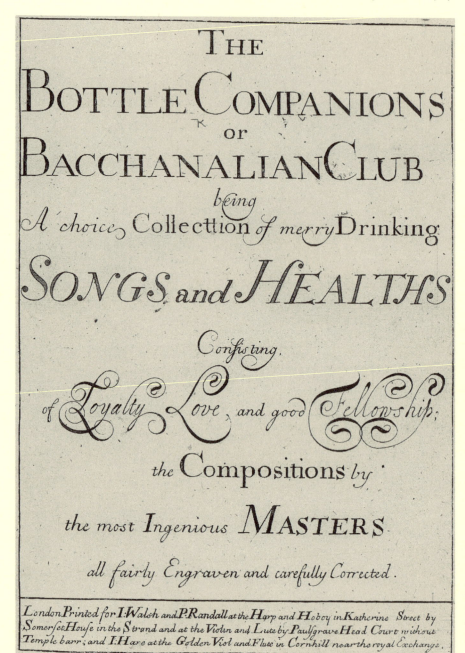

THE

BOTTLE COMPANIONS

or

BACCHANALIAN CLUB

being

A choice Collection of merry Drinking

SONGS and HEALTHS

Consisting,

of Loyalty Love, and good Fellowship;

the Compositions by

the most Ingenious MASTERS

all fairly Engraven and carefully Corrected.

London Printed for I. Walsh and P. Randall at the Harp and Hoboy in Katherine Street by
Somerset House in the Strand and at the Violin and Lute by Paulsgrave Head Court without
Temple barr; and I. Hare at the Golden Viol and Flute in Cornhill near the royal Exchange.

Caption: plate 56.1. 319 x 200 mm. Lbl: H.34.

The Bottle Companions or Bacchanalian Club being A choice Collecttion of merry Drinking Songs and Healths Consisting, of Loyalty Love, and good Fellowship; the Compositions by the most Ingenious Masters all fairly Engraven and carefully Corrected. London Printed for I: Walsh and P. Randall at the Harp and Hoboy in Katherine Street by Somerset House in the Strand and at the Violin and Lute by Paulsgrave Head Court without Temple barr; and I: Hare at the Golden Viol and Flute in Cornhill near the royal Exchange.

36 leaves. Pp. [i]□-[ii]□ □1 2□-34□.
Leaves printed on 1 side.
Tallest copy 333 x 209 mm. Vertical chain lines.

One page engraved per plate. Engraving style Walsh 1, 2, 3.
Title-page plate 225 x 159 mm.
Contents plate 261 x 171 mm.

Walsh i: 304.
Advertised in *Post Man*, 26 May 1709.

Contents: title-page [i]; contents [ii]; songs 1-34.

Songs:

No.	Page	First Line
1	1-2	If to love or good wine (m Leveridge)
2	3	Fill the glass let hautboys sound (m Leveridge, s Leveridge, D&M 1003)
3	4	Young Cupid I find, to subdue me inclin'd (m Leveridge, s Leveridge)
4	5	Come let a cheerful glass go round (m Elford)
5	6	Just coming from sea (m Leveridge, < *Britain's Happiness*)
6	7	Now comes on, the glorious year (v D'urfey, < *Modern Prophets*)
7	8-9	Fill all the glasses, fill e'm high (m Eccles, < *Harry the Fifth*)
8	10	Wine does wonders ev'ry day (m Eccles, s Gouge, Curco, Spalding, < *Morose Reformer*)
9	11	Queen of islands, victorious state
10	12	Trumpet allarms, stand, The (m Isum)
11	13	Beat the drum (m Weldon, v D'urfey, D&M 317)
12	14	Since the day of poor man (m Leveridge, s Leveridge)
13	15	Give us noble ale (m Barrett)
14	16	Make hast pierce the pipe (m Elford, v Herbert)
15	17	Fill every glass and recommend em (a D'urfey, D&M 996)
16	18	Our ordnance borde (v Estcourt, D&M 2641)
17	19	Sing mighty Marlborough's story (v D'urfey, D&M 2977)
18	20	Who now can but laugh, with a hi
19	21	You the glorious sons of honour (m Barrett, v D'urfey, D&M 4110)
20	22	Monsieur now disgorges fast (m D'urfey, v D'urfey, D&M 2212)
21	23	I'll stick to my bottle (m Garee, v Garee)
22	24	Valliant Eugene to Vienna is gone, The (m D'urfey, s Leveridge, < *Country Miss with her Furbeloe*, D&M 3541)

23	25	Boast no more of nice beautys from hence
24	26	Marlborough freedome to Brabant has brought (m Davis)
25	27	Heres a health to Queen Anne (m Roseingrave, D&M 1360)
26	28	Thou flask once filld (m Blow, D&M 3294)
27	29	Now my freedom's regain'd (m Willis, D&M 2403)
28	30	Come bring us wine in plenty (D&M 612)
29	31	Come fill up the bowl (D&M 630)
30	32	Whilst Phillis is drinking (D&M 3864)
31	33	Jolly bowle, The (D&M 1879)
32	34	Crown your bowles, loyall soul's (m Purcell, H., v D'urfey, D&M 760)

Notes:
1. Lbl: contains these additional songs, printed on lighter paper, one song to one side of a leaf, and not part of the original publication: 'Ring the barr bell of the world' (m Bradley, A.), 'Wine's a mistress gay and easy' (s Leveridge, < *Love and Wine*), 'Come let us prepare', 'Come aid me ye muses', 'Come be jolly fill your glasses' (paginated 12), 'Come all ye jolly bacchanals', 'Come charge your empty glasses', 'Come boys come, drink for the night's quite spun'.
2. Obh: p. 8 reversed.

Copies: DLC M1619.B77 Case; Lbl H.34; Obh Mus. E.116.

Plate 57.1 Scarlatti, A, *Pyrrhus and Demetrius*, 1709

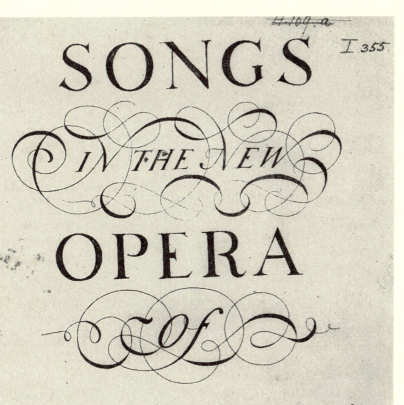

SONGS

IN THE NEW

OPERA

of

Pyrrbus and Demetrius

*With the Italian Words Grav'd under the English to such as are Sung
in Italian, & a Table for the ready finding of them .*

*Note. the Unison Songs have the entire Fiddle part to accompany the Voice ,
and those with full Symphonies are Set full, which is very proper for the Harpsi-
-chord, & yet may be perform'd on any single Instrument ; all which renders
this more Compleat and usefull·than the former Edition .*

The Whole Fairly Engrav'd on Copper Plates by T:Crofs Jun.ͬ

LONDON,

Printed for John Cullen *at the Buck between the two Temple Gates Fleet - Street,
where may be had the Newest & Correctest Editions of* Camilla & Thomyris.

57   Scarlatti, A, *Pyrrhus and Demetrius*, 25 June 1709

Caption: plate 57.1. 370 x 220 mm. Lbl: I.355.

Songs In The New Opera of Pyrrhus and Demetrius With the Italian words
Grav'd under the English to such as are Sung in Italian, & a Table for the ready
finding of them. Note. the Unison Songs have the entire Fiddlepart to
accompany the Voice, and those with full Symphonies are Set full, whick is
very proper for the Harpsi==chord, & yet may be perform'd on any single
Instrument; all which renders this more Compleat and usefull than the former
Edition. The Whole Fairly Engrav'd on Copper Plates by T: Cross Junr.
London, Printed for John Cullen at the Buck between the two Temple Gates
Fleet-Street, where may be had the Newest & Correctest Editions of Camilla
& Thomyris.

59 leaves. Pp. [i]□ 1□\□2 3□ [4]□ 1 [1A] 2□-4□ 5 [5A] 6□-15□\□16 17□-29□\□30
31□-35□\□36 37□\□38 39□-47□\□48 49□-52□ 53 [53A] 54□.
Leaves printed on 1 side.
Tallest copy 370 x 220 mm. Vertical chain lines.

One page engraved per plate. Engraving style Cross.
Title-page plate 320 x 186 mm.
Contents plate 320 x 183 mm.

Walsh i: 293.
Advertised in *Post Boy*, 25 June 1709.

Contents: title-page [i]; overture 1-3; contents and advertisement [4]; song 1; flute part
[1A]; songs 2-5; flute part [5A]; songs 6-53; flute part [53A]; song 54; advertisement
54.

Songs:

No.	Page	First Line
1	1	Come o sleep & gently ease me (Vieni o sonno) (< *Pyrrhus and Demetrius*)
2	2	Rise o sunn (s Tofts, < *Pyrrhus and Demetrius*)
3	3	Thus in a solitary grove (Tortorella) (s Tofts, < *Pyrrhus and Demetrius*)
4	4	Heal, o heal the wounds you give her (Bello tu bello sei) (s Tofts, < *Pyrrhus and Demetrius*)
5	5	If of my sorrow she has compassion (S'ha pietà del mio dolore) (s Grimaldi)
6	6	My sorrows unrelenting (m Haym, s Baroness, < *Pyrrhus and Demetrius*)
7	7	We knaves that wait upon ye great (m Haym, s Cook)
8	7	In vain ye cruell fair (s Ramondon, < *Pyrrhus and Demetrius*)
9	8	Too lovely cruel fair (m Haym, s De L'Épine, < *Pyrrhus and Demetrius*)
10	9	Tho' nature strives t' oppose (m Haym, s Baroness, < *Pyrrhus and Demetrius*)
11	10	I feel my doubtfull mind (m Haym, s De L'Épine, < *Pyrrhus and Demetrius*)
12	11	If for me the fates ordain her (Se non fosse la speranza) (m Haym, s Valentini, < *Pyrrhus and Demetrius*)
13	12	Appear all ye graces (O'gratie accorrette) (m Haym, s Valentini, < *Pyrrhus and Demetrius*)

14	13	Great love I adore thee (Belta più vezzosa) (s Valentini, < *Pyrrhus and Demetrius*)
15	14	Gentle sighs, awhile releive us (m Haym, s Tofts, < *Pyrrhus and Demetrius*)
16	15	Her bright eyes are stars that charm us (Due pupille che sono due stelle) (s Nicolini)
17	16-17	Kindly Cupid o exert thy power (s Baroness, Tofts)
18	18	Shepherds fortune who must keep, The (Per' le campagne pascendo l'agne pastor) (s Grimaldi)
19	19	Her lovely face enchains me (s Nicolini, Valentini)
20	20	Blushing violets sweetly smelling (s De L'Épine, < *Pyrrhus and Demetrius*)
21	21	No forces shall scare me (m Haym, s De L'Épine, < *Pyrrhus and Demetrius*)
22	22	Cruel charmer fair ungratefull (s Ramondon, < *Pyrrhus and Demetrius*)
23	23	In vain are sighs to move us (m Haym, s Baroness, < *Pyrrhus and Demetrius*)
24	24	Let ev'ry lover his care give over (s Ramondon, < *Pyrrhus and Demetrius*)
25	25	Thus with thirst my soul expiring (m Haym, s Tofts, < *Pyrrhus and Demetrius*)
26	26	Dying still I love (Son ferito) (m Haym, s Valentini)
27	27	Hast o sun o quickly fly (Corri o sole per pieta) (s Valentini, < *Pyrrhus and Demetrius*)
28	28	Than friendship ye are dearer (Più cara, cara del'core) (s Grimaldi)
29	29	Give or take my life my dear (s Tofts, < *Pyrrhus and Demetrius*)
30	30-31	Charmer if faithfull thou'lt beleive me (Caro se fido tu mi credi) (s Nicolini, Tofts)
31	32	Tho' ye god of love assail me (Son'guerriero, e sono amante) (s Grimaldi)
32	33	That which love denys me (m Haym, s Ramondon, < *Pyrrhus and Demetrius*)
33	34	May I tell you that I'm dying (< *Pyrrhus and Demetrius*)
34	35	O destinys, what would ye with me have (Destin che vuoi) (s De L'Épine, < *Pyrrhus and Demetrius*)
35	36	Something bloody & unexpected (Veder parmi un'ombra nera)
36	36-37	I'm contented ne'er tormented (Un contento nel'mio care)
37	38-39	O ungratefull how cou'dst thou deceive me (M'ingannasti o crudo ingrato) (s Tofts, < *Pyrrhus and Demetrius*)
38	39	Barbarous, insolent ne'er see my face again
39	40	Fortune boldly aims at all (La fortuna è un pronto ardir) (s Grimaldi)
40	41	Our hopes to joys aspiring (m Haym, s De L'Épine, < *Pyrrhus and Demetrius*)
41	42	Love thou airy vain illusion (s Ramondon, < *Pyrrhus and Demetrius*)
42	43	Ungrateful traytor go (m Haym, s Baroness, < *Pyrrhus and Demetrius*)
43	44	Furies infernal quickly come tear me (Furie del'Erebo) (s De L'Épine, < *Pyrrhus and Demetrius*)
44	45	Murm'ring zephirs sweetly singing (Sussurrando il Zefirretto) (s Grimaldi)
45	46	Moving soft breezes charm me (Sento più dolce il vento) (s Grimaldi)
46	47	Soft joys young loves gay pleasure (m Haym, s Baroness, < *Pyrrhus and Demetrius*)
47	48	Strike deep & kill a hopeless lover (s De L'Épine, < *Pyrrhus and Demetrius*)
48	48-49	I will fly, tho' I dy (Fugirò la spietata crudele)
49	50	For me love has decree'd her (m Haym, s De L'Épine, < *Pyrrhus and Demetrius*)
50	51	When o cruel fortune (Quando o'quando cruda forte)
51	51	Dear brother adieu t'ye
52	52	My heart I feel now languish (Per te già sento in petto) (s Valentini, < *Pyrrhus and Demetrius*)
53	53	My dear I feel with pleasure (Per te cara del petto) (s Grimaldi)
54	54	Live great Thames

Notes:
1. Contents correctly lists 26 songs with Italian words.
2. NjP: p. [4] bound after p. [i].
3. Ouf: - pp. [i], [4].

Copies: Cfm MU.MS.1280; Er Cupb.T. 782.2(45)THO; Lbl I.355; NjP (Ex) M1503.S28P9q; Ouf —; TWm —.

Caption: see plate 57.1.

Songs In The New Opera of Pyrrhus and Demetrius With the Italian Words
Grav'd under the English to such as are Sung in Italian, & a Table for the ready
finding of them. Note. the Unison Songs have the entire Fiddlepart to
accompany the Voice, and those with full Symphonies are Set full, which is
very proper for the Harpsi==chord, & yet may be perform'd on any single
Instrument; all which renders this more Compleat and usefull than the former
Edition. The Whole Fairly Engrav'd on Copper Plates by T: Cross Junr.
London, Printed for John Cullen at the Buck between the two Temple Gates
Fleet-Street, where may be had the Newest & Correctest Editions of Camilla
& Thomyris.

30 leaves. Pp. [i]□ 1-3 [4] 1-54.
Leaves printed on 2 sides.
Tallest copy 353 x 222 mm. Horizontal chain lines.

One page engraved per plate. Engraving style Cross.
Title-page plate 320 x 186 mm.
Contents plate 320 x 183 mm.

Contents: title-page [i]; overture 1-3; contents and advertisement [4]; songs 1-54;
advertisement 54.

Songs: see 57.

Note:
1. As the leaves are printed on both sides no flute parts are to be seen in this impression.

Copy: F-Pc Rés. V.S. 1276.

Plate 59.1   Conti, *Clotilda*, 1709

171

59   Conti, *Clotilda*, 29 November 1709

Caption: plate 59.1. 338 x 220 mm. F-Pc: Rés. V.S.1277.

[in MS.] Songs in the New Opera Called Clotilda With the Italian words Under the English to such as are Sung in Italian Note the Songs haue the Violin Parts proper For the Harpsicord [engraved label over imprint] Sold by Iohn Young Musical Instrument Seller at the Dolphin & Crown at the West end of St. Pauls Church, where you may be furnish'd with al sorts of Violins, Flutes, Hautboys Bass-Viols, Harpsicords or Spinets; likewise al sorts of Musick, Rul'd Paper & Strings, at Reasonable rates.

53 leaves. Pp. [i]□-[ii]□\□1 2□\□3 4□-24□\□25 26□-30□\□31 32□-34□\□35 36□-49□\□50 51□.
Leaves printed on 1 side.
Tallest copy 347 x 222 mm. Vertical chain lines.

One page engraved per plate. Engraving style Pippard.
Title-page plate ? x 185 mm. (See note 4.)
Contents plate 313 x 182 mm.

Advertised in *Post Man*, 29 November 1709.

Contents: title-page [i]; contents and advertisement [ii]; overture 1-4; songs 5-51.

Songs:

No.	Page	First Line
1	5	Deh venite a'consolarmi (s De L'Épine, < *Clotilda*)
2	6	Cupid go seek the rover (s De L'Épine, < *Clotilda*)
3	7	What is a crown, if you deceive me (s De L'Épine, < *Clotilda*)
4	8	Ti stringo o'mio tesoro o'mio diletto (s Valentini, < *Clotilda*)
5	9	Hor sì m'in segna'il ciel (s Nicolini, < *Clotilda*)
6	10	Fortune bright queen o'th skies (s Tofts, < *Clotilda*)
7	11	Honour is a virgins treasure (s Tofts, < *Clotilda*)
8	12	Non e'bella la vittoria (s Valentini, < *Clotilda*)
9	13	Woud yu free & easy (s Lindsey, < *Clotilda*)
10	14	Still I follow still she fly's me (s Lawrence, < *Clotilda*)
11	15	Lascia di sospirar (s Nicolini, < *Clotilda*)
12	16	Rimirarvi non amarvi (s Nicolini, < *Clotilda*)
13	17	Cease to love me (s Tofts, < *Clotilda*)
14	18	Vorrei ma'non posso (s Nicolini, < *Clotilda*)
15	19	Tho sworn to despise me (s De L'Épine, < *Clotilda*)
16	20	Pria ch'il sole s'imerga nell'onda (s Valentini, < *Clotilda*)
17	21	Cease o Cupid thus to upbraid me (s Tofts, < *Clotilda*)
18	22	Let other beauties (s Tofts, < *Clotilda*)
19	23	Ditemi dolci aureto (s De L'Épine, < *Clotilda*)
20	24	Whilst distrust my souls assailing (s De L'Épine, < *Clotilda*)
21	25-26	Luccioletta fra gl'orrori (s Nicolini, < *Clotilda*)
22	27	When loves inciting and pow'r inviteing (s Lawrence, < *Clotilda*)
23	28	Man in imagination (s Lindsey, < *Clotilda*)
24	29	Compassion leave me (s Tofts, < *Clotilda*)

25	30	Soft blessing descending (s Ramondon, < *Clotilda*)
26	31-32	Gioia e'contento (s Tofts, Valentini, < *Clotilda*)
27	33	Vieni o morte a consolarmi (s De L'Épine, < *Clotilda*)
28	24	Belle fonti che correte (s Nicolini, Valentini, < *Clotilda*)
29	35-36	La gioa m'abonda di tanto nel petto (s Valentini, < *Clotilda*)
30	37	Si crudel, barbara forte (s Nicolini, < *Clotilda*)
31	38	Dye Clotilda, thy death will secure me (s Tofts, < *Clotilda*)
32	39	How sweet is love (s Lindsey, < *Clotilda*)
33	40	Non han core (s De L'Épine, < *Clotilda*)
34	41	S'armi pur amor superbo (s Nicolini, < *Clotilda*)
35	42	La forte' ed il destin (s Tofts, < *Clotilda*)
36	43	Del fallo sul camin (s Valentini, < *Clotilda*)
37	44	Let virgins ev'ry year (s De L'Épine, Valentini, < *Clotilda*)
38	45	Del piacer ch'io sento in petto (s De L'Épine, Valentini, < *Clotilda*)
39	46	Destin se vuoi (s Nicolini, < *Clotilda*)
40	47	Non dar pui pene o cara (s Nicolini, < *Clotilda*)
41	48	Prendi l'alma prend' il core (s Tofts, Nicolini, < *Clotilda*)
42	49	Cares wn they'r over (s De L'Épine, < *Clotilda*)
43	50-51	Tutto rida in si bel

Notes:
1. Between contents list and advertisement on p. [ii] is statement: 'Musick printed for and engrav'd by L. Pippard in the year. 1709'.
2. Advertisement in *Post Man* a defence by Pippard of his printing and not directly an advertisement of *Clotilda*.
3. Cfm: - p. [i].
4. Top part of title-page is from a plate first used by Walsh in 1699 for Leveridge's *A Second Book of Songs*. The plate was subsequently used by Walsh for Graves's *Collection of Songs*, 1717 (102), and for Leveridge's *A Collection of Songs*, [1728]. For reproduction of first use see Day and Murrie, fig. 38. Label obscures lower edge of plate.

Copies: Cfm MU.MS.1279; F-Pc Rés. V.S.1277.

60   deleted (see 78a).

61   deleted (see 177).

Plate 62.1   Bononcini, *Camilla*, 1709

SONGS

IN THE NEW

OPERA,

Call'd

CAMILLA

as they are perform'd at the

Theatre Royall

Sold by I. Walsh Musicall Instrument maker in Or-
=dinary to her Majesty, & P. Randall at the Harp and Ho=boy.
in Catherine Street near Sommerset House in the strand :
and I. Hare Musick Instrument maker at ý Golden Viol and Flute in
Cornhill near ý Royal Exchange .

62   Bononcini, *Camilla*, 31 December 1709

Caption: see plate 22.1. Plate 62.1. 336 x 214 mm. MiU: RBR M1505.B72T8.

[within cartouche] ⌠ Songs in the Opera of Camilla ⌡ Berchet Inventor. H
Hulsbergh Sculpsit. [at foot] London Printed for I. Walsh Servt. to Her Matie.
at the Harp and Hoboy in Katherine Street near Somerset House in the Strand.

Songs In The New Opera, Call'd ⌠ Camilla as they are perform'd at the
Theatre Royall ⌡ Sold by I. Walsh Musicall Instrument maker in Or==dinary
to her Majesty, & P. Randall at the Harp and Ho=boy, in Catherine=Street
near Sommerset House in the Strand and I. Hare Musick Instrument maker at
ye Golden Viol and Flute in Cornhill near ye Royal Exchange.

32 leaves. Pp. [i]⬚ [ii-iii] 1-4 1-38 [38A]⬚ 39-51 [52] [53]⬚.
Leaves printed on 2 sides.
Tallest copy 336 x 214 mm. Vertical chain lines.

One page engraved per plate. Engraving style Walsh 1.
Illus. title-page plate 283 x 187 mm. Passe-partout no. 2.
Title-page plate 271 x 187 mm. Passe-partout no. 3.
Contents plate 263 x 161 mm.

Contents: illus. title-page [i]; title-page [ii]; contents [iii]; overture 1-4; songs 1-38,
[38A], 39-51, [52-53].

Songs:

No.	Page	First Line
1	1	I was born of royall race (s Tofts, < *Camilla*)
2	2	O nymph of race divine (s Boy, < *Camilla*)
3	3	Since you from death thus save me (s Boy, < *Camilla*)
4	4	Love darts are in your eyes (s Ramondon, < *Camilla*)
5	5	Fortune ever known to vary (s Tofts, < *Camilla*)
6	6	Tender maids your pity show (s Baroness, < *Camilla*)
7	7	Frail are a lovers hopes (s Hughes, < *Camilla*)
8	8	Wellcome sorrow death attending (s Baroness, < *Camilla*)
9	9	All I'le venture to restore ye (s Ramondon, < *Camilla*)
10	10	See the just gods of innocence (s Tofts, < *Camilla*)
11	11	Fair Dorinda happy may'st thou ever be (s Baroness, < *Camilla*)
12	12	Charming fair for thee I languish (s Boy, < *Camilla*)
13	13	Wretched am I, that I gain him (s Tofts, < *Camilla*)
14	14	Among women they (s Lindsey, < *Camilla*)
15	15	Aged Phillis, wanton still is (s Leveridge, < *Camilla*)
16	16	I languish, I sorrow (s Leveridge, Lindsey, < *Camilla*)
17	17	Ah never yet was known (s Hughes, < *Camilla*)
18	18	Revenge I summon (s Tofts, < *Camilla*)
19	19	In vain I fly from sorrow (s Boy, < *Camilla*)
20	20	To beauty devoted (s Boy, < *Camilla*)
21	21	I love but dare not my flame discover (s Ramondon, < *Camilla*)
22	22	Now Cupid or never be kind (s Hughes, < *Camilla*)
23	23	Fortune like a wanton gipsye (s Leveridge, < *Camilla*)

24	24	Not so much cruelty, I prethee now (s Lindsey, < *Camilla*)
25	25	No love was ever known that (s Baroness, < *Camilla*)
26	26	Joys are attending those cares (s Baroness, < *Camilla*)
27	27	Around her see Cupid flying (s Hughes, < *Camilla*)
28	28	Love leads to battle, who dares oppose (s Ramondon, < *Camilla*)
29	29	Ungratefull you fly me, unkindly (s Boy, < *Camilla*)
30	30	Love and ambition strive (s Tofts, < *Camilla*)
31	31	Tullia I feell thy charms (s Leveridge, < *Camilla*)
32	32	Something is in my face so alluring (s Lindsey, < *Camilla*)
33	33	Fly and follow your idol beauty (s Baroness, < *Camilla*)
34	34	O tyrannous jealousy, fly far away (s Hughes, < *Camilla*)
35	35	Happy I love and haste to enjoy her (s Hughes, Boy, < *Camilla*)
36	36	Fly ye virgins th' unfaithfull lover (s Baroness, < *Camilla*)
37	37	These eyes are made so killing (s Lindsey, < *Camilla*)
38	38-[38A]	Thou art he my dearest creature (s Leveridge, Lindsey, < *Camilla*)
39	39	Cupid o at lenght reward me (s Boy, < *Camilla*)
40	40	Yes t'is all I want (s Boy, < *Camilla*)
41	41	Floods shall quit the ocean, The (s Hughes, < *Camilla*)
42	42	Dangers ev'ry way surround me (s Tofts, < *Camilla*)
43	43	Be cruel and be jealous (s Turner, < *Camilla*)
44	44	Angers for war declaring (s Baroness, < *Camilla*)
45	45	Tho fierce the lightning flyes (s Ramondon, < *Camilla*)
46	46	Linco's grown another creature (s Leveridge, < *Camilla*)
47	47	Cease cruell tirannizing (s Hughes, < *Camilla*)
48	48	Cease cruell to deceive me (s Baroness, < *Camilla*)
49	49	Cease cruell tirannizing (s Hughes, Baroness, < *Camilla*)
50	50	Fate the more it does depress me (s Tofts, < *Camilla*)
51	51	Let the lightening flashing flying (s Boy, < *Camilla*)
52	[52]	Chi cede al'furore di stelle (s Valentini, < *Camilla*)
53	[53]	Amo per servir, servo per sperar (s Nicolini, < *Camilla*)

Notes:
1. Songs 52 and 53 first performed in 1709 revival.
2. DLC: - p. [i].

Copies: DLC M1508 Case; *I-BGi*; MiU RBR M1505.B72T8; *S-Skma*.

Plate 63.1   Bononcini, *Camilla*, 1709

63   Bononcini, *Camilla*, 31 December 1709

Caption: plate 63.1. 349 x 222 mm. Ob: Don. c.66(2).

[within cartouche; in MS.] ⌠ Songs in the opera of Camilla ⌡ Berchet Inventor. H Hulsburgh Sculpsit. [at foot] London Printed for I. Walsh Servt. to Her Matie. at the Harp and Hoboy in Katherine Street near Somerset House in the Strand.

60 leaves. Pp. [i]◌-[ii]◌\◌1 2◌-4◌ 1◌-37◌\◌38 [38A]◌ 39◌-51◌ [52]◌-[53]◌.
Leaves printed on 1 side.
Tallest copy 349 x 222 mm. Vertical chain lines.

One page engraved per plate. Engraving style Walsh 1.
Title-page plate 295 x 202 mm. Passe-partout no. 2.

Contents: title-page [i]; contents [ii]; overture 1-4; songs 1-38, [38A], 39-51, [52-53].

Songs: see **62**.

Notes:
1. D-Hs: p. 3 (1st sequence) reversed. MS. title within cartouche, 'The opera of Camilla'.
2. Ob: pp. 1 (1st sequence) and 38 reversed.
3. TWm: pp. [52-53] inverted.

Copies: D-Hs M C/113/3; Ob Don. c.66(2); TWm —.

Plate 64.1   Heidegger, *Almahide*, 1970

Plate 64.2   Heidegger, *Almahide*, 1710

SONGS

IN THE NEW

OPERA,

Call'd

ALMAHIDE.

The SONGS done in Italian & English
as they are Perform'd at ÿ Queens Theatre.

Sold   by I:Walsh Musicall Instrument maker in Or=
=dinary to her Majesty, &P.Randall at the Harp and Ho=boy,
in Catherine=Street   near Sommerset House in the strand'.
  and I Hare Musick Instrument maker at ÿ Golden Viol and Flute in
Cornhill near ÿ Royal Exchange.

Caption: plates 64.1-64.2. 360 x 220 mm. Lbl: H.314.

[within cartouche] ʃ Songs in ye Opera call'd Almahide ♪ London Printed for & Sold by Iohn Walsh Servant to her Majesty at the Harp and Hautboy in Katherine Street near Somerset House in the Strand

Songs In The New Opera, Call'd ʃ Almahide. The Songs done in Italian & English as they are Perform'd at ye Queens Theatre. ♪ Sold by I: Walsh Musicall Instrument maker in Or==dinary to her Majesty, & P. Randall at the Harp and Ho=boy, in Catherine=Street near Sommerset House in the Strand and I. Hare Musick Instrument maker at ye Golden Viol and Flute in Cornhill near ye Royal Exchange.

71 leaves. Pp. [i]□-[iii]□\□1 2□-4□ \□1-2□\-\□7-8□\ 9□\□10 11□\□12 13□ 14□\□15 16□-18□\□19 20□\□21 22□-28□\□29 30□-32□ \□33-34□\-\□37-38□\ 39□-40□\□41 42□-49□ \□50-51□\-\□54-55□\ 56□\□57 58□\□59 60□-62□\□63 64□.
Leaves printed on 1 side.
Tallest copy 369 x 233 mm. Vertical chain lines.

One page engraved per plate. Engraving style Walsh and Cross.
Illus. title-page plate 237 x 184 mm. Passe-partout no. 5.
Title-page plate 268 x 184 mm. Passe-partout no. 3.
Contents plate 264 x 113 mm.

Walsh i: 344.
Advertised in *Tatler*, 16 February 1710.

Contents: illus. title-page [i]; title-page [ii]; contents [iii]; overture 1-4; songs 1-64.

Songs:

No.	Page	First Line
1	1-2	Il mio core non troua riposo (Full of sorrow vexation & anguish) (s De L'Épine, < *Almahide*)
2	3-4	Per te sol perduto ho bello ('Tis for thee alone dear creature) (s De L'Épine, < *Almahide*)
3	5-6	Per render m'infelice (Proud love & cruell fortune) (s Nicolini, < *Almahide*)
4	7-8	Il peggio che sà (Let fate shew it's spite) (s Nicolini, < *Almahide*)
5	9	La speranza di giore mi consola (Ah how charming is ye blessing) (s Valentini, < *Almahide*)
6	10-11	Io non voglio vendicarmi (Tho ye crime provoke my anger) (s Valentini, < *Almahide*)
7	12-13	Non hà fortuna, il pianto mio (My tears can never, make fortune kinder) (s Girardeau, < *Almahide*)
8	14	Fato imperante (Insulting destiny) (s Girardeau, < *Almahide*)
9	15-16	Non cedero sleale (Honour all baseness scorning) (s Nicolini, < *Almahide*)
10	17	Un core innamora (Who pines with amorous passion) (s Valentini, < *Almahide*)
11	18	Non dar fede a chi t'affana (Give your love to him deserves it) (s De L'Épine, < *Almahide*)

12	19-20	A me tu nieghi amor (To slight my love ingrate) (s Girardeau, < *Almahide*)
13	21-22	Come follow boys come follow me (s Doggett, < *Almahide*)
14	23	Blessa happy creature (s Lindsey, < *Almahide*)
15	24	Good buy t'ye good night t'ye (s Lindsey, Doggett, < *Almahide*)
16	25	Ombre amiche ombre quiete (Freindly shades where peace is dwelling) (s Nicolini, < *Almahide*)
17	26	Al variar di ciel crudel (Heaven itselfe may order change) (s Nicolini, < *Almahide*)
18	27	Per salvarlo a cruda sorte (From a shamefull death to ease him) (s De L'Épine, < *Almahide*)
19	28	Un atto di vittà (Act of vile deceit, An) (s Girardeau, < *Almahide*)
20	29-30	Che'affanno tiranno (s Nicolini, Valentini, < *Almahide*)
21	31	Chi vive innamorato (s Valentini, < *Almahide*)
22	32	Si che u'adoro vezzo (Yes tis most certain your eyes) (s Nicolini, < *Almahide*)
23	33-34	Il mio cor non è più mio (No my heart is mine no longer) (s Girardeau, < *Almahide*)
24	35-36	In mirar la mia fiera suentura (See heav'n morn sure ye globe is unhinging) (s Nicolini, < *Almahide*)
25	37-39	Se t'abborro e la tua morte (s Nicolini, De L'Épine, < *Almahide*)
26	40	Who so happy as the lass is (s Cross, < *Almahide*)
27	41-42	Thou horrid monster don't think to bully (s Cross, Lindsey, Doggett, < *Almahide*)
28	43	If ere I forsake thee (s Doggett, Cross, < *Almahide*)
29	44	Did ever traytor (s Lindsey, < *Almahide*)
30	45	Oh happy choice how I rejoyce (s Cross, Doggett, < *Almahide*)
31	46	Un reo più che non credi (Guilt does of peace bereave me) (s De L'Épine, < *Almahide*)
32	47	Del suo sangue in terra sparso (When his blood in streams is flowing) (s Valentini, < *Almahide*)
33	48	Mira queste mie stille (Sorrow forbids my hopeing) (s Nicolini, < *Almahide*)
34	49	Pena ria che tiranna (Cruell sorrow feirce and raging) (s Cassani, < *Almahide*)
35	50-51	Sapran ben I tuoi lumi quanto (Rage shall thy eyes be showing how) (s Valentini, < *Almahide*)
36	52-53	Al gran tonante (Joves towring eagle) (s Nicolini, < *Almahide*)
37	54-55	Di lusinghar e fingere (With female arts and flattery) (s Girardeau, < *Almahide*)
38	56	Della morte un vil rifiuto (Death my heart is still refusing) (s De L'Épine, < *Almahide*)
39	57-58	Troppo sì troppo t'ascolto (Too well, I hear the subject) (s Nicolini, < *Almahide*)
40	59-60	Sospira pena e geme (s Nicolini, De L'Épine, < *Almahide*)
41	61	La mia fiamma (Loves dazling flame) (s Valentini, < *Almahide*)
42	62	S'uccida l'ingrato (< *Almahide*)
43	63-64	Per te porte del tormento

Notes:
1. Gu: - p. [i]; pp. 2 (1st sequence) and 3 (2d sequence) reversed; p. 4 of overture misbound next to p. 4 (second sequence); blank verso of p. 3 (1st sequence) and recto of p. 1 (2d sequence) glued together.
2. NL-DHgm: - pp. 1 (2d sequence), 17, 19, 40, 43; p. 53 reversed.
3. NRU-Mus: - p. [i].

Caption: see plates 64.1-64.2.

[within cartouche] ⌠ Songs in ye Opera call'd Almahide ⌡ [at foot] London Printed for & Sold by Iohn Walsh Servant to her Majesty at the Harp and Hautboy in Katherine Street near Somerset House in the Strand

Songs In The New Opera, Call'd Almahide. The Songs done in Italian & English as they are Perform'd at ye Queens Theatre. Sold by I: Walsh Musicall Instrument maker in Or==dinary to her Majesty, & P. Randall at the Harp and Ho=boy, in Catherine=Street near Sommerset House in the Strand and I. Hare Musick Instrument maker at ye Golden Viol and Flute in Cornhill near ye Royal Exchange.

37 leaves. Pp. [i]□ [ii-iii] □1 2-4 1-63 64□.
Leaves printed on 2 sides.
Tallest copy 361 x 232 mm. Vertical chain lines.

One page engraved per plate. Engraving style Walsh and Cross.
Illus. title-page plate 237 x 184 mm. Passe-partout no. 5.
Title-page plate 268 x 184 mm. Passe-partout no. 3.
Contents plate 264 x 113 mm.

Walsh i: 344.
Advertised in *Tatler*, 16 February 1710.

Contents: illus. title-page [i]; title-page [ii]; contents and advertisement [iii]; overture 1-4; songs 1-64.

Songs: see **64**.

Notes:
1. Cfm, Ckc, DFo: verso p. 54 blank; thus pagination after p. 53: 54 55-64.
2. CtY-Mus: p. [i] reversed.
3. Mp: - p. [1].
4. Report of a copy at CaOHM is false.

Copies: Cfm MU.MS.1277; Ckc 85.5.(2.); CSt SpC MLM118; CtY-Mus Rare M1500.B719A4+; DFo M1500.B97A6 Cage; DRc Mus.D.39; *H-Bn*; ICN Cage VM1505.S28p no.2; Lcm XCV.D.15.(2.); Lgc G.Mus.61(2); Mp BR f520Am81; NIC Rare M1505 B71 A4++; NN Drexel 4809.3; *S-Skma*.

66 and 67 deleted (see 76a).

Plate 68.1   Heidegger, *Almahide*, 1710

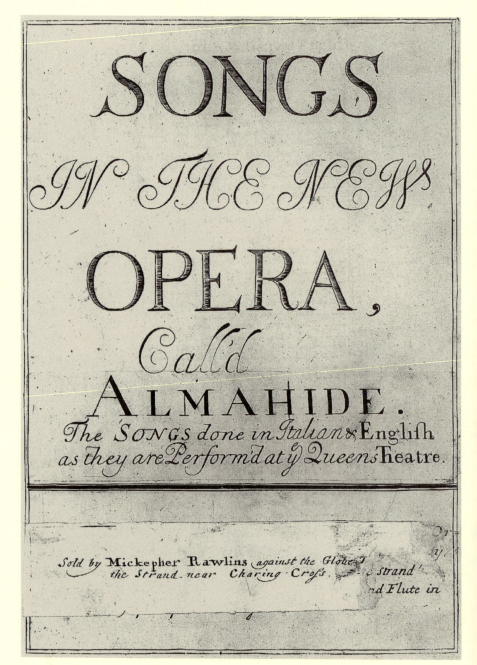

Caption: see plate 64.1. Plate 68.1. 374 x 235 mm. DLC: M1500.B7244A4
1700z Case.

[within cartouche] ⌠ Songs in ye Opera call'd Almahide ⌡ [at foot] London
Printed for & Sold by Iohn Walsh Servant to her Majesty at the Harp and
Hautboy in Katherine Street near Somerset House in the Strand

Songs In The New Opera, Call'd ⌠ Almahide. The Songs done in Italian &
English as they are Perform'd at ye Queens Theatre. ⌡ [engraved label over
Walsh, Randall and Hare imprint] Sold by Mickepher Rawlins against the
Globe T[avern] the Strand near Charing-Cross. [London.]

71 leaves. Pp. [i]□-[iii]□\□1 2□-4□ \□1-2□\-\□7-8□\ 9□\□10 11□\□12 13□ 14□\□15
16□-18□\□19 20□\□21 22□-28□\□29 30□-32□ \□33-34□\-\□37-38□\ 39□-40□\□41
42□-49□ \□50-51□\-\□54-55□\ 56□\□57 58□\□59 60□-62□\□63 64□.
Leaves printed on 1 side.
Tallest copy 374 x 235 mm. Vertical chain lines.

One page engraved per plate. Engraving style Walsh and Cross.
Illus. title-page plate passe-partout no. 5.
Title-page plate 268 x 184 mm. Passe-partout no. 3.

Contents: illus. title-page [i]; title-page [ii]; contents and advertisement [iii]; overture
1-4; songs 1-64.

Songs: see **64**.

Copy: DLC M1500.B7244A4 1700z Case.

Plate 69.1   Mancini, *Hydaspes*, 1710

Plate 69.2   Mancini, *Hydaspes*, 1710

SONGS

IN THE NEW

OPERA,

Call'd

HYDASPES,

as they are Perform'd
at the Queens Theatre.

Sold by I. Walsh Musicall Instrument maker in Or=
=dinary to her Majesty, & P. Randall at the Harp and Ho=boy.
in Catherine Street near Sommerset House in the strand
and I. Hare Musick Instrument maker at ỹ Golden Viol and Flute in
Cornhill near ỹ Royal Exchange.

Caption: plates 69.1-69.2. 367 x 224 mm. Lbl: I.282.

[within cartouche] ⌠ Songs in the Opera calld Hydaspes. ⌡ [at foot] London Printed for & Sold by Iohn Walsh Servant to her Majesty at the Harp and Hautboy in Katherine Street near Somerset House in the Strand

Songs In The New Opera, Call'd ⌠ Hydaspes, as they are Perform'd at the Queens Theatre. ⌡ Sold by I: Walsh Musicall Instrument maker in Or==dinary to her Majesty, & P. Randall at the Harp and Ho=boy, in Catherine=Street near Sommerset House in the Strand and I. Hare Musick Instrument maker at ye Golden Viol and Flute in Cornhill near ye Royal Exchange.

39 leaves. Pp. [i]◻ [ii-iii] ◻1 2-71 72◻.
Leaves printed on 2 sides.
Tallest copy 383 x 250 mm. Vertical chain lines.

One page engraved per plate. Engraving style Walsh and Cross.
Illus. title-page plate 237 x 184 mm. Passe-partout no. 5.
Title-page plate 270 x 186 mm. Passe-partout no. 3.
Contents plate 265 x 101 mm.

Walsh i: 354.
Advertised in *Post Man*, 30 May 1710.

Contents: illus. title-page [i]; title-page [ii]; contents and advertisement [iii]; overture 1-4; songs 5-72.

Songs:

No.	Page	First Line
1	5-6	Vi farà pugnando strada (s Nicolini, < *Hydaspes*)
2	7	Il timore di perder chi s'ama (s Valentini, < *Hydaspes*)
3	8-9	Lasciar d'amar chi l'ama (s Nicolini, < *Hydaspes*)
4	10-11	La gelosia di regno guerra mi moue al cor (s Valentini, < *Hydaspes*)
5	12-13	Lusinga del mio core (s Girardeau, < *Hydaspes*)
6	14	Così mi piace ch'all'ombra ancora (s Nicolini, < *Hydaspes*)
7	15	Cara si ch'ogn'or sarà (s De L'Épine, < *Hydaspes*)
8	16	In due cori un più bel foco (s Cassani, < *Hydaspes*)
9	17	Penso che non hò core (s De L'Épine, < *Hydaspes*)
10	18-19	È folle chi pretende per forza amor d'amor (s De L'Épine, < *Hydaspes*)
11	20-21	Farò che si penta d'auerti adorato (s Girardeau, < *Hydaspes*)
12	22-23	Con volto sereno già torna nel sono (s Valentini, < *Hydaspes*)
13	24-25	È uano ogni pensiero (s Nicolini, < *Hydaspes*)
14	26	Selue Ombrose io uò cercando (s De L'Épine, < *Hydaspes*)
15	27	Vieni ò sonno (s De L'Épine, < *Hydaspes*)
16	28-29	Voi bagnate ò fonti ò fiumi (s Nicolini, < *Hydaspes*)
17	30-31	Bianca man tù (s Nicolini, < *Hydaspes*)
18	32	Per punire un traditore (s Nicolini, < *Hydaspes*)
19	33	A mischiar uado le lagrime (s De L'Épine, < *Hydaspes*)

20	34-35	Non è così leggiero (s Girardeau, < *Hydaspes*)
21	36	Fammi prouar (s Valentini, < *Hydaspes*)
22	37	In felice prigioniero (s Nicolini, < *Hydaspes*)
23	38-39	Voglio morir ferita (s Nicolini, De L'Épine)
24	40-41	Empia stella nemica e rubella (s Girardeau, < *Hydaspes*)
25	42-43	Se credi ch'io non t'ami (s Girardeau, < *Hydaspes*)
26	44-45	Molto penasti ò core (s Valentini, < *Hydaspes*)
27	46-47	Torna la speme in sen mà non mi fido (s De L'Épine, < *Hydaspes*)
28	48	Vado a morir o cara (s De L'Épine, Nicolini, < *Hydaspes*)
29	49-50	Mostro crudel che fai (s Nicolini, < *Hydaspes*)
30	51-52	All'ombre alle catene (s Nicolini, < *Hydaspes*)
31	53-54	Io sento, al cor tormento (s De L'Épine, < *Hydaspes*)
32	55-56	Morà chi m'oltraggiò (s Valentini, < *Hydaspes*)
33	57-58	Vive sperando, nel petto il core (s Valentini, < *Hydaspes*)
34	59	All fiero mio tormento (s Nicolini, < *Hydaspes*)
35	60-61	Mostre dell'erebo (s Nicolini, < *Hydaspes*)
36	62-63	Ritorna già nel viso (s Girardeau, < *Hydaspes*)
37	64-65	Haura'il porto dei diletti (s Valentini, < *Hydaspes*)
38	66-69	Godrò se non m'inganna (s De L'Épine, < *Hydaspes*)
39	70-71	La costanza, del mio core (s Girardeau, Nicolini, < *Hydaspes*)
40	72	Agl amanti generosi

Notes:
1. Cfm: - pp. [i-iii].
2. Ctc, Gu, NRU-Mus: - p. [i].
3. MB: - pp. 1-3.
4. NIC: - pp. 72; p. [i] top half torn away.

Copies: BWbw —; CDp M.C.3.19; Cfm MU.MS.1282; Ckc 85.5.(1); CLU-C *fM1505.M26h; CSt SpC MLM118.(2); Ctc L.6.23; CU-MUSI M1503.M262H8 Case X; DRc Mus.D.38; Eu SpC S*17.61.(2); Gu Ca.13-y.21; ICN Case VM1505.S28p no.4; *I-Rsc*; Lbl I.282; Lcm XCV.D.15.(3.); MB **M.226.28; MiU RBR M1507.E12 v.2; Mp BR f520.Me83; NIC Lock.Pr. M1505 M26 I2++; NjP (Ex) M1503.M3H9q; NN Drexel 4809.4; NRU-Mus Vault M1500.M269I; *S-Skma*; TWm —; WaU M784.3 M312is.

Plate 70.1 *Musa et Musica*, 1710

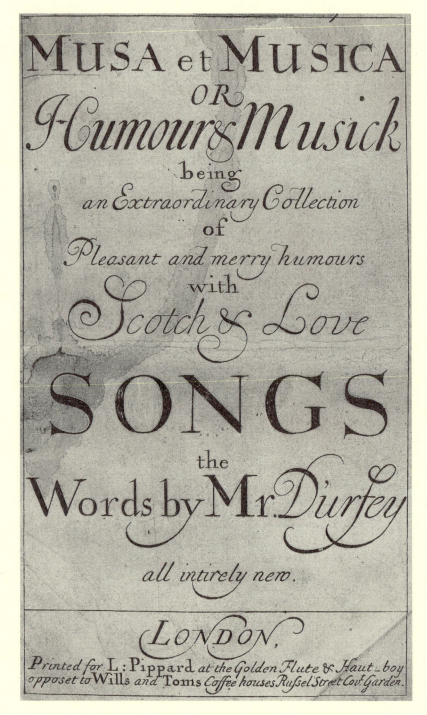

MUSA et MUSICA
OR
Humour & Musick
being
an Extraordinary Collection
of
Pleasant and merry humours
with
Scotch & Love
SONGS
the
Words by Mr. Durfey
all intirely new.

LONDON,
Printed for L: Pippard at the Golden Flute & Haut-boy
opposet to Wills and Toms Coffee houses Ruſsel Street Cov. Garden.

Plate 70.2   *Musa et Musica*, 1710

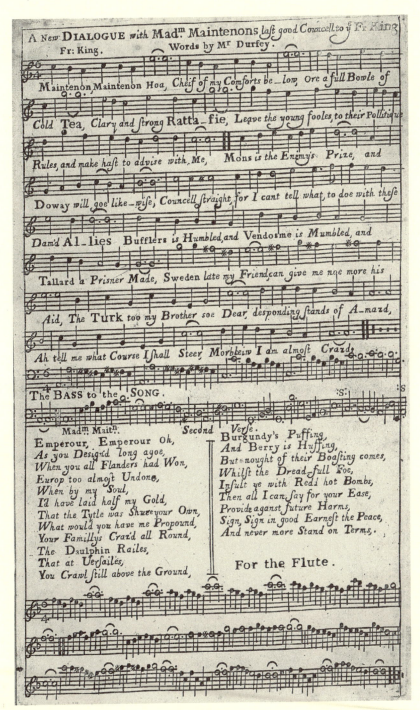

Caption: plates 70.1-70.2. 358 x 212 mm. Lbl: H.82.(1.).

Musa et Musica or Humour & Musick being an Extraordinary Collection of Pleasant and merry humours with Scotch and Love Songs the Words by Mr. D'urfey all intirely new. London, Printed for L: Pippard at the Golden Flute & Haut-boy opposet to Wills and Toms Coffee houses Russel Street Covt. Garden.

9 leaves. Pp. [i]□ [1]□-[8]□.
Leaves printed on 1 side.
Tallest copy 360 x 231 mm. Vertical chain lines.

One page engraved per plate. Engraving style Pippard.
Title-page plate 304 x 180 mm.

Walsh i: 358.
Advertised in *Post Man*, 13 June 1710.

Contents: title-page [i]; songs [1-8].

Songs:

No.	Page	First Line
1	[1]	Maintenon Hoa, cheif of my comforts below (v D'urfey)
2	[2]	Come aid me ye muses (v D'urfey)
3	[3]	Musing I late, on Windsor Tarras sate (v D'urfey, D&M 2228)
4	[4]	When smiling Flora joy prepare (v D'urfey)
5	[5]	Twanty yeares and mear (v D'urfey, D&M 3491)
6	[6]	When Phaebus dos rise (v D'urfey, D&M 3781)
7	[7]	About with the glasses
8	[8]	As tipling John (m Aldrich, v Gentleman)

Notes:
1. Lbl (H.82.(1.)): - pp. [5], [8]; + two songs, both engraved by Cross, printed on one side of one leaf each, and carrying the imprint, 'Printed for J: Cullen at ye Buck just without Temple Bar. 1710': 'Tory a Whigg & a moderate man, A' (v D'urfey, D&M 3470), 'Love the sweets of love' (m Du Ruel, D&M 2112).
2. Lbl (H.82.a.) bound with *Musa et Musica Or Humour & Musick The Second Book* (86).

Copies: Lbl H.82.(1.); Lbl H.82.a; Lsc ARC G85.0.R22.(9); SA.

Caption: see plate 72.1.

A Book Of New Songs (After the Italian manner) with Symphonies & a Through-Bass Fitted to the Harpsichord &c. All within ye Compass of the Flute, and fairly Engraven on Copper Plates, Compos'd by Mr. John Reading Organist of St. John's Hackney Educated in the Chappel-Royall under ye late Famous Dr. John Blow. Atkins scul. [at foot] London Printed for ye Author and are to be sold by him at his House in Arundel-Street in ye Strand. and by Brabazon Aylmer Bookseller at ye three Pigeons against the Royal-Exchange in Cornhill. Edward Fleetwood at the foot of ye Parliament Stairs in Westminster Hall. and at most of ye Musick Shops in town. Price Five Shillings.

27 leaves. Pp. [i]□-[ii]□ 1-4 5□ 6-9 10□ 11-18 19□ 20-23 24□ 25-28 29□ 30-43 44□. Leaves printed on 2 sides.
Tallest copy 359 x 238 mm. Vertical chain lines.

One page engraved per plate. Engraving style ?
Title-page plate 323 x 197 mm.

Price 5s.

Contents: title-page [i]; preface [ii]; songs 1-44.

Songs:

No.	Page	First Line
1	1-5	Tell my why ye cruel stars (v Person of Quality)
2	6-8	Where were the loyalty of love (v Person of Quality)
3	9-10	In lovers hearts there cannot be (v Person of Quality)
4	11-13	See whilst thou weeps't fair Cloe see (v Person of Quality)
5	14-15	Ye shady glooms, in vain you strive (v Carey)
6	16-20	Europa travel'd o'er ye main (v Person of Quality)
7	21-25	I burn with love and with desire (v Person of Quality)
8	26-30	See my Seraphina coms (v Carey)
9	31-32	Your beauties pursuing will prove my undoeing (v Person of Quality)
10	33-37	British Amphion take ye prize (v Person of Quality)
11	38-40	On a sultry summers day (v Carey)
12	41-44	Oh Phillis my freedom is gone (v Person of Quality)

Note:
1. Registered with Stationers' Company, 8 November 1710.

Copies: Ckc 110.27; Ckc Mn.18.7; CSmH 13559; *J-Tn*; Lcm I.G.20; LEp Taphouse Q784.3.R227; MiD XRMS784.R227b c.1; Ob [MS] Mus. Sch. c.191; Obh Mus. E.53; *SA*.

Plate 72.1   Reading, *Book of New Songs*, 1710

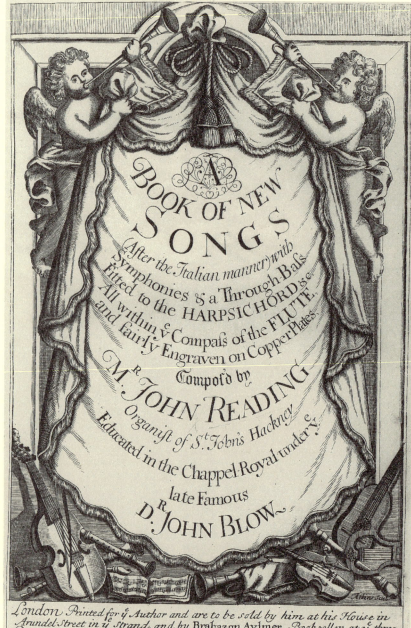

Caption: plate 72.1. 359 x 220 mm. Lbl: H.1606.

A Book Of New Songs (After the Italian manner) with Symphonies & a Through-Bass Fitted to the Harpsichord &c. All within ye Compass of the Flute, and fairly Engraven on Copper Plates, Compos'd by Mr. John Reading Organist of St. John's Hackney Educated in the Chappel-Royal under ye. late Famous Dr. John Blow. Atkins scul. [at foot] London Printed for ye Author and are to be sold by him at his House in Arundel-Street in ye Strand. and by Brabazon Aylmer Bookseller at ye three Pigeons against the Royal-Exchange in Cornhill. Edward Fleetwood at the foot of ye Parliament Stairs in Westminster Hall. and at most of ye Musick Shops in town. Price Five Shillings.

36 leaves. Pp. [i]□-[ii]□ 1□-21□ 22-23 24□ 25-28 29□ 30-43 44□.
Leaves printed on 1 side (see note 1).
Tallest copy 359 x 220 mm. Vertical chain lines.

One page engraved per plate. Engraving style ?
Title-page plate 330 x 198 mm.

Price 5s.

Contents: title-page [i]; preface [ii]; songs 1-44.

Songs: see 72.

Note:
1. Nine additional leaves, in comparison with 71, as pp. 1-4, 6-9, 11-18, 20-21 are printed on separate leaves.

Copies: Lbl H.1606; Lsc ARC G85.O.R22.

No title-page.

15 leaves. Pp. 1□-3□ 5□ 7□-12□ 14□ 17□-20□.
Leaves printed on 1 side.
Tallest copy 346 x 214 mm. Vertical chain lines.

One page engraved per plate. Engraving style Pippard.

Contents: songs: 1-3, 5, 7-12, 14, 17-20.

Songs:

No.	Page	First Line
1	1	Would you know how (m Purcell, H., D&M 4025)
2	1	Tis too late for a coach (m Purcell, H., D&M 3397)
3	2	Said Sr. John to his lady (m Brown, Robert)
4	2	Was ever mortal man so fitted
5	2	Good indeed the herb's good weed (D&M 1175)
6	3	Fy. nay prethee John (D&M 993)
7	3	Quoth Jack on a time (m Morgan, D&M 2777)
8	3	Hogshead was offer'd, A (m Reading, D&M 1383)
9	3	Whose three hoggs are these (D&M 3915)
10	5	My man John had a thing that was long (m Eccles,
11	7	Great Bacchus is mighty in giving us wine
12	8	Jack gave a kick
13	9	God preserve his majesty (m Blow, D&M 1165)
14	9	You may talk of brisk claret (D&M 4095)
15	9	Say, good master Bacchus (D&M 2853)
16	9	Aron thus propos'd to Moses
17	10	My lady's coachman John (m Purcell, H., D&M 2260)
18	10	Young John the gard'ner (m Purcell, H., D&M 4126)
19	10	Once, twice, thrice I Julia try'd (m Purcell, H., D&M 2621)
20	10	John ask'd his landlady (D&M 1877)
21	11	How shall we speak thy praise (D&M 1457)
22	11	Uds nigs! here ligs John Degs (D&M 3505)
23	11	Millers daughter riding to the fair, The (D&M 2199)
24	11	When V and I together meet (m Purcell, H., D&M 3821)
25	12	To our musical clubb (D&M 3433)
26	12	Hark! the bonny Christ-Church bells (D&M 2534)
27	12	Tom making a mantua for a lass (D&M 3458)
28	14	In drinking full bumpers (D&M 1744)
29	14	From twenty to thirty (D&M 1100)
30	14	Strange news from the Rose boys (D&M 3081)
31	14	Hark! Harry 'tis late (D&M 1251)
32	14	Peter White that never goes right (D&M 2671)
33	17	Maccedon youth, The (D&M 2147)
34	17	Taking his beer with old Anacharsis (D&M 3149)
35	17	Prithee ben't so sad and ser'ous (D&M 2759)
36	17	Tom Tory told Titus (D&M 3461)
37	18	Some write in the praise of tobacco and wine (D&M 3034)
38	18	Let the grave folks go preach (D&M 2001)
39	18	As Roger last night to Jenny lay close (D&M 234)
40	18	Once in our lives (D&M 2615)
41	19	In a cellar in s-d (D&M 1727)

42	19	Soldier take of thy wine (D&M 3020)
43	19	Sir Walter enjoying his damsel one night (D&M 2988)
44	20	Under this stone lies Gabriel John (D&M 3512)
45	20	Pale faces stand by (D&M 2656)
46	20	Had she not care enough (D&M 1220)
47	20	Confusion to the pow'r of Cupid (D&M 726)

Note:
1. Engraving style suggests Pippard probably published this collection of catches.

Copy: Lbl H.1604.

Plate 74.1   Mancini, *Hydaspes*, Additional Songs, 1711

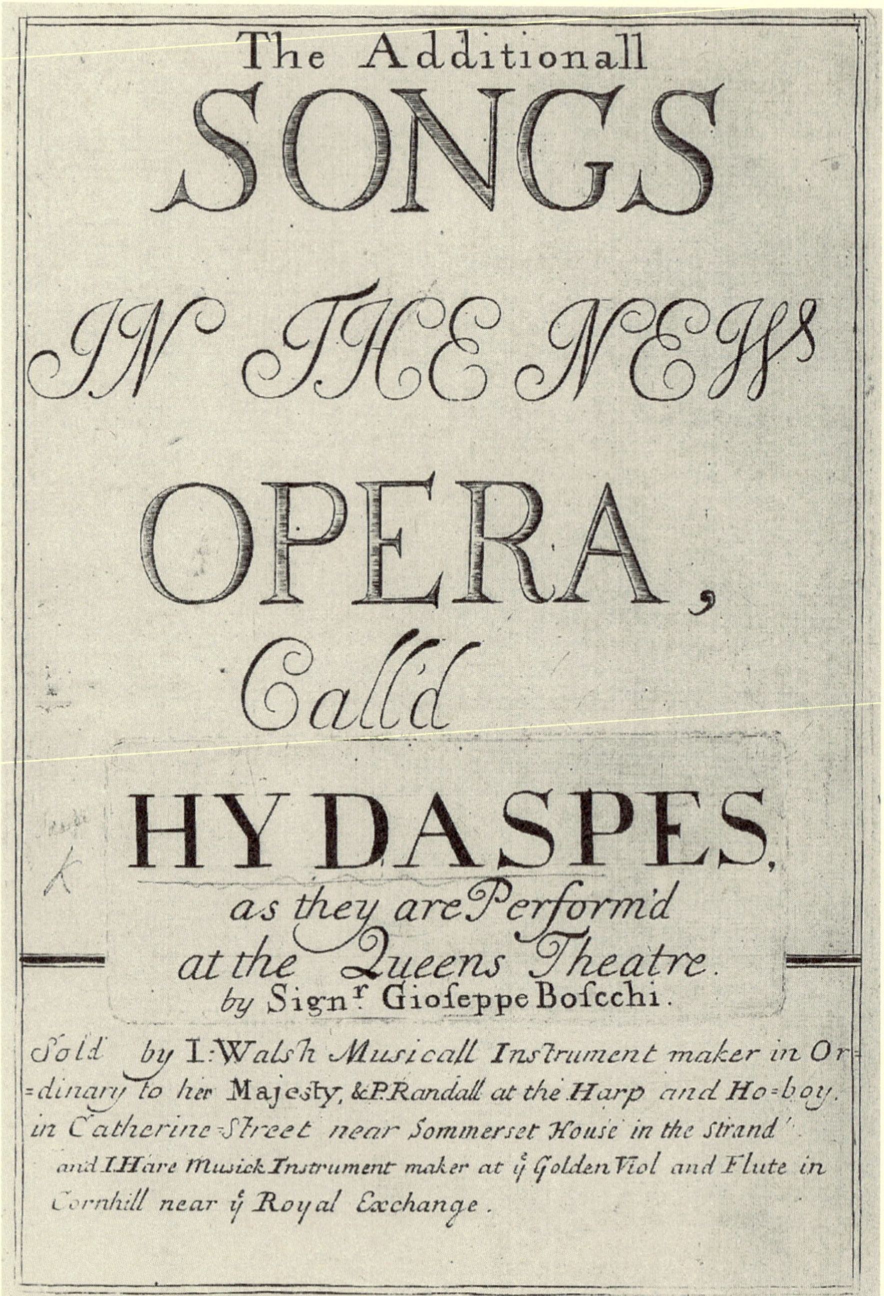

The Additionall

SONGS

IN THE NEW

OPERA,

Call'd

HYDASPES,

as they are Perform'd
at the Queens Theatre.
by Sign.r Gioseppe Boschi.

Sold by I. Walsh Musicall Instrument maker in Or=dinary to her Majesty, & P. Randall at the Harp and Ho=boy. in Catherine Street near Sommerset House in the strand and I. Hare Musick Instrument maker at ÿ Golden Viol and Flute in Cornhill near ÿ Royal Exchange.

Caption: plate 74.1. 362 x 223 mm. Lbl: H.114.(3.).

The Additionall Songs In The New Opera, call'd ⌠ Hydaspes, as they are Perform'd at the Queens Theatre. by Signr. Gioseppe Boscchi. ⌡ Sold by I: Walsh Musicall Instrument maker in Or==dinary to her Majesty, & P. Randall at the Harp and Ho=boy, in Catherine=Street near Sommerset House in the Strand and I. Hare Musick Instrument maker at ye Golden Viol and Flute in Cornhill near ye Royal Exchange.

9 leaves. Pp. [i]□ [1]□-[4]□\□[5] [6]□\□[7] [8]□.
Leaves printed on 1 side.
Tallest copy 370 x 234 mm. Vertical chain lines.

One page engraved per plate. Engraving style Walsh 1.
Title-page plate 271 x 187 mm. Passe-partout no. 3.

Walsh i: 373.
Advertised in *Daily Courant*, 27 January 1711.

Contents: title-page [i]; songs [1-8].

Songs:

No.	Page	First Line
1	[1]	Adesso e'il tempo amor (s Boschi, < *Hydaspes*)
2	[2]	Viui o cara e ti consola (s Boschi, < *Hydaspes*)
3	[3]	Crudel se mi sprezzi (s Boschi, < *Hydaspes*)
4	[4]	Vo'render sventurata (s Boschi, < *Hydaspes*)
5	[5-6]	Ho vinto, sì (s Boschi, < *Hydaspes*)
6	[7-8]	Che mi dispezza fido (s Boschi, < *Hydaspes*)

Notes:
1. Each leaf except title-page lettered in bottom right-hand corner (a-h).
2. Small title plate covers line above imprint on passe-partout title-page.
3. Boschi first performed the part of Artaxerxes in the revival on 22 November 1710.
4. Dated 1710 in Walsh i. Redating here takes Randall's partnership with Walsh and Hare into 1711.

Copies: Ckc 85.2.(1.); Lbl H.114.(3.).

74a Mancini, *Hydaspes*, 'Additional Songs', 27 January 1711

Caption: see plates 69.1, 74.1.

[within cartouche] ⌠ Songs in the Opera calld Hydaspes. ⌡ [at foot] London Printed for & Sold by Iohn Walsh Servant to her Majesty at the Harp and Hautboy in Katherine Street near Somerset House in the Strand

The Additionall Songs In The New Opera, call'd ⌠ Hydaspes, as they are Perform'd at the Queens Theatre. by Signr. Gioseppe Boscchi. ⌡ Sold by I: Walsh Musicall Instrument maker in Or==dinary to her Majesty, & P. Randall at the Harp and Ho=boy, in Catherine=Street near Sommerset House in the Strand and I. Hare Musick Instrument maker at ye Golden Viol and Flute in Cornhill near ye Royal Exchange.

39 leaves. Pp. [i]◻ [ii-iii] ◻1 2-71 72◻.
Leaves printed on 2 sides.
Tallest copy 362 x 229 mm. Vertical chain lines.

One page engraved per plate. Engraving style Walsh and Cross.
Illus. title-page plate 237 x 187 mm. Passe-partout no. 5.
Title-page plate 276 x 185 mm. Passe-partout no. 3.
Contents plate 263 x 101 mm.

Contents: illus. title-page [i]; title-page [ii]; contents and advertisement [iii]; overture 1-4; songs 5-72.

Songs: see 69.

Note:
1. Date based on use of genuine 'Additionall Songs' title-page. Compare with 80a.

Copies: DK-Kk MU 6403.1336; Lbl Hirsch II.559.

Plate 75.1   Bononcini, *Etearco*, 1711

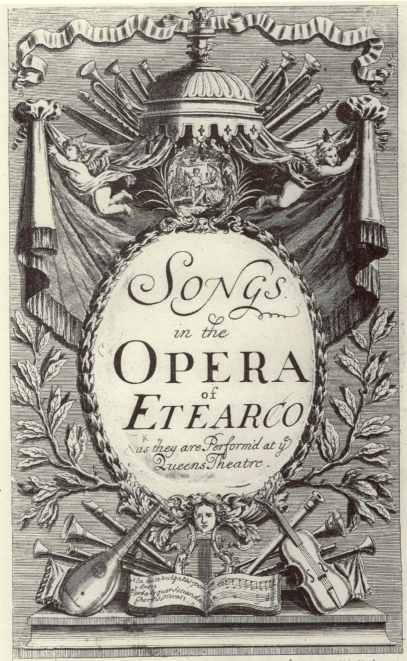

75 Bononcini, *Etearco*, 6 March 1711

Caption: plate 75.1. 366 x 227 mm. Lbl: I.354.b.

[within cartouche] ⌠ Songs in the Opera of Etearco as they are Perform'd at ye Queens Theatre. ⌡ [at foot] London Printed for J: Walsh Servant in Ordinary to her Britanick Majesty, at ye Harp & Hoboy in Katherine street, near Somerset House in ye Strand, & J: Hare at ye Viol & Flute in Cornhill near the Royall Exchange.

37 leaves. Pp. [i]◻-[ii]◻ 1-70.
Leaves printed on 2 sides.
Tallest copy 369 x 237 mm. Vertical chain lines.

One page engraved per plate. Engraving style Walsh and Cross.
Title-page plate 312 x 189 mm. Passe-partout no. 6.
Contents plate 261 x 99 mm.

Walsh i: 384.
Advertised in *Daily Courant*, 6 March 1711.

Contents: title-page [i]; contents and advertisement [ii]; overture 1-4; songs 5-70.

Songs:

No.	Page	First Line
1	5	Son figlia infelice (s Girardeau, < *Etearco*)
2	6-7	Penso di vendicarmi (s Girardeau, < *Etearco*)
3	8-10	Nume alato arcier bendato (s Nicolini, < *Etearco*)
4	11-12	Vieni ò mai dolce (s Boschi, < *Etearco*)
5	13	Io cerco à rallegrarmi (s Pilotti, < *Etearco*)
6	14	O di morte o de Mirene (s Boschi, < *Etearco*)
7	15	Doppo la notte (s Pilotti, < *Etearco*)
8	16-17	Già preparai gl'inganni (s Girardeau, < *Etearco*)
9	18-19	Dal dì che mi feri (s Nicolini, < *Etearco*)
10	20	Così m'oltraggi ingrata (s Boschi, < *Etearco*)
11	21	Alma ostinata crudele e spietata (s Boschi, < *Etearco*)
12	22	Furie terribbili (s Pilotti, < *Etearco*)
13	23-24	Sente il core acerbe (s Boschi, < *Etearco*)
14	25-26	Tormentarmi crudel (s Pilotti, < *Etearco*)
15	27-29	La mia sorte sfortunnata (s Boschi, < *Etearco*)
16	30-31	Non desio che l'idol mio (s Boschi, < *Etearco*)
17	32-33	A chi ben'ama basta il piacere (s Nicolini, < *Etearco*)
18	34-35	Io che fui Real' Donzella (s Girardeau, < *Etearco*
19	36-37	Perfida sempre altera non parlerai così (s Boschi, < *Etearco*)
20	38-39	Se mai sarà (s Pilotti, < *Etearco*)
21	40-41	O viurai bel idol mio (s Boschi, < *Etearco*)
22	42-43	Solo pietà vi chiede (s Girardeau, < *Etearco*)
23	44-45	Deh pietà di tanto ardore (s Girardeau, < *Etearco*)
24	46-47	Quella ch'adoro m'impiaga il seno (s Nicolini, < *Etearco*)
25	48-49	Empia sorte mi tradisti (s Pilotti, < *Etearco*)
26	50	Mura che mi chiudete (s Pilotti, < *Etearco*)
27	51-52	Spera non paventar (s Nicolini, Boschi)

28	53-55	Ch'io v'adori (s Nicolini, < *Etearco*)
29	56-57	La speme lusinghiera (s Girardeau, < *Etearco*)
30	58	E quando haura'mai fine il mio martiro (s Boschi, < *Etearco*)
31	59-60	Cieco amor che ben dà i lumi (s Boschi, < *Etearco*)
32	61-62	Pupille adorate con luci novelle (s Boschi, < *Etearco*)
33	63-64	Amore inganna (s Pilotti, < *Etearco*)
34	65-66	La navicella di mia speranza (s Nicolini, < *Etearco*)
35	67-68	Gode l'anima nel mirarti (s Boschi, < *Etearco*)
36	69-70	Ami pur che vuol goder

Notes:
1. Ckc and Lbl: pages are arranged [i]▯ [ii] 1-69 70▯.
2. En: - p. [i].
3. NRU-Mus: + final advertisement leaf.

Copies: Ckc 42.7.(1.); CSfst de Bellis 834; DLC M1506.B66E88 Case; En Inglis 200.(8.); *H-Bn*; ICN Case VM1505.S28p no.5; Lbl I.354.b; Lcm XCV.D.15; Lgc G.Mus.65; *MBHM*; NN Mus.Res. *MN p.v.8; NRU-Mus Vault M1500.E83; *PSt*; *S-Skma*; *TWm*.

Caption: see plate 75.1.

[within cartouche] ⌠ Songs in the Opera of Etearco as they are Perform'd at ye Queens Theatre. ⌡ [at foot] London Printed for J: Walsh Servant in Ordinary to her Britanick Majesty, at ye Harp & Hoboy in Katherine street, near Somerset House in ye Strand, & J: Hare at ye Viol & Flute in Cornhill near the Royall Exchange.

70 leaves. Pp. [i]□-[ii]□\□1-2□\□3-4□ 5□\ □6-7□\□8-9□\□11-12□ 13□-15□\□16-17□\ \□18-19□ 20□-22□ \□23-24□\-\□27-28□ 29□ \□30-31□\-\□48-49□\ 50□\□51- 52□\□53-54□ 55□\□56 57□-58□ \□59-60□\-\□69-70□\.
Leaves printed on 1 side.
Tallest copy 361 x 227 mm. Vertical chain lines.

One page engraved per plate. Engraving style Walsh and Cross.
Title-page plate 318 x 191 mm. Passe-partout no. 6.
Contents plate 263 x 101 mm.

Walsh i: 384.
Advertised in *Daily Courant*, 6 March 1711.

Contents: title-page [i]; contents and advertisement [ii]; overture 1-4; songs 5-9, 11-70.

Songs: see 75.

Note:
1. Wanting p. 10, supplied in photocopy.

Copy: CaOLU MZ.532.

Plate 76.1   Leveridge, *New Book of Songs*, 1711

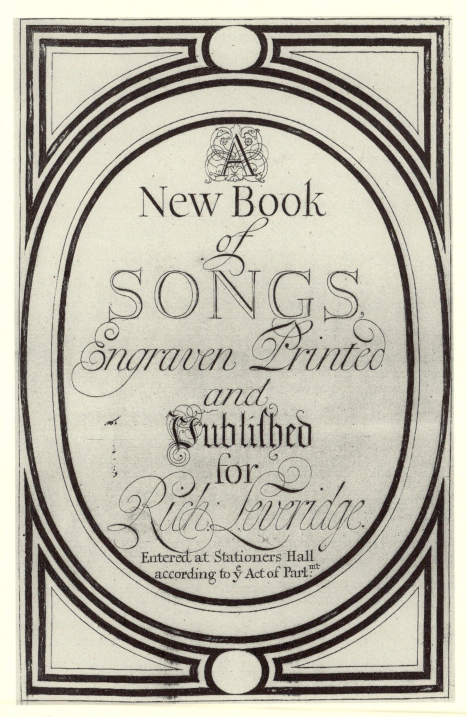

A

New Book

of

SONGS,

Engraven Printed

and

Published

for

Rich. Leveridge.

Entered at Stationers Hall
according to y͏ͤ Act of Parl.ͫᵗ

Caption: plate 76.1. 354 x 214 mm. Lbl: H.82.(2.).

[within cartouche] A New Book of Songs, Engraven Printed and Published for Rich. Leveridge. Entered at Stationers Hall according to ye Act of Parlmt:

10 leaves. Pp. [i]▢ [1]▢-[9]▢.
Leaves printed on 1 side.
Tallest copy 354 x 214 mm. Vertical chain lines.

One page engraved per plate. Engraving style ?
Title-page plate 314 x 179 mm.

Contents: title-page [i]; songs [1-9].

Songs:

No.	Page	First Line
1	[1]	Noble, generous, great, & good (v *Spectator*, no. 208, 29 October 1711)
2	[2]	Young Cupid one day wiley
3	[3]	Tis not your wealth my dear
4	[4]	Come charge your empty glasses
5	[5]	Let ye waiter bring clean glasses
6	[6]	Luff, thus, no near, that hatefull sound
7	[7-9]	Mighty love be still victorious

Notes:
1. Registered with the Stationers' Company, 29 November 1711.
2. Obh (Mus. E.28): p. [9] duplicated.
3. Copy reported at DLC actually comprises loose leaves from several Leveridge volumes.

Copies: ALb 789.99+780.3; Lbl H.41; Lbl H.82.(2.); Lcm I.G.48; Obh Mus. E.28; Obh Mus. E.29; SA.

The Additionall

SONGS

IN THE NEW

OPERA,

Call'd

ALMAHIDE

as they are Perform'd at the
Queen's Theatre.

Sold by I: Walsh Musicall Instrument maker in Or=
=dinary to her Majesty, & P. Randall at the Harp and Ho=boy.
in Catherine=Street near Sommerset House in the strand.
and I. Hare Musick Instrument maker at ÿ Golden Viol and Flute in
Cornhill near ÿ Royal Exchange.

Caption: see plate 64.1. Plate 76a.1. 337 x 230 mm. En: Inglis 173(3).

[within cartouche] ⌈ Songs in ye Opera call'd Almahide ⌡ [at foot] London Printed for & Sold by Iohn Walsh Servant to her Majesty at the Harp and Hautboy in Katherine Street near Somerset House in the Strand

The Additionall Songs In The New Opera, Call'd ⌈ Almahide as they are Perform'd at the Queen's Theatre. ⌡ Sold by I: Walsh Musicall Instrument maker in Or==dinary to her Majesty, & P. Randall at the Harp and Ho=boy, in Catherine=Street near Sommerset House in the Strand and I. Hare Musick Instrument maker at ye Golden Viol and Flute in Cornhill near ye Royal Exchange.

37 leaves. Pp. [i]☐ [ii-iii] ☐1 2-4 1-63 64☐.
Leaves printed on 2 sides.
Tallest copy 371 x 233 mm. Vertical chain lines.

One page engraved per plate. Engraving style Walsh and Cross.
Illus. title-page plate 236 x 186 mm. Passe-partout no. 5.
Title-page plate 269 x 185 mm. Passe-partout no. 3.
Contents plate 264 x 115 mm.

Contents: illus. title-page [i]; title-page [ii]; contents and advertisement [iii]; overture 1-4; songs 1-64.

Songs: see **64**.

Note:
1. DLC: 'The Additionall' faintly visible at top of title-page.

Copies: DLC M1500.B7244A4 1700zb Case; En Inglis 173(3); TWm —.

Plate 77.1   Heidegger, *Almahide*, 'Additional Songs', 1711

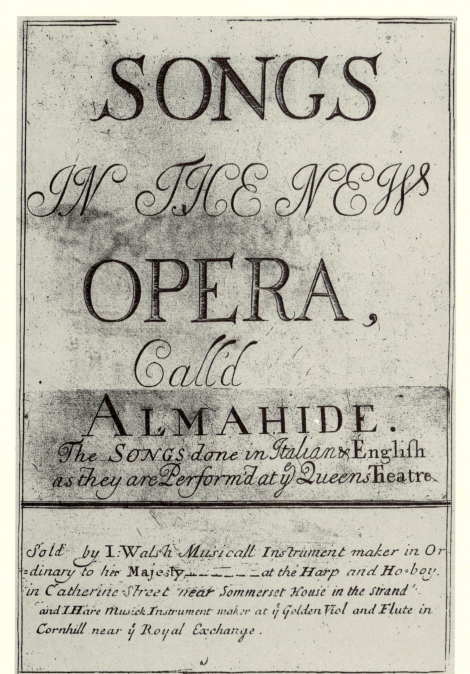

Caption: see plate 64.1. Plate 77.1. 356 x 220 mm. MB: **M.Cab.1.22.

[within cartouche] ⌠ Songs in ye Opera call'd Almahide ⌡ [at foot] London Printed for & Sold by Iohn Walsh Servant to her Majesty at the Harp and Hautboy in Katherine Street near Somerset House in the Strand

The Additionall Songs In The New Opera, Call'd ⌠ Almahide. The Songs done in Italian & English as they are Perform'd at ye Queens Theatre. ⌡ Sold by I: Walsh Musicall Instrument maker in Or==dinary to her Majesty------at the Harp and Ho=boy, in Catherine-Street near Sommerset House in the Strand and I. Hare Musick Instrument maker at ye Golden Viol and Flute in Cornhill near ye Royal Exchange.

38 leaves. Pp. [i]□-[iii]□\□1 2-4 1-63 64□.
Leaves printed on 2 sides.
Tallest copy 356 x 220 mm. Vertical chain lines.

One page engraved per plate. Engraving style Walsh and Cross.
Illus. title-page plate passe-partout no. 5.
Title-page plate 269 x 185 mm. Passe-partout no. 3.

Contents: illus. title-page [i]; title-page [ii]; contents and advertisement [iii]; overture 1-4; songs 1-64.

Songs: see **64**.

Note:
1. 'The Additionall' unprinted at top of title-page.

Copy: MB **M.Cab.1.22.

Plate 78.1   Heidegger, *Almahide*, 'Additional Songs', 1711

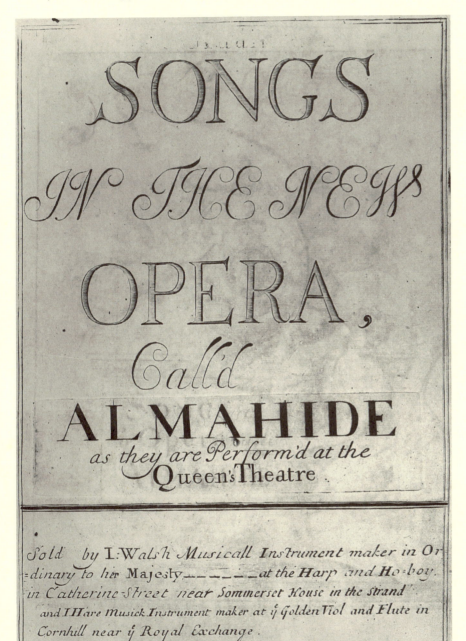

Caption: see plate 64.1. Plate 78.1. 375 x 239 mm. Obh: Mus. D.1.

[within cartouche] ⌠ Songs in ye Opera call'd Almahide ⌡ [at foot] London Printed for & Sold by Iohn Walsh Servant to her Majesty at the Harp and Hautboy in Katherine Street near Somerset House in the Strand

The Additionall Songs In The New Opera, Call'd ⌠ Almahide as they are Perform'd at the Queen's Theatre. ⌡ Sold by I: Walsh Musicall Instrument maker in Or==dinary to her Majesty------at the Harp and Ho=boy, in Catherine-Street near Sommerset House in the Strand and I. Hare Musick Instrument maker at ye Golden Viol and Flute in Cornhill near ye Royal Exchange.

38 leaves. Pp. [i]▯-[iii]▯\▯1 2-4 1-63 64▯.
Leaves printed on 2 sides.
Tallest copy 375 x 239 mm. Vertical chain lines.

One page engraved per plate. Engraving style Walsh and Cross.
Illus. title-page plate passe-partout no. 5.
Title-page plate 269 x 185 mm. Passe-partout no. 3.

Contents: illus. title-page [i]; title-page [ii]; contents and advertisement [iii]; overture 1-4; songs 1-64.

Songs: see **64**.

Note:
1. 'The Additionall' unprinted at top of title-page.

Copy: Obh Mus. D.1.

SONGS

IN THE NEW

OPERA,

Call'd

ARSINOE QUEEN *of* CYPRUS

Compos'd *by* Mr Tho. Clayton

Sold by I. Walsh Musicall Instrument maker in Or=
=dinary to her Majesty, & P. Randall at the Harp and Ho=boy,
in Catherine-Street near Sommerset House in the strand
and I. Hare Musick Instrument maker at ẏ Golden Viol and Flute in
Cornhill near ẏ Royal Exchange.

Caption: plates 78a.1-78a.2. 340 x 225 mm. DFo: M1503.C38A7 Cage.

[within cartouche] ⌠ Songs in the Opera Call'd Arsinoe Queen of Cyprus ⌡ I: Collins. sculp [at foot] London Printed for & Sould by I: Walsh Musicall Instrument maker in Ordinary to her Majesty at the Golden Harp & Ho=boy in Catherine=street near Summerset=house in ye strand and I: Hare at the Viol and Flute in Cornhill nere the Royall Exchange.

The Additionall Songs In The New Opera, Call'd ⌠ Arsino'e Queen of Cyprus Compos'd by Mr. Tho: Clayton ⌡ Sold by I: Walsh Musicall Instrument maker in Or==dinary to her Majesty, & P. Randall at the Harp and Ho=boy, in Catherine=Street near Sommerset House in the Strand and I. Hare Musick Instrument maker at ye Golden Viol and Flute in Cornhill near ye Royal Exchange.

28 leaves. Pp. [i]▯ [ii-iii] ▯1 2-7 8▯\▯9 10-49.
Leaves printed on 2 sides.
Tallest copy 346 x 234 mm. Vertical chain lines.   •

One page engraved per plate. Engraving style Walsh 1.
Illus. title-page plate 253 x 192 mm. Passe-partout no. 1.
Title-page plate 270 x 182 mm. Passe-partout no. 3.
Contents plate 205 x 145 mm.

Contents: illus. title-page [i]; title-page [ii]; contents [iii]; overture 1-2; songs 3-49.

Songs: see **26**.

Note:
1. 'The Additionall' faintly visible at head of title-page.

Copies: DFo M1503.C38A7 Cage; DRc Mus. D.40.

Caption: see plates 26.1, 78a.1.

[within cartouche] ⌠ Songs in the Opera Call'd Arsinoe Queen of Cyprus ⌡ I:
Collins. sculp [at foot] London Printed for & Sould by I: Walsh Musicall
Instrument maker in Ordinary to her Majesty at the Golden Harp & Ho=boy
in Catherine=street near Summerset=house in ye strand

The Additionall Songs In The New Opera, Call'd ⌠ Arsino'e Queen of Cyprus
Compos'd by Mr. Tho: Clayton ⌡ Sold by I: Walsh Musicall Instrument maker
in Or==dinary to her Majesty, & P. Randall at the Harp and Ho=boy, in
Catherine=Street near Sommerset House in the Strand and I. Hare Musick
Instrument maker at ye Golden Viol and Flute in Cornhill near ye Royal
Exchange.

52 leaves. Pp. [i]□-[iii]□ 1□-49□.
Leaves printed on 1 side.
Tallest copy 341 x 222 mm. Vertical chain lines.

One page engraved per plate. Engraving style Walsh 1.   .
Illus. title-page plate 255 x 195 mm. Passe-partout no. 1.
Title-page plate 272 x 188 mm. Passe-partout no. 3.
Contents plate 205 x 149 mm.

Contents: illus. title-page [i]; title-page [ii]; contents [iii]; overture 1-2; songs 3-49.

Songs: see **26**.

Note:
1. 'The Additionall' faintly visible at head of title-page.

Copy: TxDN M1500.C58A7.

Plate 79.1   Bononcini, *Camilla*, 'Additional Songs', 1711

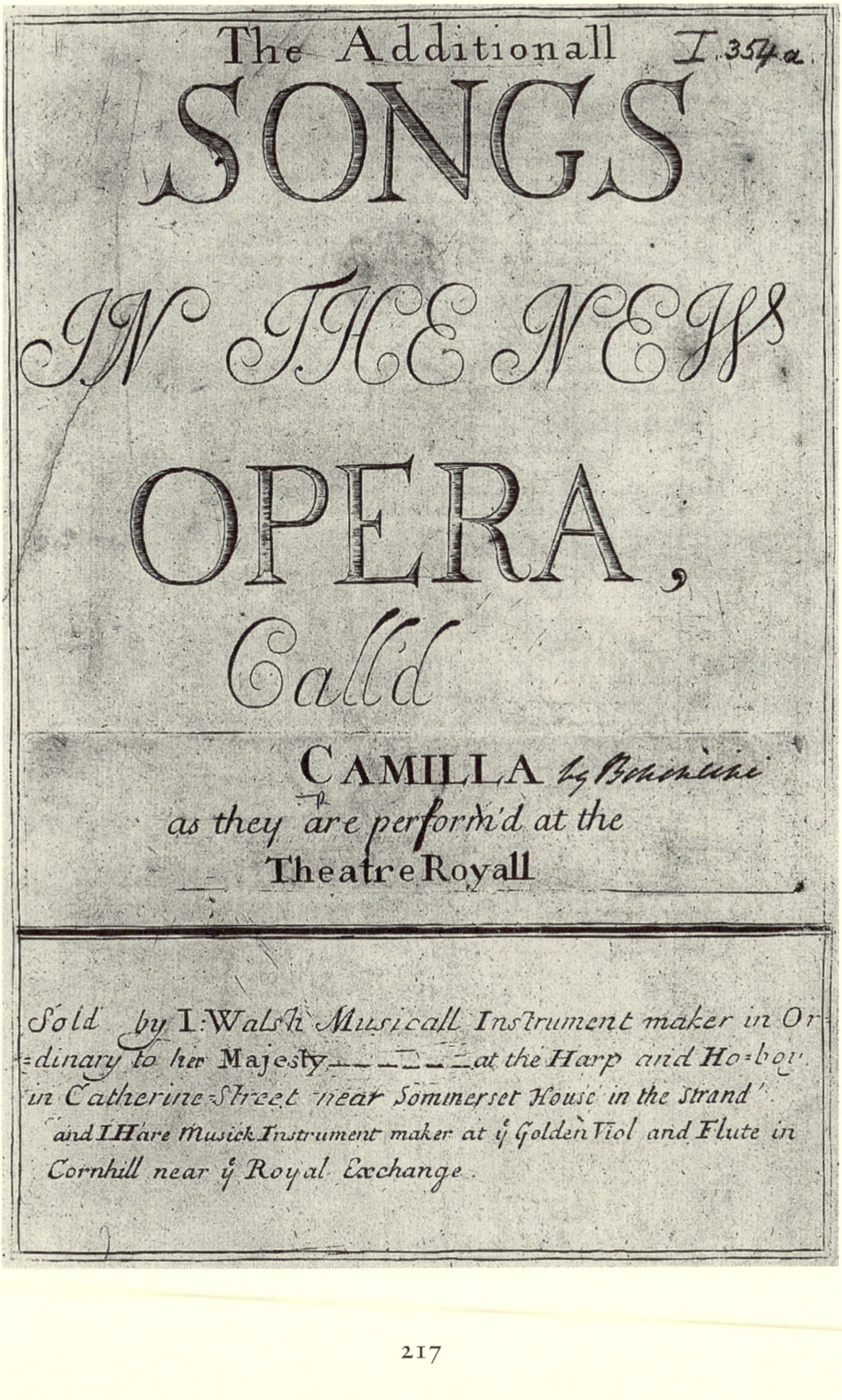

The Additionall   *I.354 a*

SONGS

IN THE NEW

OPERA,

Call'd

CAMILLA *by Bononcini*

as they are perform'd at the

Theatre Royall

Sold   by I: Walsh *Musicall Instrument maker in Or =dinary to her Majesty _ _ _ _ _ at the Harp and Ho=boy in Catherine Street near Sommerset House in the Strand and* I Hare *Musick Instrument maker at y Golden Viol and Flute in Cornhill near y Royal Exchange.*

79   Bononcini, *Camilla*, 'Additional Songs', 31 December 1711

Caption: see plate 63.1. Plate 79.1. 362 x 225 mm. Lbl: I.354.a.

[within cartouche; in MS.] ⌠ Songs in the opera of Camilla ⌡ Berchet Inventor. H Hulsbergh Sculpsit. [at foot] London Printed for I. Walsh Servt. to Her Matie. at the Harp and Hoboy in Katherine Street near Somerset House in the Strand

The Additionall Songs In The New Opera, Call'd ⌠ Camilla as they are perform'd at the Theatre Royall ⌡ Sold by I: Walsh Musicall Instrument maker in Or==dinary to her Majesty------at the Harp and Ho=boy, in Catherine-Street near Sommerset House in the Strand and I. Hare Musick Instrument maker at ye Golden Viol and Flute in Cornhill near ye Royal Exchange.

61 leaves. Pp. [i]□-[iii]□\□1 2□\□3 4□ 1□-36□ 37□\□38 [38A]□ 39□-51□ [52]□-[53]□. Leaves printed on 1 side.
Tallest copy 362 x 225 mm. Vertical chain lines.

One page engraved per plate. Engraving style Walsh 1.
Illus. title-page plate 292 x 197 mm. Passe-partout no. 2.
Title-page plate 270 x 185 mm. Passe-partout no. 3.
Contents plate 254 x 163 mm.

Walsh i: 402.

Contents: illus. title-page [i]; title-page [ii]; contents [iii]; overture 1-4; songs 1-38, [38A], 39-51, [52-53].

Songs: see 62.

Notes:
1. Lbl: - p. [1]. Pp. 1, 3 of overture reversed (1-4).
2. Copy listed in *RISM* at Ob does not exist.

Copies: ICU Rare M1508.C2; Lbl I.354.a.

SONGS
IN THE NEW
OPERA,
Call'd
CAMILLA
as they are perform'd at the
Theatre Royall

Sold   by I. Walsh Musicall Instrument maker in Or-
=dinary to her Majesty, & P. Randall at the Harp and Ho=boy.
in Catherine-Street near Sommerset House in the strand
and I. Hare Musick Instrument maker at y Golden Viol and Flute in
Cornhill near y Royal Exchange

Caption: see plate 22.1. Plate 79a.1. 343 x 220 mm. IU: xq784.2.B64c.

[within cartouche] ⌠ Songs in the Opera of Camilla ⌡ Berchet Inventor. H Hulsbergh Sculpsit. [at foot] London Printed for I. Walsh Servt. to Her Matie. at the Harp and Hoboy in Katherine Street near Somerset House in the Strand.

The Additionall Songs In The New Opera, Call'd ⌠ Camilla as they are perform'd at the Theatre Royall ⌡ Sold by I. Walsh Musicall Instrument maker in Or==dinary to her Majesty, & P. Randall at the Harp and Ho=boy, in Catherine=Street near Sommerset House in the Strand and I. Hare Musick Instrument maker at ye Golden Viol and Flute in Cornhill near ye Royal Exchange.

31 leaves. Pp. [i]□ [ii-iii] 1-4 1-38 [38A] 39-51 [52-53].
Leaves printed on 2 sides.
Tallest copy 362 x 230 mm. Vertical chain lines.

One page engraved per plate. Engraving style Walsh 1.
Illus. title-page plate 291 x 198 mm. Passe-partout no. 2.
Title-page plate 270 x 185 mm. Passe-partout no. 3.
Contents plate 250 x 162 mm.

Contents: illus. title-page [i]; title-page [ii]; contents [iii]; overture [1-4]; songs 1-38, [38A], 39-51, [52-53].

Songs: see **62**.

Notes:
1. CSt, ICN, IU: 'The Additionall' unprinted at top of title-page.
2. CU-MUSI: 'The Additionall' faintly visible at top of title-page.

Copies: CSt SpC MLM119; CU-MUSI M1505.B65T7 Case X; ICN VM1505.C62a no.2; IU xq784.2B64c.

Caption: see plate 53.1. Photograph of title-page unavailable.

[within cartouche] ⌠ Songs in the Opera Call'd Clotilda ⌡ [at foot] London Printed for & Sold by Iohn Walsh Servant to her Majesty at the Harp and Hautboy in Katherine Street near Somerset House in the Strand

The Additionall Songs In The New Opera, Call'd ⌠ Clotilda The Songs done in Italian and English as they are Perform'd at ye Queens Theatre The whole Carefully Corected ⌡ Sold by I: Walsh Musicall Instrument maker in Or==dinary to her Majesty, & P. Randall at the Harp and Ho=boy, in Catherine=Street near Sommerset House in the Strand and I. Hare Musick Instrument maker at ye Golden Viol and Flute in Cornhill near ye Royal Exchange.

31 leaves. Pp. [i]⧠ [ii-iii] ⧠1 2-4 0-52.
Leaves printed on 2 sides.
Tallest copy 359 x 227 mm. Vertical chain lines.

One page engraved per plate. Engraving style Walsh 1.
Illus. title-page plate passe-partout no. 5.
Title-page plate passe-partout no. 3.

Contents: illus. title-page [i]; title-page [ii]; contents and advertisement [iii]; overture 1-4; songs 0-52.

Songs: see 53.

Copy: TWm —.

Plate 80.1   Mancini, *Hydaspes*, 'Additional Songs', 1711

Plate 80.2   Mancini, *Hydaspes*, 'Additional Songs', 1711

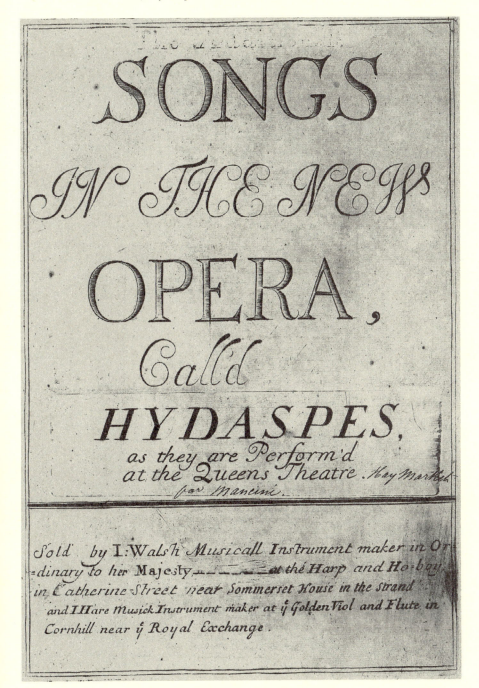

Caption: plates 80.1-80.2. 340 x 220 mm. F-Pc: Rés. V.S.1278.

[within cartouche; in MS.] (Songs in the Opera call'd Hydaspes.) [at foot] London Printed for & Sold by Iohn Walsh Servant to her Majesty at the Harp and Hautboy in Katherine Street near Somerset House in the Strand

The Additionall Songs In The New Opera, Call'd (Hydaspes, as they are Perform'd at the Queens Theatre.) Sold by I: Walsh Musicall Instrument maker in Or==dinary to her Majesty------at the Harp and Ho=boy, in Catherine=Street near Sommerset House in the Strand and I: Hare Musick Instrument maker at ye Golden Viol and Flute in Cornhill near ye Royal Exchange.

39 leaves. Pp. [i]□ [ii-iii] □1 2-71 72□.
Leaves printed on 2 sides.
Tallest copy 342 x 225 mm. Vertical chain lines.

One page engraved per plate. Engraving style Walsh and Cross.
Illus. title-page plate 239 x 188 mm. Passe-partout no. 5.
Title-page plate 272 x 188 mm. Passe-partout no. 3.
Contents plate 266 x 101 mm.

Contents: illus. title-page [i]; title-page [ii]; contents and advertisement [iii]; overture 1-4; songs 5-72.

Songs: see **69**.

Notes:
1. 'The Additionall' faintly visible at top of p. [ii].
2. CSfst: p. [iii] on own leaf; 40 leaves, pp. [i]□-[iii]□ etc.
3. En: - p. [i].

Copies: CSfst de Bellis 851; En Inglis 173; F-Pc Rés. V.S.1278; Mp BR f520.Me83a.

Caption: see plate 69.1. Photograph of title-page unavailable.

[within cartouche] (Songs in the Opera calld Hydaspes. ♪ [at foot] London Printed for & Sold by Iohn Walsh Servant to her Majesty at the Harp and Hautboy in Katherine Street near Somerset House in the Strand

The Additionall Songs In The New Opera, Call'd (Hydaspes, as they are Perform'd at the Queens Theatre. ♪ Sold by I: Walsh Musicall Instrument maker in Or==dinary to her Majesty, & P. Randall at the Harp and Ho=boy, in Catherine=Street near Sommerset House in the Strand and I. Hare Musick Instrument maker at ye Golden Viol and Flute in Cornhill near ye Royal Exchange.

39 leaves. Pp. [i]☐ [ii-iii] ☐1 2-71 72☐.
Leaves printed on 2 sides.
Tallest copy 368 x 233 mm. Vertical chain lines.

One page engraved per plate. Engraving style Walsh and Cross.
Illus. title-page plate 235 x 184 mm. Passe-partout no. 5.
Title-page plate 268 x 184 mm. Passe-partout no. 3.
Contents plate 263 x 100 mm.

Contents: illus. title-page [i]; title-page [ii]; contents and advertisement [iii]; overture 1-4; songs 5-72.

Songs: see 69.

Notes:
1. CaOLU: 'The Additionall' unprinted at top of title-page.
2. TWm: pp. 41, 44, 70 printed on one side only (40 leaves).

Copies: CaOLU MZ.528; *Obh*; TWm —.

Plate 81.1   Clayton, *Rosamond*, 1711

W: Sykes Junior Inventor.   H: Hulsbergh Fecit.

SONGS
in the New OPERA called
ROSAMOND
Compos'd by
M.ᵣ Tho: Clayton

London: Printed for I. Walsh Serv.ᵗ to Her Ma.ᵗ⁵ at the Harp and Hoboy in Catherine Street near Somerset house in ÿ Strand and I. Hare Instrument maker at the Golden Viol and Flute in Cornhill near the Royal Exchange.

Plate 81.2   Clayton, *Rosamond*, 1711

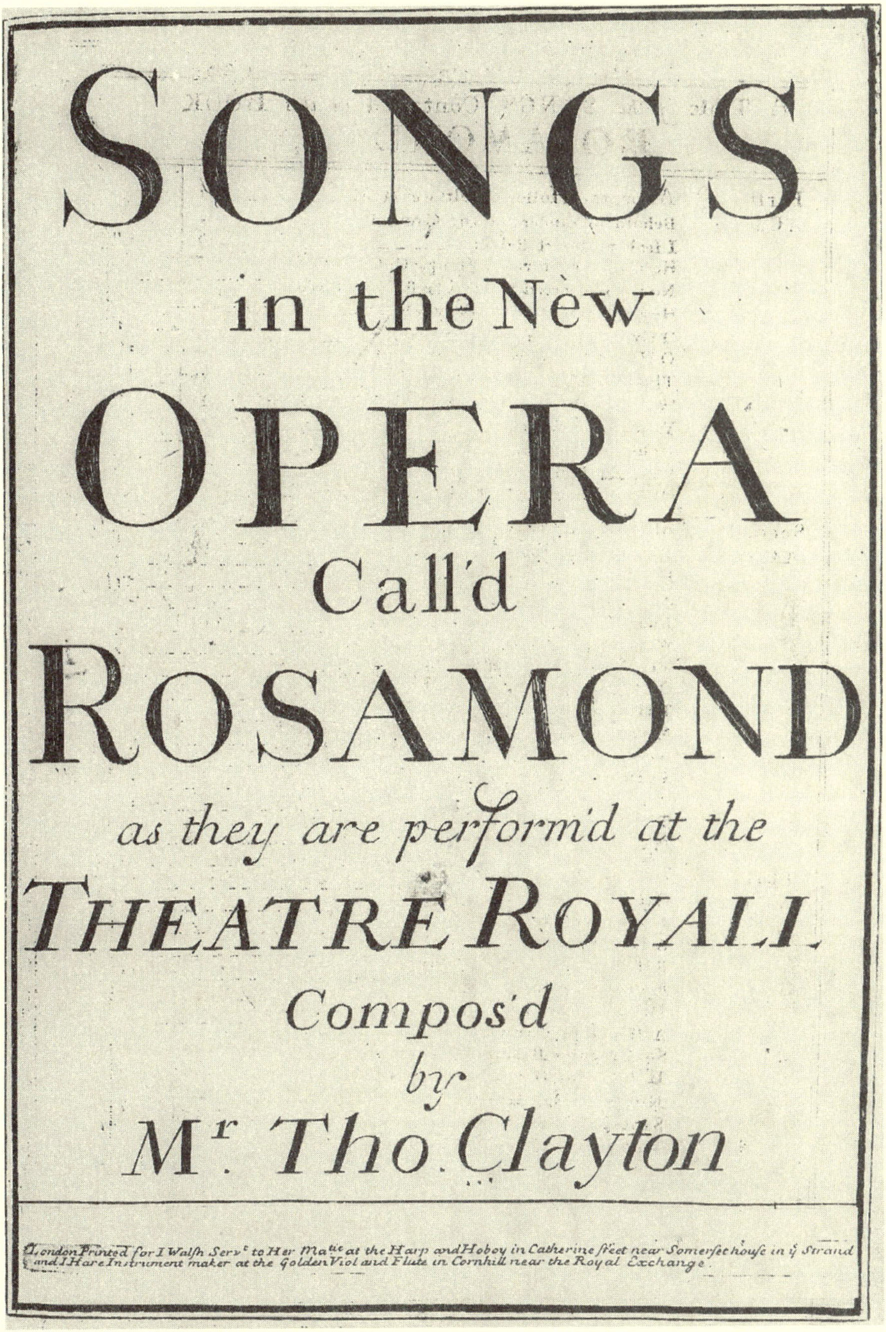

SONGS
in the New
OPERA
Call'd
ROSAMOND
as they are perform'd at the
THEATRE ROYALL
Compos'd
by
Mr Tho. Clayton

London Printed for I Walsh Servt to Her Matie at the Harp and Hoboy in Catherine Street near Somerset house in ye Strand and I Hare Instrument maker at the Golden Viol and Flute in Cornhill near the Royal Exchange

Caption: plates 81.1-81.2. 345 x 222 mm. ICN: VM1505.C62a no.5.

W: Sykes Iunior Inventor. H: Hulsbergh Fecit. [within cartouche] Songs in the New Opera Called Rosamond Compos'd by Mr. Tho: Clayton [engraved label over imprint] London Printed for I Walsh Servt to Her Matie. at the Harp and Hoboy in Catherine street near Somerset house in ye Strand, and I Hare Instrument maker at the Golden Viol and Flute in Cornhill near the Royal Exchange.

Songs In The New Opera Call'd Rosamond as they are perform'd at the Theatre Royall Compos'd by Mr. Tho. Clayton [engraved label over Walsh and Randall imprint] London printed for I Walsh Servt to Her Matie. at the Harp and Hoboy in Catherine street near Somerset house in ye Strand, and I Hare Instrument maker at the Golden Viol and Flute in Cornhill near the Royal Exchange.

49 leaves. Pp. [i]□ [ii-iii] 1□-20□ [21]□ 22□-23□ [24]□ 25□-47□.
Leaves printed on 1 side.
Tallest copy 346 x 219 mm. Mixed chain lines.

One page engraved per plate. Engraving style Walsh 1, 3.
Illus. title-page plate ? x 193 mm. (See note 1.)
Title-page plate 264 x 186 mm.

Contents: illus title-page [i]; title-page [ii]; contents [iii]; overture 1-2; songs 3-20, [21], 22-23, [24], 25-47.

Songs: see 38.

Notes:
1. Label obscures lower edge of plate.
2. ICN: pp. 3-18 unpaginated.

Copies: ICN VM1505.C62a no.5; NN Drexel 4854.2.

Plate 82.1   Pepusch, *Thomyris*, 1711

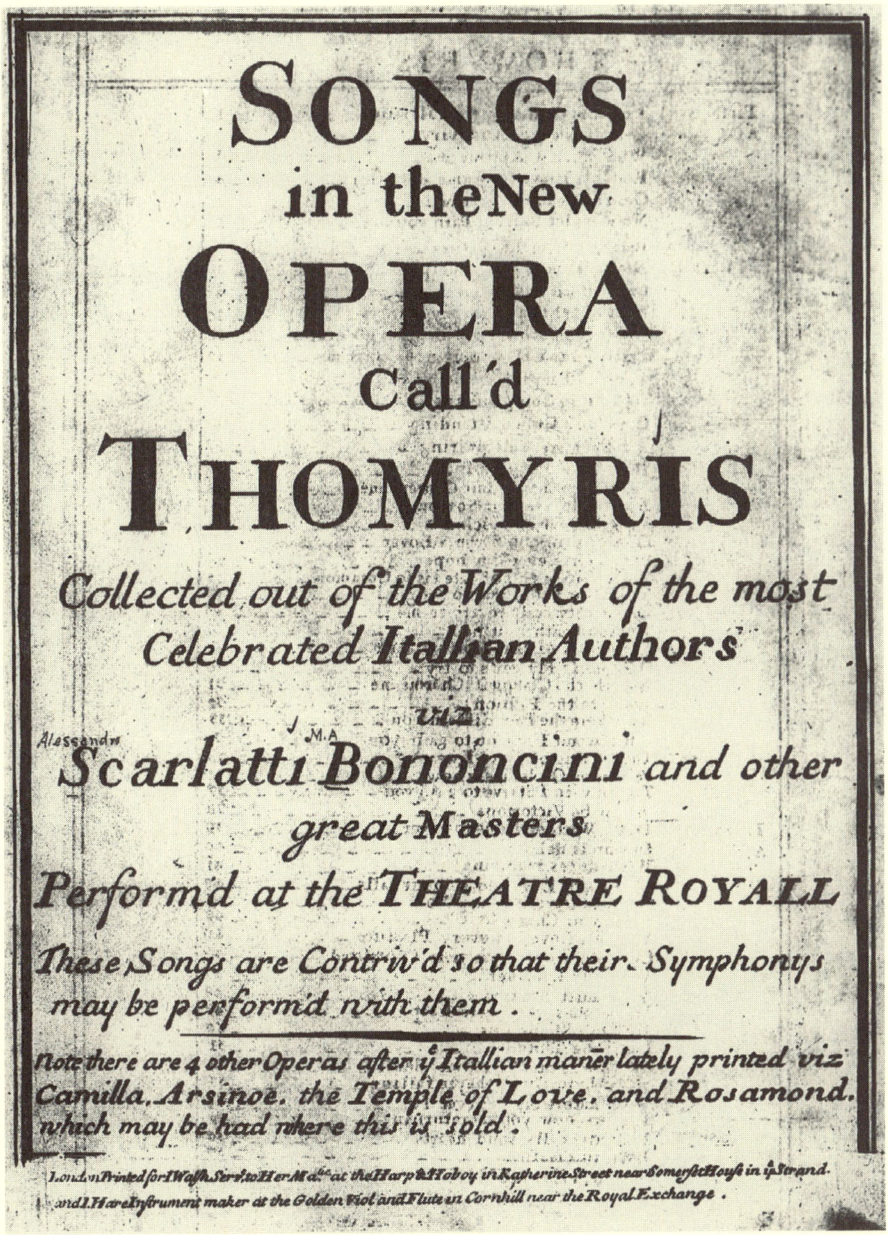

Caption: plate 82.1. 346 x 220 mm. NN: Drexel 4854.4.

Songs In The New Opera Call'd Thomyris Collected out of the Works of the most Celebrated Itallian Authors viz Scarlatti Bononcini and other great Masters Perform'd at the Theatre Royall These Songs are Contriv'd so that their Symphonys may be perform'd with them. Note there are 4 other Operas after ye Itallian maner lately printed viz Camilla, Arsinoe, the Temple of Love, and Rosamond, which may be had where this is sold. [imprint from a separate plate] London printed for I. Walsh servt. to her matie. at the Harp & Hoboy in Katherine Street near Somerset House in ye Strand. and I. Hare instrument maker at the Golden Viol and Flute in Cornhill near the Royal Exchange.

59 leaves. Pp. [i-ii] 1□-4□ 1□-2□ [3]□ 4□-14□ [15]□ 16□ 16[1.e.17]□ [18]□ 19□-44□ [45]□ 47□ 49□-56□.
Leaves printed on 1 side.
Tallest copy 346 x 220 mm. Vertical chain lines.

One page engraved per plate. Engraving style Walsh 1, 3.
Title-page plates (see note 1).

Contents: title-page [i]; contents [ii]; overture 1-4; songs 1-2, [3], 4-14, [15], 16, 16[i.e.17], [18], 19-44, [45], 47, 49-56.

Songs:

No.	Page	First Line
1	1	Freedom thou greatest blessing (s Tofts)
2	2	Ever merry gay and airy (s Lindsey, < *Thomyris*)
3	[3]	What should alarm me, no foe (s Tofts, < *Thomyris*)
4	4	Rouse yee brave for fame and glory (s De L'Épine, < *Thomyris*)
5	5	Gently treat my sorrow (s Tofts, < *Thomyris*)
6	6	No more let sorrow pain you (s De L'Épine, < *Thomyris*)
7	7	Bright wonder of nature (s Valentini, < *Thomyris*)
8	8	Never let your heart despair (s Lindsey, < *Thomyris*)
9	9	Love woud invade me (s Tofts, < *Thomyris*)
10	10	My delight, my dear my princess (s Leveridge, < *Thomyris*)
11	11	Away you rover, for shame give over (s Lindsey, < *Thomyris*)
12	12-13	Prethee leave me (s Leveridge, Lindsey, < *Thomyris*)
13	14	Joy and empire are no more (s Lawrence, < *Thomyris*)
14	[15]	In vain is complaining (s Lawrence, < *Thomyris*)
15	16	Cares on a crown attending (s De L'Épine, < *Thomyris*)
16	16[i.e.17]	Lover near despairing, A (s Valentini, Hughes, < *Thomyris*)
17	[18]	Let us fly our undoing love allures me (s Tofts, < *Thomyris*)
18	19	Ner'e torment me, but content me (s De L'Épine, < *Thomyris*)
19	20	I grieve to see your sorrow (s Hughes, < *Thomyris*)
20	21	You who for wedlock importune (s Lindsey, < *Thomyris*)
21	22	Do you think so warm a lover (s Leveridge, < *Thomyris*)
22	23	What lover ever can hope for favour (s Lindsey, < *Thomyris*)
23	24	Who can bear tho of late tis so common (s Leveridge, < *Thomyris*)

24	25	Strike me fate, now no danger allarms (s Lawrence, < *Thomyris*)
25	26	Oh in pity cease to grieve me (s Lawrence, Tofts, < *Thomyris*)
26	27-28	Say must I then despair (s Hughes, Tofts, < *Thomyris*)
27	29	Ye horrors of this hollow grave (s Lawrence, < *Thomyris*)
28	30	Oh I must fly, cease to try to charm me (s Tofts, < *Thomyris*)
29	31	While tho conquest charms me, A (s De L'Épine, < *Thomyris*)
30	32	Slaves to the fashion (s Leveridge)
31	33	Shoud er'e the fair disdain you (s Lindsey, < *Thomyris*)
32	34	What woud I not do to gain you (s Leveridge, < *Thomyris*)
33	35	Chains of love I wear, The (s Hughes, < *Thomyris*)
34	36	Yee powr's oh let me know what reason (s Tofts, < *Thomyris*)
35	37	Since in vain I strive to gain you (s Lawrence, < *Thomyris*)
36	38	Again be victorious, be glorious (s De L'Épine, < *Thomyris*)
37	39	Pretty warbler cease to hover (s Tofts, < *Thomyris*)
38	40	In vain is delay (s Tofts, < *Thomyris*)
39	41	When duty's requiring (s Tofts)
40	42	Halt when love and honour call you (s Leveridge, < *Thomyris*)
41	43	Can you leave ranging (s Lindsey, < *Thomyris*)
42	44	Woud you charme us (s Lindsey, < *Thomyris*)
43	[45]	Farewell love and all soft pleasure (s Leveridge, < *Thomyris*)
44	47	I cease to love her (s Hughes, < *Thomyris*)
45	49	When one's gone ner'e keep a pother (s Lindsey, < *Thomyris*)
46	50	Humble sheperds greif may pain you (s De L'Épine, < *Thomyris*)
47	51	Like the thunder guilt aming (s De L'Épine, < *Thomyris*)
48	52	Yee powr's my welcome death forgive (s Tofts)
49	53	Sally before you they're falling (s De L'Épine, < *Thomyris*)
50	54	Vain ambition tho still you try to soar (s Lawrence, < *Thomyris*)
51	55	I revive now you're turning (s Tofts, < *Thomyris*)
52	56	Pleasure calls fond hearts recover (s De L'Épine, < *Thomyris*)

Notes:
1. Original imprint obscured and new imprint (minus Randall) printed from separate plate.
2. Wanting pp. 46 and 48.

Copy: NN Drexel 4854.4.

Plate 83.1   Gasparini, *Antiochus*, 1712

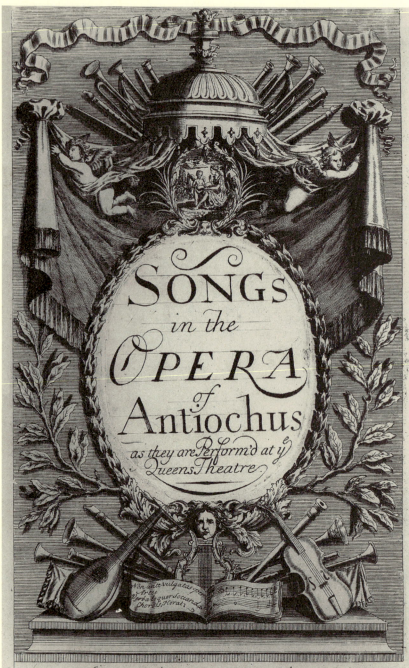

SONGs in the OPERA of Antiochus as they are Perform'd at ye Queens Theatre

London Printed for J.Walsh Servant in Ordinary to her Britanick Majesty, at ye Harp & Hoboy in Katherine street near Somerset House in ye Strand, & J.Hare at ye Viol & Flute in Cornhill near the Royall Exchange.

83 Gasparini, *Antiochus*, 21 February 1712

Caption: plate 83.1. 357 x 239 mm. Lbl: H.298.

[within cartouche] ʃ Songs in the Opera of Antiochus as they are Perform'd at ye Queens Theatre. ʃ [at foot] London Printed for J: Walsh Servant in Ordinary to her Britanick Majesty, at ye Harp & Hoboy in Katherine street, near Somerset House in ye Strand, & J: Hare at ye Viol & Flute in Cornhill near the Royall Exchange.

36 leaves. Pp. [i] [ii] 1-69.
Leaves printed on 2 sides.
Tallest copy 368 x 232 mm. Vertical chain lines.

One page engraved per plate. Engraving style Walsh and Cross.
Title-page plate 310 x 190 mm. Passe-partout title-page no. 6.
Contents plate 305 x 86 mm.

Walsh i: 417.
Advertised in *Post Man*, 21 February 1712.

Contents: title-page [i]; contents and advertisement [ii]; overture 1-6; songs 7-69.

Songs:

No.	Page	First Line
1	7-8	Fier destin di chi ben ama (s Pilotti, < *Antiochus*)
2	9-10	Sei mia gioia sei mio bene (s Barbier, < *Antiochus*)
3	11-12	Vivrò a tè fedele (s Pilotti, Barbier)
4	13-14	O morir o vendicarmi (s De L'Épine, < *Antiochus*)
5	15-16	Non cessarò d'amar (s Girardeau, < *Antiochus*)
6	17-18	Sì lietto sì contento (s Nicolini, < *Antiochus*)
7	19-20	Pensieri voi mi tormentate (s Pilotti, < *Antiochus*)
8	21-22	Rè ingrato dis pietata (s Pilotti, < *Antiochus*)
9	23	Sì candida è sì bella (s Girardeau, < *Antiochus*)
10	24-25	Al bel nume del mio amore (s Nicolini, < *Antiochus*)
11	26-28	Si cor mio confida e spera (s Nicolini, < *Antiochus*)
12	29-30	Per te bell'idol mio (s Nicolini, Pilotti)
13	31	Usignolo che col volo (s De L'Épine, < *Antiochus*)
14	32-33	Stelle spietate (s Nicolini, < *Antiochus*)
15	34-35	Tu sei l'anima mia (s Girardeau, < *Antiochus*)
16	36	Par che sia tinta in melle (s Barbier, < *Antiochus*)
17	37	Morirò per il mio bene (s Pilotti, < *Antiochus*)
18	38	Da fido vassallo (s Nicolini, < *Antiochus*)
19	39	Oh Giove che raggiri (s Nicolini, < *Antiochus*)
20	40	Di se senti (s Nicolini, < *Antiochus*)
21	41-42	Sospira il core afflitto (s Pilotti, < *Antiochus*)
22	43-44	Labro tù sei bugiardo (s Girardeau, < *Antiochus*)
23	45-46	Qual fra'l porto e'l la tempesta (s Barbier, < *Antiochus*)
24	47-48	Armateui di vezzi (s De L'Épine, < *Antiochus*)
25	49	Rozzi sassi in voi contemplo (s Nicolini, < *Antiochus*)
26	50-52	Scaccia omai s'indegna imago (s Pilotti, < *Antiochus*)
27	53	Ho un core nel petto (s De L'Épine, < *Antiochus*)

28	54-55	Questo conforto solo (s Nicolini, < *Antiochus*)
29	56-57	Vede anche il nido (s Barbier, < *Antiochus*)
30	58-59	Sento nel mio piacer (s Girardeau, < *Antiochus*)
31	60	Senti il core (s Nicolini, < *Antiochus*)
32	61-62	Al piè già ti cade la testa crudel (s Barbier, < *Antiochus*)
33	63-64	Tu sola cara sei (s Nicolini, < *Antiochus*)
34	65-66	Vuò vedermi vendicata (s De L'Épine, < *Antiochus*)
35	67-68	Lieta corre la navicella spinta (s Pilotti, < *Antiochus*)
36	69	Con danze belle scherzan

Notes:
1. B-Bc: - p. [i].
2. Ckc (42.7.(3.)): 37 leaves, [i]□-[ii]□ 1□ 2-69.
3. CSfst: - pp. [ii], 1; p. 1 supplied in photograph.
4. F-Pc: 37 leaves, [i]□-[ii]□\□1 2-69; price in MS. on title-page, '0-9-0'.
5. NN: 37 leaves, [i]□-[ii]□\□1 2-69.
6. Reports of copies at CtY, DFo, MiU and PU are false.

Copies: B-Bc 5417; CaOLU MZ.529; CDp M.C.3.18; Ckc 42.7.(3.); Ckc 85.22; CLU-C *fM1505.G24an; CSfst de Bellis 847; DLC M1500.G23A5; F-Pc D.4465; Lbl H.298; NjP (Ex) Oversize M1508 P54 1712q; NN Mus.Res. *MN p.v. 8; Ob [MS] Mus. Sch. c.189; Obh; TWm —.

Plate 84.1 Gasparini, *Hamlet*, 1712

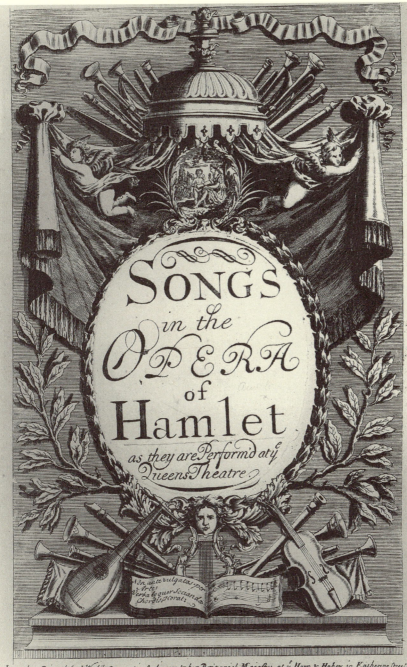

Caption: plate 84.1. 362 x 223 mm. Lbl: H.114.(1.).

[within cartouche] ⌠ Songs in the Opera of Hamlet as they are Perform'd at ye Queens Theatre. ⌡ [at foot] London printed for J: Walsh Servant in Ordinary to her Britanick Majesty, at ye Harp & Hoboy in Katherine street, near Somerset House in ye Strand, & J: Hare at ye Viol & Flute in Cornhill near the Royall Exchange.

39 leaves. Pp. [i]□-[ii]□\□1 2-73.
Leaves printed on 2 sides.
Tallest copy 368 x 232 mm. Vertical chain lines.

One page engraved per plate. Engraving style Walsh and Cross.
Title-page plate 307 x 190 mm. Passe-partout no. 6.
Contents plate 302 x 88 mm.

Walsh i: 422.
Advertised in *Spectator*, 21 April 1712.

Contents: title-page [i]; contents and advertisement [ii]; overture 1-4; songs 5-73.

Songs:

No.	Page	First Line
1	5-6	Nel tuo sen, crudel, vorrei (s Pilotti, < *Hamlet*)
2	7-8	Nel mio cor costante e forte (s Bendler, < *Hamlet*)
3	9	Empia sorte a me togliesti (s Girardeau, < *Hamlet*)
4	10	A questi occhi giunse un di (s Nicolini, < *Hamlet*)
5	11-12	Nel furor de suoi deliri (s Girardeau, < *Hamlet*)
6	13	Non sò qual sia (s Barbier, < *Hamlet*)
7	14-15	Portò piagato in petto (s Nicolini, < *Hamlet*)
8	16-17	Tromba in campo (s De L'Épine, < *Hamlet*)
9	18	Nella mia sfortunata (s Girardeau, < *Hamlet*)
10	19	Con vezzo lusinghiero (s Pilotti, < *Hamlet*)
11	20	La speme del nocchiero (s Barbier, < *Hamlet*)
12	21	Amor consolami ne più tardar' (s De L'Épine, < *Hamlet*)
13	22-23	Son vane tue minaccie (s Pilotti, < *Hamlet*)
14	24-25	Quando io torni (s Nicolini, < *Hamlet*)
15	26-31	L'una e l'altra (s Girardeau, < *Hamlet*)
16	32-33	Parto bel'idol mio (s Barbier, < *Hamlet*)
17	34-35	Ti consiglio amar un volto (s Pilotti, < *Hamlet*)
18	36-37	Cinto d'amiche rose un dì crescea (s Nicolini, < *Hamlet*)
19	38-39	Non è si fido al nido (s Girardeau, < *Hamlet*)
20	40	Vieni e mira come gira (s Nicolini, < *Hamlet*)
21	41-42	Save mia quella bella che adoro (s De L'Épine, < *Hamlet*)
22	43-44	Si ti sente l'alma mia (s Barbier, < *Hamlet*)
23	45	De la vendetta il fulmine (s Nicolini, < *Hamlet*)
24	46-47	Se un dì stringer potro (s Pilotti, < *Hamlet*)
25	48	Tu miri le mie lacrime (s Girardeau, < *Hamlet*)
26	49-50	Torna al lido la navicella (s De L'Épine, < *Hamlet*)
27	51	Godo o'cara ma d'un'diletto (s Nicolini, Girardeau)

28	52-54	Sempre in cielo Giove irato (s Girardeau, Nicolini)
29	55-56	Tu indegno sei dell'allor (s Pilotti, < *Hamlet*)
30	57	Che farai misero core (s Girardeau, < *Hamlet*)
31	57	Mi rinasce più bella (s Nicolini, < *Hamlet*)
32	58	Teneri guardi vezzi buggiardi (s Girardeau, < *Hamlet*)
33	59	Mille amplessi (s Nicolini, < *Hamlet*)
34	60-61	Beltà che sempre piace (s Barbier, < *Hamlet*)
35	62-63	Speranze più liete regnate con me (s De L'Épine, < *Hamlet*)
36	64	Qui di Bacco nella reggia
37	64	Qui d'Astrea vicino al soglio
38	65	Parto amante e parto amico (s Girardeau, < *Hamlet*)
39	66-67	D'ire armato il braccio forte (s Nicolini, < *Hamlet*)
40	68-69	Haveua l'idol mio bel volto e cor fedel (s Pilotti, < *Hamlet*)
41	70-71	Amanti voi ch'andante (s Nicolini, < *Hamlet*)
42	72-73	Godan l'alme, goda il regno

Notes:
1. Ckc and DFo (copy 1): 38 leaves, [i]□ [ii] 1-73.
2. Lgc: - p. [i]: i.e., 37 leaves, [ii] 1-73.

Copies: Bp SQ717.03 60278; Ckc 42.7.(4.); CLU-C *fM1505.G24h; DFo M1500.G9 Cage copy 1; DFo M1500.G9 Cage copy 2; F-Pc Rés. V.S.1283; Lbl H.114.(1.); Lgc G.Mus.115; NN Mus.Res. *MN p.v. 8; TWm —.

Plate 85.1   Galliard, *Calypso and Telemachus*, 1712

Songs in the OPERA of Calypso & Telemachus as they are Perform'd at the Queens Theatre. Compos'd by Mr Galliard. the Words by Mr Hughes

London Printed for J. Walsh Servant in Ordinary to her Britanick Majesty, at ye Harp & Hoboy in Katherine street. near Somerset House in ye Strand, & J. Hare at ye Viol & Flute in Cornhill near the Royall Exchange.

Caption: plate 85.1. 317 x 215 mm. Lbl: G.223.(1.).

[within cartouche] ⌠ Songs in the Opera of Calypso & Telemachus as they are
Perform'd at the Queens Theatre. Compos'd by Mr Galliard. the Words by Mr
Hughes ⌡ [at foot] London printed for J: Walsh Servant in Ordinary to her
Britanick Majesty, at ye Harp & Hoboy in Katherine street, near Somerset
House in ye Strand, & J: Hare at ye Viol & Flute in Cornhill near the Royall
Exchange.

33 leaves. Pp. [i]□ [ii] 1-61 62□.
Leaves printed on 2 sides.
Tallest copy 366 x 233 mm. Vertical chain lines.

One page engraved per plate. Engraving style Walsh and Cross.
Title-page plate 312 x 192 mm. Passe-partout no. 6.
Contents plate 265 x 99 mm.

Walsh i: 426.

Contents: title-page [i]; contents and advertisement [ii]; overture 1-4; songs 5-62.

Songs:

No.	Page	First Line
1	5-6	For thee ye rilling waters weep (s De L'Épine)
2	7	I go yet know not where (s Barbier, < *Calypso and Telemachus*)
3	8-9	Pleasing visions shall attend thee (s De L'Épine, < *Calypso and Telemachus*)
4	10-11	No you'd deceive me (s Manina, < *Calypso and Telemachus*)
5	12-13	Pursue ye flying fair (s Leveridge, < *Calypso and Telemachus*)
6	14	Thousand raptures fill my breast, A (s Barbier, < *Calypso and Telemachus*)
7	15	If in Elizian plains he roves (s Barbier, < *Calypso and Telemachus*)
8	16	No more let sorrow wound thee (s De L'Épine)
9	17	Let not pleasure's charmes undo thee (s Pearson, < *Calypso and Telemachus*)
10	18-20	Hark how the voice of fame (s Barbier, Pearson)
11	21-22	How shall I speak my secret pain (s Manina, < *Calypso and Telemachus*)
12	23	Ambition cease t'alarm me (s Barbier, < *Calypso and Telemachus*)
13	24-25	In all her charms Aurora gay (s Manina, < *Calypso and Telemachus*)
14	26-28	Fatal change! what do I see? (s Pearson, < *Calypso and Telemachus*)
15	29-30	O Cupid gentle boy (s Barbier, < *Calypso and Telemachus*)
16	31	All hail imperiall love (s De L'Épine, < *Calypso and Telemachus*)
17	32-33	From me from thee he turns his eyes (s Pearson, < *Calypso and Telemachus*)
18	34	See goddess of this happy land (s Leveridge, < *Calypso and Telemachus*)
19	35-36	Let love inspire, thee (s De L'Épine, < *Calypso and Telemachus*)
20	37-38	Hark the hollow groves resounding (s Barbier, < *Calypso and Telemachus*)
21	39-40	Amazing change what do I see (s Barbier, < *Calypso and Telemachus*)
22	41-43	My charmer, to meet thee (s Barbier, Manina)
23	44-45	Come ev'ry grace adorn me (s De L'Épine)
24	46-47	He smiles, he dreams (s Pearson, < *Calypso and Telemachus*)
25	48	Awake impending vengeance see (s De L'Épine, < *Calypso and Telemachus*)
26	49-51	Hear me love my sorrows ending (s Barbier, < *Calypso and Telemachus*)
27	52-53	Ye monsters that sleep (s Leveridge, < *Calypso and Telemachus*)

28	54-55	Cruel Cupid break thy darts (s Manina, < *Calypso and Telemachus*)
29	56	O break the charm the charmer leave (s Barbier, Pearson)
30	57	Joy forsakes me, hope is fled (s Barbier)
31	58-60	See these golden beams how bright (s Pearson, < *Calypso and Telemachus*)
32	61-62	No longer here shall nature smile (s De L'Épine, < *Calypso and Telemachus*)

Notes:
1. Registered with the Stationers' Company on 28 June 1712.
2. BWbw: - pp. [i-ii], 10-13, 18-23, 32-33, 38-43, 48-53, 58-62.
3. Ckc: + 'Cupid once in search of prey' from *Theseus* tipped in at end; printed on different paper.
4. MH-H: title within cartouche only, pasted to blank leaf.
5. NRU-Mus: - p. [i].
6. TWm: price '9^s-0^d' in MS. on title-page.

Copies: B-Br Fétis 2853; BWbw —; CDp M.C.3.30; Ckc 85.24; DFo M1500.G7C2 Cage; DLC M1500.G195C3; DRc Mus.D.35; *FMU*; F-Pc D.4451; ICU RBR M1505.G16C2; Lam —; Lbl G.223.(1.); Lcm I.G.9; MH-H *42-3780F; NN Mus.Res. *MN p.v. 8; NRU-Mus Vault M1505.G168C; Ob Mus. 22.c.196; Obh Mus. D.5; *RF-Mrg*; TWm —; WaU M1503 G35C3.

Plate 86.1   Musa et Musica, 1713

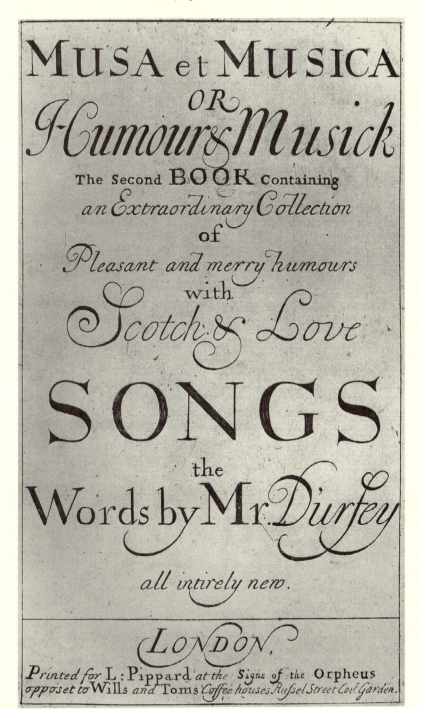

MUSA et MUSICA
OR
Humour & Musick
The Second BOOK Containing
an Extraordinary Collection
of
Pleasant and merry humours
with
Scotch & Love
SONGS
the
Words by Mr. Durfey
all intirely new.

LONDON,
Printed for L: Pippard at the Signe of the Orpheus
opposet to Wills and Toms Coffee houses Russel Street Cov. Garden.

Caption: plate 86.1. 360 x 230 mm. Lbl: H.82.a.

Musa et Musica Or Humour & Musick The Second Book Containing an Extraordinary Collection of Pleasant and merry humours with Scotch & Love Songs the Words by Mr. D'urfey all intirely new. London, Printed for L: Pippard at the Signe of the Orpheus opposet to Wills and Toms Coffee houses Russel Street Covt. Garden.

11 leaves. Pp. [i]▢ [1]▢-[10]▢.
Leaves printed on 1 side.
Tallest copy 360 x 230 mm. Vertical chain lines.

One page engraved per plate. Engraving style Pippard.
Title-page plate 307 x 180 mm.

Contents: title-page [i]; songs [1-10].

Songs:

No.	Page	First Line
1	[1]	You the glorious sons of honour (m Barrett, v D'urfey, D&M 4110)
2	[2]	When Phillida with Jockey (v D'urfey, D&M 3780)
3	[3]	Of all ye symple things we doe (m D'urfey, < *Country Wake*, D&M 2571)
4	[4]	One long Whitson holliday (v D'urfey, D&M 2629)
5	[5]	Jenny, & Molly, & Dolly (v D'urfey, D&M 1855)
6	[6]	Tho Cælia art you shew (v D'urfey, D&M 3310)
7	[7]	Spring invites the troops to warring (D&M 3052)
8	[8]	When I make a fond adresse (v D'urfey, D&M 3751)
9	[9]	Now comes joyful peace (v D'urfey, D&M 2377)
10	[10]	In a barren tree

Notes:
1. Dated on basis of reference in song 9 to 'The happy peace', i.e., the Treaty of Utrecht, 1713.
2. Bound with the first book of *Musa et Musica*, 1710 (70).

Copy: Lbl H.82.a.

Plate 87.1   Ramondon, *New Book of Songs*, 1713

Caption: plate 87.1. 326 x 207 mm. Ge: R.x.31.

[within cartouche] ⌠ A New Book of Songs the Words & Musick by Mr. Ramondon never before Publish'd ⌡ I: Collins. sculp [at foot] London Printed for & Sould by I: Walsh Musicall Instrument maker in Ordinary to her Majesty at the Golden Harp & Ho=boy in Catherine=street near Summerset=house in ye strand and I: Hare at the Viol and Flute in Cornhill nere the Royal Exchange.

10 leaves. Pp. [i]▢ 1▢-9▢.
Leaves printed on 1 side.
Tallest copy 326 x 207 mm. Vertical chain lines.

One page engraved per plate. Engraving style Walsh 1.
Title-page plate 252 x 185 mm. Passe-partout no. 1.

Walsh i: 585.

Contents: title-page [i]; songs 1-9.

Songs:

No.	Page	First Line
1	1-2	Charming Celia cruel maid (m Ramondon)
2	3	In this grove my Strephon walk'd (m Ramondon)
3	4-5	When you were fled my love (m Ramondon)
4	6	Go falsest of thy sex be gone (m Ramondon, D&M 1139)
5	7	My Cloe why d'yee slight me (m Ramondon)
6	8-9	Lissa o pitty me my Lissa (m Ramondon)

Note:
1. Dated by Smith 'c. 1720 or earlier' on the basis on advertisement in *Numitor*, 1720. Collins passe-partout title-page used by Walsh for *New Aires* in May 1712 (Walsh i, 425). Imprint suggests date between 1711, the year Randall left the business and 1714, year of Queen Anne's death.

Copy: Ge R.x.31.

Plate 88.1   Polani, *Croesus*, 1714

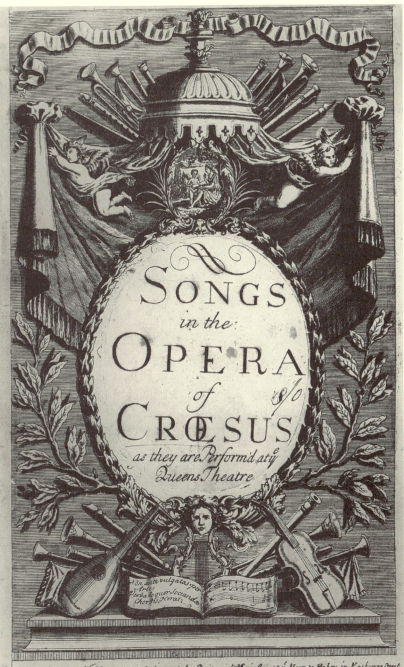

Caption: plate 88.1. 347 x 219 mm. Lbl: H.323.

[within cartouche] ⌠ Songs in the Opera of Croesus as they are Perform'd at ye Queens Theatre ⌡ [at foot] London Printed for J: Walsh Servant in Ordinary to her Britanick Majesty, at ye Harp & Hoboy in Katherine street, near Somerset House in ye Strand, & J: Hare at ye Viol & Flute in Cornhill near the Royall Exchange.

51 leaves. Pp. [1]□-[2]□ 3□-8□\□9-10□\-\□21-22□\23□\□24-25□\-\□30-31□\32□-33□ \□34-35□\-\□48-49□\ 50□-51□.
Leaves printed on 1 side.
Tallest copy 375 x 238 mm. Vertical chain lines.

One page engraved per plate. Engraving style Walsh 1.
Title-page plate 310 x 189 mm. Passe-partout no. 6.
Contents plate 309 x 88 mm.

Walsh i: 446.
Advertised in *Post Boy*, 1 May 1714.

Contents: title-page [1]; contents and advertisement [2]; overture 3-7; songs 8-51.

Songs:

No.	Page	First Line
1	8	Quanto mai son fortunato (s Barbier, < *Croesus*)
2	9-10	Un volto ch'appaga (s Barbier, Valentini)
3	11-12	Dolce speme al cor mi dice (s Robinson, A., < *Croesus*)
4	13-14	Vedersi rapire (s De L'Épine, < *Croesus*)
5	15-16	Cangia la sorte (s Galerati, < *Croesus*)
6	17-18	Un bel contento un rio tormento (s Valentini, < *Croesus*)
7	19-20	Folle e incauto mai dal lido (s Robinson, A., < *Croesus*)
8	21-22	Prende gioco il nume d'amor (s De L'Épine, < *Croesus*)
9	23	Cara bella tù di me (s Valentini, < *Croesus*)
10	24-27	Parto mà resta il core (s Robinson, A., Galerati)
11	28-29	Nei sassi ancora la pena mia (s Galerati, < *Croesus*)
12	30-31	Chi si vede inpriggionato (s Barbier, < *Croesus*)
13	32	Vanne lungi dal mio seno (s Galerati, < *Croesus*)
14	33	Sommi dei se giusti sonno (s Robinson, A., < *Croesus*)
15	34-35	Io non vorrei morir (s Valentini, < *Croesus*)
16	36-37	Si t'intendo ò core amante (s Galerati, < *Croesus*)
17	38-39	Colomba rapita d'artiglio in artiglio (s Barbier, < *Croesus*)
18	40-41	È bello il pensiero (s Robinson, A., < *Croesus*)
19	42-43	Bell'idol mio te sol desio (s Barbier, < *Croesus*)
20	44-45	Al bel idolo del mio core (s De L'Épine, < *Croesus*)
21	46-47	Idolo del mio cor (s Robinson, A., < *Croesus*)
22	48-49	Brilla o core brilla e ridi (s Galerati, < *Croesus*)
23	50	Se luggie amenità (s Barbier, < *Croesus*)
24	51	Dammi pur tormenti e pene (s Galerati, < *Croesus*)

Notes:
1. CaOLU: pp. 3 and 5 reversed.
2. Ckc: p. 26 reversed.
3. CLU-C, CtY-Mus, DFo: pp. 24 and 26 reversed.
4. Lcm: - pp. 48-51.

Copies: CaOLU MZ.701; Ckc 85.20; CLU-C *fM1508.C93; CtY-Mus Rare Mq20.C87; DFo M1500.C7 Cage; DLC M1500.C85 Case; Lbl H.323; Lcm XXXII.B.10.

Plate 89.1   Ziani, *Arminius*, 1714

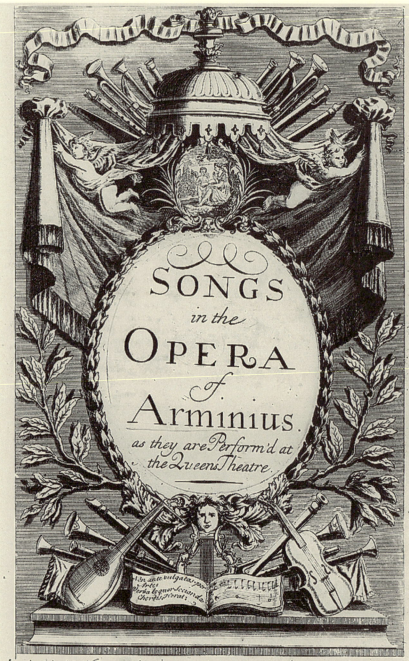

SONGS

in the

OPERA

of

Arminius

as they are Perform'd at
the Queens Theatre.

London Printed for J:Walsh Servant in Ordinary to her Britanick Majesty. at ỹ Harp & Hoboy in Katherine street.
near Somerset House in ỹ Strand. & J:Hare at ỹ Viol & Flute in Cornhill near the Royall Exchange.

Caption: plate 89.1. 347 x 218 mm. Lbl: H.322.

[within cartouche] ʃ Songs in the Opera of Arminius. as they are Perform'd at the Queens Theatre. ʃ [at foot] London Printed for J: Walsh Servant in Ordinary to her Britanick Majesty, at ye Harp & Hoboy in Katherine street, near Somerset House in ye Strand, & J: Hare at ye Viol & Flute in Cornhill near the Royall Exchange.

56 leaves. Pp. [1]□-[2]□\□3 4□ 5□\□6 7□-9□ \□10-11□\-\□16-17□\ 18□ \□19-20□\-\ □27-28□\ 29□ \□30-31□\-\□38-39□\ 40□ \□41-42□\-\□43-44□\ 45□\□46 47□\□48 49□-50□\□51 52□-53□ 54□\□55 56□.
Leaves printed on 1 side.
Tallest copy 375 x 240 mm. Vertical chain lines.

One page engraved per plate. Engraving style Walsh and Cross.
Title-page plate 314 x 190 mm. Passe-partout no. 6.
Contents plate 310 x 88 mm.

Walsh i: 447.
Advertised in *Post Boy*, 1 June 1714.

Contents: title-page [1]; contents and advertisement [2]; overture 3-5; songs 6-56.

Songs:

No.	Page	First Line
1	6-7	A tè sol bel idol mio (s Galerati, < *Arminius*)
2	8	Ho ben cor per esser forte (s Robinson, A., < *Arminius*)
3	9	Deh consola questo piante (s De L'Épine, < *Arminius*)
4	10-11	Quell'empio suenato (s Valentini, < *Arminius*)
5	12-13	Mal ferir altrui potrei (s Barbier, < *Arminius*)
6	14-15	Quanto empità (s De L'Épine, < *Arminius*)
7	16-17	Sento una bella speme (s Galerati, < *Arminius*)
8	18	Vanne in tomba (s Robinson, A., < *Arminius*)
9	19-20	Si perfida si barbara tuoi lacci vuò soffrir (s Valentini, < *Arminius*)
10	21-22	Rivo che tumido s'ingrossa d'onda (s Robinson, A., < *Arminius*)
11	23-24	Mio nume sol chiamo (s Barbier, < *Arminius*)
12	25-28	Amor accende in petto (s De L'Épine, < *Arminius*)
13	29	Quando mai spietata sorte (s Barbier, < *Arminius*)
14	30-31	Se à chiamar il caro bene (s Galerati, < *Arminius*)
15	32-33	Ombra amata del caro mio figlio (s Galerati, < *Arminius*)
16	34-35	Belle idee del'dolce figlio (s Robinson, A., < *Arminius*)
17	36-37	Io sempro appunto quel augelletto (s De L'Épine, < *Arminius*)
18	38-39	Sento già l'alma (s Valentini, < *Arminius*)
19	40	Pur dicesti ò bocca bella (s Robinson, A., < *Arminius*)
20	41-42	Tu solo sei luce (s Galerati, < *Arminius*)
21	43-45	Con rigida sembianza (s Robinson, A., Galerati, < *Arminius*)
22	46-47	Lusinghe vezzo si di speme (s Galerati, < *Arminius*)
23	48-49	Troppo crudel l'impressa (s Barbier, < *Arminius*)
24	50	Doma l'orgoglio (s Valentini, < *Arminius*)
25	51-52	Col mio cor stancai (s Galerati, < *Arminius*)

26   53   Speme gradita (s De L'Épine, < *Arminius*)
27   54   Vanne ò cara dammi ancora un altro amplesso (s Robinson, A., Galerati, < *Arminius*)
28   55-56   Che diresti a navicella (s Robinson, A., < *Arminius*)

Note:
1. Listed in the *Monthly Catalogues*, June 1714, price 10s.

Copies: CDp M.C.3.20; Ckc 85.16; Ckc 85.16.A; CSfst de Bellis 835; D-Hs M C/163; Lbl H.322; NN Mus.Res. *MN p.v. 8; TWm —.

Plate 90.1   Clayton, *Arsinoe*, 1714

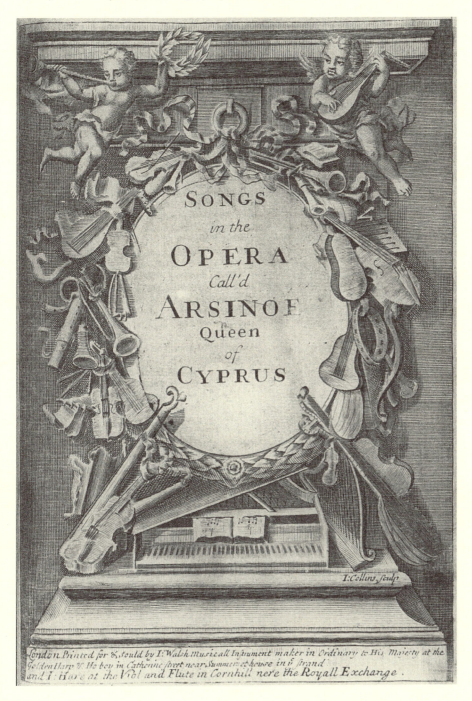

SONGS
in the
OPERA
Call'd
ARSINOE
Queen
of
CYPRUS

T:Collins *sculp*

London Printed for & sould by I: Walsh. Musicall Instrument maker in Ordinary to His Majesty at the
Golden Harp & Ho boy in Catherine street near Summerset house in y.ᵉ strand
and I: Hare at the Viol and Flute in Cornhill nere the Royall Exchange .

Caption: plate 90.1. 327 x 213 mm. Lcm: XXXII.A.1.(2).

[within cartouche] ⌠ Songs in the Opera Call'd Arsinoe Queen of Cyprus ⌡ I:
Collins. sculp [at foot] London Printed for & Sould by I: Walsh Musicall
Instrument maker in Ordinary to His Majesty at the Golden Harp & Ho=boy
in Catherine=street, near Summerset=house in ye strand and I: Hare at the
Viol and Flute in Cornhill nere the Royall Exchange.

51 leaves. Pp. [i]□-[ii]□\□1 2□-5□\□6 7□-8□\□9 10□\□11 12□-15□\□16 17□\□18
19□-26□\□27 28□-35□\□36 37□-40□\□41 42□-43□\44 45□-46□\□47 48□-49□.
Leaves printed on 1 side.
Tallest copy 327 x 213 mm. Vertical chain lines.

One page engraved per plate. Engraving style Walsh 1.
Title-page plate 251 x 181 mm. Passe-partout no. 1.
Contents plate 205 x 147 mm.

Walsh i: 600.

Contents: title-page [i]; contents [ii]; overture 1-2; songs 3-49.

Songs: see 26.

Note:
1. 1714 is the earliest year in which Collins' title-page with 'His' in imprint could have been used.

Copy: Lcm XXXII.A.1.(2).

90a   Polani, *Croesus*, 31 December 1714

Caption: photograph unavailable.

[within cartouche] ⌠ Songs in the Opera of Croesus as they are Perform'd at ye Queens Theatre ⌡ [at foot] London Printed for J: Walsh Servant in Ordinary to his Britanick Majesty, at ye Harp & Hoboy in Katherine street, near Somerset House in ye Strand, & J: Hare at ye Viol & Flute in Cornhill near the Royall Exchange.

51 leaves. Pp. [1]□-[2]□ □3 4□-8□ \□9-10□\-\□21-22□\ 23□ □24 25□-27□ \□28-29□\-\ □48-49□\ 50□-51□.
Leaves printed on 1 side.
Tallest copy 351 x 228 mm. Vertical chain lines.

One page engraved per plate. Engraving style Walsh 1.
Title-page plate passe-partout no. 6.

Contents: title-page [1]; contents and advertisement [2]; overture 3-7; songs 8-51.

Songs: see **88**.

Notes:
1. 1714 is the earliest year in which this title-page with 'his' in imprint could have been used.
2. Additional MS. thorough bass figures in overture and notes on p. 8.

Copy: WaU M1500 C75S6 1714.

SONGS in the OPERA of ETEARCO as they are Perform'd at y'e Queens Theatre

London Printed for J.Walsh Servant in Ordinary to his Britanick Majesty, at y'e Harp & Hoboy in Katherine street, near Somerset House in y'e Strand, & J.Hare at y'e Viol & Flute in Cornhill near the Royall Exchange.

90b   Bononcini, *Etearco*, 31 December 1714

Caption: plate 90b.1. 341 x 213 mm. Obh: Mus. D.10.

[within cartouche] ⌠ Songs in the Opera of Etearco as they are Perform'd at ye Queens Theatre. ⌡ [at foot] London Printed for J: Walsh Servant in Ordinary to his Britanick Majesty, at ye Harp & Hoboy in Katherine street, near Somerset House in ye Strand, & J: Hare at ye Viol & Flute in Cornhill near the Royall Exchange.

38 leaves. Pp. [i]▢-[ii]▢\▢1 2-69 70▢.
Leaves printed on 2 sides.
Tallest copy 341 x 213 mm. Vertical chain lines.

One page engraved per plate. Engraving style Walsh and Cross.
Title-page plate 312 x 189 mm. Passe-partout no. 6.

Contents: title-page [i]; contents and advertisement [ii]; overture 1-4; songs 5-70.

Songs: see 75.

Note:
1. 1714 is the earliest year in which this title-page with 'his' in imprint could have been used.

Copy: Obh Mus. D.10.

Plate 91.1   Mancini, Hydaspes, *'Additional Songs'*, 1714

Caption: plate 91.1. 368 x 241 mm. Ckc: 85.10. See plate 80.2.

[within cartouche] ⌠ Songs in the Opera calld Hydaspes. ⌡ [at foot] London Printed for & Sold by Iohn Walsh Servant to his Majesty at the Harp and Hautboy in Katherine Street near Somerset House in the Strand & I: Hare at ye Viol and Flute in Cornhill near the Royal Exchange.

The Additionall Songs In The New Opera, Call'd ⌠ Hydaspes, as they are Perform'd at the Queens Theatre. ⌡ Sold by I: Walsh Musicall Instrument maker in Or==dinary to her Majesty------at the Harp and Ho=boy, in Catherine=Street near Sommerset House in the Strand and I: Hare Musick Instrument maker at ye Golden Viol and Flute in Cornhill near ye Royal Exchange.

40 leaves. Pp. [i]□-[iii]□\□1 2-71 72□.
Leaves printed on 2 sides.
Tallest copy 368 x 241 mm. Vertical chain lines.

One page engraved per plate. Engraving style Walsh and Cross.
Illus. title-page plate 237 x 184 mm. Passe-partout no. 5.
Title-page plate passe-partout no. 3.

Contents: illus. title-page [i]; title-page [ii]; contents and advertisement [iii]; overture 1-4; songs 5-72.

Songs: see 69.

Notes:
1. 1714 is the earliest year in which p. [i] with 'his' in imprint could have been used.
2. 'The Additionall' unprinted at top of p. [ii].

Copy: Ckc 85.10.

92   Mancini, *Hydaspes*, 31 December 1714

Caption: photograph unavailable.

[within cartouche] ʃ Songs in the Opera calld Hydaspes. ♩ [at foot] London Printed for & Sold by Iohn Walsh Servant to his Majesty at the Harp and Hautboy in Katherine Street near Somerset House in the Strand & I: Hare at ye Viol and Flute in Cornhill near the Royal Exchange.

39 leaves. Pp. [i]◌-[ii]◌\◌1 2-71 72◌.
Leaves printed on 2 sides.
Tallest copy 355 x 229 mm. Vertical chain lines.

One page engraved per plate. Engraving style Walsh and Cross.
Title-page plate passe-partout no. 5.

Contents: title-page [i]; contents and advertisement [ii]; overture 1-4; songs 5-72.

Songs: see 69.

Note:
1. 1714 is the earliest year in which this title-page with 'his' in imprint could have been used.

Copy: MB **M1500.M35H9.

Plate 93.1   Dieupart, *Love's Triumph*, 'Additional Songs', 1714

Plate 93.2   Dieupart, *Love's Triumph*, 'Additional Songs', 1714

SONGS

IN THE NEW

OPERA,

Call'd

LOVE'S TRIUMPH

as they are Perform'd at the

QUEENS Theatre

Sold   by I: Walsh Musicall Instrument maker in Or=dinary to her Majesty_____at the Harp and Ho=boy. in Catherine-Street near Sommerset House in the strand, and I.Hare Musick Instrument maker at ȳ Golden Viol and Flute in Cornhill near ȳ Royal Exchange.

Caption: plates 93.1-93.2. 341 x 217mm. Lbl: H.227.

[within cartouche] ⸢ Songs in the Opera Calld Loves Triumph ⸥ [at foot] London Printed for & Sold by Iohn Walsh Servant to his Majesty at the Harp and Hautboy in Katherine Street near Somerset House in the Strand

The Additionall Songs In The New Opera, Call'd ⸢ Love's Triumph as they are Perform'd at the Queens Theatre ⸥ Sold by I: Walsh Musicall Instrument maker in Or==dinary to her Majesty------at the Harp and Ho=boy, in Catherine-Street near Sommerset House in the Strand and I. Hare Musick Instrument maker at ye Golden Viol and Flute in Cornhill near ye Royal Exchange.

74 leaves. Pp. [i]□-[iii]□ 1□-45□\□46 47□-57□\□58 [58A]□ 59□-68□\□69 70□. Leaves printed on 1 side. Tallest copy 341 x 217 mm. Vertical chain lines.

One page engraved per plate. Engraving style Walsh. Illus. title-page plate 238 x 184 mm. Passe-partout no. 5. Title-page plate 272 x 186 mm. Passe-partout no. 3. Contents plate 310 x 110 mm.

Walsh i: 450.

Contents: illus. title-page [i]; title-page [ii]; contents [iii]; songs 1-58, [58A], 59-70.

Songs: see **46**.

Notes:
1. 1714 is the earliest year in which p. [i] with 'his' in imprint could have been used.
2. A plain paper paste-over at top of title-page (p. [ii]) covers 'The Additionall'.
3. F-Pc: - p. [58A]; pp. [iii], 46, 58, 69 reversed; the title within the cartouche on p. [i] is a paste-over.
4. Lbl: pp. 46, 58, 69, reversed; + two additional title-pages, between pp. [ii-iii] and pp. 25-26 that have Randall's name in imprint (see plate 47.2), and a full contents list before p. 26. The initial contents leaf is reversed and gives only the first 25 songs.
5. Lcm: - p. [58A].

Copies: DFo M1500.G15L4 Cage; F-Pc Rés. V.S.1282; Lbl H.227; Lcm XXXII.A.2.(3.).

Plate 94.1   Scarlatti, A, *Pyrrhus and Demetrius*, 1714

94   Scarlatti, A, *Pyrrhus and Demetrius*, 31 December 1714

Caption: plate 94.1. 341 x 219 mm. Er: Tovey Coll. M78SCAR(A)-26.

[within cartouche] ⌠ Songs in the Opera Call'd Pyrrhus and Demetrius ⌡ [at foot] London Printed for & Sold by Iohn Walsh Servant to his Majesty at the Harp and Hautboy in Katherine Street near Somerset House in the Strand & I: Hare at ye Viol and Flute in Cornhill near the Royal Exchange.

59 leaves. Pp. [i]□ 1□-16□\□17 18□-19□\□20 21□-31□\□32 33□-41□\□42 43□-58□.
Leaves printed on 1 side.
Tallest copy 341 x 219 mm. Horizontal chain lines.

One page engraved per plate. Engraving style Walsh 1.
Title-page plate 237 x 184 mm. Passe-partout no. 5.

Contents: title-page [i]; songs 1-58.

Songs: see **49**.

Notes:
1. 1714 is the earliest year in which this title-page with 'his' in imprint could have been used.
2. Contains Italian texts.
3. MS. additions in red to music of some songs.

Copy: Er Tovey Coll. M78 SCAR(A)-26; *Obh*.

Plate 95.1   *New Songs with a Through Bass, 1715*

A COLLECTION

of new

SONGS

With a Through Bass to each

Song *for the* Harpficord *Compos'd by*

SEVERAL MASTERS

London

Printed for &
Sould by I: Walsh Musicall Instrument maker in Ordinary
to his Majesty ~~and Royal Duch~~ at the Harp and Hob(oy in Catherine Street near Summerset House in the Strand and I Hare
at the Viol and Flute in Cornhill nere the Royal Exchange

95   *New Songs with a Through Bass, 31 December 1715*

Caption: plate 95.1. 319 x 216 mm. Lbl: G.316.b.

A Collection of new Songs With a Through Bass to each Song for the Harpsicord. Compos'd by ʃ Several Masters ⌡ London Sould by I: Walsh Musicall Instrument maker in Ordinary to his Majesty, ▌▌▌▌▌▌▌▌▌ at the Harp and Hoboy in Cathe==rine Street, near Summerset House in the Strand and I Hare at the Viol and Flute in Cornhill nere the Royal Exchange

35 leaves. Pp. [i]□-[ii]□ [1]□-[6]□ 7□-9□ 1[0]□-1[1]□ 12□-14□ [15]□ 16□ [17]□-[18]□ 19□-20□ [2]1□ 22□-24□ [25]□-[27]□ 2[8]□ [29]□ 3[0]□ [3]1□-[3]2□ 33□.
Leaves printed on 1 side.
Tallest copy 319 x 216 mm. Vertical chain lines.

One page engraved per plate. Engraving style Walsh.
Title-page plate 253 x 168 mm. Passe-partout no. 7.
Contents plate 270 x 100 mm.

Walsh i: 464.

Contents: title-page [i], contents [ii], songs [1]-[6], 7-9, 1[0]-1[1], 12-14, [15], 16, [17]-[18], 19-20, [2]1, 22-24, [25]-[27], 2[8], [29], 3[0], [3]1-[3]2, [33].

Songs:

No.	Page	First Line
1	[1]	Beleive my sighs my tears my dear
2	[2]	As Jockey and Jenny together was laid
3	[3]	As I came down the HeyLand Town (D&M 3566)
4	[4]	As I went forth to view the spring (s Abell)
5	[5]	Gin thou wert my ene thing
6	[6]	With tuneful pipe and merry glee (s Reading, Mrs)
7	7	Bonny lad there was, A (s Prince, < *Maid in the Mill*)
8	8	Bonny northern ladd, A (m Croft)
9	9	By moonlight on the green (s Lucas, D&M 449)
10	1[0]	Celladon when spring came on (v D'urfey, s Leveridge, D&M 505)
11	1[1]	Farewell my bonny witty pretty Moggy (v D'urfey, s Leveridge, D&M 965)
12	12	Jockey was as brisk & blith a lad (m Clarke, J., s Cross, D&M 1874)
13	13	Is'e no more to shady coverts (m Clarke, J., s Temple, D&M 1653)
14	14	Ken you who comes here (s Willis, D&M 1901)
15	[15]	Pretty Moggy, why d'ye slight me
16	16	Mad loons of Albany, what ist you doe (m Corbett, v D'urfey, D&M 2148)
17	[17]	Now Jockey and Moggy are ready (D&M 2394)
18	[18]	Rosy morn lukes bleeth & gay, The (D&M 2827)
19	19	'Twas when summer was rosie (v D'urfey, D&M 3498)
20	20	Twas within a fourlong of Edinborough town (m Purcell, H., s Girl, < *Mock Marriage*, D&M 3500)
21	[2]1	Jemmey told his passion (m Keen)
22	22	Twas in the month of May Jo (m Purcell, D., D&M 3496)
23	23	When Phillida with Jockey (v D'urfey, D&M 3780)
24	24	When Sawny first did woe me (m Leveridge, D&M 3785)
25	[25]	Jockey was a dawdy lad (m Wilkins, s Wilkins, D&M 1873)

26   [26]   Ise tell the false loone (m Frances, D&M 1654)
27   [27]   Why does Willy shun his dear (m Clarke, J., s Cross, D&M 3927)
28   [28]   If my Sawny thou's but love me (m Brown, R., v Brown, R.)
29   [29]   Jenny long resisted Wully's fierce desire (s Campion, D&M 1858)
30   [30]   Blythe Jockey, young and gay (m Leveridge, s Boy, D&M 382)
31   [31]   When bonny Jenny first left me (m Corbett, < *As you find it*)
32   [32]   What garrs th' fewlish mayde complain (m Purcell, D.)
33   [33]   When Jockey first I saw (m Cox, D&M 3761)

Notes:
1. Contents' list headed: 'A table of the Scotch songs contain'd in this book.' Two songs substituted: list has as no. 1: 'Ah my fickle Jenny', and as no. 17: 'One Sunday after mass'.
2. Page numbers supplied in part or entirely in MS.: 1-6, 10-11, 15, 17-18, 21, 25-33.
3. 'Printed for &' in MS. before 'Sould by...' in imprint.
4. ∎ in title transcription = 'and P. Randall'(?) scored out.

Copy: Lbl G.316.b.

Plate 96.1 Pepusch, *Venus and Adonis*, 1716

The
SONGS
and Symphony's
in the Masque of
VENUS & ADONIS
as they are Perform'd at the
Theatre Royal.
Compos'd
by
Dr. Pepusch.
Fairly Engraven and
Carefully Corected by the
Author.

London Printed for I.Walsh Servant in Ordinary to his Britanick Majesty, at ȳ Harp & Hoboy in Katherne street,
near Somerset House in ȳ Strand, & I.Hare at ȳ Viol & Flute in Cornhill near the Royall Exchange.

Caption: plate 96.1. 350 x 220 mm. DFo: M1520 P27V4 Cage Copy 1.

[within cartouche] ⌠ The Songs and Symphony's in the Masque of Venus &
Adonis as they are Perform'd at the Theatre Royal. Compos'd by Dr: Pepusch.
Fairly Engraven and Carefully Corected by the Author. ⌡ [at foot] London
Printed for J: Walsh Servant in Ordinary to his Britanick Majesty, at ye Harp &
Hoboy in Katherine street, near Somerset House in ye Strand, & J: Hare at ye
Viol & Flute in Cornhill near the Royall Exchange.

42 leaves. Pp. [i]□ [1]□\□2 3□-7□\□8 9□-11□\□12 13□-14□\□15 16□\□17 18□\□19
20□\□21 22□-23□\□24 25□\□26 27□\□28 29□-30□\□31 32□-33□\34 35□\□36 37□-
39□\□40 41□.
Leaves printed on 1 side.
Tallest copy 384 x 250 mm. Vertical chain lines.

One page engraved per plate. Engraving style Walsh 1.
Title-page plate 312 x 189 mm. Passe-partout no. 6.
Contents plate 256 x 89 mm.

Walsh i: 492.
Advertised in *Post Man*, 10 May 1716.

Contents: title-page [i]; contents and introduction [1]; overture 2-7; songs 8-41.

Songs:

No.	Page	First Line
1	8-10	How pleasant is ranging the fields (s De L'Épine, < *Venus and Adonis*)
2	11	Ah sweet Adonis fram'd for joy (s Barbier, < *Venus and Adonis*)
3	12-13	With her alone, I'll live and dye (s De L'Épine, < *Venus and Adonis*)
4	14	Swain thy foolish sports give over (s Barbier, < *Venus and Adonis*)
5	15-16	Cease your vain teizing (s De L'Épine, < *Venus and Adonis*)
6	17-18	Cupid bend thy bow (s Barbier, < *Venus and Adonis*)
7	19-20	How silly's the heart of a woman (s De L'Épine, < *Venus and Adonis*)
8	21-23	Farewell Venus wellcome pleasure (s De L'Épine, Barbier, < *Venus and Adonis*)
9	24-25	Beauty now alone shall move him (s Turner, < *Venus and Adonis*)
10	26-27	Gentle slumbers life releiving (s De L'Épine, < *Venus and Adonis*)
11	28-30	Chirping warblers, tune your voices (< *Venus and Adonis*)
12	31-32	What heart cou'd now refuse thee (s Barbier, < *Venus and Adonis*)
13	33	Thus the brave from war returning (s Turner, < *Venus and Adonis*)
14	34-35	On love what greater curse can fall (s De L'Épine, < *Venus and Adonis*)
15	36-38	Oh believe me no I shall ever Mars adore (s Barbier, Turner, < *Venus and Adonis*)
16	39	Oh wellcome gentle death (s De L'Épine, < *Venus and Adonis*)
17	40-41	Let ev'ry tender passion feel (s Barbier, < *Venus and Adonis*)

Notes:
1. DFo (copy 1): '5s' in MS. beneath 'author' on titlepage.
2. Lcm: - p. 39; pp. 32-35 bound betweeen pp. 40-41.

Copies: DFo Bd.w. M1528.P21S4 Cage; DFo M1520.P27V4 Cage Copy 1; DLC M1520.P42
Case; DRc Mus.D.33; Lcm XXXII.B.20.(3.); Mp BR f526 Pj39; NjP (Ex) M1523.P3V5q; *Obh*.

Plate 97.1 Pepusch, *Venus and Adonis*, 1716

The
SONGS
and Symphony's
in the Masque of
VENUS & ADONIS
as they are Perform'd at the
Theatre Royal
Compos'd
by
Dr Pepusch.
Fairly Engraven and
Carefully Corected by the
Author.

London Printed for J. Walsh Servant in Ordinary to his Britanick Majesty, at ÿ Harp & Hoboy in Katherine street.
near Somerset House in ÿ Strand.

97 Pepusch, *Venus and Adonis*, 10 May 1716

Caption: plate 97.1. 328 x 215 mm. Ge: P.b.61.

[within cartouche] ⌠ The Songs and Symphony's in the Masque of Venus &
Adonis as they are Perform'd at the Theatre Royal. Compos'd by Dr: Pepusch.
Fairly Engraven and carefully Corected by the Author. ⌡ [at foot] London
Printed for J: Walsh Servant in Ordinary to his Britanick Majesty, at ye Harp &
Hoboy in Katherine street, near Somerset House in ye Strand

22 leaves. Pp. [i]▯ [1] 2-40 41▯.
Leaves printed on 2 sides.
Tallest copy 328 x 215 mm. Vertical chain lines.

One page engraved per plate. Engraving style Walsh 1.
Title-page plate 312 x 189 mm. Passe-partout no. 6.

Contents: title-page [i]; contents and advertisement [1]; overture 2-7; songs 8-41.

Songs: see **96**.

Copy: Ge P.b.61.

Plate 98.1   Pepusch, *Venus and Adonis*, 1716

The
SONGS
and Symphony's
in the Masque of
VENUS & ADONIS
as they are Perform'd at the
Theatre Royal
Compos'd
by
Dr. Pepusch.
Fairly Engraven and
Carefully Corected by the
Author.

Sold by Iohn Young Musical Instrument Seller at the Dolphin &
near Crown at the West end of St. Pauls Church, where you may be furnish'd
with al sorts of Violins, Flutes, Hautboys, Bass Viols, Harpsicords or Spinets,

Caption: plate 98.1. 319 x 210 mm. Lbl: G.222.(4).

[within cartouche] ⌠ The Songs and Symphony's in the Masque of Venus & Adonis as they are Perform'd at the Theatre Royal. Compos'd by Dr: Pepusch. Fairly Engraven and Carefully Corected by the Author. ⌡ [engraved label over Walsh & Hare imprint] Sold by Iohn Young Musical Instrument Seller at the Dolphin & Crown at the West end of St. Pauls Church, where you may be furnish'd with al sorts of Violins, Flutes, Hautboys Bass-Viols, Harpsicords or Spinets, likewise al Books of Tunes, and Directions for any of these Instruments

42 leaves. Pp. [i]□ [1]□\□2 3□-7□\□8 9□-11□\□12 13□-14□\□15 16□\□17 18□\□19 20□-23□\□24 25□\□26 27□\□28 29□-30□\□31 32□-33□\□34 35□\□36 37□-39□\□40 41□.
Leaves printed on 1 side.
Tallest copy 319 x 210 mm. Vertical chain lines.

One page engraved per plate. Engraving style Walsh 1.
Title-page plate ? x 189 mm. Passe-partout no. 6. (See note 1.)

Contents: title-page [i]; contents and advertisement [1]; overture 2-7; songs 8-41.

Songs: see **96**.

Note:
1. Young label cropped with loss of last line. Label obscures lower edge of plate.

Copy: Lbl G.222.(4.).

Plate 99.1 *Merry Musician*, v.1, 1716

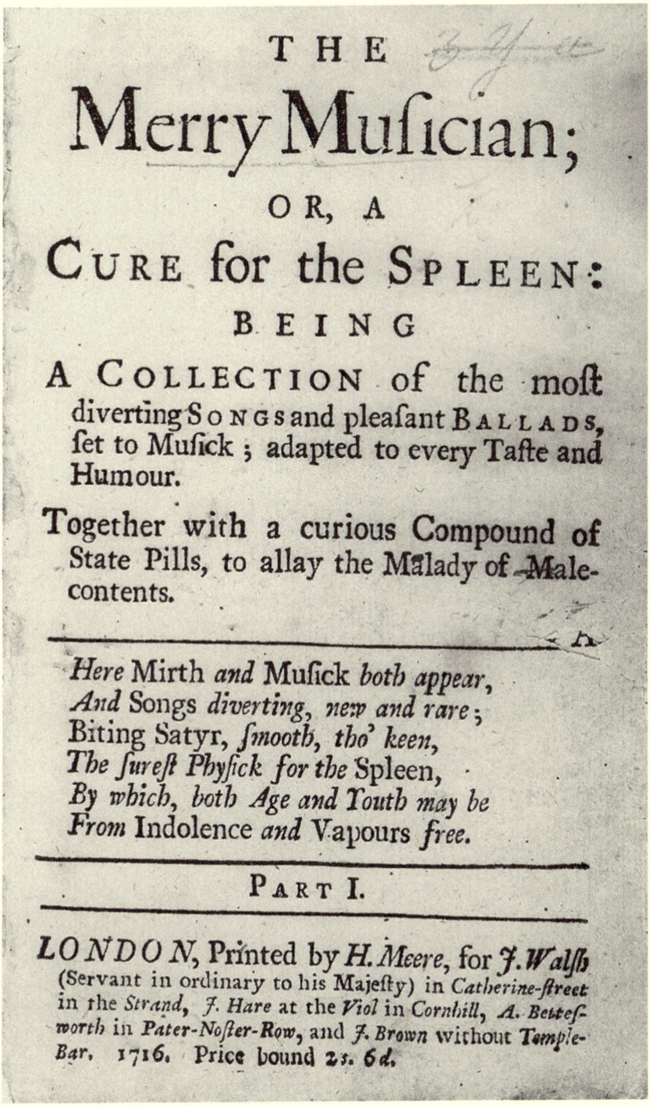

THE
Merry Musician;
OR, A
CURE for the SPLEEN:
BEING

A COLLECTION of the moſt diverting SONGS and pleaſant BALLADS, ſet to Muſick ; adapted to every Taſte and Humour.

Together with a curious Compound of State Pills, to allay the Malady of Male-contents.

Here Mirth *and* Muſick *both appear,*
And Songs *diverting, new and rare;*
Biting Satyr, ſmooth, tho' keen,
The ſureſt Phyſick for the Spleen,
By which, both Age *and* Youth *may be*
From Indolence *and* Vapours *free.*

PART I.

LONDON, Printed by *H. Meere,* for *J. Walſh* (Servant in ordinary to his Majeſty) in *Catherine-ſtreet* in the *Strand, J. Hare* at the *Viol* in *Cornhill, A. Bettes-worth* in *Pater-Noſter-Row,* and *J. Brown* without *Temple-Bar.* 1716. Price bound 2 *s.* 6 *d.*

Caption: plate 99.1. 152 x 94 mm. Lbl: B.353.

[letterpress] The Merry Musician; Or, A Cure for the Spleen: Being A Collection of the most diverting Songs and pleasant Ballads, set to Musick; adapted to every Taste and Humour. Together with a curious Compound of State Pills, to allay the Malady of Malecontents. [verse] Part I. London, Printed by H. Meere, for J. Walsh (Servant in ordinary to his Majesty) in Catherine-street in the Strand, J. Hare at the Viol in Cornhill, A. Bettes-worth in Pater-Noster-Row, and J. Brown without Temple-Bar. 1716. Price bound 2s. 6d.

174 leaves. Pp. [i-xii] 1-336.
Leaves printed on 2 sides.
Letterpress throughout. 12° A⁶ B-P¹².
Tallest copy 160 x 89 mm. Horizontal chain lines.

Walsh i: 485.
Advertised in *Post Boy*, 26 August 1721. Price 2/6.

Contents: title-page [i]; preface [iii-vi]; contents [vii-xii]; songs 1-336.

Songs:

No.	Page	First Line
1	1-5	Dear Jack, if you mean (v D'urfey, < *Hob's Wedding*, D&M 813)
2	5-7	As tipling John
3	8-9	Clasp'd in my dear Melinda's arms (v Birkhead, D&M 569)
4	9-10	Dear Catholick brother, are you come from the wars (D&M 808)
5	11-14	Farewell, Cloe, o farewell (m Ramondon, D&M 960)
6	14-16	Fill up the mightly sparkling bowl
7	17-19	Great Lord Frog to Lady Mouse (v D'urfey, D&M 1202)
8	20-21	Trifling song you shall hear, A (m Purcell, D.)
9	23-24	Go vind the vicar of Taunton Dean (v D'urfey)
10	25-27	Tory, a Whig, and a moderate man, A (v D'urfey, D&M 3470)
11	28-31	Room for the post (m Leveridge, s Leveridge)
12	32-36	Ye Jacks of the town (v D'urfey, D&M 4046)
13	36-39	At the break of morning light (m Ramondon, D&M 270)
14	39-42	To you, fair ladies, now at land (v Dorset, Charles Sackville, D&M 3453)
15	42-43	I have a tenement to lett (D&M 1526)
16	44-46	In troth, friend Harry
17	46-48	Since Tom's in the chair, and e'ery one here (D&M 2969)
18	49-52	Me send you, sir, one letter (v D'urfey, D&M 2187)
19	52-54	In a barren tree
20	54-55	There's a new set of rakes (D&M 3246)
21	56-59	Phillis, the fairest of love's powers (m Eminent Master, v Person of Quality)
22	60-61	Our Ordnance bor'd (v Estcourt)
23	62-64	Last night a dream come into my head (D&M 1927)
24	64-66	Down in the North country
25	66-68	I'll tell thee, Dick, where I have lately been (D&M 1640)
26	69-72	Come, brave boys, let's stroul it away (m Birkhead, s Birkhead < *Walking Statue*)
27	73-74	How happy are we (m Barrett, s Pack, < *Lady's Fine Airs*, D&M 1413)
28	74-76	Jenny, and Molly, and Dolly (v D'urfey, D&M 1855)

29	76-78	Now thanks to the Queen, we are rid of the war (v Motteux, s Leveridge)
30	79-80	Now comes joyful peace (v D'urfey, D&M 2377)
31	81-82	Of all the handsome ladies (D&M 2567)
32	83-87	Phillis who knows how well she is belov'd (m Wilford, v Garee)
33	87-88	In vain are the hopes of a Popish pretender
34	89-91	Tho' begging is an honest trade (D&M 3308)
35	91-93	What are these ideots doing (s Pack, < *Kingdom of the Birds*, D&M 3622)
36	94-96	You tell me, Dick, you lately read (v Estcourt, D&M 4105)
37	97-101	From grave lessons and restraint (m Weldon)
38	101-103	Musing I late on Windsor Terras sate (v D'urfey, D&M 2228)
39	104-107	Bumpers lull our cares to rest (m Barrett, < *City Ramble*)
40	107-111	Come charge your empty glasses
41	111-113	Go falsest of thy sex, be gone (m Ramondon, D&M 1139)
42	113-116	Jolly Roger Twangdillo of Plouden-Hill (v D'urfey, D&M 1881)
43	117-119	Farewell love and all soft pleasure (s Leveridge, < *Thomyris*)
44	120-122	Love in her bosom end my care (m Weldon, s Hodgson, < *Agreeable Disappointment*)
45	123-126	In a cool refreshing shade (m Purcell, D., s Davis)
46	127-129	Foolish swain, thy sighs forbear (m Leveridge, s Leveridge, D&M 1043)
47	129-132	As I was walking, I heard a maid talking (v Estcourt)
48	133-136	Madam, I'm just come from college (m Manley)
49	136-139	Hast thou not read in ancient story
50	139-144	Come all, great, small, short, tall (v D'urfey, D&M 588)
51	145-149	Boast no more of nice beauties from hence
52	149-152	Queen of islands, victorious state (m Leveridge, v Motteux)
53	153-156	If to love or good wine (m Leveridge)
54	157-159	Let burgundy flow (v D'urfey, D&M 1959)
55	159-161	Despairing beside a clear stream (D&M 841)
56	161-164	Ye winds, to whom Collin complains (m Handel)
57	164-166	Early in the dawning of a winter's morn (m Leveridge, s Pinkethman, D&M 902)
58	167-168	Elevate your joys, ye inspir'd of the town (v D'urfey, < *Modern Prophets*, D&M 903)
59	169-171	When embracing my friends (m Eminent Master, D&M 3711)
60	172-173	Britains, now let joys increase (v D'urfey, D&M 436)
61	173-175	Hark, Lewis groans, good Fader, wat ailsh him (v D'urfey, D&M 1259)
62	175-176	Suppose a man does all he can (D&M 3108)
63	177-180	Love is now become a trade (m Barrett, D&M 2104)
64	180-182	Oh the charming month of May (D&M 2535)
65	183-185	Love, the sweets of love (m Du Ruel, D&M 2112)
66	186-189	Let's drink disappointment to restless fanaticks (m Davis)
67	189-191	Maiden fresh as a rose (v D'urfey, s Pack, < *Richmond Heiress*, D&M 2153)
68	192-193	One April morn, when from the sea (v D'urfey, D&M 2624)
69	193-196	One long Whitson holiday (v D'urfey, D&M 2629)
70	196-198	We merry wives of Windsor (D&M 3580)
71	198-201	Make haste, pierce the pipe, that of racy Canary (m Elford, v Herbert)
72	201-206	Enticing love my vows has broke (m Gorton)
73	206-208	Ken you who comes here (s Willis, D&M 1901)
74	208-210	Lard, how men can claret drink (v Estcourt)
75	211-214	Now Jocky and Moggy are ready (D&M 2394)
76	214-216	Love love's a distemper that comes with high feeding (m Barrett)
77	216-218	Of all the simple things we do (< *Country Wake*, D&M 2571)
78	218-220	Of all comforts I miscarry'd (v D'urfey, D&M 2559)
79	220-222	He that marries a lass for love and a face (m Barrett, s Raynton, < *Custom of the Manor*)
80	222-224	Flatt'ring intruder, smiling deluder (v Leveridge)
81	224-227	As I came down the High-Land Town (D&M 3566)
82	227-229	At noon in a sultry summer's day (m Ramondon, D&M 268)

Notes:
1. Gm: - pp. 81-82.
2. MH-Mu: - pp. 43-44, 63-64, 131-32, 195-96, 275-76, 303-304, 325-26; pp. 41-42 and 311-12 mutilated.
3. Vols. 2, 3 and 4 were issued in 1729, 1731 and 1733 respectively. The 2d edition of vol.1 was issued in 1730 (copies at CLU-C, CU-MUSI, DLC).
4. No advertisement contemporary with the initial issue in 1716 has been traced.

Copies: Gm M8515; Lbl B.353; MH-Mu Mus 534.1 (Cage).

Plate 100.1 Marshall, *Three Songs*, 1717

Three Songs compos'd
by Mr. Marshall.
late Organist of Creed
CHURCH.

Printed for & Sold by Daniel Wright, Musical Instrument Seller, Next Door to the Sun Tavern the Corner of Brook Street in Holborn Near the Barrs

Plate 100.2   Marshall, *Three Songs*, 1717

Caption: plates 100.1-100.2. 344 x 218 mm. Lbl: H.1602.

[within cartouche] ⌠ Three Songs compos'd by Mr Marshall. late Organist of Creed Church. ⌡ [at foot] Printed for & Sould by Daniel Wright Musical Instrument Seller Next Door to the Sun Tavern the Corner of Brook Sreet in Holborn Near the Barrs

8 leaves. Pp. [i]◻\◻1 2◻\◻3 4◻-5◻\◻6 7◻.
Leaves printed on 1 side.
Tallest copy 344 x 218 mm. Vertical chain lines.

One page engraved per plate. Engraving style Wright.
Title-page plate 261 x 182 mm. Passe-partout no. 8.

Walsh i: 518.
Advertised in *Post Man*, 20 July 1717.

Contents: title-page [i]; songs 1-7.

Songs:

No.	Page	First Line
1	1-2	Earth's treasure loves delight (m Marshall, s Cook, Travers)
2	3-5	Love in her eyes triumphant plays (m Marshall, s Travers)
3	6-7	O charming Sylvia ruler of my heart (m Marshall, s Travers)

Notes:
1. CSmH: - p. [i].
2. Obh Mus. E.31 is a fragment comprising pp. 1-2 only.

Copies: CSmH 81013 v.1; Lbl H.1602.

Plate 101.1   Graves, *Twenty New Songs*, 1717

Twenty New SONGS Compos'd by Mr James Graves.

Printed & sould by Daniel Wright, next y Sun Tavern, y Corner of Brooks street, in Holborn

101 Graves, *Twenty New Songs*, 19 September 1717

Caption: plate 101.1. 313 x 220 mm. Obh: Mus. E.18.

[within cartouche] Twenty New Songs Compos'd by Mr Iames Graves. J. Cobb, scu, [at foot] Printed, & sould by Daniel Wright, next ye Sun Tavern, ye Corner of Brooks-street, in Holborn.

23 leaves. Pp. [i]☐-[ii]☐ 1☐-4☐ [5]☐-[21]☐.
Leaves printed on 1 side.
Tallest copy 313 x 220 mm. Vertical chain lines.

One page engraved per plate. Engraving style Wright.
Title-page plate 290 x 183 mm.
Contents plate 261 x 100 mm.

Walsh i: 528.
Advertised in *Post Man*, 19 September 1717. Price 3s.

Contents: title-page [i]; contents and advertisement [ii]; songs 1-4 [5-20]; contents and advertisement (Walsh edition) [21].

Songs:

No.	Page	First Line
1	1	My pritty lovely charming fair (m Graves)
2	2	Charming Silvia ever is kind, The (m Graves)
3	3	Ralph James Richard and merry Gill (m Graves)
4	4	When Chloe on the spinnet plays (m Graves)
5	[5]	Go soft spell inchant her mind (m Graves)
6	[6]	Brisk clarret and sherry (m Graves)
7	[7]	Close by a flowry fountains bank (m Graves, D&M 574)
8	[8]	In praise of musick all delight (m Graves)
9	[9]	When the shrill trumpets (m Graves)
10	[10]	Fill your glasses, and dround whineing love (m Graves)
11	[11]	High day no body here (m Graves)
12	[12]	One day being brisk (m Graves)
13	[13]	Fill your glass drink apace (m Graves)
14	[14]	Lucinda Mira give me leave (m Graves)
15	[15]	Come here honest Tim (m Graves)
16	[16]	Apollo pray tell me that is if you can sir (m Graves, < *British Apollo*)
17	[17]	Some say that marriage life is best (m Graves)
18	[18]	Musick's harmony all sorrows drown'd (m Graves)
19	[19]	Heaven first created woman to be kind (m Graves, D&M 1318)
20	[20]	How happy's the man, who do's take his cann (m Graves)

Note:
1. Copy comprises loose sheets from Wright edition and Walsh edition. Pp. 3, [8], [12], [17], [19], [21] are Walsh editions.

Copy: Obh Mus. E.18.

Plate 102.1   Graves, *Collection of Songs*, 1717

A

Collection of SONGS

Set to Muſick.

by Mr James Graves.

London Printed for I.Walſh Servt. in Ordinary to his Majeſty at the Harp and Hoboy in Catherine ſtreet in the Strand. and I.Hare at the Viol and Flute in Cornhill near the Royal Exchange.

Caption: plate 102.1. 346 x 223 mm. Obh: Mus. E.17.

A Collection of Songs Set to Musick by Mr. James Graves. London Printed for I. Walsh Servt. in Ordinary to his Majesty at the Harp and Hoboy in Catherine street in the Strand, and I. Hare at the Viol and Flute in Cornhill near the Royal Exchange.

22 leaves. Pp. [i]□-[ii]□ 1□-20□.
Leaves printed on 1 side.
Tallest copy 346 x 223 mm. Vertical chain lines.

One page engraved per plate. Engraving style Walsh.
Title-page plates 248 x 185 mm. (See note 1.)
Contents plate 262 x 100 mm.

Walsh i: 528.
Advertised in *Post Boy*, 26 October 1717.

Contents: title-page [i]; contents and advertisement [ii]; songs 1-20.

Songs:

No.	Page	First Line
1	1	My pretty lovely charming fair (m Graves)
2	2	Charming Silvia ever is kind, The (m Graves)
3	3	Ralph James Richard and merry Gill (m Graves)
4	4	When Cloe on the spinnet plays (m Graves)
5	5	Go soft spell inchant her mind (m Graves)
6	6	Brisk clarret and sherry (m Graves)
7	7	Close by a flowry fountain's brink (m Graves, D&M 574)
8	8	In praise of musick all delight (m Graves)
9	9	When the shrill trumpets (m Graves)
10	10	Fill your glasses and drown whining love (m Graves)
11	11	Hey day nobody here, no wife, no maid (m Graves)
12	12	One day being brisk (m Graves)
13	13	Fill your glass drink apace (m Graves)
14	14	Lucinda Mira give me leave (m Graves)
15	15	Come here honest Tim (m Graves)
16	16	Apollo pray tell me that is if you can sir (m Graves)
17	17	Some say that marriage life is best (m Graves)
18	18	Musick's harmony all sorrows drownd (m Graves)
19	19	Heaven first created woman to be kind (m Graves, D&M 1318)
20	20	How happy's the man who does take of his cann (m Graves)

Note:
1. Title-page comprises two plates, the illustration and the title and imprint. For an earlier use of the illustration see 59.

Copy: Obh Mus. E.17.

Plate 103.1   Galliard, *Calypso and Telemachus*, 1717

Songs
in the
OPERA
of
Calypso & Telemachus,
as they are Perform'd
at the Queens Theatre.
Compos'd by
Mr Galliard
the Words by
Mr Hughes

103 Galliard, *Calypso and Telemachus*, 31 December 1717

Caption: plate 103.1. 330 x 215 mm. ICN: Case VM1505.G16c.

[within cartouche] ⌠ Songs in the Opera of Calypso & Telemachus as they are Perform'd at the Queens Theatre. Compos'd by Mr. Galliard. the Words by Mr Hughes ⌡ London Printed for J: Walsh Servant in Ordinary to his Britanick Majesty, at ye Harp & Hoboy in Katherine street, near Somerset House in ye Strand, & J: Hare at ye Viol & Flute in Cornhill near the Royall Exchange.

33 leaves. Pp. [i]☐ [ii] 1-61 62☐.
Leaves printed on 2 sides.
Tallest copy 340 x 219 mm. Vertical chain lines.

One page engraved per plate. Engraving style Walsh and Cross.
Title-page plate 312 x 192 mm. Passe-partout no. 6.

Contents: title-page [i]; contents and advertisement [ii]; overture 1-4; songs 5-62.

Songs: see 85.

Note:
1. Revived 27 February 1717.

Copies: ICN Case VM1505.G16c; LVp 782.1; MB **M400.37.

Plate 104.1 Turner, *Twenty New Songs*, 1718

Caption: plate 104.1. 345 x 222 mm. Lbl: H.49.

[within cartouche] Twenty New Songs Of Humour Compos'd By Mr. Wm: Turner [at foot] London, Printed for the Author at the Old Post-Office in Russel-Street Covent-Garden, and Daniel Wright Musical Instrument Maker, next to the Sun-Tavern in Holborn.

28 leaves. Pp. [i]□ 1□-26□ [27]□.
Leaves printed on 1 side.
Tallest copy 345 x 222 mm. Vertical chain lines.

One page engraved per plate. Engraving style Wright.
Title-page plate 250 x 170 mm.

Advertised in *Post Man*, 29 April 1718.

Contents: title-page [i]; recitative 1; songs 2-21; cantata 22-26; flute solo [27].

Songs:

No.	Page	First Line
1	2	Is there a wretch so stupid (v Carey)
2	3	Cupid, whom great Jove obey'd
3	4	Why does my fairest Daphne fly
4	5	All the materials are the same
5	6	Variety I love 'tis true (v Wycherley)
6	7	If it be true, as wisemen say (m Turner, v Carey)
7	8	O, Cupid, I invoke to arm
8	9	Cease, you pert asses, your apish addresses
9	10	Softest charmer, do not fly me (v Huddy)
10	11	Celia's easy free and gay
11	12	Lucinda's all my joy, my treasure (v Huddy)
12	13	Look down, triumphant god of war (v Huddy)
13	14	Let braves, who to the army go (D&M 1957)
14	15	Love is all fancy, nothing more (v F., H.)
15	16	Let the nymph, who designs her amours to maintain
16	17	When first my eyes encounter'd thine (v Dyer)
17	18-19	Strict virtue guard me (< *Alexander the Great*)
18	20-21	Let courtly delights, diversion and pleasure (< *Presumptuous Love*)

Notes:
1. P. 1: 'The epistle dedicatory to the subscribers. In recitativo.'
2. P. [27]: a musical palindrome entitled 'Zenith Nadir'.

Copy: Lbl H.49.

Plate 105.1   Pepusch, *Thomyris and Camilla*, Additional Songs, 1719

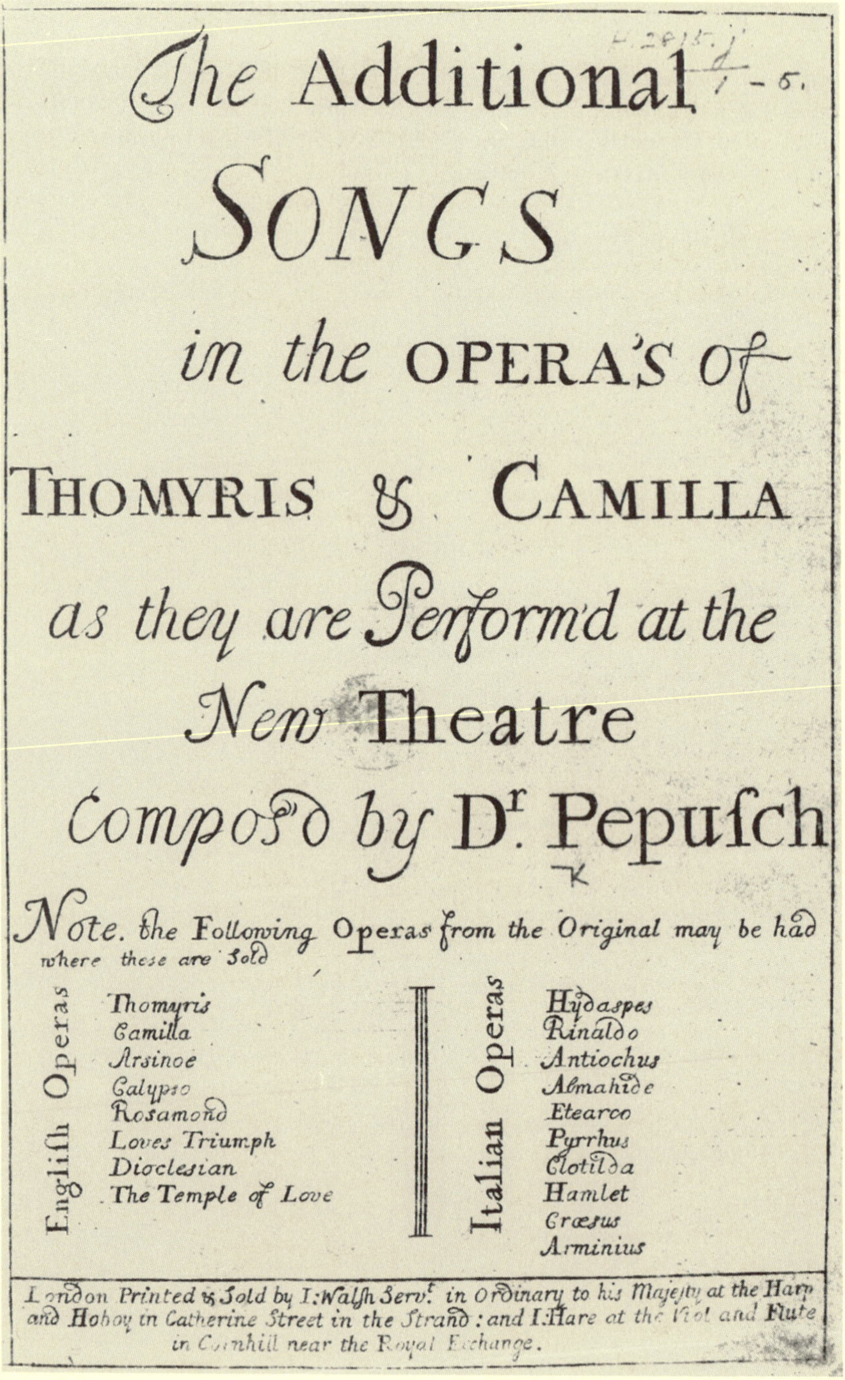

The Additional

SONGS

in the OPERA'S of

THOMYRIS & CAMILLA

as they are Perform'd at the

New Theatre

Compos'd by Dr Pepusch

Note. the Following Operas from the Original may be had where these are Sold

English Operas		Italian Operas	
	Thomyris		Hydaspes
	Camilla		Rinaldo
	Arsinoe		Antiochus
	Calypso		Almahide
	Rosamond		Etearco
	Loves Triumph		Pyrrhus
	Dioclesian		Clotilda
	The Temple of Love		Hamlet
			Cræsus
			Arminius

London Printed & Sold by I: Walsh Servt in Ordinary to his Majesty at the Harp and Hoboy in Catherine Street in the Strand: and I: Hare at the Viol and Flute in Cornhill near the Royal Exchange.

Caption: plate 105.1. 329 x 213 mm. Lbl: H.2815.j.(1.).

The Additional Songs in the Opera's of Thomyris & Camilla as they are Perform'd at the New Theatre Compos'd by Dr. Pepusch Note. the Following Operas from the Original may be had where these are Sold English Operas Thomyris Camilla Arsinoe Calypso Rosamond Loves Triumph Dioclesian The Temple of Love Italian Operas Hydaspes Rinaldo Antiochus Almahide Etearco Pyrrhus Clotilda Hamlet Croesus Arminius London printed & Sold by I: Walsh Servt. in Ordinary to his Majesty at the Harp and Hoboy in Catherine Street in the Strand: and I: Hare at the Viol and Flute in Cornhill near the Royal Exchange.

21 leaves. Pp. [i]☐ 1☐-3☐\☐4 5☐\☐6 7☐\☐8 9☐-11☐\☐12 13☐-16☐\☐17 18☐-20☐.
Leaves printed on 1 side.
Tallest copy 329 x 213 mm. Horizontal chain lines.

One page engraved per plate. Engraving style Walsh.
Title-page plate 281 x 178 mm.

Walsh i: 565.
Advertised in *Post Man*, 14 May 1719. Price 2s. 6d.

Contents: title-page [i]; songs 1-20.

Songs:

No.	Page	First Line
1	1	How blest is a soldier when listed to rove (m Pepusch, s Leveridge, < *Thomyris*)
2	2	Cares on a crown attending (m Pepusch, s Pulmon, < *Thomyris*)
3	3	Rouze ye brave for fame & glory (m Pepusch, s Pulmon, < *Thomyris*)
4	4-5	No more let sorrow pain you (m Pepusch, s Pulmon, < *Thomyris*)
5	6-7	Fop with monkey graces (m Pepusch, s Leveridge, < *Thomyris*)
6	8-11	To live nor know ye joys of love (m Pepusch, s De L'Épine, Barbier, < *Thomyris*)
7	12-16	When duty's requiring (m Pepusch, s Fletcher, Pulmon, < *Thomyris*)
8	17-20	Save me with joy posess me (m Pepusch, s Pulmon, < *Camilla*)

Note:
1. Ge: p. 16 reversed when rebound.

Copies: Ge P.b.61; Lbl H.2815.j.(1.).

Plate 106.1   *Yearly Subscription*, 1719

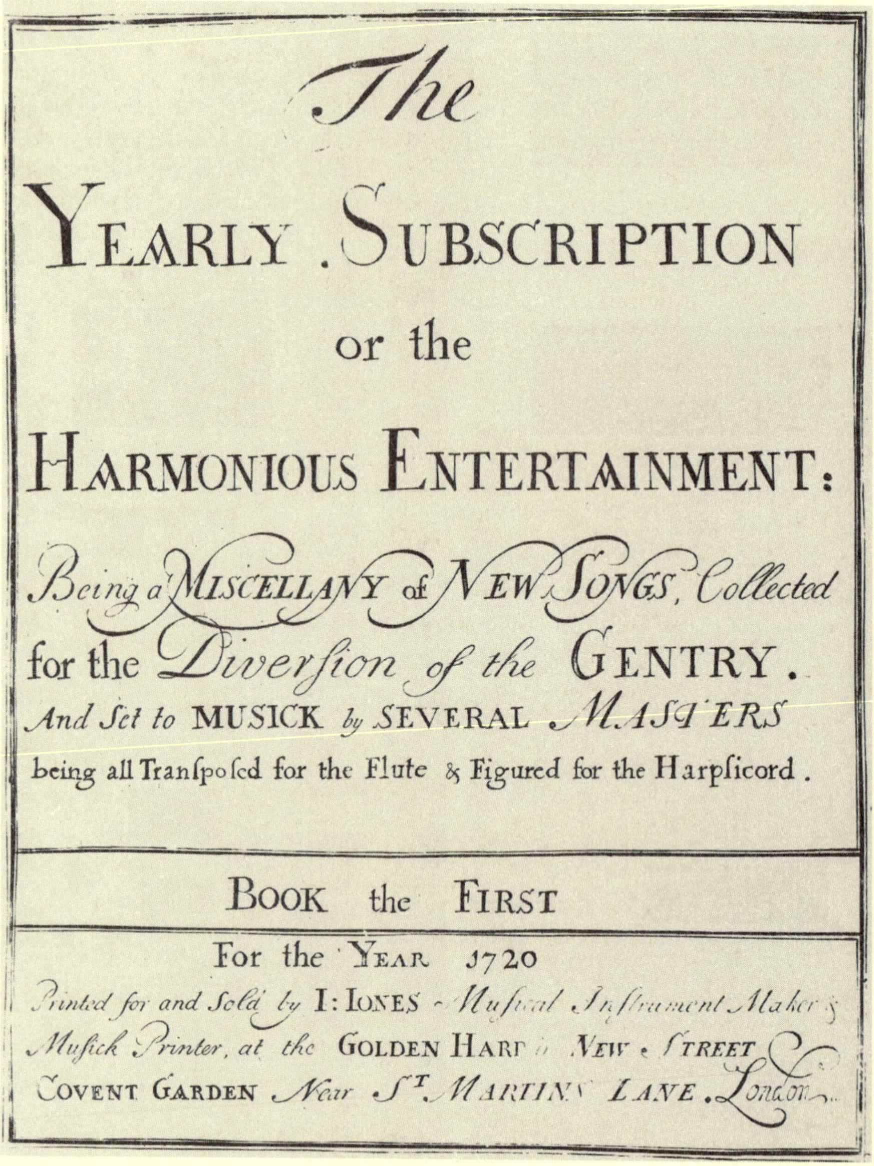

The

YEARLY . SUBSCRIPTION

or the

HARMONIOUS ENTERTAINMENT:

Being a MISCELLANY *of* NEW SONGS, *Collected*
for the *Diversion of the* GENTRY .
And Set to MUSICK *by* SEVERAL *MASTERS*
being all Transposed for the Flute & Figured for the Harpsicord .

BOOK   the   FIRST

For the YEAR 1720

Printed for and Sold by I: IONES - Musical Instrument Maker &
Musick Printer, at the GOLDEN HARP New STREET
COVENT GARDEN Near St. MARTINS LANE . London

Plate 106.2   *Yearly Subscription*, 1719

Caption: plates 106.1-106.2. 365 x 235 mm. Obh: Mus. E.143.

The Yearly Subscription or the Harmonious Entertainment: Being a Misellany of New Songs, Collected for the Diversion of the Gentry. And Set to Musick by Several Masters being all Transposed for the Flute & Figured for the Harpsicord. Book the First For the Year 1720 Printed for and Sold by I. Iones Musical Instrument Maker & Musick Printer, at the Golden Harp in New Street Covent Garden Near St Martins Lane. London.

35 leaves. Pp. [i]▢-[ii]▢\▢1 2▢\▢3 4▢\▢5 6▢-8▢\▢9-10▢\-\▢13-14▢\▢15 16▢-19▢\▢20-21▢\-\▢24-25▢\▢26 27▢-29▢ 31▢-32▢\▢33 34▢.
Leaves printed on 1 side.
Tallest copy 365 x 235 mm. Vertical chain lines.

One page engraved per plate. Engraving style Jones.
Title-page plate 296 x 208 mm.

Advertised in *Weekly Journal*, 5 December 1719.

Contents: title-page [i]; contents, preface and advertisement [ii]; songs 1-29, 31-34.

Songs:

No.	Page	First Line
1	1-2	O sacred spirit of harmony (m Sheeles)
2	3-4	Fame sound to ye farthest land (m Hayden)
3	5-6	Transporting Cloe lovely fair (m Jones)
4	7	What are crowns & scepters all (m Turner)
5	8	Di godere ha speranza (Oh, my dearest, my lovely) (m Handel)
6	9-10	While the cup walks nimbly round (m Hayden, v Anacreon)
7	11-14	See! from my arms unkind Seymora flies (m Hemming)
8	15-16	Thus when bright Luna looks from high (m Hemming)
9	17	Love and musick are such treasures (m Turner)
10	18	Oh my Corinna were I blest (m Turner)
11	19	Jove like a swan for Leda's charms (m Hemming)
12	20-21	In my triumphant chariot hurld (m Hayden)
13	22-23	Fairest charmer lovely dear (m Roseingrave)
14	24-25	While in a lovely rural seat (m Jones)
15	26-27	Boast not mistaken swain thy art (m Hemming)
16	28	See where fair Venus yields her charms (m Hemming)
17	29	Fair brillante brightest creature (m Hemming)
18	31	Musick can soften verse to song (m Turner)
19	32	Clorinda reigns as beautys queen (m Turner)
20	33-34	See how beneath ye lawrels shade (m Sheeles)

Notes:
1. No p. 30 given on contents list.
2. Walsh and Hare issued a competitive edition as the *Monthly Mask of Vocal Music* on 24 December 1719.

Copy: Obh Mus. E.143.

Plate 107.1   Porta, *Numitor*, 1720

Songs
in the
OPERA
Call'd
NUMITOR

I:Collins sculp

London Printed for & sould by I: Walsh Musicall Instrument maker in Ordinary to His Majesty at the
Golden Harp... ...atherine street near Summersethouse in ÿ strand
and I: Hare at th. ...oel and Flute in Cornhill nere the Royall Exchange.

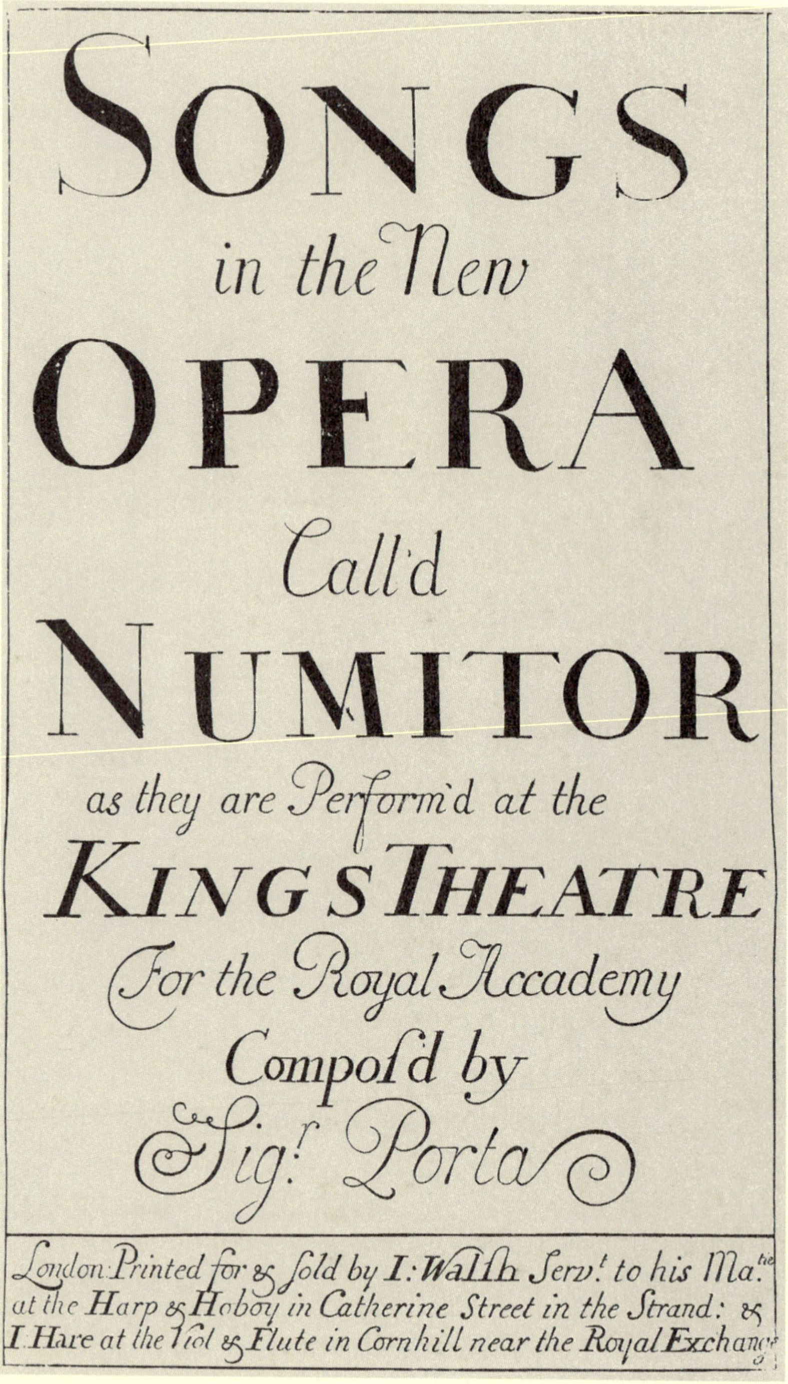

Plate 107.2   Porta, *Numitor*, 1720

SONGS

in the New

OPERA

Call'd

NUMITOR

as they are Perform'd at the

KING s THEATRE

For the Royal Accademy

Compos'd by

Sigr. Porta

London: Printed for & sold by I: Walsh Servt. to his Matie
at the Harp & Hoboy in Catherine Street in the Strand: &
I. Hare at the Viol & Flute in Cornhill near the Royal Exchange

Caption: plates 107.1-107.2. 345 x 225 mm. Lbl: H.297.

[within cartouche] ⌠ Songs in the Opera Call'd Numitor ⌡ I: Collins. sculp [at foot] London Printed for & Sould by I: Walsh Musicall Instrument maker in Ordinary to His Majesty at the Golden Harp & Ho=boy in Catherine=street near Summerset=house in ye strand and I: Hare at the Viol and Flute in Cornhill nere the Royal Exchange.

Songs in the New Opera Call'd Numitor as they are Perform'd at the Kings Theatre for the Royal Accademy Compos'd by Sigr: Porta London: Printed for & sold by I: Walsh Servt. to his Matie. at the Harp and Hoboy in Catherine Street in the Strand: & I: Hare at the Viol & Flute in Cornhill near the Royal Exchange

36 leaves. Pp. [i]◻-[iii]◻\◻1 2-65.
Leaves printed on 2 sides.
Tallest copy 362 x 236 mm. Vertical chain lines.

One page engraved per plate. Engraving style Walsh 1.
Illus. title-page plate 251 x 190 mm. Passe-partout no. 1.
Title-page plate 292 x 169 mm.
Contents plate 311 x 124 mm.

Walsh i: 588.
Advertised in *Post Boy,* 18 June 1720. Price 9s.

Contents: illus. title-page [i]; title-page [ii]; contents and advertisement [iii]; overture 1-4; songs 5-65.

Songs:

No.	Page	First Line
1	5-6	Torni o'sole (s Robinson, T., < *Numitor*)
2	7-8	Il ciel le piante i fior vien meco a rimirar (s Robinson, T., Durastanti, < *Numitor*)
3	9-10	Altro da voi non chiedo (s Robinson, A., < *Numitor*)
4	11-12	Quel piacer ch' è inaspettato (s Baldassari, < *Numitor*)
5	13-14	Chi perde ogni suo bene (s Gordon, < *Numitor*)
6	15-16	Se me fuggi l'ingrata (s Galerati, < *Numitor*)
7	17-18	Non an queste capanne (s Dennis, < *Numitor*)
8	19-20	Dolce aspetto di vaga bellera (s Durastanti, < *Numitor*)
9	21	Le dirai Dorilla bella (s Baldassari, < *Numitor*)
10	22-23	Sol m'affanna sol m'offende (s Robinson, A., < *Numitor*)
11	24-25	Il mormorio del rio lauretta (s Robinson, T., < *Numitor*)
12	26-27	Non posso dir di no (s Robinson, A., < *Numitor*)
13	28-29	Ogni asprezza di tormenti (s Durastanti, < *Numitor*)
14	30	Gran nume de pastori (s Durastanti, < *Numitor*)
15	31-33	Parto ma', oh Dio, non so (s Robinson, A., Baldassari, < *Numitor*)
16	34-35	Nascer mi sento già (s Durastanti, < *Numitor*)
17	36-37	Tal'or che un fosco velo (s Robinson, T., < *Numitor*)

18	38-39	Fiorite erbette ombrose piante (s Dennis, < *Numitor*)
19	40-41	Pensier che m'agitate (s Gordon, < *Numitor*)
20	42-43	Temo che il gran contento (s Gordon, < *Numitor*)
21	44	Per l'adorato oggetto (s Baldassari, < *Numitor*)
22	45	Si t'intendo spera la mia (s Robinson, T., < *Numitor*)
23	46	Il valor d'un nobil petto (s Durastanti, < *Numitor*)
24	47-48	Quando mai pietoso fato (s Robinson, A., < *Numitor*)
25	49	Assetato pelegrino (s Robinson, A., < *Numitor*)
26	50	Puo la forza dar dolcezza (s Galerati, < *Numitor*)
27	51	Nati al pianto occhi dolenti (s Robinson, A., < *Numitor*)
28	52	Se vuoi placarti (s Galerati, < *Numitor*)
29	53-54	Vado a pugnar (s Durastanti, < *Numitor*)
30	55	In pochi istanti ritornerò (s Baldassari, < *Numitor*)
31	56	Fuggir dal fato che vuol no'l sà (s Robinson, A., < *Numitor*)
32	57-58	Sono più care d'amor (s Robinson, T., < *Numitor*)
33	59	Virtù de pensier miei (s Durastanti, < *Numitor*)
34	60-61	Su quel trono (s Gordon, < *Numitor*)
35	62-64	Dove spiega la fama i suoi vanni (s Galerati, < *Numitor*)
36	65	Voglia tuoi figli guardo pieto

Notes:
1. CLU-C, CSfst: - p. [i].
2. DLC: p. [i] reversed.
3. Lcm: + leaf of advertisements at end.

Copies: Ckc 85.21; CLU-C *fM1505.P83n; CSfst de Bellis 894; DLC M1500.P84N8 Case; Er E162; Eu SpC S*17.61.(7.); F-Pc Rés. V.S.1284; *I-BGi*; Lbl H.297; Lcm XXXII.B.11.(1.).

Plate 108.1   Scarletti, D, and Roseingrave, *Narcissus*, 1720

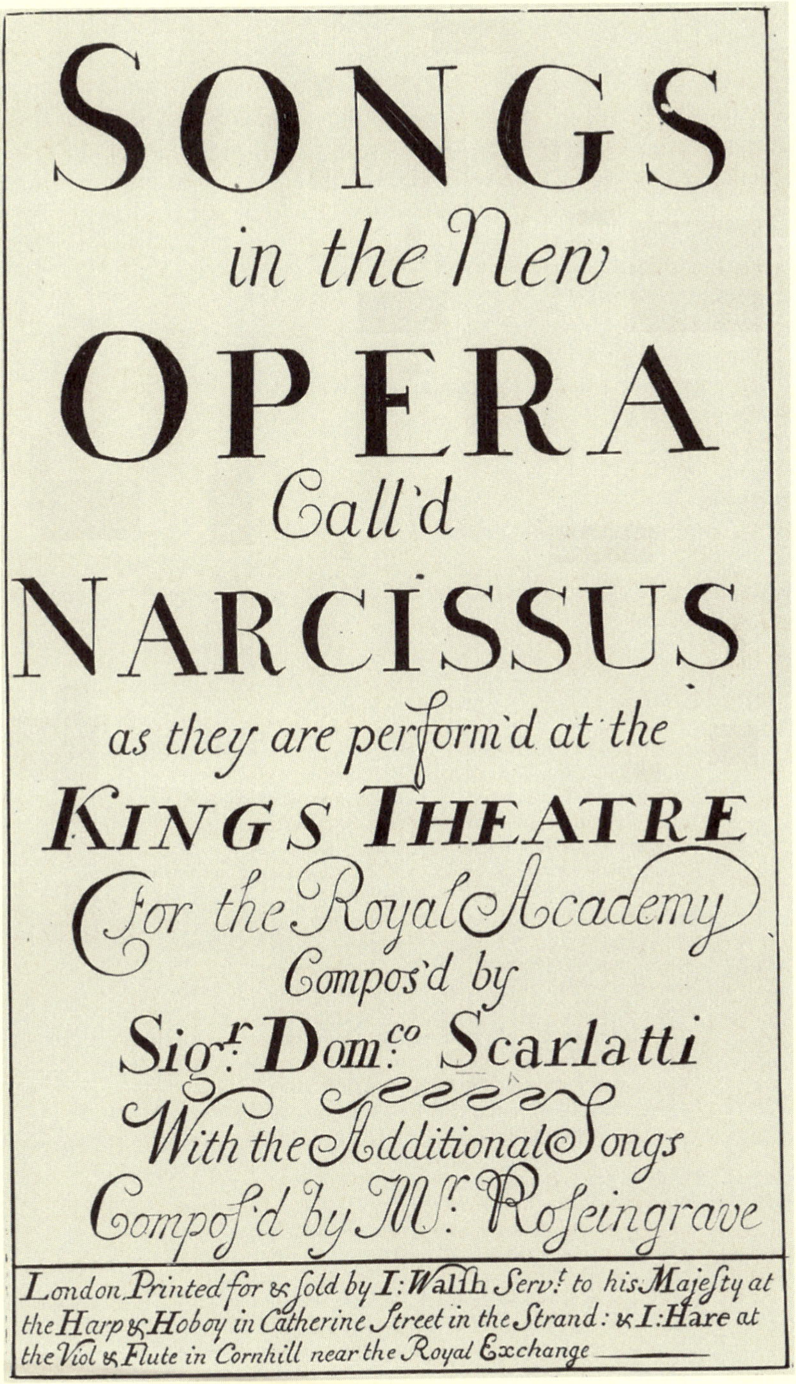

SONGS

in the New

OPERA

Call'd

NARCISSUS

as they are perform'd at the

KINGS THEATRE

(for the Royal Academy)

Compos'd by

Sigr Domco Scarlatti

With the Additional Songs

Compos'd by Mr Roseingrave

London Printed for & sold by I: Walsh Servt to his Majesty at
the Harp & Hoboy in Catherine Street in the Strand: & I: Hare at
the Viol & Flute in Cornhill near the Royal Exchange

Caption: plate 108.1. 352 x 225 mm. Lbl: H.315.

Songs in the New Opera Call'd Narcissus as they are perform'd at the Kings Theatre For the Royal Academy Compos'd by Sigr: Domco: Scarlatti With the Additional Songs Compos'd by Mr: Roseingrave London, Printed for & sold by I: Walsh Servt: to his Majesty at the Harp & Hoboy in Catherine Street in the Strand: & I: Hare at the Viol & Flute in Cornhill near the Royal Exchange

37 leaves. Pp. [i]☐-[ii]☐\☐1 2-69.
Leaves printed on 2 sides.
Tallest copy 358 x 235 mm. Vertical chain lines.

One page engraved per plate. Engraving style Walsh 1.
Title-page plate 295 x 169 mm.
Contents plate 313 x 105 mm.

Walsh i: 590.
Advertised in *Evening Post*, 6 October 1720.

Contents: title-page [i]; contents and advertisement [ii]; overture 1-5; songs 6-69.

Songs:

No.	Page	First Line
1	6-7	Ecco il ciel di luce adorno (s Robinson, A., Benedetti, Gordon, < *Narcissus*)
2	8	Caderà la belva ria (s Gordon, < *Narcissus*)
3	9-10	Dall'orror di fosco nembo (s Benedetti, < *Narcissus*)
4	11	Fuggi un tiranno si (s Robinson, T., < *Narcissus*)
5	12-13	Si tu ben lo sai (s Durastanti, < *Narcissus*)
6	14-15	Quanto è dolce quella speme (s Robinson, A., < *Narcissus*)
7	16	Sento che a poco (s Gordon, < *Narcissus*)
8	17-18	Vorrebbe la speranza (s Durastanti, < *Narcissus*)
9	19	Quel narcisso quant'e bello (s Robinson, T., < *Narcissus*)
10	20-21	Nieghi pure la speranza (s Robinson, A., < *Narcissus*)
11	22-23	No non lo credo non lo spero (s Robinson, A., < *Narcissus*)
12	24-25	Penosi tormenti (s Robinson, A., < *Narcissus*)
13	26-27	Riuolgo il passo altrove (m Roseingrave, s Durastanti, Robinson, A., < *Narcissus*)
14	28	Caro dardo gia l'alma che langue (s Robinson, A., < *Narcissus*)
15	29-30	Dentro quel cupo rio (s Benedetti, < *Narcissus*)
16	31-32	Prendi poi vanne e spera (s Robinson, T., < *Narcissus*)
17	33-34	L'ozio vil di giovinezza (m Roseingrave, s Durastanti, < *Narcissus*)
18	35-36	Perfida t'auuedrai (s Gordon, < *Narcissus*)
19	37	Dami un poco di ristoro (s Benedetti, < *Narcissus*)
20	38	Perfido traditore (m Roseingrave, s Robinson, T., < *Narcissus*)
21	39-40	Si dentro quell'onde (s Robinson, A., < *Narcissus*)
22	41-42	Lassia a me sol la pena (m Roseingrave, < *Narcissus*)
23	43-44	Un arcier che va bendata (s Durastanti, < *Narcissus*)
24	45-46	Folle tu perirai (s Robinson, A., < *Narcissus*)
25	47	Mio bel sol tu m'inuaghisti (s Durastanti, < *Narcissus*)
26	48	Dammi tregua se non pace (s Durastanti, < *Narcissus*)
27	49-51	Vieni ò cara a consolarmi (s Durastanti, < *Narcissus*)

28	52-53	Lascia ch'io vada almen (s Robinson, A., Benedetti, < *Narcissus*)
29	54	Che forse porterà (s Gordon, < *Narcissus*)
30	55	Ma di raggione armato (s Benedetti, < *Narcissus*)
31	56	Morirò mà questo morte (s Robinson, T., < *Narcissus*)
32	57	Alfin potrò morire (s Robinson, A., < *Narcissus*)
33	58-59	Dio d'amor a baciar vado lo strale (s Durastanti, Robinson, A., < *Narcissus*)
34	60-61	M'en volo contento al idolo amato (s Benedetti, < *Narcissus*)
35	62-63	Sento ch'il cor mi dice (s Gordon, < *Narcissus*)
36	64	Non è fiero nè crudele (s Robinson, A., < *Narcissus*)
37	65-66	Amorosa farfalletta (s Durastanti, < *Narcissus*)
38	67-68	In tante mie pene (s Benedetti, < *Narcissus*)
39	69	Benchè sia foco l'amore

Note:
1. Mp: p. 1 reversed.

Copies: Ckc 85.23; DLC M1500.S285N3 Case; Lbl H.315; Lbl Mad.Soc.26; Mp BR f520Sf35.

Plate 109.1   *Sea Songs, 1720*

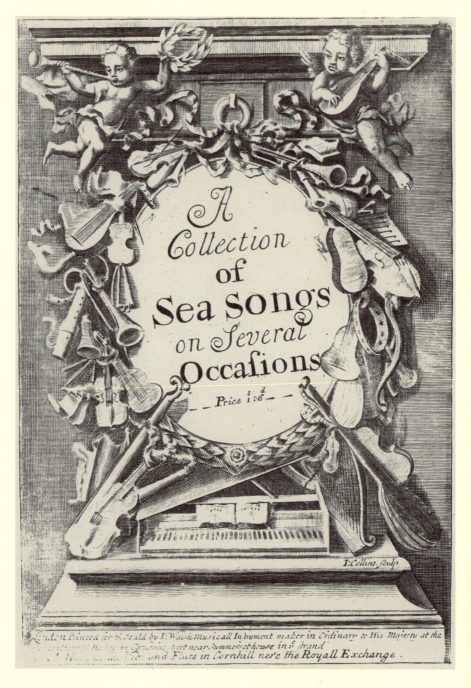

Caption: plate 109.1. 370 x 234 mm. Lbl: H.35.

[within cartouche] ⌠ A Collection of Sea Songs on Several Occasions--Price
1s: 6d--⌡ I: Collins. sculp [at foot] London Printed for & Sould by I: Walsh
Musicall Instrument maker in Ordinary to His Majesty at the Golden Harp &
Ho=boy in Catherine=street near Summerset=house in ye strand and I: Hare
at the Viol and Flute in Cornhill nere the Royall Exchange.

17 leaves. Pp. [i]□-[ii]□\□1 2□-3□ [4]□ 5 [5A] 6□-8□ [9]□ 10□-12□ [13]□\□14 15□.
Leaves printed on 1 side.
Tallest copy 370 x 234 mm. Vertical chain lines.

One page engraved per plate. Engraving style Walsh 1, 2.
Title-page plate 254 x 193 mm. Passe-partout no. 1.
Contents plate 165 x 84 mm.

Walsh i: 594.
Advertised in *Post Boy*, 1 December 1720. Price 1s. 6d.

Contents: title-page [i]; contents [ii]; songs 1-3, [4], 5, [5A], 6-8, [9], 10-12, [13],
14-15.

Songs:

No.	Page	First Line
1	1-2	Lye still ye winds, my Strephon's foe
2	3	Chear up my brave hearts (m Aldrich)
3	[4]	Haul away let your anchors be weighing (m Vanbrugh)
4	5-[5A]	All in the downs the fleet was moor'd
5	6	Blow Boreas blow (m Bradley, Robert, D&M 384)
6	7	Come my mates, letts hoist our sails (m Barrett)
7	8	Just comeing from sea (m Weldon, s Doggett, D&M 1895)
8	[9]	To you fair ladys now at land (m Dorset, Lord, D&M 3453)
9	10	Twas when the seas were roaring
10	11	I'll sail upon the Dog-star (m Purcell, H., < *Fool's Preferment*, D&M 1633)
11	12	How happy are wee now the wind is abaft (m Aldrich)
12	[13]	Farwell Cloe o farewell (m Ramondon, D&M 960)
13	14-15	Charms of bright beauty, The (m Courteville, D&M 531)

Copy: Lbl H.35.

Plate 110.1   Vanbrugh, *Modern Harmony*, 1720

Caption: plate 110.1. 357 x 224 mm. Lbl: H.1605.(1.).

[within cartouche] ⌠ Modern Harmony or a desire to Please Consisting of Vocal and Instrumental Musick as Songs and Arietts for one and two Voices and a Cantata together with a Solo for a Flute & a Bass and a Solo for a Violin & a Bass as also a Set of Lessons for the Harpsicord The whole Compos'd by Mr: Vanbrughe ⌡ [at foot] London Printed for J: Walsh Servant in Ordinary to his Britanick Majesty, at ye Harp & Hoboy in Katherine street, near Somerset House in ye Strand, & J: Hare at ye Viol & Flute in Cornhill near the Royall Exchange.

17 leaves. Pp. [1]◻\◻2 3-22 23◻ 24-31.
Leaves printed on 2 sides.
Tallest copy 357 x 224 mm. Vertical chain lines.

One page engraved per plate. Engraving style Walsh 1.
Title-page plate 318 x 192 mm. Passe-partout no. 6.

Walsh i: 583.
Price 5s.

Contents: title-page [1]; cantata 2-4; songs 5-20; instrumental solos 21-26; harpsichord lessons 27-30; flute parts 31.

Songs:

No.	Page	First Line
1	5	Why do we doat on charming Cloe's face (m Vanbrugh)
2	6-7	Let tyrants awe their humble slaves (m Vanbrugh)
3	8-9	I did but look and love a while (m Vanbrugh)
4	10-11	Cupid disarm thy self on me (m Vanbrugh)
5	12-13	Now is thy spring enjoy the flowers (m Vanbrugh)
6	14	Fickle bliss! fantastick treasure (m Vanbrugh)
7	15	Ye shady glooms in vain ye strive (m Vanbrugh)
8	16-17	At the sight of my Phillis (m Vanbrugh)
9	18	See! my Seraphina comes (m Vanbrugh)
10	19	Prithee Phillis tell me why (m Vanbrugh)
11	20	Soft god! of sleep (m Vanbrugh)

Notes:
1. Dating: advertised as 'Vanbrughes Songs. 5s. od.' in *Numitor*, 1720. Uses passe-partout title-page also employed in 1720 for Pepusch, *Six English Cantatas*.
2. Vanbrugh's other song book, *Mirth and Harmony*, was probably first published in 1730 (see Walsh ii, 1498).

Copies: CLU-C Temp; CSmH 148826; Lbl H.1605.(1.).

Plate III.1   Bononcini, *Astartus*, 1721

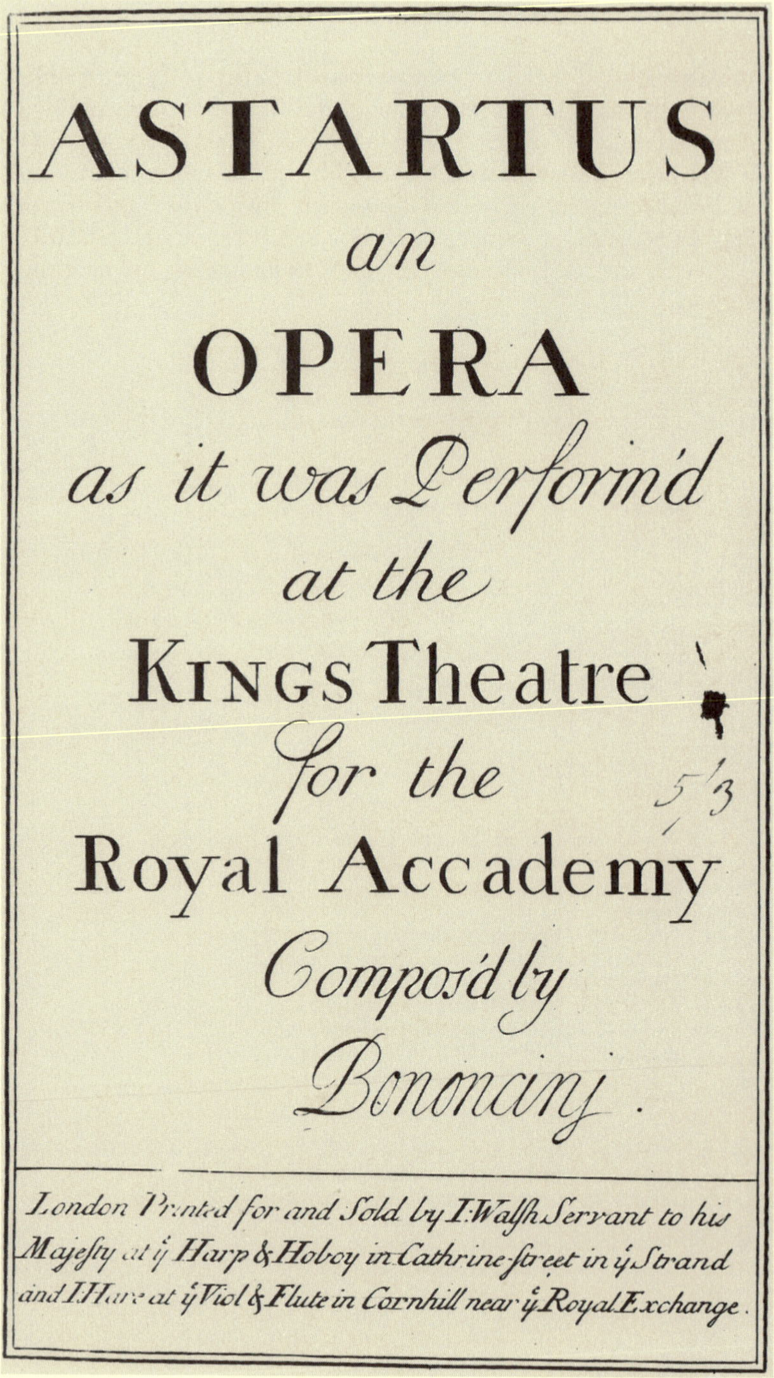

ASTARTUS

an

OPERA

*as it was Perform'd
at the*

KINGS Theatre

for the

Royal Accademy

5/3

Compos'd by

Bononcini.

*London Printed for and Sold by I.Walsh Servant to his
Majesty at y Harp & Hoboy in Cathrine street in y Strand
and I.Hare at y Viol & Flute in Cornhill near y Royal Exchange.*

Caption: plate 111.1. 360 x 227 mm. Lbl: I.296.

Astartus an Opera as it was Perform'd at the Kings Theatre for the Royal
Accademy Compos'd by Bononcini. London Printed for and Sold by I: Walsh
Servant to his Majesty at ye Harp & Hoboy in Cathrine-street in ye Strand and
I: Hare at ye Viol & Flute in Cornhill near ye Royal Exchange.

43 leaves. Pp. [i]▢-[ii]▢ 1-12 13▢ 14-81.
Leaves printed on 2 sides.
Tallest copy 366 x 217 mm. Vertical chain lines.

One page engraved per plate. Engraving style Walsh 1, 3.
Title-page plate 284 x 165 mm.
Contents plate 304 x 141 mm.

Walsh ii: 191.
Advertised in *Daily Courant*, 1 April 1721.

Contents: title-page [i]; contents and advertisement [ii]; overture 1-4; songs 5-11;
symphony 12-14; songs 15-81.

Songs:

No.	Page	First Line
1	5	Figli d'un bel valore (s Durastanti, < *Astartus*)
2	6-7	M'insegna amor l'inganno (s Galerati, < *Astartus*)
3	8-9	No più non bramo (s Berselli, < *Astartus*)
4	10-11	Se fingo se spero (s Salvai, < *Astartus*)
5	15-16	Torno alla patria (s Senesino, < *Astartus*)
6	17-18	In che peccasti (s Durastanti, < *Astartus*)
7	19-20	Stelle ingrate (s Senesino, < *Astartus*)
8	21-22	Si perirà e aura dalle nostr'armi la prima libertà (s Boschi, < *Astartus*)
9	23-24	Care pupille tra mille e mille (s Senesino, < *Astartus*)
10	25-26	Sdegni tornate (s Durastanti, < *Astartus*)
11	27-28	Mio caro ben non sospirar (s Salvai, Berselli, < *Astartus*)
12	29-31	Non mi seguir infido (s Durastanti, < *Astartus*)
13	32-34	La costanza il timore (s Senesino, < *Astartus*)
14	35-36	Sapete che in amor (s Berselli, < *Astartus*)
15	37-38	Spero ma sempre peno (s Galerati, < *Astartus*)
16	39-40	Se vuoi ch'in pace io mora (s Senesino, < *Astartus*)
17	41	Oh quanto invidia il cor (s Durastanti, < *Astartus*)
18	42-43	Non è poco credi a me (s Salvai, < *Astartus*)
19	44-45	Mi dà crudel tormento penosa gelosia (s Berselli, < *Astartus*)
20	46-49	Mi veggo solo e vinto (s Boschi, < *Astartus*)
21	50-51	Ah no non ingannar (s Durastanti, < *Astartus*)
22	52-55	Innamorar e poi mancar (s Durastanti, Senesino, < *Astartus*)
23	56-57	Sai pur s'io vivo amante (s Salvai, < *Astartus*)
24	58-60	Così fedele la mia tiranna (s Berselli, < *Astartus*)
25	61-62	Amante e sposa si gli sarai (s Senesino, < *Astartus*)
26	63-64	Coglierò la bella rosa (s Durastanti, < *Astartus*)
27	65-66	L'esperto nocchiero perchè torna (s Berselli, < *Astartus*)

28   67-68   Disciolte dal piede (s Boschi, < *Astartus*)
29   69-70   Si vedrai non son più quello (s Senesino, < *Astartus*)
30   71-72   Con disperato sdegno (s Galerati, < *Astartus*)
31   73-76   Mai non potrei goder (s Durastanti, Senesino, < *Astartus*)
32   77-79   L'onor severo brama l'offese vendicar (s Senesino, < *Astartus*)
33   80-81   Se pena se geme

Notes:
1. Songs 9, 11, 14, 15-18, 24 and 25 were reissued with additional pagination as part of *Apollo's Feast*, book 2, **172**, in 1726.
2. A-Wn, CDp, Ckc (85.18), CU-MUSI, Ob: + final advertisement leaf (see Walsh i, plate 27).
3. Cpl: + 4 leaves, cut smaller than rest of volume, 'No piu non bramo' and 'Mio caro ben' with English words 'Dear pritty maid' by 'Mr Sunderland'(two editions).
4. Lbl (Hirsch II.90.): - pp. 23-24; + final advertisement leaf (see Walsh i, plate 27).
5. Lcml: leaves with pp. 44-45, 48-49, 50-51, 52-53, 54-55, 56-57, 58-59, 60-61, 62-63 reversed.
6. MnU: - all after p. 75.
7. NRU-Mus: [i]▯-[ii]▯ 1-80 81▯.
8. Obt: sold.

Copies: A-Wn M.S.10226; B-Bc 13,393; CDp M.C.3.17; Ckc 42.8; Ckc 85.18; CLU-C Temp; Cpl —; CSfst de Bellis 824; CSt SpC MLM256; CU-MUSI M1500.B597A8 Case X; DLC M1500.B7244A8 Case; F-Pn Vm3 205; HAdolmetsch II C 45; *I-BGi*; *I-MOe*; ICN VM1500.B71a; Lam —; Lbl Hirsch II.90; Lbl I.296; Lbl R.M.II.b.18; Lcm XVIII.E.11; Lcml 111222; MiU Music RBR M1500.B72A8; MnU Music —; Mp BR f520Br31; NL-DHgm 3 L 12; NRU-Mus Vault M1500.B719A; Ob Mus. 22 c.5(1); Obt J.V.8; *RF-Mrg*; WaU M1500 B68A8 1721.

Plate 112.1   Bononcini, *Astartus*, 1721

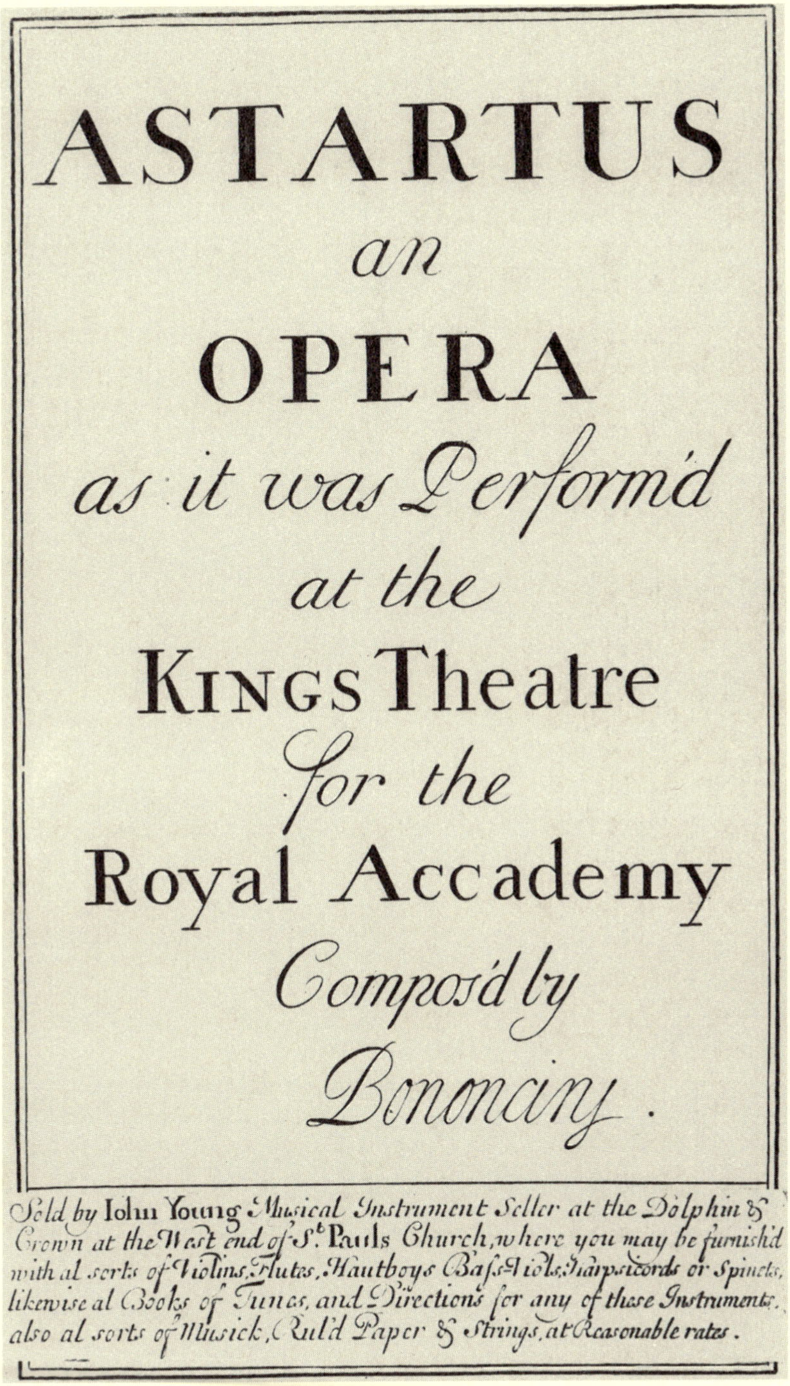

ASTARTUS

an

OPERA

as it was Perform'd

at the

KINGS Theatre

for the

Royal Accademy

Compos'd by

Bononcini.

Sold by Iohn Young Musical Instrument Seller at the Dolphin &
Crown at the West end of St Pauls Church, where you may be furnish'd
with al sorts of Violins, Flutes, Hautboys Bass Viols, harpsicords or Spinets,
likewise al Books of Tunes, and Directions for any of these Instruments,
also al sorts of Musick, Rul'd Paper & Strings, at Reasonable rates.

307

112 Bononcini, *Astartus*, 1 April 1721

Caption: plate 112.1. 380 x 241 mm. Cfm: MU.MS.500.

Astartus an Opera as it was Perform'd at the Kings Theatre for the Royal Accademy Compos'd by Bononcini. [engraved label over Walsh and Hare imprint] Sold by Iohn Young Musical Instrument Seller at the Dolphin & Crown at the West end of St. Pauls Church, where you may be funish'd with al sorts of Violins, Flutes, Hautboys Bass-Viols, Harpsicords or Spinets; likewise al Books of Tunes, and Directions for any of these Instruments, also al sorts of Musick, Rul'd Paper & Strings, at Reasonable rates.

43 leaves. Pp. [i]▯-[ii]▯ 1-12 13▯ 14-81.
Leaves printed on 2 sides.
Tallest copy 380 x 241 mm. Vertical chain lines.

One page engraved per plate. Engraving style Walsh 1, 3.
Title-page plate 284 x 165 mm.

Contents: title-page [i]; contents and advertisement [ii]; overture 1-4; songs 5-11; symphony 12-14; songs 15-81.

Songs: see 111.

Copy: Cfm MU.MS.500.

Plate 113.1   Bononcini, *Cyrus*, 1721

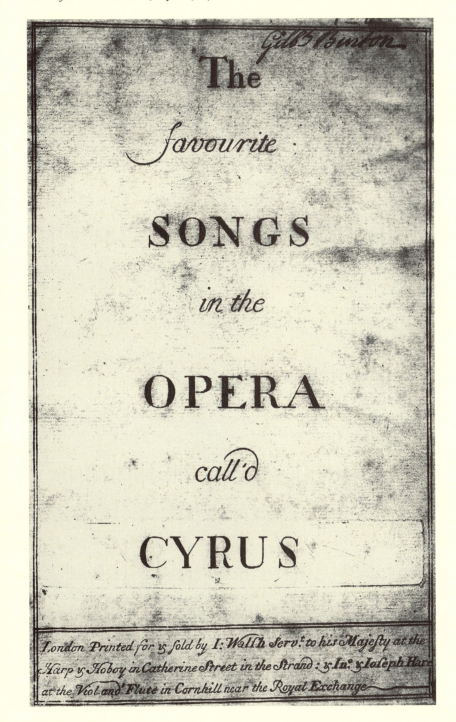

113 Bononcini, *Cyrus*, 31 December 1721

Caption: plate 113.1. 342 x 212 mm. Lcm: XXXII.B.8.(1.).

The favourite Songs in the Opera call'd ⸢ Cyrus ⸥ London Printed for & sold by I: Walsh Servt. to his Majesty at the Harp & Hoboy in Catherine Street in the Strand: & Ino. & Ioseph Hare at the Viol and Flute in Cornhill near the Royal Exchange

15 leaves. Pp. [i]☐ \☐1-2☐\ -\☐13-14☐\.
Leaves printed on 1 side.
Tallest copy 363 x 225 mm. Vertical chain lines.

One page engraved per plate. Engraving style Walsh 1.
Title-page plate 283 x 178 mm. Passe-partout no. 9.

Walsh ii: 205.

Contents: title-page [i]; songs 1-14.

Songs:

No.	Page	First Line
1	1-2	Se ponne le pene (s Robinson, A.)
2	3-4	Su questo man di latte (s Senesino)
3	5-6	Ti dò il mio sangue (s Salvai)
4	7-8	Se che mi brama aveso in petto (s Robinson, A.)
5	9-10	Amor vieni o mostrarvi (s Senesino)
6	11-12	Pupille care per farmi amare (s Durastanti)
7	13-14	Strazo sempia furia e morte (s Durastanti)

Notes:
1. All songs except 4 were reissued with additional pagination as part of *Apollo's Feast*, book 2, 172, in 1726.
2. First performed 20 May 1721. Joseph Hare joined the firm in December 1721 or January 1722.
3. Lbl: - p. [i].

Copies: Ckc 85.3.(3.); CSfst de Bellis 815; D-Hs M B/2620/4; *DLC*; Lbl H.230.f.(3.); Lcm XXXII.B.8.(1.).

Plate 114.1   Bononcini, *Griselda*, 1722

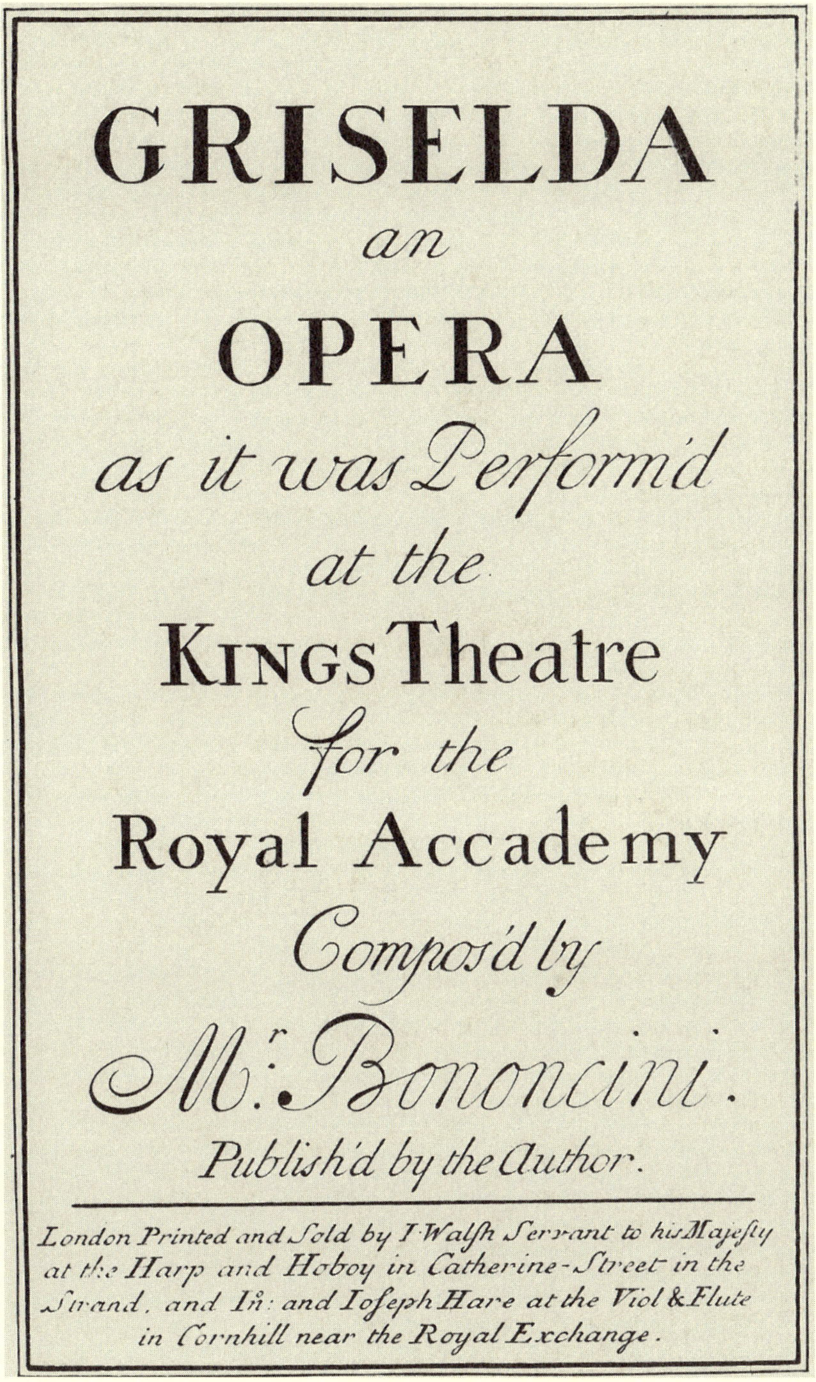

GRISELDA

an

OPERA

as it was Perform'd

at the

KINGS Theatre

for the

Royal Accademy

Compos'd by

Mr. Bononcini.

Publish'd by the Author.

London Printed and Sold by I. Walsh Serrant to his Majesty at the Harp and Hoboy in Catherine-Street in the Strand, and Ino: and Ioseph Hare at the Viol & Flute in Cornhill near the Royal Exchange.

Caption: plate 114.1. 356 x 229 mm. Lbl: Hirsch II.91.

Griselda an Opera as it was Perform'd at the Kings Theatre for the Royal Accademy Compos'd by Mr: Bononcini. Publish'd by the Author. London Printed and Sold by I: Walsh Servant to his Majesty at the Harp and Hoboy in Catherine-Street in the Strand, and Ino: and Ioseph Hare at the Viol & Flute in Cornhill near the Royal Exchange.

40 leaves. Pp. [i]☐ [ii] 1-75 76☐.
Leaves printed on 2 sides.
Tallest copy 366 x 238 mm. Vertical chain lines.

One page engraved per plate. Engraving style Walsh 1, 3.
Title-page plate 297 x 174 mm.
Contents plate 314 x 119 mm.

Walsh ii: 211.
Advertised in *Post Boy*, 22 May 1722. Price 2s.

Contents: title-page [i]; contents and advertisements [ii]; overture 1-6; songs 7-76.

Songs:

No.	Page	First Line
1	7-8	Al mio nativo prato (s Robinson, A., Senesino, < *Griselda*)
2	9-11	Parto amabile ben mio (s Robinson, A., < *Griselda*)
3	12-14	Affetto gioia e riso (s Senesino, < *Griselda*)
4	15-16	Timor e speme van combattendo (s Boschi, < *Griselda*)
5	17-19	Volgendo a me lo sguardo (s Senesino, < *Griselda*)
6	20-21	Quanto mi spiace (s Salvai, < *Griselda*)
7	22-24	Non deggio non sperare (s Benedetti, < *Griselda*)
8	25-27	Si già sento l'ardor che m'accende (s Senesino, < *Griselda*)
9	28-29	Dal mio petto ogni pace smarrita (s Robinson, A., < *Griselda*)
10	30-32	Arder per me tu poi (s Salvai, < *Griselda*)
11	33	Per la gloria d'adorarvi (s Benedetti, < *Griselda*)
12	34-36	Le fere a risvegliar (s Senesino, < *Griselda*)
13	37-38	Con si crudel beltà (s Boschi, < *Griselda*)
14	39-41	Si vieni ove il rigor (s Robinson, A., < *Griselda*)
15	42	Che giova fuggire (s Benedetti, < *Griselda*)
16	43-45	Dolce sogno deh le porta (s Senesino, < *Griselda*)
17	46-47	Se vaga pastorella (s Salvai, < *Griselda*)
18	48-49	Caro addio dal labbro amato (s Robinson, A., < *Griselda*)
19	50-52	Del offensa vendicarti (s Senesino, Robinson, A., < *Griselda*)
20	53-54	Troppo è il dolore (s Benedetti, < *Griselda*)
21	55-57	Se mai può consolarti l'amor mio (s Salvai, < *Griselda*)
22	58-59	Quel guardo di pietà (s Robinson, A., < *Griselda*)
23	60-62	Son qual face che s'accende (s Senesino, < *Griselda*)
24	63-66	Quel timoroso cervo cacciato (s Benedetti, Salvai, < *Griselda*)
25	67-68	Eterni Dei narrate (s Boschi, < *Griselda*)
26	69-70	Per te mio solo bene (s Robinson, A., < *Griselda*)
27	71-72	Sebben fu il cor severo (s Senesino, < *Griselda*)

28   73-76   Viva s'inalzi e splenda

Notes:
1. Songs 1-8, 16, 22, and 25 were reissued with additional pagination as part of *Apollo's Feast*, book 2, 172, in 1726.
2. F-Pn: cropt at fore-edge.
3. Lcm: - p. 76.

Copies: Bu M1500.B; CaOLU MZ.702; Ckc 85.17; CSt SpC MLM116; CtY-Mus Rare M1500.B719G8+; *D-BMs*; DLC M1500.B7244G7 Case; F-Pc D.1528(2); F-Pn Vm3 206; HAdolmetsch II C 46; ICN VM1500.B71g; *I-Gi(l)*; *I-Rsc*; *J-Tn*; Lbl H.321.b; Lbl Hirsch II.91; Lbl R.M.II.B.19; Lcm XVIII.E.12.(2.); MB **M431.66; Mp BR f520Br32; NL-DHgm 3 L 13; Ob Mus. 22 c.6; Obh Mus. D.16(3); WaU M1500 B68G7 1722.

114a Bononcini, *Griselda*, 22 May 1722

Caption: see plate 114.1.

Griselda an Opera as it was Perform'd at the Kings Theatre for the Royal Accademy Compos'd by Mr: Bononcini. Publish'd by the Author. London Printed and Sold by I: Walsh Servant to his Majesty at the Harp and Hoboy in Catherine-Street in the Strand, and Ino: and Ioseph Hare at the Viol & Flute in Cornhill near the Royal Exchange.

22 leaves. Pp. [i]□\□7-8□\□9 10□-11□\□12 13□-14□\□15-16□\□17 18□-19□\□20-21□\□22 23□-24□\□25 26□-27□.
Leaves printed on 1 side.
Tallest copy 339 x 218 mm. Vertical chain lines.

One page engraved per plate. Engraving style Walsh 1, 3.

Contents: title-page [i]; songs 7-27.

Songs:

No.	Page	First Line
1	7-8	Al mio nativo prato (s Robinson, A., Senesino, < *Griselda*)
2	9-11	Parto amabile ben mio (s Robinson, A., < *Griselda*)
3	12-14	Affetto gioia e riso (s Senesino, < *Griselda*)
4	15-16	Timor e speme van combattendo (s Boschi, < *Griselda*)
5	17-19	Volgendo a me lo sguardo (s Senesino, < *Griselda*)
6	20-21	Quanto mi spiace (s Salvai, < *Griselda*)
7	22-24	Non deggio non sperare (s Benedetti, < *Griselda*)
8	25-27	Si già sento l'ardor che m'accende (s Senesino, < *Griselda*)

Notes:
1. Songs 1-8 were reissued with additional pagination as part of *Apollo's Feast*, book 2, 172, in 1726.
2. Obt: at top of title-page in MS: The Favourite Songs In.

Copies: CLU-C *fM1500.B71; CSfst de Bellis 818; Obt Mus. c.33(1).

114b   Bononcini, *Griselda*, 22 May 1722

Caption: see plate 114.1.

Griselda an Opera as it was Perform'd at the Kings Theatre for the Royal Accademy Compos'd by Mr: Bononcini. Publish'd by the Author. London Printed and Sold by I: Walsh Servant to his Majesty at the Harp and Hoboy in Catherine-Street in the Strand, and Ino: and Ioseph Hare at the Viol & Flute in Cornhill near the Royal Exchange.

12 leaves. Pp. [i]❑\❑7 8-27.
Leaves printed on 2 sides.
Tallest copy 354 x 239 mm. Vertical chain lines.

One page engraved per plate. Engraving style Walsh 1, 3.

Contents: title-page [i]; songs 7-27.

Songs: See **114a**.

Notes:
1. Songs 1-8 were reissued with additional pagination as part of *Apollo's Feast*, book 2, 172, in 1726.
2. B-Bc: has last page of overture, p. 6, on recto of p. 7. At head of title-page in MS: Favourite Songs In.

Copies: B-Bc 5457; DFo M1500.B97G8 Cage.

Plate 115.1 Bononcini, *Griselda*, 1722

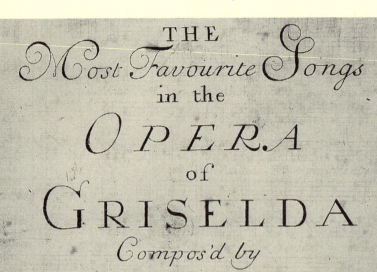

THE
Most Favourite Songs
in the
OPERA
of
GRISELDA
Compos'd by

Mr Bononcini .

LONDON,
Printed for Richd Meares, *Musical Instrument Maker, and*
Musick Printer, at the Golden Viol in St Pauls Church Yard .

Caption: plate 115.1. 329 x 210 mm. Lbl: G.192.(1.).

The Most Favourite Songs in the Opera of Griselda Compos'd by Mr. Bononcini. London, Printed for Richd. Meares, Musical Instrument Maker, and Musick Printer, at the Golden Viol in St. Pauls Church Yard.

16 leaves. Pp. [i]□ [1]□\□[2] [3]□-[4]□\□[5] [6]□\□[7] [8]□-[9]□\□[10]-[11]□\-\□[14]-[15]□\.
Leaves printed on 1 side.
Tallest copy 335 x 218 mm. Vertical chain lines.

One page engraved per plate. Engraving style Cross.
Title-page plate 190 x 184 mm.

Advertised in *Post Boy*, 26 May 1722. Price 2/6.

Contents: title-page [i]; songs [1]-[15].

Songs:

No.	Page	First Line
1	[1]	Al mio nativo prato (s Robinson, A., Senesino, < *Griselda*)
2	[2-3]	Dolce sogno deh le porta (s Senesino, < *Griselda*)
3	[4]	Quanto mi spiace (s Salvai, < *Griselda*)
4	[5-6]	Son qual face che faccende (s Senesino, < *Griselda*)
5	[7-8]	Non deggio non sperare (s Benedetti, < *Griselda*)
6	[9]	Parto amabile ben mio (s Robinson, A., < *Griselda*)
7	[10-11]	Volgendo a me lo squardo (s Senesino, < *Griselda*)
8	[12-13]	Si già sento l'ardor che m'accende (s Senesino, < *Griselda*)
9	[14-15]	Affetto gioia e riso (s Senesino, < *Griselda*)

Notes:
1. Advertised as to be published 3 June.
2. Lbl: p. [9] bound between pp. [4] and [5].

Copies: A-Wn M.S.10227; Lbl G.192.(1.).

Caption: see plate 115.1.

The Most Favourite Songs in the Opera of Griselda Compos'd by Mr. Bononcini. London, Printed for Richd. Meares, Musical Instrument Maker, and Musick Printer, at the Golden Viol in St. Pauls Church Yard.

9 leaves. Pp. [i]□ 1-16.
Leaves printed on 2 sides.
Tallest copy 346 x 220 mm. Vertical chain lines.

One page engraved per plate. Engraving style Cross.

Contents: title-page [i]; songs 1-16.

Songs:

No.	Page	First Line
1	1	Al mio nativo prato (s Robinson, A., Senesino, < *Griselda*)
2	2-3	Dolce Sogno deh le porta (s Senesino, < *Griselda*)
3	4	Quanto mi spiace (s Salvai, < *Griselda*)
4	5-6	Son qual face che faccende (s Senesino, < *Griselda*)
5	7-8	Non deggio non sperare (s Benedetti, < *Griselda*)
6	9	Parto amabile ben mio (s Robinson, A., < *Griselda*)
7	10-11	Volgendo a me lo squardo (s Senesino, < *Griselda*)
8	12-13	Si già sento l'ardor che m'accende (s Senesino, < *Griselda*)
9	14-15	Affetto gioia e riso (s Senesino, < *Griselda*)
10	16	Per la gloria d'adorarvi (s Benedetti, < *Griselda*)

Copy: DLC M1503.G719G8 Case.

Plate 117.1   Bononcini, *Griselda*, 1722

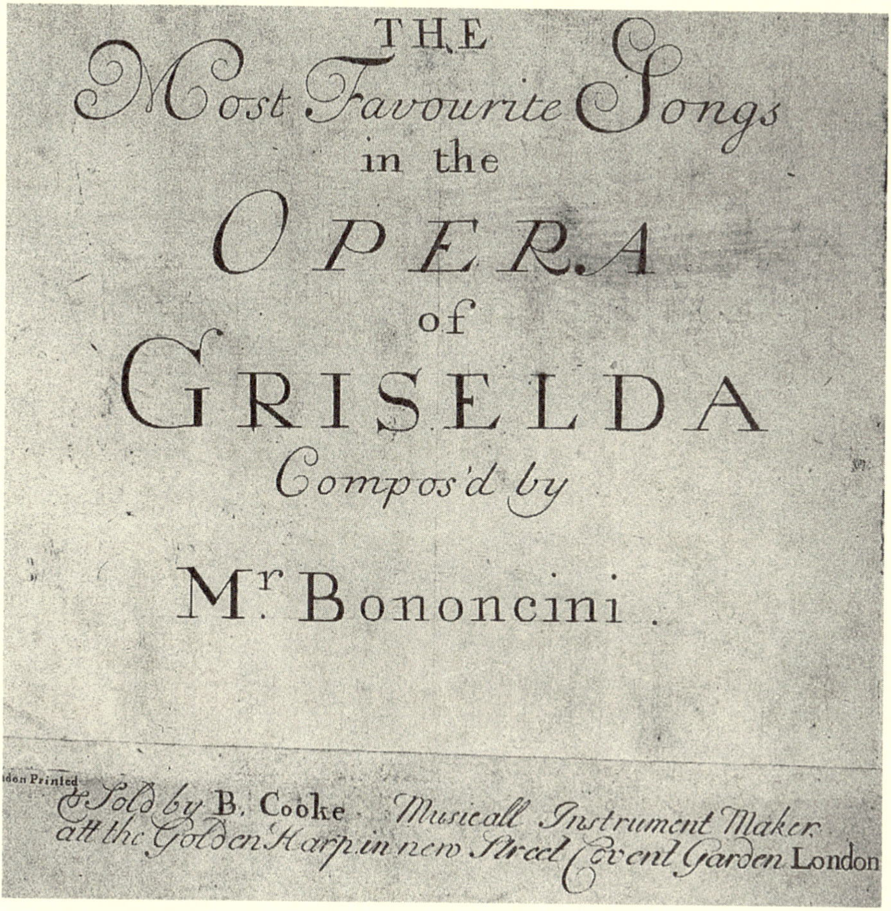

THE
Most Favourite Songs
in the
OPERA
of
GRISELDA
Compos'd by

Mr Bononcini .

Printed
& Sold by B. Cooke *Musicall Instrument Maker.*
att the Golden Harp in new Street Covent Garden London

117 Bononcini, *Griselda*, 3 June 1722

Caption: plate 117.1. 357 x 233 mm. CDp: M.C.3.16.(5).

The Most Favourite Songs in the Opera of Griselda Compos'd by Mr. Bononcini. [engraved label over Meares imprint] London Printed & Sold by B. Cooke Musicall Instrument Maker, att the Golden Harp in new Street Covent Garden London.

10 leaves. Pp. [i]□\□1 2-15 16□.
Leaves printed on 2 sides.
Tallest copy 357 x 233 mm. Vertical chain lines.

One page engraved per plate. Engraving style Cross.
Title-page plate ? x 184 mm. (See note 1.)

Contents: title-page [i]; songs 1-16.

Songs: see **116**.

Note:
1. Label obscures lower edge of plate.

Copy: CDp M.C.3.16.(5).

Plate 118.1   Bononcini, *Griselda*, 1722

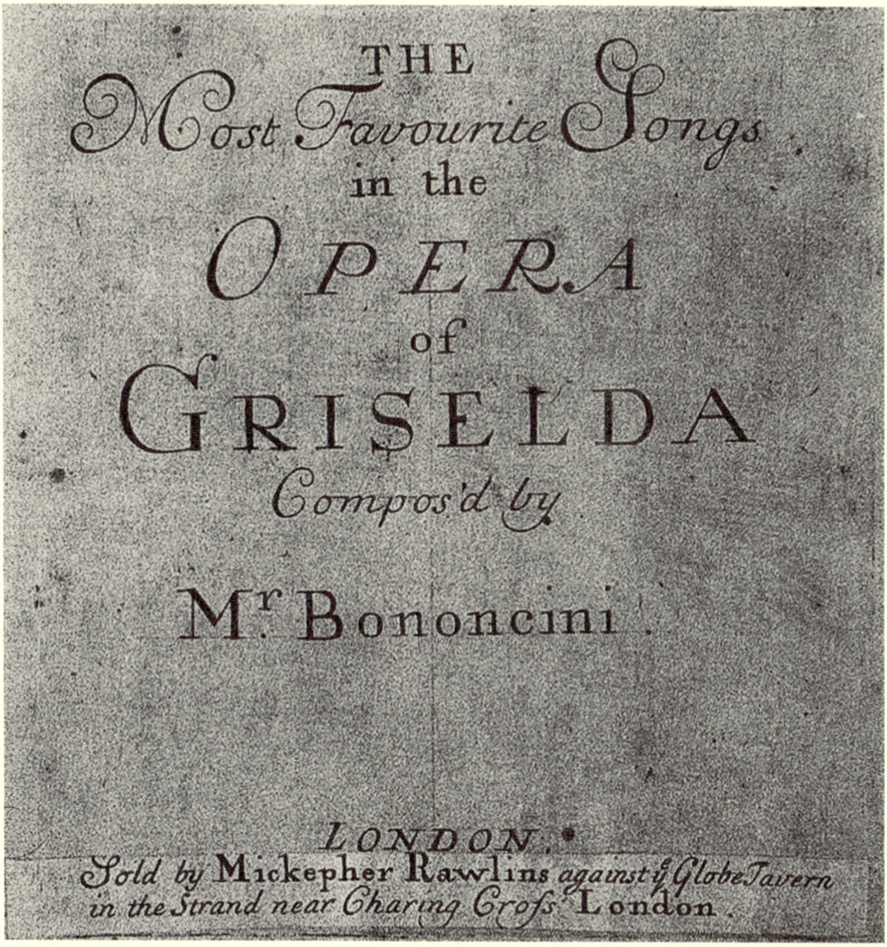

THE
Most Favourite Songs
in the
OPERA
of
GRISELDA
Compos'd by

Mr Bononcini

LONDON.
Sold by Mickepher Rawlins *against ȳ Globe Tavern*
in the Strand near Charing Crofs London.

Caption: plate 118.1. 315 x 239 mm. Lam.

The Most Favourite Songs in the Opera of Griselda Compos'd by Mr.
Bononcini. [engraved label over Meares imprint] Sold by Mickepher Rawlins
against ye Globe Tavern in the Strand near Charing Cross London.

10 leaves. Pp. [i]☐\☐1 2-15 16☐.
Leaves printed on 2 sides.
Tallest copy 315 x 239 mm. Vertical chain lines.

One page engraved per plate. Engraving style Cross.
Title-page plate 190 x 189 mm.

Contents: title-page [i]; songs 1-16.

Songs: see 116.

Copy: Lam —.

Plate 119.1   Amadei, Bononcini, and Handel, *Muzio Scaevola*, 1722

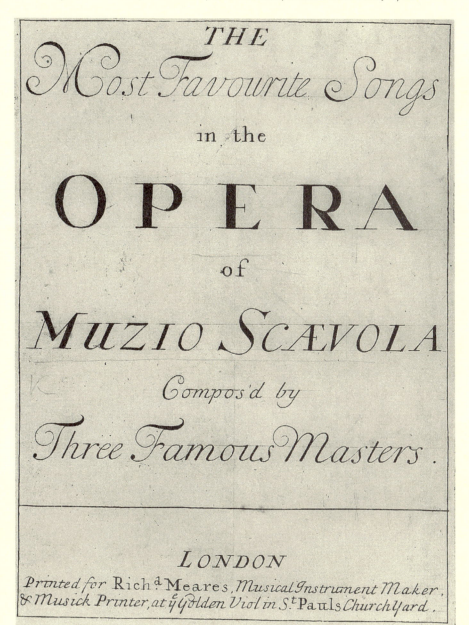

THE
Most Favourite Songs
in the
OPERA
of
MUZIO SCÆVOLA
Compos'd by
Three Famous Masters.

LONDON
Printed for Rich.d Meares, Musical Instrument Maker,
& Musick Printer, at y Golden Viol in St. Pauls Church Yard.

Caption: plate 119.1. 329 x 210 mm. Lbl: G.192.(2.).

The Most Favourite Songs in the Opera of Muzio Scævola Compos'd by Three Famous Masters. London Printed for Richd. Meares, Musical Instrument Maker, & Musick Printer, at ye Golden Viol in St. Pauls Church Yard.

23 leaves. Pp. [i]□ 1□\□2 3□-4□\□5-6□\-\□15-16□\ 17□\□18 19□-20□\□21 22□. Leaves printed on 1 side.
Tallest copy 340 x 220 mm. Vertical chain lines.

One page engraved per plate. Engraving style Cross.
Title-page plate 240 x 180 mm.

Walsh ii: 1125.
Advertised in *Flying Post*, 23 August 1722. Price 2/6.

Contents: title-page [i]; overture 1-4; songs 5-22.

Songs:

No.	Page	First Line
1	5-6	Si t'ama o cara (s Salvai, < *Muzio Scaevola*)
2	7-8	Dolce pensier forir di pace (s Robinson, A., < *Muzio Scaevola*)
3	9-10	E'pure in mezzo all'armi (s Berselli, < *Muzio Scaevola*)
4	11-12	Selvagge Deità (s Durastanti, < *Muzio Scaevola*)
5	13-14	Cedo ma pur mi chiama (s Senesino, < *Muzio Scaevola*)
6	15-17	Lungo pensar e dubitar (s Durastanti, < *Muzio Scaevola*)
7	18-20	Pupille sdegnose (s Senesino, < *Muzio Scaevola*)
8	21-22	A chi vive di speranza (s Salvai, < *Muzio Scaevola*)

Notes:
1. Plates signed 'Cross sculp': pp. 6, 10, 12, 14, 22.
2. Coke: - p. 22.
3. En: pp. 1-2 reversed.
4. Lbl: pp. 1-3 reversed (i.e., [i]□ \□1-2□\-\□15-16□\ etc.).
5. NjP copy 2: - pp. [i], 1-4.

Copies: Bu Rq M1500.M; Coke —; En BH.19; Lbl G.192.(2.); NjP (Ex) xB83.0009 copy 1; NjP (Ex) xB83.0009 copy 2.

Plate 120.1 Amadei, Bononcini, and Handel, *Muzio Scaevola*, 1722

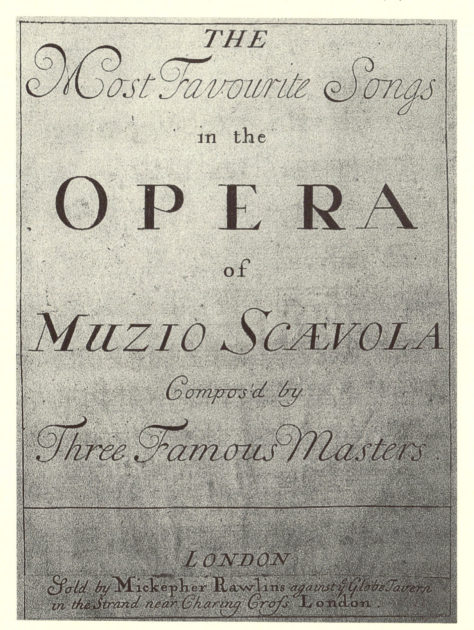

THE
Most Favourite Songs
in the
OPERA
of
MUZIO SCÆVOLA
Compos'd by
Three Famous Masters.

LONDON
Sold by Mickepher Rawlins against ye Globe Tavern
in the Strand near Charing Crofs London.

Caption: plate 120.1. 314 x 218 mm. Lam.

The Most Favourite Songs in the Opera of Muzio Scævola Compos'd by Three Famous Masters. [engraved label over Meares imprint] Sold by Mickepher Rawlins against ye Globe Tavern in the Strand near Charing Cross London.

23 leaves. Pp. [i]□ 1□-4□ \□5-6□\-\□15-16□\ 17□\□18 19□-20□\□21 22□.
Leaves printed on 1 side.
Tallest copy 314 x 218 mm. Vertical chain lines.

One page engraved per plate. Engraving style Cross.
Title-page plate 240 x 180 mm.

Contents: title-page [i]; overture 1-4; songs 5-22.

Songs: see 119.

Copy: Lam —.

Plate 121.1   Bononcini, *Crispus*, 1722

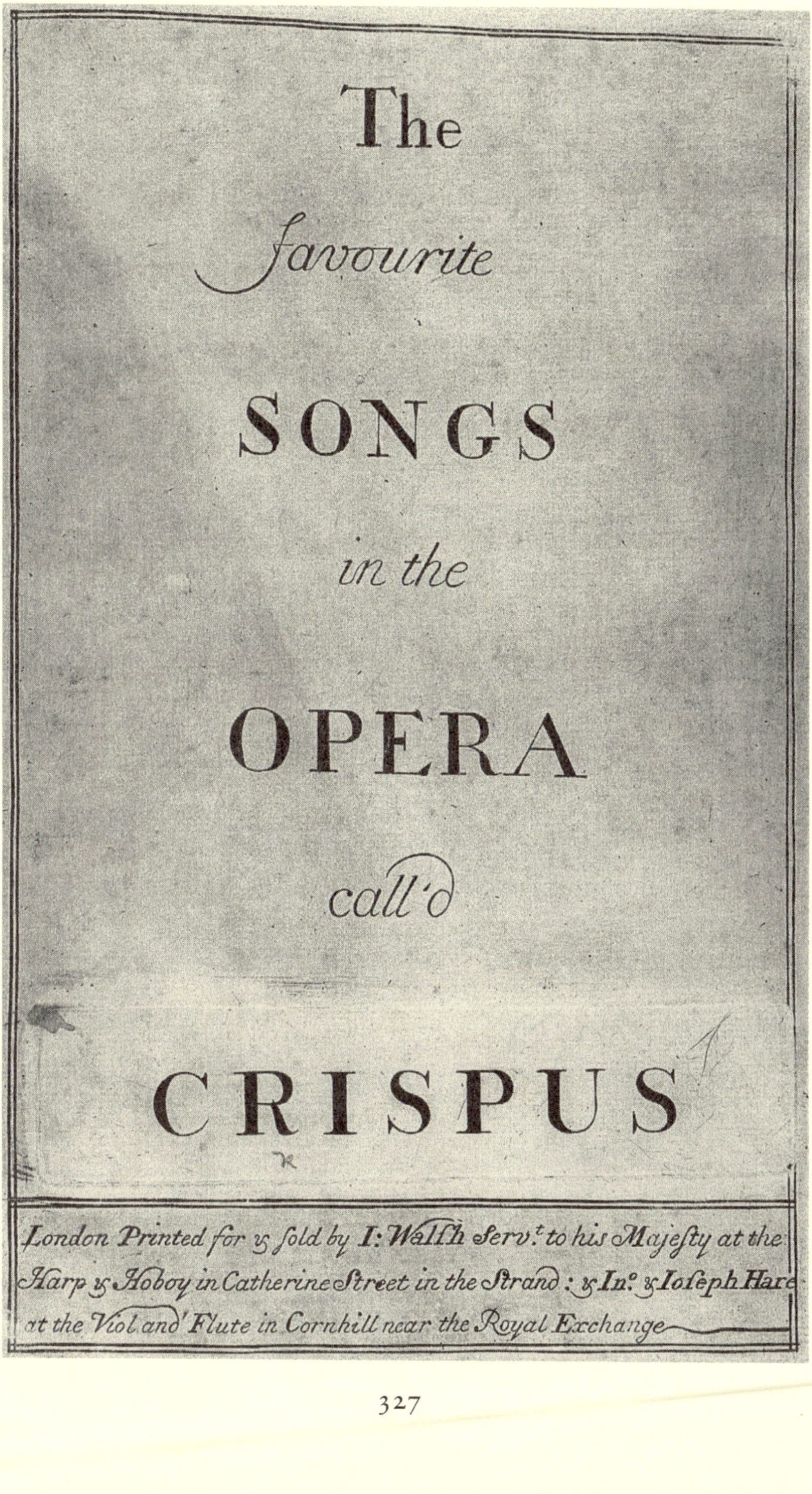

The

favourite

SONGS

in the

OPERA

call'd

CRISPUS

London Printed for & sold by I: Walsh Serv.t to his Majesty at the Harp & Hoboy in Catherine Street in the Strand : & In.o & Ioseph Hare at the Viol and Flute in Cornhill near the Royal Exchange

Caption: plate 121.1. 342 x 212 mm. Lcm: XXXII.B.8.(2.).

The favourite Songs in the Opera call'd ⌠ Crispus ⌡ London Printed for & sold by I: Walsh Servt. to his Majesty at the Harp & Hoboy in Catherine Street in the Strand: & Ino. & Ioseph Hare at the Viol and Flute in Cornhill near the Royal Exchange

21 leaves. Pp. [i]◻\◻1-2◻\-\◻19-20◻\.
Leaves printed on 1 side.
Tallest copy 360 x 224 mm. Vertical chain lines.

One page engraved per plate. Engraving style Walsh 1.
Title-page plate 283 x 170 mm. Passe-partout no. 9.

Walsh ii: 203.
Advertised in *Post Boy*, 25 August 1722.

Contents: title-page [i]; songs 1-20.

Songs:

No.	Page	First Line
1	1-2	Dille che peno (s Senesino, < *Crispus*)
2	3-4	Lo voglio lo chiede (s Robinson, A., < *Crispus*)
3	5-6	Se vedete i pensier miei (s Senesino, < *Crispus*)
4	7-8	Solo la pena mia basta a placarti (s Robinson, A., < *Crispus*)
5	9-10	Se voi m'abbandonate (s Senesino, < *Crispus*)
6	11-12	Che bella fedeltà (s Robinson, A., < *Crispus*)
7	13-14	Vaghe luci ch'il cor mi beate (s Senesino, < *Crispus*)
8	15-16	Ingrato figlio (s Robinson, A., < *Crispus*)
9	17-18	Così stanco pellegrino (s Senesino, < *Crispus*)
10	19-20	Un vezzo un guardo un riso (s Senesino, < *Crispus*)

Notes:
1. All songs except 4 and 6 were reissued with additional pagination as part of *Apollo's Feast*, book 2, 172, in 1726.
2. Lbl: - p. [i].
3. Report of a copy at B-Bc is false.

Copies: Ckc 85.1.(3.); Cpl 21.A.7; CSfst de Bellis 816; CSt SpC MLM114; *D-Gs*; D-Hs M B/2620/3; DLC M1506.B66C78 Case; *I-Rsc*; Lam —; Lbl H.230.f.(2.); Lcm XXXII.B.8.(2.); Mp BR f520Hd6292(2); Obt Mus. c.33(3).

Plate 122.1   Amadei, Bononcini, and Handel, *Muzio Scaevola*, 1722

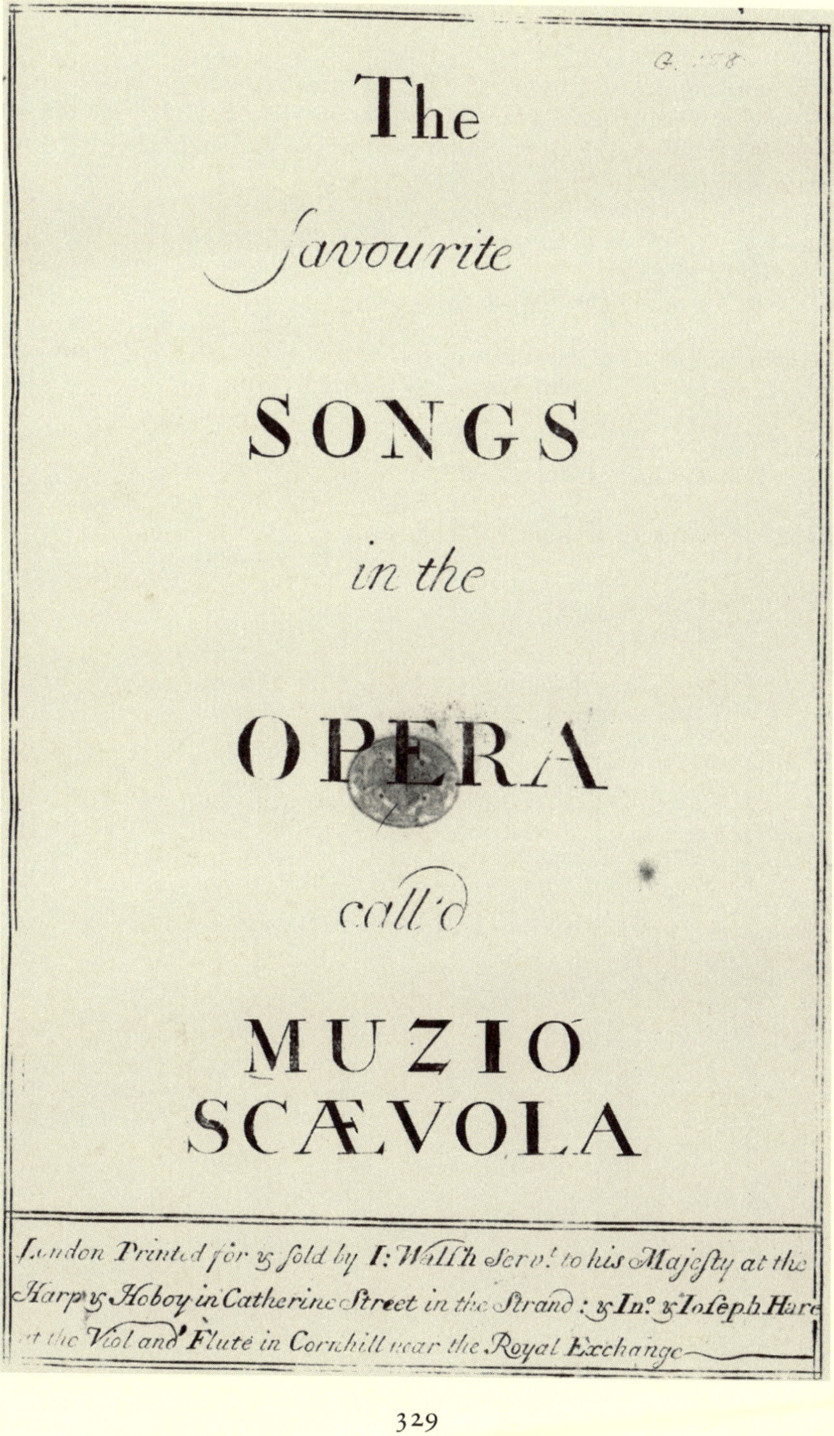

The

favourite

SONGS

in the

OPERA

call'd

MUZIO
SCÆVOLA

London Printed for & fold by I: Walfh Serv! to his Majefty at the Harp & Hoboy in Catherine Street in the Strand : & In? & Iofeph Hare at the Viol and Flute in Cornhill near the Royal Exchange

Caption: plate 122.1. 325 x 204 mm. Lbl: G.158.

The favourite Songs in the Opera call'd ⌠ Muzio Scævola ⌡ London Printed for & sold by I: Walsh Servt. to his Majesty at the Harp & Hoboy in Catherine Street in the Strand: & Ino. & Ioseph Hare at the Viol and Flute in Cornhill near the Royal Exchange

22 leaves. Pp. [i]◻ 1◻\◻2 3◻-4◻ \◻5-6◻\-\◻15-16◻\ 17◻\◻18 19◻\◻20 21◻.
Leaves printed on 1 side.
Tallest copy 359 x 225 mm. Vertical chain lines.

One page engraved per plate. Engraving style Walsh.
Title-page plate 283 x 177 mm. Passe-partout no. 9.

Walsh ii: 1125.
Advertised in *Post Boy*, 25 August 1722.

Contents: title-page [i]; overture 1-4; songs 5-21.

Songs:

No.	Page	First Line
1	5-6	Dolce pensier forir di pace (s Robinson, A., < *Muzio Scaevola*)
2	7-8	E pure in mezzo all'armi (s Berselli, < *Muzio Scaevola*)
3	9-10	Selvagge Deità (s Durastanti, < *Muzio Scaevola*)
4	11-12	Si t'ama o cara (s Salvai, < *Muzio Scaevola*)
5	13-14	Cedo ma pur mi chiama (s Senesino, < *Muzio Scaevola*)
6	15-17	Lungo pensar e dubitar (s Durastanti, < *Muzio Scaevola*)
7	18-19	Pupille sdegnose (s Senesino, < *Muzio Scaevola*)
8	20-21	A chi vive di speranza (s Salvai, < *Muzio Scaevola*)

Notes:
1. Ckc (85.2.(5.)): title plate 'Muzio Scævola' printed on blue paper wrapper.
2. Lbl: pp. 1, 2 reversed.
3. Mp: pp. 1, 14, 16 reversed.
4. NIC: - pp. [i], 20, 21.
5. DLC copy is a manuscript.

Copies: A-*Wn-h*; B-Bc 5467; B-MAR; Ckc 42.70; Ckc 85.2.(5.); Coke —; CSfst de Bellis 1169; CU-MUSI M1524.H16A2 1722 Case X; D-Hs M B/2301/4; D-Hs M B/2620/6; En BH.68; Lam —; Lbl G.158; Lcm XXXII.B.8.(3.); Mp BR f52Hd632; NIC Lock.Pr. M 1505 A48 M9++.

Plate 123.1   Conti, *Clotilda*, 1722

Caption: plate 123.1. 339 x 212 mm. Obh: Mus. D.9. See plate 53.2.

[within cartouche] ⌠ Songs in the Opera Call'd Clotilda ⌡ [at foot, engraved label over Walsh imprint] [London Printed] & Sold by B. Cooke Musicall Instrument Maker, att the Golden Harp in new Street Covent Garden London[.]

Songs In The New Opera, Call'd ⌠ Clotilda The Songs done in Italian and English as they are Performed at ye Queens Theatre The whole Carefully Corected ⌡ Sold by I: Walsh Musicall Instrument maker in Or==dinary to her Majesty, & P. Randall at the Harp and Ho=boy, in Catherine=Street near Sommerset House in the Strand and I. Hare Musick Instrument maker at ye Golden Viol and Flute in Cornhill near ye Royal Exchange.

60 leaves. Pp. [i]□-[ii]□\□[iii] □1 2□\□3 4□ 0□-12□\□13 14□-20□\□21 22□-26□\□27 28□-29□\□30 31□\□32 33□-37□\□38 39□-43□\□44 45□-47□\□48 49□-50□\□51 52□. Leaves printed on 1 side.
Tallest copy 339 x 212 mm. Vertical chain lines.

One page engraved per plate. Engraving style Walsh 1.
Illus. title-page plate ? x 185 mm. Passe-partout no. 5. (See note 2.)
Title-page plate passe-partout no. 3.

Contents: illus. title-page [i]; title-page [ii]; contents and advertisement [iii]; overture 1-4; songs 0-52.

Songs: see 53.

Notes:
1. Date is earliest year that Cooke was in operation as a publisher/seller.
2. Label cropped with loss of 'London Printed' and full stop. Label obscures lower edge of plate.

Copy: Obh Mus. D.9.

Plate 124.1   Sheeles, *Collection of Songs*, 1722

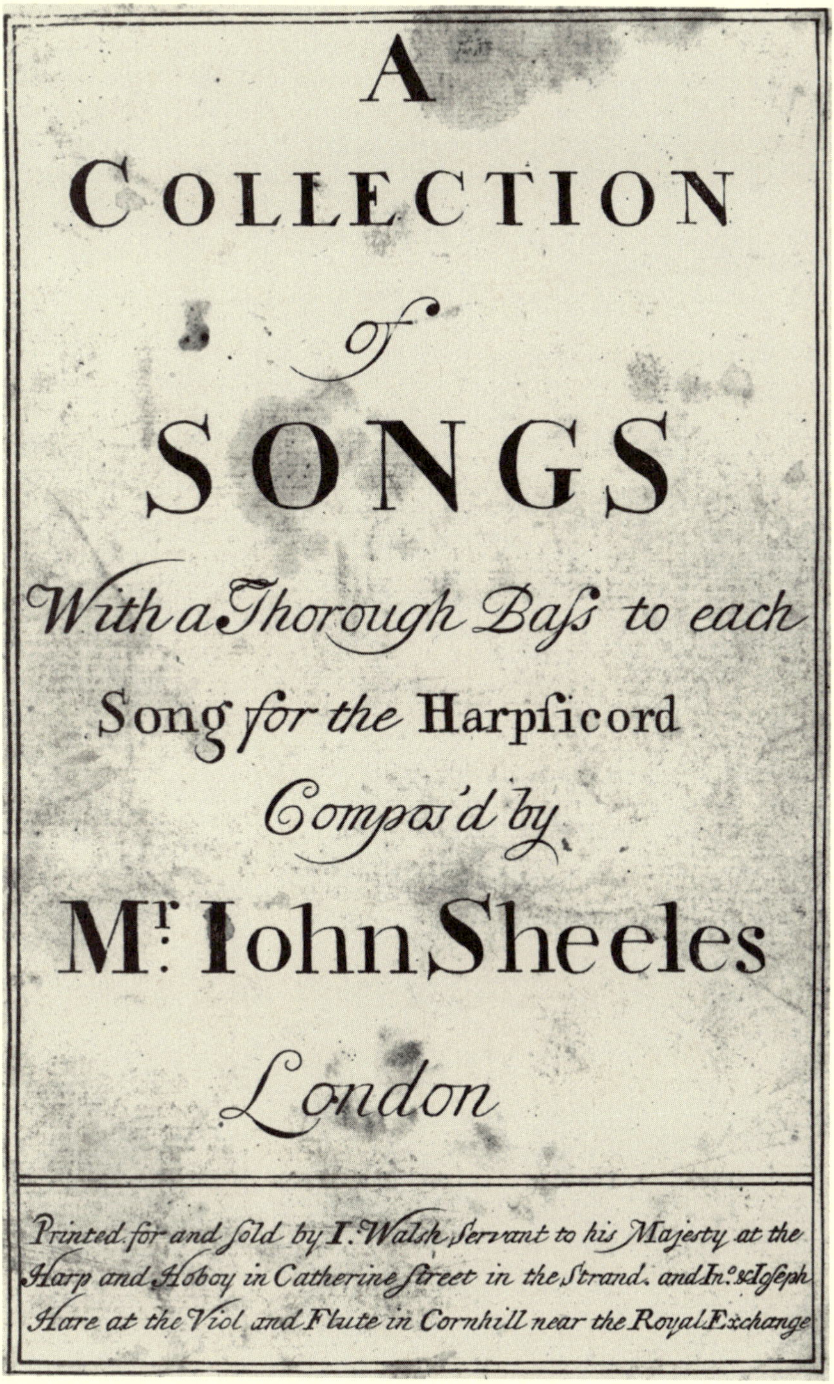

A
COLLECTION

of

SONGS

With a Thorough Bass *to each*

Song *for the* Harpsicord

Compos'd by

Mr Iohn Sheeles

London

Printed for and sold by *I. Walsh* servant to his Majesty at the
Harp and Hoboy in Catherine street in the Strand. and In.^s & Ioseph
Hare at the Viol and Flute in Cornhill near the Royal Exchange

Caption: plate 124.1. 347 x 220 mm. Obh: Mus. E.57.

A Collection of Songs With a Thorough Bass to each Song for the Harpsicord Compos'd by Mr: Iohn Sheeles London Printed for and sold by I: Walsh Servant to his Majesty at the Harp and Hoboy in Catherine street in the Strand. and Ino. & Ioseph Hare at the Viol and Flute in Cornhill near the Royal Exchange

15 leaves. Pp. [i]☐ 1☐-3☐\☐4 5☐-7☐\☐8 9☐\☐10 11☐-14☐.
Leaves printed on 1 side.
Tallest copy 347 x 220 mm. Vertical chain lines.

One page engraved per plate. Engraving style Walsh 3, 4.
Title-page plate 269 x 167 mm.

Walsh ii: 1367.

Contents: title-page [i]; songs 1-14.

Songs:

No.	Page	First Line
1	1-3	Take care ye fair (m Sheeles)
2	4-5	Lead o lead me to that charming grove (m Sheeles)
3	6-7	If a lady you doat on (m Sheeles)
4	8-9	Oh! how seraphic is Euterpe's voice (m Sheeles)
5	10-11	O sacred spirit of harmony (m Sheeles)
6	12	Hail happy day, welcome bless'd morn (m Sheeles)
7	13	Near pleasant woods on lofty mountains
8	14	When Flavia sings (m Sheeles, v Gentleman)

Notes:
1. Walsh ii date of circa 1727 revised by imprint. Walsh was in partnership with John and Joseph Hare from January 1722 to September 1725.
2. Obh copy rebound. Some leaves have stab holes at fore-edge indicating that the original leaf placement was different.

Copy: Obh Mus. E.57.

Plate 125.1   Bononcini, *Crispus*, 1722

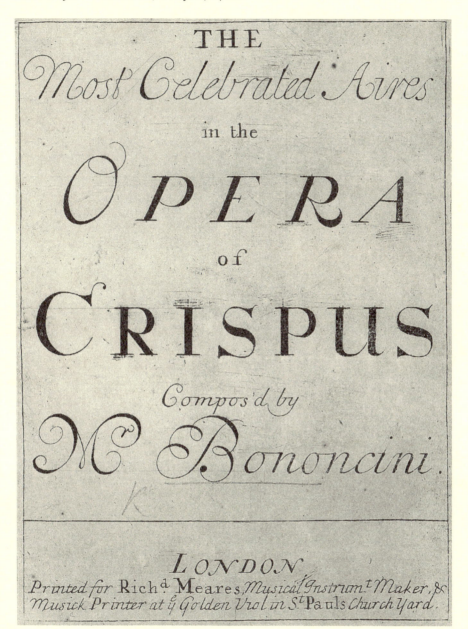

THE

Most Celebrated Aires

in the

OPERA

of

CRISPUS

Compos'd by

Mr Bononcini.

LONDON

Printed for Rich.d Meares, Musical Instrum.t Maker, &
Musick Printer at y.e Golden Viol in St Pauls Church Yard.

125   Bononcini, *Crispus*, 23 August 1722

Caption: plate 125.1. 329 x 212 mm. Lbl: G.192.(4.).

The Most Celebrated Aires in the Opera of Crispus Compos'd by Mr Bononcini. London Printed for Richd. Meares, Musical Instrumt. Maker, & Musick Printer at ye Golden Viol in St. Pauls Church Yard.

11 leaves. Pp. [i] 1-20.
Leaves printed on 2 sides.
Tallest copy 342 x 224 mm. Vertical chain lines.

One page engraved per plate. Engraving style Cross.
Title-page plate 238 x 179 mm.
Advertised in *Flying Post*, 23 August 1722. Price 2/6.

Contents: title-page [i]; songs 1-20.

Songs:

No.	Page	First Line
1	1-2	Dille che peno (s Senesino, < *Crispus*)
2	3-4	Lo voglio lo chiede (s Robinson, A., < *Crispus*)
3	5-6	Se vedete i pensier miei (s Senesino, < *Crispus*)
4	7-8	Solo la pena mia, basto a placarti (s Robinson, A., < *Crispus*)
5	9-10	Se voi m'abbandonate (s Senesino, < *Crispus*)
6	11-12	Che bella fedeltà (s Robinson, A., < *Crispus*)
7	13-14	Vaghe luci ch'il cor mi beate (s Senesino, < *Crispus*)
8	15	Ingrato figlio (s Robinson, A., < *Crispus*)
9	16-18	Cosi stanco pelegrine (s Senesino, < *Crispus*)
10	19-20	Un vezzo un guardo, un riso (s Senesino, < *Crispus*)

Note:
1. While this bibliography was at press, I found an advertisement in the *Flying Post*, which indicates that 23 August 1722 is the accurate publication date, and that the price was 2/6. The entry should be renumbered 118a.

Copies: CDp M.C.3.21(3); Lam —; Lam —; Lbl G.192.(4.).

Caption: see plate 125.1.

The Most Celebrated Aires in the Opera of Crispus Compos'd by Mr Bononcini. London Printed for Richd. Meares, Musical Instrumt. Maker, & Musick Printer at ye Golden Viol in St. Pauls Church Yard.

21 leaves. Pp. [i]□ \□1-2□\-\□13-14□\ 15□\□16 17□-18□\□19 20□.
Leaves printed on 1 side.
Tallest copy 341 x 222 mm. Vertical chain lines.

One page engraved per plate. Engraving style Cross.

Contents: title-page [i]; songs 1-20.

Songs: see 125.

Note:
1. While this bibliography was at press, I found an advertisement in the *Flying Post*, which indicates that 23 August 1722 is the accurate publication date, and that the price was 2/6. The entry should be renumbered 118b.

Copies: CaOLU MZ.704; CU-MUSI M1505.B64C7 1722 Case X.

SONGS
in the New
OPERA
Call'd
THOMYRIS

*Collected out of the Works of the most
Celebrated Itallian Authors*

viz

Scarlatti Bononcini *and other*

great Masters

Perform'd at the THEATRE ROYALL

*These Songs are Contriv'd so that their Symphonys
may be perform'd with them.*

*Note there are 4 other Operas after y Itallian maner lately printed viz
Camilla, Arsinoe, the Temple of Love, and Rosamond,
which may be had where this is sold.*

*B Cooke   Musicall Instrument Maker,
rp in new Street Covent Garden* London

338

Caption: see plate 44.1. Plate 126a.1. 334 x 211 mm. DLC: M1500.S282T4.

[within cartouche] ⌈ Songs in the Opera Call'd Thomyris Queen of Scythia ⌋
I: Collins. sculp [at foot] London Printed for & Sould by I: Walsh Musicall
Instrument maker in Ordinary to her Majesty at the Golden Harp & Ho=boy
in Catherine=street near Summerset=house in ye strand

Songs in the New Opera Call'd Thomyris Collected out of the Works of the most
Celebrated Itallian Authors viz Scarlatti Bononcini and other great Masters
Perform'd at the Theatre Royall These Songs are Contriv'd so that their
Symphonys may be perform'd with them. Note there are 4 other Operas after
ye Itallian maner lately printed viz Camilla, Arsinoe, the Temple of Love, and
Rosamond, which may be had where this is sold. [engraved label over Walsh
and Hare imprint] [London Printed & Sold by B.] Cooke Musicall Instrument
Maker, [att the Golden Ha]rp in new Street Covent Garden London.

62 leaves. Pp. [i]◻ [ii-iii] ◻1 2◻-4◻ 1◻-56◻.
Leaves printed on 1 side.
Tallest copy 334 x 211 mm. Vertical chain lines.

One page engraved per plate. Engraving style Walsh 1, 3.
Illus. title-page plate 250 x 175 mm. Passe-partout no. 1.
Title-page plate 261 x 187 mm.
Contents plate 263 x 154 mm.

Contents: illus. title-page [i]; title-page [ii]; contents [iii]; overture 1-4; songs 1-56.

Songs: see **44**.

Notes:
1. Date is earliest year that Cooke was in operation as publisher/seller.
2. Label on title-page is cropt.

Copy: DLC M1500.S282T4.

Plate 127.1 Ariosti, *Coriolano*, 1723

I L

CORIOLANO

OPERA

RAPRESENTATA NEL REGIO
TEATRO D'HAY MARKET

COMPOSTA DAL

SIG.^{RE} ATTILIO ARIOSTI.

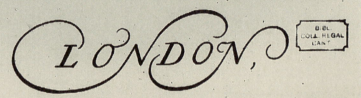

Publiſht by the Author.

Printed & Sold by **Richard Meares** *Musical Instrument Maker* and *Musick Printer* in *St Pauls Church-yard.*

Engrav'd by Tho: Croſs.

127 Ariosti, *Coriolano*, 23 May 1723

Caption: plate 127.1. 384 x 243 mm. Ckc: 85.3.(2.).

Il Coriolano Opera Rapresentata Nel Regio Teatro d'Hay Market Composta Dal Sigre, Attilio Ariosti. London, Publisht by the Author. Printed & Sold by Richard Meares Musical Instrument Maker and Musick Printer in St. Pauls Church-yard. Engrav'd by Tho: Cross.

42 leaves. Pp. [i]□\□[o] [oA] 1-79.
Leaves printed on 2 sides.
Tallest copy 384 x 243 mm. Vertical chain lines.

One page engraved per plate. Engraving style Cross.
Title-page plate 306 x 180 mm.

Advertised in *Daily Courant*, 23 May 1723.

Contents: title-page [i]; overture [o-oA]; songs 1-78; march 79.

Songs:

No.	Page	First Line
1	3-4	Rendi al padre in me la figlia (s Cuzzoni, < *Coriolano*)
2	5-7	Io spero che in quei guardi uedrò (s Senesino, < *Coriolano*)
3	8-9	E tanto graue il duolo che opprime (s Robinson, A., < *Coriolano*)
4	10-13	Sagri numi difendete (s Durastanti, < *Coriolano*)
5	14-16	Fin ch'ei stringe la spada rubella (s Boschi, < *Coriolano*)
6	17-19	Sen ua la Rondinella (s Cuzzoni, < *Coriolano*)
7	20-21	Amarti non degg'io (s Robinson, A., < *Coriolano*)
8	22-25	Perdonate o cari amori (s Senesino, < *Coriolano*)
9	26-29	E pur il gran piacer ueder il bel furor (s Durastanti, < *Coriolano*)
10	30-31	Se tu mi perdi igrato incolpane (s Robinson, A., < *Coriolano*)
11	32-34	Il suo amore intenderò (s Cuzzoni, < *Coriolano*)
12	35-37	Quella calma che a noi (s Boschi, < *Coriolano*)
13	38-40	Più benigno par che arrida (s Robinson, A., < *Coriolano*)
14	41-42	So che guarda con raggio sereno (s Senesino, < *Coriolano*)
15	43-46	Nel tuo figlio e nel tuo sposo (s Berenstadt, < *Coriolano*)
16	47-48	Più crudel si fa la sorte (s Durastanti, < *Coriolano*)
17	49-55	Si mio caro amor (s Cuzzoni, Senesino, < *Coriolano*)
18	56-57	Del cor la spene non è bastante (s Cuzzoni, < *Coriolano*)
19	58-59	Parli al tuo cor con la speranza (s Durastanti, < *Coriolano*)
20	60-62	Per combatter con lo sdegno (s Robinson, A., < *Coriolano*)
21	63-69	Spirate o iniqui marmi (s Senesino, < *Coriolano*)
22	70-72	Teco s'annodi l'alma mio caro (s Cuzzoni, < *Coriolano*)
23	73-75	Ti pentirai fra poco perfido (s Senesino, < *Coriolano*)
24	76-78	Giunse al fin quel dì bramato (s Cuzzoni, < *Coriolano*)

Notes:
1. Overture is bass part only.   2. DFo: pp. 44-45 duplicated.
3. MB, Ob: MB bound with, and Ob accompanied by, 12 additional leaves, the instrumental parts for the overture.   4. PU: - p. [i], supplied in photocopy.

Copies: *B-MAR*; Ckc 85.3.(2.); CLU-C *fM1500.A71c; D-Hs M B/2301/3; DFo M1500.A56C5 Cage; DLC M1500.A76C5; F-Pn Vm3.207; *I-MOe*; Lam —; Lbl H.319; MB **M.460.118; MBHM; Ob Mus. 22.b.26; PU RB Folio Music M1500 A7C6.

JUPITER and EUROPA

a

MASQUE

of

SONG'S

as

they were perform'd

at the Theatre

in

Lincolns Inn Fields

Publish'd for September

Price 6.^d

London Printed for and Sold by I: Walsh Servant to his Majesty at the
Harp and Hoboy in Catherine Street in the Strand and In°: & Ioseph Hare
at the Viol and Flute in Cornhill near the Royal Exchange

127a Galliard, *Jupiter and Europa*, 30 September 1723

Caption: plate 127a.1. 344 x 234 mm. Lbl: H.76.

⟨ Jupiter and Europa ⟩ a Masque of Song's as they were perform'd at the Theatre in Lincolns Inn Fields Publish'd for September Price 6d. London Printed for and Sold by I: Walsh Servant to his Majesty at the Harp and Hoboy in Catherine Street in the Strand and Ino. & Ioseph Hare at the Viol and Flute in Cornhill near the Royal Exchange

6 leaves. Pp. [i]☐ 1☐-2☐ 3-4 5☐-6☐.
Leaves printed on 1 side.
Tallest copy 344 x 234 mm. Mixed chain lines.

One page engraved per plate. Engraving style Walsh.
Title-page plate 255 x 167 mm. Passe-partout no. 10.

Walsh ii: 882.
Price 6d.

Contents: title-page [i]; songs 1-6.

Songs:

No.	Page	First Line
1	1	Europa fair, loves chiefest care (v Leveridge, < *Jupiter and Europa*)
2	2	This great world is a trouble (s Laguerre, < *Jupiter and Europa*)
3	3-5	What scenes of approaching delight (m Cobston, s Laguerre, < *Jupiter and Europa*)
4	6	Come neighbours now we've made our hay (< *Jupiter and Europa*)

Notes:
1. First performed March 1723.
2. 'Jupiter and Europa' engraved directly on plate.
3. Lbl (Ad.MS. 31,588.f.3.): + 3 leaves with different editions of songs 1, 2, and 4.
4. Lcm: + 2 songs from *Floridante*, 'Finche lo strale' and 'O cara spene', and 1 from an undetermined source, 'Vile traytor quickly leave me', composed by an eminent master (also in CLU-C copy of 172).
5. NRU-Mus: - p. 6, + different edition of song 2 following p. 5. A paste-over imprint at one time covered the original imprint.

Copies: Lbl Ad.MS. 31,588.f.3; Lbl H.76; Lcm XXXII.A.3.(3.); NRU-Mus Vault M1524.G168J.

JUPITER and EUROPA

a

MASQUE

of

SONG'S

as

they were perform'd

at the Theatre

in

Lincolns Inn Fields

Publish'd for September

Price 6.ᵈ

Sold by Iohn Young Musical Instrument Seller at the Dolphin & Crown at the West end of S.ᵗ Pauls Church, where you may be furnish'd with al sorts of Violins, Flutes, Hautboys Bass Viols, Harpsicords or Spinets, likewise al Books of Tunes, and Directions for any of these Instruments. also al sorts of Musick, Ruld Paper & Strings, at Reasonable rates.

Caption: plate 127b.1. 344 x 220 mm. CLU-C: *fM1524.G16j.

⌠ Jupiter and Europa ⌡ a Masque of Song's as they were perform'd at the
Theatre in Lincolns Inn Fields Publish'd for September Price 6d. [engraved
label over Walsh and Hares imprint] Sold by Iohn Young Musical Instrument
Seller at the Dolphin & Crown at the West end of St. Pauls Church, where you
may be furnish'd with al sorts of Violins, Flutes, Hautboys Bass-Viols,
Harpsicords or Spinets; likewise al Books of Tunes, and Directions for any
of these Instruments, also al sorts of Musick, Rul'd Paper & Strings, at
Reasonable rates.

6 leaves. Pp. [1]▯\▯2 3-4 [5]▯-[7]▯.
Leaves printed on 1 side.
Tallest copy 344 x 220 mm. Vertical chain lines.

One page engraved per plate. Engraving style ?
Title-page plate ? x 167 mm. Passe-partout no. 10. (See note 3.)

Price 6d.

Contents: title-page [1]; songs 2-4, [5-7].

Songs:

No.	Page	First Line
1	2-4	What scenes of approaching delight (m Cobston, s Laguerre, < *Jupiter and Europa*)
2	[5]	Come neighbours now we've made our hay (< *Jupiter and Europa*)
3	[6]	Europa fair, loves chiefest care (v Leveridge, < *Jupiter and Europa*)
4	[7]	This great world but a trouble (< *Jupiter and Europa*)

Notes:
1. First performed March 1723.
2. 'Jupiter and Europa' engraved directly on plate.
3. CLU-C: comprises Walsh and Hares' title-page with Young's label pasted over the imprint,
followed by non-Walsh editions of the songs. Label obscures lower edge of plate.

Copy: CLU-C *fM1524.G16j.

Plate 128.1 Bononcini, *Erminia*, 1723

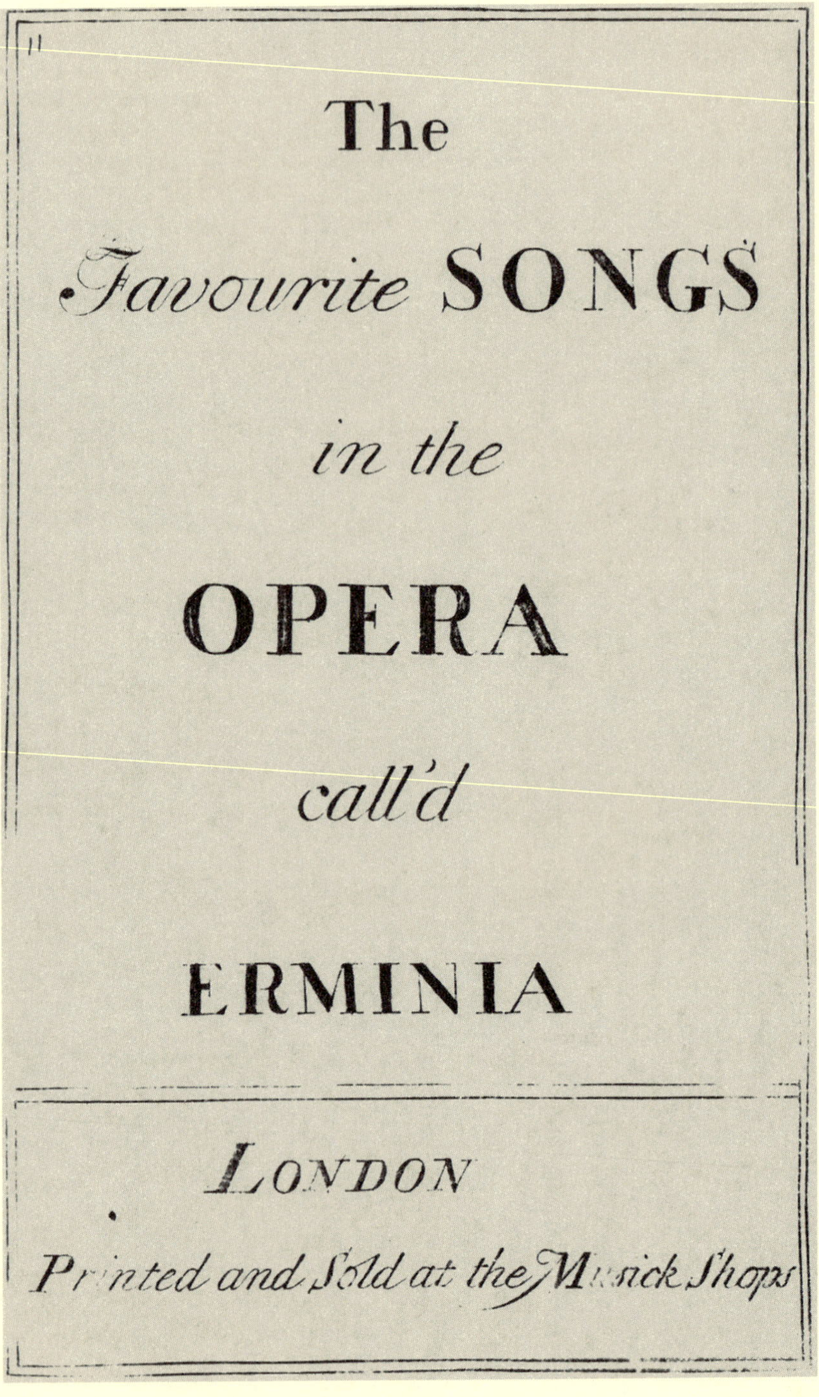

The

Favourite SONGS

in the

OPERA

call'd

ERMINIA

LONDON

Printed and Sold at the Musick Shops

Plate 128.2   Bononcini, *Erminia*, 1723

347

Caption: plates 128.1-128.2. 329 x 215 mm. Lbl: G.499.b.

The Favourite Songs in the Opera call'd ⌠ Erminia ⌡ London Printed and Sold at the Musick Shops

11 leaves. Pp. [i]□ 1□\□2 3□\□4 5□-6□\□7 8□\□9 10□.
Leaves printed on 1 side.
Tallest copy 339 x 215 mm. Vertical chain lines.

One page engraved per plate. Engraving style Musick Shops.
Title-page plate 269 x 165 mm. Passe-partout no. 11.

Contents: title-page [i]; songs 1-10.

Songs:

No.	Page	First Line
1	1	Damon cease to address me (Sol per te s'amai la pene) (< *Erminia*)
2	2-3	Vanne, disse, e chiedi (s Robinson, A., < *Erminia*)
3	4-6	Di dolce affetto io sento (s Senesino, < *Erminia*)
4	7-8	Pace almèn fra queste selve (s Senesino, < *Erminia*)
5	9-10	Dissi d'amarvi sì (s Durastanti, < *Erminia*)

Note:
1. First performed March 1723.

Copies: CaOLU MZ.1421; Lbl G.499.b.

Plate 129.1   Bononcini, *Erminia*, 1723

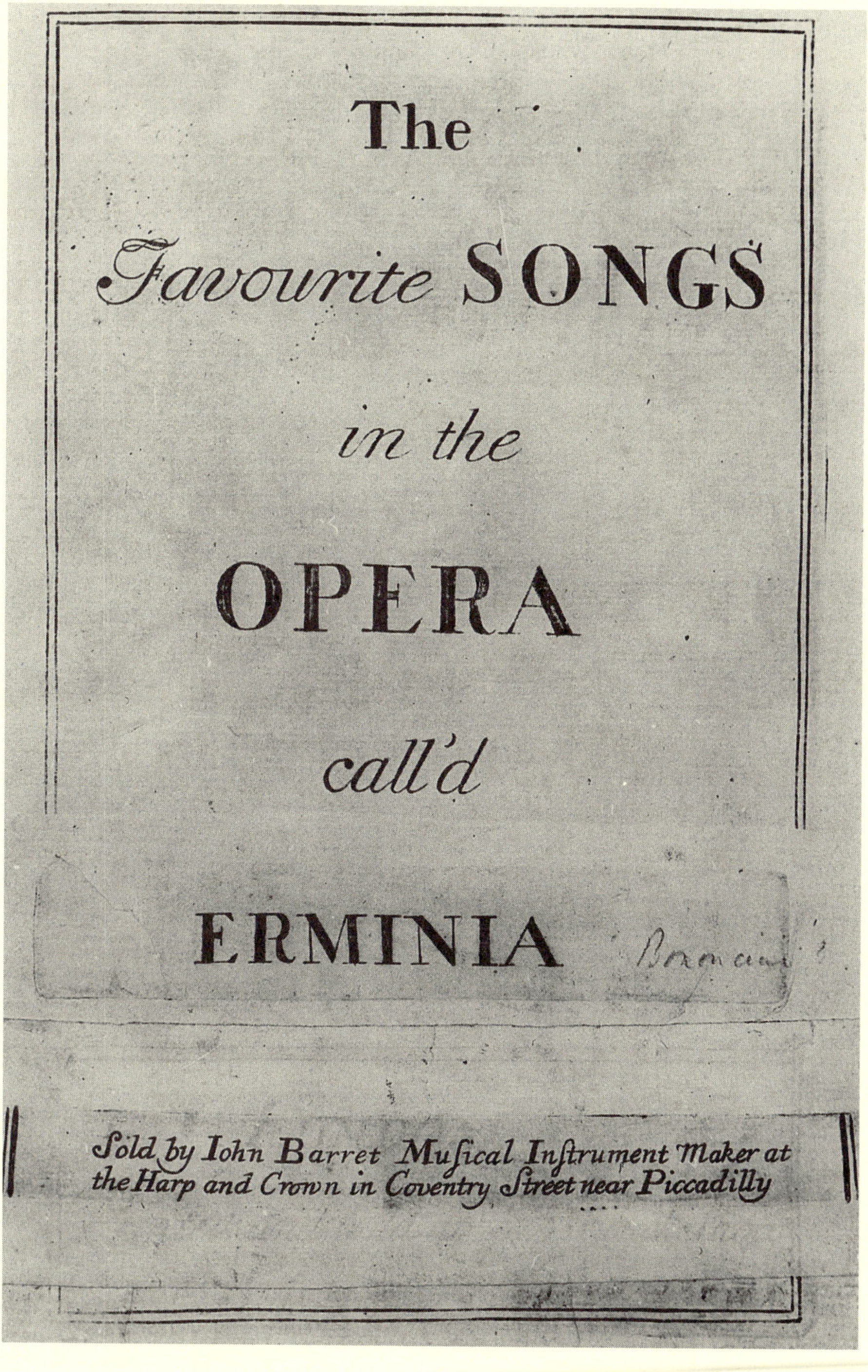

The

Favourite SONGS

in the

OPERA

call'd

ERMINIA

*Sold by Iohn Barret Muſical Inſtrument Maker at
the Harp and Crown in Coventry Street near Piccadilly*

129   Bononcini, *Erminia*, 31 December 1723

Caption: plate 129.1. 349 x 222 mm. A-Wn: M.S.10230.

The Favourite Songs in the Opera call'd ⌠ Erminia ⌡ [engraved label over Musick Shops imprint] Sold by John Barret Musical Instrument Maker at the Harp and Crown in Coventry Street near Piccadilly

11 leaves. Pp. [i]◻ 1◻\◻2 3◻\◻4 5◻-6◻\◻7 8◻\◻9 10◻.
Leaves printed on 1 side.
Tallest copy 349 x 222 mm. Vertical chain lines.

One page engraved per plate. Engraving style Musick Shops.
Title-page plate passe-partout no. 11.

Contents: title-page [i]; songs 1-10.

Songs: see **128**.

Note:
1. First performed March 1723.

Copy: A-Wn M.S.10230.

Plate 130.1   Bononcini, *Erminia*, 1723

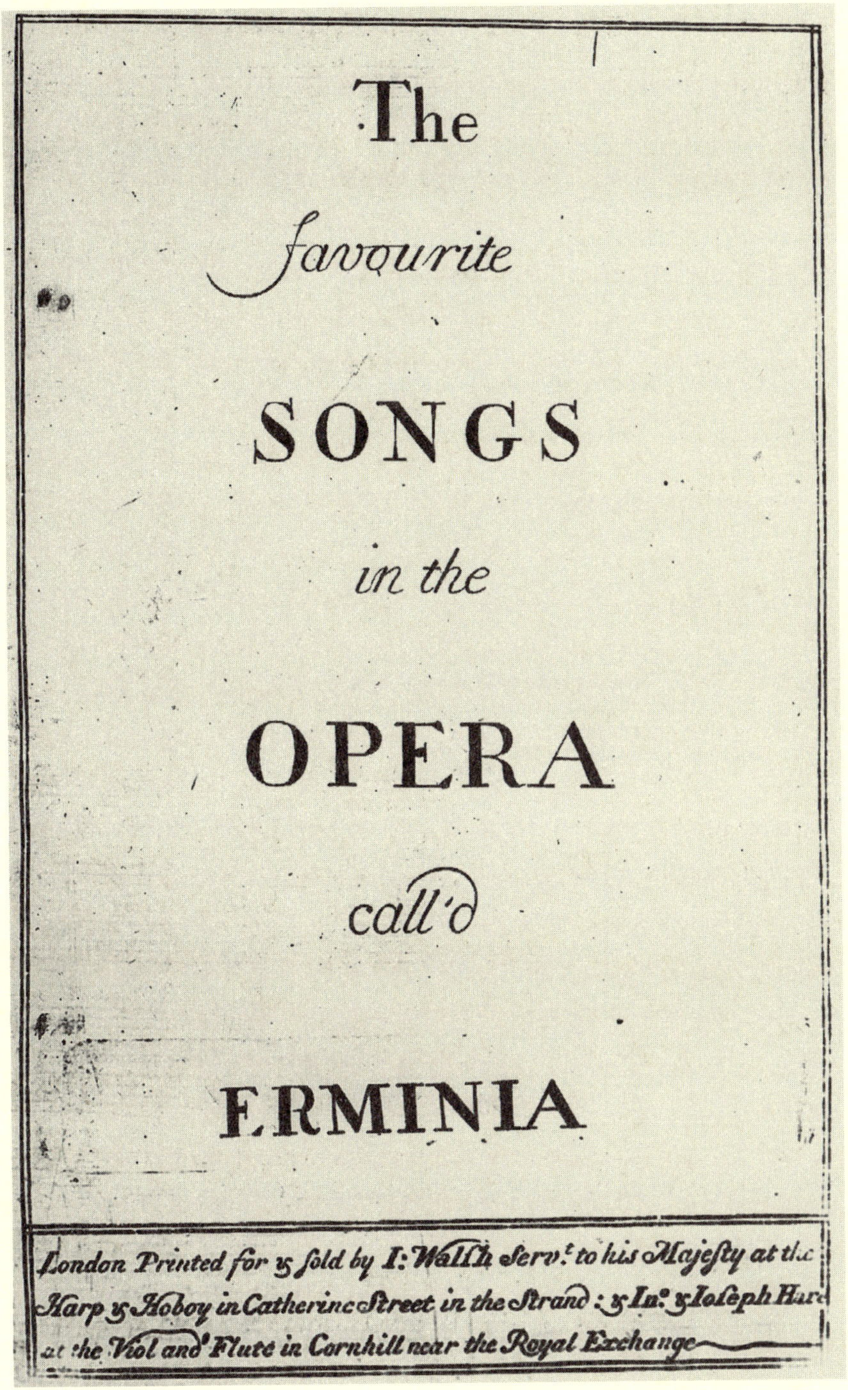

The

favourite

SONGS

in the

OPERA

call'd

ERMINIA

London Printed for & sold by I: Walsh Serv.t to his Majesty at the
Harp & Hoboy in Catherine Street in the Strand: & In.o & Ioseph Hare
at the Viol and Flute in Cornhill near the Royal Exchange

130   Bononcini, *Erminia*, 31 December 1723

Caption: plate 130.1. 363 x 230 mm. Ckc: 85.1.(4.).

The favourite Songs in the Opera call'd ⌠ Erminia ⌡ London Printed for &
sold by I: Walsh Servt. to his Majesty at the Harp & Hoboy in Catherine Street
in the Strand: & Ino. & Ioseph Hare at the Viol and Flute in Cornhill near the
Royal Exchange

11 leaves. Pp. [i]□ 1□\□2 3□\□4 5□-6□\□7 8□\□9 10□.
Leaves printed on 1 side.
Tallest copy 363 x 230 mm. Vertical chain lines.

One page engraved per plate. Engraving style Walsh 1.
Title-page plate 283 x 176 mm. Passe-partout no. 9.

Walsh ii: 207.

Contents: title-page [i]; songs 1-10.

Songs:

No.	Page	First Line
1	1	Damon cease to address me (< *Erminia*)
2	2-3	Vanne, disse, e chiedi (s Robinson, A., < *Erminia*)
3	4-6	Di dolci affetto jo sento (s Senesino, < *Erminia*)
4	7-8	Pace almèn fra queste selve (s Senesino, < *Erminia*)
5	9-10	Dissi d'amarvi si (s Durastanti, < *Erminia*)

Notes:
1. All songs except 5 reissued with additional pagination as part of *Apollo's Feast*, book 2, 172,
in 1726.
2. First performed March 1723.

Copies: Ckc 85.1.(4.); D-Hs M B/2620/5; I-Rsc.

131   deleted (see note on 55a).

132 and 133 deleted (see 127a and 127b).

Plate 134.1   Gillier, *Recueil d'airs françois*, 1723

RECUEIL

D'AIRS FRANÇOIS,

SERIEUX & à BOIRE.

A Une, Deux, & Trois PARTIES.

Compofé en ANGLETERRE,

PAR

Mr. *JEAN CLAUDE GILLIER.*

En MDCCXXIII.

A LONDRES:

Chés THOMAS EDLIN, Imprimeur & Libraire
aux Armes du Prince, vis à vis Exeter-
Exchange dans le Strand. 1723.

134   Gillier, *Recueil d'airs françois*, 31 December 1723

Caption: plate 134.1. 317 x 213 mm. Lbl: G.110.a.

[letterpress] Recueil D'airs François, Serieux & à Boire. A Une, Deux, & Trois Parties. Composé en Angleterre, Par Mr. Jean Claude Gillier. En MDCCXXIII. A Londres: Chés Thomas Edlin, Imprimeur & Libraire aux Armes du Prince, vis à vis Exeter-Exchange dans le Strand. 1723.

35 leaves. Pp. [i]☐ [ii]-[iii] [1-2] 3-4 1-62.
Leaves printed on 2 sides.
Tallest copy 338 x 228 mm. Vertical chain lines.

One page engraved per plate. Engraving style Walsh.
Title-page letterpress.

Advertised in *Daily Courant*, 4 February 1723. Price £1 1s.

Contents: title-page [i]; subscribers' list [ii-iii]; contents [1-2]; verse 3-4; songs 1-62.

Songs:

No.	Page	First Line
1	1-4	Protecteurs de l'harmonie
2	5-6	Aimer, boire, et chanter (v V)
3	7-8	Grands favoris du dieu du vin (v D—)
4	8-9	Voicy l'heure où Cloris doit combler mes desirs (v D—)
5	9-11	Cessez mes chers amis (v D—)
6	11-13	Je n'abandonne point l'amour (v D—)
7	13-15	Qui frape à la porte (v D—)
8	15-17	Souffrirons nous amis (v D—)
9	18	Ah j'ay honte des pleurs (v D—)
10	19-21	Quand j'ay bien bû tout passe (v D—)
11	22	Point de plaisir sans l'object que j'adore (v D—)
12	23-24	Amis cesses de disputer (v D—)
13	25	J'avois juré, ma Celimene (v D—)
14	26	Vous abandonnés Celimene (v D—)
15	27	On dit partout que je vous aime (v D)
16	28-29	Amour, je te croyois le souverain des coeurs (v D)
17	29-30	Amour cruel tiran des coeurs (v D)
18	31-32	Noirs enfans de l'hiuer (v Fuselier)
19	33	Liberté fy de la chaine la plus belle (v Fuselier)
20	34	Profités d'un calme si doux (v Fuselier)
21	35	L'amour est un jeune matou (v Fuselier)
22	36-37	Je resuois cette nuit
23	38	Je sens que Cupidon ce petit téméraire
24	39-40	Veux tu scavoir, ami Gregoire
25	41	Trop aimable catin votre tein
26	42	Les dieux comptent nos jours
27	43-44	Mon Iris a scu m'apprendre (v V)
28	45	Zephirs, revenés dans nos plaines (v V—)
29	46	Je ne goute jamais de plus parfait repos (v V—)
30	47	Les momens sont courts, chère Aminte (v V—)

134   Gillier, *Recueil d'airs françois*, 1723

31	48	Gregoire est yure, amis (v V)
32	49-51	Adieu troupeaux, adieu Lisete (v V)
33	51-52	Qu'un vigneron est estimable (v V)
34	53	Ma servante Margot (v V—)
35	54-55	Il est temps que la musique vienne (v Procope)
36	56	Dans notre moulin
37	57	L'amant dans ses voeux extreme
38	58-62	Laissons les allemands (v D—)

Notes:
1. Advertisement is for subscription proposal.
2. Pp. [i-iii] and [1]-4 (first series) letterpress.

Copies: B-Br II 75.598C Mus; *B-MAR*; D-Hs M B/3070/5; Lbl G.110.a.

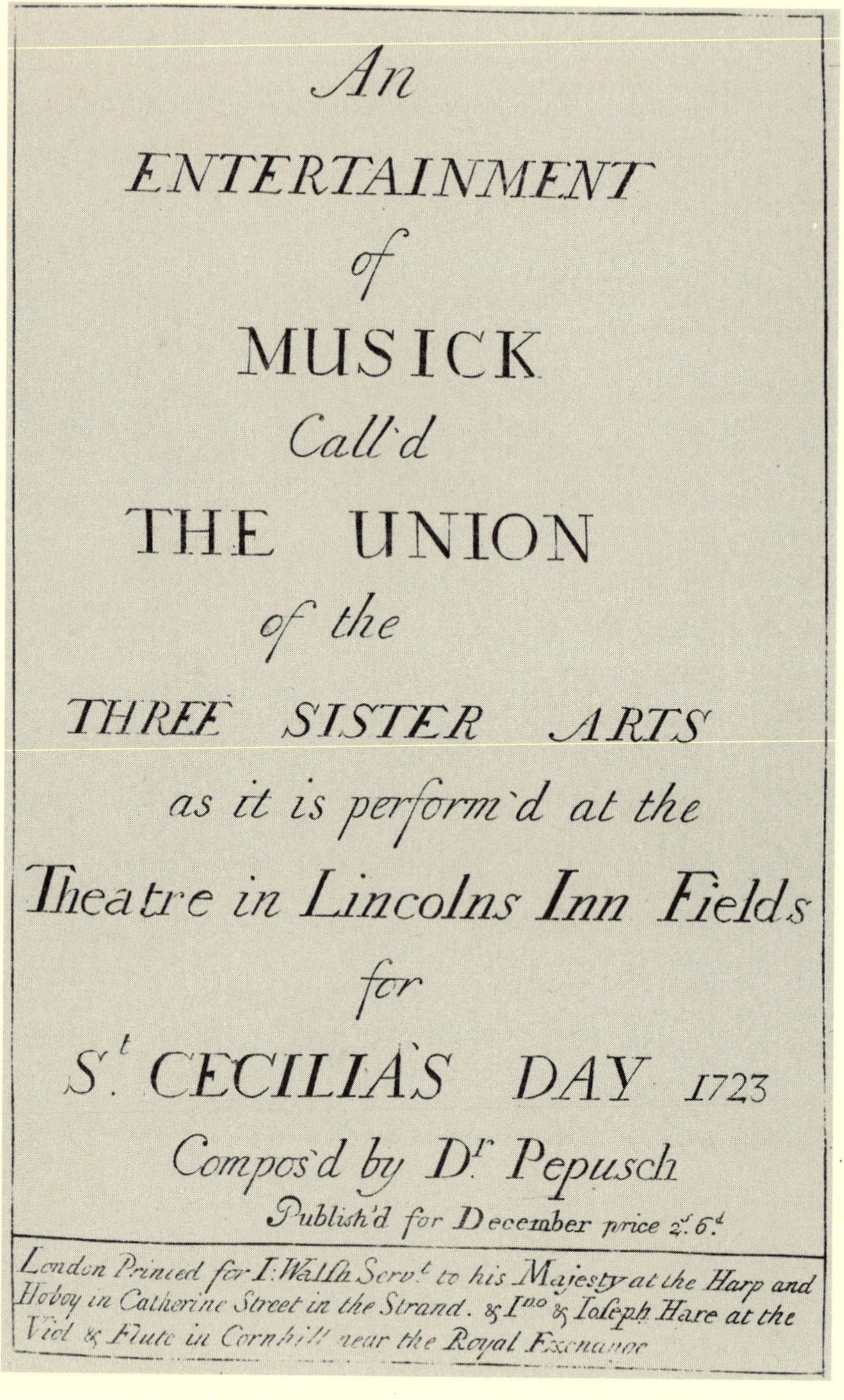

Plate 135.1   Pepusch, *Union of the Three Sister Arts*, 1723

An

ENTERTAINMENT

of

MUSICK

Call'd

THE UNION

of the

THREE SISTER ARTS

as it is perform'd at the

Theatre in Lincolns Inn Fields

for

S.t CECILIA'S DAY 1723

Compos'd by D.r Pepusch

Publish'd for December price 2.s 6.d

London Printed for I: Walsh Serv.t to his Majesty at the Harp and Hoboy in Catherine Street in the Strand. & I.no & Ioseph Hare at the Viol & Flute in Cornhill near the Royal Exchange

Caption: plate 135.1. 328 x 208 mm. Lbl: G.222.(3.).

An Entertainment of Musick Call'd The Union of the Three Sister Arts as it is perform'd at the Theatre in Lincolns Inn Fields for St. Cecilia's Day 1723 Compos'd by Dr. Pepusch Publish'd for December price 2s. 6d. London Printed for I: Walsh Servt. to his Majesty at the Harp and Hoboy in Catherine Street in the Strand. & Ino. & Ioseph Hare at the Viol & Flute in Cornhill near the Royal Exchange

15 leaves. Pp. [i]⬚ 1-28.
Leaves printed on 2 sides.
Tallest copy 385 x 240 mm. Vertical chain lines.

One page engraved per plate. Engraving style Walsh 1.
Title-page plate 269 x 168 mm.

Walsh ii: 1181.
Price 2s. 6d.

Contents: title-page [i]; overture 1-3; songs 4-28.

Songs:

No.	Page	First Line
1	4-5	Behold from my coelestial throne (s Chambers)
2	5-7	When the batt'ring Græcian thunder (s Leveridge)
3	8-11	Conqu'ring heroes fam'd in story (s Chambers, Leveridge)
4	12-13	Life and nature faults and graces (s Laguerre)
5	14-18	By great Cæcilias influ'nce fir'd (s Laguerre, Leveridge)
6	19-22	Poetry and painting with musick joyn
7	23-26	Now rise we to the mansion of the blest (s Chambers)
8	27-28	In gratefull chorus let us raise

Notes:
1. DFo, Mp: price erased from title-page.
2. Copy at Ge was published 1730 or later.

Copies: ALb 789.99+780.6; DFo Bd.W. M1528.P21S4 Cage; Lam —; Lbl G.222.(3.); Lbl Hirsch II 708; Lcm II.J.12; Mp BR f526Pj37; NRU-Mus Vault M1520.P424u; Ob Mus. 22.c.200.

THE
SONGS
in the
NECROMANCER
or
HARLEQUIN D.ᴿ FAUSTUS
as they were Perform'd
at the Theatre
in Lincolns Inn Fields

Parker Sculp.

LONDON:

Printed &ᵈ Sold by Benjamᵗ. Cooke, Musical Instrument Maker &

Musick Printer; at the Golden Harp, in New Street Covent Garden

135a   Galliard, *Necromancer*, 28 February 1724

Caption: plate 135a.1. 330 x 218 mm. Ckc: Rw.85.57.(3).

The Songs in the Necromancer or Harlequin Dr. Faustus as they were Perform'd at the Theatre in Lincolns Inn Fields Parker Sculpt. London: Printed & Sold by Benjamn. Cooke, Musical Instrument Maker & Musick Printer; at the Golden Harp, in New Street Covent Garden

9 leaves. Pp. [i]□\□[1]-[2]□ [3]□\□[4] [5]□\□[6] [7]□-[8]□.
Leaves printed on 1 side.
Tallest copy 330 x 218 mm. Vertical chain lines.

One page engraved per plate. Engraving style Parker.
Title-page plate 262 x 187 mm.

Contents: title-page [i]; songs [1-8].

Songs:

No.	Page	First Line
1	[1-2]	Arise ye subtle forms that sport (s Leveridge, < *Necromancer*)
2	[3]	Cupid god of pleasing anguish (s Chambers, < *Necromancer*)
3	[4-5]	While on ten thousand charms I gaze (s Laguerre, < *Necromancer*)
4	[6-7]	Cease injurous maids, to blame (s Chambers, < *Necromancer*)
5	[8]	Ghosts of ev'ry occupation (s Leveridge, < *Necromancer*)

Notes:
1. First performed 20 December 1723.
2. Title used in song captions is 'Dr. Faustus'.
3. Illustration of engraving style unavailable.

Copy: Ckc Rw.85.57.(3).

Dr. Faustus *or the* Necromancer

a

MASQUE

of

SONG'S

as

they were perform'd

at the Theatre

in

Lincolns Inn Fields

Publish'd for February

Price 1.s

London Printed for and Sold by I: Walsh Servant to his Majesty at the
Harp and Hoboy in Catherine Street in the Strand and In°: by Ioseph Hare
at the Viol and Flute in Cornhill near the Royal Exchange

135b Galliard, *Necromancer*, 28 February 1724

Caption: plate 135b.1. 335 x 217 mm. Lcm: XI.C.22.(2.).

⌠ Dr. Faustus or the Necromancer a ⌡ Masque of Song's as they were perform'd at the Theatre in Lincolns Inn Fields Publish'd for February Price 1s. London Printed for and Sold by I: Walsh Servant to his Majesty at the Harp and Hoboy in Catherine Street in the Strand and Ino. & Ioseph Hare at the Viol and Flute in Cornhill near the Royal Exchange

9 leaves. Pp. [i]⬚ 1⬚-2⬚ \⬚3-4⬚\-\⬚7-8⬚\.
Leaves printed on 1 side.
Tallest copy 344 x 217 mm. Vertical chain lines.

One page engraved per plate. Engraving style Walsh.
Title-page plate 257 x 169 mm. Passe-partout no. 10.

Walsh ii: 583.
Price 1s.

Contents: title-page [i]; songs 1-8.

Songs:

No.	Page	First Line
1	1	Cupid god of pleasing anguish (s Chambers, < *Necromancer*)
2	2	Ghosts of ev'ry occupation (s Leveridge, < *Necromancer*)
3	3-4	While on ten thousand charms I gaze (s Laguerre, < *Necromancer*)
4	5-6	Arise ye subtle forms that sport (s Leveridge, < *Necromancer*)
5	7-8	Cease injurious maid to blame (s Chambers, < *Necromancer*)

Notes:
1. First performed 20 December 1723.
2. Lbl: + Wright edition of song 5, 2 leaves.

Copies: B-Br Fétis 2554; Lbl Ad.MS. 31,588.f.140; Lcm XI.C.22.(2.); Ob 4.Δ.159.

The SONGS *in the*
NECROMANCER *or*
Harlequin D.r Faustus
as they were Perform'd
at the new THEATRE
in Lincolns Inn Fields

Printed for & Sold by Daniel Wright, Musical Instrument Seller, Next Door to the Sun Tavern
the Corner of Brook Street in Holborn Near the Barrs

135c   Galliard, *Necromancer*, 28 February 1724

Caption: plate 135c.1. 327 x 210 mm. Lcm: XXXII.A.3.(2).

[within cartouche] ⌠ The Songs in the Necromancer or Harlequin Dr. Faustus as they were Perform'd at the new Theatre in Lincolns Inn Fields. ⌡ [at foot] Printed for & Sold by Daniel Wright Musical Instrument Seller Next Door to the Sun Tavern the Corner of Brook Street in Holborn Near the Barrs

9 leaves. Pp. [i]□\□[1] [2]□\□[3] [4]□-[6]□\□[7] [8]□.
Leaves printed on 1 side.
Tallest copy 344 x 225 mm. Vertical chain lines.

One page engraved per plate. Engraving style Wright.
Title-page plate 262 x 184 mm. Passe-partout no. 8.

Contents: title-page [i]; songs [1-8].

Songs:

No.	Page	First Line
1	[1-2]	Arise! ye subtle forms that sport (s Leveridge, < *Necromancer*)
2	[3-4]	While on ten thousand charms I gaze (s Laguerre, < *Necromancer*)
3	[5]	Cupid! god of pleasing anquish (s Chambers, < *Necromancer*)
4	[6]	Ghosts of ev'ry occupation (s Leveridge, < *Necromancer*)
5	[7-8]	Cease injurious maids, to blame (s Chambers, < *Necromancer*)

Notes:
1. First performed 20 December 1723.
2. Title used in song captions is 'Dr. Faustus'.
3. CLU-C: p. [5] bound following p. [2], p. [6] bound following p. [8]; [i]□\□[1] [2]□ [5]□\□[3] [4]□\□[7] [8]□ [6]□.

Copies: CLU-C *fM1524.G16n; Lcm XXXII.A.3.(2).

Plate 136.1   Carey, *Cantatas*, 1724

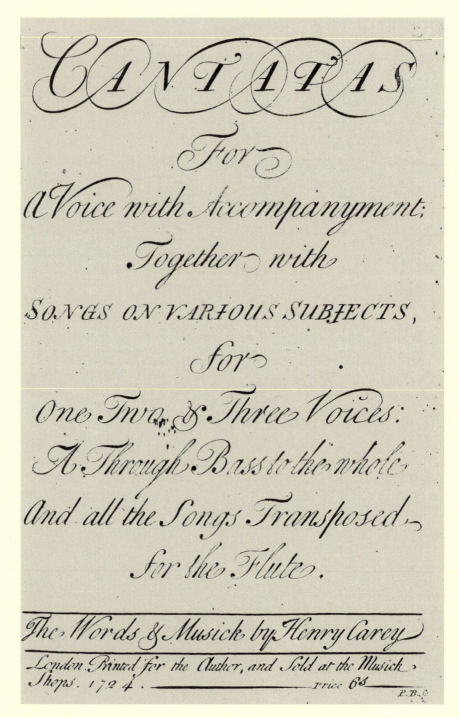

Plate 136.2   Carey, *Cantatas*, 1724

Caption: plates 136.1-136.2. 310 x 200 mm. Lbl: G.220.(2.).

Cantatas For A Voice with Accompanyment; Together with Songs On Various Subjects, for One Two & Three Voices: A Through Bass to the whole And all the Songs Transposed for the Flute. The Words & Musick by Henry Carey London. Printed for the Author, and Sold at the Musick Shops. 1724. Price 6s P.B. Sc

22 leaves. Pp. [i]□-[ii]□ 1-40.
Leaves printed on 2 sides.
Tallest copy 316 x 202 mm. Vertical chain lines.

One page engraved per plate. Engraving style Bates.
Title-page plate 283 x 171 mm.

Advertised in *Daily Post*, 3 March 1724. Price 6s.

Contents: title-page [i]; introduction [ii]; cantata 1-7; songs 8-10; cantata 11-13, songs 14-24; cantata 25-29; recitative and arias 30-32; flute parts 33-40.

Songs:

No.	Page	First Line
1	8-9	This is the day
2	9-10	Pass the glass around with pleasure
3	14-15	What shall he have that kill'd the deer (v Shakespear, s Ray, < *Love in a Forest*)
4	16-17	Turn away mine eyes
5	18	Make haste, and away mine only dear
6	19	See! the morning gives you warning
7	20	On a grassy pillow
8	21	Gardez vous bien bergere (O nymph divinely charming)
9	22-23	Come all ye jolly bacchanals
10	24	O merry land by this light

Notes:
1. P. [ii] is letterpress.
2. Recitative and arias are from 'Harlequin Doctor Faustus the words by Mr Booth'.

Copies: DFo M1529.C27C3 Cage; DLC M1620.C24C3 Cage; DLC ML30.4c no.2697 Miller; En Mus.E.l.33; Lbl G.220.(2.); Lsc ARC G84.1G13(2.); *MH-Mu*; NN Drexel 4285.1; Obh Mus. E.231.

Plate 137.1   Ariosti, *Coriolano*, 1724

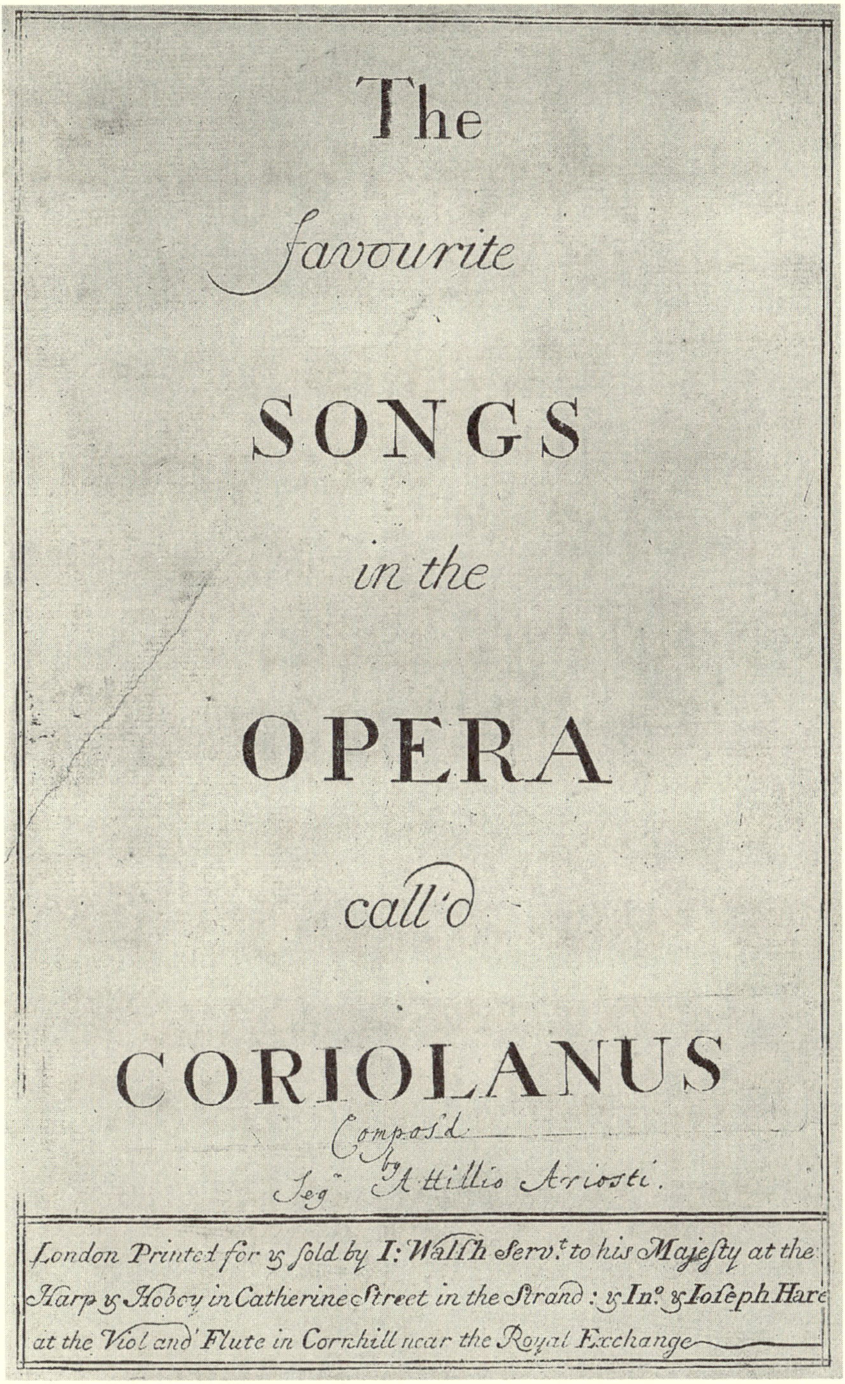

The

favourite

SONGS

in the

OPERA

call'd

CORIOLANUS

Compos'd

Seg.r Attilio Ariosti.

London Printed for & sold by I: Walsh Serv.t to his Majesty at the
Harp & Hoboy in Catherine Street in the Strand : & Ino. & Joseph Hare
at the Viol and Flute in Cornhill near the Royal Exchange

Caption: plate 137.1. 343 x 220 mm. Dfo: M1500. A56. C6 Cage.

The favourite Songs in the Opera call'd ⌠ Coriolanus ⌡ London Printed for &
sold by I: Walsh Servt. to his Majesty at the Harp & Hoboy in Catherine Street
in the Strand: & Ino. & Ioseph Hare at the Viol and Flute in Cornhill near the
Royal Exchange

29 leaves. Pp. [i]□\□1 2□\□3 4-5 \□6-7□\-\□10-11□\ □12 13-14 15□-16□\□17 18□
19□-22 23□ 24-25 26□-27□ \□28-29□\-\□32-33□\.
Leaves printed on 1 side.
Tallest copy 344 x 216 mm. Mixed chain lines.

One page engraved per plate. Engraving style Walsh 1, 4.
Title-page plate 287 x 176 mm. Passe-partout no. 9.

Walsh ii: 48.
Advertised in *Daily Courant*, 23 March 1724.

Contents: title-page [i]; songs 1-33.

Songs:

No.	Page	First Line
1	1-2	Rendi al padre in me la figlia (s Cuzzoni, < *Coriolano*)
2	3-5	Io spero che in que' guardi (s Senesino, < *Coriolano*)
3	6-7	Sacri numi difendete (s Durastanti, < *Coriolano*)
4	8-9	Fin ch'ei stringe la spada rubella (s Boschi, < *Coriolano*)
5	10-11	Perdonate o cari amori (s Senesino, < *Coriolano*)
6	12-14	Il suo amore intenderò (s Cuzzoni, < *Coriolano*)
7	15	Più benigno par che arrida (Charmer hear your faithfull lover) (s Robinson, A., < *Coriolano*)
8	16	So che guarda con raggio sereno (s Senesino, < *Coriolano*)
9	17-18	Più crudel si fa la sorte quando vede (s Durastanti, < *Coriolano*)
10	19-23	Si mio caro amor (s Senesino, Cuzzoni, < *Coriolano*)
11	24-26	Voi d'un figlio tanto misero (s Senesino, < *Coriolano*)
12	27	Teco s'annodi l'alma mio caro (s Cuzzoni, < *Coriolano*)
13	28-29	In braccio al'idol mio (s Senesino, < *Coriolano*)
14	30-31	Del cor la speme non è bastante (s Cuzzoni, < *Coriolano*)
15	32-33	Giunse al fin quel dì bramato (s Cuzzoni, < *Coriolano*)

Notes:
1. Smith and Humphries incorrectly surmise that Walsh's book is an issue of Meares' edition
(127).
2. Some leaves printed on both sides.
3. Songs 1, 2, 5-7, 9, 11, 12 reissued with additional pagination as part of *Apollo's Feast*, book 2,
172, in 1726.
4. DFo: - p. 15; + 'Per combatter con lo sdegno dal mio labbro' ([34] [35]), and the overture (19
MS. pages) bound between p. [i] and p. 1. Following 'Coriolanus' on title-page is 'Compos'd by
Senr Attillio Ariosti' in MS. Figuring and English translation added to songs in MS.

Copies: B-Bc 17,202; CSt SpC MLM Box1 Item5; DFo M1500.A56 C6 Cage.

Plate 138.1   Ariosti, *Vespasian*, 1724

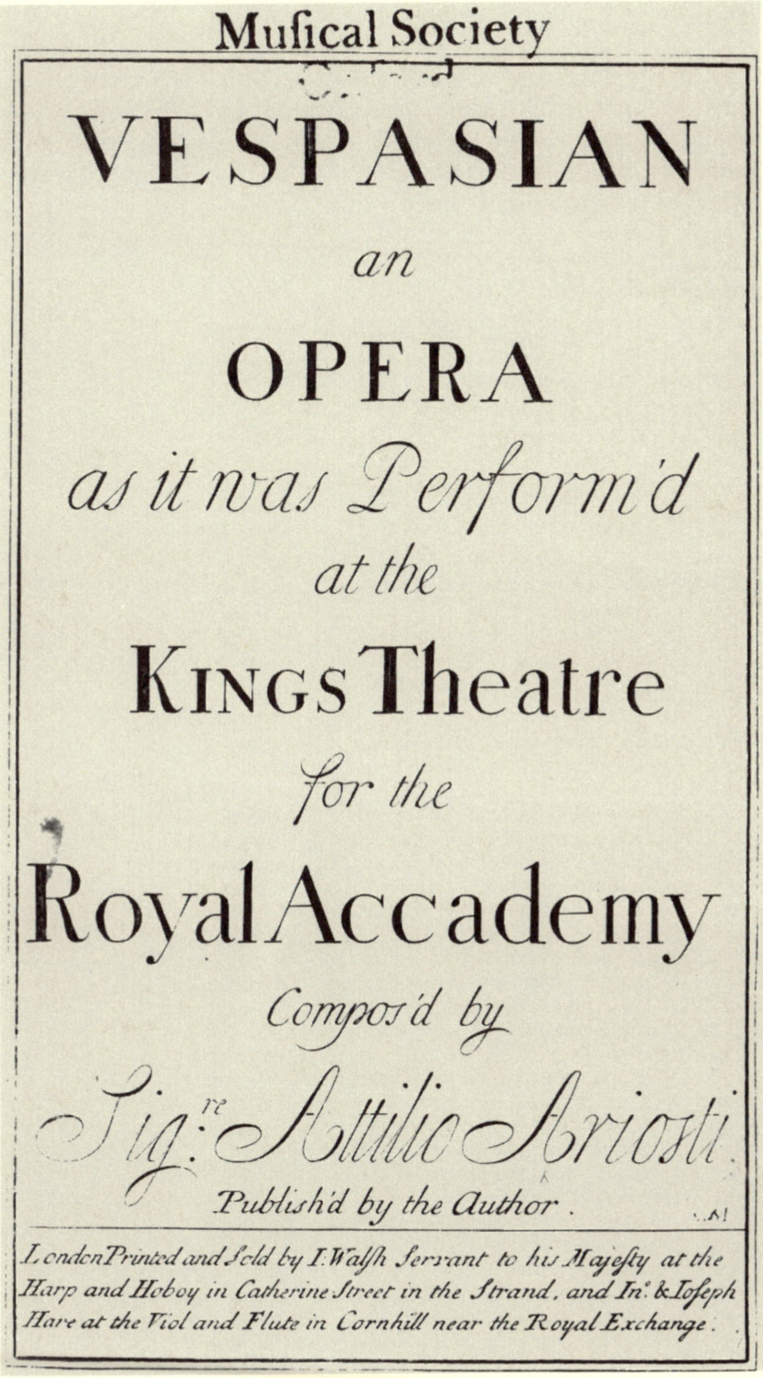

Musical Society

VESPASIAN

an

OPERA

as it was Perform'd

at the

KINGS Theatre

for the

Royal Accademy

Compos'd by

Sig.:ᵉ Attilio Ariosti.

Publish'd by the Author.

London Printed and Sold by I. Walsh Servant to his Majesty at the Harp and Hoboy in Catherine Street in the Strand, and In:ᵒ & Joseph Hare at the Viol and Flute in Cornhill near the Royal Exchange.

Caption: plate 138.1. 357 x 230 mm. Lbl: I.350.a.

Vespasian an Opera as it was Perform'd at the Kings Theatre for the Royal
Accademy Compos'd by Sigre: Attilio Ariosti. Publish'd by the Author.
London Printed and Sold by I: Walsh Servant to his Majesty at the Harp
and Hoboy in Catherine-Street in the Strand, and Ino. & Ioseph Hare at the
Viol and Flute in Cornhill near the Royal Exchange.

41 leaves. Pp. [i]▯ [ii] 1-79.
Leaves printed on 2 sides.
Tallest copy 386 x 246 mm. Vertical chain lines.

One page engraved per plate. Engraving style Walsh 1, 3.
Title-page plate 305 x 173 mm.
Contents plate 316 x 178 mm.

Walsh ii: 53.
Advertised in *Daily Courant*, 23 March 1724.

Contents: title-page [i]; contents and advertisement [ii]; overture 1-7; songs 8-79.

Songs:

No.	Page	First Line
1	8-10	Di nuovi strali armato (s Berenstadt, < *Vespasian*)
2	11-13	Prima vedrai baciarsi il lupo e l'agna (s Cuzzoni, < *Vespasian*)
3	14-15	No non piangete pupille amate (s Durastanti, < *Vespasian*)
4	16	Aure voi che m'ascoltate (s Cuzzoni, < *Vespasian*)
5	17	Con forza ascosa ne'raggi sui (s Senesino, < *Vespasian*)
6	18-19	Io sono oppressa tanto (s Robinson, A., < *Vespasian*)
7	20-21	Su fieri guerrieri vittoria o morir (s Boschi, < *Vespasian*)
8	22-23	Il dolce e bel contento (s Robinson, A., < *Vespasian*)
9	24	Lasso ch'jo t'ho'perduta (s Senesino, < *Vespasian*)
10	25	Di lieo soave e grato (s Durastanti, Cuzzoni, < *Vespasian*)
11	26-27	Del mio sen costante e forte (s Cuzzoni, < *Vespasian*)
12	28-29	Or che il sonno (s Durastanti, < *Vespasian*)
13	30-31	Al'armi a le straggi (s Boschi, < *Vespasian*)
14	32-34	Sorga pur l'opressa Roma (s Berenstadt, < *Vespasian*)
15	35	Io ti lascio amato pegno (s Robinson, A., < *Vespasian*)
16	36-38	Del caro mio tesoro (s Senesino, < *Vespasian*)
17	39-40	Come va'di fiore in fiore (s Robinson, A., < *Vespasian*)
18	41-43	S'io son schernita (s Cuzzoni, < *Vespasian*)
19	44-45	Se ben diffetto appar (s Senesino, < *Vespasian*)
20	46-47	Pur che mi sciolga il piede (s Robinson, A., < *Vespasian*)
21	48-50	La tortorella fida e costante (s Cuzzoni, < *Vespasian*)
22	51-52	Ah traditore spirar uorrei da (s Senesino, < *Vespasian*)
23	53-54	Un raggio placido di bella speme (Durastanti, < *Vespasian*)
24	55	Bella gloria sara'del mio sangue (s Boschi, < *Vespasian*)
25	56-57	Dammi sul labbro il cor (s Senesino, < *Vespasian*)
26	58-59	Su le nemiche stragi al Trono ascenderò (s Durastanti, < *Vespasian*)
27	60-61	Premerà soglio di morte (s Berenstadt, < *Vespasian*)

28	62-63	Han posto i tuoi bei lumi (s Senesino, < *Vespasian*)
29	64	Son giusti i sdegni tuoi (s Robinson, A., < *Vespasian*)
30	65-67	Combattuta navicella (s Cuzzoni, < *Vespasian*)
31	68-72	È un bel piacer l'amar (< *Vespasian*)
32	73	Non è Cupido no che mi tormenta (s Robinson, A., < *Vespasian*)
33	73-75	Nocchier che salva il legno (s Durastanti, < *Vespasian*)
34	76-77	Colomba innamorata (s Cuzzoni, < *Vespasian*)
35	78-79	Doppo oscura tempesta crudel

Notes:
1. Songs 4, 5, 9, 12, 20, 21, 23, 28, 30, 31 reissued with additional pagination as part of *Apollo's Feast*, book 2, 172, in 1726.
2. D-Hs: four leaves of songs from other editions of *Vespasian* bound following p. 17.

Copies: Ckc 85.3.(6.); Ckc 85.9; CLU-C *fM1500.A71v; D-Hs M C/152; *D-Mbs*; DLC M1500.A76V2; F-Pn Vm3.209; Lbl I.350.a; Lcm XXXII.B.11.(3.).

Plate 139.1   Ariosti, *Vespasian*, 1724

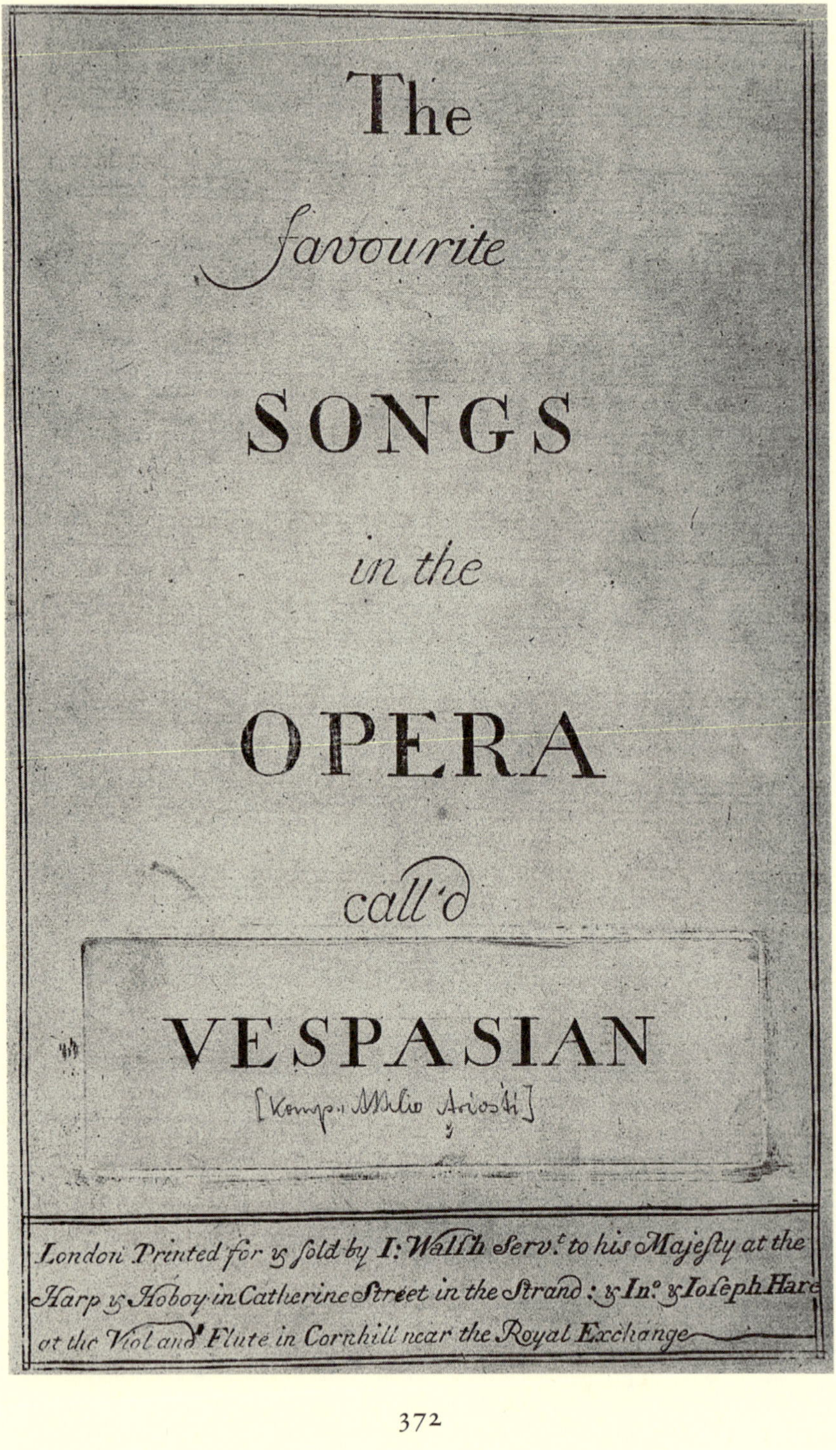

The

favourite

SONGS

in the

OPERA

call'd

VESPASIAN

[Komp. Milio Ariosti]

London Printed for & sold by I: Walsh Serv.t to his Majesty at the
Harp & Hoboy in Catherine Street in the Strand : & In.o & Ioseph Hare
at the Viol and Flute in Cornhill near the Royal Exchange

139 Ariosti, *Vespasian*, 23 March 1724

Caption: plate 139.1. 342 x 222 mm. D-Hs: M B/2620/7.

The favourite Songs in the Opera call'd ⌠ Vespasian ⌡ London Printed for &
sold by I: Walsh Servt. to his Majesty at the Harp & Hoboy in Catherine Street
in the Strand: & Ino. & Ioseph Hare at the Viol and Flute in Cornhill near the
Royal Exchange

14 leaves. Pp. [i]□ 16□-17□ 24□\□46 47□\□48 49□-50□\□53 54□\□65 66□-67□.
Leaves printed on 1 side.
Tallest copy 342 x 222 mm. Vertical chain lines.

One page engraved per plate. Engraving style Walsh 1, 3.
Title-page plate 282 x 175 mm. Passe-partout no. 9.

Contents: title-page [i]; songs 16-17, 24, 46-50, 53-54, 65-67.

Songs:

No.	Page	First Line
1	16	Aure voi che m'ascoltate (s Cuzzoni, < *Vespasian*)
2	17	Con forza ascosa ne'raggi sui (s Senesino, < *Vespasian*)
3	24	Lasso ch'jo t'ho'perduta (s Senesino, < *Vespasian*)
4	46-47	Pur che mi sciolga il piede (s Robinson, A., < *Vespasian*)
5	48-50	La tortorella fida e costante benchè (s Cuzzoni, < *Vespasian*)
6	53-54	Un raggio placido di bella speme (s Durastanti, < *Vespasian*)
7	65-67	Combattuta navicella (s Cuzzoni, < *Vespasian*)

Copy: D-Hs M B/2620/7.

Plate 140.1   Ariosti, *Vespasian*, 1724

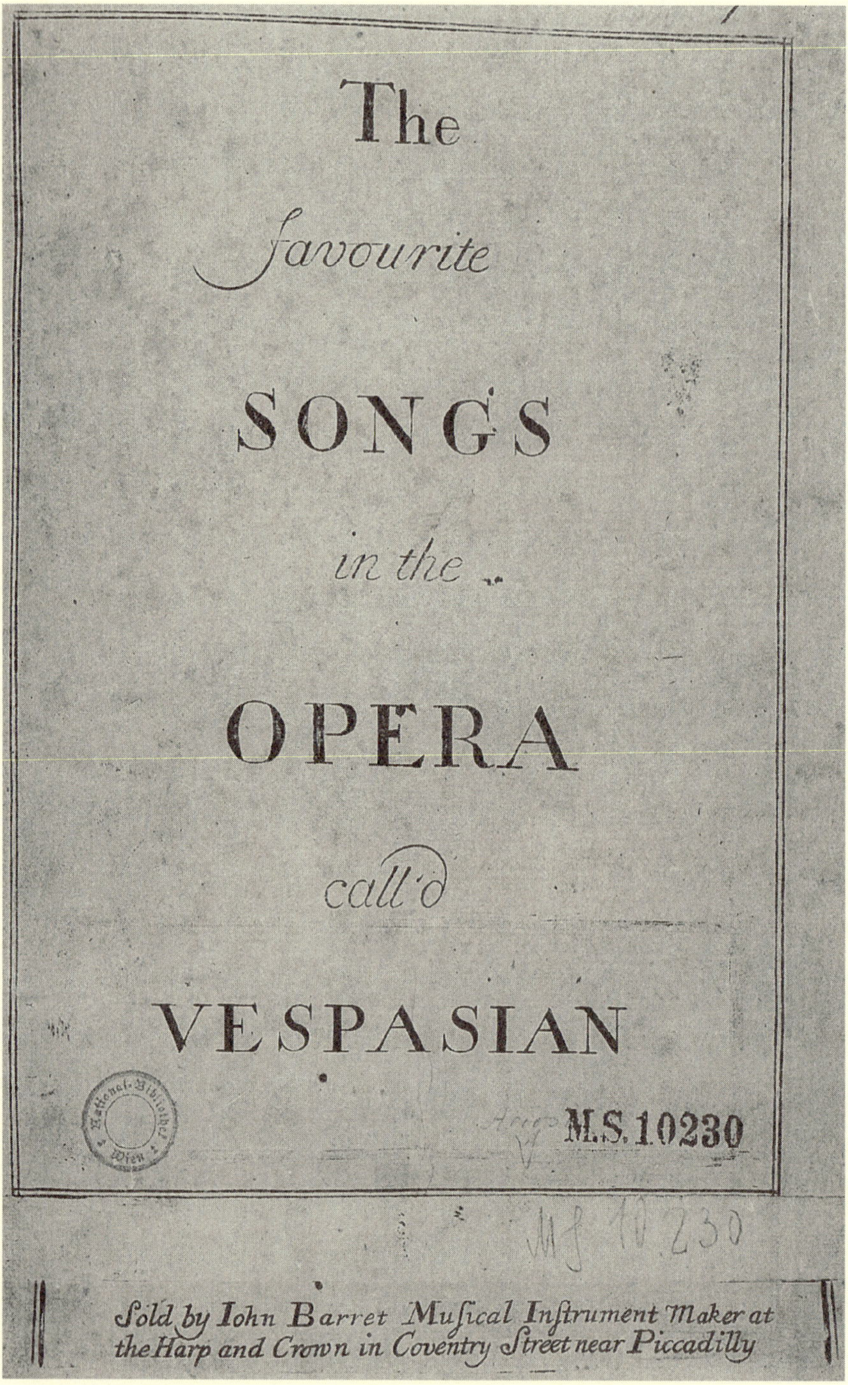

The

favourite

SONGS

in the

OPERA

call'd

VESPASIAN

M.S. 10230

Sold by John Barret *Musical Instrument Maker at the Harp and Crown in Coventry Street near Piccadilly*

Caption: plate 140.1. 349 x 220 mm. A-Wn: M.S.10230.

The favourite Songs in the Opera call'd ⌠ Vespasian ⌡ [engraved label over Walsh & Hares imprint] Sold by Iohn Barret Musical Instrument Maker at the Harp and Crown in Coventry Street near Piccadilly

14 leaves. Pp. [i]◻ 16◻-17◻ 24◻\◻46 47◻\◻48 49◻-50◻\◻53 54◻\◻65 66◻-67◻.
Leaves printed on 1 side.
Tallest copy 349 x 220 mm. Vertical chain lines.

One page engraved per plate. Engraving style Walsh 1, 3.
Title-page plate ? x 175 mm. Passe-partout no. 9. (See note 1.)

Contents: title-page [i]; songs 16-17, 24, 46-50, 53-54, 65-67.

Songs: see **139**.

Note:
1. Label obscures lower edge of plate.

Copy: A-Wn M.S.10230.

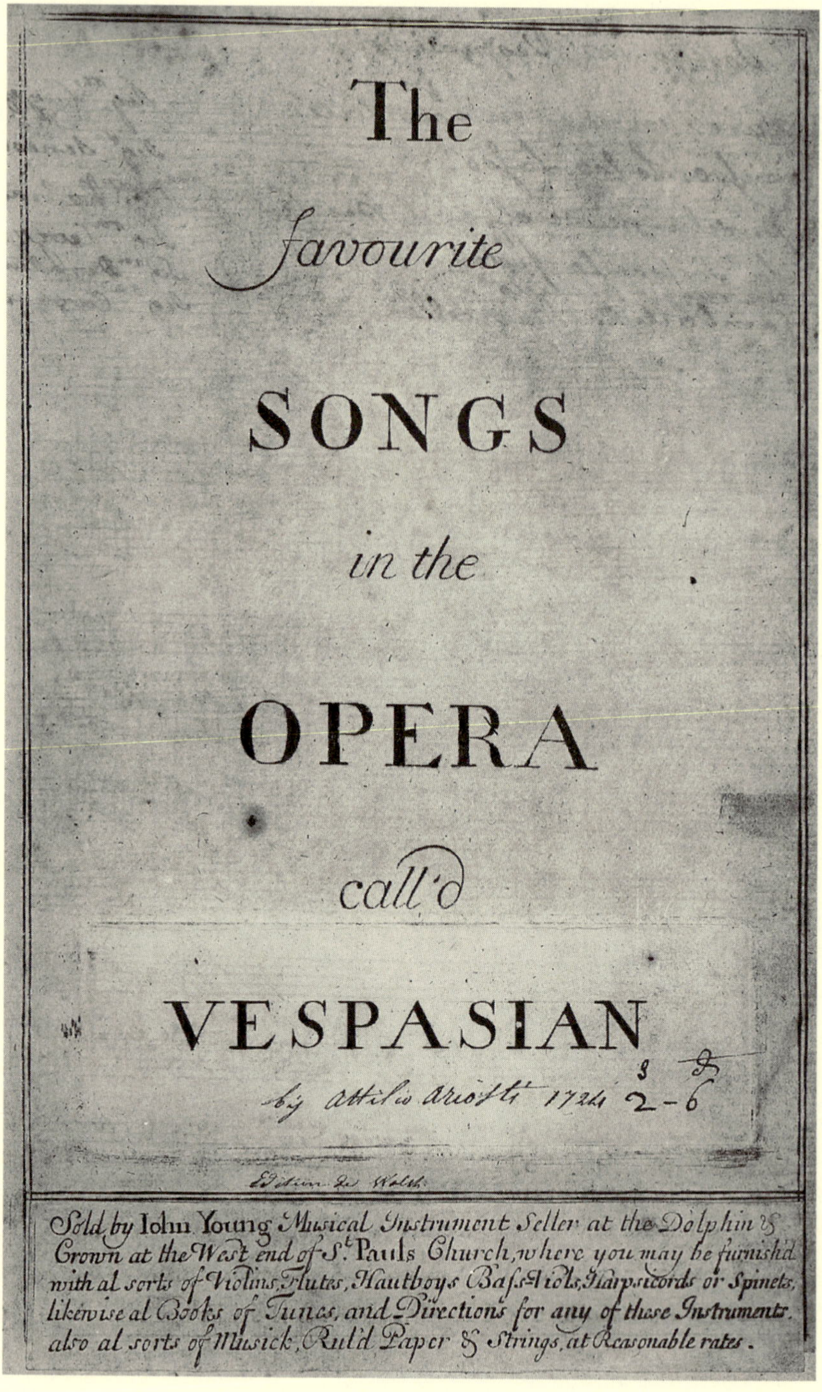

Plate 141.1   Ariosti, *Vespasian*, 1724

The

favourite

SONGS

in the

OPERA

call'd

VESPASIAN

by Attilio Ariosti 1724 2-6

Edition de Walsh

Sold by Iohn Young Musical Instrument Seller at the Dolphin &
Crown at the West end of S.t Pauls Church, where you may be furnish'd
with al sorts of Violins, Flutes, Hautboys Bass Viols, Harpsicords or Spinets,
likewise al Books of Tunes, and Directions for any of these Instruments,
also al sorts of Musick, Rul'd Paper & Strings, at Reasonable rates.

Caption: plate 141.1. 340 x 217 mm. F-Pc: Rés V.S.1289bis.

The favourite Songs in the Opera call'd ∫ Vespasian ♩ [engraved label over Walsh and Hares imprint] Sold by Iohn Young Musical Instrument Seller at the Dolphin & Crown at the West end of St. Pauls Church, where you may be furnish'd with al sorts of Violins, Flutes, Hautboys Bass-Viols, Harpsicords or Spinets; likewise al Books of Tunes, and Directions for any of these Instruments, also al sorts of Musick, Rul'd Paper & Strings, at Reasonable rates.

13 leaves. Pp. [i]⫾ 16⫾ 24⫾\⫾46 47⫾-50⫾\⫾53 54⫾\⫾65 66⫾-67⫾.
Leaves printed on 1 side.
Tallest copy 320 x 217 mm. Vertical chain lines.

One page engraved per plate. Engraving style Walsh 1, 3.
Title-page plate ? x 175 mm. Passe-partout no. 9. (See note 2.)

Contents: title-page [i]; songs 16, 24, 46-50, 53-54, 65-67.

Songs:

No.	Page	First Line
1	16	Aure voi che m'ascoltate (s Cuzzoni, < *Vespasian*)
2	24	Lasso ch'jo t'ho' perduta (s Senesino, < *Vespasian*)
3	46-47	Pur che mi sciolga il piede (s Robinson, A., < *Vespasian*)
4	48-50	La tortorella fida e costante benchè (s Cuzzoni, < *Vespasian*)
5	53-54	Un raggio placido di bella speme (s Durastanti, < *Vespasian*)
6	65-67	Combattuta navicella (s Cuzzoni, < *Vespasian*)

Notes:
1. Price in MS. on title-page: 2s. 6d.
2. Label obscures lower edge of plate.

Copy: F-Pc Rés. V.S.1289bis.

Plate 142.1   Ariosti, *Vespasian*, 1724

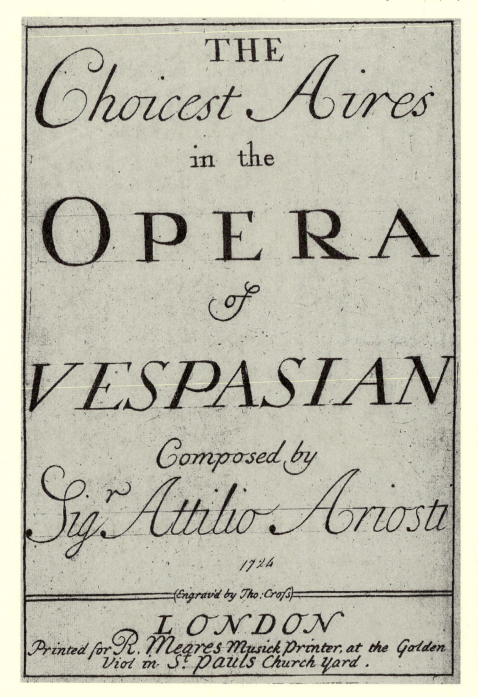

THE
Choicest Aires
in the
OPERA
of
VESPASIAN
Composed by
Sigr Attilio Ariosti
1724
(Engrav'd by Tho:Cross)
LONDON
Printed for R. Meares Musick Printer, at the Golden
Viol in St Pauls Church yard .

142 Ariosti, *Vespasian*, 28 March 1724

Caption: plate 142.1. 341 x 217 mm. F-Pc: Rés. V.S.1289.

The Choicest Aires in the Opera of Vespasian Composed by Sigr Attilio Ariosti (Engrav'd by Tho: Cross) London Printed for R. Meares Musick Printer, at the Golden Viol in St. Pauls Church Yard.

18 leaves. Pp. [i]□ \□1-2□\-\□5-6□\ 7□\□8-9□\-\□12-13□\ 14□\□15 16□-17□.
Leaves printed on 1 side.
Tallest copy 341 x 217 mm. Vertical chain lines.

One page engraved per plate. Engraving style Cross.
Title-page plate 264 x 187 mm.

Advertised in *Daily Post*, 28 March 1724. Price 2s.

Contents: title-page [i]; songs 1-17.

Songs:

No.	Page	First Line
1	1-2	Con forza ascosa ne raggi sui (s Senesino, < *Vespasian*)
2	3-4	Aure voi che m'ascoltate (s Cuzzoni, < *Vespasian*)
3	5-7	Un raggio placido di bella speme (s Durastanti, < *Vespasian*)
4	8-11	Pur che mi sciolga il piede (s Robinson, A., < *Vespasian*)
5	12-14	La tortorella fida e costante (s Cuzzoni, < *Vespasian*)
6	15-17	Combattuta nauicella (s Cuzzoni, < *Vespasian*)

Notes:
1. Each song signed at end 'T: Cross Sculp.'
2. D-Hs: p. 11 duplicated.

Copies: D-Hs M C/152Beil; F-Pc Rés. V.S.1289.

Plate 143.1   Bononcini, *Pharnaces*, 1724

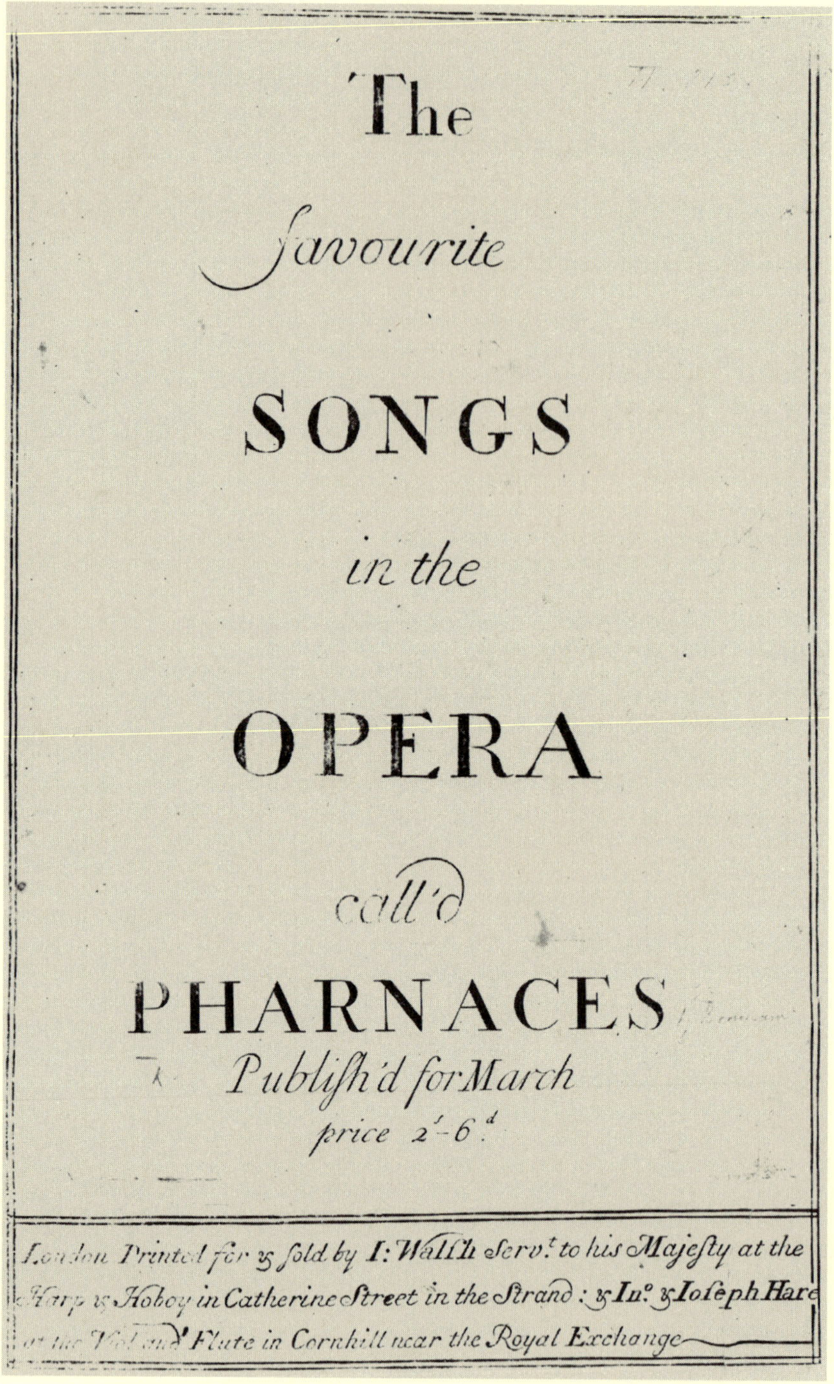

The

favourite

SONGS

in the

OPERA

call'd

PHARNACES

Publish'd for March
price 2ˢ-6ᵈ

London Printed for & sold by I: Walsh Servᵗ to his Majesty at the
Harp & Hoboy in Catherine Street in the Strand: & Inᵒ & Ioseph Hare
at the Viol and Flute in Cornhill near the Royal Exchange—

Caption: plate 143.1. 335 x 213 mm. Lbl: H.318.

The favourite Songs in the Opera call'd ⌠ Pharnaces Publish'd for March price
2s-6d. ⌡ London Printed for & sold by I: Walsh Servt. to his Majesty at the
Harp & Hoboy in Catherine Street in the Strand: & Ino. & Ioseph Hare at the
Viol and Flute in Cornhill near the Royal Exchange

21 leaves. Pp. [i]◻\◻1-2◻\-\◻19-20◻\.
Leaves printed on 1 side.
Tallest copy 366 x 228 mm. Vertical chain lines.

One page engraved per plate. Engraving style Walsh.
Title-page plate 286 x 177 mm. Passe-partout no. 9.

Walsh ii: 209.
Price 2s. 6d.

Contents: title-page [i]; songs 1-20.

Songs:

No.	Page	First Line
1	1-2	Begl'occhi lusinghieri (s Durastanti, < *Pharnaces*)
2	3-4	No chi fingere non sà in dolce affetto (s Durastanti, < *Pharnaces*)
3	5-6	Spera quest'alma (s Senesino, < *Pharnaces*)
4	7-8	Non t'inganno stretto nodo (s Cuzzoni, < *Pharnaces*)
5	9-10	Si morrò ma ancor languendo (s Cuzzoni, < *Pharnaces*)
6	11-12	Il core che pretendo (s Robinson, A., < *Pharnaces*)
7	13-14	Già col vostro rigor (s Senesino, < *Pharnaces*)
8	15-16	Nembo tal'ora porta l'aurora (s Cuzzoni, < *Pharnaces*)
9	17-18	Al par d'un fiore (s Durastanti, < *Pharnaces*)
10	19-20	Se vuol ch'io mora (s Robinson, A., < *Pharnaces*)

Notes:
1. First performed November 1723.
2. All songs except 2 and 5 reissued with additional pagination as part of *Apollo's Feast*, book 2,
172, in 1726.
3. Ckc (110.24.(1.)), Lbl (H.230.f.(4.)): - p. [i].

Copies: B-MAR; Ckc 85.2.(6.); Ckc 110.24.(1.); CSfst de Bellis 814; D-Hs M B/2620/2; Ge
P.c.36; Lam —; Lbl H.230.f.(4.); Lbl H.318.

Plate 144.1 *Pocket Companion*, [vol. 1], 1724

A Pocket-Companion
FOR
Gentlemen and Ladies.

Plate 144.2 *Pocket Companion*, [vol.1], 1724

A
Pocket Companion
FOR
Gentlemen *and* Ladies:
BEING A
COLLECTION
Of the fineſt
Opera Songs & Airs,
In Engliſh and Italian.
A Work never before attempted.
Carefully Corrected, & alſo Figur'd for ẏ Organ,
Harpſicord, and Spinet, by Mr. Rid. Neale
Organiſt of St. James's Garlick-hith.
LONDON:
Engrav'd and Printed at Cluer's *Printing-*
Office in Bow-Church-Yard, and ſold there,
and by B. Creake, *at ẏ* Bible *in Jermyn-Street*
St. James's.

Plate 144.3   *Pocket Companion*, [vol.1], 1724

Caption: plates 144.1-144.3. 160 x 104 mm. Lbl: C.491.

A Pocket Companion For Gentlemen and Ladies: Being A Collection Of the finest Opera Songs & Airs, In English and Italian. A Work never before attempted. Carefully Corrected, & also Figur'd for ye Organ, Harpsicord, and Spinet, by Mr. Rid. Neale, Organist of St. James's Garlick-hith. London: Engrav'd and Printed at Cluer's Printing-Office in Bow-Church-Yard, and sold there, and by B. Creake, at ye Bible in Jermyn-Street. St. James's.

88 leaves. Pp. ◻[i] [ii]◻-[iii]◻ [iv]-[v] i-xvi 1-152.
Leaves printed on 2 sides.
Tallest copy 173 x 124 mm. Horizontal chain lines.

Four pages engraved per plate. Engraving style Cobb.
Title-page plate: see note 1.

Advertised in *London Journal*, 2 May 1724. Price 12s.

Contents: frontispiece [i]; title-page [ii]; dedication [iii]; preface [iv]; verses [v]; subscribers' list i-xiv; advertisement xiv-xv; contents xv-xvi; songs 1-152.

Songs:

No.	Page	First Line
1	1	Sol per tè s'amai le pene (Dear charming fair, no longer teaze)
2	2-3	Ritorna o dolce amore (< *Otho*)
3	4-7	Oh lovely charmer (O cara spene) (< *Floridante*)
4	8	Se vuoi ch'io viua lascia d'amor (See how I languish, o charming fair)
5	9	'Tis my glory to adore you (< *Griselda*)
6	10-11	Più benigno par che arrida (Charmer hear your faithful lover) (< *Coriolano*)
7	12-13	Love leads to battle, who dares oppose (< *Camilla*)
8	14-15	No I will no more believe thee (No non voi più star in pene)
9	16-17	Love thou airy vain illusion (< *Pyrrhus and Demetrius*)
10	18-19	To beauty devoted (< *Camilla*)
11	20-21	Chains of love I wear, The (< *Thomyris*)
12	22-23	Too lovely cruel fair (< *Pyrrhus and Demetrius*)
13	24-25	Around her see Cupid flying (< *Camilla*)
14	26-27	Secret joy I share, A (< *Love's Triumph*)
15	28-29	So form'd to charm (< *Love's Triumph*)
16	30	Why are you kind too late (< *Love's Triumph*)
17	31	See! my Seraphina comes
18	32	Do like the rest (< *Love's Triumph*)
19	33	This great world's but a trouble (< *Jupiter and Europa*)
20	34-35	Alma mia si sol tu sei (< *Floridante*)
21	36-38	Talk no more to me of glory (Se risolvi abbandonarmi) (< *Floridante*)
22	39	Charming is your shape and air
23	40	Ye pow'rs my welcome death forgive (< *Thomyris*)
24	41	Freedom, thou greatest blessing (< *Thomyris*)
25	42-43	Appear all ye graces (O'gratie accorete) (< *Pyrrhus and Demetrius*)
26	44-45	Bright wonder of nature (< *Thomyris*)
27	46-47	Dangers ev'ry way surround me (< *Camilla*)

28	48-49	Can you leave ranging (< *Thomyris*)
29	50-51	Tutte le più vezzose armi (Cupid relieve me) (< *Arsaces*)
30	52-54	Beauty now alone shall move him (< *Venus and Adonis*)
31	55	Like the thunder guilt aming (< *Thomyris*)
32	56-59	Farewel deluding pleasure (m Eminent Master)
33	60-62	See your faithful lover (Si t'amo caro quanto un dì t'amei) (< *Theseus*)
34	63	Young Philoret and Celia
35	64	Rich Gripe does all his thoughts
36	65	Prithee Billy, be n't so silly (m Vanbrugh)
37	66-67	Vieni torna idolo mio (Turn, o turn ye, dearest creature) (< *Theseus*)
38	68-71	No non temer (< *Otho*)
39	72-74	La speranzo é giunta in porta (< *Otho*)
40	75	Con forza ascosa ne raggi sui (< *Vespasian*)
41	76-78	Benchè povera donzella (< *Flavius*)
42	79	Let monarchs fight for power & fame (m Courteville)
43	80-82	Pensa ad amare che dal tuo cor (< *Otho*)
44	83	Charmer now ease me
45	84-86	Alla fama dimi il vero (< *Otho*)
46	87	Conquering beauty 'tis I still adore
47	88-89	Cupid god of pleasing anguish (< *Necromancer*)
48	90-91	Non è Cupido nò che mi tormenta (< *Vespasian*)
49	92-93	Ghosts of ev'ry occupation (< *Necromancer*)
50	94-96	Benchè mi sia crudele (< *Otho*)
51	97	Swains wing the day (< *Love's Triumph*)
52	98	Oh my treasure, crown my pleasure (< *Floridante*)
53	99	Transported with pleasure (< *Astartus*)
54	100-101	Spare my sorrow rural pleasure (< *Love's Triumph*)
55	102-103	Dear pritty maid, don't fly me so (< *Astartus*)
56	104	Let ambition fire thy mind (m Weldon)
57	105	Lovely charming fair
58	106-107	Tu uvoi ch'io parta (< *Radamisto*)
59	108-110	Aure uoi che m'ascolta (< *Vespasian*)
60	111	Phillis the lovely, turn to your swain
61	112-115	Con raggio placido di bella (< *Vespasian*)
62	116-117	As Amoret with Phillis sat (m Dieupart)
63	118	When bright Celia on the plain
64	119	Love me no more
65	120-122	Cara sposa amato bene (< *Radamisto*)
66	123	Can you now leave me and so deceive me
67	124-126	Fenchè lo strale (< *Floridante*)
68	127	Why must I feel your dart
69	128-130	Deh non dir che mille amante (< *Otho*)
70	131	When we're young we're prone to marry (m Eminent Master)
71	132-134	Quanto dolci quanto care (< *Flavius*)
72	135	Dear charmer of my pleasure (m Eminent Master)
73	136-138	Why does my heart thus restless prove (m Eminent Master)
74	139	While I'm a pleading
75	140-142	Parte si parto si (< *Flavius*)
76	143	Lovely dear charmer
77	144-146	Gen'rous wine, and a friend (m Graves)
78	147	In love never vary
79	148-149	Qual nave smarita (< *Radamisto*)
80	150-152	Volgendo a me lo squardo (< *Griselda*)

Notes:
1. Frontispiece and title-page engraved by Cobb on a single plate approximately 165 x 206 mm.
2. First and second rectos of each gathering of songs signed ('quarto' gatherings). For pp. i-xvi, first recto of each gathering signed ('folio' gatherings), two pages per plate.

3. Ckc, NL-DHgm: - pp. xiii-xvi.
4. CtY-Mus: - p. [i], pp. i-ii misbound between pp. [ii] and [iii].
5. F-Pc: pp. 140-143 bound between pp. 137-138.
6. MH-Mu: - pp. [i]-[ii].
7. MiU: - pp. [iii]-[v].
8. Mp: - p. [i].
9. Ouf: - pp. 83-86.

Copies: ALb 789.99 + 780.2; CaOLU MZ.069; Ckc 112.41; CLU-C *M1507.P73 v.1; *Coke*;
Cpc e.7.22; CtY-Mus Rare Ms14.P751; CU-MUSI M1507.N4 Case X; DFo M1738.N45 Cage;
DLC M1507.N34P6; En BH.Add.39; En Ing.7; F-Pc Rés. V.S.1410; Ge N.d.22; *IaU*; ICN
Case VM1505.N34p; ICU Rare M1507.N34 v.1-2; *InU*; Lbl C.491; Lcm IX.F.26.a; MB
**M.129a.45; MH-Mu Mus 502.5 RBR; MiU RBR M1507.P74; Mp BR 412Nh16; *NcD*;
NjP (Ex) xB83.0224; NL-DHgm 4 H 6; Ob Mus. 9.f.1; Ouf —; TxU Ak.A100.725p2 v.1.

Plate 145.1 *Pocket Companion*, [vol.1], ed. 2, 1724

A

Pocket Companion

FOR

Gentlemen *and* Ladies:

BEING A

COLLECTION

Of the finest

Opera Songs & Airs,

In English and Italian.

A Work never before attempted.

Carefully Corrected, & also Figur'd for ỹ Organ,
Harpsicord, and Spinet, by Mr. Rid Neale
Organist of St James's Garlick-hith.

The 2d Edition.

LONDON, *Printed at* Cluer's *Printing-*
Office in Bow-Church-Yard, and fold there,
and by B. Creake, *at ỹ* Bible *in Jermyn-Street,*
St James's.

Caption: plate 145.1. 161 x 107 mm. Lbl: C.491.a.

A Pocket Companion For Gentlemen and Ladies: Being A Collection Of the finest Opera Songs & Airs, In English and Italian. A Work never before attempted. Carefully Corrected, & also Figur'd for ye Organ, Harpsicord, and Spinet, by Mr. Rid. Neale, Organist of St. James's Garlick-hith. The 2d. Edition. London, Printed at Cluer's Printing-Office in Bow-Church-Yard, and sold there, and by B. Creake, at ye Bible in Jermyn-Street. St. James's.

89 leaves. Pp. □[i] [ii]□-[iii]□ [iv]-[v] i-xvi [xvii]□ 1-152.
Leaves printed on 2 sides.
Tallest copy 165 x 113 mm. Horizontal chain lines.

Four pages engraved per plate. Engraving style Cobb.
Title-page plate: see note 1.

Advertised in *London Journal*, 6 June 1724.

Contents: frontispiece [i]; title-page [ii]; dedication [iii]; preface [iv]; verses [v]; subscribers' list i-xiv; advertisement xiv-xv; contents xv-xvi; subscribers to 2nd ed. [xvii]; songs 1-152.

Songs: see **144**.

Notes:
1. Frontispiece and title-page engraved by Cobb on plate approx. 165 x 206 mm.
2. Advertised in the *London Journal* of 6 June as to be published 8 June. A third edition was advertised in *The Monthly Apollo* of July 1724 (**146**) to be published 5 September.
3. Eu: p. [xvii] bound following p. [v]; - pp. 73-74, 79-80.
4. Gm: p. [iii] bound following p. [v].

Copies: Ckc 112.41a; Eu Dm.3.9; Gm M5571; Lbl C.491.a; Lcm IX.F.27; Mp BR 412Nh161; NN Mus.Res.*MP English; NRU-Mus Vault M1507.P739; SA.

145a Bononcini, *Calphurnia*, 31 July 1724

Caption: see plate 153.1.

The Favourite Songs in the Opera call'd ſ Calphurnia ꭍ London Printed for and sold by I: Walsh Servant to his Majesty at ye Harp and Hoboy in Catherine street in the Strand and Ino. & Ioseph Hare at the Viol and Flute in Cornhill near the Royal Exchange

21 leaves. Pp. [i]◻ 1◻\◻2-3◻\-\◻8-9◻\ ◻[10] [11]◻ 1◻\◻2-3◻\-\◻8-9◻\. Leaves printed on 1 side.
Tallest copy 369 x 220 mm. Vertical chain lines.

One page engraved per plate. Engraving style Walsh 4, 5.
Title-page plate 272 x 170 mm. Passe-partout no. 12.

Walsh ii: 199.

Contents: title-page [i]; songs 1-9, [10-11], 1-9.

Songs:

No.	Page	First Line
1	1	Se a lui dà forza il fato (s Cuzzoni, < *Calphurnia*)
2	2-3	Son nato a sospirar (s Senesino, < *Calphurnia*)
3	4-5	Un ombra di pace si mostra al mio cor (s Durastanti, < *Calphurnia*)
4	6-7	Render voglio ogn'uno amante (s Robinson, A., < *Calphurnia*)
5	8-9	Misera che fato (s Cuzzoni, < *Calphurnia*)
6	[10-11]	Se perdo il caro ben (s Cuzzoni, < *Calphurnia*)
7	1	No, oh Dio che mai farò (s Cuzzoni, < *Calphurnia*)
8	2-3	Si ch'io vuo'lasciar l'affetto lusinghier (s Cuzzoni, < *Calphurnia*)
9	4-5	Non so lasciar quel volto (s Senesino, < *Calphurnia*)
10	6-7	Pensa o bella (s Senesino, ʂ *Calphurnia*)
11	8-9	Serba fede e serba amor (s Durastanti, < *Calphurnia*)

Notes:
1. All songs except 10 were reissued with additional pagination as part of *Apollo's Feast*, book 2, 172, in 1726.
2. For later issue with continuous pagination and an English text added to song 10 see 153.
3. 'Calphurnia' engraved directly on passe-partout plate.
4. Ckc: - p. [10-11].
5. CSfst: order of songs 6-11 is 7-9, 11, 6, 10; pp. [i]◻ 1◻\◻2-3◻\-\◻8-9◻\ 1◻\◻2-3◻\-\◻4-5◻\ ◻8-9◻ ◻[10]-[11]◻ ◻6-7◻.
6. D-Hs has copy (M B/2620/1) with title-page for *Monthly Mask of Vocal Music*, July 1724, in place of regular title-page. Pagination = Ckc but the order of the songs is 7-11, 1-5.

Copies: B-Bc 5428; Ckc 85.1.(2.); CSfst de Bellis 817.

Plate 146.1   *Monthly Apollo, 1724*

Plate 146.2   *Monthly Apollo*, 1724

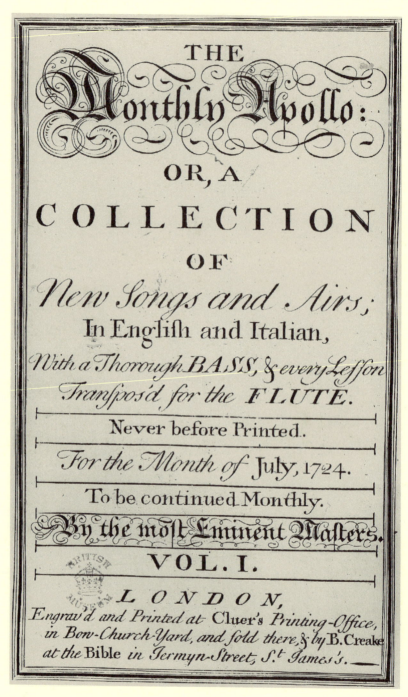

Caption: plates 146.1-146.2. 196 x 122 mm. Lbl: C.125.

The Monthly Apollo: Or, A Collection Of New Songs and Airs; In English and Italian, With a Thorough Bass, & every Lesson Transpos'd for the Flute. Never before printed. ⌠For the Month of July, 1724. [Months of Augt. & Sepr. 1724] ⌡ To be continued Monthly. By the most Eminent Masters. Vol. I. London, Engrav'd and Printed at Cluer's Printing-Office, in Bow-Church-Yard, and sold there, & by B. Creake at the Bible in Jermyn-Street, St. James's.

18 leaves. Pp. ☐[i]-☐[ii] [iii] 1-15 ☐[15A] [15B] 16-26 27☐.
Leaves printed on 2 sides.
Tallest copy 196 x 122 mm. Vertical chain lines.

Pages engraved per plate: see note 1. Engraving style Cobb.
Frontispiece plate 180 x 110 mm.
Title-page plate 180 x 110 mm. Passe-partout no. 13.

Advertised in *Daily Post*, 14 September 1724. Price 1s.

Contents: advertisement [i]; frontispiece [ii]; title-page [iii]; songs 1-15; frontispiece [15A]; titlepage [15B]; songs 16-27.

Songs:

No.	Page	First Line
July		
1	1-5	Deh serbate o giusti Dei (O preserve ye sacred powers)
2	6-9	No non piangete pupille amate (No more dear nymph complain)
3	10-14	Pensa o bella (Fairest of creatures)
4	15	Cloe you're witty Cloe you're pretty
August-September		
5	16-19	Tengo in pugno l'idol mio (While I press my idol goddess)
6	20	Commincia a respirar (My soul begins to rest)
7	21	Dear Cloe is my sole delight
8	22-25	Tu mia speranza (My hopes my pleasure)
9	26-27	Mirtilla I advice the

Notes:
1. July: pp. [i-iii] 1-15. August-September: pp. [15A-B] 16-27. July printed 2 pages to a plate. August-September apparently 1 page to a plate, every numbered page (16-27) signed (E-G4).
2. Dated on basis of advertisement for August-September issue. July issue advertised in *Evening Post*, 4 August 1724, price 1/6.
3. The August-September issue has 'Price 1s.' in MS. at foot of title-page.
4. Competitive edition issued by Walsh as *Monthly Masque of Vocal Music*. See copy at Lbl (K.7.e.4).
5. Frontispiece used later on *Pocket Companion*, v.2, 1725 (160).
6. Change of months engraved directly on plate.

Copy: Lbl C.125.

Plate 147.1   Ariosti, *Aquilio*, 1724

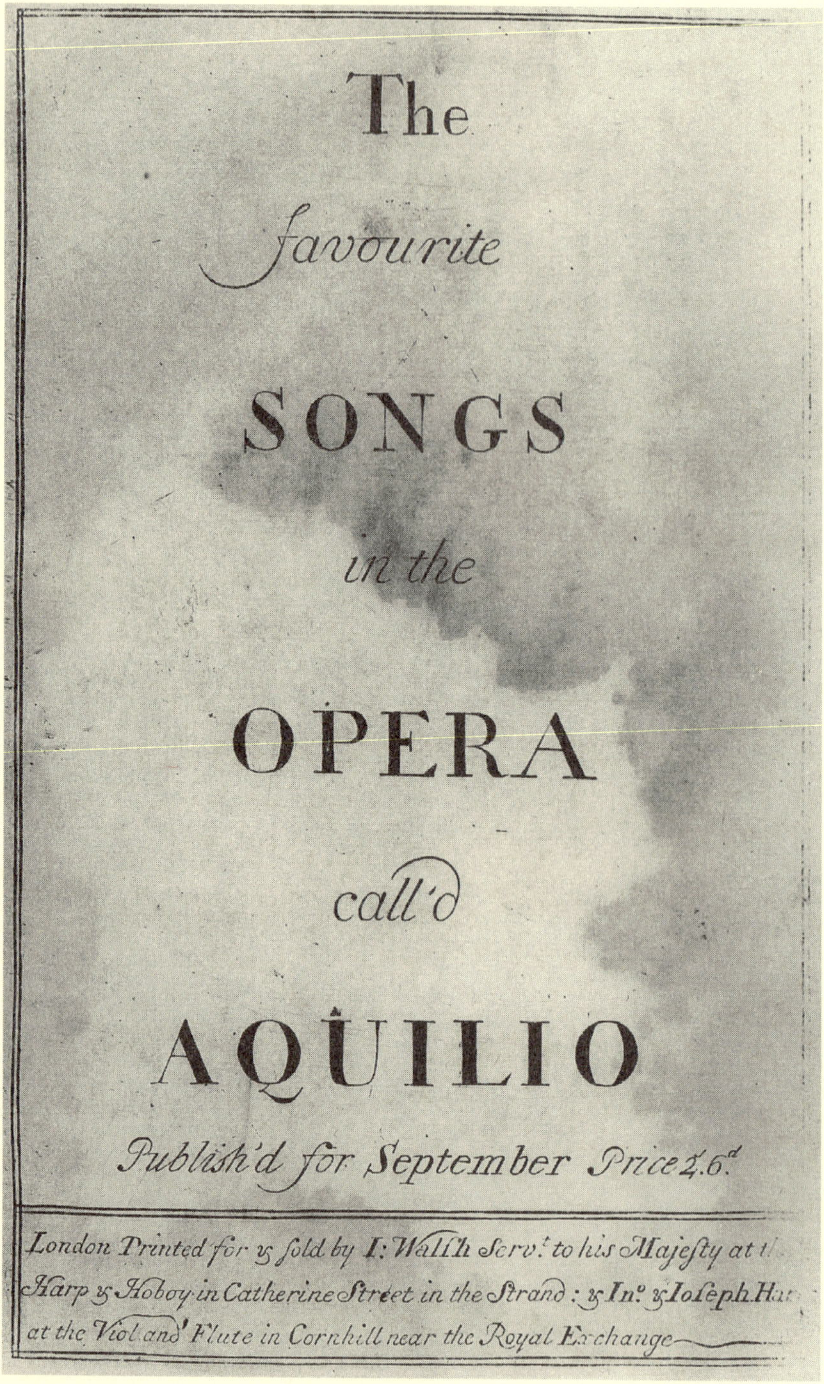

The

favourite

SONGS

in the

OPERA

call'd

AQÛILIO

Publish'd for September Price 2.6.

London Printed for ye sold by I: Walsh Serv.t to his Majesty at the
Harp ye Hoboy in Catherine Street in the Strand: ye In.o ye Ioseph Hare
at the Viol and Flute in Cornhill near the Royal Exchange

Plate 147.2   Ariossti, *Aquilio*, 1724

147 Ariosti, *Aquilio*, 30 September 1724

Caption: plates 147.1-147.2. 336 x 215 mm. Lbl: G.195.(1.).

The favourite Songs in the Opera call'd Aquilio Publish'd for September Price 2s. 6d. London Printed for & sold by I: Walsh Servt. to his Majesty at the Harp & Hoboy in Catherine Street in the Strand: & Ino. & Ioseph Hare at the Viol and Flute in Cornhill near the Royal Exchange

18 leaves. Pp. [i]▯ \▯1-2▯\-\▯7-8▯\ 9▯ \▯10-11▯\-\▯16-17▯\.
Leaves printed on 1 side.
Tallest copy 367 x 230 mm. Vertical chain lines.

One page engraved per plate. Engraving style Walsh 3, 4 (plate 147.2).
Title-page plate 284 x 177 mm. Passe-partout no. 9.

Walsh ii: 42.
Price 2s. 6d.

Contents: title-page [i]; songs 1-17.

Songs:

No.	Page	First Line
1	1-2	Se mirar potessi il core (s Cuzzoni, < *Aquilio*)
2	3-4	Lascio il solco e vengo al trono (s Durastanti, < *Aquilio*)
3	5-6	Bella non disperar (s Robinson, A., < *Aquilio*)
4	7-9	Stelle rigide placatevi (s Cuzzoni, < *Aquilio*)
5	10-13	Tutto in braccio dell'affanno (s Cuzzoni, < *Aquilio*)
6	14-17	Rinasce amor allor che amando spera (s Senesino, < *Aquilio*)

Notes:
1. All songs were reissued with additional pagination as part of *Apollo's Feast*, book 2, 172, in 1726.
2. 'Aquilio Publish'd for September Price 2s. 6d.' engraved directly on passe-partout plate.
3. Ckc: p. 12 misbound facing p. 15.
4. CSfst: p. 16 reversed.
5. DLC: - p. [i].
6. Lbl: '6d.' erased from title-page.
7. Report of copy at Lam is false.

Copies: CDp M.C.3.29(11); Ckc 85.3.(1.); CLU-C *fM1508.A65; CSfst de Bellis 836; D-Hs M B/2620/8; DLC M1500.A76A6; F-Pc Rés. V.S.1322; Lbl G.195.(1.).

Plate 148.1   Ariosti, *Aquilio*, 1724

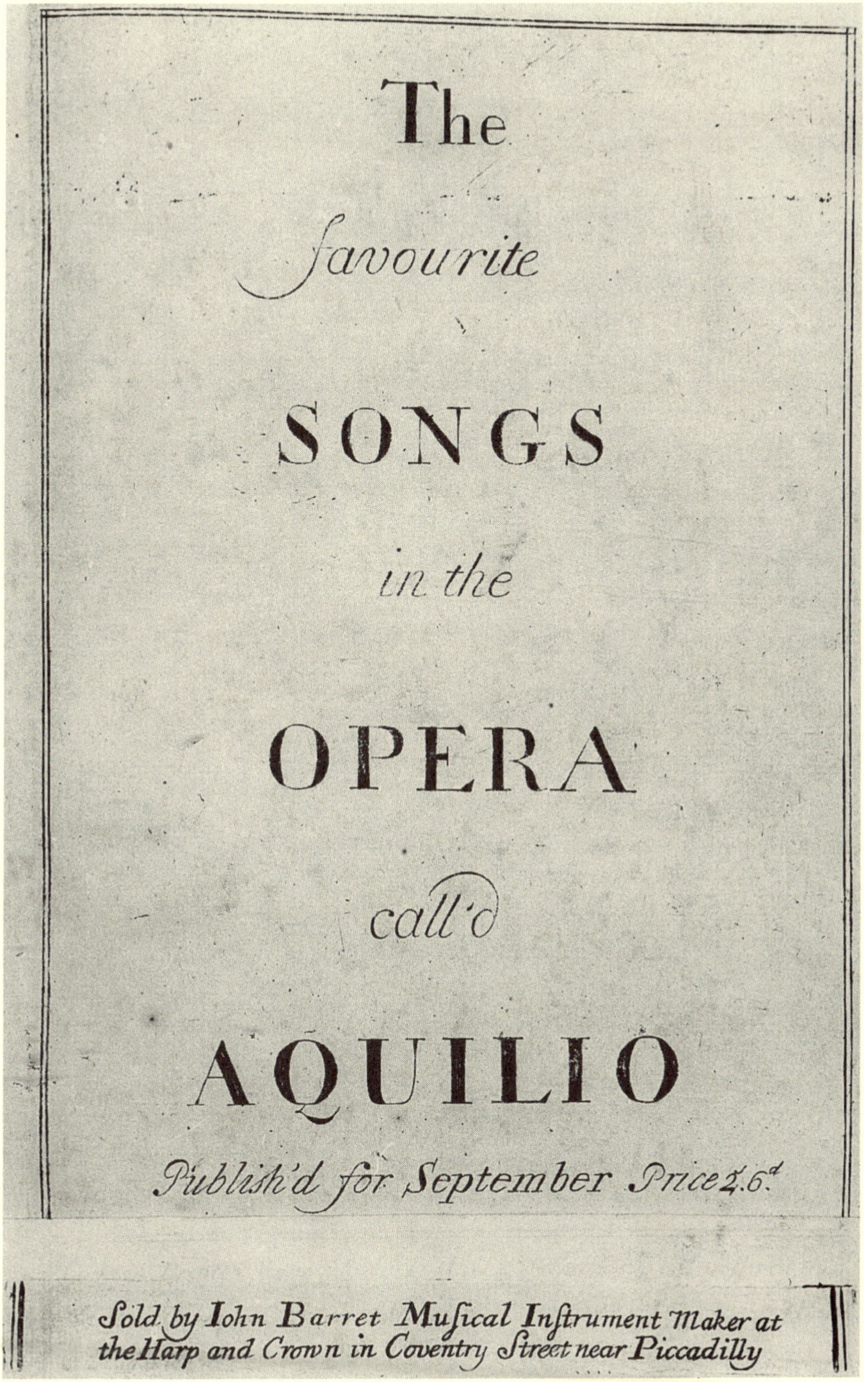

The

favourite

SONGS

in the

OPERA

call'd

AQUILIO

Publish'd for September Price 2.6ᵈ

Sold by Iohn Barret Musical Instrument Maker at the Harp and Crown in Coventry Street near Piccadilly

Caption: plate 148.1. 349 x 220 mm. A-Wn: M.S.10230.

The favourite Songs in the Opera call'd Aquilio Publish'd for September Price 2s. 6d. [engraved label over Walsh & Hares imprint] Sold by Iohn Barret Musical Instrument Maker at the Harp and Crown in Coventry Street near Piccadilly

18 leaves. Pp. [i]▯ \▯1-2▯\-\▯7-8▯\ 9▯ \▯10-11▯\-\▯16-17▯\.
Leaves printed on 1 side.
Tallest copy 349 x 220 mm. Vertical chain lines.

One page engraved per plate. Engraving style Walsh 3, 4.
Title-page plate ? x 177 mm. Passe-partout no. 9. (See note 2.)

Price 2s. 6d.

Contents: title-page [i]; songs 1-17.

Songs: see **147**.

Notes:
1. 'Aquilio Publish'd for September Price 2s. 6d.' engraved directly on passe-partout plate.
2. Label obscures lower edge of plate.

Copy: A-Wn M.S.10230.

Plate 149.1 Ariosti, *Aquilio*, 1724

The

favourite

SONGS

in the

OPERA

call'd

AQUILIO

Publish'd for September Price 2.6.ᵈ

Sold by B. Cooke *Musicall Instrument Maker.*
at the Golden Harp in new Street Covent Garden London.

399

Caption: plate 149.1. 345 x 215 mm. Lgc: G.Mus.62.(3.).

The favourite Songs in the Opera call'd Aquilio Publish'd for September Price 2s. 6d. [engraved label over Walsh and Hares imprint] [London Prin]ted & Sold by B. Cooke Musicall Instrument Maker, [a]tt the Golden Harp in new Street Covent Garden London.

14 leaves. Pp. [i]❩\❩1 2❩ 7❩-9❩ \❩10-11❩\-\❩16-17❩\.
Leaves printed on 1 side.
Tallest copy 345 x 215 mm. Vertical chain lines.

One page engraved per plate. Engraving style Walsh 3, 4.
Title-page plate ? x 177 mm. Passe-partout no. 9. (See note 3.)

Price 2s. 6d.

Contents: title-page [i]; songs 1-2, 7-17.

Songs:

No.	Page	First Line
1	1-2	Se mirar potessi il core (s Cuzzoni, < *Aquilio*)
2	7-9	Stelle rigide placatevi (s Cuzzoni, < *Aquilio*)
3	10-13	Tutto in braccio dell'affanno (s Cuzzoni, < *Aquilio*)
4	14-17	Rinasce amor allor che amando spera (s Senesino, < *Aquilio*)

Notes:
1. 'Aquilio Publish'd for September Price 2s. 6d.' engraved directly on passe-partout plate.
2. Presumably incomplete; wanting pp. 3-6.
3. Label obscures lower edge of plate.

Copy: Lgc G.Mus.62.(3.).

Plate 150.1   Ariosti, *Artaxerxes*, 1724

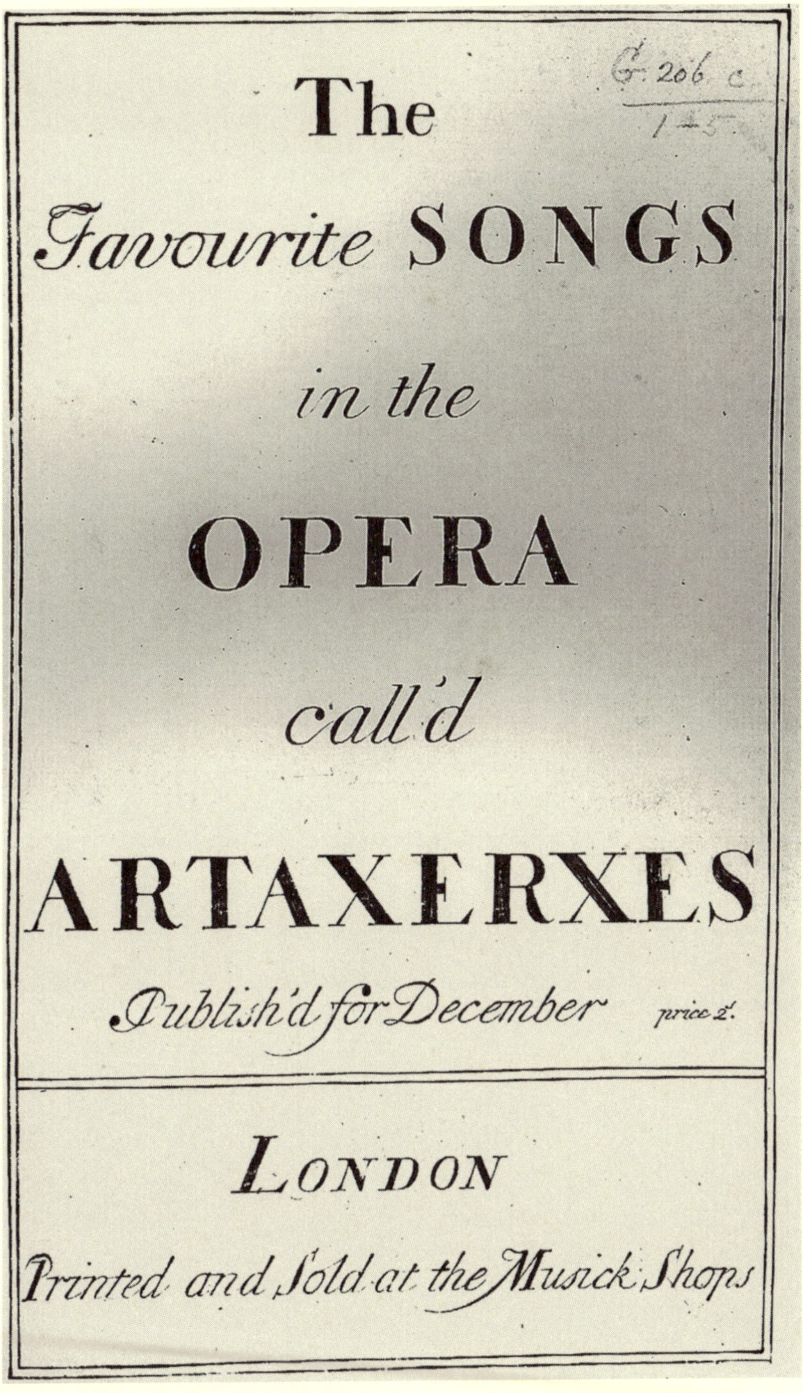

The

Favourite SONGS

G. 206 c
145

in the

OPERA

call'd

ARTAXERXES

Publish'd for December   *price 2ˢ.*

LONDON

Printed and Sold at the Musick Shops

Caption: plate 150.1. 320 x 210 mm. Lbl: G.206.c.(1.).

The Favourite Songs in the Opera call'd Artaxerxes Publish'd for December
price 2s. London Printed and Sold at the Musick Shops

17 leaves. Pp. [i]□\□1 2□-3□\□4 5□\□6 7□-8□\□9 10□-11□\□12 13□\□14 15□-16□.
Leaves printed on 1 side.
Tallest copy 361 x 233 mm. Vertical chain lines.

One page engraved per plate. Engraving style Musick Shops.
Title-page plate 273 x 157 mm.

Walsh ii: 47.
Price 2s.

Contents: title-page [i]; songs 1-16.

Songs:

No.	Page	First Line
1	1-3	Son come navicella in mar turbato (s Cuzzoni, < *Artaxerxes*)
2	4-5	Deh m'ascolto ferma oh dio (s Cuzzoni, < *Artaxerxes*)
3	6-8	Un figlio crudele ti chiama al rigore (s Dotti, < *Artaxerxes*)
4	9-11	Nel suo duol così si lagra sospirando (s Cuzzoni, < *Artaxerxes*)
5	12-13	Nel mirarui se spietati vaghirai (s Senesino, < *Artaxerxes*)
6	14-15	Sinque che piaque amai (s Borosini, < *Artaxerxes*)
7	16	T'amo tanto o mio tesoro (s Senesino, < *Artaxerxes*)

Notes:
1. Probably issued by Walsh as all songs except 6 were reissued with additional pagination as
part of *Apollo's Feast*, book 2, 172, in 1726.
2. First performed December 1, 1724.
3. Lbl: pp. 9, 14 reversed.
4. Copy reported at B-Bc is Hasse's version.

Copies: CaOLUMZ.707; CLU-C*fM1621.A71; D-HsMB/2620/9; F-PcRés.V.S.1288; Lam —;
Lbl G.206.c.(1.).

Plate 151.1   Ariosti, *Artaxerxes*, 1724

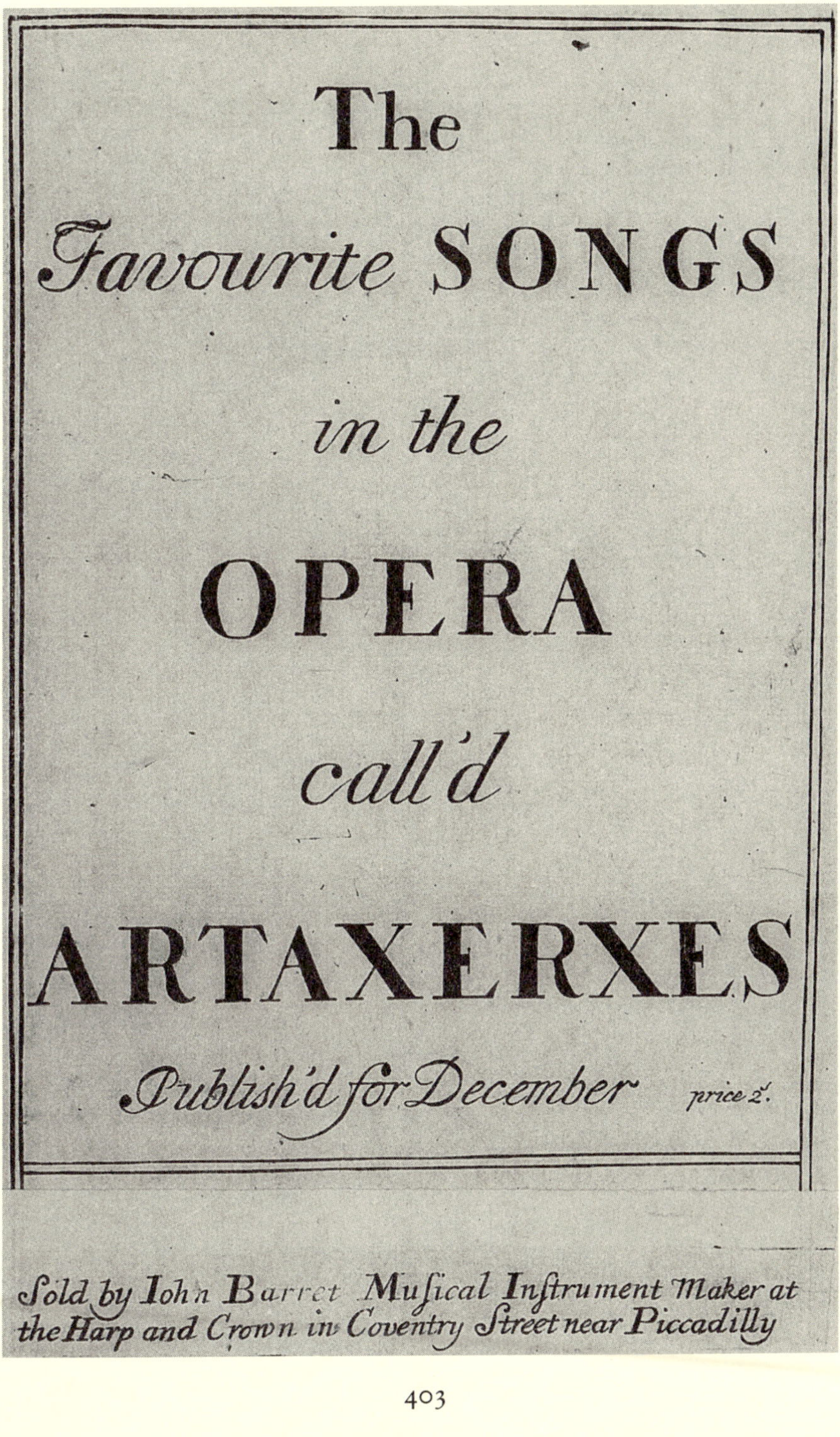

The

Favourite SONGS

in the

OPERA

call'd

ARTAXERXES

Publish'd for December   *price 2.*

*Sold by John Barret Musical Instrument Maker at
the Harp and Crown in Coventry Street near Piccadilly*

151 Ariosti, *Artaxerxes*, 31 December 1724

Caption: plate 151.1. 349 x 222 mm. A-Wn: M.S.10230.

The Favourite Songs in the Opera call'd Artaxerxes Publish'd for December price 2s. [engraved label over Musick Shops imprint] Sold by Iohn Barret Musical Instrument Maker at the Harp and Crown in Coventry Street near Piccadilly

16 leaves. Pp. [i]□\□1 2□-3□\□4 5□\□6 7□-8□\□9 10□-11□\□12 13□\□14 15□. Leaves printed on 1 side.
Tallest copy 349 x 222 mm. Vertical chain lines.

One page engraved per plate. Engraving style Musick Shops.
Title-page plate ? x 157 mm. (See note 2.)

Price 2s.

Contents: title-page [i]; songs 1-15.

Songs:

No.	Page	First Line
1	1-3	Son come navicella in mar turbato (s Cuzzoni, < *Artaxerxes*)
2	4-5	Deh m'ascolto ferma oh dio (s Cuzzoni, < *Artaxerxes*)
3	6-8	Un figlio crudele ti chiama al rigore (s Dotti, < *Artaxerxes*)
4	9-11	Nel suo duol così si lagra sospirando (s Cuzzoni, < *Artaxerxes*)
5	12-13	Nel mirarui se spietati vaghirai (s Senesino, < *Artaxerxes*)
6	14-15	Sinque che piaque amai (s Borosini, < *Artaxerxes*)

Notes:
1. Presumably incomplete, wanting p. 16.
2. Label obscures lower edge of plate.

Copy: A-Wn M.S.10230.

Plate 152.1   Bononcini, *Calphurnia*, 1724

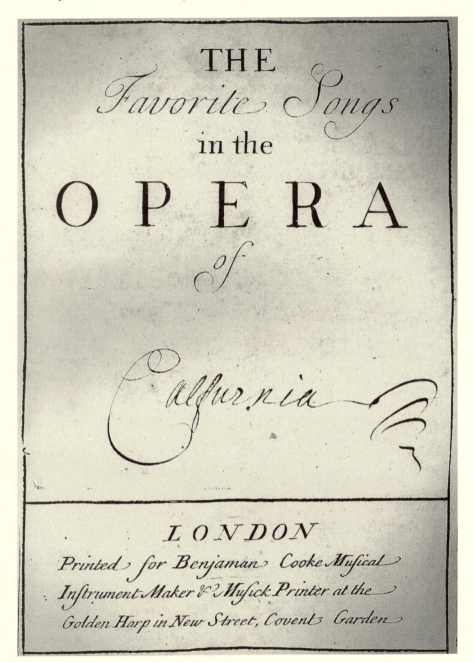

THE
Favorite Songs
in the
OPERA
of
Calfurnia

LONDON
Printed for Benjaman Cooke Musical
Instrument Maker & Musick Printer at the
Golden Harp in New Street, Covent Garden

152 Bononcini, *Calphurnia*, 31 December 1724

Caption: plate 152.1. 320 x 209 mm. Lbl: G.499.a.

The Favorite Songs in the Opera of ʃ [in MS., Calfurnia] ʃ London Printed for Benjamin Cooke Musical Instrument Maker & Musick Printer at the Golden Harp in New Street, Covent Garden

15 leaves. Pp. [1]▯ 2▯ \▯3-4▯\ -\▯11-12▯\ 1▯\▯2-3▯.
Leaves printed on 1 side.
Tallest copy 350 x 222 mm. Vertical chain lines.

One page engraved per plate. Engraving style Bates.
Title-page plate 265 x 189 mm. Passe-partout no. 14.

Contents: title-page [1]; songs 2-12; flute parts 1-3.

Songs:

No.	Page	First Line
1	2	No, oh Dio che mai farò (s Cuzzoni, < *Calphurnia*)
2	3-4	Si ch'io vuo'lasciar l'affetto lusinghier (s Cuzzoni, < *Calphurnia*)
3	5-6	Non so lasciar quel volto (s Senesino, < *Calphurnia*)
4	7-8	Pensa o bella (s Senesino, < *Calphurnia*)
5	9-10	Serba fede e serba amor (s Durastanti, < *Calphurnia*)
6	11-12	Misera che fato (s Cuzzoni, < *Calphurnia*)

Notes:
1. First performed May 1724.
2. Er: - p. [1], 2, 1-3 (final sequence).
3. Lgc: p. 9 reversed.

Copies: DLC M1506.B66C32 Case; Er E162; Lbl G.499.a; Lgc G.Mus.62.(2).

Plate 153.1   Bononcini, *Calphurnia*, 1724

The

Favourite

SONGS

in the

OPERA

call'd

CALPHURNIA

London Printed for and sold by I. Walsh Servant to his Majesty, at ÿ
Harp and Hoboy in Catherine street in the Strand and Inº & Ioseph Hare
at the Viol and Flute in Cornhill near the Royal Exchange

Plate 153.2   Bononcini, *Calphurnia*, 1724

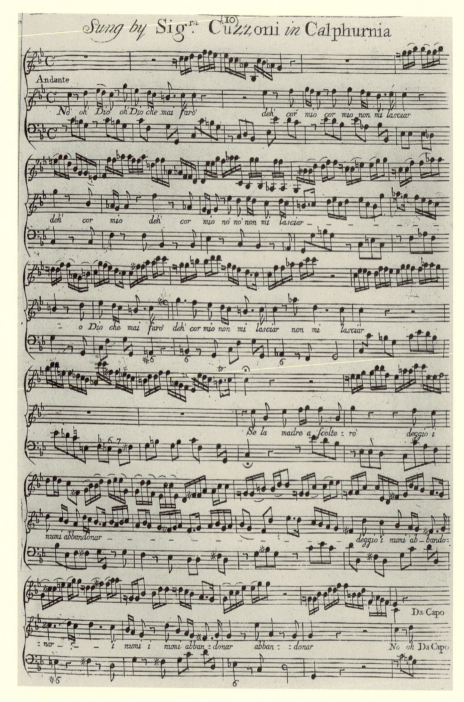

Caption: plates 153.1-153.2. 350 x 218 mm. Lbl: H.230.f.(1.).

The Favourite Songs in the Opera call'd ⌠ Calphurnia ⌡ London Printed for and sold by I: Walsh Servant to his Majesty at ye Harp and Hoboy in Catherine street in the Strand and Ino. & Ioseph Hare at the Viol and Flute in Cornhill near the Royal Exchange

21 leaves. Pp. [i]▯ 1▯ \▯2-3▯\-\▯8-9▯\ 10▯ \▯11-12▯\-\▯19-20▯\.
Leaves printed on 1 side.
Tallest copy 364 x 225 mm. Vertical chain lines.

One page engraved per plate. Engraving style Walsh 4, 5 (plate 153.2).
Title-page plate 270 x 166 mm. Passe-partout no. 12.

Walsh ii: 199.

Contents: title-page [i]; songs 1-20.

Songs:

No.	Page	First Line
1	1	Se a lui dà forza il fato (s Cuzzoni, < *Calphurnia*)
2	2-3	Son nato a sospirar (s Senesino, < *Calphurnia*)
3	4-5	Un ombra di pace si mostra al mio cor (s Durastanti, < *Calphurnia*)
4	6-7	Render voglio ogn'uno amante (s Robinson, A., < *Calphurnia*)
5	8-9	Misera che fato (s Cuzzoni, < *Calphurnia*)
6	10	No, oh Dio che mai farò (s Cuzzoni, < *Calphurnia*)
7	11-12	Si ch'io vuo'lasciar l'affetto lusinghier (s Cuzzoni, < *Calphurnia*)
8	13-14	Non so lasciar quel volto (s Senesino, < *Calphurnia*)
9	15-16	Serba fede e serba amor (s Durastanti, < *Calphurnia*)
10	17-18	Se perdo il caro ben (s Cuzzoni, < *Calphurnia*)
11	19-20	Pensa o bella (Fairest of creatures) (s Senesino, < *Calphurnia*)

Notes:
1. All songs except 11 were reissued with additional pagination as part of *Apollo's Feast*, book 2, 172, in 1726.
2. Separate impression from 145a indicated by repagination and addition of English to song 11.
3. 'Calphurnia' engraved directly on passe-partout plate.
4. CDp (M.C.3.29(14)): - p. 10.
5. Lam (1 copy): price '2s. 0' in MS. on title-page.

Copies: CDp M.C.3.21(2); CDp M.C.3.29(14); CSt SpC MLM113; CU-MUSI M1505.B64C25 1724 Case B; F-Pc D.1528(3); I-Rsc; I-Vc; Lam —; Lam —; Lbl H.230.f.(1.); Lcm XXXII.B.8.(4.).

154, 155, and 156 deleted (see 135a, 135b, and 135c).

Plate 157.1   Purcell, H, *Orpheus Brittanicus*, 1724

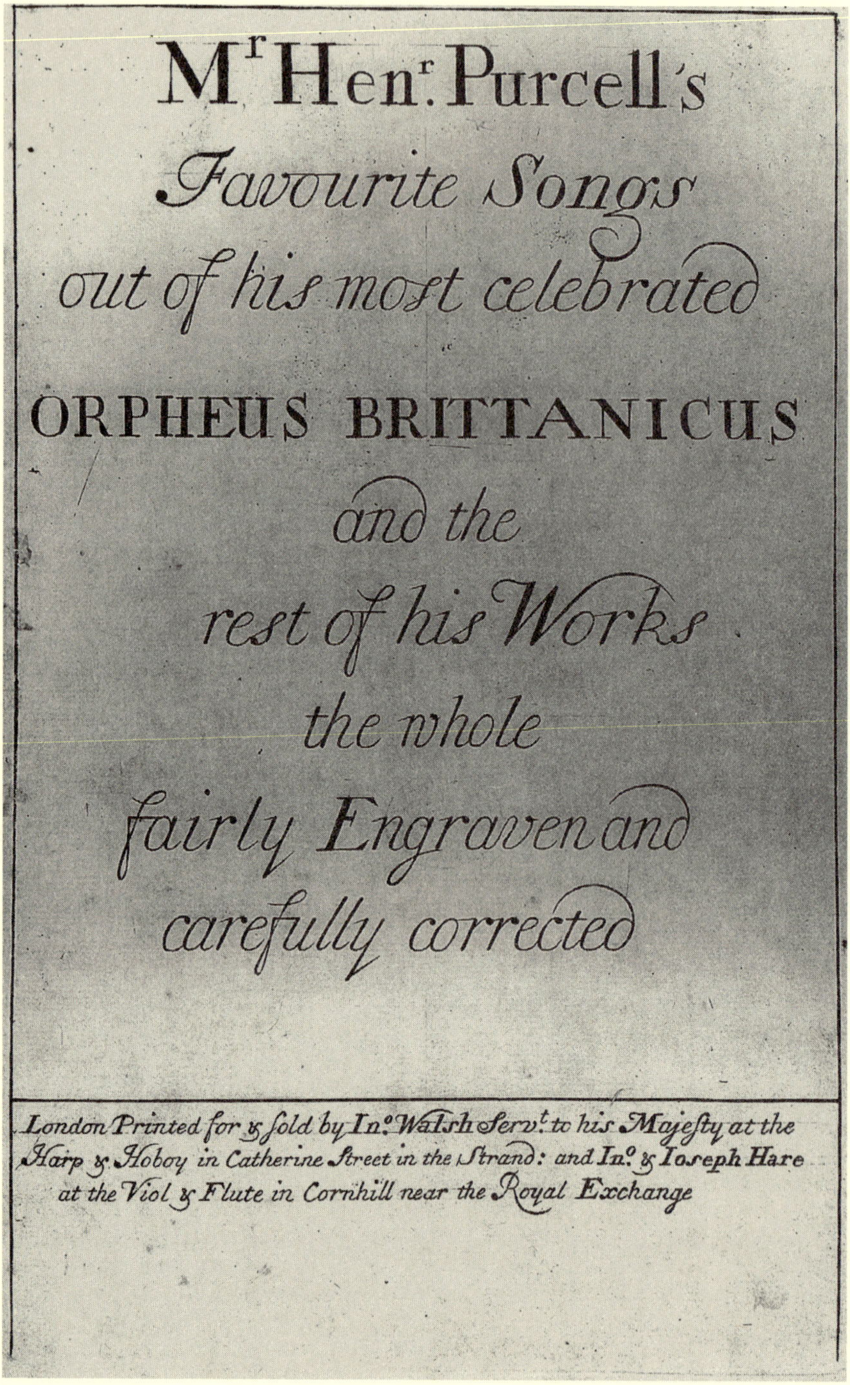

Mr Hen^r. Purcell's

Favourite Songs

out of his most celebrated

ORPHEUS BRITTANICUS

and the

rest of his Works

the whole

fairly Engraven and

carefully corrected

London Printed for & sold by In.° Walsh Serv.t to his Majesty at the
Harp & Hoboy in Catherine Street in the Strand: and In.° & Joseph Hare
at the Viol & Flute in Cornhill near the Royal Exchange

157 Purcell, H, *Orpheus Brittanicus*, 31 December 1724

Caption: plate 157.1. 335 x 214 mm. Lbl: G.102.a.(1.).

Mr. Henr. Purcell's Favourite Songs out of his most celebrated Orpheus Brittanicus and the rest of his Works the whole fairly Engraven and carefully corrected London Printed for & sold by Ino. Walsh Servt. to his Majesty at the Harp & Hoboy in Catherine Street in the Strand: and Ino. & Ioseph Hare at the Viol & Flute in Cornhill near the Royal Exchange

54 leaves. Pp. [i]□ [1]□ 2□-5□ 6-11 12□-13□ \□14-15□\ -\□20-21□\ 22□-23□\□24 25□-27□□28 29□-32□\□33-34□\ -\□41-42□\ 43-46 □47 48□\□49 50□ 51-52 53□ 54-55 56□ 57-58 59□ 60-61 62□.
Leaves printed on 1 and 2 sides (see note 1).
Tallest copy 351 x 215 mm. Mixed chain lines.

One page engraved per plate. Engraving style Walsh and Cross.
Title-page plate 273 x 172 mm.
Contents plate 311 x 117 mm.

Walsh ii: 1248.

Contents: title-page [i]; contents and advertisement [1]; songs 2-62.

Songs:

No.	Page	First Line
1	2	Ah! how sweet it is to love (m Purcell, H., s Ayliff, < *Tyrannic Love, or the Royal Martyr*, D&M 59)
2	3	Celia has a thousand charms (m Purcell, H., D&M 511)
3	4	Celebrate this festival (m Purcell, H., D&M 506)
4	5	Dear pretty youth (m Purcell, H., < *Tempest*, D&M 821)
5	6-9	From rosie bow'rs where sleeps the god of love (m Purcell, H., D&M 1091)
6	10-12	Fly swift ye hours (m Purcell, H., D&M 1029)
7	13	Forth from my dark and dismall cell (D&M 1064)
8	14-15	From silent shad's and the elizium groves (m Purcell, H., D&M 1093)
9	16-17	Genius of England, from thy pleasant bow'r (m Purcell, H., < *Don Quixote*, D&M 1111)
10	18-19	I see she flyes me (m Purcell, H., s Ayliff, < *Aureng-Zebe*, D&M 1596)
11	20-21	If musick be the food of love (m Purcell, H., D&M 1695)
12	22	I'll sail upon the Dog-star (m Purcell, H., < *Fool's Preferment*, D&M 1633)
13	23	I look'd and saw within the book of fate (m Purcell, H., D&M 1550)
14	24-25	Let the dreadfull engines of eternall will (m Purcell, H., D&M 1998)
15	26	Oh lead me to some peacefull gloom (m Purcell, H., < *Bonduca*, D&M 2486)
16	27	Sound fame, thy brazen trumpet sound (m Purcell, H., < *Dioclesian*, D&M 3040)
17	28-29	You twice ten hundred deities (m Purcell, H., D&M 4111)
18	30	And in each track of glory (m Purcell, H., D&M 168)
19	31	Come let us agree (m Purcell, H., < *Timon of Athens*, D&M 663)
20	32	Come let us leave the town (m Purcell, H., D&M 673)
21	33-34	Dulcibella when e're I sue for a kiss (m Purcell, H., D&M 899)
22	35-36	Fair Cloe my breast so alarms (m Purcell, H., D&M 933)
23	37-38	Let Hector Achilles, and each brave commander (m Purcell, H., D&M 1971)
24	39-40	Lost is my quiet for ever (m Purcell, H., D&M 2086)

411

25	41-42	Sound a parly ye fair and surrender (m Purcell, H., < *King Arthur*, D&M 3039)
26	43-46	Sing all ye muses (m Purcell, H., v D'urfey, D&M 2973)
27	47-48	To arms your ensigns strait display (m Purcell, H., < *Bonduca*, D&M 3411)
28	48	Britains strike home (< *Bonduca*, D&M 437)
29	49-50	When Myra sings (m Purcell, H., D&M 3774)
30	51-53	Behold the man that with gigantick might (m Purcell, H., s Leveridge, Lindsey, D&M 345)
31	54-56	Now the maids and the men are making their hay (m Purcell, H., s Reading, J., Pate, < *Fairy Queen*, D&M 2419)
32	57-59	Since times are so bad (m Purcell, H., < *Don Quixote*, D&M 2968)
33	60-62	Tell me why my charming fair (m Purcell, H., < *Prophetess*, D&M 3175)

Notes:
1. Pp. 6-7, 8-9, 10-11, 43-44, 45-46, 51-52, 54-55, 57-58, 60-61 printed on single leaves.
2. BWbw: - pp. 54-56.
3. Mp: - pp. [1], 60-62.
4. NN: - pp. 57-59.
5. Copies reported at Lam and Ooc are of 'second edition with additions'. As the Lam copy has the publisher's numbering on the title-page I have dated the Ooc copy *c.* 1729 and the Lam copy post-1730. DCU also has a copy of this second edition; it lacks the publisher's number (M1497.P98 F3 1700).

Copies: BWbw —; DFo M1491.P9708 Cage; Lbl G.102.a.(1.); Mp —; NN Drexel 4285.

Plate 158.1 Ariosti, *Vespasian*, 1724

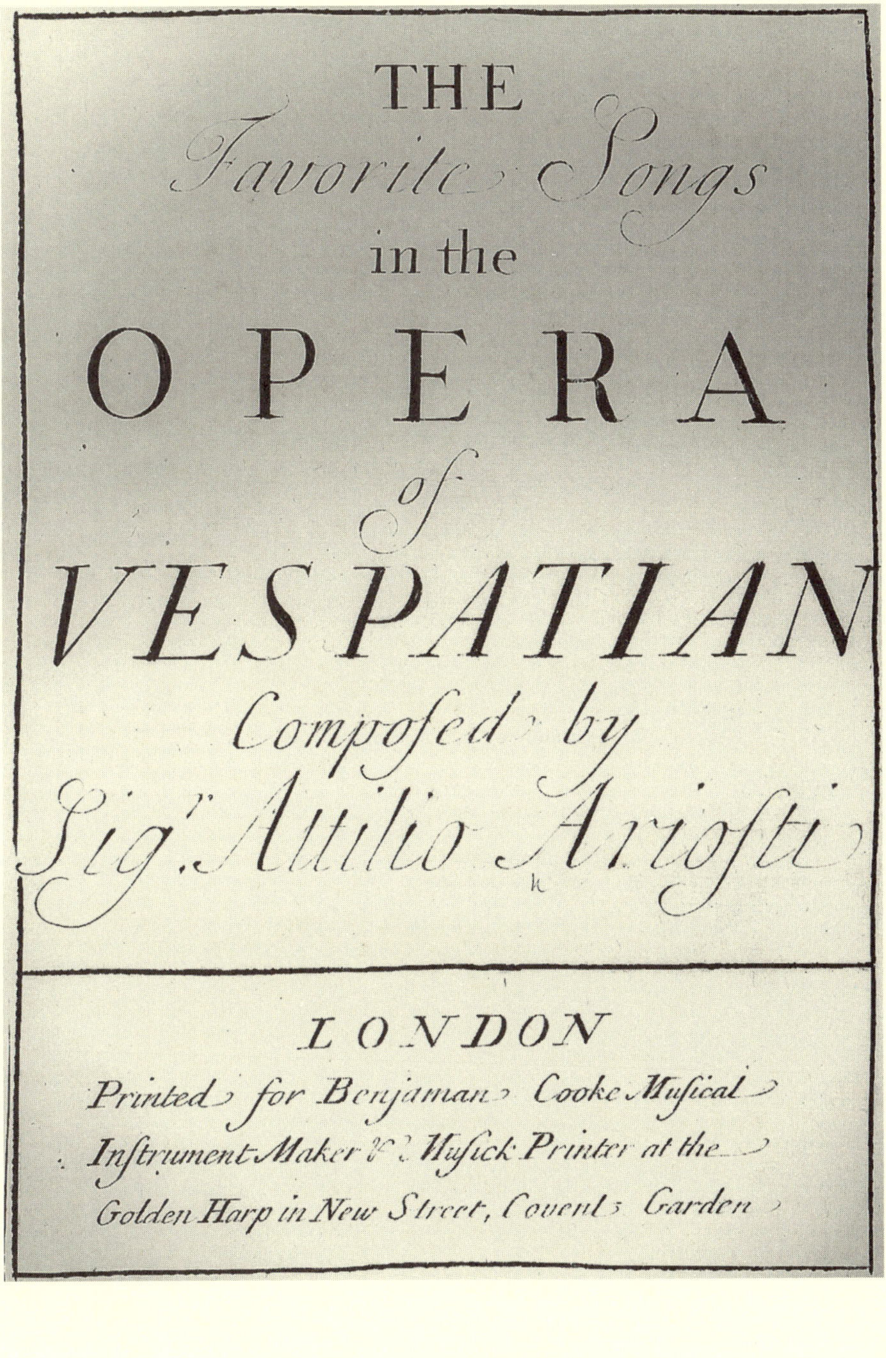

THE
Favorite Songs
in the
OPERA
of
VESPATIAN
Composed by
Sigᵣ Attilio Ariosti

LONDON
Printed for Benjaman Cooke Musical
Instrument Maker &ᶜ Musick Printer at the
Golden Harp in New Street, Covent Garden

413

Caption: plate 158.1. 344 x 218 mm. Lbl: H.319.b.

The Favorite Songs in the Opera of ʃ Vespatian Composed by Sigr. Attilio Ariosti ʃ London Printed for Benjamin Cooke Musical Instrument Maker & Musick Printer at the Golden Harp in New Street, Covent Garden

17 leaves. Pp. [i]□\□1 2□\□3 4□\□5 6-7 □8 9-10 11□\□12 13-14 □15 16□-17□\□18 19□. Leaves printed on 1 and 2 sides (see note 1).
Tallest copy 345 x 219 mm. Vertical chain lines.

One page engraved per plate. Engraving style Bates.
Title-page plate 266 x 188 mm. Passe-partout no. 14.

Contents: title-page [i]; songs 1-19.

Songs:

No.	Page	First Line
1	1-2	Con forza ascosa ne raggi sui (s Senesino, < *Vespasian*)
2	3-4	Aure voi che m'ascoltate (s Cuzzoni, < *Vespasian*)
3	5-7	Un raggio placido di bella speme (s Durastanti, < *Vespasian*)
4	8-11	Pur che mi sciolga il piede (s Robinson, A., < *Vespasian*)
5	12-14	La tortorella fida e costante (s Cuzzoni, < *Vespasian*)
6	15-17	Combattuta nauicella (s Cuzzoni, < *Vespasian*)
7	18	Lasso ch'io t'ho'perduta (s Senesino, < *Vespasian*)
8	19	Non è Cupido (s Robinson, A., < *Vespasian*)

Notes:
1. Pp. 6-7, 9-10, 13-14 printed on single leaves.
2. P. 17 signed 'P. Bates, Sculp.'
3. Title-page used as passe-partout on *Calphurnia*, 152. 'Vespatian Composed by Sigr. Attilio Ariosti' engraved directly on passe-partout plate.

Copies: CLU-C *fM1624.7.A71; Lbl H.319.b; Lgc G.Mus.62(5).

Plate 159.1 *Opera Miscellany*, 1725

Plate 159.2 *Opera Miscellany*, 1725

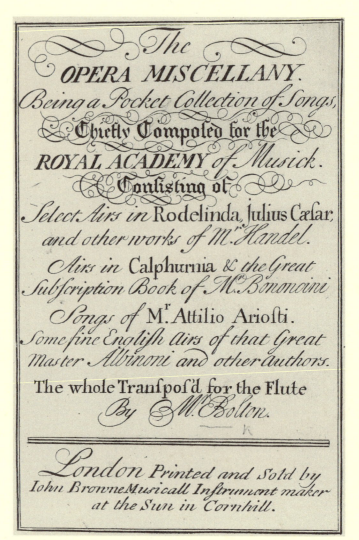

The
OPERA MISCELLANY.
Being a Pocket Collection of Songs,
Chiefly Composed for the
ROYAL ACADEMY of Musick.
Consisting of
Select Airs in Rodelinda, Julius Cæsar,
and other works of M.r Handel.
Airs in Calphurnia & the Great
Subscription Book of M.r Bononcini
Songs of M.r Attilio Ariosti.
Some fine English Airs of that Great
Master Albinoni and other Authors.
The whole Transpos'd for the Flute
By M.r Bolton.

London Printed and Sold by
Iohn Browne Musicall Instrument maker
at the Sun in Cornhill.

Caption: plates 159.1-159.2. 160 x 105 mm. Lbl: A.416.

The Opera Miscellany. Being a Pocket Collection of Songs, Chiefly Composed for the Royal Academy of Musick. Consisting of Select Airs in Rodelinda, Julius Cæsar, and other works of Mr. Handel. Airs in Calphurnia & the Great Subscription Book of Mr. Bononcini Songs of Mr. Attilio Ariosti. Some fine English Airs of that Great Master Albinoni and other Authors. The whole Transpos'd for the Flute By Mr. Bolton. London Printed and Sold by Iohn Browne Musicall Instrument maker at the Sun in Cornhill.

59 leaves. Pp. □[i] [ii]□ [iii-iv] 1-83 [84] [o] 1-27.
Leaves printed on 2 sides.
Tallest copy 160 x 105 mm. Horizontal chain lines.

Four pages engraved per plate. Engraving style Cross.
Title-page plate 140 x 93 mm.

Advertised in *Daily Post*, 27 April 1725.

Contents: frontispiece [i]; title-page [ii]; subscription list [iii-iv]; overture 1-8; songs 9-83; index [84]; section title [o]; flute parts 1-27.

Songs:

No.	Page	First Line
1	9	S'ho lasso il piè (s Dotti, Cuzzoni, < *Darius*)
2	10-11	Soffro in pace (m Bononcini)
3	12-13	È forza l'amore (m Eminent Master)
4	14-15	Lungi da te ben mio (m Bononcini)
5	16	Gently touch the warb'ling lyre (m Geminiani)
6	17	T'amo tanto o mio tesoro (s Senesino, < *Artaxerxes*)
7	18-19	I'm tormented when I see (m Albinoni)
8	20-21	Appear all ye gods on ye plain (m Humphries)
9	22-23	Ah what forebodes this prodigie (m Albinoni)
10	24-25	No you charm me with your rage (s Borosini, < *Tamerlane*)
11	26-27	Virgins if your peace you prize (m Albinoni)
12	28-30	No more complain (s Cuzzoni, < *Tamerlane*)
13	31	Of my own heart I shou'd be jealous (m Albinoni)
14	32-33	Ah! how happy were ye days (m Albinoni)
15	34-35	Non credo instabile chi mi piango (s Durastanti, < *Flavius*)
16	36-37	Ritorna o caro dolce mio tesoro (s Cuzzoni, < *Rodelinda*)
17	38-39	Figurati estinti (< *Arsaces*)
18	40	Celia my dearest no longer depress me (< *Vespasian*)
19	41	Play of love is now begun, The (s Leveridge)
20	42-43	Dal mio bando si veda (< *Julius Caesar*)
21	44-45	Di quel bel che m'innamora (s Berenstadt, < *Flavius*)
22	46-47	Serba fede e serba amor (s Durastanti, < *Calphurnia*)
23	48-50	Mio caro bene (s Cuzzoni, < *Rodelinda*)
24	51	When Cloe we ply (s Reading, Mrs)
25	52-53	Falsa imagine m'ingannasti (s Cuzzoni, < *Otho*)
26	54-55	Dove sei amato bene (s Senesino, < *Rodelinda*)

27	56	As buxom Susan milk'd ye brindl'd cow
28	57	Ye little love that hourly wait
29	58-59	Nel mirarvi sì spietati (m Ariosti)
30	60-61	Navicella che lungi dal porto (m Bononcini)
31	62-63	Where shall I find ye lovely fair (m Handel)
32	64-65	Se ti piace di farmi morire (m Bononcini)
34	68-69	Misera che fato (s Cuzzoni, < *Calphurnia*)
35	70-71	Teco s'annodi l'alma mio caro (s Cuzzoni, < *Coriolano*)
36	72-73	No, oh dio che mai farò (s Cuzzoni, < *Calphurnia*)
37	74-75	Wine's a mistress gay & easy (s Leveridge, < *Love and Wine*)
38	76-79	Scacciata dal suo nido (s Senesino, < *Rodelinda*)
39	80	Wanton Cloe young & charming
40	81	Thus mighty eastern kings
41	82-83	I come my fairest treasure (s Senesino, < *Julius Caesar*)

Notes:
1. Section title, p. [0]: 'Here follow the aires transposed for the flute. Ingraved by T: Cross.' 'T. Cross Ingraver of this book' was one of the subscribers.
2. Recto of first two and last two leaves of each octavo gathering signed; e.g., C, C2, —, —, —, —, C2, C.
3. The 'Great Subscription Book of Mr. Bononcini' was his *Cantate e Duetti* published in December 1721 or January 1722.

Copies: Coke —; DLC M1505.A2B7; F-Pc Y.605; Lbl A.416.

Plate 160.1   *Pocket Companion*, v.2, 1725

Plate 160.2   *Pocket Companion*, v.2, 1725

C.491.

A

Pocket Companion

FOR

Gentlemen and Ladies.

BEING

A Collection of Favourite Songs,

out of the most Celebrated Opera's

Compos'd by

Mr Handel, Bononcini, Attilio, &c.

In English and Italian

To which is Added

Several Choice Songs of Mr Handel's,

never before Printed

VOL. II.

Carefully Corrected and Figur'd for the Harpsicord

The whole Transpos'd for the FLUTE in the

most proper KEYS.

LONDON,

Engrav'd & Printed at Cluer's Printing Office in Boro Church Yard

and Sold there, and by B. Creake at the Bible in Jermyn Street

St James's: Where the first Volume may be had

Note, They have just publish'd the 2d Pack of Musical playing Cards.

420

Caption: plates 160.1-160.2. 194 x 124 mm. Lbl: C.491.

A Pocket Companion For Gentlemen and Ladies. Being A Collection of Favourite Songs, out of the most Celebrated Opera's Compos'd by Mr. Handel, Bononcini, Attilio, &c. In English and Italian To which is Added Several Choice Songs of Mr. Handel's, never before Printed Vol. II. Carefully Corrected and Figur'd for the Harpsicord The whole Transpos'd for the Flute in the most proper Keys. London, Engrav'd & Printed at Cluer's Printing Office in Bow Church Yard and Sold there, and by B. Creake at the Bible in Jermyn Street St. James's: Where the first Volume may be had Note, They have just publish'd the 2d. Pack of Musical playing Cards.

91 leaves. Pp. □[i] [ii]□-[iii]□ [iv-xi] [xii]□ 1-164 165□.
Leaves printed on 2 sides.
Tallest copy 207 x 137 mm. Vertical chain lines.

Four pages engraved per plate. Engraving style Cobb.
Frontispiece plate 180 x 110 mm.
Title-page plate 170 x 106 mm.

Advertised in *Daily Post*, 23 December 1725.

Contents: frontispiece [i]; title-page [ii]; dedication [iii]; subscribers' list [iv-xi]; contents [xii]; songs 1-165.

Songs:

No.	Page	First Line
1	1	S'ho lassa il piè (Oh cruel fair) (< *Darius*)
2	2-7	Scacciata dal suo nido (< *Rodelinda*)
3	8-10	Dove sei amato bene (< *Rodelinda*)
4	11-14	Pupille sdegnoso (< *Muzio Scaevola*)
5	15-19	Dolce pensier ferrier (< *Muzio Scaevola*)
6	20-22	No, oh Dio che mai farò (< *Calphurnia*)
7	23-27	Tengo inpugno l'idol mio (While I press my idol goddess) (a Carey, < *Theseus*)
8	28-32	S'ei non mi vuol amar (Since thus you slight my pain) (a Carey, < *Tamerlane*)
9	33-36	Non è si vago e bello (I come my fairest treasure) (< *Julius Caesar*)
10	37-40	Pupillette vezzosette (< *Elpidia*)
11	41-45	Non ha più che temere (My life my only treasure) (a Carey, < *Julius Caesar*)
12	46-48	Cara speme questo core (Cruel creature can you leave me) (< *Julius Caesar*)
13	49-53	Doni premio amica sorte (< *Titus Manlius*)
14	54-59	Sperai nè m'ingannai (< *Julius Caesar*)
15	60-65	La speranza all'alma mia (Hopes beguiling pleasures smiling) (a Carey, < *Julius Caesar*)
16	66-71	Chi perde un momento (While Celia is flying) (a Carey, < *Julius Caesar*)
17	72-75	Misera che faro (< *Calphurnia*)
18	76-81	Venere bella per un istante (Gazing on my idol treasure) (a Carey, < *Julius Caesar*)
19	82-84	Parto bell'idol mio (Must I then leave my treasure) (< *Elpidia*)
20	85-87	No il tuo sdegno mi placo (Go leave me thou faithless perjur'd man) (< *Tamerlane*)

21	88-93	Tortura che il suo bene (See how the amious turtles) (a Carey, < *Elpidia*)
22	94-99	Mio caro bene (< *Rodelinda*)
23	100-105	Non sa temere questo mio petto (< *Amadis*)
24	106-111	Già doppo l'orrore (< *Darius*)
25	112-117	Se potessi un dì placare (Cruel stars could I appease you) (a Carey, < *Tamerlane*)
26	118-123	Se pietà di me non senti (Welcome death oh end my sorrow) (a Carey, < *Julius Caesar*)
27	124-129	Amante stravagante (See my charmer flyes me) (a Carey, < *Flavius*)
28	130-132	V'adoro pupille (Lamenting complaining) (< *Julius Caesar*)
29	133-136	Ma chi punir desio (< *Flavius*)
30	137-139	Più non cerca libertà (< *Theseus*)
31	140-145	S'armi il fato (Ever lovely ever charming) (a Carey, < *Theseus*)
32	146-151	Non disperar chi sa (O what a fool was I) (a Carey, < *Julius Caesar*)
33	152-154	Amarti si vorrei (O Cupid gentle Cupid) (< *Theseus*)
34	155-159	Con un vezzo con un riso (< *Flavius*)
35	160-161	Se condaste al fine o stelle (In those eyes I see my ruin) (< *Pastor fido*)
36	162-165	Non è più tempo (No more complain) (s Cuzzoni, < *Tamerlane*)

Notes:
1. Subscribers' list, pp. [iv-xi], signed A on p. [iv], B on p. [viii].
2. Frontispiece first used on *Monthly Apollo*, 1724 (**146**).
3. ALb: 'Vol.II.' erased from title-page.
4. CLU-C: - p. [xii].
5. NjP: - pp. [iii], [xii]; + an 8-page letterpress section 'A succinct method for the right reading and pronouncing the Italian tongue' (pp. 1-6) and an unnumbered page of advertisements for Cluer and Creake, bound between the verso of p. [ii] and p. [iv].
6. TxU: + the 8-page letterpress section, bound in at end.

Copies: ALb 789.99 + 780.2; A-Wn M.S. 16812; Cfm Mu MS 1274; Ckc Mn.23.7; Ckc 112.42; CLU-C *M1507.P73 v.2; En BH.Add.39; ICU Rare M1507.N34 v.2; Lbl C.491; Lcm IX.F.26.b; NjP (Ex) xB83.0223; TxU Ak.A100.725p2 v.2.

Plate 161.1   Ariosti, *Darius*, 1725

The

Favourite SONGS

in the

OPERA

call'd

DARIUS

LONDON

Printed and Sold at the Musick Shops

Caption: plate 161.1. 338 x 217 mm. Lbl: H.319.a.

The Favourite Songs in the Opera call'd ⌈ Darius ⌋ London Printed and Sold at the Musick Shops

22 leaves. Pp. [i]□-[ii]□ \□1-2□\-\□13-14□\ 15□\□16 17□\□18 19□-20□.
Leaves printed on 1 side.
Tallest copy 368 x 230 mm. Vertical chain lines.

One page engraved per plate. Engraving style Musick Shops.
Title-page plate 270 x 164 mm. Passe-partout no. 11.
Contents plate 150 x 180 mm.

Walsh ii: 50.

Contents: title-page [i]; contents and advertisement [ii]; songs 1-20.

Songs:

No.	Page	First Line
1	1-2	Pastorel ch'in folta selva (s Sorosina, < *Darius*)
2	3-4	Dite voi o giuste stelle (s Senesino, < *Darius*)
3	5-6	Fate voi ancor così (s Borosini, < *Darius*)
4	7-8	Se non folse ingrannatrice (s Sorosina, < *Darius*)
5	9-10	Che bel piacere poter godere (s Borosini, < *Darius*)
6	11-12	Voi del ciel pietosi numi (s Pacini, < *Darius*)
7	13-15	Cara oh dio almen potessi (s Cuzzoni, Senesino, < *Darius*)
8	16-17	Qual fra'l porto e la tempesta (s Pacini, < *Darius*)
9	18-19	Pia dapo l'orrore d'un fato (s Cuzzoni, < *Darius*)
10	20	S'ho lasso il piè (s Dotti, Cuzzoni, < *Darius*)

Notes:
1. Probably issued by Walsh as all songs except 4 were reissued with additional pagination as part of *Apollo's Feast*, book 2, 172, in 1726.
2. First performed May 1725.
3. B-Bc: - pp. [i], 20.
4. Ckc: title name printed on blue wrapper.
5. CLU-C: bass figures added in MS.
6. F-Pn: pp. 16, 18 mis-rebound (reversed).

Copies: B-Bc 17,199; Ckc 85.3.(4.); CLU-C *fM1508.D215; F-Pn Vmg 15717; Lbl H.319.a; Lcm XXXII.B.20.(5.); NIC Lock.Pr. M1508 A71 D2++; Obt Mus. c.33(2).

Plate 162.1   Ariosti, *Darius*, 1725

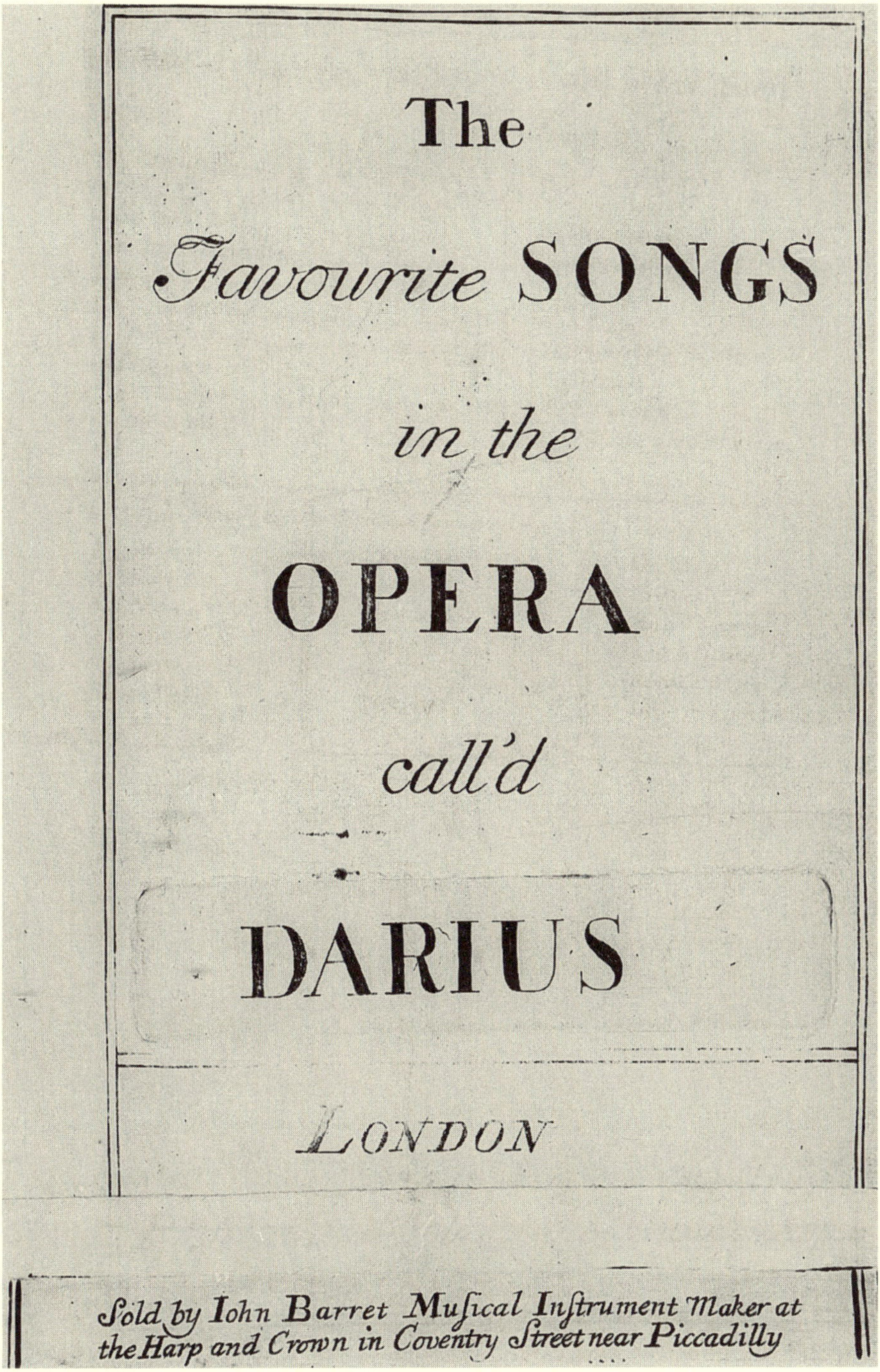

The

Favourite SONGS

in the

OPERA

call'd

DARIUS

London

Sold by Iohn Barret Muſical Inſtrument Maker at the Harp and Crown in Coventry Street near Piccadilly

Caption: plate 162.1. 349 x 222 mm. A-Wn: M.S.10230.

The Favourite Songs in the Opera call'd ⌠ Darius ⌡ [engraved label over Musick Shops imprint] Sold by Iohn Barret Musical Instrument Maker at the Harp and Crown in Coventry Street near Piccadilly

22 leaves. Pp. [i]□-[ii]□ \□1-2□\-\□13-14□\ 15□\□16 17□\□18 19□-20□.
Leaves printed on 1 side.
Tallest copy 349 x 222 mm. Vertical chain lines.

One page engraved per plate. Engraving style Musick Shops.
Title-page plate ? x 164 mm. Passe-partout no. 11. (See note 1.)

Contents: title-page [i]; contents and advertisement [ii]; songs 1-20.

Songs: see 161.

Note:
1. Label obscures lower edge of plate.

Copy: A-Wn M.S.10230.

Plate 163.1   Vinci, *Elpidia*, 1725

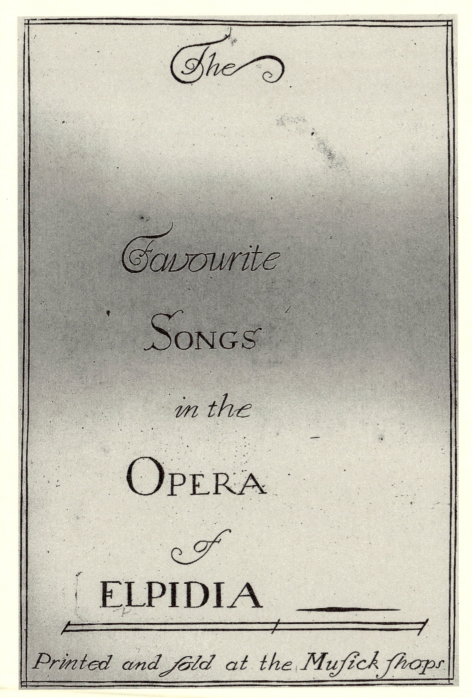

The

Favourite

Songs

in the

Opera

of

ELPIDIA

Printed and sold at the Musick shops

Caption: plate 163.1. 320 x 210 mm. Lbl: G.206.c.(2.).

The Favourite Songs in the Opera of ⸢ Elpidia ⸥ Printed and sold at the Musick shops

14 leaves. Pp. [1]□ \□2-3□\-\□8-9□\ 10□\□11 12□\□13 14□.
Leaves printed on 1 side.
Tallest copy 342 x 223 mm. Vertical chain lines.

One page engraved per plate. Engraving style Musick Shops.
Title-page plate 270 x 165 mm. Passe-partout no. 15.

Contents: title-page [1]; songs 2-14.

Songs:

No.	Page	First Line
1	2-3	Dì pur ch'io sono ingrato (s Senesino, < *Elpidia*)
2	4-5	Dolce error che vezzegiando (s Cuzzoni, < *Elpidia*)
3	6-7	Pupillette vezzosette (s Cuzzoni, < *Elpidia*)
4	8-10	Un vento lusingier tal (s Senesino, < *Elpidia*)
5	11-12	Dea triforme astra seconda (s Cuzzoni, < *Elpidia*)
6	13-14	Men superba andria la sorte (s Pacini, < *Elpidia*)

Notes:
1. First performed May 1725.
2. Er: [1]□\□2 3□\□6 7□\□4 5□\□11 12□\□8 9□-10□\□13 14□.

Copies: CDp M.C.3.21(4); Er E162; Lbl G.206.c.(2.).

Plate 164.1   Vinci, *Elpidia*, 1725

The

Favourite SONGS

in the

OPERA

call'd

ELPIDIA

LONDON

Printed and Sold at the Musick Shops

164   Vinci, *Elpidia*, 31 December 1725

Caption: plate 164.1. 337 x 218 mm. CLU-C: *fM1505.V77e.

The Favourite Songs in the Opera call'd ∫ Elpidia ♩ London Printed and Sold at the Musick Shops

23 leaves. Pp. [i]□-[ii]□\□1-2□\-\□9-10□\11□-12□\□13-14□\-\□17-18□\19□\□20 21□. Leaves printed on 1 side.
Tallest copy 377 x 228 mm. Vertical chain lines.

One page engraved per plate. Engraving style Musick Shops.
Title-page plate 270 x 165 mm. Passe-partout no. 11.
Contents plate 142 x 182 mm.

Walsh ii: 1508.

Contents: title-page [i]; contents and advertisement [ii]; songs 1-21.

Songs:

No.	Page	First Line
1	1-2	Pupillette vezzosette (s Cuzzoni, < *Elpidia*)
2	3-4	Barbara mi schernisci (s Senesino, < *Elpidia*)
3	5-6	Tortora che il suo bene (s Cuzzoni, < *Elpidia*)
4	7-8	Parto bel idol mio (s Senesino, < *Elpidia*)
5	9-11	Un vento lusinghier tal (s Senesino, < *Elpidia*)
6	12	Deh caro Olindo non mi tradir (s Cuzzoni, Senesino, < *Elpidia*)
7	13-14	Addio dille e da quel labro (s Senesino, < *Elpidia*)
8	15-16	Vanne e spera (s Borosini, < *Elpidia*)
9	17-19	Di pur ch'io sono ingrato (s Senesino, < *Elpidia*)
10	20-21	Dea triforme astro secondo (s Cuzzoni, < *Elpidia*)

Notes:
1. Probably issued by Walsh as songs 1-3, 5, 7-10 were reissued with additional pagination as part of *Apollo's Feast*, book 2, 172, in 1726.
2. First performed May 1725.
3. CDp: pp. 1-6 cut out.
4. Lbl: - p. [i].

Copies: B-Bc 17,231; CDp M.C.3.29(15); Ckc 85.1.(10.); CLU-C *fM1505.V77e; F-Pc Rés. V.S.1285; ICN VM1503.V77e; Lbl H.230.f.(7.); MiU RBR M1505.V78E5; NIC Lock.Pr. M1505 E48 F3++.

165   deleted (see 164).

No title-page.

14 leaves. Pp. \[]1-2[]\-\[]13-14[]\.
Leaves printed on 1 side.
Tallest copy 349 x 222 mm. Vertical chain lines.

One page engraved per plate. Engraving style Mixed.

Contents: songs 1-14.

Songs:

No.	Page	First Line
1	1-2	Più non so dirti spera (s Cuzzoni, < *Elpidia*)
2	3-4	Vaga risplende d'amor (s Senesino, < *Elpidia*)
3	5-6	Sorge qual luccioletta (s Dotti, < *Elpidia*)
4	7-8	Con nodi più tenaci (s Dotti, < *Elpidia*)
5	9-10	Parte il pie'ma teco resta (s Balti, < *Elpidia*)
6	11-12	Ahi nemico e'al nostro affetto (s Balti, < *Elpidia*)
7	13-14	Amor deh lasciami (s Tenori, < *Elpidia*)

Notes:
1. Contains the 'Additional Songs in Elpidia', published in another edition by Walsh and Hare as *The Quarterly Collection of Vocal Musick* (167). The songs were first performed on November 30, 1725.
2. A-Wn: a bound-with; other items carry title-pages with Barret's label on them.
3. Ckc: in volume that contains portions of other song books; song order 2, 4, 3, 1, 7, 6, 5.

Copies: A-Wn M.S.10230; Ckc 110.24.

Plate 167.1   *Quarterly Collection of Vocal Musick, 1725*

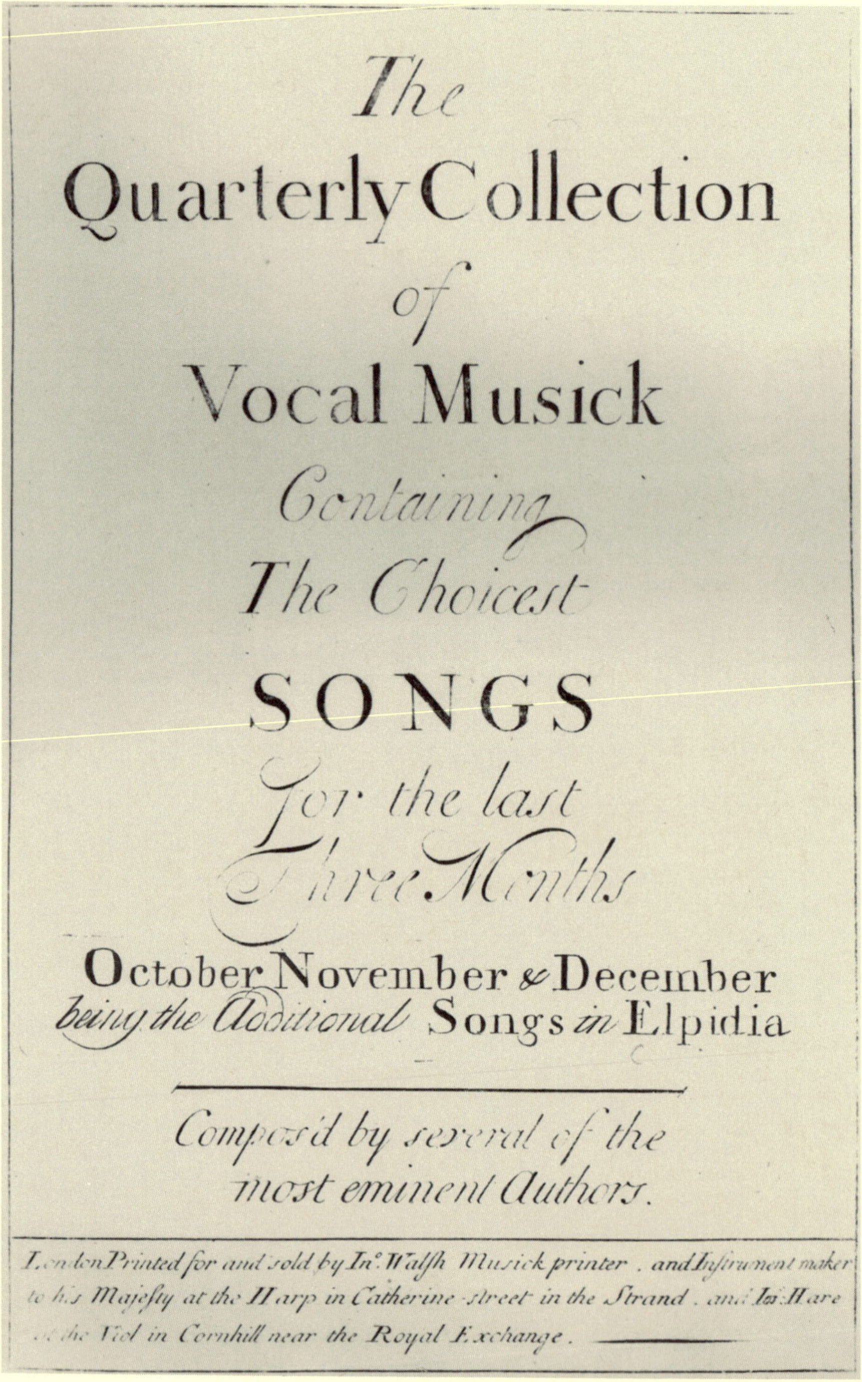

The

Quarterly Collection

of

Vocal Musick

Containing

The Choicest

SONGS

for the last

Three Months

October November & December

being the Additional Songs *in* Elpidia

Compos'd by several of the

most eminent Authors.

London Printed for and sold by Jn°. Walsh Musick printer . and Instrument maker to his Majesty at the Harp in Catherine street in the Strand . and Jn° Hare at the Viol in Cornhill near the Royal Exchange . _____

Plate 167.2 *Quarterly Collection of Vocal Musick*, 1725

Caption: plates 167.1-167.2. 330 x 220 mm. Lbl: G.316.r.

The Quarterly Collection of Vocal Musick Containing The Choicest Songs For the last Three Months ⌠ October November & December being the Additional Songs in Elpidia ⌡ Compos'd by several of the most eminent Authors. London Printed for and sold by Ino. Walsh Musick printer. and Instrument maker to his Majesty at the Harp in Catherine-street in the Strand. and Ios: Hare at the Viol in Cornhill near the Royal Exchange.

15 leaves. Pp. [i]◻ \◻1-2◻\ -\◻13-14◻\.
Leaves printed on 1 side.
Tallest copy 343 x 223 mm. Vertical chain lines.

One page engraved per plate. Engraving style Walsh 4, 6 (plate 167.2).
Title-page plate 270 x 174 mm. Passe-partout no. 16.

Walsh ii: 1266.

Contents: title-page [i]; songs 1-14.

Songs:

No.	Page	First Line
1	1-2	Più non so dirti spera (s Cuzzoni, < *Elpidia*)
2	3-4	Vaga risplende d'amor (s Senesino, < *Elpidia*)
3	5-6	Sorge qual luccioletta (s Dotti, < *Elpidia*)
4	7-8	Con nodi più tenaci (s Dotti, < *Elpidia*)
5	9-10	Parte il pie'ma teco resta (s Balti, < *Elpidia*)
6	11-12	Ahi nemico e'al nostro affetto (s Balti, < *Elpidia*)
7	13-14	Amor deh lasciami (s Tenori, < *Elpidia*)

Notes:
1. Songs 1, 4, 6, 7, were reissued with additional pagination as part of *Apollo's Feast*, book 2, 172, in 1726.
2. The additional songs in *Elpidia* were first performed on 30 November 1725.
3. The *Quarterly Collection of Vocal Musick* was also published for January-March 1726 containing additional songs from Handel's 'Otho' (copies at Coke, En, Lbl and Lcm; the first two lack title-pages). A copy of the 'Otho' songs at F-Pc has *Monthly Mask of Vocal Music* title-pages.
4. En: + 2 songs from *Alexander*.
5. Lbl: bound with the January-March 1726 issue.

Copies: En BH.Add.42; Lbl G.316.r.

Plate 168.1   Thomson, *Orpheus Caledonius*, 1726

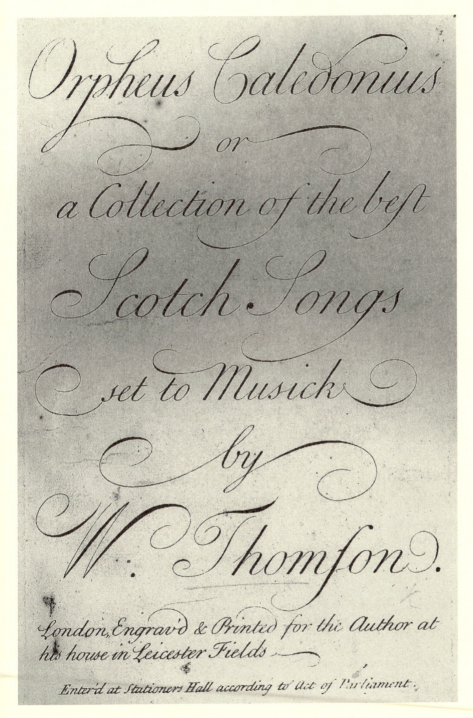

435

Caption: plate 168.1. 364 x 238 mm. Lbl: I.367.b.

Orpheus Caledonius or a Collection of the best Scotch Songs set to Musick by W. Thomson. London, Engrav'd & Printed for the Author at his house in Leicester Fields Enter'd at Stationers Hall according to Act of Parliament.

64 leaves. Pp. [i]⬚-[ii]⬚ [1] 2-4 [5]⬚ {1-2} 1⬚-58⬚.
Leaves printed on 1 side.
Tallest copy 402 x 248 mm. Vertical chain lines.

One page engraved per plate. Engraving style Mixed.
Title-page plate 308 x 184 mm.

Contents: title-page [i]; dedication [ii]; subscribers' list [1] 2-4; contents [5]; verses {1-2}; songs 1-50; flute parts 51-58.

Songs:

No.	Page	First Line
1	1	Lass of Paties Mill, sae bony, The
2	2	O Bessie Bell and Mary Gray, they are
3	3	Hear me, ye nymphs, and every swain
4	4	As early I walk'd on the first of sweet May
5	5	Blest as th' immortal gods is he
6	6	Last time I came o'er the moor, The
7	7	In April when primroses paint the sweet plain
8	8	Ye gales that gently wave the sea
9	9	With broken words and downcast eyes
10	10	O the broom, the bonny broom
11	11	O Bell thy looks have kill'd my heart
12	12	How sweetly smells the summer green
13	13	Nansy's to the green wood gane
14	14	O my bonny highland laddie
15	15	As gentle turtle doves
16	16	What beauties does Flora disclose
17	17	By a murmuring stream a fair shepherdess lay
18	18	Loves goddess in a myrtle grove said
19	19	Happy's the love that meets return
20	20	Beneath a green shade I fand a fair maid
21	21	Tho' for seven years and mair
22	22	As walking forth to view the plain
23	23	Ann thou were my ain thing
24	24	At Polwart on the green
25	25	O let us swim in blood of grapes
26	26	Cock=laird fu' Caigie with Jenny did meet, A
27	27	And gin ye meet a bonny lassie
28	28	Harken and I will tell you how
29	29	As from a rock past all relief
30	30	There's auld Rob Morris that wins in yon glen
31	31	Should auld acquaintance be forgot
32	32	'Twas forth in a morning
33	33	My dady's a delver of dykes

34	34	And wale' up yon bank
35	35	By smooth winding Tay a swain was reclining
36	36	Come fye let us a' to the bridal
37	37	Come let's ha'e mair wine in
38	38	While some for pleasure pawn their health
39	39	Meal was dear short sine, The
40	40	There was an a May and she lo'ed na men
41	41	Ah the poor shepherd's mournfull fate
42	42	Betty early gone a maying
43	43	Pauky auld Carle came o'er the lee, The
44	44	Collier has a daughter, The
45	45	Come lassie, lend me your braw hemp heckle
46	46	Carle he came o'er the craft, The
47	47	I will awa' wi' my love
48	48	Pain'd with her slighting Jamie's love
49	49	When all was wrapt in dark midnight
50	50	When trees did bud and fields were green

Notes:
1. { } = [ ] on page.
2. Pp. [ii], [1], 2-4, [5], {1-2} printed letterpress.
3. Advertised in *Daily Post* on December 24 and 31, 1725 as 'Tomorrow will be published'. Registered at the Stationers' Company on 5 January 1726.
4. The attribution of the verbal text of songs 1-3, 8, 23, 30, 50 to 'David Rezzio' (Rizzio or Riccio, d. 1566) in the contents list is more likely an attempt to increase sales through sensationalism than the transmission of accurate oral tradition concerning the songs' origins. Thirty-eight of the verbal texts are from Allan Ramsay, *Tea-table Miscellany*, 1723.
5. En (Inglis 220): - pp. [1], 13, 32; pp. 13 and 32 supplied in MS.
6. En (Inglis 219): - p. 1.
7. Gm: - p. 10, supplied in MS.
8. Lam, Lbl (H.1630.a), LVp: p. [5] bound after p. [ii].
9. Copy reported at Lcs is of 2nd edition.

Copies: *CaB VaU*; Ckc 110.151; DU Wighton 3254; En Glen. 371; En Inglis 219; En Inglis 220; En Inglis 241; En Inglis 242; F-Pc Fol.Y.41; Ge N.a.2; Gm M8214; IU xq784.8T383 1726; Lam —; Lbl H.1630.a; Lbl I.367.b; Lbl R.M.14.a.19; Lcm II.K.5; Lcm II.K.2.(1.); LVp 784.81; MH-H 25261.36*; *Ob*; P O.6.

Plate 169.1   *Delightful Musical Companion*, 1726

Il Teatro dell'Opera di Londra

Barbiton hic paries habebit

Cheron delin:

E. Kirkall sculp.

Plate 169.2   *Delightful Musical Companion, 1726*

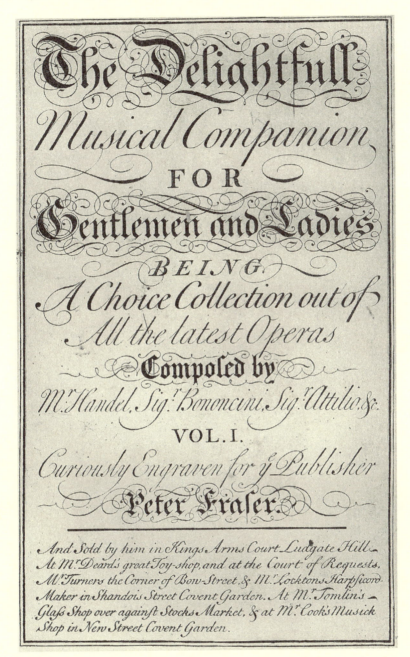

The Delightfull Musical Companion FOR Gentlemen and Ladies BEING A Choice Collection out of All the latest Operas Compoſed by Mr. Handel, Sigr. Bononcini, Sigr. Attilio, &c. VOL. I. Curiously Engraven for ye Publisher Peter Fraſer.

And Sold by him in Kings Arms Court Ludgate Hill. At Mr. Deard's great Toy-shop, and at the Court of Requests. Mr. Turners the Corner of Bow-Street, & Mr. Locktons Harpſicord-Maker in Shandois Street Covent Garden. At Mr. Tomlin's Glaſs Shop over against Stocks Market, & at Mr. Cook's Muſick Shop in New Street Covent Garden.

Plate 169.3   *Delightful Musical Companion*, 1726

Caption: plates 169.1-169.3. 194 x 122 mm. Lbl: C.370.

The Delightfull Musical Companion For Gentlemen and Ladies Being A Choice Collection out of All the latest Operas Composed by Mr: Handel, Sigr: Bononcini, Sigr: Attilio, &c. Vol. I. Curiously Engraven for ye Publisher Peter Fraser. And Sold by him in Kings Arms Court Ludgate Hill At Mr. Deard's great Toy-shop, and at the Court of Requests, Mrs Turners the Corner of Bow-Street, & Mr. Locktons Harpsicord-Maker in Shandois Street Covent Garden. At Mr. Tomlin's Glass Shop over against Stocks Market, & at Mr. Cook's Musick Shop in New Street Covent Garden.

89 leaves. Pp. □[i] [ii]□-[iii]□ [iv-xii] 1-87 88□ [90] 91-151 152□ [154]□ 156-161 162□. Leaves printed on 2 sides.
Tallest copy 201 x 127 mm. Mixed chain lines.

Two pages engraved per plate. Engraving style Cole.
Frontispiece plate 186 x 111 mm.
Title-page plate 170 x 110 mm.

Advertised in *Daily Journal*, 8 January 1726.

Contents: frontispiece [i]; title-page [ii]; dedication [iii]; preface [iv-vii]; subscribers' list [viii-xi]; contents [xii]; songs 1-88; contents [90]; songs 91-152; section title [154]; flute parts 156-162.

Songs:

No.	Page	First Line
1	1-4	Fals'imagine m'ingannasti (s Cuzzoni, < *Otho*)
2	5-8	Venere bella per un istante (s Cuzzoni, < *Julius Caesar*)
3	9-12	Non è più tempo no (s Cuzzoni, < *Tamerlane*)
4	13-16	Aure voi che m'ascoltate (s Cuzzoni, < *Vespasian*)
5	17-20	Dal fulgor di questa spada (s Boschi, < *Julius Caesar*)
6	21-24	Se potessi un dì placare (s Cuzzoni, < *Tamerlane*)
7	25-28	No, oh Dio che mai farò (s Cuzzoni, < *Calphurnia*)
8	29-32	Sapete che in amor (s Berselli, < *Astartus*)
9	33-36	Chi può mirare (s Berenstadt, < *Flavius*)
10	37-40	Bell'Asteria il tuo cor mi diffenda (s Senesino, < *Tamerlane*)
11	41-44	Pupille sdegnose (s Senesino, < *Muzio Scaevola*)
12	45-48	Ciel e terr'armi di sdegno (s Borosini, < *Tamerlane*)
13	49-52	Se una stella a me rubella (m Gasparini)
14	53-56	Non è sì vago e bello (s Senesino, < *Julius Caesar*)
15	57-60	Dì pur ch'io sono ingrato (< *Elpidia*)
16	61-64	V'adoro pupile saette d'amore (s Cuzzoni, < *Julius Caesar*)
17	65-68	Cessa o mai di sospirar (s Robinson, A., < *Julius Caesar*)
18	69-72	Si ch'io vuo lasciar l'affetto (s Cuzzoni, < *Calphurnia*)
19	73-76	Quanto dolci quanto care (s Cuzzoni, < *Flavius*)
20	77-78	Mio caro bene (s Cuzzoni, < *Rodelinda*)
21	81-86	Deh fuggi un traditore (< *Radamisto*)
22	87-88	Con forz'ascosa (< *Vespasian*)

23	91-96	A suoi piedi padre esangue (s Borosini, < *Tamerlane*)
24	97-100	Se risolvi abbandonarmi (< *Floridante*)
25	101-104	Alla fama dimmi il vero (s Cuzzoni, < *Otho*)
26	105-108	Serba fede e fede amor (s Durastanti, < *Calphurnia*)
27	109-112	No più non bramo no (s Berselli, < *Astartus*)
28	113-116	Son come navicella in mar turbato (s Cuzzoni, < *Artaxerxes*)
29	117-120	Se vuoi ch'in pace io moro (s Senesino, < *Astartus*)
30	121-126	Tu sei'l cor di questo cuore (s Boschi, < *Julius Caesar*)
31	127-132	Se sol la mia morte (s Senesino, < *Arsaces*)
32	133-137	Stelle ingrate (s Senesino, < *Astartus*)
33	138	T'amo tanto o mio tesoro (s Senesino)
34	139-144	Da tempeste il legno infranto (s Cuzzoni, < *Julius Caesar*)
35	145-148	Se'l mio duol non è si forte (s Cuzzoni, < *Rodelinda*)
36	149-152	Non mi seguir infido (s Durastanti, < *Astartus*)

Notes:
1. Ckc: + proposal, printed letterpress, for second volume and English volume, pp. 1-4, bound at end.
2. CU-MUSI: - p. [i]; pp. 32-35 misbound between pp. 27-28.
3. DLC: - pp. 42-43.
4. En: - pp. [viii-xi].
5. F-Pc: p. [ii] bound after p. [iii].
6. ICN: - p. [i].
7. Lbl (R.M.15.g.1): - p. [i]; with label pasted to p. [163]: 'Sould by [Jo]hn Walsh musicall instrument [ma]ker in ordinary to his majesty; at ye [Go]lden Harpe & Haut Boy against Summerset=House water gate in Cathe=[rine] street in ye Strand London'.
8. MB: - pp. [i-vii].
9. Report of copy at DU is false.

Copies: Ckc 112.30; Coke —; CU-MUSI M1507.F7 Case X; DLC M1507.A2F84; En BH.Add.40; F-Pc Y.606; ICN VM1505.D35; I-Rsc; Lbl C.370; Lbl R.M.15.g.1; MB**M145.22.

Plate 170.1   *Delightful Musical Companion, 1726*

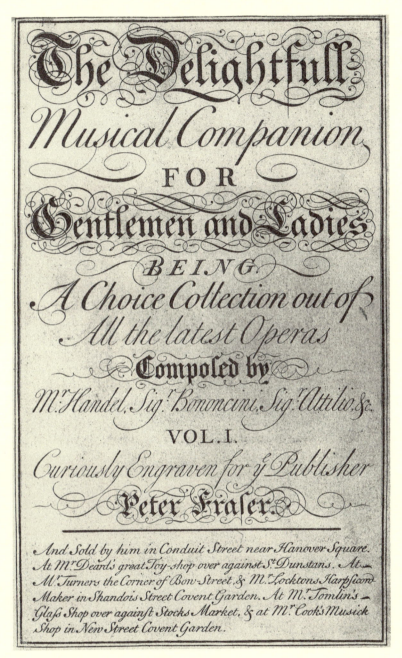

443

Caption: plate 170.1. 186 x 124 mm. CLU-C: *M1507.D35.

The Delightfull Musical Companion For Gentlemen and Ladies Being A Choice Collection out of All the latest Operas Composed by Mr: Handel, Sigr: Bononcini, Sigr: Attilio, &c. Vol. I. Curiously Engraven for ye Publisher Peter Fraser. And Sold by him in Conduit Street near Hanover Square. At Mr. Deard's great Toy-shop over against St. Dunstans. At Mr. Turners the Corner of Bow-Street, & Mr. Locktons Harpsicord-Maker in Shandois Street Covent Garden. At Mr. Tomlin's Glass Shop over against Stocks Market, & at Mr. Cook's Musick Shop in New Street Covent Garden.

89 leaves. Pp. π[i] [ii]π-[iii]π [iv-xii] 1-87 88π [90] 91-151 152π [154]π 156-161 162π. Leaves printed on 2 sides.
Tallest copy 201 x 127 mm. Mixed chain lines.

Two pages engraved per plate. Engraving style Cole.
Title-page plate 173 x 108 mm.

Walsh ii: 547.

Contents: frontispiece [i]; title-page [ii]; dedication [iii]; preface [iv-vii]; subscribers' list [viii-xi]; contents [xii]; songs 1-88; contents [90]; songs 91-152; section title [154]; flute parts 156-162.

Songs: see **169**.

Notes:
1. CLU-C: cropt at head with loss of some page numbers.
2. Coke: - p. [i]; 'Vol. I.' erased from title-page.
3. Mp: pp. [iv-vii] and [viii-xi] inverted; 'Vol. I.' erased from title-page; cropt at head with loss of some page numbers.

Copies: CLU-C *M1507.D35; Coke —; Mp BR412 Dh45.

Plate 171.1   Carey, *Diamonds Cut Diamonds*, 1726

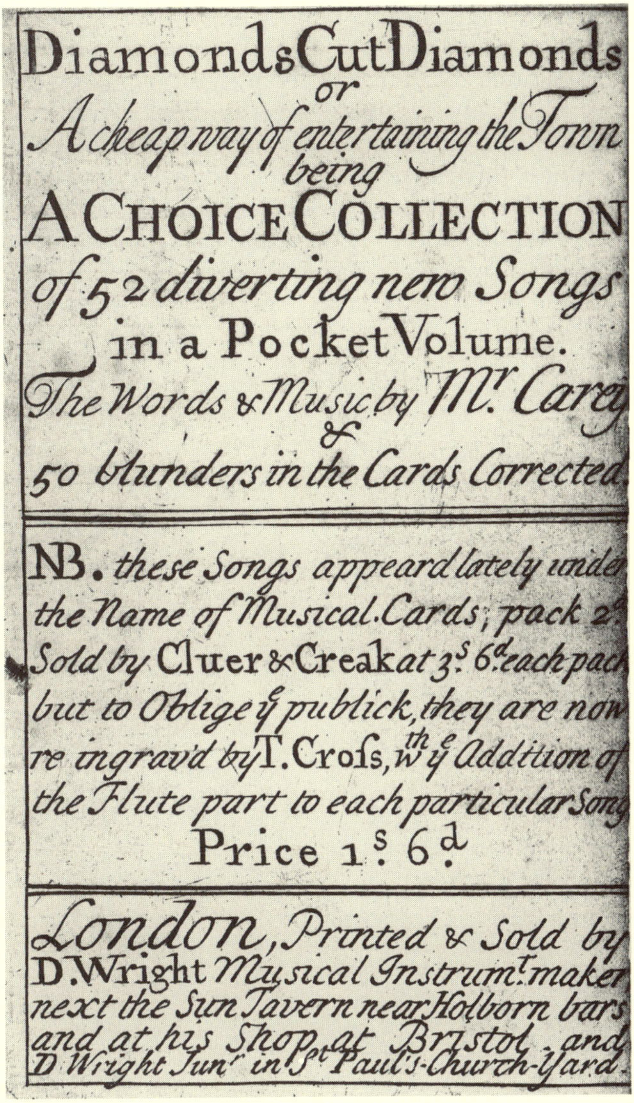

Caption: plate 171.1. 154 x 96 mm. Obh: Mus. E.730.

Diamonds Cut Diamonds or A cheap way of entertaining the Town being A Choice Collection of 52 diverting new Songs in a Pocket Volume. The Words & Music by Mr. Carey & 50 blunders in the Cards Corrected. NB. these Songs appeared lately under the name of Musical Cards, pack 2d. Sold by Cluer & Creak at 3s. 6d. each pack but to Oblige ye publick, they are now re ingrav'd by T. Cross wth ye Addition of the Flute part to each particular Song Price 1s. 6d. London, Printed & Sold by D. Wright Musical Instrumt. maker, next the Sun Tavern near Holborn bars and at his Shop at Bristol. and D Wright Junr in St. Paul's-Church-Yard.

27 leaves. Pp. [1]◻ 1-52.
Leaves printed on 2 sides.
Tallest copy 154 x 96 mm. Vertical chain lines.

Four pages engraved per plate. Engraving style Cross.
Title-page plate 151 x 90 (?) mm. (See note 2.)

Price 1/6.

Contents: title-page [i]; songs 1-52.

Songs:

No.	Page	First Line
1	1	Don't call me joy & treasure
2	2	Charmer if I ever leave you
3	3	Cuckold it is thought, A
4	4	Follow, nymphs & swains
5	5	My mother calls me harmless maid
6	6	As I was a walking all round cross ye park
7	7	Masons & the gormagons, The
8	8	Hur Winnifred was pretty
9	9	No longer I'll despair
10	10	Why Molly what's the reason
11	11	See that abject nasty queen
12	12	Ever scolding, never holding
13	13	Kind consenting charming fair, The
14	14	Tom Mixum's spouse
15	15	To banish care wn stoks were sinking
16	16	My Jockeys grown a faithless loon
17	17	See the turtles how they wooe
18	18	Madam you (or your diamonds
19	19	Queen of my heart
20	20	To see a wither'd fair
21	21	Worst of plagues, The
22.	22	Treachrous knave, A
23	23	King & ruler of my heart

24	24	Squemish prude, The
25	25	Clorinda do not grumble
26	26	Keep away, oh hateful day
27	27	Thus gayly advancing
28	28	See yt dirty groom
29	29	Great god of love oh set me free
30	30	I will not bear it
31	31	Must I still languish
32	32	Let whimsical monarchs of state
33	33	Come my dearest Sylvia
34	34	See the smiling fair
35	35	Men are all ungrateful
36	36	Fair are soonest pierc'd wth golden darts, The
37	37	Why, my lady in a fluster
38	38	Tell me not of a wife
39	39	Oh I'll have a husband ah marry
40	40	Knave's a knave, A
41	41	Toby Swill, has ne'er his fill
42	42	Empty bottle's such a curse, An
43	43	Alone by a lonely willow
44	44	Tell me Sylvia tell me why
45	45	No diamonds are so bright
46	46	Your heart alone is all I prize
47	47	What is the reason thou of late
48	48	What should a merry
49	49	Pretty country lass, A
50	50	I hate a sot yt at his pot
51	51	Oh happy pair
52	52	Clorinda has such killing eyes

Notes:
1. Cluer and Creake advertised an edition in *Evening Post*, 18 January 1726, and as the genuine edition in *London Journal*, 22 January 1726.
2. Closely trimmed, with slight loss of text at fore-edge.

Copy: Obh Mus. E.730.

Plate 172.1   *Apollo's Feast*, vol.2, 1726

Plate 172.2   *Apollo's Feast, vol.2, 1726*

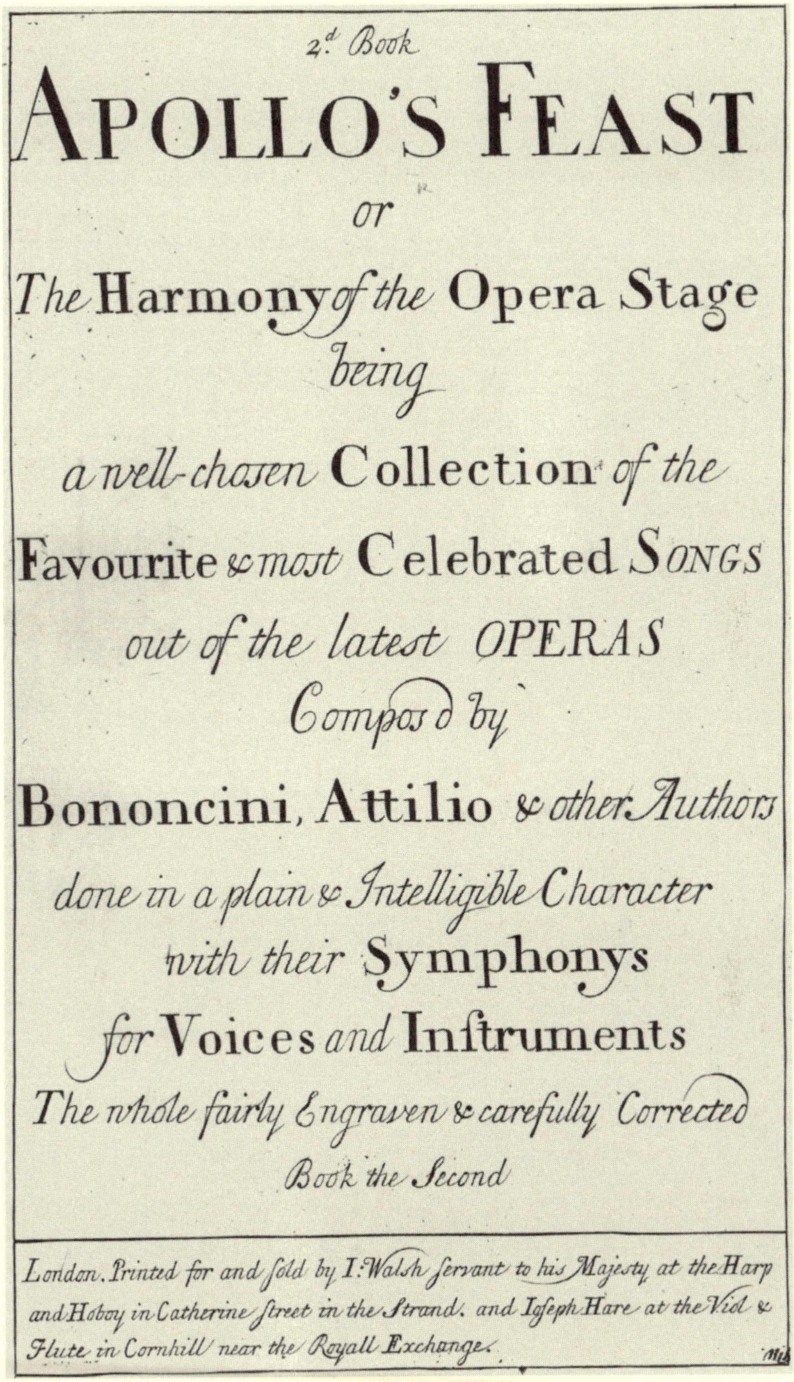

2.ᵈ Book

APOLLO'S FEAST

or

The Harmony of the Opera Stage

being

a well-chosen Collection of the

Favourite & most Celebrated Songs

out of the latest OPERAS

Compos'd by

Bononcini, Attilio & other Authors

done in a plain & Intelligible Character

with their Symphonys

for Voices and Instruments

The whole fairly Engraven & carefully Corrected

Book the Second

London. Printed for and sold by I: Walsh servant to his Majesty at the Harp and Hoboy in Catherine street in the Strand. and Joseph Hare at the Viol & Flute in Cornhill near the Royall Exchange.

Caption: plates 172.1-172.2. 364 x 231 mm. Lbl: R.M.13.d.24.

2d. Book Apollo's Feast or The Harmony of the Opera Stage being a well-chosen Collection of the Favourite & most Celebrated Songs out of the latest Operas Composed by Bononcini, Attilio & other Authors done in a plain & Intelligible Character with their Symphonys for Voices and Instruments The whole fairly Engraven & carefully Corrected Book the Second London. Printed for and sold by I: Walsh servant to his Majesty at the Harp and Hoboy in Catherine street in the Strand. and Ioseph Hare at the Viol & Flute in Cornhill near the Royall Exchange.

117 leaves. Pp. ☐[i] [ii]☐-[iii]☐\☐1 2-135 136☐ 137-226.
Leaves printed on 2 sides.
Tallest copy 365 x 237 mm. Vertical chain lines.

One page engraved per plate. Engraving style Walsh.
Frontispiece plate 293 x 200 mm. Passe-partout no. 2.
Title-page plate 305 x 178 mm.
Contents plate 308 x 181 mm.

Walsh ii: 41.
Advertised in *Daily Courant*, 16 September 1726.

Contents: frontispiece [i]; title-page [ii]; contents [iii]; songs 1-226.

Songs:

No.	Page	First Line
1	1-2	Al mio nativo prato (s Robinson, A., Senesino, < *Griselda*)
2	3-5	Affetto gioia e riso (s Senesino, < *Griselda*)
3	6	Aure voi che m'ascoltate (s Cuzzoni, < *Vespasian*)
4	7-8	Amor vieni o mostrarvi (s Senesino)
5	9-10	Amante e sposa si gli sarai (s Senesino, < *Astartus*)
6	11-12	Al pard'un fiore (s Durastanti, < *Pharnaces*)
7	13-14	Amor deh lasciami (s Tenori, < *Elpidia*)
8	15-16	Ahi nemico e'al nostro affetto (s Balti, < *Elpidia*)
9	17-18	Addio dille e da quel labro (s Senesino, < *Elpidia*)
10	19-20	Begl'occhi lusinghieri (s Durastanti, < *Pharnaces*)
11	21-22	Barbara mi schernisci (s Senesino, < *Elpidia*)
12	23-24	Bella non disperar (s Robinson, A., < *Aquilio*)
13	25-26	Care pupille tra mille e mille (s Senesino, < *Astartus*)
14	27-29	Così fedele la mia tiranna (s Berselli, < *Astartus*)
15	30-32	Cara oh dio almen potessi (s Cuzzoni, Senesino, < *Darius*)
16	33-35	Combattuta navicella (s Cuzzoni, < *Vespasian*)
17	36	Con forza ascosa ne'raggi sui (Fly me not Silvia) (s Senesino, < *Vespasian*)
18	37-38	Così stanco pelegrino (s Senesino, < *Crispus*)
19	39-40	Che bel piacere poter godere (s Borosini, < *Darius*)
20	41-42	Con nodi più tenaci (s Dotti, < *Elpidia*)
21	43-44	Dille che peno (s Senesino, < *Crispus*)
22	45-46	Dite voi o giuste stelle (s Borosini, < *Darius*)

23	47-48	Deh m'ascolto ferma oh dio (s Cuzzoni, < *Artaxerxes*)
24	49-50	Dea triforme astro secondo (s Cuzzoni, < *Elpidia*)
25	51-53	Dolce sogno deh le porta (s Senesino, < *Griselda*)
26	54-56	Di dolce affetto jo sento (s Senesino, < *Erminia*)
27	57-59	Di pur ch'io sono ingrato (s Senesino, < *Elpidia*)
28	60-64	È un bel piacer l'amar (< *Vespasian*)
29	65-66	Eterni dei narrate (s Boschi, < *Griselda*)
30	67-68	Fate voi ancor così (s Borosini, < *Darius*)
31	69-70	Già col vostro rigor (s Senesino, < *Pharnaces*)
32	71-72	Han posto i tuoi bei lumi (s Senesino, < *Vespasian*)
33	73-74	Ingrato figlio (s Robinson, A., < *Crispus*)
34	75-76	Il core che pretendo (s Robinson, A., < *Pharnaces*)
35	77-78	Il suo amore intenderò (s Cuzzoni, < *Coriolano*)
36	79-81	Io spero che in que'guardi (s Senesino, < *Coriolano*)
37	82-84	La tortorella fida e costante (s Cuzzoni, < *Vespasian*)
38	85	Transported with pleasure (L'esperto nocchiero) (< *Astartus*)
39	86	Lasso ch'jo t'ho'perduta (s Senesino, < *Vespasian*)
40	87-88	Lo voglio lo chiede (s Robinson, A., < *Crispus*)
41	89-90	Lascio il solco e vengo (s Durastanti, < *Aquilio*)
42	91-92	Mio caro ben non sospirar (s Salvai, Berselli, < *Astartus*)
43	93-94	Misera che fato (s Cuzzoni, < *Calphurnia*)
44	95-96	Non è poco credi a me (s Salvai, < *Astartus*)
45	97-99	Non deggio non sperare (s Benedetti, < *Griselda*)
46	100-102	Nel suo duol così si lagra (s Cuzzoni, < *Artaxerxes*)
47	103-104	Non t'inganno stretto nodo (s Cuzzoni, < *Pharnaces*)
48	105-106	Nembo tal'ora (s Cuzzoni, < *Pharnaces*)
49	107-108	Non so lasciar quel volto (s Senesino, < *Calphurnia*)
50	109-110	Nel mirarui se spietati (s Senesino, < *Artaxerxes*)
51	111	No, oh dio che mai farò (s Cuzzoni, < *Calphurnia*)
52	112	Oh quanto invidia il cor (s Durastanti, < *Astartus*)
53	113-114	Or che il sonno (s Durastanti, < *Vespasian*)
54	115-117	Parto amabile ben mio (s Robinson, A., < *Griselda*)
55	118	Tis my glory to adore you (Per la gloria d'adorarvi) (< *Griselda*)
56	119-120	Pupille care per farmi amare (s Durastanti)
57	121-122	Pace almen fra queste selve (s Senesino, < *Erminia*)
58	123-124	Pastorel ch'in folta selva (s Sorosina, < *Darius*)
59	125-126	Pia dapo l'orrore d'un fato (s Cuzzoni, < *Darius*)
60	127-128	Pur che mi sciolga il piede (s Robinson, A., < *Vespasian*)
61	129-130	Pupillette vezzosette (s Cuzzoni, < *Elpidia*)
62	131-132	Più non so dirti spera (s Cuzzoni, < *Elpidia*)
63	133-134	Perdonate o cari amori (s Senesino, < *Coriolano*)
64	135-136	Più crudel si fa la sorte (s Durastanti, < *Coriolano*)
65	137	Più benigno par che arrida (Charmer hear your faithfull lover) (s Robinson, A., < *Coriolano*)
66	138-139	Quanto mi spiace (s Salvai, < *Griselda*)
67	140-141	Quel guardo di pietà (s Robinson, A., < *Griselda*)
68	142-143	Qual fra'l porto e la tempesta (s Pacini, < *Darius*)
69	144-145	Render voglio ogn' uno amante (s Robinson, A., < *Calphurnia*)
70	146-149	Rinasce amor allor che amando spera (s Senesino, < *Aquilio*)
71	150-151	Rendi al padre in me la figlia (s Cuzzoni, < *Coriolano*)
72	152-153	Sapete che in amor (s Berselli, < *Astartus*)
73	154-156	Si già sento l'ardor che m'accende (s Senesino, < *Griselda*)
74	157	Damon cease to address me (Sol per te s'amai la pene) (< *Erminia*)
75	158-159	Se vedete i pensier miei (s Senesino, < *Crispus*)
76	160-161	Se voi m'abbandonate (s Senesino, < *Crispus*)
77	162-163	Se ponne le pene (s Robinson, A.)
78	164-165	Su questo man di latte (s Senesino)
79	166-167	Strazo sempia furia e morte (s Durastanti)

Notes:

1. Frontispiece: [within cartouche] ⌠ Apollo's Feast ⌡ Berchet Inventor. H. Hulsbergh Sculpsit. [at foot] London Printed for I. Walsh Servt. to Her Matie. at the Harp and Hoboy in Katherine Street near Somerset House in the Strand.

2. A reissue of songs from 14 books first published by Walsh and Hares or by Walsh under Musick Shops imprint: *Astartus* 111, *Cyrus* 113, *Griselda* 114, *Crispus* 121, *Erminia* 130, *Coriolano* 137, *Vespasian* 138, *Pharnaces* 143, *Calphurnia* 145a and 153, *Aquilio* 147, *Artaxerxes* 150, *Darius* 161, *Elpidia* 164, *Quarterly Collection of Vocal Music* ('Additional Songs in Elpidia') 167.

3. Page numbering is in top centre of each page. Pagination of initial edition remains in top right-hand corner.

4. Songs 17, 38, 55, 65 have English text and song 74 has Italian text added in comparision with initial publication.

5. CLU-C: + 4 additional songs (9 leaves), 'Vile traytor' (see also 127a), 'Deh serbate', 'No non piangete', 'Fairest of creatures', and the flute parts to 'Deh serbate' and 'Fairest of creatures' (1 leaf).

6. D-Hs, Lbl: 'Her' in imprint of frontispiece altered to 'His' in MS.

7. Copies at Lcm (XXXII.D.26 and XXXII.D.27.b), NjP and NN are 1730 or later.

Copies: CLU-C *fM1505.A64 1726; D-B; D-DL; D-Hs M C/86; D-SWl; En BH.203; F-Pn Vm3.216bis; Lbl R.M.13.d.24; MiU; Mp BR f412Ar53.

Plate 173.1 *Monthly Collection of Songs*, 1726

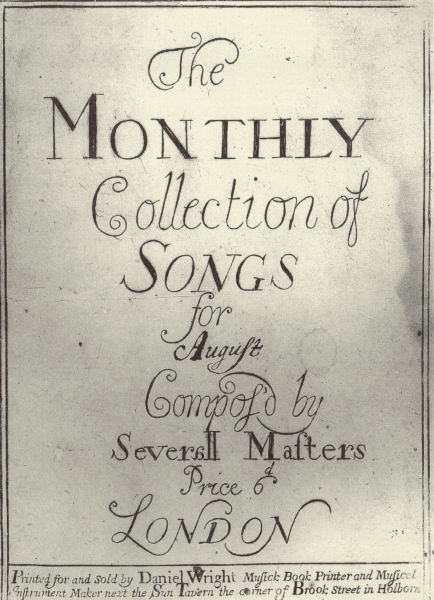

Caption: plate 173.1. 338 x 227 mm. Obh: Mus. E.124.

The Monthly Collection of Songs for ⌠ [August/Septembar/Octobar] ⌡ Compos'd by Severall Masters Price 6d London Printed for and sold by Daniel Wright Musick Book Printer and Musical Instrument Maker next the Sun Tavern the corner of Brook street in Holborn

11 leaves. Pp. August [i]☐ [1]☐-[2]☐; September [i]☐ [1]☐-[3]☐; October [i]☐ [1]☐-[3]☐. Leaves printed on 1 side.
Tallest copy 338 x 227 mm. Vertical chain lines.

One page engraved per plate. Engraving style Mixed.
Title-page plate 273 x 194 mm. Passe-partout no. 17.

Price 6d. per month.

Contents: title-page [i]; songs [1-2]; title-page [i]; songs [1-3]; title-page [i]; songs [1-3].

Songs:

No.	Page	First Line

August
| 1 | [1] | Dimmi cara tu dei morir (s Senesino, < *Scipio*) |
| 2 | [2] | Strephon in vain, thou courtest occasion (s Laguerre, < *Capricious Lover*) |

September
3	[1]	See the yielding fair protesting (s Laguerre, Leveridge, < *Capricious Lover*)
4	[2]	Whine not pine not tell me no more (s Leveridge, Chambers, < *Capricious Lover*)
5	[3]	No thou vain deceiver (s Leveridge, < *Fickle Fair One*)

October
6	[1]	Dum spectas fugio (m Young, C., v Monlass)
7	[2]	Ye gentle gale that fan ye air (m Webb)
8	[3]	Now come love's plagues (s Platt)

Notes:
1. Obh: Mus. E.124 comprises August and October, Mus. E.125 September. Copies are disbound.
2. *The Capricious Lovers* was first performed 8 December 1725. *Scipio* was first published in 1726.

Copies: Obh Mus. E.124; Obh Mus. E.125.

Plate 174.1   Galliard, *Apollo and Daphne*, 1726

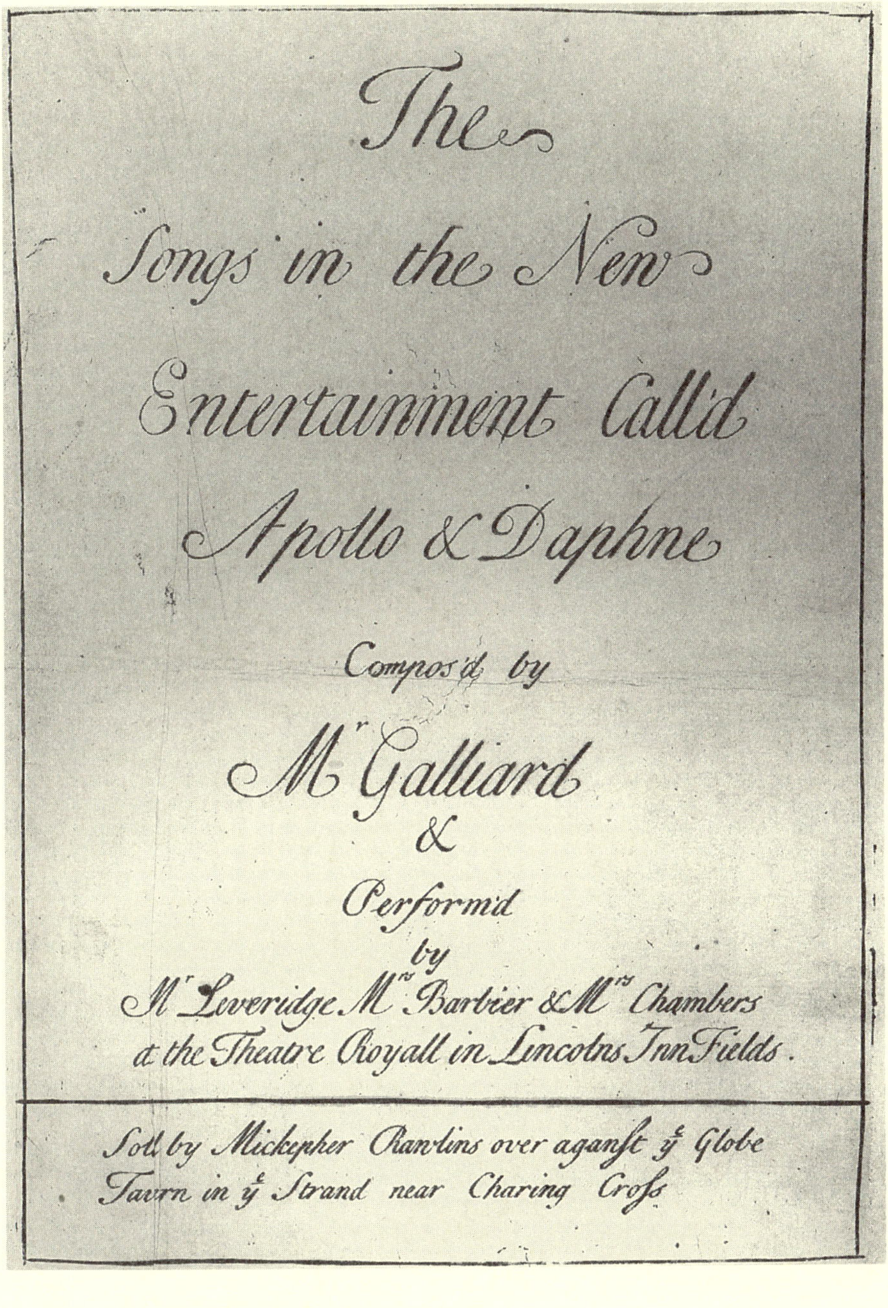

The
Songs in the New
Entertainment Call'd
Apollo & Daphne

Compos'd by

Mr Galliard
&
Perform'd
by
Mr Leveridge Mrs Barbier & Mrs Chambers
at the Theatre Royall in Lincolns Inn Fields.

Sold by Mickepher Rawlins over aganst ye Globe
Tavrn in ye Strand near Charing Cross

Plate 174.2   Galliard, *Apollo and Daphne*, 1726

Caption: plates 174.1-174.2. 348 x 221 mm. Ob: [MS] Mus. Sch. c.97(20).

The Songs in the New Entertainment Call'd Apollo & Daphne Compos'd by Mr Galliard & Perform'd by Mr Leveridge Mrs Barbier & Mrs Chambers at the Theatre Royall in Lincolns Inn Fields. Sold by Michepher Rawlins over aganst ye Globe Tavern in ye Strand near Charing Cross

9 leaves. Pp. [i]▯ [1]▯\▯[2] [3]▯\▯[4] [5]▯-[6]▯ [7] [7A] [8]▯.
Leaves printed on 1 side.
Tallest copy 378 x 241 mm. Vertical chain lines.

One page engraved per plate. Engraving style Rawlins.
Title-page plate 269 x 189 mm.

Contents: title-page [i]; songs [1-7]; flute part [7A]; song [8].

Songs:

No.	Page	First Line
1	[1]	Vain were graces blooming faces (s Barbier, < *Apollo and Daphne*)
2	[2-3]	Daphne shine the queen of love (s Barbier, < *Apollo and Daphne*)
3	[4-5]	Smiling graces plesures gay (s Barbier, < *Apollo and Daphne*)
4	[6]	Tho' envious old age (s Leveridge, < *Apollo and Daphne*)
5	[7-7A]	Farewell mountain lawns & fountains (s Chambers, < *Apollo and Daphne*)
6	[8]	Am'rous kisses lover's pleasure (s Barbier, Chambers, < *Apollo and Daphne*)

Notes:
1. First performed January 1726.
2. NN: p. [6] bound at end.

Copies: NN Berg + Theobald; Ob [MS] Mus. Sch. c.97(20); *RF-Mrg*.

Plate 175.1   Galliard, *Apollo and Daphne*, 1726

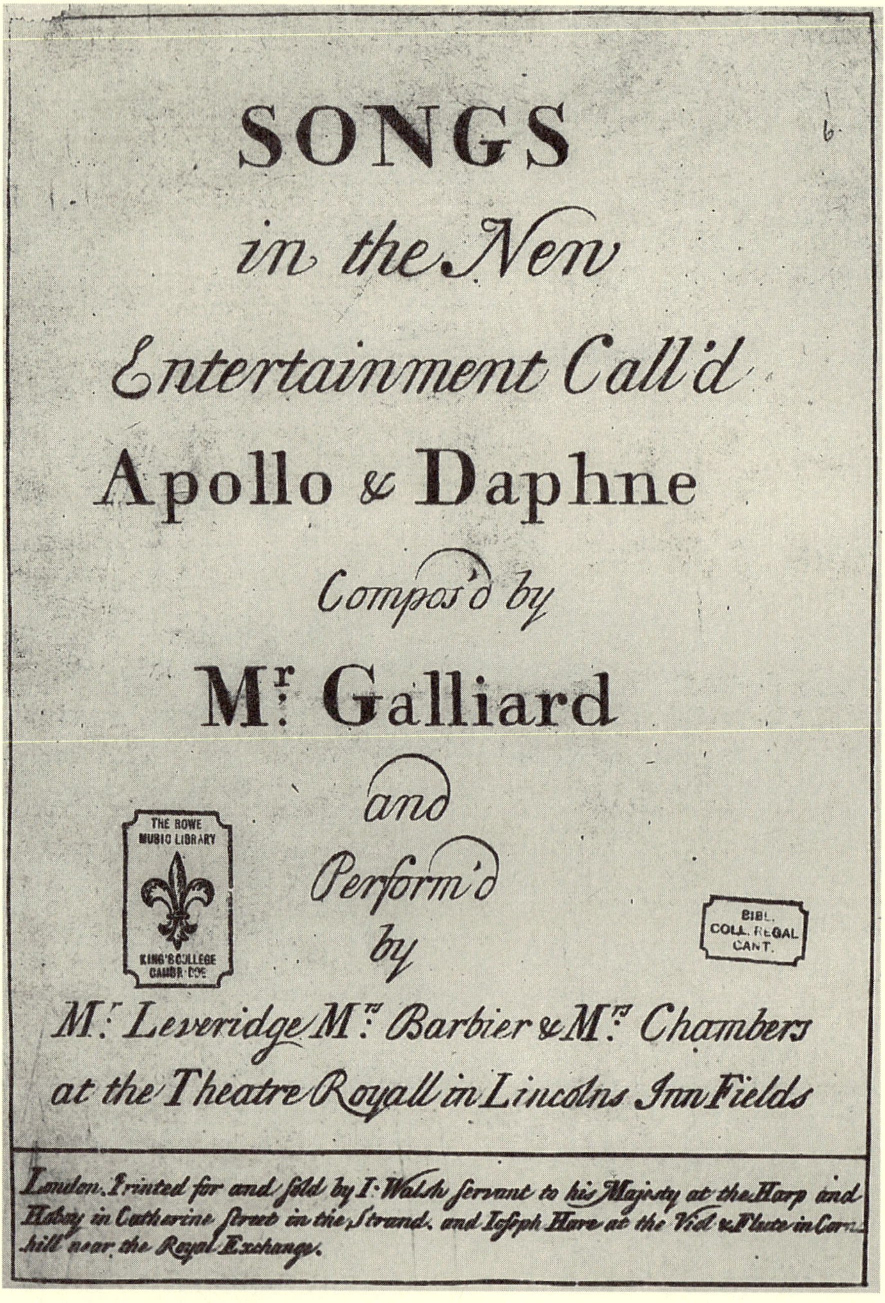

SONGS

in the New

Entertainment Call'd

Apollo & Daphne

Compos'd by

Mr Galliard

THE ROWE
MUSIC LIBRARY

KING'S COLLEGE
CAMBRIDGE

and

Perform'd

by

BIBL.
COLL. REGAL
CANT.

Mr Leveridge Mrs Barbier & Mrs Chambers

at the Theatre Royall in Lincolns Inn Fields

London. Printed for and sold by I. Walsh servant to his Majesty at the Harp and Hoboy in Catherine street in the Strand. and Ioseph Hare at the Viol & Flute in Cornhill near the Royal Exchange.

Caption: plate 175.1. 371 x 230 mm. Ckc: 85.1.(6.).

Songs in the New Entertainment Call'd Apollo & Daphne Compos'd by Mr: Galliard and Perform'd by Mr: Leveridge Mrs: Barbier & Mrs: Chambers at the Theatre Royall in Lincolns Inn Fields London. Printed for and sold by I: Walsh servant to his Majesty at the Harp and Hoboy in Catherine street in the Strand. and Ioseph Hare at the Viol & Flute in Corn-hill near the Royal Exchange.

10 leaves. Pp. [i]□ 1□ \□2-3□\ -\□6-7□\ 8□-9□.
Leaves printed on 1 side.
Tallest copy 371 x 230 mm. Vertical chain lines.

One page engraved per plate. Engraving style Walsh.
Title-page plate 265 x 197 mm.

Walsh ii: 652.

Contents: title-page [i]; songs 1-9.

Songs:

No.	Page	First Line
1	1	Vain were graces blooming faces (s Barbier, < *Apollo and Daphne*)
2	2-3	Daphne shine the queen of love (s Barbier, < *Apollo and Daphne*)
3	4-5	Smiling graces pleasures gay (s Barbier, < *Apollo and Daphne*)
4	6-7	Farewell mountains lawns & fountains (s Chambers, < *Apollo and Daphne*)
5	8	Am'rous kisses lover's pleasure (s Barbier, Chambers, < *Apollo and Daphne*)
6	9	Tho' envious old age (s Leveridge, < *Apollo and Daphne*)

Notes:
1. Lbl: price in MS. on title-page: 0-1-0.
2. Obh: [i]□ 1□-9□. With additional songs 'Hark the huntsman sounds his horn' (p. [10]) and 'Wild as despair the tim'rous Daphne flew' (pp. [11-12]), which has the caption title '(Apollo and Daphne) A Cantata Compos'd by Mr Whichello, The Words by Mr Carey'.
3. Copy at Bp lost.

Copies: Ckc 85.1.(6.); Lbl Ad.MS. 31,588.f.130; Obh Mus. D.3.

Caption: see plate 111.1.

Astartus an Opera as it was Perform'd at the Kings Theatre for the Royal Accademy Compos'd by Bononcini. London Printed for and Sold by I: Walsh Servant to his Majesty at ye Harp & Hoboy in Cathrine-street in ye Strand and I: Hare at ye Viol & Flute in Cornhill near ye Royal Exchange.

43 leaves. Pp. [i]□-[ii]□ 1-80 81□.
Leaves printed on 2 sides.
Tallest copy 347 x 221 mm. Vertical chain lines.

One page engraved per plate. Engraving style Walsh 1, 3.

Contents: title-page [i]; contents and advertisement [ii]; overture 1-4; songs 5-11; symphony 12-14; songs 15-81.

Songs: see 111.

Notes:
1. Pp. 23-24, 27-28, 35-36, 41-43, 58-62 renumbered in top centre 25-26, 91-92, 152-153, 112, 95-96, 27-29, 9-10. Renumbered pages reissued as part of *Apollo's Feast*, book 2, 172, in 1726.
2. F-Pc: pp. 35-36, 41-43 not renumbered; + different edition of 'Amante e sposa' (song 25, pp. 61-62) tipped in between pp. 62-63, and of 'Mio caro ben' (song 11) with English words 'Dear pritty maid' by 'Mr Sunderland' (see 111, Cpl copy) at end.

Copies: D-Hs M C/113/2; F-Pc D.1528(1); F-Pn Vm3.204.

Plate 177.1   Bononcini, *Camilla*, and *Camilla*, Additional Songs, 1726

Berchet Inventor.   H.Hulfbergh Sculpfit.

London Printed for I.Walfh Serv.t to Her Ma.ty at the Harp and Hoboy in Katherine Street near Somerfet Houfe in the Strand.

Plate 177.2 Bononcini, *Camilla*, and *Camilla*, Additional Songs, 1726

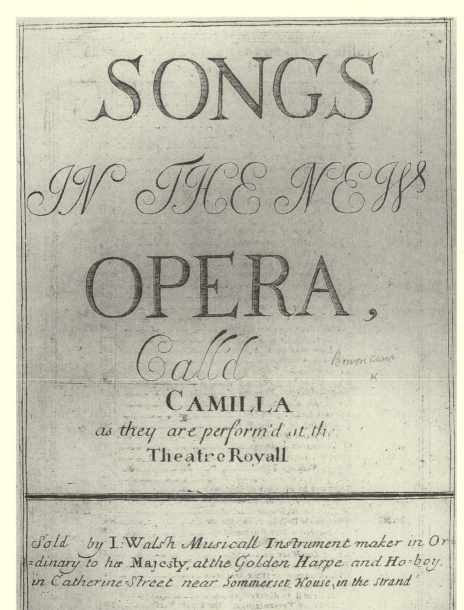

Plate 177.3 Bononcini, *Camilla*, and *Camilla*, Additional Songs, 1726

2

The

Additional

SONGS

in the

OPERA

Bononcini

call'd

CAMILLA

*as it was perform'd at the Theatre
in Lincolns Inn Fields*

London Printed for & sold by I: Walsh Serv.t to his Majesty at the
Harp & Hoboy in Catherine Street in the Strand: ___ and Ioseph Hare
at the Viol and Flute in Cornhill near the Royal Exchange.

463

Caption: plates 177.1-177.3. 321 x 198 mm. Lbl: R.M.11.b.20.

[within cartouche; in MS.] ⌠ Opera of Camilia by Bononcini ⌡ Berchet Inventor. H Hulsbergh Sculpsit. [at foot] London Printed for I. Walsh Servt. to Her Matie. at the Harp and Hoboy in Katherine Street near Somerset House in the Strand.

Songs In The New Opera, Call'd ⌠ Camilla as they are perform'd at the Theatre Royall ⌡ Sold by I. Walsh Musicall Instrument maker in Or==dinary to her Majesty, at the Golden Harpe and Ho=boy, in Catherine-Street near Sommerset House in the Strand

The Additional Songs in the Opera call'd ⌠ Camilla as it was perform'd at the Theatre in Lincolns Inn Fields ⌡ London Printed for & sold by I: Walsh Servt. to his Majesty at the Harp & Hoboy in Catherine Street in the Strand:— and Ioseph Hare at the Viol and Flute in Cornhill near the Royal Exchange

66 leaves. Pp. [i]□ [ii-iii] [1-2] [3]□ 1□-38□ [38A]□ 39□-51□ [52]□-[53]□ [iv]□\□1 2□-3□\□4 5□\□6 7□.
Leaves printed on 1 side.
Tallest copy 322 x 199 mm. Vertical chain lines.

One page engraved per plate. Engraving style Walsh 1, Cross; Walsh 5, 6.
Illus. title-page plate passe-partout no. 2.
Title-page plate 270 x 186 mm. Passe-partout no. 3.
Contents plate 253 x 163 mm.
Second title-page 285 x 179 mm. Passe-partout no. 9.

Walsh i: 298. Walsh ii: 184.

Contents: illus. title-page [i]; title-page [ii]; contents [iii]; overture [1-3]; songs 1-51 [52-53]; second title-page [iv]; songs 1-7.

Songs:

No.	Page	First Line
1	1	I was born of royall race (s Tofts, < *Camilla*)
2	2	O nymph of race divine (s Boy, < *Camilla*)
3	3	Since you from death thus save me (Bononcini, s Boy < *Camilla*)
4	4	Love darts are in your eyes (s Ramondon, < *Camilla*)
5	5	Fortune ever known to vary (s Tofts, < *Camilla*)
6	6	Tender maids your pity show (s Baroness, < *Camilla*)
7	7	Frail are a lovers hopes (s Hughes, < *Camilla*)
8	8	Wellcome sorrow death attending (s Baroness, < *Camilla*)
9	9	All I'le venture to restore ye (s Ramondon, < *Camilla*)
10	10	See the just gods of innocence (s Tofts, < *Camilla*)
11	11	Fair Dorinda happy may'st thou ever be (s Baroness, < *Camilla*)
12	12	Charming fair for thee I languish (s Boy, < *Camilla*)
13	13	Wretched am I, that I gain him (s Tofts, < *Camilla*)

14	14	Among women they for certain know (s Lindsey, < *Camilla*)
15	15	Aged Phillis, wanton still is (s Leveridge, < *Camilla*)
16	16	I languish, I sorrow (s Leveridge, Lindsey, < *Camilla*)
17	17	Ah never yet was known (s Hughes, < *Camilla*)
18	18	Revenge I summon (s Tofts, < *Camilla*)
19	19	In vain I fly from sorrow (s De L'Épine, < *Camilla*)
20	20	To beauty devoted (s Boy, < *Camilla*)
21	21	I love but dare not my flame discover (s Ramondon, < *Camilla*)
22	22	Now Cupid or never be kind (s Hughes, < *Camilla*)
23	23	Fortune like a wanton gipsye (s Leveridge, < *Camilla*)
24	24	Not so much cruelty, I prethee now (s Lindsey, < *Camilla*)
25	25	No love was ever known that (s Baroness, < *Camilla*)
26	26	Joys are attending those cares (s Baroness, < *Camilla*)
27	27	S'en vola il dio d'amore (m Bononcini, s De L'Épine, < *Camilla*)
28	28	Love leads to battle, who dares oppose (s Ramondon, < *Camilla*)
29	29	Ungratefull you fly me, unkindly (s Boy, < *Camilla*)
30	30	Love and ambition strive (s Tofts, < *Camilla*)
31	31	Tullia I feell thy charms (s Leveridge, < *Camilla*)
32	32	Something is in my face so alluring (s Lindsey, < *Camilla*)
33	33	Fly and follow your idol beauty (s Baroness, < *Camilla*)
34	34	O tyrannous jealousy, fly far away (s Hughes, < *Camilla*)
35	35	Happy I love and haste to enjoy her (s Hughes, Boy, < *Camilla*)
36	36	Fly ye virgins th' unfaithfull lover (s Baroness, < *Camilla*)
37	37	These eyes are made so killing (s Lindsey, < *Camilla*)
38	38-[38A]	Thou art he my dearest creature (s Leveridge, Lindsey, < *Camilla*)
39	39	Cupid oh at length reward me (s De L'Épine, < *Camilla*)
40	40	Yes t'is all I want (s Boy, < *Camilla*)
41	41	Floods shall quit the ocean, The (s Hughes, < *Camilla*)
42	42	Dangers ev'ry way surround me (s Tofts, < *Camilla*)
43	43	Be cruel and be jealous (s Turner, < *Camilla*)
44	44	Angers for war declaring (s Baroness, < *Camilla*)
45	45	Tho fierce the lightning flyes (s Ramondon, < *Camilla*)
46	46	Linco's grown another creature (s Leveridge, < *Camilla*)
47	47	Cease cruell tirannizing (s Hughes, < *Camilla*)
48	48	Cease cruell to deceive me (s Baroness, < *Camilla*)
49	49	Cease cruell tirannizing (s Hughes, Baroness, < *Camilla*)
50	50	Fate the more it does depress me (s Tofts, < *Camilla*)
51	51	Let the lightening flashing flying (s Boy, < *Camilla*)
52	[52]	Chi cede al' furore di stelle (s Valentini, < *Camilla*)
53	[53]	Amo per servir, servo per sperar (s Nicolini, < *Camilla*)

Additional Songs:

54	1-3	O tyrannous iealosye (s Barbier, < *Camilla*)
55	4-5	O fear complying and ne'er beleive (s Chambers, < *Camilla*)
56	6-7	Guardian pow'rs descend (s Fletcher, < *Camilla*)

Notes:

1. Performers of the *Additional Songs* are those of the revival that began on 19 November 1726.
2. Passe-partout title-page to *Additional Songs* is reworking of Walsh and Hares' 'The favourite Songs' passe-partout title-page first used in 1721.
3. No dimensions are given for the illustrated title-page plate as the image in the Lbl copy is slightly cropped.
4. Lbl: - pp. 3 (2nd sequence). Pp. 1-3 (1st sequence), 5-8, 10, 12-18, 20, 22-24, 26-28, 30-31, 33-36, 38, 39-41, 44, 47-51 numbered in MS. Pp. 11, 19, 21, and 39 are from the Cullen edition engraved by Cross.
5. TWm: - p. [38A]; + p. 39 in the Cullen edition engraved by Cross, following p. 39. Pp. 5-10, 12-14, 16-18, 20-22, 24, 26-28, 30-31, 35-36, 38-39, 39-41, 43-44, 47-51 numbered in MS. Pp. 33-34 printed on a single leaf.
6. Copy listed in *RISM* at Ob does not exist.

Copies: *B-MAR*; Lbl R.M.11.b.20; TWm —.

The

favourite SONGS

in the new OPERA

Call'd ELISA

as also

the Additional Songs

in the OPERA *of*

RODELINDA

Compos'd by

M.r Handel

BIBL.
COLL. REGAL
CANT.

as they are perform'd at the

KINGS THEATRE

for the Royal Accademy

London. Printed for and sold by In.o Walsh servant to his Majesty at the Harp &
Hoboy in Catherine street in the Strand, and Joseph Hare at the Viol and Flute in
Cornhill near the Royal Exchange.

Caption: plate 178.1. 374 x 234 mm. Ckc: 85.1.(7.).

The favourite Songs in the new Opera Call'd Elisa as also the Additional Songs in the Opera of Rodelinda Compos'd by Mr: Handel as they are perform'd at the Kings Theatre for the Royal Accademy London. Printed for and sold by Ino. Walsh servant to his Majesty at the Harp and Hoboy in Catherine street in the Strand. and Ioseph Hare at the Viol and Flute in Cornhill near the Royal Exchange.

24 leaves. Pp. [i]□-[ii]□ \ □1-2□\ - \□5-6□\ 7□ \ □8-9□\ - \□14-15□\ 16□ \ □17-18□\ - \□21-22□\.
Leaves printed on 1 side.
Tallest copy 374 x 234 mm. Vertical chain lines.

One page engraved per plate. Engraving style Walsh 4, 6.
Title-page plate 271 x 196 mm.
Contents plate 150 x 180 mm.

Walsh ii: 598.

Contents: title-page [i]; contents and advertisement [ii]; songs 1-22.

Songs:

No.	Page	First Line
1	1-2	Per te nel caro nido (s Cuzzoni, < *Elisa*)
2	3-4	Va lusingando amore (s Cuzzoni, < *Elisa*)
3	5-6	Timada pastorella (s Cuzzoni, < *Elisa*)
4	7	Per voi care pupille di nobille (s Senesino, < *Elisa*)
5	8-9	Apre il seno (s Cuzzoni, < *Elisa*)
6	10-13	Nobil onda (s Cuzzoni, < *Elisa*)
7	14-15	Vivi tiranno (s Senesino, < *Rodelinda*)
8	16	Ahi perchè quisto ciel, (s Cuzzoni, < *Rodelinda*)
9	17-18	D'ogni crudel martir (s Cuzzoni, < *Rodelinda*)
10	19-20	So no i colpi della sorte (s Cuzzoni, < *Rodelinda*)
11	21-22	Si rivedrò (s Senesino, < *Rodelinda*)

Note:
1. En: - p. [i].

Copies: Ckc 85.1.(7.); En BH.90.

178a   Porpora, Handel, *Elisa,* and *Additional Songs to Rodelinda,*
31 December 1726

Caption: see plate 178.1.

The favourite Songs in the new Opera Call'd Elisa as also the Additional Songs in the Opera of Rodelinda Compos'd by Mr: Handel as they are perform'd at the Kings Theatre for the Royal Accademy London. Printed for and sold by Ino. Walsh servant to his Majesty at the Harp and Hoboy in Catherine street in the Strand. and Ioseph Hare at the Viol and Flute in Cornhill near the Royal Exchange.

14 leaves. Pp. [i]⬚ \⬚1-2⬚\-\⬚5-6⬚\ 7⬚ \⬚8-9⬚\-\⬚12-13⬚\.
Leaves printed on 1 side.
Tallest copy 342 x 222 mm. Vertical chain lines.

One page engraved per plate. Engraving style Walsh 4, 6.

Walsh ii: 598.

Contents: title-page [i]; songs 1-13.

Songs:

No.	Page	First Line
1	1-2	Per te nel caro nido (s Cuzzoni, < *Elisa*)
2	3-4	Va lusingando amore (s Cuzzoni, < *Elisa*)
3	5-6	Timada pastorella (s Cuzzoni, < *Elisa*)
4	7	Per voi care pupille di nobille (s Senesino, < *Elisa*)
5	8-9	Apre il seno (s Cuzzoni, < *Elisa*)
6	10-13	Nobil onda (s Cuzzoni, < *Elisa*)

Notes:
1. In comparison with **178** omits content and advertisement page and songs from *Rodelinda*.
2. A-Wn has similar copy of *Elisa* only but with *Monthly Mask of Vocal Music* title-page and Barret label (M.S.10230).

Copy: D-Hs M B/2620/14.

Caption: see plate 114.1.

Griselda an Opera as it was Perform'd at the Kings Theatre for the Royal Accademy Compos'd by Mr: Bononcini. Published by the Author. London Printed and Sold by I: Walsh Servant to his Majesty at the Harp and Hoboy in Catherine-Street in the Strand, and Ino: and Ioseph Hare at the Viol & Flute in Cornhill near the Royal Exchange.

40 leaves. Pp. [i]□ [ii] 1-75 76□.
Leaves printed on 2 sides.
Tallest copy 346 x 215 mm. Vertical chain lines.

One page engraved per plate. Engraving style Walsh 1, 3.

Contents: title-page [i]; contents and advertisement [ii]; overture 1-6; songs 7-76.

Songs: see 114.

Note:
1. Of the 11 songs (nos. 1-8, 16, 22, and 25) from *Griselda* that were reissued as part of *Apollo's Feast*, book 2, 172, on September 16, 1726, with additional pagination at the top centre of the page, 7 songs in this copy carry all or part of that additional pagination. The affected pages are: 8-11, 14-17, 22-27, which have the numbers 2, 115-117, 5, 190-191, 204, 97-99, 154-156, respectively, in the top centre of the page.

Copy: D-Hs M C/113/1.

Plate 180.1   Carey, *Works*, 1726

THE

WORKS

OF

Mr. Henry Carey.

The Second Edition.

LONDON:
Printed in the Year MDCCXXVI.

Caption: plate 180.1. 330 x 235 mm. Lbl: H.1619.

[letterpress] The Works Of Mr. Henry Carey. The Second Edition. London: Printed in the Year MDCCXXVI.

26 leaves. Pp. [i]☐-[ii]☐ 1-32 [33-46] [47]☐.
Leaves printed on 2 sides.
Tallest copy 330 x 235 mm. Mixed chain lines.

One page engraved per plate. Engraving style Bates, Walsh.
Title-page letterpress.

Contents: title-page [i]; dedication [ii]; cantata 1-7; songs 8-10; cantata 11-13; songs 14-24; cantata 25-29; recitative and arias 30-32; songs [33-47].

Songs:

No.	Page	First Line
1	8-9	This is the day
2	9-10	Pass the glass around with pleasure
3	14-15	What shall he have that kill'd the deer (v Shakespear, s Ray)
4	16-17	Turn away mine eyes
5	18	Make haste, and away mine only dear
6	19	See! the morning gives you warning
7	20	On a grassy pillow
8	21	Gardez vous bien bergere (O nymph divinely charming)
9	22-23	Come all ye jolly bacchanals
10	24	Merry land by this light, A
11	[33]	Saw you the nymph whom I adore (m Carey)
12	[34-35]	Flocks are sporting doves are courting (m Carey, v Carey, s Carey)
13	[36]	Come my dainty doxies (m Carey)
14	[37]	All in the downs the fleet was moor'd (m Carey)
15	[38]	Waft me, some soft and cooling breeze (m Carey)
16	[39]	Tho' cruel you seem to my pain (m Carey, v Carey)
17	[40]	Sad Musidora all in woe (m Carey, v Lady)
18	[41]	Of all the girls that are so smart (m Carey, v Carey)
19	[42]	Twas when the sun began to shine (m Carey, v Carey)
20	[43]	Here's to thee my boy (m Carey, v Gentleman)
21	[44]	Happy the youthfull swain (m Carey, v Carey)
22	[45]	I'll range arround the shady bowrs (m Carey, v Carey)
23	[46]	Farewell the fatal pleasures (m Carey, v Lady)
24	[47]	Young Philoret and Celia met (m Carey, v Wilks)

Notes:
1. Recitative and arias are from 'Harlequin Doctor Faustus the words by Mr Booth'.
2. The first edition was published as *Cantatas*, 136, in 1724.
3. P. 19 plate in different state from 136; tempi have been added.

Copy: Lbl H.1619.

Indexes

1 First lines and translations

References are to entry numbers followed by song numbers in brackets. Original spelling maintained except in cases of differences between editions when the most correct form printed is used. English initial articles are inverted to end of line. In filing, initial apostrophes and medial punctuation are ignored.

Alass you strive to heal in vain 5 (383)
Albacinda, drew the dart 5 (8)
Alfin potrò morire 108 (32)
All beauty were a foolish toy 5 (382),
8-11 (18)
All fiero mio tormento 69 (34), 80-80a (34),
91-92 (34)
All hail imperiall love 85 (16), 103 (16)
All I'le venture to restore ye 13 (14), 16 (9), 18
(14), 19-23 (9), 33a-35 (9),
62-63 (9), 79-79a (9), 177 (9)
All in the downs the fleet was moor'd 109 (4),
180 (14)
All in the land of cyder 99 (101)
All the materials are the same 104 (4)
All the world's in strife and hurry 99 (87)
All things seem deaf to my complaints 5
(244), 8-11 (9)
All wee here whose names sir 55-55a (17)
All ye pleasures Himen brings 5 (246)
All you that must take a leap in the dark 99
(85)
Alla fama dimi il vero 144-45 (45),
169-70 (25)
All'ombre alle catene 69 (30), 80-80a (30),
91-92 (30)
Alma mia si sol tu sei 144-45 (20)
Alma ostinata crudele e spietata 75-75a (11),
90b (11)
Alone by a lonely willow 171 (43)
Altro da voi non chiedo 107 (3)
Amante e sposa si gli sarai 111-12 (25), 172
(5), 176 (25)
Amante stravagante 160 (27)
Amanti voi ch'andante 84 (41)
Amarti non degg'io 127 (7)
Amarti si vorrei 160 (33)
Amazing change what do I see 85 (21), 103
(21)
Ambition cease t'alarm me 85 (12), 103 (12)
Ami pur che vuol goder 75-75a (36), 90b (36)
Amis cesses de disputer 134 (12)
Amo per servir, servo per sperar 62-63 (53),
79-79a (53), 177 (53)
Among women they for certain know 15 (3),
16 (14), 19-23 (14), 33a-35 (14), 62-63
(14), 79-79a (14), 177 (14)
Amongst the pure ones all 5 (19), 33 (5)
Amor accende in petto 89 (12)
Amor consolami ne più tardar' 84 (12)
Amor deh lasciami 166-67 (7), 172 (7)
Amor vieni o mostrarvi 113 (5), 172 (4)
Amore inganna 75-75a (33), 90b (33)
Amorosa farfalletta 108 (37)
Amorous swain to Juno pray'd, An 5 (1)
Amour cruel tiran des coeurs 134 (17)
Amour, je te croyois le souverain des coeurs
134 (16)
Am'rous kisses lover's pleasure 174 (6), 175
(5)

And gin ye meet a bonny lassie 168 (27)
And in each track of glory 5 (18), 157 (18)
And wale' up yon bank 168 (34)
And you Dorisbe 26 (6), 29-31 (6), 78a-b (6),
90 (6)
Angers for war declaring 15 (17), 16 (44),
19-23 (44), 33a-35 (44), 62-63 (44),
79-79a (44), 177 (44)
Ann thou were my ain thing 168 (23)
Ape, a lyon, a fox and an ass, An 55-55a (43)
Apollo pray tell me that is if you can sir
101-102 (16)
Appear all ye gods on ye plain 159 (8)
Appear all ye graces 48a-52 (13), 57-58 (13),
94 (13), 144-45 (25)
Appointed hour of promis'd bliss, The 5 (180)
Apre il seno 178-78a (5)
Arder per me tu poi 114 (10), 179 (10)
Arise ye subtle forms that sport 135a-c (1)
Armateui di vezzi 83 (24)
Aron thus propos'd to Moses 73 (16)
Around her see Cupid flying 15 (9), 16 (27),
19-23 (27), 33a-35 (28), 62-63 (27),
79-79a (27), 144-45 (13)
As Amoret with Phillis sat 144-45 (62)
As buxom Susan milk'd ye brindl'd cow 159
(27)
As Cupid rogishly one day 5 (16), 8-11 (89)
As early I walk'd on the first of sweet May 168
(4)
As from a rock past all relief 168 (29)
As gentle turtle doves 168 (15)
As I came down the High-Land Town 95 (3),
99 (81)
As I walk'd forth to view the plain 99 (111)
As I was a walking all round cross ye park 171
(6)
As I was walking, I heard a maid talking 99
(47)
As I went forth to view the spring 95 (4)
As Jockey and Jenny together was laid 95 (2)
As o'er the hollow valts we walk 37-38 (1), 81
(1)
As Oyster Nan stood by her tub 5 (20), 33 (4)
As Roger last night to Jenny lay close 73 (39)
As roses shew more pale with dew 12a (18),
26 (3), 29-31 (3),
78a-b (3), 90 (3)
As tipling John 70 (8), 99 (2)
As walking forth to view the plain 168 (22)
Assetato pelegrino 107 (25)
Assist ye furys from the deep 26 (20), 29-31
(20), 78a-b (20), 90 (20)
Astrea by her conqu'ring charms 24-24a (5)
At noon in a sultry summer's day 5 (17), 99
(82)
At Polwart on the green 168 (24)
At the break of morning light 99 (13)
At the sight of my Phillis 110 (8)
Aure voi che m'ascoltate 138 (4), 139-41 (1),

By those pigsneyes that starrs do seem 8-11 (96), 33 (111)

Caderà la belva ria 108 (2)
Cælia let not pride undoe you 5 (31)
Cælia with mournful pleasure hears 5 (311)
Cælia, hence with affectation 99 (108)
Calms appear when storms are past 5 (247)
Can life be a blessing or worth the possessing 8-11 (80)
Can you leave ranging 40 (9), 40a (40), 42 (40), 44-45 (41), 82 (41), 126a (41), 144-45 (28)
Can you now leave me and so deceive me 144-45 (66)
Cangia la sorte 88 (5), 90a (5)
Cara bella tù di me 88 (9), 90a (9)
Cara oh dio almen potessi 161-62 (7), 172 (15)
Cara si ch'ogn'or sarà 69 (7), 80-80a (7), 91-92 (7)
Cara speme questo core 160 (12)
Cara sposa amato bene 144-45 (65)
Care is fled dispairs no more 33a-35 (17)
Care pupille tra mille e mille 111-12 (9), 172 (13), 176 (9)
Cares on a crown attending 40a (15), 42 (15), 43 (4), 43a (8), 44-45 (15), 82 (15), 105 (2), 126a (15)
Cares when they'r over 53-54 (42), 59 (42), 79b (42), 123 (42)
Carle he came o'er the craft, The 168 (46)
Caro addio dal labbro amato 114 (18), 179 (18)
Caro dardo gia l'alma che langue 108 (14)
Caro se fido tu mi credi 49-52 (30), 57-58 (30), 94 (30)
Cease cruel tyrannising 5 (394), 14 (5, 7), 16 (47, 49), 19-23 (47, 49), 33a-35 (47, 49), 62-63 (47, 49), 79-79a (47, 49), 177 (47, 49)
Cease cruell to deceive me 5 (395), 14 (6), 16 (48), 19-23 (48), 33a-34a (48), 35 (50), 62-63 (48), 79-79a (48), 177 (48)
Cease injurious maids, to blame 135a (4), 135b-c (5)
Cease o Cupid thus to obraid me 53-54 (17), 59 (17), 79b (17), 123 (17)
Cease of Cupid to complain 5 (236), 8-11 (1), 33 (17)
Cease that inchanting song 5 (370)
Cease to love me 53-54 (13), 59 (13), 79b (13), 123 (13)
Cease, you pert asses, your apish addresses 104 (8)
Cease your amrous pipes, and flutes 5 (41)
Cease your vain teizing 96-98 (5)
Cedo ma pur mi chiama 119-20 (5), 122 (5)
Celebrate this festival 5 (47), 157 (3)
Celemene is both fair and young 5 (314)
Celemene, pray tell me 5 (282)

Celestiall harmony is in her tongue 5 (49)
Celia has a thousand charms 5 (46), 157 (2)
Celia is soft, she's charming too 5 (281)
Celia my dearest no longer depress me 159 (18)
Celia my heart has often rang'd 5 (44)
Celia now is all my song 5 (367)
Celia you in vain deceive me 5 (45)
Celias bright beautys all other's transcend 5 (39), 33 (9)
Celia's charms are past expressing 24-24a (9)
Celia's easy free and gay 104 (10)
Celia's smiles will quite undoe me 33 (15)
Celinda's beauty voice and witt 5 (51)
Celladon when spring came on 5 (30), 33 (21), 95 (10)
Cessa o mai di sospirar 169-70 (17)
Cessez mes chers amis 134 (5)
Chains of love I wear, The 40a (32), 42 (32), 43 (19), 44-45 (33), 82 (33), 126a (33), 144-45 (11)
Charmer at last be kind 46-47a (35), 93 (35)
Charmer hear your faithful lover 137 (7), 144-45 (6), 172 (65)
Charmer if faithfull thou'lt beleive me 48a-52 (30), 57-58 (30), 94 (30)
Charmer if I ever leave you 171 (2)
Charmer now ease me 144-45 (44)
Charmer why do you fly me 46-47a (15), 93 (15)
Charming Celia cruel maid 87 (1)
Charming creature, every feature 5 (389), 12-12a (2), 26 (14), 29-31 (14), 78a-b (14), 90 (14)
Charming creature look more kindly 5 (38)
Charming, fair Amoret 5 (310)
Charming fair for thee I languish 5 (393), 14 (3), 16 (12), 19-23 (12), 33a-35 (12), 62-63 (12), 79-79a (12), 177 (12)
Charming is your shape and air 144-45 (22)
Charming Phyllis brisk and gay, The 5 (272)
Charming roses flowry treasures 32-32a (1)
Charming Silvia ever is kind, The 101-102 (2)
Charms of bright beauty, The 5 (179), 109 (13)
Che bel piacere poter godere 161-62 (5), 172 (19)
Che bella fedeltà 121 (6), 125-26 (6)
Che diresti a navicella 89 (28)
Che farai misero core 84 (30)
Che forse porterà 108 (29)
Che giova fuggire 114 (15), 179 (15)
Che mi dispezza fido 74-74a (6)
Che'affanno tiranno 64-65 (20), 68 (20), 76a-78 (20)
Chear up my brave hearts 99 (96), 109 (2)
Chi cede al'furore di stelle 62-63 (52), 79-79a (52), 177 (52)
Chi perde ogni suo bene 107 (5)
Chi perde un momento 160 (16)

Fair are soonest pierc'd wth golden darts, The 171 (36)

Fair Aurelias gon astray, The 5 (187)

Fair brillante brightest creature 106 (17)

Fair Cloe my breast so alarms 5 (72), 157 (22)

Fair Dorinda happy may'st thou ever be 13 (9), 16 (11), 18 (9), 19-23 (11), 33a-35 (11), 62-63 (11), 79-79a (11), 177 (11)

Fairest charmer lovely dear 106 (13)

Fairest of creatures 146 (3), 153 (11)

Falsa imagine m'ingannasti 159 (25), 169-70 (1)

Fame sound to ye farthest land 106 (2)

Fammi prouar 69 (21), 80-80a (21), 91-92 (21)

Fan me ye gentle zephyrs 53-54 (19), 79b (19), 123 (19)

Far from thee be anxious care 5 (284)

Farewel deluding pleasure 144-45 (32)

Farewell, Cloe, o farewell 99 (5)

Farewell love and all soft pleasure 40 (17), 40a (42), 42 (42), 43a (24), 44-45 (43), 82 (43), 99 (43), 126a (43)

Farewell mountains lawns & fountains 174-75 (4)

Farewell my bonny, witty pretty, Moggy 5 (59), 33 (31), 95 (11)

Farewell the fatal pleasures 180 (23)

Farewell vaine nymph 5 (65), 33 (92)

Farewell Venus wellcome pleasure 96-98 (8)

Farò che si penta d'auerti adorato 69 (11), 80-80a (11), 91-92 (11)

Farwell Cloe o farewell 109 (12)

Fatal change! what do I see? 85 (14), 103 (14)

Fate the more it does depress me 15 (18), 16 (50), 19-23 (50), 33a-35 (51), 62-63 (50), 79-79a (50), 177 (50)

Fate voi ancor così 161-62 (3), 172 (30)

Fato imperante 64-65 (8), 68 (8), 76a-78 (8)

Fear no danger to insue 5 (238), 33 (30)

Fear not mortall none shall harm thee 5 (286), 8-11 (37)

Fenchè lo strale (see Benchè)

Fickle bliss! fantastick treasure 110 (6)

Fier destin di chi ben ama 83 (1)

Figli d'un bel valore 111-12 (1), 176 (1)

Figurati estinti 159 (17)

Fill all the glasses, fill e'm high 5 (71), 8-11 (73), 33 (90), 56 (7)

Fill every glass and recommend em 56 (15)

Fill the glass let hautboys sound 56 (2)

Fill up the mightly sparkling bowl 99 (6)

Fill your glass drink apace 101-102 (13)

Fill your glasses, and dround whineing love 101-102 (10)

Fin ch'ei stringe la spada rubella 127 (5), 137 (4)

Find me a lonely cave 8-11 (20)

Fiorite erbette ombrose piante 107 (18)

Firm as a rock above the ocean seen 6 (5), 8-11 (56)

Fixt on ye fair Miranda's eies 5 (62)

Flatt'ring intruder, smiling deluder 99 (80)

Flocks are sporting doves are courting 180 (12)

Floods shall quit the ocean, The 15 (2), 16 (41), 19-23 (41), 33a-35 (42), 62-63 (41), 79-79a (41), 177 (41)

Fly and follow your idol beauty 14 (1), 16 (33), 19-23 (33), 33a-35 (34), 62-63 (33), 79-79a (33), 177 (33)

Fly from Dorinda's beauteous face 5 (317)

Fly from his charming language fly 5 (68)

Fly me not Silvia 172 (17)

Fly swift ye hours 157 (6)

Fly ye happy shepherds fly 8-11 (94)

Fly ye lazy hours 5 (60), 8-11 (74)

Fly ye virgins th' unfaithfull lover 14 (9), 16 (36), 19-23 (36), 33a-35 (37), 62-63 (36), 79-79a (36), 177 (36)

Fly ye winged cupids fly 5 (320)

Folle e incauto mai dal lido 88 (7), 90a (7)

Folle tu perirai 108a (24)

Follow, nymphs & swains 171 (4)

Fond love has gain'd my heart 46-47a (48), 93 (48)

Fond moments false pleasure 46-47a (52), 93 (52)

Fond woman with mistaken art 5 (69), 33 (26)

Fool me fond hope no more 53-54 (11), 79b (11), 123 (11)

Foolish swain, thy sighs forbear 99 (46)

Fop with monkey graces 105 (5)

For Iris I sigh and hourely dye 5 (319)

For me love has decreed her 48a-52 (48), 57-58 (49), 94 (48)

For mighty Loves unerring dart 5 (318)

For rurall and sincerer joys 5 (70)

For thee ye rilling waters weep 85 (1), 103 (1)

For thy ferry boat Charon 26 (5), 29-31 (5), 78a-b (5), 90 (5)

For you who are rid by the fury, love 8-11 (90), 33 (89)

Forbear o goddess of desire 5 (285)

Forth from my dark and dismall cell 5 (63), 157 (7)

Fortune boldly aims at all 48a-52 (36), 57-58 (39), 94 (36)

Fortune bright queen o'th skies 53-54 (6), 59 (6), 79b (6), 123 (6)

Fortune ever known to vary 14 (4), 16 (5), 19-23 (5), 33a-35 (5), 62-63 (5), 79-79a (5), 177 (5)

Fortune like a wanton gipsy 13 (11), 16 (23), 18 (11), 19-23 (23), 33a-35 (24), 62-63 (23), 79-79a (23), 177 (23)

Frail are a lovers hopes 14 (16), 16 (7), 19-23 (7), 33a-35 (7), 62-63 (7), 79-79a (7), 177 (7)

Frank what shall we do 5 (64), 33 (28), 55-55a (10)

Freedom thou greatest blessing 40-40a (1), 42 (1), 44-45 (1), 82 (1), 126a (1), 144-45 (24)

Freindly shades where peace is dwelling 64-65 (16), 68 (16), 76a-78 (16)

From a shamefull death to ease him 64-65 (18), 68 (18), 76a-78 (18)

From Aud'nard fam'd battel 55-55a (7)

From grave lessons and restraint 5 (399), 99 (37)

From love from thought from business free 24-24a (12)

From me from thee he turns his eyes 85 (17), 103 (17)

From rosie bow'rs where sleeps the god of love 5 (61), 157 (5)

From silent shad's and the Elizium groves 5 (66), 157 (8)

From this happy day 6 (3), 8-11 (8)

From twenty to thirty 73 (29)

Fuggi un tiranno si 108 (4)

Fuggir dal fato che vuol no'l sà 107 (31)

Fugirò la spietata crudele 49-52 (49), 57-58 (48), 94 (49)

Full of sorrow vexation & anguish 64-65 (1), 68 (1), 76a-78 (1)

Furie del'Erebo, sù laceratemi 49-52 (43), 57-58 (43), 94 (43)

Furie terribbili 75-75a (12), 90b (12)

Furies infernal quickly come tear me 48a-52 (43), 57-58 (43), 94 (43)

Fy nay prithee John 55-55a (23), 73 (6)

Fye Amarillis cease to greive 5 (58), 8-11 (28)

Fye, Damon leave this foolish passion 5 (67), 33 (27)

Gardez vous bien bergere 136 (8), 180 (8)

Gay kind and airy 46-47a (23), 93 (23)

Gazing on my idol treasure 160 (18)

Gen'rous wine, and a friend 144-45 (77)

Genius of England, from thy pleasant bow'r 157 (9)

Gentle sighs awhile releive us 48a-52 (15), 57-58 (15), 94 (15)

Gentle slumbers life releiving 96-98 (10)

Gentle warmth comes o're my heart, A 5 (3)

Gently touch the warb'ling lyre 159 (5)

Gently treat my sorrow 40-40a (5), 42 (5), 44-45 (5), 82 (5), 126a (5)

Germano addio 49-52 (51), 94 (51)

Ghosts of ev'ry occupation 135a (5), 135b (2), 135c (4), 144-45 (49)

Già col vostro rigor 143 (7), 172 (31)

Già doppo l'orrore 160 (24)

Già preparai gl'inganni 75-75a (8), 90b (8)

Gin thou wert my ene thing 95 (5)

Gioia e contento 53-54 (26), 59 (26), 79b (26), 123 (26)

Giunse al fin quel dì bramato 127 (24), 137 (15)

Give or take my life my dear 48a-52 (29), 57-58 (29), 94 (29)

Give us noble ale 56 (13)

Give way to pleasure 46-47a (13), 93 (13)

Give your love to him deserves it 64-65 (11), 68 (11), 76a-78 (11)

Gloriana is engaging fair 5 (73)

Glory our martial paradice 5 (241)

Glory strives the field is won 38 (31), 81 (31)

Go falsest of thy sex be gone 87 (4), 99 (41)

Go leave me thou faithless perjur'd maid 160 (20)

Go perjur'd man 5 (287), 33 (93)

Go sheperd you're a rover 46-47a (18), 93 (18)

Go soft spell inchant her mind 101-102 (5)

Go vind the vicar of Taunton Dean 99 (9)

God preserve her Majesty 55-55a (61)

God preserve his majesty 73 (13)

Godan l'alme, goda il regno 84 (42)

Gode l'anima nel mirarti 75-75a (35), 90b (35)

Godo o'cara ma d'un'diletto 84 (27)

Godrò se non m'inganna 69 (38), 80-80a (38), 91-92 (38)

Good buy t'ye good night t'ye 64-65 (15), 68 (15), 76a-78 (15)

Good indeed the herb's good weed 55-55a (4), 73 (5)

Gran nume de pastori 107 (14)

Grands favoris du Dieu du vin 134 (3)

Great Bacchus is mighty in giving us wine 73 (11)

Great Cæsar is crown'd 99 (88)

Great god of love oh set me free 171 (29)

Great Jove look down 5 (250)

Great Lord Frog to Lady Mouse 99 (7)

Great love I adore thee 48a-52 (14), 57-58 (14), 94 (14)

Great love is immortal 53-54 (14), 79b (14), 123 (14)

Greatness leave me, undeceive me 5 (400), 12-12a (6), 26 (29), 29-31 (29), 78a-b (29), 90 (29)

Gregoire est yure, Amis 134 (31)

Guardian pow'rs descend 177 (56)

Guilt does of peace bereave me 64-65 (31), 68 (31), 76a-78 (31)

Ha! well hast thou done 5 (371)

Had she not care enough 55-55a (55), 73 (46)

Hail happy day, welcome bless'd morn 124 (6)

Hail happy pair, great Pelops and Arsinoe 26 (36), 29-31 (36), 78a-b (36), 90 (36)

Halt when love and honour call you 40 (15), 40a (39), 42 (39), 44-45 (40), 82 (40), 126a (40)

Han posto i tuoi bei lumi 138 (28), 172 (32)
Happy Britains, seated here 33 (94)
Happy ever, happy wee 5 (252)
Happy he who void of love 26 (7), 29-31 (7),
78a-b (7), 90 (7)
Happy I love and haste to enjoy her 15 (13),
16 (35), 19-23 (35), 33a-35 (36), 62-63
(35), 79-79a (35), 177 (35)
Happy mansions pleasant shades 5 (251)
Happy page, the lovely boy, The 5 (358)
Happy the youthfull swain 180 (21)
Happy thou of human race 8-11 (38)
Happy wee who free from love 5 (77)
Happy's the love that meets return 168 (19)
Hark Harry tis late 55-55a (9), 73 (31)
Hark how the muses call aloud 1-3 (1), 8-11
(91)
Hark how the voice of fame 85 (10), 103 (10)
Hark, Lewis groans, good Fader, wat ailsh
him 99 (61)
Hark Prince Eugine com's along 5 (84), 33
(34)
Hark the bonny Christ Church bells 55-55a
(21), 73 (26)
Hark the cock crow'd 5 (76), 33 (35)
Hark the hollow groves resounding 85 (20),
103 (20)
Hark the trumpet sounds alarms 5 (75)
Harken and I will tell you how 168 (28)
Hast thou not read in ancient story 99 (49)
Hast o sun, o quickly fly 48a-52 (27), 57-58
(27), 94 (27)
Haste, give me wings 8-11 (76)
Hated strife, and rebells life, A 26 (16), 29-31
(16), 78a-b (16), 90 (16)
Haul away let your anchors be weighing 109
(3)
Haura'il porto dei diletti 69 (37), 80-80a (37),
91-92 (37)
Haveua l'idol mio bel volto e cor fedel 84 (40)
He comes victorious Henry comes 37-38 (4),
81 (4)
He led her by the milk-white hand 5 (254)
He smiles, he dreams 85 (24), 103 (24)
He that has whom he lov'd possest 5 (86),
8-11 (50)
He that marries a lass for love and a face 99
(79)
Heal o heal the wounds you gave her 48a-52
(4), 57-58 (4), 94 (4)
Hear me love my sorrows ending 85 (26), 103
(26)
Hear me, ye nymphs, and every swain 168 (3)
Hear ye midnight fantomes 5 (74), 8-11 (48),
33 (95)
Heart so unrepenting, A 38 (37), 81 (37)
Heaven first created woman to be kind
101-102 (19)
Heaven itselfe may order change 64-65 (17),
68 (17), 76a-78 (17)

Hee, oh! pray father 5 (323)
Help oh help ye powr's divine 8-11 (49)
Hence ye curst infernal train 5 (324)
Her bright eyes are starrs that charm us
48a-52 (16), 57-58 (16), 94 (16)
Her eyes are like the morning bright 5 (321),
8-11 (27)
Her lovely face enchains me 48a-52 (19),
57-58 (19), 94 (19)
Her pow'rfull foes she thus alarms 8-11 (83)
Here are the rarities of the whole fair 55-55a
(60)
Here Tom here's a health 5 (239), 33 (29),
55-55a (11)
Here where is my landland 55-55a (47)
Here's a health to Queen Anne 55-55a (12),
56 (25)
Here's a health to the Queen 5 (240)
Here's that will challenge all the fair 55-55a
(24)
Here's to thee my boy 180 (20)
Hey day nobody here, no wife, no maid 102
(11)
Hey hoe the clock has just struck four 8-11
(40)
Hide me in some lonely den 33 (32)
High day no body here 101 (11)
Him I love, no longer try me 46-47a (14), 93
(14)
Hither turn thee 5 (401)
Ho ben cor per esser forte 89 (2)
Ho un core nel petto 83 (27)
Ho vinto, sì 74-74a (5)
Hogshead was offer'd, A 55-55a (49), 73 (8)
Hold and no further advance 5 (322)
Hold Iohn e're you le've me 5 (83)
Honour all baseness scorning 64-65 (9), 68
(9), 76a-78 (9)
Honour is a virgins treasure 53-54 (7), 59 (7),
79b (7), 123 (7)
Hopes beguiling pleasures smiling 160 (15)
Hor sì m'insegna il ciel 53-54 (5), 59 (5), 79b
(5), 123 (5)
How bless'd are shepherds when they see 99
(109)
How blest is a soldier when listed to rove 105
(1)
How calm Elesa are these groves 5 (78)
How great is my blessing 46-47a (16), 93 (16)
How happy are we 99 (27)
How happy are wee now the wind is abaft
109 (11)
How happy's the man who does take of his
cann 101-102 (20)
How insipid were life 5 (85), 33 (33)
How inviting how smiling a rose 46-47a (33),
93 (33)
How long I thought the nights and days 99
(113)
How long shall I pine, for love 5 (82)

How pleasant is ranging the fields 96-98 (1)
How severe is my fate 5 (81)
How shall a lover come to know 5 (253)
How shall I speak my secret pain 85 (11), 103 (11)
How shall we speak thy praise 55-55a (63), 73 (21)
How silly's the heart of a woman 96-98 (7)
How sweet how lovely when return'd 8-11 (7), 33 (91)
How sweet is love 53-54 (32), 59 (32), 79b (32), 123 (32)
How sweetly smells the summer green 168 (12)
How unhappy is he 37-38 (6), 81 (6)
How vain and false a woman is 5 (79)
How wretched is our fate, to love 5 (80)
Humble sheperds greif may pain you 40a (47), 42 (47), 43 (30), 44-45 (48), 82 (46), 126a (48)
Hur Winnifred was pretty 171 (8)

I am a poor shepherd undone 99 (99)
I am come to lock all fast 5 (327)
I attempt from love's sickness to fly 5 (332)
I bles'd his memory that first 5 (329)
I burn, my brain consumes to ashes 5 (94), 8-11 (84)
I burn with love and with desire 71-72 (7)
I cannot see my lord repine 38 (19), 81 (19)
I cease to love her 40a (44), 42 (44), 43 (27), 43a (25), 44-45 (45), 82 (44), 126a (45)
I come my fairest treasure 159 (41), 160 (9)
I did but look and love a while 110 (3)
I feel my doubtfull mind 48a-52 (11), 57-58 (11), 94 (11)
I feel my heart relent 37-38 (3), 81 (3)
I gently toucht her hand 5 (90), 8-11 (87)
I go yet know not where 85 (2), 103 (2)
I grasp thee 32-32a (18)
I grieve to see your sorrow 40a (19), 42 (19), 43 (7), 44-45 (19), 82 (19), 126a (19)
I hate a sot yt at his pot 171 (50)
I have a tenement to lett 99 (15)
I humbly intreat you for charity's sake 5 (325)
I know brother tar 55-55a (59)
I languish for whom 33a-35 (16)
I languish, I sorrow 15 (4), 16 (16), 19-23 (16), 62-63 (16), 79-79a (16), 177 (16)
I lately vow'd but 'twas in haste 41 (8)
I look'd and saw within the book of fate 157 (13)
I love a plain lass 46-47a (5), 93 (5)
I love but dare not my flame discover 13 (13), 16 (21), 18 (13), 19-23 (21), 33a-35 (23), 62-63 (21), 79-79a (21), 177 (21)
I revive now you're turning 40a (52), 42 (52), 43 (35), 44-45 (53), 82 (51), 126a (53)
I see she flyes me 5 (402), 157 (10)
I thought you'd charms but now I find 24-24a (13)

I was born of royall race 13 (1), 16 (1), 18-23 (1), 33a-35 (1), 62-63 (1), 79-79a (1), 177 (1)
I will awa' wi' my love 168 (47)
I will fly tho I dye 48a-52 (49), 57-58 (48), 94 (49)
I will not bear it 171 (30)
Idolo del mio cor 88 (21), 90a (21)
Ienny long resisted Wully's fierce desire 5 (92)
If 'tis joy to wound a lover 38 (39), 81 (39)
If a lady you doat on 124 (3)
If all be true that I do think 55-55a (42)
If Celia you had youth at will 5 (91)
If doubts and fears my passion feed 5 (328)
If ere I forsake thee 64-65 (28), 68 (28), 76a-78 (28)
If ever tis my fortune 46-47a (31), 93 (31)
If for me the fates ordain her 48a-52 (12), 57-58 (12), 94 (12)
If I ever encline to complying 32-32a (13)
If I hear Orinda swear 5 (100), 8-11 (85)
If in Elizian plains he roves 85 (7), 103 (7)
If it be true, as wisemen say 104 (6)
If love claims no return 32-32a (16)
If loves a sweet passion 5 (330)
If musick be the food of love 157 (11)
If my Sawny thou's but love me 95 (28)
If of my sorrow she has compassion 48a-52 (5), 57-58 (5), 94 (5)
If to love or good wine 56 (1), 99 (53)
If wine and musick have the pow'r 5 (87), 8-11 (35)
Il ciel le piante i fior vien meco a rimirar 107 (2)
Il core che pretendo 143 (6), 172 (34)
Il dolce e bel contento 138 (8)
Il est temps que la musique vienne 134 (35)
Il mio cor non è più mio 64-65 (23), 68 (23), 76a-78 (23)
Il mio core non troua riposo 64-65 (1), 68 (1), 76a-78 (1)
Il mormorio del rio lauretta 107 (11)
Il peggio che sà 64-65 (4), 68 (4), 76a-78 (4)
Il suo amore intenderò 127 (11), 137 (6), 172 (35)
Il timore di perder chi s'ama 69 (2), 80-80a (2), 91-92 (2)
Il valor d'un nobil petto 107 (23)
I'll ever be loving 32-32a (3)
I'll hurry thee hence 5 (102), 33 (40)
I'll range arround the shady bowrs 180 (22)
I'll sail upon the Dog-star 109 (10), 157 (12)
I'll stick to my bottle 33 (37), 56 (21)
I'll tell thee, Dick, where I have lately been 99 (25)
I'm contented ne'er tormented 57-58 (36)
I'm like inconstant chance 5 (99)
I'm tormented when I see 159 (7)
I'm vex'd to think that Damon woes me 5 (331)

I'me contented, nere tormented 48a-52 (39), 94 (39)

In a barren tree 86 (10), 99 (19)

In a cellar in s-d 73 (41)

In a cool refreshing shade 99 (45)

In a groves forsaken shade 5 (103)

In all her charms Aurora gay 85 (13), 103 (13)

In April when primroses paint the sweet plain 168 (7)

In braccio al idol mio 137 (13)

In che peccasti 111-12 (6), 176 (6)

In Cloes sparkling eyes 5 (403)

In Cynthia's face and brightest eyes 5 (373)

In drinking full bumper there is no deceit 55-55a (57), 73 (28)

In due cori un più bel foco 69 (8), 80-80a (8), 91-92 (8)

In felice prigioniero 69 (22), 80-80a (22), 91-92 (22)

In gratefull chorus let us raise 135 (8)

In love never vary 144-45 (78)

In lovers hearts there cannot be 71-72 (3)

In mirar la mia fiera suentura 64-65 (24), 68 (24), 76a-78 (24)

In my brest what disorder so rages 46-47a (27), 93 (27)

In my triumphant chariot hurld 106 (12)

In pochi istanti ritornerò 107 (30)

In praise of musick all delight 101-102 (8)

In seventeen hundred, and three 55-55a (45)

In spring time Beau monde to Hide-Park repairs 99 (127)

In tante mie pene 108 (38)

In Taunton Dean che were bore and a bred 99 (115)

In the fields in frost and snows 25 (2)

In the pleasant month of May 5 (288)

In this grove my Strephon walk'd 87 (2), 99 (106)

In those eyes I see my ruin 160 (35)

In troth, friend Harry 99 (16)

In vain are sighs to move us 48a-52 (23), 57-58 (23), 94 (23)

In vain are the hopes of a Popish pretender 99 (33)

In vain I fly from sorrow 13 (3), 16 (19), 18 (3), 19-23 (19), 33a-35 (21), 62-63 (19), 79-79a (19), 177 (19)

In vain I seek for ease 5 (97)

In vain I strive my flame to hide 5 (105)

In vain is complaining 40-40a (14), 42 (14), 44-45 (14), 82 (14), 126a (14)

In vain is delay 40a (37), 42 (37), 43 (24), 44-45 (38), 82 (38), 126a (38)

In vain poor Damon prostrate lies 5 (289)

In vain we dispair 33 (38)

In vain we say, that love's the best 4 (5), 5 (368), 7 (5)

In vain ye cruel fair 48a-52 (9), 57-58 (8), 94 (9)

In vain ye god I ask 24-24a (7)

In vain you keep a pother 46-47a (37), 93 (37)

In vain you tell me love is sweet 5 (104)

Ingrato figlio 121 (8), 125-26 (8), 172 (33)

Innamorar e poi mancar 111-12 (22), 176 (22)

Inspire me love to raise thee 5 (404)

Inspire us genius of the day 6 (1), 8-11 (12)

Instruct me gentle Cupid 24-24a (4)

Insulting destiny 64-65 (8), 68 (8), 76a-78 (8)

Insulting rivall doe not boast 5 (89)

Intombed here lyes good Sr Harry 55-55a (27)

Io cerco à rallegrarmi 75-75a (5), 90b (5)

Io che fui Real' Donzella 75-75a (18), 90b (18)

Io non voglio vendicarmi 64-65 (6), 68 (6), 76a-78 (6)

Io non vorrei morir 88 (15), 90a (15)

Io sempre appunto quel augelletto 89 (17)

Io sento, al cor tormento 69 (31), 80-80a (31), 91-92 (31)

Io sono oppressa tanto 138 (6)

Io spero che in que' quardi uedrò 127 (2), 137 (2), 172 (36)

Io ti lascio amato pegno 138 (15)

I'o Victoria 5 (88)

Iocky (see Jocky)

Iogging (see Jogging)

Is innosence so void of cares 5 (106)

Is there a wretch so stupid 104 (1)

Is'e no more to shady coverts 5 (95), 33 (43), 95 (13)

Ise tell the false loone 95 (26)

It tis not that I love you less 5 (98), 33 (42)

Jack gave a kick 73 (12)

Jack thou'rt a toper 55-55a (51)

J'avois juré, ma Celimene 134 (13)

Je n'abandonne point l'amour 134 (6)

Je ne goute jamais de plus parfait repos 134 (29)

Je resuois cette nuit 134 (22)

Je sens que Cupidon ce petit téméraire 134 (23)

Jemmy told his passion, in a courtly phrase 5 (101), 95 (21)

Jenny long resisted 33 (45), 95 (29)

Jenny, & Molly, & Dolly 86 (5), 99 (28)

Joan has been galloping 55-55a (62)

Jockey loves his Moggey dearly 5 (372)

Jockey was a dawdy lad 5 (255), 95 (25)

Jockey was as brisk & blith a lad 5 (96), 33 (41), 95 (12)

Jogging on from yonder green 5 (93), 33 (44)

John ask'd his landlady 73 (20)

Jolly bowle, The 5 (199), 56 (31)

Jolly breeze that comes whistling, The 5 (182), 8-11 (14)

(51), 19-23 (51), 33a-35 (52), 62-63 (51), 79-79a (51), 177 (51)

Let the nymph, who designs her amours to maintain 104 (15)

Let the trumpet sound loud 5 (117)

Let the waiter bring clean glasses 99 (98)

Let thus thy prosp'rous minutes glide 1-3 (6), 8-11 (26)

Let tyrants awe their humble slaves 110 (2)

Let us fly, our undoing love allures me 40 (16), 40a (17), 42 (17), 43a (10), 44-45 (17), 82 (17), 126a (17)

Let us revel and roar 5 (334), 8-11 (93), 33 (96)

Let virgins ev'ry year 53-54 (37), 59 (37), 79b (37), 123 (37)

Let whimsical monarchs of state 171 (32)

Let ye waiter bring clean glasses 76 (5)

Let's drink disappointment to restless fanaticks 99 (66)

Lets drink to all our wives 55-55a (67)

Lets laugh, and dance, & play 46-47a (2), 93 (2)

Lets live good honest lives 55-55a (35)

Let's sing of stage coaches 5 (118), 33 (48)

Liberia's all my thought and dream 5 (115)

Liberté fy de la chaine la plus belle 134 (19)

Lieta corre la navicella spinta 83 (35)

Life and nature faults and graces 135 (4)

Like the thunder guilt aming/alarming 40a (48), 42 (48), 43 (31), 43a (28), 44-45 (49), 82 (47), 126a (49), 144-45 (31)

Like you the goddess thus replies 1-3 (3), 8-11 (63), 33 (46)

Lillies roses pearly dew 12a (17), 26 (2), 29-31 (2), 78a-b (2), 90 (2)

Linco's grown another creature 13 (8), 16 (46), 18 (8), 19-23 (46), 33a-35 (46), 62-63 (46), 79-79a (46), 177 (46)

Lissa o pitty me my Lissa 87 (6)

Live Charles, King Williams friend 5 (336)

Live great Thames 48a-52 (54), 57-58 (54), 94 (54)

Lo voglio lo chiede 121 (2), 125-26 (2), 172 (40)

Long has Pastora rul'd the plain 5 (374)

L'onor severo brama l'offese vendicar 111-12 (32), 176 (32)

Look down, triumphant god of war 104 (12)

Look from your window, my dear 99 (123)

Lord! what's come to my mother 5 (116), 33 (49)

Lost is my quiet for ever 157 (24)

Love and ambition strive 15 (10), 16 (30), 19-23 (30), 33a-35 (31), 62-63 (30), 79-79a (30), 177 (30)

Love and Hymen are combining 46-47a (60), 93 (60)

Love and musick are such treasures 106 (9)

Love darts are in your eyes 13 (5), 16 (4), 18

(5), 19-23 (4), 33a-35 (4), 62-63 (4), 79-79a (4), 177 (4)

Love in her bosom end my care 5 (113), 99 (44)

Love in her eyes triumphant plays 100 (2)

Love is a god whose charming sway 5 (333)

Love is all fancy, nothing more 104 (14)

Love is an empty airy name 5 (406), 8-11 (51)

Love is lost, nor can his mother 5 (110)

Love is now become a trade 99 (63)

Love is now out of fashion grown 5 (109)

Love leads to battle, who dares oppose 14 (8), 16 (28), 19-23 (28), 33a-35 (29), 62-63 (28), 79-79a (28), 144-45 (7), 177 (28)

Love love's a distemper that comes with high feeding 99 (76)

Love may plead 38 (32), 81 (32)

Love me no more 144-45 (64)

Love oh spare me 46-47a (39), 93 (39)

Love the sweets of love 70 (10), 99 (65)

Love thou airy vain illusion 48a-52 (41), 57-58 (41), 94 (41), 144-45 (9)

Love thou art best of human joys 5 (297)

Love thou tyrant of the fair 5 (407)

Love woud invade me 40a (9), 42 (9), 43 (3), 43a (6), 44-45 (9), 82 (9), 126a (9)

Lovely charmer, dearest creature 5 (111)

Lovely charming fair 144-45 (57)

Lovely dear charmer 144-45 (76)

Lover discover no sorrow 46-47a (44), 93 (44)

Lover near despairing, A 40a (16), 42 (16), 43 (5), 43a (9), 44-45 (16), 82 (16), 126a (16)

Lovers for their harvest staying 32-32a (14)

Loves blind and strikes our heart's 32-32a (12)

Love's but the frailty of the mind 5 (259), 8-11 (62)

Loves dazling flame 64-65 (41), 68 (41), 76a-78 (41)

Love's fire in my eyes is shining 32-32a (6)

Loves goddess in a myrtle grove said 168 (18)

L'ozio vil di giovinezza 108 (17)

Luccioletta fra gl'orrori 53-54 (21), 59 (21), 79b (21), 123 (21)

Lucinda is bewitching fair 5 (335)

Lucinda Mira give me leave 101-102 (14)

Lucinda's all my joy, my treasure 104 (11)

Luff, thus, no near, that hatefull sound 76 (6)

L'una e l'altra 84 (15)

Lungi da te ben mio 159 (4)

Lungo pensar e dubitar 119-20 (6), 122 (6)

Lusinga del mio core 69 (5), 80-80a (5), 91-92 (5)

Lusinghe vezzo si di speme 89 (22)

Lusty young smith at his vice stood afiling, A 5 (10), 33 (6)

Lye still ye winds, my Strephon's foe 109 (1)

Ma chi punir desio 160 (29)

Ma di raggione armato 108 (30)

My mother calls me harmless maid 171 (5)
My poor heart says dally 46-47a (21), 93 (21)
My pretty lovely charming fair 101-102 (1)
My sorrows unrelenting 48a-52 (6), 57-58 (6), 94 (6)
My soul begins to rest 146 (6)
My tears can never, make fortune kinder 64-65 (7), 68 (7), 76a-78 (7)
My wishing eyes 5 (120)
Mysterious love uncertain treasure 38 (35), 81 (35)

Nansy's to the green wood gane 168 (13)
Nascer mi sento gia 107 (16)
Nati al pianto occhi dolenti 107 (27)
Nature fram'd thee sure for loveing 5 (131)
Nature her gifts us'd wisely to dispense 5 (342)
Navicella che lungi dal porto 159 (30)
Near pleasant woods on lofty mountains 124 (7)
Ne'er deceive me 32-32a (11)
Ne'er leave me more my treasure 32-32a (4)
Ne'er torment me 40a (18), 42 (18), 43 (6), 43a (11), 44-45 (18), 82 (18), 126a (18)
Nei sassi ancora la pena mia 88 (11), 90a (11)
Nel furor di suoi deliri 84 (5)
Nel mio cor costante e forte 84 (2)
Nel mirarvi se spietati vaghi rai 150-51 (5), 159 (29), 172 (50)
Nel suo duol così si lagra sospirando 150-51 (4), 172 (46)
Nel tuo figlio e nel tuo sposo 127 (15)
Nel tuo sen, crudel, vorrei 84 (1)
Nella mia sfortunata 84 (9)
Nembo tal'ora porta l'aurora 143 (8), 172 (48)
Neptune frown, and Boreas roar 5 (130)
Ne're complain tho' ne're contented 46-47a (59), 93 (59)
Ner'e torment me (see Ne'er)
Never let your heart despair 40-40a (8), 42 (8), 43a (5), 44-45 (8), 82 (8), 126a (8)
New reformation, begins thro the nation 5 (341)
Nieghi pure la speranza 108 (10)
No Albion thou canst ner'e repay 6 (4), 8-11 (53)
No chi fingere non sà in dolce affetto 143 (2)
No diamonds are so bright 171 (45)
No, ev'ry morning my beauties renew 5 (343)
No forces shall scare me 48a-52 (21), 57-58 (21), 94 (21)
No I shan't envy him who e'er he be 5 (344)
No I will no more believe thee 144-45 (8)
No il tuo sdegno mi placo 160 (20)
No let the loitring goddess 8-11 (21)
No longer here shall nature smile 85 (32), 103 (32)
No longer I'll despair 171 (9)

No love was ever known that 16 (25), 19-23 (25), 33a-35 (27), 62-63 (25), 79-79a (25), 177 (25)
No more complain 159 (12), 160 (36)
No more dear nymph complain 146 (2)
No more his brain possess 5 (345)
No more I'le change 38 (40), 81 (40)
No more let Damons eyes persue 33 (51)
No more let sorrow pain you 40a (6), 42 (6), 43 (2), 43a (4), 44-45 (6), 82 (6), 105 (4), 126a (6)
No more let sorrow wound thee 85 (8), 103 (8)
No more thou dearest creature 53-54 (40), 79b(40), 123 (40)
No more tryall, nor deniall 46-47a (20), 93 (20)
No my heart is mine no longer 64-65 (23), 68 (23), 76a-78 (23)
No non lo credo non lo spero 108 (11)
No non piangete pupille amate 138 (3), 146 (2)
No non temer 144-45 (38)
No non voi più star in pene 144-45 (8)
No, oh Dio che mai farò 145a (7), 152 (1), 153 (6), 159 (36), 160 (6), 169-70 (7), 172 (51)
No più non bramo 111-12 (3), 169-70 (27), 176 (3)
No sorrow we discover 46-47a (45), 93 (45)
No thou vain deceiver 173 (5)
No 'tis decreed the traytress shall bleed 37-38 (5), 81 (5)
No you charm me with your rage 159 (10)
No you'd deceive me 85 (4), 103 (4)
Nobil onda 178-78a (6)
Noble, generous, great, & good 76 (1)
Nocchier che salva il legno 138 (33)
Noirs enfans de l'hiuer 134 (18)
Non an queste capanne 107 (7)
Non cedero sleale 64-65 (9), 68 (9), 76a-78 (9)
Non cessarò d'amar 83 (5)
Non credo instabile chi mi piango 159 (15)
Non dar fede a chi t'affana 64-65 (11), 68 (11), 76a-78 (11)
Non dar pui pene o cara 53-54 (40), 59 (40), 79b (40), 123 (40)
Non deggio non sperare 114-14b (7), 115-18 (5), 172 (45), 179 (7)
Non desio che l'idol mio 75-75a (16), 90b (16)
Non disperar chi sa 160 (32)
Non è bella la vittoria 53-54 (8), 59 (8), 79b (8), 123 (8)
Non è così leggiero 69 (20), 80-80a (20), 91-92 (20)
Non è Cupido no che mi tormenta 138 (32), 144-45 (48), 158 (8)
Non è fiero nè crudele 108 (36)

Queen of islands, victorious state 56 (9), 99 (52)
Queen of my heart 171 (19)
Quel guardo di pietà 114 (22), 172 (67), 179 (22)
Quel narcisso quant'e bello 108 (9)
Quel piacer ch' è inaspettato 107 (4)
Quel timoroso cervo cacciato 114 (24), 179 (24)
Quell'empio suenato 89 (4)
Quella calma che a noi 127 (12)
Quella ch'adoro m'impiaga il seno 75-75a (24), 90b (24)
Questo conforto solo 83 (28)
Qui d'Astrea vicino al soglio 84 (37)
Qui di Bacco nella reggia 84 (36)
Qui frape à la porte 134 (7)
Quoth Jack on a time 55-55a (13), 73 (7)
Qu'un vigneron est estimable 134 (33)

Racking thoughts of what is past 5 (152)
Rage shall thy eyes be showing how 64-65 (35), 68 (35), 76a-78 (35)
Ralph James Richard and merry Gill 101-102 (3)
Rè ingrato di spietata 83 (8)
Reason what art thou 5 (156)
Releive, the fair Belinda said 5 (153), 8-11 (29)
Remember o disembler 46-47a (28), 93 (28)
Render voglio ogn'uno amante 145a (4), 153 (4), 172 (69)
Rendi al padre in me la figlia 127 (1), 137 (1), 172 (71)
Restless in thought disturb'd in mind 8-11 (2)
Revenge I summon 14 (13), 16 (18), 19-23 (18), 33a-35 (19), 62-63 (18), 79-79a (18), 177 (18)
Rich Gripe does all his thoughts 144-45 (35)
Rimirarvi e non amarvi 53-54 (12), 59 (12), 79b (12), 123 (12)
Rinasce amor allor che amando spera 147-48 (6), 149 (4), 172 (70)
Ring the barr bell of the world 56 (33)
Rise Alecto, rise rejoyce and see with me 26 (10), 29-31 (10), 78a-b (10), 90 (10)
Rise glory rise in all thy charms 38 (34), 81 (34)
Rise o sunn 48a-52 (2), 57-58 (2), 94 (2)
Ritorna già nel viso 69 (36), 80-80a (36), 91-92 (36)
Ritorna o caro dolce mio tesoro 159 (16)
Ritorna o dolce amore 144-45 (2)
Riuolgo il passo altrove 108 (13)
Rivo che tumido s'ingrossa d'onda 89 (10)
Room for a rover 5 (155), 33 (62)
Room for th'express 55-55a (46)
Room for the post 99 (11)
Rosy morn lukes bleeth & gay, The 95 (18)
Rouse ye gods of the main 5 (154)

Rouse yee brave for fame and glory 40a (4), 42 (4), 43 (1), 43a (3), 44-45 (4), 82 (4), 126a (4)
Rouze ye brave for fame & glory 105 (3)
Rozzi sassi in voi contemplo 83 (25)

Sacri numi difendete 137 (3)
Sad Musidora all in woe 180 (17)
Sagri numi difendete 127 (4)
Sai pur s'io vivo amante 111-12 (23), 176 (23)
Said Sr John to his lady 55-55a (2), 73 (3)
Sally before you they're falling 40a (50), 42 (50), 43 (33), 44-45 (51), 82 (49), 126a (51)
Sapete che in amor 111-12 (14), 169-70 (8), 172 (72), 176 (14)
Sapran ben I tuoi lumi quanto 64-65 (35), 68 (35), 76a-78 (35)
S'armi il fato 160 (31)
S'armi pur amor superbo 53-54 (34), 59 (34), 79b (34), 123 (34)
Saturnia wife of thundring Jove 8-11 (86)
Save me with joy posess me 105 (8)
Save mia quella bella che adoro 84 (21)
Saw you the nymph whom I adore 99 (122), 180 (11)
Say, good master Bacchus 55-55a (58), 73 (15)
Say must I then despair 40a (25), 42 (25), 43-43a (13), 44-45 (26), 82 (26), 126a (26)
Scaccia omai s'indegna imago 83 (26)
Scacciata dal suo nido 159 (38), 160 (2)
Sdegni tornate 111-12 (10), 176 (10)
Se à chiamar il caro bene 89 (14)
Se a lui dà forza il fato 145a (1), 153 (1), 172 (82)
Se ben diffetto appar 138 (19)
Se che mi brama aveso in petto 113 (4)
Se condaste al fine o stelle 160 (35)
Se credi ch'io non t'ami 69 (25), 80-80a (25), 91-92 (25)
Se fingo se spero 111-12 (4), 176 (4)
Se luggie amenità 88 (23), 90a (23)
Se mai può consolarti l'amor mio 114 (21), 179 (21)
Se mai sarà 75-75a (20), 90b (20)
Se me fuggi l'ingrata 107 (6)
Se mirar potessi il core 147-49 (1), 172 (90)
Se non folse ingrannatrice 161-62 (4)
Se non fosse la speranza 49-52 (12), 57-58 (12), 94 (12)
Se pena se geme 111-12 (33), 176 (33)
Se perdo il caro ben 145a (6), 153 (10), 172 (87)
Se pietà di me non senti 160 (26)
Se ponne le pene 113 (1), 172 (77)
Se potessi un dì placare 160 (25), 169-70 (6)
Se risolvi abbandonarmi 144-45 (21), 169-70 (24)

Si t'intendo spera la mia 107 (22)
Si ti sente l'alma mia 84 (22)
Si tu ben lo sai 108 (5)
Si vedrai non son più quello 111-12 (29), 176 (29)
Si vieni ove il rigor 114 (14), 179 (14)
Silvia how cou'd you e're mistrust 8-11 (25)
Since Celia 'tis not in our power 5 (166)
Since conjugal passion 38 (41), 81 (41)
Since heav'n & earth combine 53-54 (35), 79b (35), 123 (35)
Since in vain I strive to gain you 40a (34), 42 (34), 43 (21), 43a (19), 44-45 (35), 82 (35), 126a (35)
Since Momus comes to laugh below 5 (376)
Since now the worlds turn'd upside down 25 (4)
Since the day of poor man 56 (12)
Since thus you light my pain 160 (8)
Since times are so bad 5 (157), 157 (32)
Since Tom's in the chair, and e'ery one here 99 (17)
Since ungratefull still you shun me 53-54 (30), 79b (30), 123 (30)
Since you from death thus save me 13 (6), 16 (3), 18 (6), 19-23 (3), 33a-35 (3), 62-63 (3), 79-79a (3), 177 (3)
Sing all ye muses 5 (163), 157 (26)
Sing mighty Marlborough's story 56 (17)
Sing ye muses 5 (162)
Sinque che piaque amai 150-51 (6)
S'io son schernita 138 (18)
Sir Walter enjoying his damsel one night 73 (43)
Slaves to London I'll deceive you 5 (161)
Slaves to the fashion 40a (27), 42 (27), 43 (17), 44-45 (30), 82 (30), 126a (30)
Sleep in body, wake in mind 32-32a (7)
Sleep Ormondo void of fear 5 (411), 12-12a (11), 26 (33), 29-31 (33), 78a-b (33), 90 (33)
Sleep shepherd sleep 5 (352)
Smile then with a beam devine 5 (354)
Smiling graces pleasures gay 174-75 (3)
So bright a bloom 38 (38), 81 (38)
So che guarda con raggio sereno 127 (14), 137 (8)
So form'd to charm 46-47a (32), 93 (32), 144-45 (15)
So no i colpi della sorte 178 (10)
So sweet an air 26 (4), 29-31 (4), 78a-b (4), 90 (4)
So well Corinna likes the joy 5 (412), 8-11 (24)
Soffro in pace 159 (2)
Soft blessing descending 53-54 (25), 59 (25), 79b (25), 123 (25)
Soft god! of sleep 110 (11)
Soft ioys young loves gay pleasure 48a-52 (47), 57-58 (46), 94 (47)
Softest charmer, do not fly me 104 (9)

Sol m'affanna sol m'offende 107 (10)
Sol per te s'amai la pene 128-29 (1), 144-45 (1), 172 (74)
Soldier take off thy wine 55-55a (54), 73 (42)
Solo la pena mia, basto a placarti 121 (4), 125-26 (4)
Solo pietà vi chiede 75-75a (22), 90b (22)
Some say that marriage life is best 101-102 (17)
Some write in the praise of tobacco and wine 73 (37)
Something bloody and unexpected 48a-52 (35), 57-58 (35), 94 (35)
Something is in my face so alluring 13 (15), 16 (32), 18 (15), 19-23 (32), 33a-35 (33), 62-63 (32), 79-79a (32), 177 (32)
Sommi dei se giusti sonno 88 (14), 90a (14)
Son come navicella in mar turbato 150-51 (1), 169-70 (28), 172 (88)
Son ferito e cerco i dardi 49-52 (26), 57-58 (26), 94 (26)
Son figlia infelice 75-75a (1), 90b (1)
Son giusti i sdegni tuoi 138 (29)
Son nato a sospirar 145a (2), 153 (2), 172 (84)
Son qual face che s'accende 114 (23), 115-18 (4), 179 (23)
Son vane tue minaccie 84 (13)
Son'guerriero e son amante 49-52 (31), 57-58 (31), 94 (31)
Sono più care d'amor 107 (32)
Sorga pur l'opressa Roma 138 (14)
Sorge qual luccioletta 166-67 (3)
Sorrow forbids my hopeing 64-65 (33), 68 (33), 76a-78 (33)
Sospira il core afflitto 83 (21)
Sospira pena e geme 64-65 (40), 68 (40), 76a-78 (40)
Souffrirons nous amis 134 (8)
Sound a parly ye fair and surrender 157 (25)
Sound fame, thy brazen trumpet sound 5 (160), 157 (16)
Sound thy loudest trumpet fame 1-3 (4), 8-11 (78)
Spare my sorrow rurall pleasure 46-47a (1), 93 (1), 144-45 (54)
Speme gradita 89 (26)
Spera non paventar 75-75a (27), 90b (27)
Spera quest'alma 143 (3), 172 (80)
Sperai nè m'ingannai 160 (14)
Speranze più liete regnate con me 84 (35)
Spero ma sempre peno 111-12 (15), 176 (15)
Spirate o iniqui marmi 127 (21)
Spring invites the troops to warring 86 (7)
Squemish prude, The 171 (24)
Stay, ah stay, ah turn, ah whither wou'd you fly 5 (159), 8-11 (5)
Stay lovely youth, delay thy choice 5 (167)
Stelle ingrate 111-12 (7), 169-70 (32), 176 (7)
Stelle rigide placatevi 147-48 (4), 149 (2), 172 (89)

Tho' fierce love ye war is waging 53-54 (34), 79b (34), 123 (34)

Tho' for seven years and mair 168 (21)

Tho' yon waters 53-54 (33), 79b (33), 123 (33)

Thou art he my dearest creature 15 (14), 16 (38), 19-23 (38), 33a-35 (39), 62-63 (38), 79-79a (38), 177 (38)

Thou art ugly and old 37-38 (9), 81 (9)

Thou flask once filld 5 (189), 56 (26)

Thou gay, thou cruel maid 5 (170)

Thou horrid monster don't think to bully 64-65 (27), 68 (27), 76a-78 (27)

Thou only goddess first could'st tell 8-11 (3)

Thou soft machine, that dost her hand obey 5 (416)

Thousand fairy scenes appear, A 38 (18), 81 (18)

Thousand raptures fill my breast, A 85 (6), 103 (6)

Thus Damon knock't at Celias door 5 (198)

Thus gayly advancing 171 (27)

Thus in a solitary grove 48a-52 (3), 57-58 (3), 94 (3)

Thus mighty eastern kings 159 (40)

Thus sinking mariners 5 (414), 12-12a (3), 26 (24), 29-31 (24), 78a-b (24), 90 (24)

Thus the brave from war returning 96-98 (13)

Thus when bright Luna looks from high 106 (8)

Thus while the eight goes merrily round 55-55a (64)

Thus with thirst my soul expiring 48a-52 (25), 57-58 (25), 94 (25)

Thus you may be as happy as we 8-11 (6)

Thy voice oh harmony 8-11 (15)

Ti consiglio amar un volto 84 (17)

Ti dò il mio sangue 113 (3), 172 (96)

Ti pentirai fra poco perfido 127 (23)

Ti stringo o mio tesoro o mio diletto 53-54 (4), 59 (4), 79b (4), 123 (4)

Till now I suppress'd, the fire in my breast 5 (357)

Timada pastorella 178-78a (3)

Timor e speme van combattendo 114-14b (4), 172 (91), 179 (4)

Tinking Tom was an honest man 55-55a (56)

Tis done, the pointed arrow's in my heart 5 (183)

'Tis for thee alone dear creature 64-65 (2), 68 (2), 76a-78 (2)

'Tis my glory to adore you 144-45 (5), 172 (55)

'Tis not your wealth, my dear 76 (3), 99 (107)

Tis pitty poor Barnet a vigilant curr 55-55a (8)

Tis sultry weather pretty maid 5 (181)

Tis the fashion, without passion 12-12a (15), 26 (8), 29-31 (8), 78a-b (8), 90 (8)

Tis too late for a coach 55-55a (32), 73 (2)

'Tis vain fond Strephon to complain 24-24a (11)

To arms your ensigns strait display 5 (418), 157 (27)

To banish care wn stoks were sinking 171 (15)

To beauty born a willing slave 33 (65)

To beauty devoted 14 (2), 16 (20), 19-23 (20), 33a-35 (22), 62-63 (20), 79-79a (20), 144-45 (10), 177 (20)

To convent streams and shady groves 5 (301)

To cullies and bullies of country and town 5 (300)

To Cynthia then our homage pay 5 (270)

To joys that delight us 53-54 (26), 79b (26), 123 (26)

To little or no purpose I spent many days 8-11 (41)

To live nor know ye joys of love 105 (6)

To meet her Mars, the queen of love 5 (178), 8-11 (75)

To our musical clubb 73 (25)

To see a wither'd fair 171 (20)

To slight my love ingrate 64-65 (12), 68 (12), 76a-78 (12)

To thee o gentle sleep alone 5 (191)

To touch your heart 5 (190)

To warr my thoughts to warr 5 (415), 12a (19), 26 (27), 29-31 (27), 78a-b (27), 90 (27)

To you, fair ladies, now at land 99 (14), 109 (8)

To you I gave a virgin heart 5 (377)

Toby Swill has ne'er his fill 171 (41)

Tom making a manteua for a lass 55-55a (31), 73 (27)

Tom Mixum's spouse 171 (14)

Tom Tory told Titus 73 (36)

Too lovely cruel fair 48a-52 (8), 57-58 (9), 94 (8), 144-45 (12)

Too well, I hear the subject 64-65 (39), 68 (39), 76a-78 (39)

Tormentarmi crudel 75-75a (14), 90b (14)

Torna al lido la navicella 84 (26)

Torna la speme in sen mà non mi fido 69 (27), 80-80a (27), 91-92 (27)

Torni o'sole 107 (1)

Torno alla patria 111-12 (5), 176 (5)

Tortora che il suo bene 164 (3), 172 (95)

Tortorella 49-52 (3), 57-58 (3), 94 (3)

Tortura che il suo bene 160 (21)

Tory, a Whig, and a moderate man, A 5 (295), 99 (10)

Transported with pleasure 144-45 (53), 172 (38)

Transporting Cloe lovely fair 106 (3)

Transporting pleasure who can tell it 38 (21), 81 (21)

Treachrous knave, A 171 (22)

Trifling song you shall hear, A 99 (8)

Tromba in campo 84 (8)

Trop aimable catin votre tein 134 (25)

Troppo crudel l'impressa 89 (23)
Troppo è il dolore 114 (20), 179 (20)
Troppo sì troppo t'ascolto 64-65 (39), 68 (39), 76a-78 (39)
True English men drink a good health 55-55a (38)
True love alone can never cloy 46-47a (68), 93 (68)
Trumpet allarms, stand, The 56 (10)
Trust not to oath, that subtle snare 99 (128)
Tu indegno sei dell'allor 84 (29)
Tu mia speranza 146 (8)
Tu miri le mie lacrime 84 (25)
Tu sei l'anima mia 83 (15)
Tu sei'l cor di questo cuore 169-70 (30)
Tu sola cara sei 83 (33)
Tu solo sei luce 89 (20)
Tu uvoi ch'io parta 144-45 (58)
Tullia I feell thy charms 15 (11), 16 (31), 19-23 (31), 33a-35 (32), 62-63 (31), 79-79a (31), 177 (31)
Turn away mine eyes 136 (4), 180 (4)
Turn, o turn ye, dearest creature 144-45 (37)
Tutte le più vezzose armi 144-45 (29)
Tutto in braccio dell'affanno 147-48 (5), 149 (3), 172 (94)
Tutto rida in si bel 53-54 (43), 59 (43), 79b (43), 123 (43)
Twanty yeares and mear 70 (5)
'Twas forth in a morning 168 (32)
Twas in the month of May Jo 5 (193), 33 (67), 95 (22)
'Twas when summer was rosie 5 (175), 33 (69), 95 (19)
'Twas when the seas were roaring 99 (112), 109 (9)
Twas when the sheep were shearing 5 (356)
Twas when the sun began to shine 180 (19)
Twas within a fourlong of Edenborough town 5 (194), 33 (66), 95 (20)
Twelve hundred years at least 5 (169)
Two nymphs insulted Damon's heart 5 (271)

Uds nigs! here ligs John Degs 73 (22)
Ulme is gon, but basely won 5 (200)
Un arcier che va bendata 108 (23)
Un atto di vittà 64-65 (19), 68 (19), 76a-78 (19)
Un bel contento un rio tormento 88 (6), 90a (6)
Un contento nel'mio care 57-58 (36)
Un core innamora 64-65 (10), 68 (10), 76a-78 (10)
Un figlio crudele ti chiama al rigore 150-51 (3), 172 (99)
Un ombra di pace si mostra al mio cor 145a (3), 153 (3), 172 (102)
Un raggio placido di bella speme 138 (23), 139-40 (6), 141 (5), 142 (3), 158 (3), 172 (104)

Un reo più che non credi 64-65 (31), 68 (31), 76a-78 (31)
Un vento lusinghier tal 163 (4), 164 (5), 172 (107)
Un vezzo un guardo un riso 121 (10), 125-26 (10), 172 (100)
Un volto ch'appaga 88 (2), 90a (2)
Under this stone lies Gabriel John 55-55a (40), 73 (44)
Underneath a gloomy shade 5 (202)
Ungratefull cruel maid 53-54 (5), 79b (5), 123 (5)
Ungratefull so to deceive me 26 (11), 29-31 (11), 78a-b (11), 90 (11)
Ungratefull traytor go 48a-52 (42), 57-58 (42), 94 (42)
Ungratefull you fly me, unkindly 13 (7), 16 (29), 18 (7), 19-23 (29), 33a-35 (30), 62-63 (29), 79-79a (29), 177 (29)
Unhappy lovers are ne'er contented 40a (43), 42 (43), 44-45 (44), 126a (44)
Usignolo che col volo 83 (13)

V'adoro pupille 160 (28), 169-70 (16)
Va lusingando amore 178-78a (2)
Vado a morir o cara 69 (28), 80-80a (28), 91-92 (28)
Vado a pugnar 107 (29)
Vaga risplende d'amor 166-67 (2)
Vaghe luci ch'il cor mi beate 121 (7), 125-26 (7), 172 (97)
Vain ambition tho still you try to soar 40a (51), 42 (51), 43 (34), 43a (30), 44-45 (52), 82 (50), 126a (52)
Vain is my art 46-47a (42), 93 (42)
Vain were graces blooming faces 174-75 (1)
Valliant Eugene to Vienna is gone, The 5 (176), 56 (22)
Vanne, disse, e chiedi 128-30 (2), 172 (101)
Vanne e spera 164 (8), 172 (105)
Vanne in tomba 89 (8)
Vanne lungi dal mio seno 88 (13), 90a (13)
Vanne ò cara dammi ancora un altro amplesso 89 (27)
Variety I love 'tis true 104 (5)
Vede anche il nido 83 (29)
Veder parmi un'ombra nera 49-52 (35), 57-58 (35), 94 (35)
Vedersi rapire 88 (4), 90a (4)
Venere bella per un istante 160 (18), 169-70 (2)
Veux tu scavoir, ami Gregoire 134 (24)
Vi farà pugnando strada 69 (1), 80-80a (1), 91-92 (1)
Vieni e mira come gira 84 (20)
Vieni o cara a consolarmi 108 (27)
Vieni o mai dolce 75-75a (4), 90b (4)
Vieni o morte a consolarmi 53-54 (27), 59 (27), 79b (27), 123 (27)
Vieni o sonno 69 (15), 80-80a (15), 91-92 (15)

Vieni o sonno e l'alma in petto 49-52 (1),
57-58 (1), 94 (1)
Vieni torna idolo mio 144-45 (37)
Virgins if your peace you prize 159 (11)
Virtù de pensier miei 107 (33)
Virtumnus Flora you that bless the feilds 5
(201)
Viui o cara e ti consola 74-74a (2)
Viva s'inalzi e splenda 114 (28), 179 (28)
Vive sperando, nel petto il core 69 (33),
80-80a (33), 91-92 (33)
Vivi tiranno 178 (7)
Vivrò a tè fedele 83 (3)
Vo'render sventurata 74-74a (4)
Voglia tuoi figli guardo pieto 107 (36)
Voglio morir ferita 69 (23), 80-80a (23),
91-92 (23)
Voglio morir ma voglio 53-54 (2), 79b (2),
123 (2)
Voi bagnate ò fonti ò fiumi 69 (16), 80-80a
(16), 91-92 (16)
Voi del ciel pietosi numi 161-62 (6), 172 (103)
Voi d'un figlio tanto misero 137 (11), 172
(106)
Voicy l'heure où Cloris doit combler mes
desirs 134 (4)
Volgendo a me lo sguardo 114-14b (5),
115-18 (7), 144-45 (80), 172 (98), 179 (5)
Vorrebbe la speranza 108 (8)
Vorrei ma non posso 53-54 (14), 59 (14), 79b
(14), 123 (14)
Vous abandonnés Celimene 134 (14)
Vuò vedermi vendicata 83 (34)

Waft me, some soft and cooling breeze 180
(15)
Wake Britain wake, 'tis high time 8-11 (43)
Wakefull nightingale that takes no rest, The 5
(177)
Wanton Cloe young & charming 159 (39)
Wanton rovers winds now sporting 46-47a
(26), 93 (26)
Wanton zephy'rs softly blowing 5 (420),
12-12a (9), 26 (31), 29-31 (31), 78a-b
(31), 90 (31)
Warbling the birds enjoying 32-32a (15)
Warr and battle, now no more 5 (360)
War's angry voice be heard no more 1-3 (5),
8-11 (34)
Was ever fate so hard as mine 26 (23), 29-31
(23), 78a-b (23), 90 (23)
Was ever mortal man so fitted 55-55a (3), 73
(4)
Was ever nymph like Rosamond 37-38 (13),
81 (13)
Was ever passion cross'd like mine 37-38 (10),
81 (10)
Was it a dream or did I hear 5 (207)
Wasted with sighs I sigh'd & pin'd 5 (363),
8-11 (54)

We knaves that wait upon the great 48a-52
(7), 57-58 (7), 94 (7)
We merry wives of Windsor 99 (70)
We with coldness and disdain 5 (277)
Wee catts when assembl'd at midnight 55-55a
(65)
Welcome death oh end my sorrow 160 (26)
Wellcome sorrow death attending 14 (15), 16
(8), 19-23 (8), 33a-35 (8), 62-63 (8),
79-79a (8), 177 (8)
What are crowns & scepters all 106 (4)
What are these ideots doing 25 (3), 99 (35)
What beauties does Flora disclose 168 (16)
What beauty doe I see 5 (208), 33 (105)
What beauty is, let Strephon tell 5 (359)
What garrs th' feulish mayde complain 5
(224), 95 (32)
What heart cou'd now refuse thee 96-98 (12)
What is a crown, if you deceive me 53-54 (3),
59 (3), 79b (3), 123 (3)
What is the reason thou of late 171 (47)
What life can compare with the jolly town
rakes 5 (380)
What lover ever can hope for favour 40a (21),
42 (21), 43 (10), 44-45 (22), 82 (22), 126
(22)
What pain Corinna he endures 5 (203)
What put off with one denial 41 (11)
What scenes of approaching delight 127a (3),
127b (1)
What shall he have that kill'd the deer 136 (3),
180 (3)
What should a merry 171 (48)
What should alarm me, no foe 40-40a (3), 42
(3), 43a (2), 44-45 (3), 82 (3), 126a (3)
What ungrateful devil moves you 5 (361)
What wou'd Europa whose shrill cryes 5
(213), 33 (82)
What woud I not do to gain you 40a (31), 42
(31), 43 (18), 43a (17), 44-45 (32), 82
(32), 126a (32)
What's love 8-11 (59), 33 (101)
When a blind unhappy passion 53-54 (21),
79b (21), 123 (21)
When all was wrapt in dark midnight 168
(49)
When bonny Jenny first left me 95 (31)
When bright Celia on the plain 144-45 (63)
When Celia was learning 33 (75), 55-55a (44)
When charming Teraminta sings 5 (421)
When Chloe on the spinnet plays 101-102
(4)
When Cloe I your charms survey 5 (205)
When Cloe sings 5 (212), 33 (102)
When Cloe we ply 159 (24)
When Cupid from his mother fled 5 (210)
When Daphne first her shepherd saw 5 (216)
When duty's requiring 40a (38), 42 (38), 43
(25), 43a (22), 44-45 (39), 82 (39), 105
(7), 126a (39)

Why shou'd women be so coy 33 (79)
Why so fast, why in haste 46-47a (54), 93 (54)
Why vainly am I calling 46-47a (61), 93 (61)
Why will Clemene when I gaze 5 (221)
Wild and frantick is my grief 38 (20), 81 (20)
Will you go by water 55-55a (30)
Wine does wonders ev'ry day 5 (222), 8-11 (33), 33 (100), 56 (8)
Wine's a mistress gay & easy 56 (34), 159 (37)
Wise nature owns, thy undisputed sway 8-11 (66), 33 (103)
With broken words and downcast eyes 168 (9)
With female arts and flattery 64-65 (37), 68 (37), 76a-78 (37)
With her alone, I'll live and dye 96-98 (3)
With horns, & with hounds 5 (225)
With how much grace her swelling sighs 24-24a (1)
With tuneful pipe and merry glee 95 (6)
Within an arbor of delight 5 (226), 33 (77)
Worst of plagues, The 171 (21)
Wou'd bright Celinda favour me 5 (215)
Wou'd the jolly old Bacchus look sparkling and fine 99 (83)
Wou'd you charme us 40a (41), 42 (41), 43 (26), 43a (23), 44-45 (42), 82 (42), 126a (42)
Wou'd you free and easy 53-54 (9), 59 (9), 79b (9), 123 (9)
Would you know how we meet 55-55a (18), 73 (1)
Wounded I, and sighing lye 26 (12), 29-31 (12), 78a-b (12), 90 (12)
Wretched am I, that I gain him 15 (15), 16 (13), 19-23 (13), 33a-35 (13), 62-63 (13), 79-79a (13), 177 (13)
Wully and Georgy now beath are gean 5 (378)

Ye birds that in our forrests sing 5 (278)
Ye Commons and Peers 99 (95)
Ye gales that gently wave the sea 168 (8)
Ye gentle gales that fan the air 5 (229), 8-11 (60), 173 (7)
Ye horrors of this hollow grave 40a (26), 42 (26), 43-43a (14), 44-45 (27), 82 (27), 126a (27)
Ye jacks of the town 99 (12)
Ye little love that hourly wait 159 (28)
Ye loves and pleasure 46-47a (67), 93 (67)
Ye men and maids who cut the ear 5 (243)
Ye minutes bring ye happy hour 5 (230)
Ye monsters that sleep 85 (27), 103 (27)
Ye pow'rs I rave, I bleed, I dye 37-38 (11), 81 (11)
Ye pow'rs my welcome death forgive 40a (49), 42 (49), 43 (32), 43a (29), 44-45 (50), 82 (48), 126a (50), 144-45 (23)

Ye shady glooms, in vain you strive 71-72 (5), 110 (7)
Ye winds, to whom Collin complains 99 (56)
Yee gods I only wish to die 5 (423), 12-12a (7), 26 (17), 29-31 (17), 78a-b (17), 90 (17)
Yee powr's my welcome (see Ye powr's)
Yee powr's oh let me know what reason 40a (33), 42 (33), 43 (20), 43a (18), 44-45 (34), 82 (34), 126a (34)
Yee stars that rule my birth 5 (422), 12-12a (4), 26 (25), 29-31 (25), 78a-b (25), 90 (25)
Yes 'tis all I want 14 (14), 16 (40), 19-23 (40), 33a-35 (41), 62-63 (40), 79-79a (40), 177 (40)
Yes tis most certain your eyes 64-65 (22), 68 (22), 76a-78 (22)
You damzells who sleep, devoid of all care 8-11 (61), 33 (108)
You fair but peevish 41 (2)
You fly and yet you love me too 5 (232)
You ladyes who are young and gay 5 (228)
You laugh to see me fond appear 5 (234)
You may talk of brisk claret 55-55a (22), 73 (14)
You say you love me 46-47a (65), 93 (65)
You scorn a tender heart 46-47a (56), 93 (56)
You tell me, Dick, you lately read 99 (36)
You the glorious sons of honour 5 (233), 33 (84), 56 (19), 86 (1)
You twice ten hundred deities 5 (227), 157 (17)
You who for wedlock importune 40a (20), 42 (20), 43 (8), 44-45 (20), 82 (20), 126a (20)
You're so pretty airy witty 46-47a (55), 93 (55)
Young and charming 46-47a (12), 93 (12)
Young Collen cleaving of a beam 55-55a (33)
Young Corydon and Phyllis 5 (231), 33 (85)
Young Cupid I find, to subdue me inclin'd 56 (3)
Young Cupid one day wiley 76 (2)
Young John the gard'ner 73 (18)
Young Mirtillo brisk and gay, The 4 (1), 5 (195), 7 (1)
Young Philoret and Celia 144-45 (34), 180 (24)
Young Ursley, in a merry mood 99 (124)
Your beauties pursuing will prove my undoeing 71-72 (9)
Your hay it is mow'd and your corn is reap'd 5 (303)
Your heart alone is all I prize 171 (46)
You've been with dull prologues here banter'd so long 5 (279)

Zephirs, revenés dans nos plaines 134 (28)

2 Composers, librettists, adaptors

Persons named on title-pages or songs, or in Table V.
References are to entry numbers followed, when appropriate, by song numbers in brackets, or by the equals sign and entry numbers in brackets when song numbers are identical to earlier entries.

Akeroyde, Samuel 5 (208, 254, 273, 378), 33 (105), 55-55a (56)
Albinoni 159 (7, 9, 11, 13-14)
Aldrich, Bedford 70 (8), 99 (96), 109 (2, 11)
Amadei, Filippo 119-120, 122
Ariosti, Attilio 127, 137-42, 147-51, 158-62, 169-70, 172
Armstrong 48a-52

Barrett 5 (38, 51, 73, 79-80, 109, 115, 121, 123, 130, 133, 212, 232-33, 288, 309, 360), 33 (84, 102), 56 (13, 19), 86 (1), 99 (27, 39, 63, 76, 79, 84, 90-91, 100, 108), 109 (6)
Berenclow, Bernard 5 (75, 117, 161), 33 (32, 47)
Birkhead, Matthew 99 (26, 89)
Biron, Lord 5 (293)
Blow, John 5 (189, 265, 287), 33 (93), 55-55a (59-63), 56 (26), 73 (15), 99 (104)
Bolton 159
Bononcini, Giovanni 13-16, 18-23, 33a-35, 62-63, 75-75a, 79-79a, 90b, 111-22, 125-26, 128-30, 143, 145a, 152-53, 159-60, 169-70, 172, 176-77, 179
Bradley, A 56 (33)
Bradley, Robert 5 (27), 33 (10), 109 (5)
Brown, Richard 5 (325, 329, 344, 372), 55-55a (2-3, 5-8, 15-17, 26-27, 65), 95 (28)
Brown, Robert 73 (3)

Carey, Henry 136, 171, 180
Clarke, Jeremiah 5 (3, 14, 33, 76, 95-96, 116, 140, 169, 181, 196, 200, 204, 207, 231, 249, 255, 261, 281, 331, 354, 362, 364, 370, 374, 384), 33 (22, 35, 41, 43, 49, 83, 85), 55-55a (12, 57), 95 (12-13, 27)
Clarke, Thomas 5 (15, 122), 33 (3, 50)
Clayton, Thomas 5 (385-86, 389-92, 400, 411, 414-15, 423), 12-12a, 26, 29-31, 37-38, 78a-b, 81, 90
Cobston 132 (3), 133 (1)
Conti, Francesco 53-54, 59, 79b, 123
Corbett, William 5 (328, 355), 95 (16, 31)
Courteville, Richard 5 (5, 152, 179, 190, 201, 276, 297, 299, 301, 320, 366), 109 (13), 144-45 (42)

Cox, Robert 5 (98, 141, 379), 33 (42, 55, 61), 95 (33)
Croft, William 5 (11-12, 81, 85, 215, 340, 388, 403, 407, 416), 33 (33), 95 (8)
D'urfey, Thomas 5 (176), 33 (77), 56 (20, 22), 86 (3)
Damascene, Alexander 99 (103)
Davis, William 33 (15), 56 (24), 99 (66)
Day, George 55-55a (28)
Dieupart, Charles 46-47a, 93, 144-45 (62)
Dorset, Lord 109 (8)
Du Ruel 70 (10), 99 (65)

Eccles, John 1-3, 5 (13, 16, 25, 37, 58, 60, 71, 74, 86-87, 90, 94, 100, 102, 118, 126, 131, 153, 159, 167, 172, 178, 182, 222, 228-29, 236, 244, 259, 262, 286, 302, 311, 316, 321, 323, 333-34, 339, 343, 348-49, 351, 357, 359, 363, 397, 406, 412), 6, 8-11, 33 (8, 40, 48, 100), 55-55a (1, 9, 45, 48), 56 (7-8), 73 (11), 99 (83, 128)
Eccles, Henry 33 (51)
Elford, Richard 5 (191, 306-07, 346), 56 (4, 14), 99 (71)
Eminent Master 5 (151), 33 (59), 99 (21, 59), 144-45 (32, 70, 72-73), 159 (3)

Farinel, Michael 5 (162)
Fedelli, Giuseppe 32-32a
Finger, Gottfried 5 (88, 247, 266, 275)
Frances 95 (26)
Franck, Johann 5 (336)

Galliard, Johann 85, 103, 127a-b, 135a-c, 174-75
Garee, John 5 (314), 33 (37), 56 (21)
Gasparini, Francesco 83-84, 169-70 (13)
Geminiani, Francesco 159 (5)
Gillier, Jean Claude 5 (65, 97, 315, 317-18), 33 (92), 134
Gorton, William 5 (56), 99 (72)
Graves, James 5 (256, 322), 101-102, 144-45 (77)

Hall, Henry 5 (105, 310), 55-55a (14, 64)
Handel, George Frederic 99 (56, 107), 106

(5), 119-20, 122, 159-60, 169-70, 178
(7-11)
Hayden, George 33 (74), 106 (2, 6, 12)
Haym, Nicola 48a-52 (7-8, 10-13, 15, 19,
21-23, 25-28, 32, 40, 42-43, 47-48),
57-58 (6-7, 9-13, 15, 21, 23, 25-26, 32,
40, 42, 46, 49), 94 (=48a)
Heidegger, John 64-65, 68, 76a-78
Hemming 106 (7-8, 11, 15-17)
Hickes 33 (98)
Humphries 159 (8)

Isum (or Isham), John 5 (269), 24 (2, 5-7, 9,
12), 24a (2, 5, 7, 9-10, 12), 33 (75), 55-55a
(44), 56 (10)

Jones, Richard 106 (3, 14)

Keen, Edward 5 (39, 101), 33 (9), 95 (21)
King, Robert 99 (102)

Lane 33 (64)
Leveridge, Richard 5 (6, 10, 34, 68, 83,
92-93, 112, 125, 138-39, 142, 164,
187-88, 197, 205-206, 214, 223, 257,
279, 289), 33 (6, 12, 44-45, 56-57, 63, 68,
76, 78), 56 (1-3, 5, 12), 76, 95 (24, 30), 99
(11, 46, 52-53, 57, 95)

Mancini, Francesco 69, 74-74a, 80-80a,
91-92
Manley, Cornelius 99 (48)
Marshall 100
Martin, George 5 (219), 33 (81)
Morgan, Thomas 5 (313, 356), 55-55a (13),
73 (7)
Morley, William 24 (1, 3-4, 8, 10-11), 24a
(1, 3-4, 6, 8, 11)
Motley, Richard 5 (55), 33 (25)

Neale, Richard 144-45
Nickson, John 5 (375)
Nicola (i.e., Nicola Matteis) 5 (373, 377)

Paisible, James 5 (155), 33 (62)
Pepusch, Johann 40-40a, 42-45, 82, 96-98,
105, 126a, 135
Person of Quality 5 (300)
Polani, Girolamo 88, 90a
Porpora, Nicola 178 (1-6), 178a
Porta, Giovanni 107
Purcell, Daniel 5 (28, 35, 40-41, 49, 69, 70,
103-104, 111, 114, 124, 127, 132, 134,
147-48, 154, 166, 170, 183-84, 193, 202,
216, 218, 224-25, 230, 234, 241-43, 246,
248, 251-52, 267, 268, 270, 277-78,
284-85, 291, 294, 298, 305, 324, 338,

345, 353, 358, 361, 369, 371, 376, 380),
33 (20, 26, 60, 67, 99, 106-107), 95 (22,
32), 99 (8, 45)
Purcell, Henry 5 (7, 18, 24, 36, 46-48, 52, 54,
61-62, 66, 72, 136, 157, 160, 171, 194,
211, 227, 238, 260, 274, 282, 290, 303,
312, 319, 327, 332, 335, 337, 341, 347,
387, 402, 405, 408, 418-19), 33 (19, 24,
30, 66, 73), 55-55a (18-20, 24-25, 29,
31-43, 46, 51-54), 56 (32), 73 (1-2, 19-21,
26), 95 (20), 109 (10), 157

Ramondon, Littleton 87, 99 (5, 13, 41, 82,
85, 92, 106, 113), 109 (12)
Reading, John 55-55a (49), 71-72, 73 (8)
Robart, William 5 (245, 253, 263-64,
271-72, 308)
Roseingrave, Thomas 56 (25), 106 (13), 108
(13, 17, 20, 22)

Scarlatti, Alessandro 48a-52, 57-58, 94
Scarlatti, Domenico 108
Sheeles, John 106 (1, 20), 124
Shore, William 5 (84), 33 (34)
Simmons 5 (304)
Smith, John 25
Sweet 5 (2)

Thomson, William 168
Townsend, James 33 (7)
Tudway, Thomas 55-55a (22)
Turner, William 104, 106 (4, 9, 10, 18, 19)

Vanbrugh, George 99 (124), 109 (3), 110,
144-45 (36)
Vinci, Leonardo 163-64

Webb, Kelly 173 (7)
Weldon, John 4, 5 (1, 17, 29, 31-32, 42,
44-45, 89, 113, 119-20, 128, 144,
149-50, 156, 158, 168, 177, 180, 192,
195, 203, 209, 221, 368, 383, 399, 401,
404, 409, 413, 417, 421), 7, 33 (36, 94,
97), 56 (11, 37, 44), 109 (7), 144-45 (56)
White 33 (23)
Wilford, John 5 (350), 33 (18, 38), 99 (32)
Wilkins 95 (25)
Williams 5 (342)
Willis 5 (64, 129, 239), 33 (28, 52-53),
55-55a (10-11), 56 (27)

Ximenes, Charles 33 (65, 79)

Young, Anthony 41
Young, Charles 173 (6)

Ziani, Marc'Antonio 89

3 Singers

References are to entry numbers followed by song numbers in brackets, or by the equals sign and entry numbers in brackets when song numbers are identical to earlier entries.

Abell, John 95 (4), 99 (125)
Allinson 5 (210)
Ayliff, Mrs 5 (7, 301, 402), 8-11 (49), 157 (1, 10)

Baldassari, Benedetto 107 (4, 9, 15, 21, 30) 108 (1, 3, 10, 15, 19, 28, 30, 34, 38), 114 (7, 11, 15, 20, 24), 114a-114b (7), 115 (5), 116-118 (5, 10), 172 (45), 179 (=114)
Baldwin, Mary 5 (135), 8-11 (89), 33 (58)
Balti 166-67 (5-6), 172 (8)
Barbier, Jane 83 (2-3, 16, 23, 29, 32), 84 (6, 11, 16, 22, 34), 85 (2, 6-7, 10, 12, 15, 20-22, 26, 29-30), 88 (1-2, 12, 17, 19, 23), 89 (5, 11, 13, 23), 90a (=88), 96-98 (2, 4, 6, 8, 12, 15, 17), 103 (=85), 105 (6), 174 (1-3, 6), 175 (1-3, 5), 177 (54)
Baroness (i.e., Joanna Maria Lindelheim) 13 (9), 14 (1, 6-7, 9, 12, 15), 15 (8, 17), 16 (6, 8, 11, 25-26, 33, 36, 44, 48-49), 18 (9), 19-23 (=16), 33a-35 (6, 8, 11, 26-27, 34, 37, 44), 46-47a (1, 4, 14-15, 27, 30, 40-41, 47-48, 57), 48a-52 (6, 10, 17, 23, 42, 47, 51), 57-58 (6, 10, 17, 23, 42, 46), 62-63 (=16), 79-79a (=16), 93 (=46), 94 (=48a), 177 (=16)
Bendler, Salomon 84 (2)
Benedetti (see Baldassari, Benedetto)
Berenstadt, Gaetano 127 (15), 138 (1, 14, 27), 159 (21), 169-70 (9)
Berselli, Matteo 111-12 (3, 11, 14, 19, 24, 27), 119-20 (3), 122 (2), 169-70 (8, 27), 172 (14, 42, 72), 176 (=111)
Birkhead, Matthew 99 (26, 84)
Boman, Elizabeth 5 (244, 262, 406), 8-11 (23, 51, 67), 32-32a (7, 104)
Boman, John 5 (290, 321), 8-11 (79), 25 (6), 33 (110)
Borosini, Francesco 150-51 (6), 159 (10), 161-62 (3, 5), 164-65 (8), 169-70 (12, 23), 172 (19, 22, 30, 105)
Boschi, Giuseppe Maria 74 (1-6), 75-75a (4, 6, 10-11, 13, 15-16, 19, 21, 27, 30-32, 35), 90b (=75), 99 (107), 111-12 (8, 20, 28), 114, (4, 13, 25), 114a-114b (4), 127 (5, 12), 137 (4), 138 (7, 13, 24), 169-70 (5, 30), 172 (29, 91), 176 (=111), 179 (=114)
Bourdon, [Gabriel?] 5 (208), 33 (105)
Bowen, James 5 (28, 62, 170, 305)
Boy 5 (22, 246, 252, 261, 265, 270, 278, 282, 291, 323, 393), 13 (2-4, 6-7), 14 (2-3, 11,

14), 15 (13), 16 (2-3, 12, 19-20, 29, 35, 39-40, 51), 18 (=13), 19-23 (=16), 33 (12), 33a-35 (41), 62-63 (=16), 79-79a (=16), 95 (30), 177 (=16)
Boy, Little 5 (412)
Boy, Mr Magnus' 5 (364)
Boy, New 5 (298)
Bracegirdle, Anne 5 (13, 60, 100, 102, 126, 236-7, 316, 339, 343, 357), 8-11 (1, 36, 41, 52, 58, 65, 67-69, 74, 76, 84-85, 88, 96), 32-32a (4, 8, 11), 33 (17, 40, 104, 111)
Bradshaw, Lucretia 5 (399), 25 (1)
Butler, Charlotte 5 (319)

Campion, Mary Anne 4 (1, 3-4), 5 (44, 92, 112, 149, 168, 195, 197, 230, 247, 254-5, 273, 364, 374, 413, 417), 7 (1, 3-4), 33 (45), 95 (29)
Carey, Henry 180 (12)
Cassani, Giuseppe 64-65 (34), 68 (34), 69 (8), 76a (34), 77-78 (34), 80-80a (8), 91-92 (8)
Chambers, Isabella 135 (1, 3, 7), 135a (2, 4), 135b (1, 5-6), 135c (3, 5), 173 (4), 174 (5-6), 175 (4-5), 177 (55)
Church, John 8-11 (21, 31, 45)
Cibber, Mrs 5 (292)
Cook, Mr 1-3 (5), 5 (74, 397, 408), 6 (1, 3, 5), 8-11 (8, 12, 31, 34, 44, 48, 56), 32-32a (9), 33 (8, 95, 98), 48a-52 (7), 57-58 (7), 94 (7), 100 (1)
Cooper, Mr 5 (40)
Crofts, Miss 5 (361)
Cross, Letitia 5 (96, 249, 332, 352, 354-5, 391-2), 12-12a (4, 12, 14), 26 (9-10, 19-20, 25, 34, 41), 29-31 (=26), 64-65 (26-28, 30), 68 (=64), 76a (=64), 77-78 (=64), 78a-b (=26), 90 (=26), 95 (12, 27)
Curco, Mr 5 (222, 334), 33 (100), 56 (8)
Cuzzoni, Francesca 127 (1, 6, 11, 17-18, 22, 24), 137 (1, 6, 10, 12, 14-15), 138 (2, 4, 10-11, 18, 21, 30, 34), 139-40 (1, 5, 7), 141 (1, 4, 6), 142 (2, 5-6), 143 (4-5, 8), 145a (1, 5-8), 147-48 (1, 4-5), 149 (1-3), 150-51 (1-2, 4), 152 (1-2, 6), 153 (1, 5-7, 10), 158 (2, 5-6), 159 (1, 12, 16, 23, 25, 34-36), 160 (36), 161-62 (7, 9-10), 163 (2-3, 5), 164 (1, 3, 6, 10), 166 (1), 167 (1), 169-70 (1-4, 6-7, 16, 18-20, 25, 28, 34-35), 172 (3, 15-16, 23-24, 35, 37, 43, 46-48, 51, 59, 61-62, 71, 82-83, 85,

87-90, 93-95), 178 (1-3, 5-6, 8-10), 178a
(1-3, 5-6)

Damascene, Alexander 6 (1), 8-11 (12)
Davis 5 (74), 8-11 (48), 33 (14, 95, 98), 41
(6), 99 (45)
De L'Épine, Margaritta 33a-35 (2-3, 12,
21-22, 30, 40, 52), 40a (4, 6, 15, 18, 29,
35, 47-48, 50, 53), 42 (=40a), 43 (1-2, 4,
6, 16, 22, 30-31, 33), 43a (3-4, 8, 11, 15,
20, 28, 31), 44-45 (4, 6, 15, 18, 29, 36,
48-49, 51, 54), 46-47a (10, 12, 14, 32,
34-35, 42-43, 45, 49-50, 62-63, 68),
48a-52 (8, 11, 20-21, 33-34, 40, 43, 46,
48), 53-54 (1-3, 15, 20, 27, 33, 37-38, 42),
57-58 (9, 11, 20-21, 34, 40, 43, 47-48), 59
(1-3, 15, 19-20, 27, 33, 37-38, 42), 64-65
(1-2, 11, 18, 25, 31, 38, 40), 68 (=64), 69
(7, 9-10, 14-15, 19, 23, 27-28, 31, 38), 74a
(=69), 76a-78 (=64), 80-80a (=69), 82 (4,
6, 15, 18, 29, 36, 46-47, 49, 52), 83 (4, 13,
24, 27, 34), 84 (8, 12, 21, 26, 35), 85 (1, 3,
8, 16, 19, 23, 25, 32), 88 (4, 8, 20), 89 (3,
6, 12, 17, 26), 90a (=88), 91-92 (=69), 93
(=46), 94 (=48a), 96-98 (1, 3, 5, 7-8, 10,
14, 16), 103 (=85), 105 (6), 123 (=53),
126a (=44), 177 (19, 27, 39)
Dennis, Mrs 107 (7, 18)
D'Legard (see Laguerre)
Doggett, Thomas 5 (118, 348, 356), 8-11 (22,
79, 96), 33 (36, 48, 110-11), 64-65 (13,
15, 27-28, 30), 68 (=64), 76a-78 (=64),
109 (7)
Dotti, Anna 150-51 (3), 159 (1), 161-162
(10), 166-67 (3-4), 172 (20, 83, 99)
Durastanti, Margherita 107 (2, 8, 13-14, 16,
23, 29, 33), 108 (5, 8, 13, 17, 23, 25-27,
33, 37), 111-12 (1, 6, 10, 12, 17, 21-22,
26, 31), 113 (6-7), 119-20 (4, 6), 122 (3,
6), 127 (4, 9, 16, 19), 128-30 (5), 137 (3,
9), 138 (3, 10, 12, 23, 26, 33), 139-40 (6),
141 (5), 142 (3), 143 (1-2, 9), 145a (3, 11),
147 (2), 148 (2), 152 (5), 153 (3, 9), 158
(3), 159 (15, 22), 169-70 (26, 36), 172 (6,
10, 41, 52-53, 56, 64, 79, 86, 102, 104),
176 (=111)
Dyer, Mrs 5 (327, 330)

Edwards, Thomas 5 (380)
Elford, Richard 1-3 (1-4), 5 (203, 388), 6
(1-2, 4), 8-11 (10, 12, 16, 30-31, 43, 53,
63, 78, 83, 91-92), 33 (46)
Erwin, Mrs 5 (41, 69, 103-4, 124, 225, 251,
277, 281), 33 (26)

Faire 33 (5)
Fletcher, Maria 105 (7), 177 (56)
Fowell 5 (302)
Freeman, John 5 (81, 147, 241, 248, 362,
369, 376)

Galerati, Catterina 88 (5, 10-11, 13, 16, 22,
24), 89 (1, 7, 14-15, 20-22, 25, 27), 90a
(=88), 107 (6, 26, 28, 35), 111-12 (2, 15,
30), 176 (2, 15, 30)
Gallia, Maria Margherita 32-32a (1, 3, 10,
12-13, 15, 17-18), 37 (10-12), 38 (10-12,
15-16, 21-23, 25-26), 81 (=38)
Girardeau, Isabella 64-65 (7-8, 12, 19, 23,
37), 69 (5, 11, 20, 24-25, 36, 39), 74a
(=69), 75-75a (1-2, 8, 18, 22-23, 29),
76a-78 (=64), 80-80a (=69), 83 (5, 9, 15,
22, 30), 84 (3, 5, 9, 15, 19, 25, 27-28, 30,
32, 38), 90b (=75), 91-92 (=69)
Girl 5 (194, 282, 323, 353), 33 (66), 95 (20)
Girl, Mrs Willis's 25 (2)
Good 12 (16), 26 (26), 29-31 (26),
78a-b (26), 90 (26)
Gordon, Alexander 107 (5, 19-20, 34), 108
(1-2, 7, 18, 29, 35)
Gouge, Mrs 5 (25, 222, 328), 8-11 (47, 71,
95), 33 (100), 56 (8)

Haines, Mrs 5 (229, 315), 8-11 (60)
Harris, Mrs 5 (114)
Hodgson, Mrs 5 (58, 86-87, 113, 123, 159,
178, 191, 228, 259, 266, 306, 311, 318,
337, 351, 359, 382, 384, 396, 403, 408),
8-11 (2, 5, 13, 17-18, 20, 25, 28, 35, 39,
50, 62, 75, 77), 99 (44)
Holcomb, Henry 37 (2, 4), 38 (2, 4, 18), 81
(=38)
Hughes, Francis 5 (128, 134, 166, 190, 258,
389, 394, 410, 414), 12 (1-3), 12a (1-3,
17, 18), 14 (5, 7, 16), 15 (2, 5-6, 9, 12-13),
16 (7, 17, 22, 27, 34-35, 41, 47, 49), 19-23
(=16), 26 (1-4, 6, 9, 11, 14-16, 18, 21-24,
35, 37), 29-31 (=26), 33 (97), 33a-34a (7,
18, 20, 28, 35, 42, 47), 35 (7, 18, 20, 28,
35, 42, 49), 37 (13-14), 38 (13-15, 33-34,
36-38, 40, 42), 40a (32, 44), 42 (=40a), 43
(5, 7, 13, 19, 27), 43a (9, 13, 25), 44-45
(16, 19, 26, 33, 45), 62-63 (=16), 78a-b
(=26), 79-79a (=16), 81 (=38), 82 (16,
19, 26, 33, 44), 90 (=26), 126a (=44), 177
(7, 17, 22, 34-35, 41, 47, 49)

Isabella (see Giradeau)

Knapp, Mr 5 (333)
Knight, Frances Maria 5 (347)

Laguerre, John 127a (2-3), 127b (1), 135
(4-5), 135a-b (3), 135c (2), 173 (2-3)
Laroche, James 5 (349), 8-11 (64)
Laroon, Marcellus 4 (6), 5 (128, 145), 7 (6),
32 (5-6, 14, 18), 33 (97, 99)
Lawrence, Mr 32 (2, 16), 38 (30-32), 40 (4,
13-14), 40a (13-14, 23, 26, 34, 43, 51), 42
(=40a), 43 (12, 14, 21, 34), 43a (7, 12, 14,
19, 30), 44-45 (13-14, 24-25, 27, 35, 44,

52), 53-54 (10, 22), 59 (=53), 81 (=38), 82 (13-14, 24-25, 27, 35, 50), 123 (=53), 126a (=44)

Lee, Mr 33 (109)

L'Épine (see De L'Épine)

Leveridge, Richard 5 (24, 30, 33, 59, 83, 138, 142, 171, 176, 181, 186, 198, 213, 218, 234, 279, 362, 386, 423), 12-12a (5, 7), 13 (8), 14 (10), 15 (4, 11, 14), 16 (15-16, 23, 31, 38, 46), 18 (8, 11), 19-23 (=16), 26 (7, 11, 16-17, 28, 36), 29-31 (=26), 33 (21-22, 31, 57, 63, 73, 82, 107), 33a-35 (15, 24, 32, 46), 37 (6-7, 9), 38 (6-7, 9, 28, 41), 40 (10, 12, 15, 17), 40a (10, 22, 27, 31, 39, 42), 42 (=40a), 43 (9, 11, 17, 18), 43a (17, 24), 44-45 (10, 12, 21, 23, 30, 32, 40, 43), 46-47a (2-3, 5, 7, 20, 24, 38, 53-54, 56, 58, 64, 66), 56 (2-3, 12, 22, 34), 62-63 (=16), 78a-b (=26), 79-79a (=16), 81 (=38), 82 (=44), 85 (5, 18, 27), 90 (=26), 93 (=46), 95 (10-11), 99 (11, 29, 43, 46, 123, 126), 103 (5, 18, 27), 105 (1, 5), 126a (=44), 135 (2-3, 5), 135a (1, 5), 135b (2, 4), 135c (1, 4), 157 (30), 159 (19, 37), 173 (3-5), 174 (4), 175 (6), 177 (=16)

Lindsey, Mary 4 (2, 5), 5 (24, 68, 77, 78, 93, 119, 121, 145, 158, 181, 188, 207, 242-43, 250, 261, 294, 324, 338, 368), 7 (2, 5), 12-12a (15-16), 13 (10, 15), 15 (3-4, 7, 14), 16 (14, 16, 24, 32, 37, 38), 18 (10, 15), 19-23 (=16), 26 (8, 26), 29-31 (=26), 33 (44, 99), 33a-35 (14, 25, 33, 38), 37 (8-9), 38 (8-9, 17, 41), 40 (2, 6, 8-9, 11-12), 40a (2, 8, 11, 20-21, 30, 40-41, 46), 42 (=40a), 43 (8, 10, 26, 29), 43a (1, 5, 16, 23, 27), 44-45 (2, 8, 11-12, 20, 22, 31, 41-42, 47), 46-47a (6-7, 13, 21, 23-25, 31, 37, 54-55, 65-66), 53-54 (9, 23, 32), 59 (=53), 62-63 (=16), 64-65 (14-15, 27, 29), 68 (=64), 76a-78 (=64), 78a-b (=26), 79-79a (=16), 79b (=53), 81 (=38), 82 (2, 8, 11-12, 20, 22, 31, 41-42, 45), 90 (=26), 93 (=46), 99 (108), 123 (=53), 126a (=44), 157 (30), 177 (=16)

Lucas, Jane 5 (21, 116, 208), 33 (13, 49, 105), 95 (9)

Magnus, Mrs 5 (270)

Manina, Maria 85 (4, 11, 13, 22, 28), 103 (=85)

Margaretta (see De L'Épine)

Mills, Margaret 5 (139), 33 (56)

Nicolini (i.e., Nicola Grimaldi) 48a-52 (1, 5, 16, 18-19, 28, 30-31, 35-36, 39, 44-45, 50, 53), 53-54 (5, 11-12, 14, 19, 21, 28, 30, 34, 39-41), 57-58 (5, 16, 18-19, 28, 30-31, 39, 44-45, 53), 59 (=53), 62-63 (53), 64-65 (3-4, 9, 16-17, 20, 22, 24-25, 33, 36, 39-40), 68 (=64), 69 (1, 3, 6, 13,

16-18, 22-23, 28-30, 34-35, 39), 74a (=69), 75-75a (3, 9, 17, 24, 27, 28, 34), 76a-78 (=64), 79-79a (53), 79b (=53), 80-80a (=69), 83 (6, 10-12, 14, 18-20, 25, 28, 31, 33), 84 (4, 7, 14, 18, 20, 23, 27-28, 31, 33, 39, 41), 90b (=75), 91-92 (=69), 94 (=48a), 99 (98), 123 (=53), 177 (53)

Pacini, Andrea 161-162 (6, 8), 163 (6), 172 (68, 103)

Pack, George 25 (1, 3, 6, 27), 99 (35, 67)

Pate, John 5 (83, 154, 218, 260, 267-68, 345, 371), 8-11 (70), 33 (107), 157 (31)

Pearson, Mrs 85 (9-10, 14, 17, 24, 29, 31), 103 (=85)

Pilotti, Elizabetta 75-75a (5, 7, 12, 14, 20, 25-26, 33), 83 (1, 3, 7-8, 12, 17, 21, 26, 35), 84 (1, 10, 13, 17, 24, 29, 40), 90b (=75)

Pinkethman, WIlliam 5 (57), 99 (57)

Platt, Bartholomew 173 (8)

Prince, Mrs 5 (4, 37, 82, 99), 33 (1, 16), 95 (7)

Pulmon, Mrs 105 (2-4, 7-8)

Ramondon, Littleton 13 (5, 12-14), 14 (8), 16 (4, 9, 21, 28, 45), 18 (=13), 19-23 (=16), 26 (5), 29-31 (5), 33a-34a (4, 9, 23, 29, 45), 35 (9, 23, 29, 45), 48a-52 (9, 22, 24, 32, 41), 53-54 (25), 57-58 (8, 22, 24, 32, 41), 59 (25), 62-63 (=16), 78a-b (5), 79-79a (=16), 79b (25), 90 (5), 94 (=48a), 123 (25), 177 (16)

Ray, John 136 (3), 180 (3)

Raynton, Mr 99 (79)

Reading, John 5 (260, 334), 33 (109), 157 (31)

Reading, Mrs 38 (30-32), 81 (=38), 95 (6), 159 (24)

Robert 1-3 (1, 6), 6 (3), 8-11 (8, 26, 91)

Robert, Mrs 5 (299)

Robinson, Anastasia 88 (3, 7, 10, 14, 18, 21), 89 (2, 8, 10, 16, 19, 21, 27-28), 90a (=88), 107 (3, 10, 12, 15, 24-25, 27, 31), 108 (1, 6, 11-14, 21, 24, 28, 32-33, 36), 113 (1, 4), 114 (1-2, 9, 14, 18-19, 22, 26), 114a-b (1-2), 115-118 (1, 6), 119-120 (2), 121 (2, 4, 6, 8), 122 (1), 125-126 (=121), 127 (3, 7, 10, 13, 20), 128-129 (2), 130 (2), 137 (7, 16), 138 (6, 8, 15, 17, 20, 29, 32), 139-140 (4), 141 (3), 142 (4), 143 (6, 10), 145a (4), 147-148 (3), 153 (4), 158 (4, 8), 169-70 (17), 172 (1, 12, 33, 34, 40, 54, 60, 65, 67, 69, 77, 81, 101), 179 (=114)

Robinson, T 107 (1-2, 11, 17, 22, 32), 108 (4, 9, 16, 20, 31)

Salvai, Maria Maddalena 111-12 (4, 11, 18, 23), 113 (3), 114 (6, 10, 17, 21, 24), 114a-b (6), 115-118 (3), 119-20 (1, 8),

122 (4, 8), 172 (42, 44, 66, 96), 176 (=111), 179 (=114)
Senesino (i.e., Francesco Bernardi) 111-12 (5, 7, 9, 13, 16, 22, 25, 29, 31-32), 113 (2, 5), 114 (1, 3, 5, 8, 12, 16, 19, 23, 27), 114a-b (1, 3, 5, 8), 115-118 (1-2, 4, 7-9), 119-120 (5, 7), 121 (1, 3, 5, 7, 9-10), 122 (5, 7), 125-26 (=121), 127 (2, 8, 14, 17, 21, 23), 128-30 (3-4), 137 (2, 5, 8, 10-11, 13), 138 (5, 9, 16, 19, 22, 25, 28), 139-40 (2-3), 141 (2), 142 (1), 143 (3, 7), 145a (2, 9, 10), 147-48 (6), 149 (4), 150 (5, 7), 151 (5), 152 (3-4), 153 (2, 8, 11), 158 (1, 7), 159 (6, 26, 38, 41), 161-62 (2, 7), 163 (1, 4), 164 (2, 4-7, 9), 166 (2), 167 (2), 169-70 (10-11, 14, 29, 31-33), 172 (1-2, 4, 5, 9, 11, 13, 15, 17-18, 21, 25-27, 31-32, 36, 39, 49-50, 57, 63, 70, 73, 75-76, 78, 80, 84, 92, 97-98, 100, 106-7), 173 (1), 176 (=111), 178 (4, 7, 11), 178a (4), 179 (=114)
Shaw 5 (70, 127, 183, 202, 289)
Sorosina, Benedetta 161-62 (1, 4), 172 (58)
Spalding, Mr 5 (222), 33 (100), 56 (8)

Temple 5 (95), 33 (43), 95 (13)
Tenori 166-7 (7), 172 (7)
Tofts, Catherine 5 (385, 400, 411, 415, 420), 12 (6, 8-9, 11, 13), 12a (6, 8-9, 11, 13, 19), 13 (1, 11), 14 (4, 13), 15 (1, 10, 15, 18), 16 (1, 5, 10, 13, 18, 30, 42, 50), 18 (1), 19-23 (=16), 26 (4, 12-13, 21-23, 27, 29-33, 35), 29-31 (=26), 33a-35 (1, 5, 10, 13, 19, 31, 43, 51), 37 (1, 3, 5), 38 (1, 3, 5, 19-20, 24, 27, 29, 35, 37, 39-40, 42), 40 (1, 3, 5, 16), 40a (1, 3, 5, 9, 17, 28, 33, 36-37, 45, 49, 52), 42 (=40a), 43 (3, 12, 13, 15, 20, 23-25, 28, 32, 35), 43a (2, 6, 10, 13, 18,

21-22, 26, 29), 44-45 (1, 3, 5, 9, 17, 25-26, 28, 34, 37-39, 46, 50, 53), 46-47a (11, 16-18, 22, 26, 28, 33, 35, 44, 46, 52, 59, 61, 62), 48a-52 (2-4, 15, 17, 25, 29, 30, 37-38), 53-54 (6-7, 13, 17-18, 24, 26, 31, 35, 41), 57-58 (2-4, 15, 17, 25, 29-30, 37), 59 (=53), 62-63 (=16), 78a-b (=26), 79-79a (=16), 79b (=53), 81 (1, 3, 5, 19-20, 24, 27, 29, 35, 37, 39-40, 42), 82 (1, 3, 5, 9, 17, 25-26, 28, 34, 37-39, 48, 51), 90 (=26), 93 (=46), 94 (=48a), 123 (=53), 126a (=44), 177 (=16)
Travers, G 100 (1-3)
Turner, William 15 (16), 16 (43), 19-23 (43), 33a-34a (50), 35 (48), 62-63 (43), 79-79a (43), 96-98 (9, 13, 15)

Valentini (i.e., Valentini Urbani) 40 (7), 40a (7, 16, 19), 42 (=40a), 43 (5), 43a (9), 44-45 (7, 16), 46-47a (8-9, 16, 19, 29, 36, 39, 51, 57-58, 67), 48a-52 (12-14, 19, 26-27, 39, 49, 52), 53-54 (4, 8, 16, 26, 28-29, 36, 38), 57-58 (12-14, 19, 26-27, 51), 59 (=53), 62-63 (52), 64-65 (5-6, 10, 20-21, 32, 35, 41), 68 (=64), 69 (2, 4, 12, 21, 26, 32-33, 37), 76a-78 (=64), 79-79a (52), 79b (=53), 80-80a (=69), 82 (=44), 88 (2, 6, 9, 15), 89 (4, 9, 18, 24), 90a (=88), 91-92 (2, 4, 12, 21, 26, 32-33, 37), 93 (=46), 94 (=48a), 123 (=53), 126a (=44), 177 (52)

Wilford, John 33 (18)
Wilkins, Mr 95 (25)
Willis, Elizabeth 5 (19, 108, 196, 214), 25 (4), 33 (5, 9), 95 (14, 73)
Wiltshire, John 5 (312, 363), 8-11 (54)

4 Literary or dramatic works, operas, occasions

For short-titles of books see next index.
References are to entry numbers followed, when appropriate, by song numbers in brackets.

Abdelazar, or the Moor's Revenge 5 (335)
Aesope 5 (164)
Agreeable Disappointment 5 (37, 113), 33
   (16), 99 (44)
Alexander the Great 5 (148, 267), 33 (60),
   104 (17)
Almahide 64-65, 68, 76a-78
Amadis 160 (23)
Amalasont 5 (103, 324)
Amphitryon 5 (319)
Antiochus 83
Apollo and Daphne 174-75
Aquilio 147-49, 172 (12, 41, 70, 89, 90, 94)
Arminius 89
Arsaces 144-45 (29), 159 (17), 169- 70 (31)
Arsinoe 5 (385-86, 389-92, 400, 410- 11,
   414-15, 420, 423), 12-12a, 26, 29-31,
   78a-b, 90
Artaxerxes 150-51, 159 (6), 169-70 (28), 172
   (23, 46, 50, 88, 92, 99)
As you Find it 5 (86), 8-11 (50), 95 (31)
Astartus 111-12, 144-45 (53, 55), 169-70 (8,
   27, 29, 32, 36), 172 (5, 13-14, 38, 42, 44,
   52, 72), 176
Aureng-Zebe 5 (402), 157 (10)

Bath, or the Western Lass 5 (116, 208), 33
   (49, 105)
Beau Defeated 5 (153), 8-11 (29)
Beau Demolished 99 (123, 126)
Birthday Songs 6
Biter 5 (397), 33 (8)
Bonduca 5 (136, 387, 419), 157 (15, 27, 28)
Britain's Happiness 33 (94), 56 (5)
British Apollo 101 (16)

Calphurnia 145a, 152-53, 159 (22, 34, 36),
   160 (6, 17), 169-70 (7, 18, 26), 172 (43,
   49, 51, 69, 82, 84-87, 102)
Calypso and Telemachus 85, 103
Camilla 5 (393-94), 13-16, 18-23, 33a-35,
   62-63, 79-79a, 105 (8), 144-45 (7, 10, 13,
   27), 177
Campaigners 5 (255, 298, 338, 341)
Capricious Lover 173 (2-4)
Cecilia song 1701 8-11 (3, 15, 19, 46, 66), 33
   (103)
Chances 5 (363), 8-11 (54)
City 8-11 (18)
City Bride 8-11 (64)

City Lady 5 (382, 406), 8-11 (51)
City Ramble 99 (39)
Clotilda 53-54, 59, 79b, 123
Committee 5 (33), 33 (22)
Conquest of Granada 5 (282)
Constant Couple or a Trip to the Jubilee 5
   (147)
Coriolano 127, 137, 144-45 (6), 159 (35),
   172 (35-36, 63-65, 71, 93, 106)
Country Miss with her Furbeloe 5 (30, 176),
   56 (22)
Country Wake 5 (351), 8-11 (39), 86 (3), 99
   (77)
Crispus 121, 125-26, 172 (18, 21, 33, 40,
   75-76, 97, 100)
Croesus 88, 90a
Custom of the Manor 99 (79)
Cynthia and Endymion 5 (356)
Cyrus 113
Cyrus the Great 8-11 (65)

Darius 159, 160 (1), 161-62, 172 (15, 19, 22,
   30, 58-59, 68, 83, 103)
Dioclesian (see also Prophetess) 5 (160), 157
   (16)
Don Quixote 5 (94, 157, 290, 337), 8-11
   (84), 157 (9, 32)
Duchess of Malfey 8-11 (81), 33 (87)
Duke and no Duke 5 (301)

Elisa 178-78a
Elpidia 160 (10, 19, 21), 163-64, 166, 169-70
   (15), 172 (7-9, 11, 20, 24, 27, 61-62, 95,
   105, 107)
Erminia 128-30, 172 (26, 57, 74, 101)
Esquire Brainless 99 (90)
Etearco 75-75a, 90b

Fair Example 4 (1), 5 (195), 7 (1)
Fair Penitent 5 (74, 159), 8-11 (5, 48)
Fairy Queen 5 (260, 327, 330), 157 (31)
Fate of Capua 5 (359)
Female Gallants 8-11 (42)
Female Wits 5 (355)
Fickle Fair One 173 (5)
Fickle Shepherdess 8-11 (76)
Flavius 144-45 (41, 71, 75), 159 (15, 21), 160
   (27, 29, 34), 169-70 (9, 19)
Floridante 144-45 (3, 20-21, 52, 67), 169-70
   (24)

5 Short-titles, publishers, dates

References are to entry numbers.

Almahide, Rawlins, 16 February 1710 68
  Walsh, Randall, Hare, 16 February 1710
    64-65
  Walsh, Randall, Hare, 31 December 1711
    76a
Almahide, 'Additional Songs', Walsh, Hare,
    31 December 1711 77-78
Antiochus, Walsh, Hare, 21 February 1712 83
Apollo and Daphne, Rawlins, 31 December
    1726 174
  Walsh, Hare 31 December 1726 175
Apollo's Feast, Book 2, Walsh, Hare, 16
    September 1726 172
Aquilio, Barret, 30 September 1724 148
  Cooke, 30 September 1724 149
  Walsh, Hares, 30 September 1724 147
Arminius, Walsh, Hare, 1 June 1714 89
Arsinoe, Rawlins, 5 October 1706 31
  Walsh, 5 October 1706 26
  Walsh, Hare, 5 October 1706 29
  Walsh, Hare, 31 December 1714 90
  Young, 5 October 1706 30
Arsinoe, 'Additional Songs', Walsh, Randall,
    Hare, 31 December 1711 78a-b
Arsinoe, [First Collection], Walsh, 2 April
    1706 12-12a
Artaxerxes, Barret, 31 December 1724 151
  Musick Shops [Walsh?], 31 December
    1724 150
Astartus, Walsh, Hare, 1 April 1721 111
  Walsh, Hare, 31 December 1726 176
  Young, 1 April 1721 112

Birthday Songs, Walsh, 4 November 1703 6
Book of New Songs, Author, 8 November
    1710 71-72
Bottle Companions, Walsh, Randall, Hare,
    26 May 1709 56

Calphurnia, Cooke, 31 December 1724 152
  Walsh, Hares, 31 July 1724 145a
  Walsh, Hares, 31 December 1724 153
Calypso and Telemachus, Walsh, Hare, 28
    June 1712 85
  Walsh, Hare, 31 December 1717 103
Camilla, Cullen, 1 March 1707 34-34a
  [Cullen], 22 February 1707 33a
  Rawlins, 1 March 1707 35
  Walsh, 11 May 1706 19
  Walsh, 16 May 1706 20
  Walsh, 31 December 1709 63

  Walsh, Hare, 16 May 1706 22-22a
  Walsh, Randall, Hare, 31 December 1709
    62
  Young, 16 May 1706 23
Camilla, Additional Songs, Walsh, Hare, 31
    December 1726 177
Camilla, 'Additional Songs', Walsh, Hare, 31
    December 1711 79
  Walsh, Randall, Hare, 31 December 1711
    79a
Camilla, [First Collection], Walsh, 2 April
    1706 13
  Walsh, 11 May 1706 18
Camilla, Second Collection, Walsh, 17 April
    1706 14
Camilla, 'Second Collection', Walsh, 1 May
    1706 16
Camilla, [Third Collection], Walsh, 30 April
    1706 15
Camilla, 'Third Collection', Walsh, Hare, 16
    May 1706 21-21a
Cantatas, Author, 3 March 1724 136
Clotilda, Cooke, 31 December 1722 123
  Walsh, Randall, Hare, 15 April 1709
    53-54
  Young, 29 November 1709 59
Clotilda, 'Additional Songs', Walsh, Randall,
    Hare, 31 December 1711 79b
[Collection of Catches], [Pippard], 31
    December 1710 73
Collection of Choicest Songs & Dialogues,
    Walsh, 31 October 1703 5
Collection of New Songs, (Young) Author, 5
    June 1707 41
  (Morley & Isum) Authors, 1 August 1706
    24
  (Weldon) Walsh, 31 December 1703 7
Collection of Songs, (Eccles) Walsh, 14
    November 1704 8-9
  (Eccles) Walsh, Hare, 14 November 1704
    10
  (Graves) Walsh, Hare, 26 October 1717 102
  (Sheeles) Walsh, Hares, 31 December
    1722 124
  (Eccles) Young, 14 November 1704 11
Comical Songs, Walsh, 31 December 1706 33
Coriolano, Author, 23 May 1723 127
  Walsh, Hares, 23 March 1724 137
Crispus, Meares, 23 August 1722 125-26
  Walsh, Hares, 25 August 1722 121
Croesus, Walsh, Hare, 1 May 1714 88

6 Printers, publishers, sellers, with short-titles and dates

References are to entry numbers.

Walsh, Hares, *Aquilio*, 30 September 1724
147
Calphurnia, 31 July 1724 145a
Calphurnia, 31 December 1724 153
Collection of Songs, 31 December 1722
124
Coriolano, 23 March 1724 137
Crispus, 25 August 1722 121
Cyrus, 31 December 1721 113
Erminia, 31 December 1723 130
Griselda, 22 May 1722 114-114b
Griselda, 31 December 1726 179
Jupiter and Europa, 30 September 1723
127a
Muzio Scaevola, 25 August 1722 122
Necromancer, 28 February 1724 135b
Orpheus Brittanicus, 31 December 1724
157
Pharnaces, 31 March 1724 143
Union of the Three Sister Arts, 31
December 1723 135
Vespasian, 23 March 1724 138-39
Walsh, Randall, *Rosamond*, 29 April 1707 38
Rosamond, [First Collection], 10 March
1707 37
Thomyris, 12 June 1707 43a
Thomyris, 19 June 1707 44-44a
Walsh, Randall, Hare, *Almahide*, 16
February 1710 64-65
Almahide, 31 December 1711 76a
Arsinoe, 'Additional Songs', 31 December
1711 78a-b
Bottle Companions, 26 May 1709 56
Camilla, 31 December 1709 62
Camilla, 'Additional Songs', 31 December
1711 79a
Clotilda, 15 April 1709 53-54
Clotilda, 'Additional Songs', 31 December
1711 79b

Hydaspes, 30 May 1710 69
Hydaspes, Additional Songs, 27 January
1711 74
Hydaspes, 'Additional Songs', 27 January
1711 74a
Hydaspes, 'Additional Songs', 31
Decmeber 1711 80a
Jovial Companions, 20 May 1709 55-55a
Love's Triumph, 28 April 1708 47-47a
Pyrrhus and Demetrius, 20 January 1709
48a-b
Pyrrhus and Demetrius, 9 February 1709
49, 51
Wright, *Monthly Collection of Songs*, 31
October 1726 173
Necromancer, 31 December 1724 156
Three Songs, 20 July 1717 100
Twenty New Songs, 19 September 1717
101
Wright and author (Turner), *Twenty New
Songs*, 29 April 1718 104
Wrights, *Diamonds Cut Diamonds*, 31
January 1726 171

Young, *Arsinoe*, 5 October 1706 30
Astartus, 1 April 1721 112
Camilla, 16 May 1706 23
Clotilda, 29 November 1709 59
Collection of New Songs, 1 August 1706
24a
Collection of New Songs, 5 June 1707
41
Collection of Songs, 14 November 1704
11
Jupiter and Europa, 31 December 1723
127b
Thomyris, 19 June 1707 45
Venus and Adonis, 10 May 1716 98
Vespasian, 23 March 1724 141

7 Engravers and engraving styles

References are to entry numbers. Bold=entries with an illustration of the engraving style.

? 71-72, 76, 127b
Bates **136**, 152, 158
Bates and Walsh 180

Cobb **144**-45, 146, 160
Cole **169**-70
Cross 24-24a, 33a-35, 40a, 42, 57-58, 115-
   20, 125-26, 127, 142, 159, 171.
   See also combinations with Walsh.

Jones **106**

Mixed 166, 168, 173
Musick Shops 128-29, 150-51, 161-64

Parker 135a
Pippard 59, 70, 73, 86

Rawlins **174**

Walsh 46-47a, 93, 95, 102, 105, 122-23,
   127a, 134, 135b, 143, 172, 175
Walsh 1 1-4, 6-7, 12-16, 18-23, 25-26,
   29-32a, 48a-54, 62-63, 74, 78a-79b,
   87-88, 90, 90a, 94, 96-98, 107-108, 110,
   113, 121, 123, 130, 135
Walsh 1 and 2 8-11, 109
Walsh 1, 2 and 3 56
Walsh 1 and 3 37-38, 40, 43-45, 81-82,
   111-12, 114-14b, 126a, 138-41, 176, 179
Walsh 1 and 4 137
Walsh 3 and 4 124, **147**-49
Walsh 4 and 5 145a, 153
Walsh 4 and 6 **167**, 178-78a
Walsh and Cross 5, 33, 64-65, 68-69,
   74a-75a, 76a-78, 80-80a, 83-85, 89,
   90b-92, 103, 157
Walsh 1, 3 and Cross 55-55a
Walsh 1, 5, 6, and Cross 177
Wright 100-101, 104, 135c

8 Passe-partout title-page uses

Passe-partout number	Entries
1	1-2, 4-7, 26, 29, 33, 44-45, 78a-b, 87, 90, 107, 109, 126a
2	8-10, 19, 21-23, 62-63, 79-79a, 172, 177
3	12-12a, 13-16, 18-23, 25, 29-32a, 46-54, 62, 64-65, 68-69, 74-74a, 76a-80a, 91, 93, 123, 177
4	32-32a
5	46-54, 64-65, 68-69, 74a, 76a-78, 79b-80a, 91-94, 123
6	75-75a, 83-85, 88-89, 90a-90b, 96-98, 103, 110
7	95
8	100, 135c
9	113, 121-122, 130, 137, 139-41, 143, 147-49, 177
10	127a-b, 135b
11	128-29, 161-62, 164
12	145a, 153
13	146
14	152, 158
15	163
16	167
17	173

9 Books published in versions with one or both sides of each leaf printed

Arranged by entry numbers of initial one-side printed version.

Title (publisher)	Entry numbers (one side / both sides)
Collection of Songs	9, 11 / 8, 10
Camilla (Walsh)	16, 19-23, 63, 177 / 62, 79a
Arsinoe	26, 29-31, 78b, 90 / 78a
Love's Triumph	46-47, 93 / 47a
Pyrrhus and Demetrius (Walsh)	48a-50, 52, 94 / 51
Clotilda	53, 123 / 54, 79b
Pyrrhus and Demetrius (Cullen)	57 / 58
Almahide	64, 68 / 65, 76a-78
Book of New Songs	72 / 71
Etearco	75a / 75, 90b
Venus and Adonis	96, 98 / 97
Griselda (Walsh)	114a / 114, 114b, 179
Griselda (Meares)	115 / 116-18
Crispus	126 / 125
Vespasian (Walsh)	139-41 / 138

10 Libraries

References are to entry numbers. Italics indicate unvisited libraries or collections and unexamined copies. Assignment of unexamined copies to particular entries is provisional. Parentheses indicate copies not included in the main part of the description due to their being lost, sold, fragmentary, an out of scope issue, or part of the *Monthly Mask of Vocal Music*. The location of such copies is given in the Notes area of the descriptions. The number of copies is indicated following x if greater than one.

A-Wn   Musiksammlung, Nationalbibliothek, Vienna, Austria 111, 115, 129, 140, 148, 151, 160, 162, 166, (178)

A-Wn-h   Hoboken Collection, Musiksammlung, Nationalbibliothek, Vienna, Austria *122*

ALb   Britten-Pears Library, Aldeburgh, England (1), 76, 135, 144, 160

B-Bc   Conservatoire Royal de Musique, Brussels, Belgium 5, 44, 83, 111, 114b, (121), 122, 137, 145a, (*150*), 161, 164

B-Br   Bibliothèque Royale Albert 1er, Brussels, Belgium 29, 32, 38, 47, 85, 134, 135b

B-MAR   Abbaye de Maredsous, Denée, Belgium *49, 122, 127, 134, 143, 177*

Bp   Birmingham Public Library, England (7), 84, (*175*)

Bu   Barber Institute, University of Birmingham, England 114, 119

BWbw   Baldwin-Wilson, private collection, Brentwood, England 12a, 22, 38, 46, 54, 69, 85, 157

CaBVaU   University of British Columbia, Vancouver, Canada *168*

CaOHM   McMaster University, Hamilton, Ontario, Canada 44, (*65*)

CaOLU   University of Western Ontario, London, Canada 12a, 21a, 44, 49, 53, 75a, 80a, 83, 88, 114, 126, 128, 144, 150

CDp   Cardiff Public Library, Wales (now at the University of Wales, College of Cardiff Library) 46, 69, 83, 85, 89, 111, 117, 125, 147, 153x2, 163, 164

Cfm   Fitzwilliam Museum, Cambridge, England 29, 34, 38, 42, 57, 59, 65, 69, 112, 160

Ckc   Rowe Music Library, King's College, Cambridge, England 12x2, 19, 21a, 26, 29, 32, 34, 38, 44x2, 44a, 46x2, 48a, 49x2, 54, 65, 69, 71x2, 74, 75, 83x2, 84, 85, 88, 89x2, 91, 107, 108, 111x2, 113, 114, 121, 122x2, 127, 130, 135a, 138x2, 143x2, 144, 145, 145a, 147, 160x2, 161, 164, 166, 168, 169, 175, 178

CLU-C   Clark Library, University of California, Los Angeles, CA, USA 23, 26, 32, 34a, 39, 44, 46, 48a, 53, 55a, 64, 69, 83, 84, 88, (99), 107, 110, 111, 114a, 127, 127b, 135c, 138, 144, 147, 150, 160, 161, 164, 170, 172

Coke   Coke, private collection, Bentley, England 119, *122*, 144, *159*, (*167*), *169, 170*

Cpc   Pembroke College, Cambridge, England 144

Cpl   Pendlebury Library, Music Faculty, Cambridge, England 111, 121

CSfst   De Bellis Collection, San Francisco State University, San Francisco, CA, USA 22ax2, 32, 34, 44, 44a, 47, 49, 53x2, 64, 75, 80, 83, 89, 107, 111, 113, 114a, 121, 122, 143, 145a, 147

CSmH   Huntington Library, San Marino, CA, USA 5, 29, 71, 100, 110

CSt   Stanford University, Stanford, CA, USA   44, 49, 65, 69, 79a, 111, 114, 121, 137, 153

Ctc   Trinity College, Cambridge, England   69

CtY   Yale University, New Haven, CT, USA   (*83*)

CtY-Mus   Music Library, Yale University, New Haven, CT, USA   8, 29, 47, 49, 65, 88, 114, 144

Cu   Cambridge University Library, England   8

CU-MUSI   Music Library, University of California, Berkeley, CA, USA   5, 12a, 20, 38, 44, 46, 48a, 69, 79a, (99), 111, 122, 126, 144, 153, 169

CZ-Pu   Music Department, University of Prague, Czech Republic   26, 32

D-B   Staatsbibliothek zu Berlin–Preussischer Kulturbesitz, Berlin, Germany   22, 26, 32, *38*, 44, *172*

D-BMs   Staats- und Universitätsbibliothek, Bremen, Germany   *114*

D-DL   Bibliothek, Museum, Delitzsch, Germany   *172*

D-Gs   Staats- und Universitätsbibliothek, Göttingen, Germany   *121*

D-Hs   Staats- und Universitätsbibliothek, Hamburg, Germany   63, 89, 113, 121, 122x2, 127, 130, 134, 138, 139, 142, 143, (145a), 147, 150, 172, 176, 178a, 179

D-Mbs   Musiksammlung, Bayerische Staatsbibliothek, Munich, Germany   *138*

D-SWl   Wissenschaftliche Allgemeinbibliothek, Schwerin, Germany   *172*

DCU   Catholic University, Washington, DC, USA   (*157*)

DFo   Folger Shakespeare Library, Washington, DC, USA   5, 8, 9, 38, 44, 53, 55a, 65, 78a, (*83*), 84x2, 85, 88, 93, 96x2, 114b, 127, 135, 136, 137, 144, 157

DK-Kk   Royal Library, Copenhagen, Denmark   74a

DLC   Library of Congress, Washington, DC, USA   5, 8, 16, (22), 24, 29, 32, 38, (49), 56, 62, 68, 75, (76), 76a, 85, 88, 96, (99), 107, 108, 111, *113*, 114, 116, 121, (122), 126a, 127, 136x2, 138, 144, 147, 152, 159, 169

DRc   Durham Cathedral Library, England   (3), 38, (46), 49, 65, 69, 78a, 85, 96

DU   Dundee Public Library, Scotland   (99), 168, (*169*)

En   National Library of Scotland, Edinburgh, Scotland   12a, 19, 46, 55a, 75, 76a, 80, 119, 122, 136, 144x2, 160, 167, (167), 168x5, 169, 172, 178

Er   Reid Music Library, University of Edinburgh, Scotland   42, 57, 94, 107, 152, 163

Eu   Rare Book Room, University of Edinburgh, Scotland   48b, 53, 69, 107, 145

F-Pc   Fonds du Conservatoire, Bibliothèque nationale, Paris, France   22x2, 26, 32a, 38, 44, 58, 59, 64, 80, 83, 84, 85, 93, 107, 114, 141, 142, 144, 147, 150, 153, 159, 164, (167), 168, 169, 176

F-Pn   Bibliothèque nationale, Paris, France   44, 111, 114, 127, 138, 161, 172, 176

FMU   University of Miami, Coral Gables, FL, USA   *85*

Ge   Euing Music Library, University of Glasgow, Scotland   2, 8, 22, 31, 87, 97, 105, (135), 143, 144, 168

Gm   Mitchell Library, Glasgow, Scotland   99, 145, 168

Gu   Special Collections, University of Glasgow, Scotland   32a, 48a, 64, 69

H-Bn   National Library, Budapest, Hungary   *53*, *65*, *75*

HAdolmetsch   Dolmetsch, private collection, Haslemere, England   43a, 111, 114

I-BGi   Civico Istituto Musicale, Bergamo, Italy   62, *107*, *111*x2

I-Gi(l) Biblioteca dell'Istituto (Liceo) Musicale 'Paganini', Genova, Italy   *114*

I-MOe	Biblioteca Estense, Modena, Italy *111, 127*
I-Rsc	Conservatorio di Santa Cecilia, Rome, Italy *8, 69, 114, 121, 130, 153, 169*
I-Vc	Biblioteca del Conservatorio 'Benedetto Marcello', Venice, Italy *153*
IaU	University of Iowa, Iowa City, USA *144*
ICN	Newberry Library, Chicago, IL, USA 29, 32a, 44, 47, 49, 53, 65, 69, 75, 79a, 81, 103, 111, 114, 144, 164, 169
ICU	University of Chicago, IL, USA 5, 79, 85, 144, 160
INS	Illinois State University, Normal, IL, USA 49
InU	Indiana University, Bloomington, IN, USA *44, 144*
IU	University of Illinois, Urbana, IL, USA 22, 44a, 79a, 168
J-Tn	Nanki Library, Tokyo College of Music, Japan *34, 71, 114*
Lam	Royal Academy of Music, London, England (3), 8, 42, 85, 111, 118, 121, 122, 125x2, 127, 135, 143, (147), 150, 153x2, (157), 168
Lbl	British Library, London, England 2, 3, 4, 5x3, 6, 7, 8x2, 12, 14, 15, 18, 22x2, 24, 24a, 25, 26, 32x3, 33, 35, 38, 40, 41, 42, 44, 49x2, 53, 55, 56, 57, 64, 69, 70x2, 72, 73, 74, 74a, 75, 76x2, 79, 83, 84, 85, 86, 88, 89, 93, 95, 98, 99, 100, 104, 105, 107, 108x2, 109, 110, 111x3, 113, 114x3, 115, 119, 120, 121, 122, 125, 127, 127ax2, 128, 134, 135x2, 135b, 136, 138, 143x2, 144, 145, 146, 147, 150, 152, 153, 157, 158, 159, 160, 161, 163, 164, 167, 168x3, 169x2, 172, 175, 177, 180
Lcm	Royal College of Music, London, England 1, 4, 6, 7, 8, 9, 21, 24a, 32, 38, 41, 42, 44a, 51, 53, 54, 65, 69, 71, 75, 76, 85, 88, 90, 93, 96, 107, 111, 113, 114, 121, 122, 127a, 135, 135b, 135c, 138, 144, 145, 153, 160, 161, (167), 168x2, (172x2)
Lcml	Westminster Music Library, London, England 111
Lco	Royal College of Organists, London, England (69)
Lcs	Vaughan Williams Library, Cecil Sharp House, London, England 11, (168)
LEp	Leeds Public Library, England 44a, 71
Lgc	Gresham College Collection, Guildhall Library, London, England 29, 34, 42, 54, 55a, 65, 75, 84, 149, 152, 158
Lsc	Sion College, London, England 70, 72, 136
LVp	Liverpool Public Library, England 26, 103, 169
MB	Boston Public Library, MA, USA 10, 33a, 44, 54, 55a, 69, 77, 92, 103, 114, 127, 144, 169
MBMH	Harvard Musical Association, Boston, MA, USA *75, 127*
MdBPC	Peabody Conservatory, Baltimore, MD, USA 22
MH-H	Houghton Library, Harvard University, Cambridge, MA, USA 19, 38, (55a), 85, 168
MH-Mu	Music Library, Harvard University, Cambridge, MA, USA 26, 42, 52, 99, *136*, 144
MiD	Detroit Public Library, MI, USA 71
MiU	University of Michigan, Ann Arbor, MI, USA 38, 44, 47, 48b, 53, 62, 64, 69, (83), 111, 144, 164, 172
MnU	Music Library, University of Minnesota, Minneapolis, MN, USA 111
Mp	Henry Watson Music Library, Manchester Public Library, England 8, 32a, 49, 53, 64, 65, 69, 80, 96, (99), 108, 111, 114, 121, 122, 135, 144, 145, 157, 170, 172